Education in America

Education

in America

3rd edition

JAMES MONROE HUGHES

Harper & Row, Publishers
New York · Evanston · London

EDUCATION IN AMERICA, Third Edition
Copyright © 1960, 1965, 1970 by James Monroe Hughes.

*Printed in the United States of America. All rights
reserved. No part of this book may be used or
reproduced in any manner whatsoever without
written permission except in the case of brief
quotations embodied in critical articles and reviews.
For information address Harper & Row, Publishers,
Inc., 49 East 33rd Street, New York, N.Y. 10016.*

Library of Congress catalog card number: 79–96230

Contents

Aims and Methods in America

Preface

Education in America is directed to a particular kind of reader, one who is interested in learning what education in America is, how it came to be what it is, and, so far as we can tell now, what its future is likely to be. The book is intended to be both helpful and interesting to two broad types of readers: college students who are considering entering the teaching profession and those citizens who are directly or indirectly concerned about the course of education in this country. For instance, taxpayers who question the present policies of financial support of education and wish to study the whole problem will find several sections of the book helpful.

As explained in the first chapter, the presentation is in the form of an overview; this kind of approach has been proven during long experience to be most appropriate for beginning students in education. Some reasons for the success of what can also be called a broad-view presentation should be mentioned. First, an over-all, general course is particularly suitable as an introduction to the professional study of education because it provides the beginning student with a foundation on which to build his later professional courses which are, necessarily, more specialized. It is assumed in such professional courses that the student has an orientation to education in America—a frame of reference into which he can fit specialized professional study. Obviously, specialized courses by their very nature cannot provide this basic orientation; they are usually taught by specialists whose objectives must be quite circumscribed. Second, an over-all view acquired at the beginning of a professional education sequence builds and fosters the student's interest in teaching and helps him to decide early about joining forces with the teaching profession—making teaching his life's career. Third, when a student, early in his career, becomes knowledgeable about America's educational undertaking, he also becomes intelligently realistic about both its strengths and its weaknesses; this informed realism tends to protect him from later disillusionment, even discouragement. Fourth, when a student becomes knowledgeable about education in America early in his professional career, he also becomes able to make intelligent decisions about the role or roles he himself will play in the profession; he becomes qualified to plan more wisely a preparational program suited to the realization of his own aims.

.   .   .

A few words about this new edition seem indicated. The book was first published in the summer of 1960; changes in the educational picture then came so rapidly that a revised printing was issued in the spring of 1962. In 1965, a complete revision, the second edition, was published. This, the third edition but fourth issue of the book, has been written with the collaboration of my wife, Kathleen Pye Hughes, a seventh-grade team leader at Chute Junior High School, Evanston, Illinois, and, for some years, head of social studies in the Evanston junior high schools. Many sections of the book have been rewritten to present an up-to-date, faithful picture of education in America. For instance, Unit III, ''The Schools in America,'' has been extensively rewritten to reflect current trends more accurately.

The organization of the book in four fairly independent units has been retained because this plan has been generally approved by those who have used the book as a text, mostly because it permits flexibility. The instructor may vary the sequence of the units as he desires without detracting from the presentation of the principal theme of the book. Some instructors, for example, have begun their study with Unit II, ''Ideas Influential in America.'' Others have preferred to postpone Unit I until the end of the course and have combined it with Unit IV.

The readings listed at the close of each unit do not constitute a bibliography in the sense that a bibliography is a list of works referred to in the text or consulted by the author. The readings are, instead, suggestions for individual or group activity leading to personal papers or oral discussion or presentation. An effort has been made to confine the suggestions to books and periodicals found in practically all college libraries. In many cases, the readings are from periodicals designed for a wide, lay audience, not limited to those in professional education (for example, the monthly education issue of the *Saturday Review*). It is expected that the suggested readings will be an incentive to the student to find other similar current material. Certainly there is much to find in general periodicals and newspapers. The readings on subject matter and methods in the schools include a number in professional publications in various fields. Most of them are nontechnical, however. In fact, the student will find it valuable and interesting to explore outside his area of major interest. For instance, the potential English teacher could at least browse through articles or books that show something about what the science people or the mathematics people are thinking about and working on.

The reader will discover that many "open-ended" questions are raised throughout the book; they concern topics about which there is much disagreement and often much misunderstanding. Each is discussed as it arises in context, at the point where the text sheds some light on the nature and origin of the specific problem. In some cases, a brief analysis of some of the pros and cons of proposed answers and solutions to problems and issues is included. In some cases, an opinion is expressed, together with the reasons behind it. Various views and attitudes toward the questions and issues are found in the readings suggested. I hope the reader will be stimulated to think about these "open-ended" questions, will explore current attitudes, and will ponder and discuss his findings.

Pictures are included throughout the text to make each chapter vivid and meaningful. Looking at the pictures carefully and reading the captions may often be a good way to start a stimulating critical discussion. The charts and figures also add to the concreteness of the material. In addition, they invite comparisons among the states in terms of policies toward education and generalizations about the national effort.

It is obvious that many persons and organizations have contributed significantly to this edition and the previous editions of the book. I am grateful for this very generous help from sources too numerous to mention individually. Special appreciation, however, is expressed to the Research Division of the National Education Association and the National Center for Educational Statistics of the U. S. Office of Education for their help in supplying me with a great deal of specific data. I hope that those who have assisted will find recompense in the knowledge that they have made a very worthwhile contribution to education in America.

J. M. H.

Acknowledgments

The photographs in this book are used by courtesy of the individuals and organizations listed below. When there are two or more photographs on a page, the credits are listed in order, top to bottom and left to right.

iii: *Chicago Public Schools; Teachers College, Columbia University; St. Louis Board of Education; Kansas State Historical Society.* 4: *National School Boards Association.* 5: *Saturday Review, Inc.,* © 1968 *(Pageant Studios).* 10: *Niagara Mohawk Power Corporation.* 13: *Ford Foundation (Roy Stevens).* 14: *National Congress of Parents and Teachers.* 21: *University of Wisconsin, Milwaukee; Wilmington Public Schools; Shelton from Monkmeyer; St. Louis Board of Education; University of Wisconsin, Milwaukee.* 26: *Hays from Monkmeyer.* 32: *Chicago Public Schools.* 42: *Seattle School District; Merrim from Monkmeyer.* 50: *Southern Illinois University.* 57: *Seattle School District; University of South Florida; Seattle School District (four lower photos).* 65: *Indiana State University.* 77: *Schenectady Public Schools; Shelton from Monkmeyer; Merrim from Monkmeyer.* 90: *National Education Association (left and top center); American Federation of Teachers (other three photos).* 91: *National Education Association (upper left and lower right); American Federation of Teachers (other three photos).* 113: *Peace Corps; Departmento de Instrucción, P.R.; Peace Corps; Ewing Galloway.* 118: *The Lutheran Church, Missouri Synod.* 124: *Atlantic Monthly Press.* 127: *Teachers College, Columbia University.* 128: *Ford Foundation (Arthur Leipzig).* 131: *Borough School District, Anchorage, Alaska.* 139: *Shelton from Monkmeyer (two top photos); Monkmeyer; Bloom from Monkmeyer.* 153: *Milwaukee Public Schools (top and center left); Seattle School District; Chicago Public Schools; Better Schools Advertising Council.* 171: *Department of Administration, State of Minnesota.* 173: *Merrim from Monkmeyer; Chicago Public Schools.* 175: (no credit). 176: *Pio Istituto di S. Spirito, Rome.* 177: (no credit); *Chicago Public Schools; Children's Bureau, Department of Health, Education, and Welfare; Seattle School District.* 186: (no credit). 191: *Slavonic Division, New York Public Library.* 198: *Prints Division, New York Public Library.* 203: *Swiss National*

Tourist Office, New York.   204: Wisconsin State University, Superior (both).   209:
Prints Division, New York Public Library.   211: Indiana State University, Terre
Haute; Chicago Public Schools.   214: (no credit).   219: Prints Division, New
York Public Library.   225: Kansas State Historical Society.   229: New-York His-
torical Society.   235: New-York Historical Society (both left photos); L. Downs,
Grand Rapids Public Library.   243: Wisconsin State Historical Society; Chicago
Public Schools.   253: UNESCO.   256: United Nations.   267: St. Louis Board of
Education (top right and lower left); American Seating Company; IBM; New York
Board of Education.   307: La Porte Community School Corporation; Kansas State
Historical Society.   312: National Safety Council; (no credit).   323: Department
of Education, State of New Jersey.   327: St. Louis Board of Education; National
Education Association.   339: (no credit); Ford Foundation (Arthur Leipzig).   345:
Berkley, Michigan, Public Schools; Ford Foundation (William R. Simmons).   351:
Berkley, Michigan, Public Schools (lower left); Seattle School District (other three
photos).   365: Seattle School District.   367: Chicago Public Schools (upper three
photos); Seattle School District.   371: Larry D. Miller (all four photos).   377:
Berkeley Unified School District; Chicago Public Schools; New York Board of Education.
399: The Lutheran Church, Missouri Synod (top two photos); Sacred Heart High School,
Pittsburgh; (no credit).   401: Lexington School for the Deaf, New York; Hadley School
for the Blind, Winnetka, Illinois.   407: Chrysler Corporation (both).   413: The
Phillips Exeter Academy, Exeter, New Hampshire.   419: Southern Illinois University.
423: Chicago Public Schools (all three photos).   427: Chicago Public Schools.
438: New York School of Printing; Pasadena City College; Indiana University,
Bloomington; Seattle School District.   439: Chicago Public Schools; Bellflower, Cali-
fornia, Unified School District; Indiana University, Bloomington.   462: (no credit).
466: Stanford University.   473: Chicago Public Schools (top and lower right); St.
Louis Board of Education; Chute Junior High School, Evanston; Seattle School District;
American Seating Company.   486: Teachers College, Columbia University.   498:
National Congress of Parents and Teachers; Evanston Photographic Service; New York
Board of Education (center and lower left); Greenberg from Monkmeyer.   499: National
Congress of Parents and Teachers (upper left); Merrim from Monkmeyer (other two
photos).   507: (no credit).   516: (no credit).   525: Seattle School District.   533:
Lincoln, Nebraska, Public Schools; New York Board of Education; St. Louis Board of
Education; Seattle School District; American Seating Company; Wide World (upper
right).   547: St. Louis Board of Education.   557: Wide World; Evanston Photo-
graphic Service; Kranzten Studio (center right and lower left); Chicago Public Schools.
564: Kranzten Studio.   570: Los Angeles City Board of Education; Kranzten Studio.
579: IBM; Frink from Monkmeyer; Kranzten Studio; Chicago Public Schools; Lincoln,
Nebraska, Public Schools; Digital Equipment Corporation; Grolier, Inc.   592: Seattle
School District.   595: Lincoln, Nebraska, Public Schools; Evanston Photographic
Service.   601: Teachers College, Columbia University; Ford Foundation (William
Simmons).   603: Indiana University, Bloomington.   611: Southern Illinois Univer-
sity, Carbondale; University of South Florida; Ford Foundation (Arthur Leipzig);
Seattle School District; University of South Florida.   614: Encyclopaedia Britannica;
American Seating Company.

Education in America

1
Introduction

At the beginning of a study of education in America, it is important to decide on the meaning of the word "education," because it has a number of meanings; they are, broadly, divided into two categories: the act or process of educating and the science of teaching and learning. The word, of course, is only one of many in the English language that do have a number of different meanings—a situation that leads to the kind of confusion in communication that has been ascribed to "the tyranny of words."

Before we choose the limited meaning of "education" that will guide subsequent discussions in this book, we should note a few of the different ways the word is commonly used. A person may be referred to as one with a high school or a college education. A student may say that he is taking a course in education or that he is enrolled in a department or school or college of education. Some writers use the term to encompass all and any activities by which children learn the techniques, sentiments, and customs of the society in which they live.

Popular usage indicates that all these meanings are correct. To make this study of education in America reasonably logical and consistent, however, we have chosen a meaning of the word "education" that best serves the purpose of this text. Throughout the book the word will be used to refer to the deliberate and formal learning that is organized and directed by the people of the United States. Most of the learning we will be concerned with in this book is that which takes place in the schools. (Whenever, as will sometimes be the case, a broader, more inclusive meaning of the word is intended, the distinction will be made clear.)

I

Magnitude of the educational undertaking

Education is the largest undertaking in America and, perhaps, the most important. Hence it is *Big Business*. America spent more than $58 billion on education in 1968–1969, and this was far from sufficient to finance education that was good enough. Teacher shortages, obsolete buildings, and other unmet needs attest to this. The very size of the educational establishment, one that includes well over two and a half million classroom teachers, indicates that the problems related to educating, attracting, and supervising educational personnel are tremendous.

Every September more than 50 million people of all ages enter some kind of school, many to attend full time, some to attend part time. As Figs. 1.1 and 1.2 show, this number increases markedly each year. If we add to the full-time students at all levels, the teachers, principals, and instructional specialists, and the cooks, bus drivers, and custodians, and the people engaged in selling or producing something for the schools, the total is 30 percent of this country's population. In terms of numbers of persons involved, education is by far this country's No. 1 enterprise. In terms of business and the nation's economy, it may displace national defense when the war in Vietnam ends. Other people are involved in schools in a variety of ways— parents of school children, members of school boards, school trustees, school architects, builders of school buildings, investors in school bonds. If the payers of school taxes and the voters on school matters are included, almost everyone in the United States is a participant in the vast undertaking. Whether viewed in terms of its extent or its importance, the magnitude of America's educational undertaking is immense.

Education and an enlightened citizenry

A prerequisite to providing good education is citizens who are informed about the needs of education. Also, in the United States, where citizens control education, it is important that there be intelligent leaders who, in turn, will organize the citizenry for effective

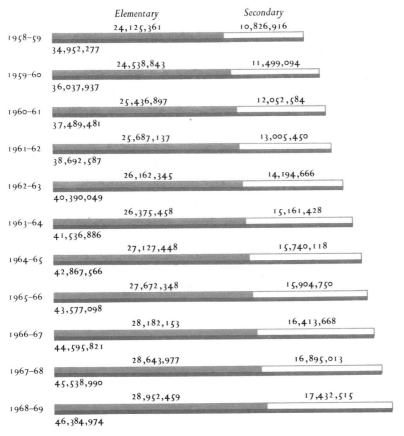

	Elementary	Secondary
1958–59	24,125,361	10,826,916
	34,952,277	
1959–60	24,538,843	11,499,094
	36,037,937	
1960–61	25,436,897	12,052,584
	37,489,481	
1961–62	25,687,137	13,005,450
	38,692,587	
1962–63	26,162,345	14,194,666
	40,390,049	
1963–64	26,375,458	15,161,428
	41,536,886	
1964–65	27,127,448	15,740,118
	42,867,566	
1965–66	27,672,348	15,904,750
	43,577,098	
1966–67	28,182,153	16,413,668
	44,595,821	
1967–68	28,643,977	16,895,013
	45,538,990	
1968–69	28,952,459	17,432,515
	46,384,974	

Fig. 1.1 Public school enrollments, 1958–1959 to 1968–1969. (Data from NEA Research Report 1968-R16)

1958–59	...
1959–60	3.1
1960–61	7.3
1961–62	10.7
1962–63	15.6
1963–64	18.8
1964–65	22.6
1965–66	24.7
1966–67	27.6
1967–68	30.3
1968–69	32.7

Fig. 1.2 Public school enrollments, percentage increases over 1958–1959. (Data from NEA Research Report 1968-R16)

This 27th annual convention of the National School Boards Association attracted 9,039 members of public school boards, each representing one board. Each was a lay citizen interested in giving intelligent lay leadership to public education in America. Board members spend a startling amount of time on this work.

action. Herein lies a great challenge faced by any segment of a democratic government controlled by the lay public. What this implies will become clearer as we proceed.

The schools in the United States are particularly the special responsibility of the citizens. Even privately controlled schools exist and perform a valuable function only because of public policy. Even they must meet certain regulatory standards established by the public. Placing the educational destiny of the nation in the hands of its people requires an intelligent and well-informed public.

The American people are fully cognizant of the power of education and, hence, are concerned that their power over education not be minimized. They are aware that education received in the schools may change a whole social viewpoint in a single generation. As we shall see later, the American people shrewdly exercise their power

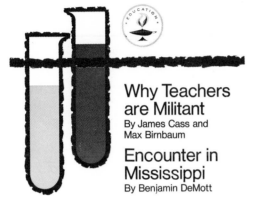

Saturday Review

January 20, 1968   35¢

The Chemistry of Learning
By David Krech

Why Teachers are Militant
By James Cass and Max Birnbaum

Encounter in Mississippi
By Benjamin DeMott

Current educational topics and issues are receiving an increasing amount of space in general magazines and newspapers. In fact, the Saturday Review—a weekly magazine read by educated, influential people who have wide interests—devotes one issue each month to education.

over the schools in a short, direct line by establishing their basic control over the schools from the home, the community, and the local school district, and by dictating—often through school elections—who shall be in charge of the schools and how, and how much, money shall be spent. This means that it would be very difficult for any single political group in the United States ever to seize control over education throughout the nation. It is readily apparent that people who are inclined to keep their hands tightly on the reins and who insist on occupying the driver's seat should, if the schools are to achieve good results, themselves be enlightened about the needs of education and have a clear concept of the general direction education should take.

Education and well-informed teachers

The public depends mainly on the trained professional teaching group for a mature and intelligent interpretation of what education in the United States should be, what its principal needs are, and what is

*F*ew *if any thoughtful people have denied that the art of teaching can be developed by practice, under suitable conditions. Thus, the members of the Massachusetts Board of Education, before they established the first normal school in the United States, subscribed to the statement that "No one can entertain a doubt that there is a mastery in teaching as in every other art. Nor is it less obvious that within reasonable limits this skill and this mastery may themselves be made the subject of instruction and be communicated to others." These words were written in 1838. The question then was: What is this skill and how can one communicate it to others? This question remains the hard core·of the issue. . . .*

At the outset, I think we can identify four components of the intellectual equipment that would be a prerequisite to the development of teaching skill. The first I shall call the "democratic social component." The second is an interest in the way behavior develops in groups of children and some experience of this development. A third is a sympathetic knowledge of the growth of children, by which I mean far more than physical growth, of course. A fourth might be called the principles of teaching. This last is almost equally applicable to a teacher with only one pupil (the tutor of a rich family in former times) as to a person attempting to develop an intellectual skill in a group of children.

My phrase "democratic social component" may need an explanation. To understand what I mean, we must consider everything that is involved in teaching in our elementary or secondary schools. We must constantly bear in mind that the schools in every nation have been and continue to be involved in more than imparting knowledge and developing skills. . . .

The second of my four components, which has to do with the development of behavior in groups of children, is not unrelated to the first. A concern with the values inherent in a "democratic social system" has intruded itself into questions that some social scientists might say should involve only predictive generalizations based upon observations or experience. At all events, a teacher must know something about the processes by which social behavior emerges in groups of children. *Technically one ought to be able to study this process dispassionately as a problem in social psychology. In fact, however, it has proved incredibly difficult to separate this question from one of another type: "What kind of social behavior do we wish to develop?"*

My third and fourth components, a knowledge of the growth of children and the principles of teaching, emerge most clearly if one notes what good school teachers do. Let me ask you to run through a list of such "doings." First of all, obviously the teacher disseminates information, and it goes without saying that this information should be accurate and significant. . . .

But the elementary teacher, and to a lesser extent the secondary teacher, must select and organize materials without the guidelines marked by university research fields ; that is, he teaches "science" not "qualitative analysis," "social studies" not "history of England in the seventeenth century." Moreover, the information must be presented in a form understandable by the very young ; the conceptual and verbal skill of the educated adult cannot be assumed.

The public school teacher is also expected to adjust his methods of instruction to a student group that is highly heterogeneous with respect to intellectual ability, motivation, and previous educational achievement. This means that he must select from a wide range of instructional materials those most suited to the intellectual maturity of each youngster, and this maturity may vary as much as two or three years in normal development. . . .

James B. Conant, *The Education of American Teachers.* New York: McGraw-Hill, 1963, pp. 113, 115, 116. Quoted by permission of McGraw-Hill Book Company.

necessary for the maintenance of an excellent system of schools. Only a well-informed, responsible teaching profession can supply this kind of information.

Furthermore, all theories of education—progressive or reactionary, liberal or conservative—assume that the classroom teacher is always in direct control. The dependence on the instructor's initiative and discretion justifies the expectation that classrooms be manned by teachers who are well informed about the entire educational venture.

While teachers play a role that requires considerable individual initiative, they also play a role that calls for a close relationship with many other persons. Throughout the day teachers are in close contact not only with the pupils in their own classrooms, but also with the pupils taught by other teachers. Further, they have personal relationships with other teachers, with principals and supervisors, with the pupils' parents, and with boards of education. In no other profession do roles interlock so intimately; maintaining good relationships in all of these roles is an important factor in achieving marked teaching success. This demands that the teacher be well informed about education in general. It is not enough to know subject matter and to master methods and problems related only to the classroom. He must be

The Magnitude of the American Educational Establishment, 1968–1969

More than 60,400,000 Americans are engaged full-time in the nation's educational enterprise as students, teachers, or administrators. Nearly another 140,000 make education a time-consuming avocation as trustees of local school systems, state boards of education, or institutions of higher learning. The breakdown is given here:

THE INSTITUTIONS

Elementary schools	88,556
Secondary schools	31,306
Universities, colleges, and junior colleges	2,374
Total institutions	122,236

SCHOOL DISTRICTS 21,990

THE LEARNERS

Pupils in elementary schools (kindergarten through Grade 8)	
Public schools	32,100,000
Nonpublic (private and parochial)	4,600,000
Total elementary	36,700,000
Secondary school students	
Public high schools	12,800,000
Nonpublic	1,400,000
Total secondary	14,200,000
College and university full- and part-time students enrolled for credit toward degrees	
Public institutions	4,600,000
Nonpublic institutions	2,100,000
Total higher	6,700,000
Grand total students enrolled	57,600,000

THE TEACHERS

Public school teachers	
Elementary	1,070,000
Secondary	856,000
Nonpublic school teachers	
Elementary	157,000
Secondary	90,000

College and university teachers

Public institutions	299,000
Nonpublic institutions	205,000
Total teachers	2,677,000

ADMINISTRATORS AND SUPERVISORS

Superintendents of schools	13,313
Principals and supervisors	112,583
College and university presidents	2,374
Other college administrative and service staff	82,000
Total	210,270

BOARD MEMBERS

Local school board members	110,380
State board members	500
College and university trustees	25,000
Total	135,880

THE COST (in billions)

Current expenditures and interest

Elementary and secondary schools

Public	$29.0
Nonpublic	3.7

Higher

Public	9.8
Nonpublic	7.2

Capital outlay

Elementary and secondary schools

Public	4.5
Nonpublic	0.6

Higher

Public	2.4
Nonpublic	1.0
Total	$58.2

SOURCE: *Saturday Review*, November 16, 1968. Copyright 1968 by Saturday Review, Inc. Figures are based on latest available estimates from the U. S. Office of Education and the National Education Association.

Business concerns recognize that good schools are essential to successful operation of industry and business.

equipped to recognize, adjust to, and influence the many forces at play in the process of education.

The overview approach

Research concerning the relative effectiveness of various approaches to introductory college courses in specialized fields reveals that, for most specialized fields, the overview approach is superior. "Overview" as applied to introductory courses carries the idea that the coverage is extensive and that the topics selected are basic and fundamental to later study. In many colleges students pursue one-year or one-semester introductory courses, each of which delineates a field of study, reveals the nature of major problems included in the field, describes the methods used, and elaborates on the principal basic ideas. Above all, the purpose is to present the field of study so that the student may obtain accurate insights into its foundational elements. The approach, then, is sweeping and general rather than technical and specialized; the treatment is simple rather than complicated; the subject matter is introductory rather than terminal. Such an approach is particularly appropriate to an introduction to the study of education.

The overview technique followed in this book is designed to meet the needs of intelligent citizens who may wish to be well informed about education in America, those who are playing a part or who expect to play a part in controlling or influencing education. The overview also will meet the needs of the college student who, as a prospective teacher, expects to become an active participant in American education. For the student, the book explores basic concepts that all members of the teaching profession need to understand and, further, it examines certain basic concepts that are fundamental to later professional study.

Selection of material

Certain principles have guided in the selection and rejection of both topics and materials.

First, it is assumed that the reader is taking his first systematic look at education in the United States. Perhaps he is a citizen who wishes to be informed enough about education to function as an intelligent parent or voter. Perhaps he is a taxpayer who wishes to know more about the educational venture he is obligated to support. The materials are selected and the discussions are fashioned with these kinds of readers in mind.

Second, those phases of education have been selected that will give students of education the information and understanding they need to assist in making a vocational choice or some related decision.

Third, in some states a general, introductory education course is required for state certification for all who enter a teacher education program. The requirement is usually imposed by the state educational authority, an agency that will be described later. Even where such a

If the earth were struck by one of Mr. Wells's comets, and if, in consequence, every human being now alive were to lose all the knowledge and habits which he had acquired from preceding generations (though retaining unchanged all his own powers of invention, and memory, and habituation), nine tenths of the inhabitants of London or New York would be dead in a month, and 99 percent of the remaining tenth would be dead in six months. They would have no language to express their thoughts, and no thoughts but vague reverie. They could not read notices, or drive motors or horses. They would wander about, led by the inarticulate cries of a few naturally dominant individuals, drowning themselves, as thirst came on, in hundreds at the riverside landing places, looting those shops where the smell of decaying food attracted them, and perhaps at the end stumbling on the expedient of cannibalism. Even in the country districts, men could not invent, in time to preserve their lives, methods of growing food, or taming animals, or making fire, or so clothing themselves as to endure a northern winter. An attack of constipation or measles would be invariably fatal. After a few years mankind would almost certainly disappear from the northern and temperate zones. The white races would probably become extinct everywhere. A few primitive races might live on fruit and small animals in those fertile tropical regions where the human species was originally evolved, until they had slowly accumulated a new social heritage. After some thousands of generations they would probably possess something which we should recognize as a language, and perhaps some art of taming animals and cultivating land. They might or might not have created what we should call a religion, or a few of our simpler mechanical inventions and political expedients. They probably would not have recreated such general ideas as "Law" or "Liberty"; though they might have created other general ideas which would be new to us.

Graham Wallas, *Our Social Heritage*. New Haven, Conn.: Yale University Press, 1921, pp. 16–17. Quoted by permission of Yale University Press.

course is not required for state certification, it is assumed that every teacher will have some knowledge of the fundamental features of education as they are incorporated in the various school systems throughout America.

Fourth, the materials of the book are selected to serve as a foundation for more advanced study in professional education.

Other teachers, administrators, and specialists of various kinds can help teachers grow in knowledge and techniques. Here a teaching team at an inner-city school in Pittsburgh is at one of its weekly meetings with a mental health group—a psychiatrist, psychologist, and social worker. Their topic is the development of new teaching methods especially suited to underprivileged children.

Plan of the book

The materials of the book are organized around four aspects of education referred to as "units." Each unit can be studied more or less independently of the others. Unit I focuses on the classroom teacher—describing what he does, how he qualifies, how he is related to his profession, how he formulates his professional philosophy, and how he is affected by being part of an institution.

Unit II focuses on ideas that have been influential in shaping the course of American education. Discussed first are the ideas that were propagated by three significant European social movements—the Athenian cultural movement, the Christian religious movement, and the broad-scale intellectual movement, the Renaissance, particularly

The Teacher in America

Our discussion of education in America begins with a focus on the classroom teacher as an individual. After all, it is the classroom teachers who, in the last analysis, largely determine what and how effective education will be. Following the study of the teacher as an individual we shall, in later units, broaden our perspective to include many other features that influence the teacher and have a bearing on the entire educational picture.

The individual teacher in the classroom is the key to education; it is obvious, therefore, that teachers must be well informed. The most appropriate time to increase one's enlightenment about education is at the time of choosing, or considering, teaching as a career—the very time when the entire career, which may prove to be a lifetime one, lies ahead. A starting point is information about and understanding of the duties and responsibilities of a teacher, his place in the profession and in his institution, the sources and functions of his philosophy in terms of which he, as an individual teacher, will operate.

In this focus on the teacher as an individual, we consider the nature of a teacher's work, how he becomes qualified to teach, personality traits he must have, the responsibilities he assumes in accepting membership in the profession, and the rewards he may expect. How will the formulation of a personal educational philosophy help him? How does he go about building his philosophy? How does teaching in an educational institution affect what he does? How will an institution serve him?

Such questions, of course, cannot be answered categorically; indeed, they cannot even be analyzed completely. Nevertheless, questions centering around the teacher as an individual serve as a point of departure, something on which to build. Throughout the rest of the book additional information and understandings will gradually emerge to add other insights.

In the closing unit of the book, "Aims and Methods in America," we return to the work of classroom teachers as a professional group, emphasizing then the broader aspects of their over-all instructional responsibilities.

2
What Teachers Do

We begin with a study of the work of the key figure in the educational picture—the teacher. In Unit I five questions about the teacher are considered. What do teachers do? How must they qualify? What are the principal characteristics of the profession to which they belong? How does a teacher formulate his professional philosophy? And how are his obligations affected by the nature of the institution in which he works? Since none of the questions lends itself to brief analysis, a chapter is devoted to each. First, what do teachers do?

The basic function of a teacher

The familiar statement that the principal function of the teacher is to stimulate and direct learning activities constitutes a fairly accurate, simple, and definitive description of what teachers do. Though it must be followed with a more detailed analysis if we are to acquire an adequate description of the occupation, the statement, nevertheless, is helpful as a point of departure from which our analysis may proceed. It conveys the idea that the teacher is the key figure in the drama of the education of a child. He is in control of many of the manageable features of the educative process. The results of the process certainly are determined by the wisdom of his control.

The word "stimulation" is equally as significant as the word "direction." A teacher may be in control of the classroom and may greatly influence what is learned. What any child learns depends on how he, personally, interacts with his environment. "Stimulation" emphasizes that a teacher's job is not limited to guidance and direction and control. It also includes inciting the pupils to action. It involves providing a foundation on which is built self-direction and the advance toward a higher level of maturity. The teacher's job is to modify the stimuli in the environment so that they have a favorable educational impact on the learners.

Complex nature of the work of teachers

The work of teachers is complex because of the complex nature of the human organisms they teach. Such scientists as the physiologists, psychologists, and social biologists, who devote their lives to a study of the human organism and the factors that influence its growth, emphasize the intricacies involved in their searches for a fuller under-standing of the human individual. Not only is the human organism complex, but the social environment that so directly influences the development of the individual also is complex and is constantly in-creasing in complexity. Influencing large numbers of these rapidly growing, complex systems of living energy to develop in desirable, worthwhile directions can, by no possible stretch of the imagination, be considered a simple task, a task that can be performed satisfactorily by almost any normal person. A study of what classroom teachers do must be approached with these complexities in mind.

Limitations on interpretations of teachers' work

GAPS IN KNOWLEDGE

One factor that limits our interpretation of what teachers do and should do is a lack of fundamental knowledge about the nature of the human organism. It is significant, for instance, that those who work in the fields referred to as the life sciences have never adequately defined what life is. Their efforts to measure the amount of life an organism possesses have been unsatisfactory. They are resigned to describing life and, sometimes, to measuring some of its manifestations. Life and death and cell growth and the nature of individuality and emotions can

Influencing "these rapidly growing, complex systems of living energy" to develop in desirable directions is a complex task. Teachers help children in many ways—instruction, guidance, testing. In one classroom, a teacher works with a group. In another, a teacher gives individual guidance to one of her pupils. The two teacher-clinicians are working privately with pupils who have particular problems. Such specialists can be employed when there is adequate school support. By helping children referred to them, they lighten the teaching load of classroom teachers and they can do much to prevent the emotional problems that arise in children frustrated by learning inadequacies. (Such children used to be called "disciplinary" problems.) The other teacher is helping a boy keep up with his school work at home. Many school systems provide home and hospital instruction for pupils with extended illness. It is obvious that teaching requires specialized skills and natural as well as trained ability.

be cited as only a few of the many unknowns. Furthermore, complete explanations of such processes as learning, perceiving, reasoning, and imagining aren't available to the educator.

Voids in knowledge are, of course, common to all fields of study. For example, when Newton stated the laws of gravitation, he exempted certain natural phenomena such as light, electricity, and magnetism from his interpretation. What gravitation is remains an unknown. The whole field of cosmology, the general science of the universe, is characterized by much that is unexplained. Since such gaps exist in our knowledge of the physical aspects of human environment—aspects that can be measured—it is not surprising that so many gaps exist in our knowledge of human organisms, an area that does not lend itself to experimentation and quantification.

Despite the gaps and the many obstacles to narrowing them, useful knowledge of human behavior has been accumulated. The gaps are stressed here because students are sometimes disturbed when final answers cannot be given to some educational problems. Beginning teachers, particularly, are apt to be confused by the tendency among those who teach education to reason along theoretical lines. Where one does not have facts and the principles or "laws" abstracted from facts, one must turn to theories. Yet it is the presence of unsolved problems that helps make teaching such an intriguing occupation.

INFLUENCE OF PAST EXPERIENCE

The individual's interpretation of what he reads about education and the generalizations he makes about the teacher's work are inevitably colored by his own past school experiences. This fact both helps and limits an attempt to understand what a teacher does or should do. Personal school experiences provide only a partial view of all that a teacher does. In addition, any individual has been taught by a sampling of teachers that would not be considered statistically representative. Furthermore, from decade to decade, the role of the teacher is modified because of various continuing changes. Nevertheless, because certain more or less persistent attitudes of the student toward teachers and teaching, favorable and unfavorable, have been acquired through an individual's own experiences in school, we necessarily begin our study of what teachers do with certain varied, individual predispositions. It is important to be aware of and take into account these predispositions in our study of the work of a teacher.

TENDENCY TO OVERSIMPLIFY

The student is taught to rely on the *simplicity postulate* when working on a problem in the field of physics. This postulate asserts that of two alternatives the one that can be more simply stated is likely to be more acceptable. The principle of simplicity is often applied to our thinking about problems of teaching. When two educational theories are proposed, we tend to accept the one that is simpler, that more nearly accords with our previous experiences, and that promises to be more fruitful in its application. The simplicity postulate holds in education as it does in other fields of learning, but oversimplification sometimes presents the teaching profession with its most frustrating situations. Simplification is desirable only when it follows careful and expert analysis. The tendency generally leads to good habits of thinking. In interpreting the work of the teacher, however, it can be unwisely used and lead to harmful results.

Often influential citizens who are relatively uninformed about education will make statements such as, "I am opposed to federal aid to education" or "Teachers should fail more pupils in the interest of higher achievement standards." Their statements appeal to many partly because they are simple, positive, direct answers about what schools should be and what teachers should do. Those who have carefully and diligently studied the problems, however, are not always sure of the solutions. They wish to weigh various alternatives with thoughtful care.

UNOBSERVABLE ELEMENTS

Interpretations based on studies of teachers' work must recognize that there are elements in this work that are not revealed by any form of investigation. One is the qualitative factor. This will be discussed after an examination of the nature and extent of teachers' duties.

Classifying teachers' duties

NEED FOR CLASSIFICATION

Classification is a basic method used for studying the similarities and differences among objects in the universe. Those objects that have similar characteristics are assigned to the same category. This is perhaps the oldest and simplest method for arriving at order in the world of knowledge.. By noting similarities among the activities in which teachers engage, we can, in some measure, reduce many of them to a class and then speak of them as a single activity. Thus we can discuss guidance as a single activity even though we know that guidance actually includes a large number of individual activities.

Exactness in classification of a teacher's duties would be helpful but does not seem possible. Educational terminology is not fully standardized, and, even more important, teaching activities do not fall into readily classifiable categories. Lines of demarcation between classifications are often blurred. They frequently overlap. No classification is, therefore, to be considered final or authoritative.

If we had generally accepted definitions of educational terms, more uniform classifications of activities would be possible. In an effort to promote a kind of standardization of terms to be helpful not only in classifying but in the education field generally, a dictionary of the specialized vocabulary of professional education has been produced.[1] Such standardization is particularly important to the student who needs to know that professional writers and instructors in education use the same words to convey like meanings. More work is needed in this area of standardization. There is, however, more or less general agreement with respect to some of the classifications of teacher activities.

CLASSIFICATIONS

In general, teacher functions have been broadly grouped into five classifications: (1) classroom instruction, (2) guidance, (3) staff functions,

[1] Carter V. Good, *Dictionary of Education*, 2nd ed. New York: McGraw-Hill, 1959, 704 pp.

(4) community duties, and (5) professional activities. The classifications
are, of course, arbitrary. Everything a teacher does might be classified as related to classroom instruction or to guidance.

1. Classroom instruction

This is the foremost duty of the teacher; it comprises the bulk of his activities. It involves all the duties that the teacher performs in directing group and individual learning. Teachers direct discussions, make assignments, listen to reports and recitations, direct reading, show films, check workbooks, and plan and check work, often at home in the evenings. You know from your own experiences that this most important function is discharged in a great variety of ways, and you can appreciate better now that it reflects most accurately the philosophy of the teacher and of the school and that it is most readily modified by the social environment of the teacher and by the physical resources made available to him. Extended observation of classroom instruction is necessary if one is to get a complete picture that reflects this aspect of the total school situation.

2. Guidance

Every teacher is a counselor to his pupils. Duties in this classification consume much time and energy. Often they are incidental to instruction. Sometimes they are definitely scheduled (perhaps weekly conferences with an individual pupil over a period of time). The teacher may find it necessary to counsel pupils outside of school hours. Counseling may also involve parent conferences, home visits, or interviews with supervisors, principals, or other teachers. The teacher must be adept at group guidance, too. Almost every day he must assist the entire class, a committee group, or some other group in making choices and decisions.

In some schools teachers devote a number of periods a week to counseling. Some schools provide special help for teachers in the performance of this function—deans, social caseworkers, school psychologists, testing departments, and others.

Regardless of the organizational plan, however, most guidance is directed by the classroom teacher. It is the teacher who must work with the specialist in helping a pupil make an adjustment. It is the teacher who must utilize what the specialists supply to help guide and counsel a pupil. It is the teacher who does most of the investigating, testing, interviewing, follow-up, and record-making that are involved. But the satisfactions that accrue to the teacher as a result of success in pupil guidance are commensurate with the effort involved.

Teaching and guidance are inseparable functions. When the teacher directs a pupil in developing a chemistry project for a contest, he instructs the pupil in the necessary chemistry and guides him in making a mature approach to a competitive situation, in independently completing self-assigned work, and in developing good study habits. The distinction between instruction and guidance cannot be a sharp one. When a teacher reprimands a pupil for discourteous behavior, is he directing classroom instruction or engaging in guidance? Much guidance is incidental. No guidance is unimportant.

3. Staff functions

The classroom teachers, collectively, are responsible for the greatest part of the administration of a school. The classroom is the administrative unit in the school, and the teacher is primarily responsible for the administration of its affairs. But classrooms are not isolated independent units of school administration. The school is the larger unit, an organization with a principal who is responsible for achieving a reasonable measure of coordination of the staff members' efforts. Teachers are organized into a system to work as a unit and to plan together.

As a member of an organized staff the teacher is obliged to attend faculty, departmental, or grade-level meetings; to work on curriculum committees; and to assist with such school functions as plays, parties,

At the end of a long day, teachers gather in their lounge—not to relax and chat, but to record grades.

and concerts. The teacher must make announcements, issue bulletins, collect fees. In schools that do not have modern data processing equipment, the teacher must still keep attendance records, make monthly enrollment reports, prepare report cards, and record health, behavior, and achievement data. He must make inventories; order, distribute, and collect supplies; and assign lockers. He must supervise play periods and lunchrooms and proctor children in the halls. These are just examples of the kinds of duties added to the teacher's work because his classroom is the unit of administration and he is a member of a staff whose work must be coordinated. Many of the duties are routine and mechanical. All of them are time-consuming.

It is in the area of these auxiliary activities that teachers tend to be most vocal in their complaints. The complaints arise not because the importance of the work is unrecognized but because the duties tend to be numerous and exceedingly time-consuming. Usually they must be made to fit into a rigid schedule. Sometimes the teacher cannot see that certain records are utilized sufficiently to warrant the time they take to make them out. Often meetings are held after school hours and seem unduly prolonged to a tired teacher. At times responsibilities such as lunchroom supervision and hall proctoring seem to be unfairly distributed.

Parents or mature students are sometimes used to assist the teacher with such duties. Lay readers, paraprofessionals, and student teachers often relieve the teacher of some paper work, recording, collecting fees, setting up teaching aids, etc. Teachers have more time for classroom instruction and guidance functions when the load of other duties is lightened.

4. Community duties

The typical elementary or secondary school in the United States is a community institution, whose teachers are valued members of the community. The responsibility for the education of the pupils is shared by the school with the community. The community largely controls the school. It decides who is to be educated. By controlling the purse strings it determines, for instance, whether there will be summer schools, nursery schools, and classes for various atypical children. The community influences what the schools can attempt to do. For instance, if community mores are opposed to social dancing, the school cannot offer instruction in it. The people connected with the school can, of course, by exerting influence on the Parent-Teacher Association and other community groups, work to change community attitudes.

As we have said before, all the classifications of duties overlap. Perhaps producing the concert is the music teacher's job because he is a faculty member—but perhaps it falls on his shoulders because he is a member of a community of interested lay people. Certain teaching duties, such as participating in the Parent-Teacher Association, seem to be related to the teacher's community membership. In many communities the teacher is expected to have a church affiliation. He might very well have many of the community relationships regardless of his teaching connection. The point is that, as a teacher, he is *expected* to have them, to be a community participant. His free choice is somewhat curtailed.

Besides the responsibility for contributing to the community, the teacher usually has the opportunity and privilege of using various community resources. Individuals with unique skills, special talents, or interesting backgrounds of experience can, at appropriate times, be enlisted to supplement the regular work of the classroom or to contribute to some professional activity, perhaps curriculum planning. Museums, historical societies, courts, and industrial organizations are examples of another kind of community resource that can also be used. Teachers feel free to use suitable and available human and material community resources because they, as well as their schools, are a part of the community.

5. Professional activities

Certain other tasks fall to teachers because they are affiliated with various local, regional, state, and national professional organizations— organizations dedicated to promoting good education and to advancing teacher welfare. A teacher may add markedly to his work load by sharing in the preparation of a study of salaries and a faculty salary schedule for the local board of education; by participating in the development of a state convention program for English teachers; by writing an article for a professional journal describing his success in the classroom with some novel approach or device; or by serving as a discussion member on a program for a local professional organization. This kind of work is usually assumed voluntarily by the teacher, and the extent of an individual's time and energy invested varies with his interest, zeal, and ability. Even those who take no responsibility for leadership devote considerable time to attending meetings and reading professional publications. All teachers are interested in aspects of their own welfare related to teaching load, retirement, pensions, salaries, certification, and tenure.

As a rule, teachers also are expected to advance professionally by participating in various kinds of workshops or by pursuing college study, either after school hours during the year or during the summer vacation period. A master's degree is not a terminal point. In some places advancement on a salary scale depends on the accumulation of specified hours of additional college credit.

Allocation of time

To a teacher each school day is a challenge, not only because of the constancy of important and varied activity, but also because of the element referred to earlier as the unobservable, but nevertheless real, qualitative factor. A teacher must learn many things about each pupil and, in terms of these, formulate daily aims, select subject matter, decide on procedures to follow, and choose appropriate teaching aids. One who teaches effectively with a free and easy grace has expended considerable time and energy in achieving the background that makes his performance possible.

No two days' work are precisely the same for any teacher, nor is a day's work for each of two teachers ever identical. This is evident from the descriptions on pages 33–36 of the work of six different teachers. Certain broad classifications of duties are, however, common to most teachers.

That teachers have a short working day is a myth. Teachers are required to be at school before the pupils arrive and must remain for stated periods after the pupils leave. In 1966, the median length of the required school day for teachers was 7 hours and 20 minutes. Most teachers stay longer than the "required" period and many take work home to be completed. The number of hours per week devoted to teaching duties, therefore, averages about 47½ hours. Teachers average about six hours a day with pupils and spend nearly 30 percent as much time in school work beyond the school day as they do during official school hours.

Figs. 2.1 and 2.2 show how, on the average, elementary and high school teachers divide the school week. Such practices as lengthening the school day, requiring additional study by teachers for promotional credit, enlarging class size, increasing pupils' home study, and expecting teachers to share more in formulating administrative policies that closely concern them have inevitably added to the teacher's work day; this is true in spite of attempts to alleviate the situation by providing such help as expert supervision, paraprofessional aides, lay readers, special classes for slow learners, and opportunity rooms for the handicapped. There is little evidence to indicate that the teacher's working day will be lighter in the future. Indeed, recent teacher strikes reflect a growing concern among teachers about teacher loads.

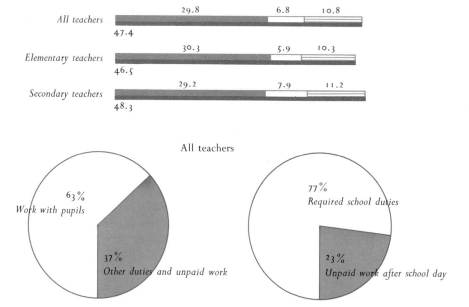

Fig. 2.1 How the teacher divides the week; average hours shown in three different ways. (Data from NEA Research Monograph 1967-R4)

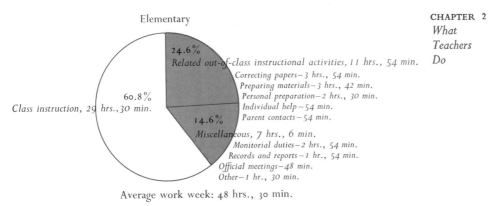

Elementary

24.6%
Related out-of-class instructional activities, 11 hrs., 54 min.
Correcting papers—3 hrs., 54 min.
Preparing materials—3 hrs., 42 min.
Personal preparation—2 hrs., 30 min.
Individual help—54 min.
Parent contacts—54 min.

60.8%
Class instruction, 29 hrs., 30 min.

14.6%
Miscellaneous, 7 hrs., 6 min.
Monitorial duties—2 hrs., 54 min.
Records and reports—1 hr., 54 min.
Official meetings—48 min.
Other—1 hr., 30 min.

Average work week: 48 hrs., 30 min.

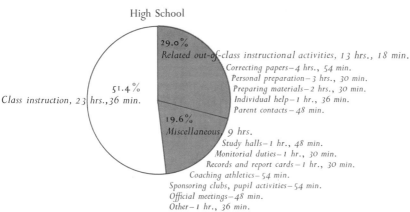

High School

29.0%
Related out-of-class instructional activities, 13 hrs., 18 min.
Correcting papers—4 hrs., 54 min.
Personal preparation—3 hrs., 30 min.
Preparing materials—2 hrs., 30 min.
Individual help—1 hr., 36 min.
Parent contacts—48 min.

51.4%
Class instruction, 23 hrs., 36 min.

19.6%
Miscellaneous, 9 hrs.
Study halls—1 hr., 48 min.
Monitorial duties—1 hr., 30 min.
Records and report cards—1 hr., 30 min.
Coaching athletics—54 min.
Sponsoring clubs, pupil activities—54 min.
Official meetings—48 min.
Other—1 hr., 36 min.

Average work week: 45 hrs., 54 min.

Fig. 2.2 How the elementary school teacher and the high school teacher divide the week—a detailed breakdown. (Data from NEA Research Monograph 1963-M2)

Study of teachers' work

There are two approaches to a study of the work of teachers. The first is an intensive study of the work of one teacher or of a few teachers. This approach has certain advantages. It enables one to study the work of a highly skilled teacher who works at a given level of education, who teaches a special subject, or who works in a particular kind of environmental setting. The second approach is an extensive study of the work of a large sampling of teachers teaching at several levels of

The classroom is where the teacher is. These high school pupils are studying American history from an urban-oriented viewpoint. An incidental but important benefit: since these students are enrolled on a city-wide basis, such a class provides valuable opportunities for social group interaction.

education and in many kinds of situations. This approach also has certain advantages. It gives breadth to the findings, reveals the possible range of duties, and gives, perhaps, a more accurate picture of the kinds of duties performed by teachers. A more realistic and complete account of what teachers do results from a combination of both methods of study. Therefore, we shall first note the results of studying the work of individual teachers and then follow with the more extensive findings of a wider sampling.

STUDYING INDIVIDUALS

Two procedures may be followed in studying the work performed by a selected individual or individuals: directly observing what they do, and obtaining from the teachers themselves verbal descriptions of what they have done over a definite period of time. The two procedures lead to slightly different conclusions. Both methods contribute useful information.

1. Direct observation

By observing a teacher at work for several successive days, one may secure a more vivid and realistic picture of what he does than by any other method. This is especially true if many of his activities are observed.

It is important to realize that this method has its limitations. In learning about the work done by one teacher, we may not directly observe all that he does, such as preparing for the day's teaching, counseling with pupils or parents, or reading the written assignments handed in by pupils. Also the value of the observation is related to the maturity, the insights, and the understandings of the observer. What an experienced teacher concludes from an observation tends to be quite different from what a novice or a layman concludes.

Still, this method is especially helpful to the beginning student, for thus he can learn what and how to observe. He learns to discriminate, to get a feeling for what the teacher's job is in a particular subject, at a given level of teaching, or in a single aspect of his work.

2. Verbal description

Some of the shortcomings of direct observation are overcome by having teachers describe their work in simple, direct statements. This method has certain advantages. A teacher can accurately describe his own work and he is more likely to select what is most important in his job. A description of the work of individual teachers tends also to emphasize the many differences in the work that various teachers do. Descriptions also are valuable in revealing some of the subtle, more qualitative aspects of the teacher's work. The following examples illustrate some of the features of teaching.

A first-grade teacher says:

> There are 38 children in my room. It would take 38 pages of type-written material to describe the work I do. [A lengthy, although condensed, description of classroom work then follows, closing with this statement.]
> Now a few words about the "extras." I attend faculty meetings,

committee meetings, meetings of the Parent-Teacher Association, district meetings and, well, just meetings. These are always held during school time.

I operate the movie projector, the slide projector, and the hectograph machine. I prepare the seat work by hand and run it off on the hectograph, and sometimes I make drawings from typewritten material which I prepare. I keep records of daily attendance, daily work, test grades, and monies collected. I prepare monthly summary sheets of attendance, monthly supply orders, lists of supplies to be put away, and book inventories. I fill out health records, quarterly report cards, cumulative records, and other office records required at the end of the semester and, occasionally, make special reports. I also prepare plan books for the work of each day.

A third-grade teacher writes:

No two days of work are ever alike. I view my job as that of working with children—all kinds of children—striving to help them make worthwhile progress each day. In order to do this I try to understand each child and try to find ways of helping him adjust to me and to his many classmates. I try also to know all of the parents, to find out how they live and what their interests are. Yes, I even enjoy talking to Mrs. Hill, who insists that her son has a right to break other children's crayons whenever his heart desires. It is only by being able to talk to her that I have hopes of showing her what our common problems are. Teaching is such a natural, easy way of living, in spite of the many things there are to teach and do, like making impromptu talks to parents, selling taffy apples, growing a community garden, and learning about the insects that are garden pests. . . .

A junior high school teacher says:

My functions are to teach music to four classes on the sixth-, seventh-, and eighth-grade levels. Each of these music classes meets twice a week, eight periods of music in all. The remainder of the teaching week is spent with my homeroom, the eighth grade. I teach the following subjects in my homeroom: arithmetic, social studies, reading, composition and related language arts, and health. The school day begins at 8:30 and runs until 3:15. Sometimes it merely creeps. The genuine teaching duties are stimulating and highly rewarding, for the most part. The numerous nonteaching duties and clerical duties definitely take the edge off the pleasure of being a teacher. . . .

A physical education teacher describes her work:

> I teach physical education to boys and girls, 8 to 14 years of age.
> I teach 35 class periods a week, 28 of which are devoted to regular
> physical education activities, four to co-recreational programs for the
> seventh- and eighth-grade pupils, one to a gymnastics class, one to the
> school safety patrol which I sponsor, and one to keeping my records
> and equipment in good order. In addition I assist with the annual paper
> drive, present an assembly program once a year, direct the color guard,
> take charge of the boys' entrance, and serve as a member of the audio-
> visual aids committee, as cochairman of the community resources com-
> mittee, as chairman of the standards of achievement committee, and
> as instructor at our school's after-school social center. I also serve as
> recording secretary and member of the executive board of the teachers'
> union. My listing of duties might leave the impression that teachers do
> quite a bit. They do!

Another teacher writes:

> I am a teacher of industrial arts in an industrial arts department in a
> high school of 2,600 pupils. I teach two classes of industrial arts pupils.
> The shop is general shop, each experience extending over six weeks.
> The two classes alternate experiences. I also teach two classes of sopho-
> more printing of 22 pupils each. There are some juniors and seniors in
> these two groups. The pupils are of all kinds of abilities and offer all
> kinds of reasons for being in the class—from an intense interest to
> nothing-else-to-take. I also have an advanced vocational class which does
> much of the production printing of the school. . . .
>
> The linotypes and presses require repair and maintenance that must
> be done by the teacher. The costs of jobs must be figured, charged,
> and recorded. Supplies of paper, ink, and other materials must be re-
> plenished as needed. Telephone calls on the status of the newspaper and
> other jobs frequently interrupt the work of the classes. Club sponsors
> and office personnel come into the shop often. Copy is handed in late,
> and finished jobs are expected overnight.
>
> I like printing and I like teaching. There are no boring moments.
> . . . Each week I take home some work—papers to be corrected, orders
> to write, costs to be figured, jobs and projects to be planned. Each week
> I return to the school for an average of three hours to keep abreast of
> the work at the school shop that cannot be done during the day and,
> of course, cannot be taken home.
>
> Before entering college I worked at the printing trade and I still do

during the summer months. I keep in touch with the trade, earn additional income, and have the assurance that I can tell the principal "good-by" tonight and go out tomorrow and take my pick of 10 jobs which pay more than teaching and require less work. But, then, I wouldn't be helping young people! I'd just be helping myself!

A team teacher writes:

As a member of a seventh-grade teaching team charged with fulfilling curriculum requirements in social studies, language arts, and mathematics on an interdisciplinary basis, my teaching week includes a significant allocation of time for team planning. Even so, I meet with the group regularly and frequently during the lunch period, carrying a tray to a vacant classroom. Every week I share in drawing up a weekly schedule in terms of activities planned for each of the fields. Some weeks I am responsible for presenting a large group lesson related to the social studies curriculum. This involves a 30-minute presentation four times to groups of 60 or 90 children. Before the lesson I prepare appropriate transparencies for use on the overhead projector, locate and have on hand maps, film strips, or other visual aids, and prepare follow-up textbook, study, and enrichment material to be used when I, and others on the team, meet with boys and girls in smaller groups. I also decide on such related language arts activities as paragraph writing, outlining, and reading biographies or poetry.

Inasmuch as team teaching seems to mean something different wherever it is used, I have had to make certain decisions in terms of trial and error and to spend time individually and in group meetings evaluating procedures and materials. In addition to large group presentations, at certain times I work with small groups in subject-matter areas and also for group guidance and enrichment activities. Of course, I have the regular responsibilities for attendance, collecting fees, etc. I have individual pupil conferences, team-teacher group conferences with pupils, and team-teacher group conferences with nonteam teachers who teach seventh-graders in nonteam areas like foreign language or science. I share in regular parent conferences where the parent meets with the child and the three teachers who have the main responsibility for the child's instruction in language arts, social studies, and mathematics. In addition, I hold other parent conferences as they are requested by the parent or as I decide they would be helpful. From my experience I conclude that a team teacher's day is a full one, and that all of the team teacher's work cannot be done in the "required" hours of the school day.

Personal description of a teacher's duties shows that the work of an individual teacher is unique. Instead of emphasizing similarities in the work of teachers, such descriptions tend to bring out the differences. Even when the same activitiy is reported, the approach, the time invested, and the manner of performing it tend to vary. One teacher, as a result of his interests, may emphasize some activities far more than others. The teacher's philosophy, interests, and abilities are related to the proportion of time invested in any activity. Usually the more favored activities are more efficiently performed.

A carefully written and fairly complete description of the work of a single teacher sets forth what the teacher believes important to report, not what the investigator thinks is important to observe. It gives a reasonably accurate picture of each teacher's work, but does not afford as definite a summation of duties as some of the other methods of study.

STUDYING LARGE SAMPLINGS BY THE METHOD OF VOCATIONAL ANALYSIS

This method has been borrowed from industry and the armed services where it has been used as a sort of measuring stick to select individuals who, in terms of personality and training, have the greatest promise of success with certain kinds of work.

In general, the method consists of three steps:(1) the duties involved in a particular vocation are itemized; (2) the relative difficulty of performing each of the duties is determined; and (3) the knowledge, skills, and habits necessary to a successful pursuit of the vocation are then determined. Appropriate instructional materials can then be prepared to teach an individual to meet successfully the demands of the job. Each of the steps calls for considerable interpretative skill. The method has proved very valuable for providing information about all the vocations—information that has been especially useful to those who formulate training programs.

The method should be used, however, with full recognition of its limitations. One shortcoming can be illustrated from the findings of one vocational analysis project. This project analyzed reports from over 6,000 classroom teachers who enumerated what they did while on their jobs. The activities reported numbered around 200,000!

Those activities considered to be most significant were selected for more intensive study. They still numbered 1,001 items. They could not be further reduced and still give a realistic picture of the work of teachers. The list of duties is so extensive that it is of little value in providing a typical picture.

Although largely inappropriate for studying the work of any given teacher, the vocational analysis method has revealed certain general features of the work of teachers as a group. It has shown that the range of activities teachers engage in is enormous and that many of these activities are difficult and time-consuming. It has made clear why teachers, if they desire to become expertly proficient, must continue to study throughout their professional careers. Competence is not quickly developed. There is a continuously mounting hierarchy among the skills to be acquired. One competence becomes the foundation for building another, higher level of competence. Skills, however, are not accumulated as one fits bricks into a rising wall.

Incidentally, educators have applied the vocational analysis method to the activities in which adults generally engage. These activities have then been classified and the results made the basis for planning the school curriculum. In Unit IV, in the study of aims, this approach is examined in more detail.

In enlarging the sampling, the various investigators have not found it practicable to make a complete vocational analysis. The various studies have used certain specialized techniques, each of which gives an incomplete but nevertheless helpful picture of the teacher's work. The more common techniques include the questionnaire, direct observation, verbal description, and time analysis.

1. The questionnaire

The questionnaire is a device frequently used in the analysis of teaching. Many carefully selected and skillfully phrased questions are directed to the teacher. Each question can be answered simply, sometimes with a single word like *yes* or *no* or a number. The questions are prepared in advance by the investigator and cover those aspects of the teacher's work that the investigator selects for study.

Questionnaire studies are convenient to tabulate, record, and summarize. The questionnaire is especially appropriate in determining what practices are current. Because of this, studies of teacher activities based on questionnaires are often called *status* studies. They have been helpful in revealing what activities give most difficulty, recur most often, and seem to persist over long periods of time. They are well adapted to showing what problems are peculiar to teaching a given subject or to teaching at a given grade level. The English teacher, the shop teacher, the kindergarten teacher, the eighth-grade teacher— each encounters a range of varying problems. Even when the problems are approximately the same at different educational levels, dealing with each of them involves a different kind of teacher activity.

Questionnaires, like each of the other techniques, have certain weaknesses of which one must be aware when interpreting the information they provide. For example, if a teacher has a behavior problem in his classroom he cannot by a simple answer tell how he solved it. He may report how many behavior problems he has had, but his answer gives no indication of how serious each of them has been or how much time and energy he has given to the solution of each. If an English teacher makes a vivid presentation of a beautiful poem and gives it a striking interpretation, he cannot report on a questionnaire precisely what he did. Nor can he accurately report all the time he spent in preparation. The findings of a good questionnaire are revealing, but the picture provided is never complete.

2. Direct observation

Direct observation may be applied to a group of teachers in much the same way that it is applied to an individual teacher. In this case an observer may extend the number of direct observations, or a team of observers may observe teachers working at different levels and in varying situations. Direct observation of the group has the same limitations as direct observation of the individual. As a method of mass study it suffers further because it is exceedingly time-consuming.

3. Verbal description

The method of obtaining individual descriptions can be expanded to include any number of teachers teaching at any level of education or teaching any given subject. It is somewhat difficult to summarize verbal descriptions, and the interpretation of the results presents a special problem. The sampling, however, may be as wide as the investigator wishes to make it.

4. Time analysis

The time analysis of activities may be used as an extension of the questionnaire, direct observation, or the analysis of individual descriptions. The time given to the performance of a certain activity is recorded. As an observer notes what activity a teacher engages in, for instance, he also uses a stop watch and makes a record of the exact time spent on the activity. Or teachers may report on questionnaires their estimates of time they devote to the various activities they perform.

The qualitative element

Each of the techniques of discovering and reporting what a teacher does gives a picture of the work from a somewhat different perspective. In all the information gathered, however, one important element of the teacher's work, perhaps the most important feature, is more or less omitted—is almost simplified out of existence. This is the qualitative factor mentioned earlier. It is the one element that is, in large part, responsible for the great differences in what teachers do. Two teachers covering the same subject may make identical assignments, but the two assignments are not qualitatively the same and may have differing effects on how the pupils feel and what they learn. The same is true of giving tests, assigning marks, or any other activity.

Through observation we may sense this qualitative characteristic, or teachers' descriptions may reveal its presence; but no statistical tabulation, classification, or report can completely capture it. In making conclusions about what teachers do, using all the sources of information, we must recognize the importance of this factor and avoid oversimplification.

Qualitative differences stem from many factors, some of which do not lend themselves to ready analysis. The freedom that teachers in American schools have to use their own judgment about what shall

*F*rom *earliest times to the present, great thinkers have directed their thinking toward the education of children. In 1416, a renowned discoverer of ancient learning, Poggio, found the complete text of Quintilian's* On the Training of an Orator *in a dump heap in one of the abbey towers at a Swiss monastery. This great work, written in the first century* A.D., *was in form a manual on the training of a public speaker, but it was actually the outline of a liberal education. It came to be viewed as summarizing all the pedagogical wisdom of the ancients. The following quotation from Quintilian shows the trend of his thinking about the successful qualities of the good teacher.*

> *Let him therefore adopt a parental attitude to his pupils, and regard himself as the representative of those who have committed their children to his charge. Let him be free from vice himself and refuse to tolerate it in others. Let him be strict but not austere, genial but not too familiar : for austerity will make him unpopular, while familiarity breeds contempt. Let his discourse continually turn on what is good and honorable ; the more he admonishes, the less he will have to punish. He must control his temper without however shutting his eyes to faults requiring correction : his instruction must be free from affectation, his industry great, his demands on his class continuous but not extravagant.*

Reprinted by permission of the publishers from Marcus Fabius Quintilianus, *The Institutio Oratoria of Quintilian*, with English translation by H. E. Butler. Cambridge, Mass.: Harvard University Press, Loeb Classical Library edition, 1921, Vol. I, Book II, ii, paragraph 5, p. 213.

be taught, how it shall be taught, and how the classroom should be managed is but one example. Teachers differ greatly in personality and in the kind of personal and professional philosophy that guides their teaching. They differ in social background, in education, and in many other ways. They teach in vastly different situations. All such factors contribute to the encouragement of the qualitative differences so characteristic of teaching. As we discuss such topics as the philosophy and aims of the teacher, subject matter, methods, and other aspects of teaching, we shall become increasingly conscious of the causes and effects of the ever-present qualitative differences that are characteristic of teachers' work.

The teacher's role involves many interrelationships, and energy and enthusiasm are essential in all of them. The teacher tutoring a small group radiates vigor and interest in her pupils. The teacher greeting a pupil and his mother shows warmth and friendliness—a good start toward a mutually profitable association.

Summary

What knowledge of the work of the teacher has Chapter 2 revealed? In commencing our overview of education in the United States, what details about what school teachers do can we now fill in?

In seeking to discover what teachers do, studies that use the method of vocational analysis are one source of information. We get a picture with a different perspective by turning to a teacher's own description of what he does. Another readily available source of fruitful information is direct observation, which allows us to capture some of the "feel" of the teaching, to get an appreciation of the essence of the pupil-teacher relationship and other classroom relationships that elude tabulation and reporting, and to focus our study on a single teacher or particular factor.

From the many studies made we discover that the work of the teacher is highly complex and that his duties cover a great range. For convenience, we group teacher activities into five classifications: (1) classroom instruction, (2) guidance, (3) staff functions, (4) community duties, and (5) professional activities. Such classifications are neither definite nor rigid in their boundaries. They are made in order to facilitate our thinking and to simplify our understanding.

It is evident that in reporting what teachers do it has not been possible to include the qualitative differences that mark the activities of any two or more teachers. This elusive and intangible element is present in all features of the entire school picture. It is influenced most dramatically by the teacher's philosophy, personality, training, and experience as manifest in his values, beliefs, and ideals. Because this factor is elusive and because, perhaps, the current tendency in many subject-matter fields is to stress quantification, many studies that bear on education have omitted this subjective element entirely.

In conclusion, then, we recognize that teaching is a collective name for many kinds of work and that it involves many kinds of activities. Describing the work that teachers do is somewhat analogous to analyzing the constituents of a bowl of soup. The soup is a mixture of a large number of ingredients. Not only are the ingredients separate; they are also heterogeneous in character. Each ingredient changes its original characteristic when it becomes part of the final dish. The ingredients that go to make up teaching are numerous, and, like the ingredients in the soup, they are heterogeneous in character. The work of the teacher, then, does not lend itself to a simple description of the kind that would suffice in telling how a cook bakes a cake or how a machinist uses a lathe.

This study of what teachers do in American schools can be no more than preliminary—preliminary to further study, to a more detailed analysis, and to a broadening of interpretation that will continue throughout the book. (In Unit IV, "Aims and Methods in America," teacher responsibilities are explored from another angle.)

Questions

1. What are some reasons why the work of one teacher is never exactly like the work of another?

2. How do your own experiences in school contribute to or limit your better understanding of the work of a classroom teacher? In what respects are your experiences probably atypical?
3. In describing a teacher's work, how can one give due recognition to the factor of excellence of performance?
4. What attitude should a beginning teacher assume toward the performance of routine duties?
5. What are some purposes served by classifying all that teachers do into broad categories? What undesirable effects may also result?
6. In the school, what are the functions of such specialists as the supervisor, guidance director, and school psychologist? How is the teacher's work affected by specialists in the school?
7. What has caused recent tendencies to increase the work load of classroom teachers?

Projects

1. Interview a classroom teacher concerning the kind and amount of work he has done over a period of one week.
2. Observe a teacher teaching a single class and describe the kind of preparation you think he made before teaching the class.
3. Write an essay of not more than 500 words explaining why most teachers find teaching school an interesting and challenging occupation.
4. Write a letter to some highly successful teacher asking him to explain to you and the class the aspects of teaching he finds most challenging and the aspects he finds least challenging. Ask what advice he would like to give to one seriously considering entering the teaching profession.

The association has not concerned itself with standards for elementary education; these standards have remained completely under state control. Since the North Central Association and similar regional associations include colleges and secondary schools only, their accreditation practices have tended to add to the prestige of high school teachers and thus, to some extent, to lower the prestige of elementary teachers. In general, however, the effect of accrediting associations of this kind has been salutary. They have not attempted to infringe on the states' rights to set standards. They have sought only to raise the standards of education given in public and nonpublic schools.

In 1949, the presidents of a number of colleges and universities became concerned about the growing number of accrediting agencies for higher institutions and they established the National Commission on Accrediting. In the words of the executive secretary, "the commission is serving as a coordinating agency through the labyrinth of accreditation; it is continually making suggestions for improvement in this frequently misunderstood educational activity. . . ." In 1968, the members of the commission included more than 1,200 colleges and universities located in many sections of the United States and seven national organizations, such as the Association of American Universities. Serving as a coordinating agent, the commission recognizes six regional associations and 23 professional associations.

Among the professional associations recognized is the influential National Council for Accreditation of Teacher Education (usually called the NCATE), which was established by the NEA in 1952. In 1967, 28 states had reciprocity accreditation through the NCATE. Currently, more than 450 of America's foremost teacher education institutions, the prime source of the new supply of teachers each year, are members. In 1956, the National Commission on Accrediting officially recognized the NCATE as most directly responsible for determining the accreditation procedures for teacher education programs. The plan is to have this association evaluate and accredit each qualified teacher education program. The states would then automatically license all graduates who successfully complete an accredited program.

All the problems of accreditation have not been solved, nor can a complete analysis of the issues be made here. For example, why is a plan of accreditation that is successful for secondary schools not logically extended to the elementary schools? Efforts are being made on a broad scale to discover proper ways to guarantee academic standards, to encourage, even coerce, institutions to maintain certain minimum standards in the education of teachers, and to coordinate and approve the activities of the many voluntary agencies involved in accreditation of teacher education programs.

Teacher preparation

For years all the states have attempted to improve the quality of education by improving the programs of teacher training, by assuming the authority for accrediting teacher education institutions, and by imposing more demanding certificate requirements. A college degree has, in most states, become a requirement for entrance to teaching. Furthermore, degree candidates must take specific courses deemed essential for teacher preparation.

Since 1952, the degrees in education awarded by American colleges have far exceeded in number the degrees conferred in other areas of concentration. One might conclude from this that there is a surplus of teachers. That is not true, however, partly because of the rapid attrition during the early years.

Although there is some difference of opinion concerning the details of a desirable program of teacher education, there is general agreement that it should be at least four years in length and, ideally, that it should be a five-year program. There is also general agreement that the program should be *balanced*—made up of three broad classifications of subject matter: (1) background education—the broad cultural

Many facilities are needed for the education of teachers, and most of the state universities have schools of education that are adequately housed, staffed, and equipped. The Wham Education Building at Southern Illinois University contains classrooms, offices, laboratories, and an auditorium.

setting, (2) specialized subject matter, and (3) courses in professional education.

BACKGROUND EDUCATION

There is no disagreement about the fact that a prospective teacher should pursue a program designed to give him a broad cultural background—contribute to making him a "cultured person." There are, however, different schools of thought as to how best this may be achieved.

Until about 1940, the teacher-in-preparation typically pursued traditional courses in subject-matter fields and planned his study around required majors and minors. Since then, early specialization has become progressively more generally required. More recently, the necessity for mastering skills of quantification has been extended beyond fields like mathematics, chemistry, and physics to such areas as economics, geography, and biology. Emphasis on study in depth in an area necessarily limits the possibilities for study in breadth. For instance, it may be assumed now by a college that courses in chemistry, physics, calculus, and statistics are prerequisites to a first course in biology, to provide a necessary background for a biologist. Are such requirements, however, necessary for a good biology teacher who must also have that first course in biology? Will requirements of this kind actually operate as selective factors and limit the number of students who study to prepare for teaching in certain important subject-matter areas? At present, colleges and universities are educating more teachers than are needed in some fields and a scant few in others. It seems that refined specialization and emphasis on quantification skills have a relationship to the imbalance in teacher supply as well as to difficulties in providing the desired broad cultural background for teachers.

Most colleges recognize the weaknesses of the traditional approach and are attempting through different kinds of courses to provide students with a broad cultural background. It is agreed that the enlightenment and refinement of taste acquired through formal intellectual and esthetic training can be cultivated in more than a single pattern of education. The experimental, new courses are based on the belief that the desired cultural background can be achieved through courses that are general rather than specialized. For instance, often a course is offered that encompasses subject matter from a group of closely related fields. The professors from these related fields combine their talents in a kind of team teaching, utilizing the resources of their individual departments—visual aids, laboratories, and the like. "An Introduction to the Behavioral Sciences," "Modern Society," "Basic Science," "The Use of English" are examples of courses offered where the broader approach is followed. In some colleges this kind of course is given for all beginning students, except for those who specialize immediately. A student is expected to achieve an understanding of the basic concepts common to all the subject-matter fields included.

It is not possible to evaluate accurately the success of colleges in providing the broad cultural background necessary for the prospective teacher. Obviously, however, regardless of the approach, the teacher-to-be will profit most when he is taught by highly skilled teachers in all his college-level courses. Furthermore, as the student plans his program with an adviser, he, too, may influence the quality of his own learning situation. Most colleges allow the student considerable leeway in choice in this background education.

SPECIALIZED SUBJECT MATTER

For prospective high school teachers, specialization in a particular field is obligatory. The state usually requires from 24 to 36 semester hours of work in a given subject or field for certification. This amounts to from three to four years of continuous study. Leaders concerned with improving present high school programs urge states to require that teachers prepare themselves in broad fields corresponding to the major areas taught in secondary schools. Some colleges have responded to such requests. Some of them, for instance, permit students to complete majors in areas like general science and social studies. These subjects harmonize with the classifications of subject matter found in secondary and elementary schools. Some offer courses like "Mathematics for the Intermediate Teacher" or "Basic Mathematics," "Physics for Teachers," "Chemistry for Teachers," and the like. They are taught by specialists, but not for the purpose of preparing specialists. Often the subject matter is designed to complete the education received by the teacher-in-training, to fill in gaps. The aim of the courses is strictly vocational but not for the preparation of professional mathematicians, physicists, chemists, or biologists. Such courses may carry graduate credit in a graduate school for those who are in the teaching profession but not for specialists following other programs in the graduate school. Vocational need is one criterion for the selection of the subject matter taught.

Deciding on the best type of specialized preparation for elementary teachers presents special difficulties to the colleges. School officials frequently expect an elementary teacher to be prepared in every basic and special field of the elementary curriculum, besides being competent in the areas of child growth and development and human relations. Some state authorities have made the elementary school certification requirements so specific that the curriculum of the colleges has been practically dictated by a state educational authority.

Whatever the final answer to the question of required specialized training, there is wide agreement that the fields included in the teacher education program should be carefully selected for the purpose of improving potential teaching competence. In other words, although the specialized content of the teacher education program should be balanced in relation to the broad cultural courses and the professional courses, it should also be designed to give the teacher professional competence in those special fields of study in which he intends to teach.

PROFESSIONAL PREPARATION

While the academic education of a teacher, including general and specialized courses, is basic, it is not the whole of his essential preparation. Much of the professional knowledge and skill that is necessary for starting to teach must be acquired in professional courses given in college. These courses are, in many states, specified in state regulations; thus some uniformity in this portion of the prospective teacher's program is assured. However, there is much difference of opinion about what part of the total time of training should be devoted to professional education and whether courses should begin with the freshman year or at some later stage in the program. Professional courses are sometimes considered to be so theoretical as to make them more suitable for graduate than undergraduate study.

The Commission on Teacher Education recommends that "strictly professional elements should be allocated from one-eighth to one-sixth of the time available in a four- or five-year program of teacher preparation." Most colleges accept this division of time. Usually out of the total of 120 semester hours of college work required for graduation, from 15 to 20 semester hours of professional courses, including special methods and student teaching, are required for high school teachers and from 20 to 30 hours for elementary school teachers. Colleges differ, however, in their specific requirements and in the nature of the content and organization of professional courses.

In the area of teacher preparation perhaps the greatest agreement is in the matter of practical experience. It is uniformly agreed that the individual and class assignments of a prospective teacher should include observation in classrooms, that the prospective teacher should participate in a wealth of activities with children in both school and community situations, and that he should engage in actual student teaching. It is only through supervised full-time work with pupils over a period of time that a student gains a "feel" for the teacher's task and can assess his own potentialities in relation to the task. Despite agreement that teaching should be included in a prospective teacher's program, there is no general agreement on how much time students should spend teaching, in which fields they should teach, and when they should begin teaching. (Usually, however, student teaching starts during the senior year.)

Sometimes, usually during a fifth year of preparation and as a part of graduate study, a program of teaching internship is offered. This is teaching, full- or part-time, in a regular public school classroom with the approval and under the close supervision of the teacher education institution. The program provides an opportunity to combine theoretical with practical work while completing requirements for a master's degree. Some feel, however, that a beginning teacher who has complete teaching responsibility for a group of children needs to give all his time to teaching during his initial years and that the effort to combine teaching with graduate study and seminar attendance works to the disadvantage of both the practical and theoretical phases of an internship plan. Whether an internship plan is a part of the teacher program or not, the trend is toward planning the total teacher preparation program in terms of five years' work.

Selection of prospective teachers

The current shortage of teachers is much more serious in some areas than in others; nevertheless, it means that a consideration of selection is somewhat theoretical. One cannot make choices when the number of suitable candidates is too limited. In the long run, the number of capable people who will be attracted to teaching will increase only if teaching standards are high enough to win respect and if the prestige, security, and financial rewards are attractive to qualified people.

Unfortunately, research has provided neither the measures for making predictions of success nor a scientific basis for deciding how selections should be made. We cannot, for instance, with accuracy define what successful teaching is, or specifically identify the personality traits that are the attributes of the successful teacher. Our selection must therefore be largely subjective and must be based on such sources of information as interviews, letters of recommendation, standard tests, physical examinations, marks in college courses, and the like. Even with data concerning scholastic achievement, special aptitudes, attitude toward teaching, and experience with youth groups, we still cannot, with assurance, predict in advance what teaching ability an individual possesses. Subjective judgments are liable to considerable error. This does not mean, however, that we cannot recognize that some factors are more favorable to producing teaching success than others.

Perhaps the most important qualifying factor in determining success is the individual's interest in teaching. Unfortunately, it cannot be measured. A student who has an interest in teaching, ideally founded on some kind of firsthand experience in working with children and youth, will be motivated to plan wisely with his advisers in selecting the most fruitful teacher education program. He will be alert to the opportunities to develop necessary basic abilities appropriate to the field of his choice. If his institution does not offer the necessary opportunities, he will discover them in some other institution.

The selection of students to pursue the teaching profession is a process that continues during the entire period of preparation. It is not one act completed when the student is admitted to college. Continuous study *by* the student is accompanied with continuous study *of* the student so that a redirection of the student's program can be made at any time when warranted. The student's welfare is kept in mind but so also is the welfare of all those whom he may teach. Counseling by the professional staff is an important aspect of selection. An attempt is made to aid the student in matching his potentialities with his choice of teaching field and to eliminate only those who obviously possess disabling qualifications such as, for instance, emotional instability or low ability to succeed in academic work. In selection, the college staff emphasizes positive factors related to the growth and education of the student rather than the negative factor of denial of the right to continue.

Although all higher institutions have admissions officers, the process of making a reasonable selection of potential teachers is a responsibility of the staffs that actually prepare them. In this way the professors themselves influence the standards applied to the selection of those who will qualify for and enter teaching.

Placement of teachers

After completing the teacher preparation program and qualifying for certification, the prospective teacher faces the important step of placement. All teacher education institutions counsel their students about placement and recommend them for positions. Most of them maintain placement bureaus. Graduates are assisted in writing letters of application and in making personal applications. It is, however, the superintendent of a local school system, a school trustee, or someone else officially charged by a local school system with the responsibility of employing the staff who makes the final offer.

Commercial teachers' agencies, organizations that make a business of placing teachers and that charge a commission for their services, also may be utilized by the student. If a candidate wishes to teach in a certain school system, it is considered ethical to write a letter of inquiry that includes information about his training, experience, and interests.

Learning to teach must involve actual teaching situations. It must also begin at an early age—and it should never stop. In-service teachers learn by observing the techniques of a skilled teacher. Prospective teachers learn by doing what they will later have their pupils do. Future teachers who are themselves still in high school learn by helping younger children— working with Head Start children and tutoring elementary school pupils. Student teachers learn by teaching under the supervision of experienced teachers. Here a student teaches a chemistry course for the first time. (Student teaching is one of the most valued of college professional courses.) Formal study is essential for a teacher, but equally essential are observing, acting, practicing, performing.

Personal qualifications

PROBLEM OF GENERALIZATION

We have indicated that it is impossible to define in detail the personality characteristics of the successful teacher. One must use terms that are general, that call for considerable subjective interpretation, and that are related more or less to standard virtues about which there can be little disagreement. We can, for instance, agree that a sympathetic personality is desirable. Can we define a sympathetic personality? Can we agree on the specific traits that must always, or generally, be identified with such a personality? Numerous studies of what constitutes first-rate teaching have resulted in a list of virtues expressing more of a hope than an expectation.

The difficulty of defining personal qualifications necessary to teaching success is further compounded because, strictly speaking, teaching is not a single occupation. It is a large family of occupations. Opportunities for specialization in teaching are numerous. Obviously the requirements for a third-grade teacher will not be identical with those for a teacher at the graduate school level, for a teacher-librarian, or for a teacher of physically handicapped children. Even positions that appear, at first, to be the same may make widely varying demands depending on variations in total school responsibilities and the composition of the pupil enrollment.

Minimum personal qualifications required are influenced, too, by the times. In one generation, one set of qualifications is deemed sufficient, while in another, such qualifications are considered inadequate. Radio, television, films, new electronic aids, maps, globes, improved textbooks—all help to change the character of teaching and to modify teacher requirements. New knowledge about such matters as individual differences, special abilities, or the nature of growth changes the nature of teaching, modifies the standards of successful teaching, and influences the personal qualifications needed.

STUDIES

Despite the difficulties, numerous studies have been made in an effort to shed some light on our understanding of what characteristics,

*Applying for a Teaching Post
1871*

"*W*ant to be a school-master, do you? You? Well what would you do in Flat Crick deestrick, I'd like to know? Why, the boys have driv off the last two, and licked the one afore them like blazes. You might teach a summer school, when nothin' but children come. But I 'low it takes a right smart man to be a school-master in Flat Crick in the winter. They'd pitch you out of doors, sonny, neck and heels, afore Christmas.*"
. . . *The impression made by these ominous remarks was emphasized by the glances which he received from Jack Means' two sons. The older one eyed him from the top of his brawny shoulders with that amiable look which a big dog turns on a little one before shaking him. Ralph Hartsook had never thought of being measured by the standard of muscle. This notion of beating education into young savages in spite of themselves dashed his ardor.*

From Edward Eggleston, *The Hoosier Schoolmaster: A Story of Backwoods Life in Indiana*, 1871.

Today

While the policies with respect to employment vary considerably from district to district, the following practices are not uncommon:

1. Most teacher education institutions now help the student to obtain his initial appointment. Many colleges have placement offices that specialize in teacher placement. They collect information about the student, counsel him, and direct him in his attempts to obtain his first teaching position.

2. Some superintendents of schools visit the colleges and personally seek out and employ the student. Many administrators look upon this as their best opportunity to improve the quality of teaching in their school systems.

3. Many school systems print attractive brochures about the schools and the community that are sent to all applicants for teaching positions. The administrative policies of the school system are plainly set forth.
The trend in the employment of teachers is toward the school seeking the teacher, rather than the teacher seeking the school.

in general, seem to be related to teaching success. The studies have been principally of two kinds—those that approach the problem by asking pupils to report the characteristics of the teachers they considered most successful and those that base conclusions on reports from school administrators and professors of school administration.

One early investigator analyzed the opinions of a total of 30,000 pupils.[1] He discovered that those characteristics most persistently cherished by pupils were: fairness, cheerfulness, businesslike procedures when teaching, ability to obtain pupil response, and skillful methods of teaching. Under the classification of fairness, for example, the pupils hoped that praise and criticism would be based on fact, that the teacher would show no favoritism, that grading would be fair, that the opinions of pupils would be respected, and that the teacher would reveal at all times a willingness to help pupils. Pupils did not like teachers who consistently found fault, nagged, scolded, used sarcasm and otherwise reacted negatively to what the pupils were attempting to do. They seemed greatly to appreciate the teacher who had what they thought to be a wholesome sense of humor.

Studies based on reports from school administrators and professors of school administration are legion. In general, the most impressive fact emphasized by the findings is that only a very low correlation between any single personality trait and teaching success can be discovered.

Studies by psychologists have been devoted to the relation of personality traits to success in various lines of endeavor. They have emphasized that a combination of traits is vitally related to performance. However, it is not always possible to state what this combination actually is. Indeed, many different combinations may be equally successful. A weakness in one trait may be compensated for by strength in another. In focusing attention on the individual it is easy to forget this and to overemphasize the importance of some one outstanding personality trait.

CLASSIFICATION OF QUALITIES

Because it is impossible to identify any single ability or trait that is principally responsible for success or to determine whether training will lead to the development of some required combination of abilities, our discussion of personal qualifications is developed in terms of five broad classifications of qualities: (1) native intelligence, (2) social intelligence, (3) facility of expression, (4) special abilities, and (5)

[1] Dwight E. Beecher, *The Evaluation of Teaching*. Syracuse, N.Y.: Syracuse University Press, 1949, pp. 41–63.

*M*any studies have been made to discover what traits or personal qualities pupils consider characteristic of the teachers they like best and those they like least. A pioneering investigation by Professor Frank William Hart (1881–1968) of the responses of 10,000 high school seniors is summarized in the following table.

Highest Ranking Traits of the "Best Liked" Teachers

1. Is helpful with school work, explains lessons and assignments clearly and thoroughly, and uses examples in teaching.
2. Cheerful, happy, good-natured, jolly, has a sense of humor and can take a joke.
3. Human, friendly, companionable, "one of us."
4. Interested in and understands pupils.
5. Makes work interesting, creates a desire to work, makes class work a pleasure.
6. Strict, has control of the class, commands respect.
7. Impartial, shows no favoritism, has no "pets."
8. Not cross, crabby, grouchy, nagging, or sarcastic.
9. "We learned the subject."
10. A pleasing personality.

Highest Ranking Traits of the "Least Liked" Teachers

1. Too cross, crabby, grouchy, never smiles, nagging, sarcastic, loses temper, "flies off the handle."
2. Not helpful with school work, does not explain lessons and assignments, not clear, work not planned.
3. Partial, has "pets" of favored students, and "picks on" certain pupils.
4. Superior, aloof, haughty, "snooty," overbearing, does not know you out of class.
5. Mean, unreasonable, "hard boiled," intolerant, ill mannered, too strict.
6. Unfair in marking and grading, unfair in tests and examinations.
7. Inconsiderate of pupils' feelings, bawls out pupils in the presence of classmates, pupils are afraid and ill at ease and dread class.
8. Not interested in pupils and does not understand them.
9. Unreasonable assignments and home work.
10. Too loose in discipline, no control of class, does not command respect.

F. W. Hart, *Teachers and Teaching.* New York: Macmillan, 1934, pp. 131, 250–251.

physical traits. These classifications have often been divided and subdivided. They are, however, fairly representative of classifications generally accepted.

1. Native intelligence

Intelligence tests, perhaps the best measure of native ability known to us, seem to measure the individual's aptitude for scholastic work, verbal learning, and problem-solving. Teaching involves considerable mental work. Other things being equal, then, it may be assumed that native intelligence is related to success in teaching. Studies indicate that, at least to some extent, this is true. The degree of relationship, however, is unknown. The most that can be said is that success in teaching is related to a number of factors of which intelligence seems to be one.

As discussed in Chapter 16, intelligence tests are applicable only to children under 16 years of age. It is the custom to supplement them in the early years with achievement tests, and after the elementary school, to rely wholly on various kinds of standardized achievement tests, the assumption being, of course, that test scores on achievement tests are closely related to native intelligence.

The importance of native intelligence, or of any other trait, is always relative to the total personality. Perhaps scores on intelligence tests can be best used to establish a critical minimum point, say the point that marks the average of the intelligence scores made by the population at large. The higher the scores one makes on such a scale, the more certain it is that he possesses enough intelligence to succeed at teaching. Below a certain minimum point other personality factors cannot sufficiently compensate.

In deciding the level or field of teaching in which one has the best chances of success, those fields that call for a higher level of scholastic work, that demand greater facility in expression, and that call for a greater application of ability at problem-solving will tend to require a higher minimum native intelligence.

Scholastic achievement as revealed in marks received in school is related to native intelligence and will give a prospective teacher a clue to his native intelligence. One who has great difficulty in his own school work probably should not teach.

2. Social intelligence

Teaching is always concerned with helping people to grow in maturity and develop desirable responses to various social situations. Behavior is primarily social. The one who teaches others must himself, to a reasonable degree, possess what the psychologists call social intelligence. He must exhibit social competence. Social intelligence cannot, of course, be separated from native intelligence or from any of the other personality traits.

The social competences associated with successful teaching include capacity for leadership, tactfulness in working closely with others, sensitivity to the needs and wants of those with whom one works. There are no techniques to measure the degree to which an individual possesses social intelligence. Only through intimate personal acquaintance can one make a subjective appraisal of what the effectiveness of training and experience in developing this qualification might be.

3. Facility of expression

Regardless of the field or the level of a teacher's work, he is always aided by his fluency in the use of symbols or what is sometimes called verbal ability. The demand for this ability is almost constant, although some teaching positions place a higher premium on it than others. Explaining, expressing original thought, interpreting, advising, giving directions—the effectiveness of these and many other activities depends, in part, on the teacher's facility of expression. This is an ability that can be developed, largely through training and persistent practice. The teacher who is apt in his choice of words and phrases, who gives vivid illustrations, who speaks ''trippingly on the tongue'' is a teacher who has a quality among his repertoire of qualifications that is valuable indeed.

4. Special abilities

It is not difficult to recognize individuals who have unusual artistic ability, musical ability, mathematical ability, mechanical ability, or some other similar special ability. Certain people, for example, delight in working with numbers and develop mathematical skills with ease.

Obviously, a special ability would enhance an individual's interest and success in teaching any subject related to this ability.

5. Physical traits

Because teaching taxes physical strength, it is generally accepted that physical vigor and good health are necessary to teaching effectiveness. Supply of energy, appearance, and quality of voice are all believed to have some bearing on the quality of teaching. There is little evidence, however, that any particular type of physical structure or amount of physical vigor is essential to success in teaching. As is true with all the other traits, various physical traits must all be considered in relation to each other and to the entire personality.

Combination of abilities

None of the abilities classified above and designated basic in teaching is an entity. Success in teaching seems to be related to all of them, but the degree of relationship for all teachers can only be guessed. The relationship undoubtedly varies with the entire teaching situation, including the teaching field and the grade level. In some teaching situations a woman of small stature and great intelligence would have less chance of success than a less intelligent man built like a professional heavyweight boxer. Situation makes a difference. The concept of what a skilled teacher is continuously takes on new meaning in different times and places.

Predicting teaching success

In considering whether it would be wise for an interested individual to enter teaching, it is well to consider all the qualities—native intelligence, social intelligence, facility of expression, special abilities, and physical traits. Four years of college study, carefully planned to meet the individual's particular needs and earnestly pursued, can contribute significantly to improving the combination of traits that characterize the student when he first enters the program.

The most accurate way to predict success in teaching and to test abilities and combinations of abilities is through experience in student teaching or in activities closely related to teaching—working with

These second-graders are acting from a "script" they themselves have created. A teacher must become prepared to teach many types of activities, and for this professional training is essential. In the case of dramatics, the training must include specialized emphasis on speech and creative dramatics.

children in clubs, teaching Sunday school, or counseling in boys' or girls' camps. How one works in the classroom and shoulders teaching responsibility will, in say three years' time, establish whether one possesses the basic abilities needed for successful teaching. Even here, however, an initial failure does not prove that success is impossible. Some great teachers have been failures in their initial attempts.

Summary

By setting standards for teachers as a condition for granting teaching certificates, the state attempts to protect the public against substandard education and the teaching profession from infiltration by the inferior and the poorly prepared. States also control the quality of teaching through their accreditation policies for teacher education institutions. In addition, schools themselves have banded into voluntary associations that cut across state lines and that have established standards for the schools to meet as conditions to membership. Their standards do not apply to levels of education below the high school.

In qualifying, the prospective teacher receives his college education through three classifications of subject matter. One is referred to as courses for background education. Another is made up of specialized courses that are related to what the teacher will teach. In the third are professional courses that point directly to the vocation of teaching.

While progress has been made toward improving courses pursued by prospective teachers, marked agreement as to what the curriculum should be has yet to be reached.

Native intelligence, social intelligence, facility of expression, special abilities, and physical traits seem to be positively related to success in teaching. There is, however, no sterotype of the successful teacher. The key to success is not found in one or several personality traits but in the combination of all the traits in a total personality.

Questions

1. What advantages may accrue to the teaching profession from the imposition of minimum standards of qualification by society?
2. When may minimum standards of qualification be inimical to the cause of good education?
3. In what ways may a state legislature misuse its authority to establish minimum standards of qualification for teachers?
4. How can the legislatures of the various states deal with the problem of encouraging a free interflow of teachers between states?
5. Why have voluntary accrediting agencies arisen in the different geographical sections of the country?
6. Why have voluntary accrediting agencies concerned themselves mainly with standards at the high school and college levels? How has the teaching profession been affected by this policy?
7. Why have the colleges in America not agreed upon what constitutes a satisfactory background education?
8. What are some of the difficulties colleges face in offering suitable content courses for elementary teachers? For junior high school teachers? For, say, teachers of social studies in senior high schools?
9. What are the principal differences between the content of a professional education course and a specialized content course?
10. How can stricter selective policies be made effective in the occupational field of teaching?
11. What is the responsibility of American society in upgrading its teaching profession?

12. In view of the fact that there are more than two million teachers in the teaching profession, how selective, in your opinion, can teacher education institutions become?

13. Considering the number of teachers in the teaching profession, what responsibilities do college teachers need to assume for the development of outstanding teaching skills?

Projects

1. Study the official certification requirements for teaching in your state. Give your personal evaluation of the requirements in: (a) background education, (b) specialized subject matter, (c) professional subject matter.

2. Describe an outstanding teacher you have known in terms of his personal qualifications for teaching.

3. For one week note your own speech inadequacies. Outline for yourself a speech improvement program. Follow this program for one week and make a note of the results. You may substitute another qualification if you desire.

4. Write your reactions to the Conant recommendation which reads as follows:

    For certification purposes the state should require only (a) that a candidate hold a baccalaureate degree from a legitimate college or university . . . ; (b) that he hold a specially endorsed teaching certificate from a college or university which, in issuing the official document, attests that the institution as a whole considers the person adequately prepared to teach in a designated field and grade level.

5. a. Explain how a graduate of an institution holding membership in NCATE would qualify for a teaching certificate in any one of the participating states.

    b. Explain how he would qualify if the institution from which he had been graduated was not accredited by NCATE.

    c. State how you believe the problem of reciprocity in certification among the states should be resolved.

6. How are required standards of competence and a shortage of teachers related? Explain what is involved in any practical solution.

4

The Teacher
and His
Profession

Anyone who is considering the teaching profession as an extended career needs to know details about the profession. This chapter is concerned with a few of the more important of these: What is a profession? How does the teaching profession differ from other professions? What standards must one meet to enter teaching? How does the teaching profession compare with other professions in size, and what does this imply concerning one's responsibilities to the profession? What must be done to attract able young people to teaching as a career? To what degree do teachers enjoy the respect of American citizens? How is a reasonable degree of security provided for teachers? How are these security provisions obtained? What is a satisfactory salary scale, and how do teachers share in determining it? The answers to such questions in any particular school district—whether public, elementary or secondary, private, or a whole state—are vital to a teacher's feeling of well-being, to the satisfactions he will experience over the years.

America's social well-being and its future progress depend, in considerable degree, on that small proportion of its population that is commonly classified as professional. While no one of the professions is more important to the national welfare than any of the others, it is certainly true that the achievements of all are dependent on how efficiently the teaching group performs its functions. All, including the teaching profession, must rely on the education their members receive from the teachers in the schools.

The American public and its teachers are "natural partners." And as teachers must be aware of the implications of membership in their profession, so the public must recognize the impact that the profession has on the general welfare. Together, they must work toward policies that strengthen both.

What is a profession?

DIFFICULTIES OF DEFINITION

In attempting to define a profession, to set up criteria to distinguish a profession from other occupational groups, significant difficulties are encountered. The word "profession" is loosely used. Even in a college textbook in sociology, for instance, the gambling "profession" and other illicit "professions" are mentioned. When we speak of certain professions as "full-fledged," we imply that some are more professional than others. Many vocational groups claim professional status, and the number continues to increase. The oldest of the professions—medicine, law, and the ministry—have been joined by other groups seeking and achieving, in varying degrees, recognition as professions: teachers, engineers, pharmacists, dentists, nurses, social workers, architects, and, more recently, scientists, journalists, accountants, and others. The boundary between professional and non-professional occupational groups is, in fact, so hazy that the Bureau of the Census has refrained from defining the term "profession."[1]

The attitudes of the American people toward a vocational group, like the journalists, for instance, determine whether the desires and efforts of the group to be accorded professional status will be successful. If the public recognizes the importance of the group, has an uncommon regard for the training, knowledge, and skill that membership in the group requires, and highly respects the relatively few people who engage in the occupation, then they may accord with the desire of the occupation to have the title of profession.

In one sense, then, the public decides when a group is a profession. The number of groups recognized as professions changes somewhat in

[1] For an able explanation of the elements common to professions and other leading occupations, see Talcott Parsons, *Essays in Sociological Theory*, rev. ed. New York: Macmillan, 1954, chap. 2, "The Professions and Social Structure."

relation to the demands for particular services. For instance, national statistics on employment opportunities reveal current shortages in engineering and an unfilled demand for physicists and chemists. Members of these fields are striving for recognition of their fields as professions. That their services are in strong demand adds to the promise of success in achieving professional status.

Despite the confusion over the meaning of the word ''profession,'' there are certain characteristics typical of, and more or less unique to, professions.

ORGANIZATION

In this discussion we think of education as a learned profession, defined in the dictionary as ''any profession in the preparation for or practice of which academic learning is held to play an important part.'' Historically, professions have been initiated when those practicing a technique or craft that required special training desired to be set apart and identified as the persons so specially equipped. For this purpose they formed associations, limiting membership to individuals with minimum qualifications. By excluding the unqualified, they guaranteed their own competence and secured public recognition of their competence. In addition, they set up standards of conduct required for continued membership. In this way they sought to guarantee honor and exclude not only the incompetent but also the unscrupulous. Having established their membership, the professions sought next to improve the status of their members. Since the relation between status and remuneration is a close one, the professions gave attention to remuneration, among other factors.

In the teaching profession members exert their powers over standards for membership and influence over benefits through various organizations, mainly the national organizations AFT and NEA. Today one may be a member of a profession without the organizational affiliation. To exercise the historical prerogatives of the profession, however, a member of the teaching profession acts through the national organization just as, for instance, a doctor works through the AMA to influence controls and standards in the medical profession.

NATURE OF WORK

Persons in a profession are engaged in work that involves special mental and other attainments. In general, a profession is related to a vocation that summons or appeals to those who enter because they recognize the social importance of the work to be done. This recognition helps them to do the work better and to get satisfaction from doing it well. We see that the line of demarcation between a profession and another vocational group need not be clear-cut. Certainly a vocational group may also be social-minded; on the other hand, a professional group may de-emphasize its social responsibility. In general, however, it is the professional group that gives greatest deliberate stress to its opportunities and responsibilities to render services that contribute to the public welfare.

The teacher-to-be is willing to devote much time and thought and money to adequate preparation partly because he recognizes that the work of the teaching profession is socially significant. A profession should seek improvements of benefit to the public as zealously as it seeks improvements of benefit only to the profession or to individuals within the profession. A profession is distinguished from other vocational groups in this stress on social perspective, in its emphasis on the dedication of its members to public service.

A profession is somewhat distinguished also because it involves work that is generally more mental than manual. Members of a profession must seek a constant flow of ideas from the seminar, from the laboratory, from communication within the profession. Such intellectual demands call for a liberal education as a part of the pre-service preparation. Teachers and those in other professions, too, must have broad and basic understandings. Every teacher should strive to secure a broad cultural education, not only in order to live a rich, meaningful personal life, but also in order to be intellectually prepared for professional membership.

ENTRANCE REQUIREMENTS

Certain standards must be met by those who seek entrance to a profession. In licensed vocational groups and in the professions, including the teaching profession, standards for entrance are, in the final phase, established by the state and embodied in certification laws. In determining admission to the teaching profession, the state educational authority works closely with leaders in the profession and with those in higher institutions responsible for administering teacher education programs.

The nation has had to learn that in order to provide the manpower necessary in certain professional fields, concerted efforts are required to maintain reasonable standards of admission as well as to make the conditions of work attractive to able personnel. Throughout the United States there is, potentially, adequate and capable manpower to answer the national demand for teachers and, at the same time, to maintain high standards of admission. But the American public has not been sufficiently concerned to eliminate those conditions that disparage a teaching career in the eyes of some capable men and women who can meet high professional qualifications.

How is the teaching profession different?

While all the professions have some features in common, they differ in the amounts and kinds of preparation required, in personnel, remuneration, security provisions, and the like. The teaching profession has certain unique characteristics related to function, control, support, size, and the sex of its membership. These differences necessitate a special approach by the profession to the attainment of a higher level of professionalization.

FUNCTION

The primary function of the teaching profession is stated in its name—teaching. The schools of the nation are structured to encourage good teaching. Teachers are selected in terms of their potential ability to perform well, school buildings are planned to encourage expert teaching, and citizens devote much time and spend much money to promote and encourage the best possible discharge of this function.

CONTROL

The legal control of education lies *outside* the profession, in the hands of the public. What the teaching profession is, therefore, and what it develops into depend partly on what those in control want it to be or, perhaps, to put this a little more strongly, on what the public will permit it to be. That the American public firmly holds the reins is evidence that they have a deep and abiding concern for education. It also means, however, that teachers must continually strive to keep the public intelligently informed about their problems and needs. Public control over the schools is continuing and extensive. Hence teachers, as a group, must interact with the public in a more direct and vigorous manner than is necessary for other groups.

SUPPORT

Closely linked with control is the matter of financial support. He who holds the purse strings wields the power. Public education in the United States is financed through public taxes. Private education is privately financed, largely by fees and tuition. Those who establish the polices of school support determine the status of members of the teaching profession. Adequacy or inadequacy of support, for example, has a bearing on the number of applicants for entrance to the profession and thereby affects selection policies. It influences teachers' living conditions, affects the amount and kind of education that can be required, and raises or lowers prestige. A generation of citizens that places a low priority on teaching, and that wishes to get good teaching but does not wish it strongly enough to pay well for it, is a generation that will impede the progress of the teaching profession toward desirable professional goals. Generally speaking, a narrow-minded community, whose support of its schools is niggardly, is likely also to be niggardly in granting the degree of freedom that is necessary to good teaching. The result is professional regression rather than progression.

SIZE

The teaching profession has far more members than any other profession. Its instructional membership numbers well over two and a

half million. In 1969 more than two million persons were members of
the instructional staff of the public schools alone. Size has a special
bearing on selection and, conversely, selective policies have an effect on
size. Size dictates that standards for selection be moderate. In order for
any selective policy to operate, there must be considerably more
applicants than openings.

Public school classroom teachers	1,838,000
Professional nurses	659,000
Lawyers	317,000
Physicians	309,000
Dentists	115,000

*Fig. 4.1 Approximate membership in five selected professional groups, 1968. (Data from
national professional organizations)*

Since the profession is large, it is impossible to limit membership
to a very select group. The state cannot adopt selective procedures for
admitting members to the teaching profession comparable to those
followed, for instance, in the medical profession. The number who
must be admitted makes a great difference. In 1969, the medical
profession included only 315,000 persons. Also, the ratio between the
number of professionals needed and the number who have the abilities,
interest, and desire to enter the profession and who possess the capacity
to bear the cost of training for the profession influences the policies of
selection. To continue the comparison, perhaps the medical profession
must be more selective, because while it may be considered better to have
an inexpert teacher than none, an inexpert medical diagnosis or bungled
surgery may be worse than none. It is well to remember that, for the
benefit of the students and the community, schools are desperately
trying to make the supply of teachers meet the demand. Great reliance
must therefore be placed on superior pre-service and in-service
training to obtain teachers of superior quality. Efforts to increase the
attractiveness of the profession so that a measure of selection is possible
are necessarily directed toward making working conditions attractive.

RATIO OF THE SEXES

Although the proportion of men among classroom teachers rose
from 27.3 percent in 1958–1959 to 31.9 percent in 1968–1969,

women continue to outnumber men in the teaching profession; as these figures indicate, about 68 percent of the classroom teachers in 1969 were women. This preponderance of women seems to decrease as the grades ascend, however. According to an NEA research study of American public school teachers, in 1968–1969, though only 14.7 percent of the elementary school teachers were men, in the secondary schools, men made up 53.5 percent of the teaching personnel. Prestige, higher salaries for high school teachers in independent high school districts with larger taxing power, and the opportunity to do specialized teaching contribute to the greater attraction of men to the secondary schools. Also, a man teacher may well feel out of place in a lower grade elementary school where the teachers are mostly women (there is a vicious circle here).

The predominance of women does differentiate the teaching profession from most other professions. It is both a result and a cause of some basic economic and social factors. Traditionally, in America, women have constituted the most important economic minority group. There has always been an unwritten policy in the United States to pay women less than men and to deny them those positions that are most lucrative. In the past, women elementary teachers typically received less salary than men elementary teachers. The effect of artificial barriers resulting from deeply embedded social attitudes toward women in the other professions is also significant. Restrictions on the entry of women to some fields, e.g., law and medicine, have led to a disproportionate representation of women in others, e.g., teaching and nursing.

In summary, then, the teaching profession differs from other professions in its primary function, in the nature of its control and support, in size, and in the ratio of men to women in its membership. Any program of improvement initiated by the public or by the profession must be planned with these differences in mind. They have a bearing on procedures used in the selection of members for the profession, on the specialized training that is required, and on other qualifications for admission.

Teacher recruitment

It is important that an adequate supply of teachers come into the profession regularly. As we have said, selection occurs at the time of admission to teacher preparation in college and is continued at the time of admission to student teaching, at the time of employment, and again before granting tenure. With the recent rapid growth of the school population, the demand for teachers has been great, making selection very difficult. The problem of recruiting and retaining capable young people in teaching has become so acute as to demand the attention not only of the profession but also of numerous lay groups.

Recruitment is conducted through publicity, through direct personal conference, through opportunities for exploratory experiences, and through scholarships. The NEA has been actively engaged in teacher recruitment through all these channels. Every April the NEA conducts a "Teaching Career Month." During this time national broadcasting networks, the magazines, and the nation's press focus the spotlight of public attention on the American teacher—how he is recruited, prepared, and retained in the classroom, and the importance of his position in a free society. Special posters, leaflets, booklets, and films on such subjects as the current problem of teacher dropout, certification practices, and teacher education are channeled through the local branches of the NEA or the AFT to students considering careers in teaching, to parents and citizens who can help recruit promising youngsters, and to the general public.

Since 1938 the NEA has sponsored the Future Teachers of America, an organization with local clubs in every high school and junior high school in the country where there is sufficient interest and leadership. In addition there are "chapters" of the organization on the campuses of teacher education institutions.

Teachers are encouraged to promote interest in teaching by providing exploratory experiences for their pupils. Children in the upper grades, for instance, may be allowed to read stories to younger children. High school pupils may be assigned as "aides" in the kindergarten. It is important that high school counselors have an appreciation of the great possibilities open in the teaching field and have an interest in pointing these out to capable young people.

Perhaps the vital key to teacher recruitment lies within the community. If the public pays teachers adequate salaries and provides for teacher security and teacher welfare, and if teachers are respected and have prestige, conditions are favorable for interesting the young people of the community to go into teaching. Many organizations of lay people,

Who are the people in teaching?
How do others help them decide to
become teachers? How do they help
themselves? The people are of all
types. The man with his elementary
school class is one of them, but as
an elementary teacher he
unfortunately belongs to a minority
group. A fairly even balance
between men and women in the
elementary schools would create a
more natural learning atmosphere.
Better salaries and the adoption of a
single salary scale will, hopefully,
attract more men. A high school
student interested in becoming a
teacher discusses her future with a
counselor, whose advice will help

her. Every progressive high school
provides individual consultation
about careers. Another high school
student, farther along on the road
to a definite decision, is "trying
out" teaching under the Future
Teachers of America program as
she tutors her contemporaries in
French (she is second from the left).

like the American Association of University Women and the Optimist Club, offer scholarships and conduct essay contests to promote teacher recruitment. Scholarships frequently are offered by local teachers' organizations, by the PTA, by state teacher organizations, and by state governments.

The prestige factor

When an individual assumes membership in the teaching profession, he not only accepts the obligation to render certain services and to play a certain role according to established rules but he also accepts the social status associated with people who fulfill that role. Prestige is the distinction or reputation that people attach to individuals or groups. It has a great deal to do with determining those who will be attracted to a profession and how long they stay in it.

Does the public regard teachers highly? Does it value intellectual endeavor highly? Do the positive and sympathetic features of the social climate in the United States assure the kind of prestige status to teachers that will encourage a desire to enter the profession? The qualified answers to these questions mean that effective teacher recruitment must include efforts to improve the social status and the prestige of teachers.

THE SCALE OF SOCIAL PRESTIGE

Prestige is, of course, related to income and education. It is determined also by a combination of other factors, including what the public thinks of the kind of service rendered to humanity; the special training, intelligence, and ability needed; and the morality of the group. In more than 30 studies of occupations made in the United States between 1925 and 1947, the consistency in the way occupations were scored was remarkable. The table here gives the scores of 88 occupations made by 2,290 people in 1947. The study shows that a college professor outranks others in the teaching profession, that school teachers are above average in prestige in that they outrank members of such occupational groups as radio announcers, newspaper columnists, insurance agents, and traveling salesmen. But teachers are outranked by physicians, lawyers, airline pilots, state governors, and captains in the army. (Judging from later studies, the prestige of classroom teachers has not changed significantly since then.)

Other studies show that teachers score higher as credit risks than clergymen, lawyers, judges, musicians, and some others. Morally and ethically, school teachers rank high. College teachers and school administrators, predominantly men, as well as high school teachers, have a higher position on the prestige scale than teachers in the lower grades. That the teaching profession establishes levels of stratification within its own group will be discussed later.

Although a combination of factors determines prestige, when other factors are equal, higher income means higher prestige. Inasmuch as the public determines teacher income, what the public does in the matter adds to or detracts from the prestige status of the teacher. To the extent that members of the profession suffer financially in comparison with other groups, they also suffer in comparison on the social status scale. It must be remembered, though, that the amount of money spent for schools must be judged in terms of complete community spending. An economically poor community may pay low teacher salaries but show that it places high values on teaching by spending a relatively large proportion of its total funds for classroom teaching.

Prestige ratings of selected vocations obtained through public opinion polls give a picture of the average of comparative ranks only. Such a rank does not reveal the level of public acceptance in any specifically designated public elementary or secondary school district. In those districts where the citizens give a low priority to public education, the prestige of teachers usually suffers accordingly. In other districts where education is more highly respected, the community probably will accord its teachers a higher degree of respect. While ratings such as those in the table do not tell the whole story, they nevertheless are significant enough to justify a critical self-examination by the profession.

Prestige, on the whole, is determined outside the profession. It is true, however, that a rank lower than the importance of the services rendered justifies may be at least partly based within the profession itself. It follows that any improvements that result from efforts within the profession add to the public's respect for teaching. A prospective teacher should recognize that his over-all worth to the profession, as well as his own personal welfare, can be enhanced by sharing in successful efforts to promote desirable changes within the profession.

Prestige for the teaching profession suffers because it is characterized by an unhealthy, excessively high mobility. For instance, according to the best available information, in 1966–1967 the rate of attrition for elementary school teachers was 8.1 percent; for secondary school teachers, it was 8.6 percent. It was estimated that in that year there were almost 82,000 elementary teachers who had not completed the bachelor's degree. It is apparent that many children in affluent America's public schools are taught by teachers who have not served long enough to have attained a favorable degree of public acceptance. Some, perhaps, have not remained in the profession long enough to become personally identified with it. The standing of the profession suffers further when children have to be taught for long periods by substitute teachers or by teachers with substandard training. The high proportion of new and inexperienced teachers may be in part the result of the expansion of the school population. Unfortunately, the percentage of the new and inexperienced tends to be larger among the faculties of schools in less affluent communities.

The prestige of the teaching profession may be influenced also by the fact that two large, highly influential, but competitive associations represent the profession—the American Federation of Teachers and the

The Ratings of Occupations

U. S. Supreme Court Justice	96	Head of a department in a state	
Physician	93	government	8?
State governor	93	Minister	8?
Cabinet member in the federal government	92	Architect	8(
Diplomat in the U. S. Foreign Service	92	Chemist	8(
Mayor of a large city	90	Dentist	8(
College professor	89	Lawyer	8(
Scientist	89	Member of the board of directors of a	8(
U. S. Representative in Congress	89	large corporation	8(
Banker	88	Nuclear physicist	8(
Government scientist	88	Priest	8(
County judge	87	Psychologist	8?

Occupation	Score	Occupation	Score
Civil engineer	84	Railroad conductor	67
Airline pilot	83	Mail carrier	66
Artist who paints pictures that are exhibited in galleries	83	Carpenter	65
		Plumber	63
Owner of a factory that employs about 100 people	82	Garage mechanic	62
		Local official of a labor union	62
Sociologist	82	Owner-operator of lunch stand	62
Accountant for a large business	81	Corporal in the regular army	60
Biologist	81	Machine operator in a factory	60
Musician in a symphony orchestra	81	Barber	59
Author of novels	80	Clerk in a store	58
Captain in the regular army	80	Fisherman who owns his own boat	58
Building contractor	79	Streetcar motorman	58
Economist	79	Milk route man	54
Public school teacher	78	Restaurant cook	54
County agricultural agent	77	Truck driver	54
Railroad engineer	77	Lumberjack	53
Farm owner and operator	76	Filling station attendant	52
Official of an international labor union	75	Singer in a night club	52
Radio announcer	75	Farm hand	50
Newspaper columnist	74	Coal miner	49
Owner-operator of a printing shop	74	Taxi driver	49
Electrician	73	Railroad section hand	48
Trained machinist	73	Restaurant worker	48
Welfare worker for a city government	73	Dock worker	47
Undertaker	72	Night watchman	47
Reporter on a daily newspaper	71	Clothes presser in a laundry	46
Average	70	Soda fountain clerk	45
Manager of a small store in a city	69	Bartender	44
Bookkeeper	68	Janitor	44
Insurance agent	68	Sharecropper—one who owns no livestock or equipment and does not manage a farm	40
Tenant farmer—one who owns livestock and machinery and manages a farm	68		
		Garbage collector	35
Traveling salesman for a wholesale concern	68	Street sweeper	34
		Shoe shiner	33
Playground director	67		
Policeman	67		

SOURCE: *Opinion News*, Vol. IX, September 1, 1947. Reproduced by permission of the National Opinion Research Center, University of Chicago. Drs. Cecil North and Paul Hatt designed the study upon which these data are based.

*D*oc once said to me :

> *You don't know how it feels to grow up in a district like this. You go*
> *to the first grade—Miss O'Rourke. Second grade—Miss Casey. Third*
> *grade—Miss Chalmers. Fourth grade—Miss Mooney. And so on. At*
> *the fire station it is the same. None of them are Italians. The police*
> *lieutenant is an Italian, and there are a couple of Italian sergeants,*
> *but they never have made an Italian captain in Cornerville. In the*
> *settlement houses, none of the people with authority are Italians.*
> *Now you must know that the old-timers here have a great respect for*
> *schoolteachers and anybody like that. When the Italian boy sees that*
> *none of his own people have the good jobs, why should he think he is as*
> *good as the Irish or the Yankees? It makes him feel inferior. If I had*
> *my way, I would have half the schoolteachers Italians and three-quarters*
> *of the people in the settlement. Let the other quarter be there just to*
> *show that we're in America. . . .*

Willam Foote Whyte, *Street Corner Society.* Chicago: University of Chicago Press,
1943, p. 276. Copyright 1943 by the University of Chicago and quoted by
permission of the University of Chicago Press.

National Education Association. Both have served the profession with
distinction, especially in those school districts where one or the other
is the dominant representative of the profession. In some areas,
however, there is rivalry. The prestige of the profession would, it
seems, become higher if the strengths of these two organizations were
combined. At the present writing there is only scant evidence that
such an amalgamation may be achieved some time in the future. Once
the profession becomes organizationally united and so organized within
itself as to have a greater degree of unity among its three levels—local,
state, and national—than is now apparent, the public image of the
profession will be elevated.

Within the profession, the prestige of classroom teachers as a
group has traditionally been the lowest. In districts where the educational organization includes a great many functionaries, a hierarchy,
the classroom teacher is traditionally at the bottom. When classroom
teachers are recognized as the most important pivot in the educational
structure and are given greater importance in the educational affairs of
the school district, the prestige of teachers within the profession is
raised.

Security provisions

SECURITY DEFINED

Security is a basic personality need, a frame of mind, an attitude defined by psychologists as a persistent state of readiness to use the self for motive satisfaction. All attitudes have an emotional core. They are related to the affective aspects of our lives. A teacher with a sense of security feels protected, is free from fear of unfair dismissal or unjust and unwarranted treatment. But security does not imply complacency. Rather, it builds confidence. The teacher becomes more sure of his own personal and professional adequacy, is encouraged to improve, to become more proficient. Insecurity has the opposite effect. The teacher who is insecure tends to feel inadequate to meet his assignments and lacks confidence in his ability to achieve.

State and local school systems and the teaching profession strive to provide teachers with a suitable degree of security. Certain security features, like tenure, retirement, and salary scales, are illustrative of the provisions intended to avoid the ill effects of insecurity. Also, it is now true (as it was not in earlier years) that most of America's teachers—both men and women—are or have been married. Many, of course, have children of their own. Married or not, they expect to maintain a manner and standard of living appropriate to their status as professionals. Thus their homes or apartments, distance of residence from place of employment, and other aspects of their way of life are much the same as for other career people. These facts naturally influence their attitude toward the number and type of security provisions they wish and need to have.

ASSOCIATIONS

So numerous and so influential are associations in this country that the United States is sometimes described as an "associational" society. Organizations of both private and public employees have become accepted as an important phase of American life. As many as 340 different kinds of local teachers' organizations have been identified. Some are entirely local, some are affiliated with a state-wide group, and many are units in an organization of national scope, the NEA or the AFT.

The fact that school teachers are prolific organizers may be an indication of their deep-seated desire for greater personal security. Their numerous organizations indicate confidence in affiliation and association. The relationship between the individual teachers and the profession may be better understood by a brief look at some of these associations.

1. National Education Association

Founded in 1857, the National Education Association of the United States (NEA) is now the world's largest professional association. Its headquarters is an eight-story building in the nation's capital, with a full-time staff of more than 300 people. It has more than a million members, from all types of schools, in all types of educational positions, and at all levels in the educational program; by far the largest group is composed of classroom teachers, about 92 percent. The NEA differs from the other large educational association, the American Federation of Teachers, in that the NEA is not allied with labor. The NEA states its purpose thus: "to elevate the character and advance the interests of the profession of teaching, and to promote the cause of education in the United States." In seeking to achieve this purpose, the NEA engages in such activities as these: issuing reports dealing with important issues, making the results of research available in popular form, holding conferences, providing consultative and other field services, working with members of Congress and federal agencies to promote and protect the interests of children, working for higher standards for the teaching profession and for more reciprocal certification requirements, aiding school systems with salary problems, seeking improved personnel practices, and promoting working professional relationships in the profession and between the profession and the public. The NEA states that it urges the improvement of the quality of teachers in order that the public will be well served. Likewise, it protects members of the teaching profession in the discharge of their duties, and it urges that only proper dismissal procedures be employed if teachers are found unworthy.

As a coercive measure the NEA has used *sanctions*. The sanction is said to have advantages over the strike in that it is legal—it does not

*I*n June, 1961, the Representative Assembly of the NEA passed the following
resolution defining the policy it believes should be adhered to in teacher-school
board relationships. This resolution is historical; it marked the beginning of
a new era. It opened the door to teacher negotiating or bargaining with
boards of education concerning matters related to teacher welfare. It also led
the way to such subsequent coercive measures as sanctions and strikes.

Teacher-Board of Education Relationships. *Since boards of
education and the teaching profession have the same ultimate aim of
providing the best possible educational opportunity for children and
youth, relationships must be established which are based upon this
community of interest and the concept of education as both a public
trust and a professional calling.*

*Recognizing both the legal authority of boards of education and
the educational competencies of the teaching profession, the two groups
should view the consideration of matters of mutual concern as a joint
responsibility.*

*The National Education Association believes, therefore, that pro-
fessional education associations should be accorded the right, through
democratically selected representatives using appropriate professional
channels, to participate in the determination of policies of common
concern including salary and other conditions for professional service.*

*The seeking of consensus and mutual agreement on a professional
basis should preclude the arbitrary exercise of unilateral authority by
boards of education and the use of the strike by teachers as a means for
enforcing economic demands.*

*When common consent cannot be reached, the Association recom-
mends that a Board of Review consisting of members of professional and
lay groups affiliated with education should be used as the means of
resolving extreme differences.*

From NEA Research Division Memo 1961-31; revised, August, 1961.

violate teachers' contractual relationships with school boards. When
everything else has been tried and has failed, sanctions are imposed as a
last resort. The procedure involves: (1) factual study and a report on
conditions in the specific system or district; (2) widespread publicity
on the profession's dissatisfaction with existing conditions; (3) a
warning to NEA members that accepting a position in the system will

be considered unethical; (4) messages to colleges and university placement agencies asking them not to recommend teachers to the system. The *NEA Journal* for December, 1966, reported:

> One of the most remarkable and surprising effects of sanctions is their impact on business and industry. The profession gets quick action once the bankers and industrialists begin to question the wisdom of investing within the borders of a state under NEA sanctions. Many politicians have learned for the first time that good schools are an essential commodity in any community or state.

At its annual convention in the summer of 1967, the NEA passed this resolution about teacher strikes:

> The NEA recognizes that under conditions of severe stress, causing deterioration of the educational program, and when good-faith attempts at resolution have been rejected, strikes have occurred and may occur in the future. In such instances, the NEA will offer all of the services at its command to the affiliate concerned to help resolve the impasse.

However, the resolution gave major attention to a series of steps which "should make the strike unnecessary." These were mediation, fact-finding, arbitration, political action, and sanctions. It was made clear that every effort should be made to avoid a strike.[2]

2. State teachers' associations

The NEA has 59 state and territory and 8,264 local affiliated associations. The state organizations, sometimes referred to as the state education associations, are among the most effective of all organized teachers' groups. Each enrolls a majority of the teachers in the state. Generally, each has a well-paid executive secretary who is an able and experienced professional educator. Most state associations have well-equipped offices and able personnel. Many of them publish a monthly journal that compares well with the best professional magazines.

State teachers' organizations are generally effective in their

[2] For an analysis of negotiation procedures, see *Formal Grievance Procedures for Public School Teachers, 1965–66*, NEA Research Report 1967-R10.

relationship with the state education authority and with the state legislatures. It is through the state organization that local groups or individuals can make known the specific nature of the security provisions needed to improve education in a particular state. Teachers indicate confidence in this kind of association through their financial support and their participation.

Teachers in fields such as English or social studies, those working at a particular educational level such as nursery or elementary, and educators in special fields such as guidance or administration have their own associations. Typically, these comprise local or regional units that are part of state organizations that, in turn, hold membership in a national unit more or less directly affiliated with the parent organization, the NEA.

3. Local or city-wide teachers' organizations

Local teachers' organizations are the oldest, the most numerous, and the most varied of all teachers' organizations. Their number attests to general confidence in their worth. They provide most individual teachers with an opportunity for participation in the affairs of the profession that is not possible in the groups covering a broader geographical area. The individual teacher, through the local organization, has the opportunity to experience the satisfaction of actively helping to protect his and his profession's security. Local organizations also serve a significant social function in some communities by providing a common meeting place for teachers.

Local organizations have a variety of patterns. Some admit all the teachers in a system; some admit only those working in a given field or at a specific level or those discharging a common specialized function, like guidance or administration. The aims are always broader than that of providing security for the members, but security for the members is an implied complement to all the other stated aims. Local associations strengthen group loyalty and reinforce the members' efforts to protect the organization's and the profession's reputation for the benefit of the membership.

Local associations enable teachers to become better acquainted with each other, with their school systems, and with their more urgent local problems. Thus they can learn more directly what the community is like and what the attitudes of its citizens are toward the maintenance of good schools. Local organizations open paths of communication by functioning as liaison between teachers, teachers and the public, and teachers and school administrators.

Should a local teachers' organization have the same rights as organizations in private industry, the right to call a strike, for example? The American tradition is that the public interest should come first, that the servants of the people may not strike against the people. In some instances this principle has been recognized by the courts, although both the NEA and the AFT support the teachers' right to strike. However, since teachers, in general, are reluctant to strike or to ask the NEA to impose sanctions, those who administer the schools have a responsibility to establish fair and positive personnel procedures and working conditions. Teachers in local organizations should have the right to organize for bargaining purposes, the right of free discussion, the right to appeal over the decisions of local administrations, and, ultimately, the right to take their case to the people.

> The typical teacher in today's schools is vastly different from the typical teacher of two or three decades ago. He is younger, better educated, and more highly skilled, but also more impatient, more demanding, and more courageous than ever before. He goes to bat for what he believes in, even at the risk of losing his job. And, he is determined to get for himself a better economic break in this era of two- and three-car families and electric toothbrushes.[3]

One of the thorniest problems concerns the right of organized teachers to engage in political activity. While studies of the past voting records of all elementary and secondary public school teachers show that well above 90 percent of them have voted regularly, fewer than 7 percent of them participated actively as members of a political organization and only 2 percent had ever been candidates for elective public office.

Perhaps the future welfare of the profession will depend in large part on how wisely teachers exercise their right to organize. It seems likely that in the future, local teacher groups will seek to advance the interests of the profession by increasing their activities through

[3] Sam M. Lambert, executive secretary, NEA, in a speech before the 10th Annual Convention, NEA, July, 1967.

organizational channels. In other words, the teacher will act less as an individual and more as a member of an association. Questions of rights, privileges, and teacher welfare, for example, will be answered in terms of a mature, carefully planned policy presented to the public or its representatives by an organized education group. In order that these policies might be more expertly formulated and effectively presented to the public or its representatives, local teachers' organizations in larger school districts are employing specially qualified executive secretaries who spend their full time representing the interests of the local teaching group.

The more successful local teachers' associations seek to protect the standards of performance within the schools from unwarranted encroachments from outside interest groups that are unfavorable to the cause of good education. They seek to enforce upon the membership a reasonable regard for their own professional code. They disapprove of the individual who would advance his interest at the expense of the group. They seek to promote the welfare of the group through advocating carefully formulated policies concerning salaries, retirement, sick leave, and the like. They seek to alter any community condition that is considered inimical to the cause of good education. Finally, while guarding the interests of individual teachers, they function to guard the interests of the professional organization itself by being alert to those influences that operate to weaken it.

Effective local teachers' organizations show various organizational patterns. A qualified, salaried executive on a full-time or part-time basis can be a significant asset to a local organization. In most local organizations, however, appropriate committees carry out self-assumed functions. Perhaps careful study of a problem basic to policy formulation is done by a research committee. A welfare committee might function in the interest of any individual member; a public relations committee may channel communication between teachers and the public; a legislative committee may keep the membership informed about impending state or federal legislation of interest to the profession. The local teachers' organization is instituted to meet the problems peculiar to the local district. An important committee serving a local organization may include representatives of teachers, administrators, and the school board (TAB).

The NEA is encouraging a trend toward unification of local, state,

''The status of the profession will not rise perceptibly unless the profession itself exerts its energies . . . '' The size of the NEA's headquarters in Washington reflects the size of the staff needed to carry on its many activities. Three intent teachers are shown at a conference, sponsored by the NEA, of the National Commission on Teacher Education and Professional Standards. AFT members often make direct contact with the public to try to achieve their aims. Here some of them protest a reduction in funds for art education; others hand out leaflets urging support of a proposed bond issue. This kind of action has saved many bond issues from defeat at the polls. The AFT also organizes tours to inform interested citizens about the schools; the members of one such group are shown with children in a classroom. Sometimes more drastic measures seem to be necessary. In California, AFT members demonstrate against the governor's efforts to cut state funds for colleges. Both the NEA and the AFT feel that strikes should be a last resort, but sometimes teachers do strike. These striking teachers are members of an AFT local in Chicago. In such a case, the local association receives advice and active help from national headquarters.

"*P*rofessional negotiation must mean something more than the right to
be heard. Most teachers' associations have had this right for years. The
right only to be heard might be simply an annual supplicatory pilgrimage
to the board of education, resulting only in warm expressions of gratitude
and good-will by both parties. This routine could consist of a polite
presentation by the teachers, blank stares from the board, and a polite
'thank you.' Then follows an interminable wait by the teachers ; finally,
reading of the board's action in the local newspaper or via the superintendent's
bulletin, with any connection between teachers' requests and board action
strictly coincidental. This, of course, is not professional negotiation.''
There seems to be little doubt that true professional negotiation, based
on a series of orderly procedures, officially adopted by the school board and
the recognized local association, is necessary and is becoming more common.*

Saturday Review. September 17, 1966, p. 89 (quoting from T. M. Stinnett,
Jack H. Kleinmann, and Martha L. Ware, *Professional Negotiation in Public
Education.* New York: Macmillan, 1966).

and national organizations. Oregon is an example of a state that has
achieved this through unification of dues. Instead of allowing a teacher
to choose among the organizations at the three levels, membership has
been made mandatory, and a single collection of dues pays for membership in all three. Such unification markedly increases organizational
strength and effectiveness while eliminating waste in collecting dues for
separate organizations. It is through their organizations—local, state,
and national—that the teachers claim their rights to professional
autonomy like that granted by the American people to other professions.

4. American Federation of Teachers

The organization that competes with the NEA for the privilege
of representing teachers is the American Federation of Teachers, a
national union of classroom teachers affiliated with the American
Federation of Labor-Congress of Industrial Organizations. The AFT
limits its membership to classroom teachers because it believes that
classroom teachers can and should speak for themselves and that school
superintendents, principals, and other administrators therefore should
not be admitted. Within the AFT organization are local, state, and
national affiliates. Dues in each local union of the AFT are determined
by its members and depend on the demands of the local's program,

which is also member-determined. The average dues range between $4 and $6 a month and include local, state, and national affiliation. As its brochure, "Questions and Answers About AFT," states, "Because the AFT believes in action—in 'getting things done' rather than issuing reports, letting someone else do the 'doing'—a powerful, cohesive structure is necessary." The AFT includes more than 650 local unions of teachers, has state federations in most of the states, and maintains a national headquarters in Washington. The AFT is currently working for improved teacher salaries; recognition of the rights of teachers everywhere to organize, negotiate, and bargain collectively; a "more effective schools" program; state tenure laws; elimination of overcrowding in classrooms, excessive class interruptions, and the use of students as teacher substitutes; state laws requiring free and uninterrupted lunch periods for all teachers; better teacher pensions; adequate, cumulative sick leave pay; and hospitalization and medical insurance paid from school funds. The organization states that strikes should be a last resort when all other means to bring about a fair settlement of a serious controversy have failed.

A president of AFT has written in its official publication:

> The days ahead will present many additional occasions to test the integrity, the selflessness, the devotion to a common cause, of the two teacher organization giants. There is no use denying that the AFT and the NEA are engaged in dire competition for the membership of the teachers of America. But we must do this without giving aid and power to the governmental authorities, boards of education, and superintendents with whom we are contending. And then, let us keep the door open; let us look forward to the day when AFT-NEA unity may become a reality. Heaven knows, we badly need a strong, unified, militant, and labor-oriented teachers' union to fight the great battles that lie ahead. Teacher welfare, a sound educational system, and the good of society as a whole require nothing less.[4]

5. National Congress of Parents and Teachers

The largest organization connected with education in the United States is the National Congress of Parents and Teachers, with a mem-

---

[4] Charles Cogen, "Teacher Militancy: Bridge to AFT-NEA Unity?" *American Teacher*, 52 (No. 7), March, 1968.

bership of more than 11 million. As the name implies, members are both lay and professional, with the lay membership far outnumbering the professional. This organization represents one of the greatest educational movements in history. It operates largely through state congresses, which in turn reach down into the local community through local parent-teacher associations. It is influential and provides for active, direct participation at local, state, and national levels. The state and national congresses speak with authority to legislatures. The National Congress of Parents and Teachers, recognizing that security is linked with the other aims of the organization, has consistently and effectively advocated policies favorable to improving teacher security.

6. World Organization of the Teaching Profession

A constitution for the World Organization of the Teaching Profession (WOTP) was adopted when 56 delegates from 38 national education associations and nine professional and intergovernmental organizations concerned with education met in Scotland in 1947. The purposes of the WOTP as stated in its constitution are:

> To make the highest standards of full and free education available to all without discrimination;
> To improve the professional status of the teachers of the world and to promote their intellectual, material, social and civic interests and rights;
> To promote world-wide peace through the building of good will founded upon co-operation between nations in educational enterprises, based upon pertinent and accurate information;
> To advise the appropriate organs of the United Nations and of other international bodies on educational and professional matters.[5]

THE TEACHER AND TEACHER ASSOCIATIONS

Teacher associations reflect the collective judgment of school teachers as to the goals of education. The large number of unrelated organizations is partial evidence that the teaching profession, nationally, is not fully unified to achieve these goals.

A well-informed profession is one safeguard to education. The individual teacher becomes informed about current educational needs

[5] As listed in Walter S. Monroe, ed., *Encyclopedia of Educational Research*. New York: Macmillan, 1950, p. 1446.

through periodicals and yearbooks that are issued by most state, regional, and national organizations. Speakers and consultants are sent out from headquarters to local groups. Many of the organizations have regular state or regional and national conventions. Often teachers are released from teaching in order to attend meetings, e.g., the annual convention of the National Council of Teachers of English. Frequently, planning and executing a program for special days called "institute days" is delegated to a regional or state organization.

Through associations teachers gain a reasonable degree of autonomy of action that would otherwise be denied them. This is essential to securing and maintaining a satisfactory degree of professional solidarity. Because control of the schools lies outside the profession this is especially important to classroom teachers. Teachers, unless well organized, are vulnerable to all kinds of external influences, some of them inimical to the cause of education and threats to the individual teacher. Influential groups throughout the United States consistently oppose state and community efforts to improve education and to improve the welfare of teachers. For instance, an organized group may be dedicated to reducing taxes. Such an aim will usually lead to opposition to any teacher association program that requires tax money for the improvement of teacher welfare. Individual teachers cannot be alert to all such organizations and pressure groups in the community or in the state, but teacher association officers are trained to recognize and to recommend action to deal with such situations.

SECURITY POLICIES IN SCHOOL ADMINISTRATION

Local policies of educational administration, especially those related to security provisions for teachers, vary strikingly throughout the United States. Not all state school authorities agree on what security provisions are appropriate. Policies toward contracts, promotion, tenure, retirement, pensions, and salary scales illustrate rather vividly some of the concrete problems in procuring reasonable security provisions.

1. Contracts

"Contract" is the legal term for a binding agreement between two parties. A teacher's contract is prepared by the local school district and is a statement of terms and conditions of employment. It generally stipulates that he shall receive a certain salary for his services for a period of time. Contracts vary all the way from a simple, oral agreement to extended technical statements of terms. What is said in the contract is a fairly good expression of the attitude of the school officers toward the individual teacher.

The present trend is greatly to simplify teachers' contracts. Frequently, school policies, as they pertain to teachers, are worked out with the help of the teachers' associations. The school system may publish the policies, including specific statements relating to teacher welfare, in a handbook. When the teacher accepts a position he then knows precisely the commitments of the school system. Large school systems, and most smaller ones, make the community's commitments to its teachers unmistakably clear and binding on the community.

2. Tenure

Tenure refers specifically to the period of time a teacher is entitled to hold his position—the length of his term of appointment. A teacher beginning in a school system ordinarily serves a probationary period before receiving what are called continuing contracts, indefinite contracts, or permanent contracts. Tenure provisions, as they are stated in official pronouncements of school district policy, vary from community to community and from state to state, and there is some disagreement within the profession about what constitutes the best manner of stating the terms of tenure. In most states the circumstances under which teachers are entitled to permanent tenure are defined by law.

Tenure is an important security provision. Free from any fear of unfair dismissal, the teacher is relieved of a strain which might impair his teaching effectiveness. This means, however, that three steps in the selection of teachers are especially important.

The initial selection comes when application is made for admission to teacher training. It is impossible to state definitely the qualifications of a successful teacher, much less to assess an individual's possession of potential powers for good teaching. It is possible, however, at the time of original application to eliminate some individuals who because of intellectual, physical, or social factors seem poor prospects for teaching. Some institutions select again when students apply for the privilege of student teaching.

After a student has completed the training requirements and has

received his college degree, an employing official, perhaps a superintendent of schools, makes another evaluation of potential success. If
the applicant is given a teaching position, the initial contract is typically
for one year. Sometimes a teacher beginning in a system has three of
these one-year contracts. During the period of the one-year contracts
he is "on probation." At the end of each year, often in joint conference
with an administrator, the teacher's work is reviewed and direction and
advice given. At the end of any one year a teacher's contract may be not
renewed.

The most important point of selection comes at the close of the
probationary period. At this time the teacher is eligible for a permanent
contract—for tenure. He also is eligible for an extension of the
probationary period, or he may be dismissed. The employing official
faces a significant responsibility. If only those of proven competence are
allowed to have permanent contracts, the virtue of the tenure provisions for teachers will not be questioned and most future dissatisfaction
with the tenure laws will be avoided.

When a teacher has permanent tenure, when he has passed the
selection barriers, his tenure then is for *a* position in the school
system—not for *the* position that he holds at any particular time. For
instance, a principal could, without loss of salary, be shifted to a
class room teaching position without any violation of his tenure
privileges, although this would be most unusual.

The burden of the proof of incompetence or misbehavior rests
with the school officials. A teacher who is "on tenure," who has
permanent employment in a school district, cannot be dismissed
because of the personal whim of an administrator, school board
member, or political manipulator. The protection of tenure, however,
as well as any of the other security provisions provided teachers, does
not relieve the teacher of responsibility to fulfill his obligations to the
school system to the best of his ability. He has been judged the kind of
individual who has the qualifications for professional membership.
He owes it to himself and to the profession to merit this confidence.
The tenure laws are not intended to protect the incompetent.

3. Promotion

In joining the profession and in affiliating with a local school
district it is important to know what lies ahead, what the avenues for

advancement are. One may decide advancement lies in leaving classroom teaching and entering some specialized educational field. There are many such opportunities—e.g., special teaching, supervision, and school administration. Outside-the-classroom positions often offer such rewards that the individual decides early in his career to prepare for one of them. Unfortunately, a skillful teacher is all too frequently rewarded with an appointment to such a position rather than to a position that fully utilizes his teaching skill. *This policy reflects a tendency in the profession itself to depreciate the importance of teaching, to attach greater significance to nonteaching functions.* It would seem logical that an outstanding teacher who prefers to remain in the classroom should be given the same recognition and salary that would be his in an administrative or supervisory post. But practice within the profession itself does not encourage this.

Many excellent teachers who, at considerable sacrifice, have stayed with classroom teaching have been resourceful in supplementing their salaries with other employment. Part-time services of teachers have always been in great demand. The poorer the school district, the more likely it is that the more competent classroom teachers will be encouraged to move up to other positions or to seek other teaching positions which offer financial inducements. Partly as a result of policies of this kind, teaching is an excessively mobile profession. And for this, education in the United States pays an enormous price. Preparing prospective teachers and orienting new teachers are expensive operations. Too rapid personnel turnover results in diminished returns from this investment. The turnover also is educationally wasteful, not only from the viewpoint of the pupils who suffer from lack of educational continuity over a period of years, but also from the viewpoint of a personnel handicapped in its long-term plans and frustrated in carrying on activities designed to be built up over the years. Rapid turnover is costly in terms of group morale and is detrimental to teacher prestige because a transient group usually does not command the respect afforded a stable, continuing, professional group.

4. Retirement

Admission to the teaching profession assumes the candidate intends to serve the profession and devote his energies to improving it during all his employed years. At the age of 70, or thereabouts, he will be expected to retire from teaching. The problem of income for the rest of his life must be solved. Because education is a state function, each state has the responsibility to establish laws regarding public school teacher retirement policies. All the states have done this with characteristic variations consistent with differing points of view about educational policy.

In general, retirement provisions are developed in terms of three plans. The state may establish its own system—define its own policy toward retirement and retirement pay. When this plan is followed, the teacher usually contributes a share toward retirement pay. By basing the plan on actuarial predictions, the system adopted tends to be sound. In some cases, special provisions are made for survivors' benefits to protect a teacher's dependents, as well as for those becoming disabled before retirement age and for those who for personal reasons desire to retire at an earlier age.

The second plan is for the state to join the federal government in providing for old-age benefits. It conforms to the current tendency to shift state and local financial burdens to the national government. Teachers' associations, however, are generally opposed to this. A pension plan set up within a state for teachers is usually also a savings plan. A teacher may withdraw funds invested at any time he leaves teaching, regardless of his age. The plan provides some flexibility in that the age of retirement is determined partly in terms of years of service and is not set at a chronological age point. Teachers' associations contend also that a pension fund worked out for them specifically is unifying for the teachers and is more within their own control. For a career teacher, the benefits of a state teacher retirement plan tend to be much more generous than those offered under a federal plan for old-age security.

The third general plan is for the local school district to gain state permission to administer its own pension program. A few larger cities continue to support local teacher retirement plans established years ago. New adoptions of this plan are rare.

Programs of retirement have some weaknesses. Differing state policies make it difficult for a teacher to transfer to another state without sacrificing some accrued pension benefits. The question of what percentage teachers should contribute to the costs is difficult to decide. What to do about disability insurance and what the age of retirement should be are points of disagreement. Survivors' benefits have not always been made clear. But improvements in retirement provisions are gradually being made. The NEA, the AFT, state teachers' associations, local teachers' unions, and other organizations are working on the problem.

5. Leaves of absence

Teachers who have some good reason for enforced absence, who may become ill, are given further security through a policy providing sick leaves. It is usual for a school system to grant two weeks' leave a year for enforced absence, to permit these leaves of absence to be cumulative, and to inflict no loss of pay. Such a policy does not jeopardize the teacher's pension status. Some systems grant extended leaves on full- or part-time pay or without pay. These leaves may be for a semester or more to be devoted to study or travel or something else that will enhance a teacher's worth to the community.[6]

6. Salary

Two factors in a teacher's situation do much to influence the feeling of satisfaction that he derives from a conscientious discharge of his responsibilities: the salary structure and scale and the teaching load. A too-heavy teaching load either leads a teacher to work beyond his strength or forces him to make adjustments in the interest of self-protection that are, from an educational standpoint, undesirable. Substandard salaries limit the number of capable people attracted to teaching and the number willing to stay in the profession. With inadequate salaries, those dedicated to teaching are forced into "moon-lighting" and summer employment in other lines of work in order to maintain a comfortable standard of living. In better communities, therefore, much thought is given to establishing a salary *structure* and a

[6] For an over-all picture of this aspect of security provisions, see *Leaves of Absence for Classroom Teachers, 1965–66*, NEA Research Report 1967-R5.

Fig. 4.2 Estimated average annual salaries of public school classroom teachers, 1968–1699. Note: In terms of actual purchasing power, the Alaska figure would be $7,820, which would rank Alaska as No. 21. (Data from NEA Research Report 1969-R1)

State	Rank	Value
Alaska	1	$10,427
California	2	9,500
Michigan	3	9,288
Illinois	4	9,100
New York	5	9,000
Maryland	6	8,815
Connecticut	7	8,500
New Jersey	8	8,425
Nevada	9	8,330
Washington	10	8,250
Arizona	11	8,240
Delaware	12	8,200
Florida	13	8,130
Massachusetts	14	8,100
Hawaii	14	8,100
Indiana	14	8,100
Rhode Island	17	8,070
Minnesota	18	8,000
Wisconsin	18	8,000
Oregon	20	7,965
UNITED STATES		7,908
Pennsylvania	21	7,858
Iowa	22	7,781
Ohio	23	7,750
Virginia	24	7,300
Wyoming	25	7,252
Colorado	26	7,150
New Mexico	27	7,133
Missouri	28	7,108
Utah	29	7,100
Kansas	30	7,062
New Hampshire	31	7,058
Georgia	32	7,002
Louisiana	33	6,978
Montana	34	6,900
North Carolina	35	6,852
Vermont	36	6,700
Oklahoma	37	6,641
Texas	38	6,619
Maine	39	6,600
Nebraska	40	6,585
Kentucky	41	6,550
West Virginia	42	6,400
Tennessee	43	6,365
Idaho	44	6,245
Arkansas	45	6,155
North Dakota	46	6,050
South Carolina	47	5,875
Alabama	47	5,875
South Dakota	49	5,800
Mississippi	50	5,772

salary *scale* that provide incentive and encouragement for a satisfied and relatively stable professional corps of teachers.

At this point, two aspects of the salary situation will be of interest to the prospective teacher—the over-all salary situation throughout the country and the part played, or that should be played, in determining and paying salaries by school districts (not always local districts).

Fig. 4.2 compares the average annual salaries of the classroom teachers in the public schools of each state. Since each state in America is the legal unit of public school administration and since the states vary greatly in their ability to raise revenues, variations in the salaries paid by different states are marked—perhaps surprisingly so. Fig. 4.3 graphically shows that the states differ in the importance they attach to the problem of improving salaries. This figure shows the relative efforts the states are putting forth, but what it would be *possible* for them to do can be deduced from the data in Fig. 11.6 (page 331), which show the money spent on public schools as a percentage of personal income. The data show that some of the states making the greatest efforts are simply unable to pay good salaries. Variations in such factors as birth rate, personal income, and taxable wealth make the problem more difficult in some states than in others. Mississippi, for example, ranked fiftieth in average instructional salaries in 1968, when in salary *increase* over a 10-year period, the state ranked sixth. In 1968, Mississippi ranked sixteenth in the percentage of personal income expended on education. Although Mississippi is making a great effort to improve its educational situation, it has been unable to reach a desirable salary level.

The salary situation among the more than 20,000 school districts in the United States is, perhaps, of more immediate personal importance to the individual seriously considering entering the profession. After all, the teacher will probably be employed by an independent school district, and the policy of that district toward paying teachers will have much to do with his future satisfactions in teaching.

Local salary policy is reflected in the salary structure and in the salary scale for a given year. Since the salary structure and salary scale are developed and formulated to attract and retain capable teachers,

Fig. 4.3 Percentage increases in instructional staff salaries, 1958–1959 to 1968–1969. (Data from NEA Research Report 1969-R1)

Kentucky	1	102.1
Georgia	2	92.0
Arkansas	3	87.8
Iowa	4	87.0
Virginia	5	86.1
Mississippi	6	85.6
Nebraska	7	84.8
Tennessee	8	84.3
Hawaii	9	80.6
North Carolina	10	80.5
South Carolina	11	80.4
South Dakota	12	78.4
Illinois	13	77.1
Alabama	14	76.9
West Virginia	14	76.9
Maryland	16	75.8
North Dakota	17	75.0
New Hampshire	18	72.4
Vermont	19	71.3
Florida	20	71.0
Wisconsin	21	70.5
Kansas	22	69.1
Missouri	23	68.8
Alaska	24	67.5
Michigan	25	66.5
Massachusetts	26	66.2
UNITED STATES		65.9
Maine	27	65.2
Nevada	28	64.5
Rhode Island	29	63.6
Indiana	30	62.4
Washington	30	62.4
Wyoming	32	62.1
California	33	62.0
Ohio	34	61.8
Oregon	35	61.3
Arizona	36	59.2
Connecticut	37	58.9
Montana	38	58.4
Pennsylvania	39	57.0
Minnesota	40	55.6
New Jersey	41	55.3
Utah	42	53.9
Colorado	43	53.3
Idaho	44	52.4
Louisiana	44	52.4
Delaware	46	50.7
New York	47	49.2
Texas	48	47.6
Oklahoma	49	47.5
New Mexico	50	44.0

taken together they constitute a fairly reliable criterion for judging the value a given school district places upon good teaching.

The salary structure, usually printed or mimeographed, is a written statement of the policies that govern salaries in a given school district. The policies adopted by the board of education include salary differentials for preparation and experience—and sometimes for so-called "merit" differences—allowances for sick leave, for dependents, for health insurance, sabbaticals, pensions, extra pay for extra work like coaching, and other matters related to teacher welfare. The salary structure specifically states the principles on which the plan for paying teachers is based. For example, in a 58-page booklet issued to teachers in 1968–1969, the San Francisco Unified School District states:

> The salary schedule of the San Francisco Unified School District for teachers is a single salary schedule of the preparational type. Every teacher is in his proper place on the schedule according to his preparational qualifications, his years of experience in the San Francisco public schools and such additional outside teaching experience as has been approved by the Board of Education for salary increment credit.

Besides stating the policies that govern the payment of teachers, the booklet explains how the policies were formulated and states the minimum and maximum salaries for the current year as well as the salary increments for each year. Inasmuch as each school district in the American school system has considerable autonomy, each district formulates its own salary structure.

Both the NEA and the AFT view the formulation of a salary structure as a matter for mutual consideration by both the teaching personnel and the school board. Research studies are made regularly by the NEA, and the results are disseminated throughout the profession.[7] In their report on the economic status of teachers in 1966–1967, the NEA's research staff said: "It can be concluded from the data presented here that teachers' salaries, though much improved in recent years, are still far below the levels of compensation attainable by college graduates in other professional occupations." The NEA and the AFT provide expert help to local organizations in formulating salary scales. By using an "index" system, allotting a value of 1.0 to the

---

[7] See, for example, *Economic Status of Teachers*, NEA Research Report 1967-R8.

salary paid beginning teachers with a bachelor's degree and no experience and assigning value increases in terms of training and years of experience, the entire scale is geared to the amount that must be paid to the beginning teacher in the competitive market.

The AFT advocates a single salary schedule for teachers at the bachelors level, based on training and experience, starting at $8,500 and reaching $17,000 in five annual increments. Additional substantial differentials are recommended for teachers with training above the bachelor's level, to more nearly equal the incomes in other professions requiring comparable education and training. The AFT and also the NEA oppose "merit-rating" systems of pay for teachers on the basis that such systems cannot operate without the injection of personal bias and preferment.

For the 1968–1969 school year, the *average* annual salary of classroom teachers in the elementary schools was approximately $7,676 and of secondary school teachers, $8,160.[8] Although elementary school teachers' salaries have traditionally been below those of secondary school teachers, the difference has grown smaller during the past decade. (By comparison, in 1969 the *beginning* salary was $9,816 in engineering for men with bachelor's degrees, $8,844 in accounting, and $8,028 in sales-marketing.)

Remuneration for teaching may be expected to improve to a point where teaching will attract more of the abler college graduates and keep them in the profession. Salary structures and salary scales alone will not, of course, bring all this to pass. They are, however, important elements.

Summary

Membership in a social group has striking effects on the individual. Assuming membership in a professional group implies acceptance of standards of behavior adopted by the group. The standards not only protect the teachers but also guarantee children a satisfactory quality of education.

Opportunity to improve the profession is afforded teachers

[8] NEA Research Report 1969-R1, pp. 22, 23.

through membership in teacher associations that influence both local and state governments. The status of the profession will not rise perceptibly unless the profession itself exerts its energies to bring this about. The problem of improvement is different from other professions because of the differences in functions, control, support, and the ratio of the sexes in the teaching profession, and also because teaching is a tax-supported profession.

The prestige status of teachers is well above the average. A measure of the value placed on education by a state or by a community is reflected in the security provisions made for teachers. Salary scales are especially important. Often teachers, through their associations, participate in determining their security provisions.

An NEA research publication shows that most teachers would enter the teaching profession again if they had to make the choice once more. The professional features of teaching help to make it very desirable work.

Questions

1. How can an individual teacher contribute to upgrading the teaching profession?
2. How do social attitudes toward the teaching profession affect the level of professionalization the membership of the profession is capable of achieving?
3. What are some of the adjustments an individual must make when he becomes a member of the teaching profession?
4. How does social stratification within the teaching profession affect the prestige of the membership?
5. What considerations would help you to decide whether to join the AFT or the NEA? Both associations?
6. What evidence is there to support the contention that a reasonable degree of security is essential to the development of a healthful personality?
7. What do you consider legitimate pressure-group methods that a teachers' association is justified in using to obtain what it considers to be rightful ends?

8. What are some of the benefits a teacher may expect to receive from belonging to a local teachers' association?
9. What security provisions do you hope to find provided for the teachers by the community in which you begin your teaching?
10. How would your own obligations be affected by a liberal policy toward teachers?
11. Which policy do you prefer—including school administrators in the local teachers' association, or excluding them?
12. Why do the secondary schools attract more men teachers than the elementary schools?

Projects

1. Evaluate the features of a salary scale that has been adopted in some school system. If possible, compare this salary scale with that of another school system.
2. Describe the activities engaged in by the National Congress of Parents and Teachers. Evaluate its services.
3. Analyze the contents of a recent issue of the NEA journal, *Today's Education*, and evaluate the contribution the magazine makes to the membership of the NEA.
4. Analyze the contents of a current issue of the journal of the state education association in your home state and evaluate the contribution it makes to the membership.
5. Analyze a recent NEA research publication related to the economic status of teachers.
6. Analyze the contents of the teachers' handbook issued by a local school district. List the kind of information it supplies.
7. To bring pressure on local school boards the NEA has worked out a policy for "sanctions." Explain what sanctions are, how they are to be applied, where they have been used, and with what results.

5

The Teacher
and His
Philosophy

From this book and from other books about education and also from teachers of education, the student receives advice on how to answer many of the perplexing questions he must face as a teacher. The advice is abundant, often positive, frequently diverse, and sometimes reflects deep-seated prejudice.

Education, like parenthood, religion, and politics, is a subject on which every man thinks himself something of an authority, even though recognized experts seldom approach consensus. Faced, then, with numerous contradictions, how is the student to answer his own questions, to think his way through to his own conclusions with clarity and with what seems to be some reliability? To what sources may he turn for help?

Some of the questions that confront the teacher are the center of public debates about education: What should the role of the federal government be in improving education? Traditionally, the role of the states has been relatively clear, but is the federal government causing a modification in the states' role? How may educational leadership be improved, be divorced from the machinations of professional politicians? What subject matter should be taught in the elementary and secondary curriculums? How can America's schools meet the challenges of rapidly advancing technology throughout the world? On all such questions the classroom teacher is expected to have a well-formulated point of view.

Other questions that the teacher faces are of more immediate and direct personal concern. The teacher asks himself: What kinds of rewards and positive incentives can I use in the classroom to encourage desirable forms of behavior? How shall I take into account the special problems of the pupils? Shall I judge the work of each pupil relative to the achievements of the rest of the class or in terms of his individual efforts? How do I determine a reasonable standard to apply in judging the work of pupils? How much weight should I give to the differences in learning ability of my pupils?

There are also questions of another kind that the teacher must answer. These center around the relationships of a teacher with the community, the parents of the pupils, fellow teachers, and administrators. A teacher must answer such questions as: What responsibility should I take in the total program of the school? What should my relationships be with my fellow teachers and with school administrators? If there is a teachers' union in my city, should I belong? In what ways should I participate in the administration of my school? In the programs of the PTA?

The answers teachers give to these questions and to others like them are reflected in classroom teaching. Great variation in teaching methods and procedures stems from varying answers.

Differences on an educational issue

The variations among answers given to questions revolving around an educational issue may be illustrated by analyzing the use of motivation in classroom teaching. Practices related to motivation are selected as illustrative because there are few subjects in the field of teaching that lead to more heated controversy than pupil motivation. From the following descriptions of the practices of three conscientious and intelligent teachers, it is apparent that each teacher has asked and answered in radically different ways such questions as: What teaching methods will motivate pupils to learn what I think they should learn? What degree of coercion is appropriate to motivate children to learn? What kinds of coercion are most likely to lead to the best results? Are grades, examinations, credits, graduation requirements, and the like, the most promising tools for motivating learning? To move to a set of broader and, in the long run, more significant questions: How can I motivate pupils to be strong and self-respecting? To have wholesome relationships with their classmates? To resist exploitation? To avoid gullibility in the face of constant streams of propaganda? To put the questions in still more comprehensive terms: How can I so motivate pupils that my whole educative influence will be oriented toward encouraging pupil growth—growth toward what the psychologists call self-actualization of the pupil?

Teacher A exacts strict obedience from his pupils. He tells the pupils all they need to know and expects them to be able to repeat what he has told them. He makes daily assignments to be completed before the next class meeting. He gives frequent tests based on the assignments; they are objective and rigorously graded. His methods of teaching are founded on the principle of authority. Pupils are trained to "behave" and to study "because the teacher says so." Teacher A relies heavily on coercion, rewards for merit, definite assignments, and the like to motivate the pupils to learn what he expects them to learn.

In Teacher B's class the pupils all study the same assignment. Learning is a contest. Pupils compete with one another, with the awards and approval consistently going to the winners. Pupils are graded on a curve of probability. The highest grade is awarded to the pupil at the top, with the lowest going to the pupil at the bottom. In the minds of the pupils, certain children are consistently "good," others are habitually "bad." The teacher believes that motivation stems from rivalry and that the race for mastery is a fair one even though those who are required to compete are unequally endowed. He acts as a referee, making and enforcing the rules of the game. The strong survive. The weak fail—"as in life," Teacher B observes. Success and failure, as measured against classmates' performances, are the primary sanctions.

Teacher C emphasizes group accomplishments and tries to build confidence in each pupil and goodwill among all of them. He encourages each pupil to contribute what he can to class projects. There is an exchange of ideas among pupils between pupils and teacher, a sharing of responsibility. The theme of class work is cooperation. Grading is considered to be of minor importance. The teacher strives to encourage each pupil to develop along lines that are in accordance with his natural talents, to build confidence and self-respect, to develop a feeling of responsibility, and to be resistant to exploitation either of himself or of others. Sanctions lie in the success of the group and in the individual's acceptance by the group. Methods that motivate the pupils to learn allow the pupils considerable freedom of choice.

Let us assume that the three teachers are equally capable of being effective teachers. Why do they differ so markedly in their procedures? Fundamentally, they have different educational philosophies that lead them to teach differently. They give different answers to the question of what is good education. An analysis of their teaching reveals several kinds of disagreement. There is, of course, the initial disagreement about the most successful way of motivating pupils—to put it briefly, whether authority, rivalry, or cooperation can best stimulate pupils to achieve the desired ends. But there are also disagreements about the ends themselves—whether, for example, learning academic subjects is more worthwhile than learning to compete with others, or learning to get along with others, and whether all are desirable goals for the teacher in the classroom. There are also disagreements about the justice of judging pupils according to a single standard. There are disagreements about the relative value of directed and nondirected inquiry. Further, among teachers who might agree that cooperation is the most desirable basis for motivation, there will be many differences about what cooperation means in practice, and to what extent the restrictions of a classroom situation allow cooperation to be put into practice at all. There are just as many disagreements about the meaning and practicability of authority and rivalry.

Sources of differences

The kind of wide differences discerned in the examples illustrating questions related to motivation may be discovered in many educational situations. Why are there such differences? What differences are typical? Where do differences originate?

We must not be led into the error of thinking that the differences that teachers have in answers to questions of an educational nature can be explained in terms of differences in intelligence or sincerity. Wide differences on many issues and problems may be expected of teachers who are all fully capable and all deeply concerned for the welfare of their pupils. If a teacher is not intelligent or interested, the decisions he makes may be wrong; but for a teacher to make what others conclude is a wrong decision does not imply that he *is* dull or insensitive.

That teachers cannot turn to a single unquestioned authority for established answers to their questions explains in part the variations in their responses. If psychologists, for instance, knew a great deal more than they now know about the behavior of human beings, they might develop an authoritative theory that would be an accepted guide to teaching practice and thereby encourage uniformity.

But the answers of the experts often are in conflict. Teachers must choose among them. In answering questions related to motivation, for instance, it is generally agreed that the purposive activity a child engages in originates in his instincts and is expressed through learned incrustation of cultural derivation. Psychologists disagree as to what the instincts are and as to how they are molded by culture in determining the whole pattern of a child's behavior.

The answers to educational questions tend to be relative, not absolute. May a teacher use coercion? Perhaps the answer is a qualified *yes*. Coercion, yes, but coercion that is reasonable. What is reasonable coercion? Is there an ethical implication? Is good taste involved? Answers are also relative in terms of their setting. As new situations arise, not only do new questions arise, but the old ones take new forms. What was once considered a correct answer may, at another time, be thought incorrect.

Where, then, does the teacher turn for answers to his questions? What can he use as a guide to bring reasonable consistency into his educational practices? The title of the chapter indicates our answer: the teacher develops an educational philosophy that serves him as a frame of reference in terms of which he solves educational problems or answers educational questions. This chapter explains how a teacher develops his philosophy, explores the sources to which he may turn, suggests how he may put his philosophy to practical use. *No attempt is made to provide the student with an educational philosophy.* Developing an educational philosophy is a personal and individual responsibility that cannot be delegated to someone else. Nevertheless, as we shall see as we proceed, there are sources of help in fulfilling this responsibility.

No matter where or when a teacher
teaches, his philosophy influences
what and how he teaches. Two
Peace Corps volunteer teachers are
shown—one with her kindergarten
class in western Africa, the other
teaching in Peru in a school he
himself built of bamboo matting.
Peace Corps teachers are sought as
teachers here after their return; the
traits that led them to volunteer in
the first place, plus their experience,
make them particularly sympathetic
and skilled as teachers. Teaching
and learning in two other parts of

the world are also shown. Elementary
school pupils in Puerto Rico are
preparing original stories in book
form. High school students on a
Navajo reservation in Arizona are
in a mathematics class.

What is philosophy?

What is this base in terms of which educational questions are answered and educational practices patterned? This intellectually derived source that helps a teacher answer questions? Where does it come from? A *practical* philosophy—which in contrast to a speculative philosophy is what we are concerned with here—is a thoughtful and critical view of the world that carries implications for action. This meaning of philosophy is in direct contrast to that which the term carries in popular usage, such as when any set of beliefs, unexamined and uncriticized, is spoken of as a philosophy—or as a philosophy of life— thus overextending a term that etymologically means a love of wisdom. Everyone holds a set of beliefs that guides his actions; not everyone has, by study and reflection, systematized those beliefs into a consistent philosophy.

A philosophy used by the teacher as a guide in handling the problems that face him in his professional work is his philosophy of education.

Sources of a teacher's philosophy

The more prominent sources from which philosophical truth has been derived are: personal experience, common sense, religion, science, and systematic philosophy. These terms, obviously, are not mutually exclusive. All of them, for example, include something of experience. We treat them separately because in common usage they are spoken of as though they were entities. In examining each of these sources we shall note that each has contributed to man's search for philosophical truth. We shall also discover that no one of these sources in itself is sufficient to serve as the sole base for an educational philosophy.

EXPERIENCE

How does experience, one's self-conscious interaction with one's environment, contribute to one's educational philosophy? A child's experiences, from the beginning, make impressions on him concerning the kind of world he lives in and the worth of people and things, including himself. He can develop a feeling, for instance, that he lives in a world that allows him to satisfy himself and to explore; or he can come to feel that he must constantly guard against threats to himself and his private belongings. Such feelings may remain as unformulated— sometimes unrecognized—attitudes, or they may be translated into conscious convictions. Some of the child's most lasting beliefs come from what people tell him. His parents, his teachers, and his peers make pronouncements with various degrees of authority. Some of their statements, to the extent that his experiences do not contradict them, are accepted by the child as fundamental truths. He develops deep-seated beliefs, too, based on his emotional needs. If, for example, he has a strong need for rules to guide him in all his actions, he might invent such rules and come to regard them as moral laws. On the other hand, if he has an antipathy to authority he might flagrantly defy authority and rationalize his behavior. Some of his beliefs are based on his explorations of the world itself, still others on projecting analogies from what he has experienced to what is beyond his experience.

As his experience broadens, he comes in time to see that he cannot depend entirely on his past experiences as a basis for his beliefs. He becomes conscious that beliefs based on past experience are in need of constant critical examination and, perhaps, continual modification. He comes to realize that some of his beliefs picked up haphazardly from so many random sources, conflict with one another. Stories he was told as a toddler are contradicted by what he is told in school. Earlier experiences are contradicted by newer experiences. New authorities may replace older ones. Reliance on the findings of the senses may grow stronger, and confidence in the discoveries of the imagination may weaken. When a person's beliefs conflict, he strives to resolve the dissonance. This attempt may lead him to drop or to ignore those beliefs that clash with more strongly held beliefs or to find ways of modifying the conflicting beliefs so that none needs to be completely relinquished. As experience and reflection add new data and new interpretations, new conflicts arise and some of the older beliefs fade into the background. In a continuous process, a person's system of beliefs ever evolves, becoming more and more complex.

Regardless of their range, an individual cannot depend solely on his personal experiences to provide him with wholly reliable guides to action. If we look upon philosophy as a thoughtful and critical view of the world with implications for action, then our own experiences and the beliefs derived from them cannot be exempted from that critical view. A teacher's experiences, for example, do not provide him with answers to such educational questions as: What reason do I have for believing that a classroom with an atmosphere of democracy is to be preferred over one with an atmosphere of autocracy? One in which the teaching procedures are humane rather than harsh? How do I know that one kind of social arrangement in the classroom provides pupils with a more worthwhile experience than some other? What criteria shall I use to judge the educative values of certain kinds of classroom experiences? And where do I go to find those criteria? Although the student will raise many such questions as he proceeds with serious professional study, we shall not attempt to answer them here. We cite them to illustrate that beliefs derived from experience, while valuable, cannot answer every question that can legitimately be raised.

COMMON SENSE

Aristotle is credited with having first used the term "common sense" to include the beliefs and knowledge people gain through their senses and reactions in the process of ordinary day-by-day living. In America "common sense" is generally used to denote the fund of knowledge growing out of ordinary experience in solving practical questions. Common sense is frequently used carelessly to mean shrewdness and sharpness in practical matters. We use common sense to mean the accumulated body of knowledge that has been gained through common daily experience. Our generalizations from common experience include such patent rules as "food satisfies hunger," "fire burns," or "lightning strikes." The range of common-sense beliefs in time becomes great, and such beliefs become important determinants in our day-to-day decisions.

It would be a mistake for teachers to place undue reliance on common sense for wise solutions to educational problems, for dependable answers to questions about teaching. Knowledge that is shared by all must be based on the most elementary kinds of human experience.

In fact, no knowledge can be more elementary, no beliefs more simple, than those classified as common sense, because that is the knowledge and those are the beliefs that are derived from the simple, common experiences of daily living. Any educational belief that is said to be sanctioned by common sense, therefore, is a belief that is accepted at face value by a person who has received no training whatever, because no training was necessary to its formulation. Common sense cannot answer questions that call for specialized, technical knowledge.

Critical scrutiny is a preliminary requisite for most of the beliefs incorporated in an educational philosophy. The beliefs growing out of common sense tend to be accepted without critical scrutiny. Einstein pointed out that common sense is nothing more than a deposit of prejudices laid down in the mind before the age of 18. Often they are mistaken beliefs.

Excessive reliance on common sense as the source of an educational philosophy may have unfortunate effects. It minimizes the importance of a methodical, cultivated philosophical foundation for educational beliefs. This means that the importance of extended training, thoughtful study, and serious pursuit of educational understanding is likewise minimized. If teaching problems could be solved by the application of common sense, then every citizen who believes he possesses common sense is justified in believing himself an educational expert. The opinions of the man on the street, the parents of the children, the popular journalist, the lecturer who talks on all subjects—opinions that may be expressions of biases and prejudices gained from simple experiences—would carry as much weight with the public as the opinions of the wisest educators.

What, then, is the contribution of common sense to the teacher's educational philosophy? How does it help him to answer educational questions, to make decisions related to his teaching practices? Common sense—good common sense—is essentially reliable. Danger lies in *undue* reliance on common sense. Common sense is one good source of beliefs, but it must be utilized in proper relationship to the other sources. It must not blind the teacher to the importance of seeking more training and experience, of utilizing the experts. The teacher must diligently seek help from sources that extend far beyond the sphere of common sense.

This classroom, though it looks like one in any modern elementary school, is actually in a Lutheran parochial school. The teaching and other activities in such a school are profoundly influenced by the religious philosophy adhered to by the teachers and the pupils' parents.

RELIGION

The universality and continuity of religion throughout history are evidence of its strength. Religious beliefs have had a pronounced influence on all the major trends of human events.

Religion, being concerned with basic beliefs, has relevance to a teacher's educational philosophy. Religion includes an unquestioned faith, indeed, an unshakeable conviction, about certain matters. In terms of these—man's highest values—man evaluates all else. Religious principles are not derived solely from experience past or current; they also originate in mystical insight. Religion is concerned with the ultimate end of man. It is also concerned with questions related to the good life. It is in this second of its concerns that it contributes most significantly to educational philosophy. Since both religion and education seek to promote the good life, religion contributes to the philosophy of education.

To say that one concern of religion is to promote the good life is not to say that every guide or signpost to the good life is furnished by religion. There may be several good answers to a particular problem, all of them acceptable from a religious standpoint. Another problem may have no religious implications at all. While the lessons of personal experience and common sense tend to help a teacher over familiar ground, the lessons of religion help him never to forget the ultimate goals of education and life.

SCIENCE

In our modern world of atomic energy and space exploration, science is probably the most highly respected source for educational beliefs and practices. Can science provide the answers to all our educational problems? Does an available fund of scientific knowledge obviate the need for a teacher to formulate an educational philosophy? Or does science serve as a ready reference in the development of a philosophy rather than as a substitute for a philosophy? In order that we may see clearly that science, undoubtedly, has an important relationship to philosophical thinking, but that science cannot provide answers to all of our educational problems, we shall briefly consider the nature of science, observing the subjects with which science deals.

From training in science in high school one gains an idea of what science is like. Perhaps one already knows, for instance, that science has customarily been subdivided into two categories—formal science and natural science; that mathematics is the classic example of formal science; that the natural sciences are those concerned with nature, such as biology, astronomy, and physics. Let us look more closely at each of the classifications.

Formal science, as the name indicates, is a science of form. It is an outcome of logical reasoning. Formal science begins with hypotheses or axioms that are assumed to be true. Following the dictates of certain rules and definitions, the formal scientist reasons from these hypotheses and determines other truths that logically follow. If the hypothesis is true, the subsequent statements *have* to be true. The last statement in the sequence logically follows from the first. It is true, providing the first statement or hypothesis is true.

Euclidean geometry, more commonly called demonstrational geometry, is an example of a formal science. Algebra, too, is a formal science. It begins with a set of axioms thought to be true; that is, the truth is thought to be self-evident. Reasoning logically from these axioms leads to other truths.

A pure formal science is an exercise in logic in which the original statements are *assumed* to be true. The primary concern of the formal scientist is not with the truth of the original assumptions but with the logic followed while reasoning from the basic assumptions.

To what extent can we depend on formal science to furnish answers to educational problems? We may be justified in answering, "Very little." Formal science is normally and ethically *neutral* toward all human issues. When, for instance, the mathematician proves a theorem, he accepts his proof as true because he rigorously followed certain rules and applied certain principles in arriving at that proof. He does not assume any responsibility for explaining to people how they should use the theorems he deduces and the formulas he accumulates. This he leaves to others.

The natural sciences are, in the order of their historical development, astronomy, physics, chemistry, biology, and sociology. This is a very broad classification that will serve the purpose of our discussion. For sake of simplification it omits such modern divisions as history, political science, psychology, and zoology, each of which may be considered a branch of one of the five basic classifications.

Can all our fundamental educational questions be answered from what is supplied by the natural sciences? Can we develop from the findings of the natural scientists a complete and harmonious educational philosophy? Note the kind of problems the natural sciences deal with and consider the principal characteristics of a field of knowledge that carries the distinction of qualifying as a science.

Alfred North Whitehead in his Lowell Lectures, given at Harvard University in 1925, expressed in very few words the underlying principle upon which the natural sciences are developed:

> The faith in the order of nature which has made possible the growth of science is a particular example of a deeper faith. This faith cannot be justified by any inductive generalization. It springs from the direct inspection of the nature of things as disclosed in our own immediate present experience. There is no parting from our shadow.[1]

This inexpugnable faith of mankind that there is an order of nature defines the principal, if not the single, aim of natural science. The aim

[1] Alfred North Whitehead, *Science and the Modern World*. New York: Macmillan, 1926, p. 27.

of the natural sciences is to discover the laws to which events in nature conform. It is this aim that motivates the natural scientists to strive so energetically to discover the pattern of natural events.

> The raw material of every science must always be an accumulation of facts. . . . But, as Poincaré remarked, an accumulation of facts is no more a science than a heap of stones is a house. When we set to work . . . to create a science we must first coordinate and synthesize the accumulated piles of facts. It is then usually found that a great number of separate facts can be summed up in a much smaller number of general laws. . . . These express the pattern of events for which we are searching.[2]

It should be noted that the natural scientists make no claim to a discovery of the causes of natural events. They are content to learn, with the limited tools at their disposal, what the pattern of events is and to describe the pattern as accurately as they can. Whatever discoveries they make seem to be in answer to man's insatiable curiosity to learn the pattern of the natural events that govern the universe in which he must live. The primary aim of natural science, namely, to discover the pattern of natural events, leaves to the province of others the task of deciding what is to be done with their findings.

The development of science, of course, is inherently dynamic. Its findings have positive and immediate effects on men's lives in untold ways. Particularly does science lead to a progressive modification of many of man's traditional beliefs. Education is not exempt from its tremendous influence. Sociology, mathematics, biology, political science, psychology, history—all make notable contributions. They do not, however, provide an authoritative base for educational decisions or serve as a substitute for educational philosophy.

The aims of both natural and formal science render them philosophically neutral and impersonal. Science endeavors to tell us what is. Science does not claim to tell us what should be. Educational philosophy utilizes the knowledge of formal and natural science, but its concern extends beyond the limitations of the sciences.

[2] Sir James Jeans, *Physics and Philosophy*. New York: Cambridge University Press, 1943, p. 8.

If we wish to discover the truth about nature . . . the only sound method is to go out into the world and question nature directly, and this is the long established and well-tried method of science. Questioning our own minds is of no use ; just as questioning nature can tell us truths only about nature, so questioning our own minds will tell us truths only about our own minds. The general recognition of this has brought philosophy in closer relations with science, and this approach has coincided with a change of view as to the proper aims of philosophy. The ancient philosophers pursued their studies in the hope of finding a lantern which should guide their feet along the best path in their journey through this life, the philosophers of the seventeenth and eighteenth centuries in a fixed determination to find evidence that this journey ended in a life to come. This humanistic tinge has taken a long time to disappear, but has almost done so in recent years ; philosophy has become less concerned with ourselves and more concerned with the universe outside ourselves. . . .

This may seem to suggest that philosophy should have not only the same methods but also the same aims and also, broadly speaking, the same field of work as science. . . . The tools of science are observation and experiment ; the tools of philosophy are discussion and contemplation. It is still for science to try to discover the pattern of events, and for philosophy to try to interpret it when found. . . .

Sir James Jeans, *Physics and Philosophy*. New York: Cambridge University Press, 1943, pp. 80–81. Quoted by permission of Cambridge University Press.

PHILOSOPHIC DOCTRINE

In philosophic doctrine, in the particular principles advocated or taught by the various so-called "systems" of philosophy or "schools" of philosophy, we have another resource that is valuable in formulating an educational philosophy.

Professional philosophers over the years have thought about man's problems in the light of knowledge from various specialized fields and have developed solutions and drawn conclusions about how solutions can be derived. A philosopher may have selected a particular problem or a particular hypothesis regarding the solution of a particular problem. By studying the main lines of relationships among all the facts that have a bearing on the making of human decisions, the philosopher finally has arrived at a generalization, a particular world view, a potential guide in making such decisions. If the process of reasoning leads logically to a statement of a philosophy that advocates a particular viewpoint, one that is consistent in all its parts and in the relationships between the facts used, and if the principles derived and the bearing they have on arriving at human decisions are set forth in logical order, the philosophy is said to be a systematic one, an expression of a philosophic doctrine.

Some of the better known philosophic doctrines have been classified in terms of their general characteristics and are thus described by such names as dualism, eclecticism, idealism, realism, rationalism, pragmatism, or existentialism. Sometimes a philosophic doctrine is identified with the name of the man who developed it. Taking the German philosophers, for example, we have doctrines identified with Kant, Fichte, Schelling, Hegel, Schopenhauer, Fechner, Lotze, Hartmann, Nietzsche, and Wundt. Sometimes a doctrine may relate to a single area of knowledge. A scholar may, for instance, develop a systematic philosophy of history. This has been done by such writers as Toynbee, Mannheim, Niebuhr, Frankel, and Maritain. One may find a philosophy of physics, of law, of religion, of biology, of government, of psychology, of education. Great thinkers are concerned with the development of philosophic doctrine. They do not bother with problems of little significance.

Charles S. Peirce (1839–1914) was a graduate of Harvard University and the Lawrence scientific school. As a member of the staff of the U. S. Coast Survey, he did work on the problems of geodesy and researches on the pendulum that received wide recognition. In 1880 and 1881 he gave a series of lectures at John Hopkins University on philosophical logic, expanding on the ideas he had advanced in an article in the January, 1878, Popular Science Monthly. *Although he had not used the word "pragmatism" in his article, he is credited with having formulated the idea generally referred to as Peirce's Principle and to have connected the name "pragmatism" with the idea. According to William James, the principle of pragmatism lay unnoticed for 20 years until he, in 1898, in a lecture at the Univeristy of California, reintroduced the term. Said James, "By that date [1898] the times seemed ripe for its reception. The word 'pragmatism' spread, and at present it fairly spots the pages of the philosophic journals."
Peirce was the first of the famous trio of American pragmatists—Peirce, James, and Dewey. The combined influence of the three on education in America has been very great indeed.*

As discussed in this chapter, the responsibility for developing one's philosophy lies within oneself. In developing a personal philosophy one often turns for help to the writings of the professional philosophers. Whether one accepts or rejects, in whole or in part, the philosophy in these writings, one will discover the professional philosopher's point of view, his line of reasoning that led to his beliefs about the solutions of various human problems.

As the teacher turns to science for scientific knowledge, he turns to philosophic doctrine for scholarly conclusions about philosophic matters. The philosophic doctrine expounded by a scholar like John Dewey, for example, is a helpful guide to a teacher in forming his own philosophy. How a specific doctrine affects a teacher will depend on the teacher's understanding of and response to the philosophic doctrine. His response will be conditioned by his understanding and by his entire thoughtful, critical view of the world.

Characteristics of a teacher's philosophy

A teacher's philosophy reflects his experience, his common sense, his religion, science, and philosophic doctrine. Some characteristics are clear in the definition of an educational philosophy: a thoughtful and

William James, about 1885.

It is generally accepted that William James (1842–1910) has no peer among the philosophers of America. He received the M.D. degree at Harvard University in 1870 and taught at Harvard from 1872 until his death, first teaching anatomy and physiology, then psychology, and finally, in the latter stages of his academic life, philosophy. In 1891, James published a monumental work in two volumes, The Principles of Psychology. *The book was immediately recognized as innovating and definitive, and it can still be read with enjoyment and profit. This work completed, James turned to that most profound of subjects—philosophy—for which he now believed himself prepared. After 1900 most of his writing was done in this field. Like Peirce, by whom he was influenced, James was trained as a scientist. It is not strange, therefore, that in harmony with Peirce's Principle, he constructed a philosophy that was a generalization of the scientific attitude toward the whole of life. James believed that philosophy, like science, should follow the method of finding the facts and of then harmonizing the facts to provide man with a basis for reasoning out answers to his perplexing problems, for solving his enigmas, and for making his distinctions, and to supply man with more or less valid principles to use as instruments with which to think. Using the descriptive term first used by Peirce, James referred to the method of pragmatism as "a new name for some old ways of thinking." In December, 1906, and January, 1907, James developed his understandings of the meaning of the pragmatic movement in a series of eight lectures given at Columbia University.*

> *A number of tendencies that have always existed in philosophy have all at once become conscious of themselves collectively, and of their combined mission ; and this has occurred in so many countries, and from so many different points of view, that much unconcerted statement has resulted. I have sought to unify the picture as it presents itself to my own eyes, dealing in broad strokes, and avoiding minute controversy.*

James not only stated that he was not expounding a new philosophy ; he even questioned the propriety of calling the method of pragmatism a philosophy. After these lectures, however, throughout the English-speaking world, he became the leader, if not of a new philosophy, at least of a new philosophical viewpoint.

Although James died in 1910, it is still too early to estimate the influence of his philosophy. It is, however, obvious that his high place among philosophers is secure. While he assiduously avoided erecting a new philosophy for others to repeat, he nevertheless supplied the seed and the soil that germinated new thought in all who considerately weighed what he said.

critical view of the world that carries implications for educational action. Two important specific characteristics are, in a sense, an amplification of this definition. An educational philosophy is personal. An educational philosophy is socially conditioned.

PERSONAL

A teacher's educational philosophy grows out of his own experiences and is modified by his own re-examination based on the principles of criticism that he chooses to apply. His developed philosophy is a description, explanation, and evaluation of the world as seen from his unique perspective. He can turn for help to many sources, but no matter how many sources he may draw upon or how many authorities he may listen to, the decision is his to accept or reject the would-be truths presented to him. His decision is free; it is shaped by his attitudes and presuppositions.

Although a teacher may not get outside himself to develop a purely objective view of the world, he can broaden himself by expanding the area of his experience, by trying to understand other people's senses of values, and by developing the habit of analyzing problems from various perspectives. He can also cultivate the practice of subjecting his own cherished beliefs to a critical cross-examination. The quality of his educational philosophy rests on his willingness continuously to explore and criticize.

Take as example a teacher who, let us assume, has come from a middle-class urban background and who, before and during his teaching

John Dewey (1859–1952) developed the pragmatic philosophy from an educational and social focus. He was a native of Vermont and a graduate of the University of Vermont and later of Johns Hopkins University. After graduation from Johns Hopkins he went west to teach philosophy, first at the University of Minnesota (1888–1889), then Michigan (1889–1894), and then Chicago (1894–1904). As director of the School of Education at the University of Chicago, he established an experimental school that carried out his ideas of the new pedagogy. It was through this work and his writings in connection with it that he won national fame. In 1904 he became professor of philosophy at Columbia University. It was here that his philosophy began to influence the social and philosophical thought of his time. His numerous writings have had a profound influence on the theory and practice of

John Dewey.

education in American schools. One of Dewey's students, William Heard Kilpatrick (1871–1965), wrote of Dewey's influence on education as follows:

> Possibly no service of John Dewey to American education, in fact to American thinking in general, has been greater than his help in better methods of thinking. The America of his youth was on the whole content to think in terms of unexamined terms most of which meant entities where in fact there were no entities but processes. Will, consciousness, faculties as memory, reasoning and the like, instincts, intelligence, mind—these are but samples of processes masquerading as entities. James's pragmatism (following Peirce) and Dewey's experimentalism here joined hands with the rising army of scientific thinkers to question everything that could be questioned.
>
> For teachers Dewey's How We Think, and particularly the seventh chapter (of the original edition) on "The Analysis of a Complete Act of Thought," has directly and indirectly brought great tonic effect. Through these, as stated earlier, American education discovered, so to speak, "the problem approach" as a teaching device. The effect has been very great. . . . It is . . . easy to assert that this one book has brought a wide emphasis on problems and the conscious use of problems in school work.

Paul Schilpp, ed., *The Philosophy of John Dewey*, 2nd ed. New York: Tudor, 1955, pp. 469–470. Quoted by permission of The Library of Living Philosophers, Inc.

career, has had experience only with children of one fairly homogenous ethnic, social, and economic group. Assume that he is assigned to teach children in a depressed area who, throughout most of their lives, have experienced deprivation. They speak their own characteristic language and have their own concepts of acceptable behavior. Technically speaking, the social distance between teacher and pupils is wide indeed. What shall the teacher do about his preconceived beliefs about standards of conduct, of learning, of wholesome social attitudes? Obviously, he will make little progress if he does not take fully into account the great differences between how he would like to proceed and how conditions indicate that he must proceed. Will his belief that it is essential to nurture dignity and feelings of personal worth among students, to meet a wide range of individual personal and social needs, be sacrificed? Or, are there guides to new and radically different points of view, to revised notions about academic standards, about what is to be learned at certain grade levels, about the way in which pupils are to be graded and promoted, and the like?

Because his educational philosophy is personal, it will not be static as long as the teacher continues to grow. A broadening of

In-migrant specialists in Milwaukee plan programs to assist teachers who teach the culturally deprived. One of the most important responsibilities of such a staff is to help teachers develop a workable philosophy. It seems obvious now, but only in recent years has it come to be generally realized that the philosophy of a teacher who teaches in one cultural area may be entirely unsuited to teaching in a different kind of cultural area.

experience and a critical evaluation of it will result in a constantly evolving and improving educational philosophy. We observed earlier that a person's collection of beliefs develops gradually with experience. Similarly, the critical examination of beliefs, called philosophizing, is not a temporally bounded event that should come to a final solution. It, too, is a continuing process. A person does not overhaul his entire set of beliefs at one time. Modifications are made under the impulses of observed conflict.

It is important for the teacher to regard his beliefs, and particularly his educational beliefs, as tentative, properly subject to re-examination whenever facts or other beliefs challenge them. To fail to recognize the imperfect foundations on which all beliefs are built is to endorse the delusions of dogmatism. Equally dangerous is the contrary fault, indecision, which is often an attempt to avoid commitment to a belief until irreproachable grounds for it are discovered. A measure of positive conviction is essential to prudent and courageous action even though objective certainty is not within human reach. Holding beliefs as tentative does not necessarily lead to a lack of conviction. A teacher can arrive at his conclusions on the best evidence available to him but can be prepared to change them when better evidence arises.

SOCIALLY CONDITIONED

The sources of a teacher's educational philosophy—the areas of experience and knowledge that are open to him—are contingent on the society and the groups in which he lives. He speaks the language of his society and develops his ideas in its terms. He tends to adopt the customs of his society as his own habits and to value what his society approves. Even the methods of critical reflection by which he can re-evaluate his beliefs are limited by what he learns from his environment. To the extent that a person is a creature of his society, so also is his philosophy.

Thus, in a society dominated by a single set of values, a teacher has little opportunity to make an independent choice of values. But where, as in America, ranges of values exist, the teacher, while not entirely free, is able to exercise considerable leeway in his choice of values. This requires him to take greater responsibility for making his value choices intelligently. Value choice means, in simplest terms, the act of choosing between what is thought to be good education and what is believed to be bad. Education that is good is a value; so, likewise, is bad education.

Throughout discussions on educational practice we find almost continual reference made to terms implying values such as purposes, goals, preferences, interests, correctness, character, duties, ideals, freedom, truth, beauty, self-actualization—to list a few. Each of these terms implies that choice must be made. What purposes are most worthy? What goals are most desirable? What interests are the most wholesome? In American education, no one set of values can be considered dominant, as one will discover when he attempts to satisfy any group of educators with answers to the questions just raised. Different teachers make different value choices. Fortunately for the teaching profession, in America, more than in most societies, there are both public and official toleration of diversity and dissent, as well as opportunities for varied experiences and frequent exposures to many value systems. This is perhaps because American society comprises many groups who have differing traditions, who live in greatly varied circumstances, and who cherish differing sets of values, many in transition and many displaying the internal conflicts that result from eclectic development. The multiple origins of the American people, the social mobility characteristic of a democracy, and the rapid changes of a technological age are responsible for diversity and flux both in basic beliefs and in value systems.

Among the conflicts that beset a socially conditioned educational philosophy is the conflict between traditional and emergent beliefs. Values on which the American society was once in substantial agreement—hard work, personal success, planning for the future, an emphasis on the good of the individual, a deep-seated respect for moral law—are being challenged by emerging value systems that stress sociability, sensitivity to others, present values in contrast to deferred values, group harmony, and a relativistic attitude toward morals. Other conflicts are caused by differences among ethnic groups and economic classes. Yet, with all the diversities in values and beliefs, there exists in America a pragmatic unity, especially in political life, and a willingness to compromise and cooperate. For example, democratic processes are uniformly held in deep respect. This unity in viewpoint

Cross-country ski training is part of the regular physical education program at an Anchorage, Alaska, high school. The first U. S. Olympic girls' cross-country ski team is likely to be dominated by girls from this school. What part does educational philosophy play in helping a school to make subject-matter choices? What part do goals and rewards play in good teaching? What other questions of a philosophical nature are suggested by this picture?

stems in part from an orientation to action rather than to theory, and from a recognition that disagreement in philosophy does not preclude agreement in practice.

Over-all unity and internal diversity of value systems carry numerous implications for teaching. The unity tends to bring practical agreement on educational questions and to make persuasion effective where disagreement exists. Teachers strongly desire consensus before making final group decisions. Efforts are made to reason questions through to a point where concensus is reached. Teachers, for example, may agree that good citizenship is a worthy goal, but what good citizenship is when judged in terms of specific schoolroom situations may be a matter of some disagreement. Even so, the teaching staffs of individual schools can and do arrive at intelligent agreement about matters calling for practical action. This is partly because the individual school in American education is a subsociety in which the range of differences is normally smaller than in the whole society. The more intimate interaction among the teachers, strengthened, perhaps, by similar backgrounds, leads in time to a degree of homogeneity in

*Booker T. Washington (1859–1915) ranks among the most influential
American educational leaders. He founded Tuskegee Institute at Tuskegee,
Alabama, in 1881 and remained as its head until his death. Under his
leadership the institute became an outstanding educational institution in the
fields of teacher education, nursing and hospital education, industrial arts,
and household arts. He excelled in the arts of teaching, writing, and public
speaking, through which avenues he influenced countless numbers of people.
He propagated a definite educational philosophy. The educational program
at Tuskegee was built on the principle that education would be more
meaningful "if it stuck close to the common and familiar things—things
that concern the greater part of the people the greater part of the time."
His emphasis was on solving problems that arose in connection with the
practical needs of those who were being educated. Thus he provided an
outstanding example of how a philosophy of education could be incorporated
in institutional practice.*

basic beliefs. This core of common beliefs makes it easier for teachers
in an individual school to communicate with one another, with pupils
and parents, and to understand the problems of individual pupils.
Thus teachers are able to develop a healthy degree of teamwork as they
face educational situations.

Diversity, of course, makes communication and agreement somewhat more difficult. At the same time, however, it opens the way to
an enriched education for pupils through teachers who have outgrown
the provincialism of limited experience and unquestioning acceptance
of early beliefs. Diversity entails a contrast among traditions that is
necessary if pupils are to appreciate fully the worth of their own
traditions and those of others. It also causes a conflict among ideas, a
conflict that is necessary and desirable if ideas are to be judged on their
merit rather than on their orthodoxy. But the actualization of the
more valued of the possibilities requires a teacher with intellectual
toleration.

A teacher, then, should always be aware that diversity leads to
conflict, not only between groups, but within the growing individual
who borrows beliefs from various groups and thereby internalizes
intergroup conflict. Cultural diversity is thus responsible for some of
the inconsistencies a person discovers on examining his own beliefs.
A teacher may find, for example, that his belief in the importance of
group harmony both as a principle and as a guide to classroom conduct

conflicts with his belief in the importance of individual development. Conceivably he can find ways of eliminating or reducing such conflicts. The first step, of course, is to become aware of important conflicts and conscious of the major issues. Subsequently, as the teacher analyzes his problems and decides on his course of action, he will use his personal yet socially conditioned educational philosophy to help resolve his problems and to decide on his plans of action.

Summary

The task of developing his educational philosophy belongs to the individual teacher. As he develops his philosophy, and he will do this continuously throughout his professional life, he will seek help from many sources, even though the philosophy will be his own. It will be consonant with him and with everything that has made him what he is. He will use his philosophy in choosing his ideals and in deciding on educational aims. His educational philosophy will be a practical help in answering questions related to the selection of subject matter, in choosing teaching procedures, and in determining relationships with associates in the school.

In actual teaching one does not constantly and consciously call on one's philosophy in making ordinary day-to-day decisions. Institutionalization, for example (discussed in the following chapter), reduces many day-to-day decisions to the commonplace, assigns some actions to the level of habit, minimizes the need to exercise measured judgment.

There are, however, critical points in one's teaching career (with which one is sometimes confronted quite unexpectedly) that demand a conscious re-examination of one's cherished beliefs, beliefs that had heretofore constituted a taken-for-granted sound background on which to base decisions. It is at these critical points that one must consciously and carefully think a problem through. This means, to borrow a phrase from William James, "the habit of always seeing an alternative, of not taking the usual for granted, of making conventionalities fluid again, of imagining foreign states of mind." It is at these relatively critical points that one's educational philosophy becomes a ready instrument with which to think out answers to one's more important or serious problems.

Questions

1. What, in your opinion, should be the relationship between philosophical thinking and educational practice?
2. Why is it that one's educational philosophy must, perforce, be one's own?
3. What is there about educational philosophy that makes it impossible for one to state one's educational philosophy once and for all? What kinds of experiences should a teacher seek in order to broaden his educational philosophy?
4. What is a value? How does one decide that one value is better than another?
5. What is the difference between the word "principle" used in the scientific sense and the same word used in the ethical sense?
6. Referring to the three teachers described in this chapter, choose the one you think is best. What is the basis for your choice?
7. Why is it not possible for one to make his educational practice conform at all times to the dictates of the more recent findings of physiology and psychology?
8. Why have the educational philosophies that have evolved from past philosophical thinking differed so markedly from one another?

Projects

1. Give an example that will illustrate how each of the following contributes to the formulation of one's educational philosophy: (a) personal experience, (b) common sense, (c) religion, (d) science, and (e) systematic philosophy.
2. (a) State an educational question the answer to which cannot be found in your past personal experience; (b) the answer to which cannot be supplied by common sense; (c) the answer to which is not supplied by science.
3. State an educational principle you believe to be true. Locate the sources that led you to believe in its validity.

4. Give a number of concrete examples that illustrate how one's educational philosophy is socially conditioned.
5. List a few of your cherished beliefs and comfortable patterns of living that have undergone modification in recent years. Explain what caused you to modify your beliefs.
6. Explain how educational philosophy and innovating practices are related.

We have examined what a teacher does, how he qualifies, what his relationships to the profession are, and why his philosophy is important. It is also important to interpret what he does and should do in terms of his reciprocal relations with the total personnel of a school or a school system. For an accurate picture of the total work of the teacher we must take into account the institutional character of the school and recognize the impact of the school as an institution on what the teacher does and how he does it.

When you accept a teaching position, you join forces with an institution, an institution that will affect your life in professional and personal ways. At the time of your first appointment, you will raise a basic question: What should I expect the institution to do for me? There is a difference among institutions regarding opportunity for personal growth and advancement offered, standing of the institution in the community, morale among the personnel, fringe benefits like sick leaves and hospital insurance. You will want to know if the teaching load is reasonable so that you will have time to confer with pupils and parents, if meetings are held after or during school time, if the teachers are represented by and have an opportunity to participate in an effective organization. The school board employs a teacher to render services to the institution; the institution is also expected to contribute to the teacher.

Schools as institutions

WHAT AN INSTITUTION IS

In order to understand how the institutionalization of education dictates to a considerable degree what education shall be and conditions somewhat the work of teachers, we turn to the question of what an institution is and then discuss some of its effects.

"Institution" is defined with slightly different emphasis by the social philosopher, the social psychologist, and the sociologist. We turn to the definitions of the latter because it is the sociologists who, more than the highly specialized philosophers or social psychologists, deal with the fundamental laws of social relations and institutions and who concern themselves with basic social phenomena.

One sociologist writes:

> More commonly the term *institution* is applied to those features of social life which outlast biological generations or survive drastic changes that might have been expected to bring them to an end. . . . Institutions are the established forms of procedure by which group activity is carried on.[1]

Another sociologist states:

> Institutions . . . are patterns governing behavior in social relationships which have become interwoven with a system of common moral sentiments which in turn define what one has a "right to expect" of a person in a certain position.
>
> . . . the essential aspect of social structure lies in a system of patterned expectations defining the *proper* behavior of persons playing certain roles, enforced both by the incumbent's own positive motives for conformity and by the sanctions of others. Such systems of patterned expectations, seen in the perspective of their place in a total social system and sufficiently thoroughly established in action to be taken for granted as legitimate, are conveniently called "institutions."[2]

[1] R. M. MacIver, *Society: A Textbook of Sociology*. New York: Holt, Rinehart and Winston, 1937, pp. 14, 15–16.

[2] Talcott Parsons, *Essays in Sociological Theory*, rev. ed. New York: Macmillan, 1954, pp. 143, 231. Quoted by permission of the publisher.

Another sociologist gives still a slightly different emphasis in his definition of "institution."

> The real component units of culture which have a considerable degree of permanence, universality and independence are the organized systems of human activities called institutions. Every institution centers around a fundamental need, permanently unites a group of people in a cooperative task and has its particular body of doctrine and its technique or craft. . . . But institutions show a pronounced amalgamation of functions and have a synthetic character. Each of them satisfies a variety of needs.[3]

From these general definitions it is not difficult to identify the characteristics of a school that qualify the school and various features of the school as an American institution. As society felt the need for ordered, systematic fulfillment of the educational requirements of children, the school came into being. As it acquired the qualities of permanence, universality, and independence, the institution emerged.

We note that an institution possesses the characteristic of persistency. Even if some technical advance were invented that might achieve a desired end, the institution and its established practices of achieving the end tend to persist.

The definitions also stress continuity in conscious forms of group behavior. The history of the school is, in one sense, a history of a continuous form of collective behavior. When we think of the school, just as when we think of the family or the church, we immediately summon certain images of definite forms of collective behavior which are characteristic of the institution—forms of behavior continuous from generation to generation. An individual within the school realizes that the institution is older than he and is expected to outlive him. He fits into the stream of continuity. He expects to behave, within limits, as have his predecessors.

Another idea carried by the definitions is that the institution exercises a degree of restraint on the individual. Participants are subjected to a degree of control. The school, for instance, furnishes the pupils, personnel, and, to an extent, also the parents with a routine of life, with patterns of expected behavior by which they will be judged, and with objectives and ambitions towards which they may strive. The

---

[3] Bronislaw Malinowski, "Culture," *Encyclopedia of the Social Sciences*, 1931, p. 626.

"We see the school as a social institution playing its part in a total pattern of institutions . . ."

The school is a civic center : here citizens are voting, as they do in schools throughout the country. The school is an adult education center : at a gourmet cooking class, mothers learn how to decorate a ham for buffet serving. In cities there are extensive day and evening adult education programs attended by many people. The school is a health center : people line up to receive polio vaccine in a high school. The school is a social center : the annual senior mother-daughter tea is held in a school cafeteria. Other social events, such as dances and dinners, often take place in the schools.

school encompasses recognized rules, formal procedures for their application, and a structure consisting of persons acting officially. The school and all other institutions are subject in some measure to the common mores. In addition, the school is a vehicle of conscious and formal control over the years when children are enrolled (whether the enrollment is compulsory or voluntary). School personnel often attempt to bring to explicit formulation matters that have been subject to the mores, and to apply to them the formal procedures of the school. Insofar as teachers and other school personnel successfully set themselves up as the proper persons to define and enforce the mores, these take on the qualities of the law. Identification with the established rights and duties growing out of society's deliberate organization of knowledge and techniques to fulfill the need for education is part of the process by which a teacher becomes a person with a social identity.

Institutionalization embraces the concept that human relationships within an organization are structured, that they are consistent with a fairly well-defined pattern. A school—an institution—has a basic structure, and he who functions within the school fulfills a fairly definite role—a role that fits into the total pattern of roles played by all the participants. As Parsons expresses it, "His role is defined by the normative expectations of the members of the group as formulated in its social traditions."[4]

On a wider perspective we see the school as a social institution playing its part in a total pattern of institutions and contributing to a total system of social integration of which it is a part. Along with other institutions the school contributes to uniting human beings in a stable system. It shares in regulating and establishing the rules that determine the relations of individuals to one another. Also, in common with the other social institutions, the schools make such adaptations to the environment and such internal adjustments as seem necessary to advance a well-ordered social life.

The school shares in the fulfillment of unique and significant functions. It is vitally responsible for teaching children the techniques and rules of society, the particular ways of doing all the things society cherishes. The school is interrelated with other institutions, for example, the family. It is also interrelated with informal parts of our culture

[4] Op. cit., p. 230.

such as community attitudes. The school's functions are to be understood only in relation to the total social system. The same is true of any institution.

WHY EDUCATION IS INSTITUTIONALIZED

The education of the young in any country could, conceivably, be carried on without the establishment of schools. It could be left, for example, to the family or to the church or to industry, or it could be shared by all these. Why have various societies chosen to institutionalize education? Why do the schools in the United States have a kind of organization, rules, regulations, customs, traditions, and practices that are now associated with them? How do these common understandings among many people about the functions of the schools influence the work of the teachers in the schools?

Basically, the reason for the institutionalization of education is the same as the reason for the institutionalization of other large group interests. There has been first of all a felt need. Driving on the right side of the street became an institution in the United States because of a widely recognized need for traffic order. Institutionalization was the solution to a perplexing social problem. When people felt the need for children to be educated in a deliberate fashion, their common response was the organized school, eventually with the rules, organization, and customs that are attached to it.

The school was established for a particular purpose—as an answer to a felt need. This does not mean, however, that originally there was unanimity as to how, specifically, this need should be met. Eventually a pattern, conforming in general to the broad outlines of what most people desired, was evolved. In time the pattern became standardized and ultimately the word "school" meant approximately the same thing to everyone. The school had become an institution as the result of a degree of unity of beliefs about what it should be and should do. Once established, the school served to further the degree of unanimity of belief.

EFFECTS OF INSTITUTIONALIZATION

The institutionalization of education brings many benefits to the individual pupil and to the individual teacher. It preserves cultural

Institutions are viewed in their educative effect :—with reference to the type of individuals they foster. The interest in individual moral improvement and the social interest in objective reform of economic and political conditions are identified. And inquiry into the meaning of social arrangements gets definite point and direction. We are led to ask what the specific stimulating, fostering, and nurturing power of each specific social arrangement may be. . . . Just what response does this *social arrangement, political or economic, evoke, and what effect does it have upon the disposition of those who engage in it? Does it release capacity? If so, how widely? Among a few, with a corresponding depression in others, or in an extensive and equitable way? Is the capacity which is set free also directed in some coherent way, so that it becomes a power, or is its manifestation spasmodic and capricious? Since responses are of an indefinite diversity of kind, these inquiries have to be detailed and specific. Are man's senses rendered more delicately sensitive and appreciative, or are they blunted and dulled by this and that form of social organization? Are their minds trained so that the hands are more deft and cunning? Is curiosity awakened or blunted? What is its quality : is it merely aesthetic, dwelling on the forms and surfaces of things, or is it also an intellectual searching into their meaning? Such questions as these . . . become the starting-points of inquiries about every institution of the community when it is recognized that individuality is not originally given but is created under the influences of associated life.*

John Dewey, *Reconstruction in Philosophy*. New York: Holt, Rinehart and Winston, 1920, pp. 196–198. Quoted by permission of the publisher.

values in customs and traditions. As an institution the school has qualities of endurance and stability. It benefits from being universally accepted. Conformity to and continuance of accepted practices result in universal familiarity and encourage understanding and sharing.

The characteristic of continuity in educational institutions may sometimes have adverse effects. When practices, customs, and traditions become deeply ingrained, pressure is exerted on schools to maintain what people have come to regard as almost sacred or, at least, a revered part of the status quo. Under such conditions originality may be curbed, wholesome freedom for creativeness may be restricted, and expertly planned innovations may encounter serious obstacles, some, even, from within the profession itself. For example, older school buildings, designed somewhat like boxes, have proved obstacles to changing class size, deterrents to wise use of teaching aids, to services from resource centers, to some changes in kinds of subject matter taught, to such innovations as team teaching. Later discussions will focus on causes and kinds of changes desired. What we wish to emphasize here is that institutions, including schools, have not always encouraged or been friendly to change. The school is an institution based on cultural values, and, therefore, functions in part to preserve these values. As a result schools, in some measure, tend to resist change.

As the story of education in the United States unfolds, we become conscious that so-called "cultural lag" and "institutional lag" apply to education. For example, technological advances may indicate the desirability of changing techniques in teaching science and mathematics. Certain well-established traditions, however, may be a bulwark sufficiently strong to perpetuate techniques inconsistent with the contemporary life picture or inadequate in terms of current social demands. Sometimes practices in the schools lag behind those in other institutions or do not keep pace with the needs of pupils. There is a tendency for the school, since it is a social institution with the characteristics of permanence and continuity, to lag behind the point of advancement indicated by social understanding and professional theory. The degree of lag varies with communities, with states, and with sections of the country.

It is important that a teacher be conscious that he is part of an institution. He makes decisions and acts in terms of a superstructure that has both a regulatory and a protective effect on everything he does. The institution is embedded in customs and traditions that have origins historically remote. However, it is also currently dynamic, an organization that contributes to a teacher in many ways and, conversely, to which a teacher contributes in many ways.

IDEAS AND THE INSTITUTION

The current pattern of American schools and school systems and the contemporary traditions in educational practices have resulted from a recombination of ideas and from institutional accommodations to ideas some of which have been influencing social institutions for thousands of years and some of which are very recent. Because this topic justifies a more extended discussion, a study of the impact of the contemporary social scene and its influence on present-day institutional patterns of education in the United States is pursued in Unit II. Obviously, no adequate interpretation of education can be made if regulations, rules, customs, and typical practices are considered apart from the ideas and social values they are supposed to reflect.

The teacher as a group member

VARIETY OF MEMBERSHIPS

In studying the work of the teacher we indicated certain duties and responsibilities which were added because the teacher is a member of an organized group that shares certain common tasks and whose work has to be coordinated with the work of others. Besides being associated in an institution established for the education of the young, a teacher is part of a variety of other groups also, by virtue of his employment in the school.

The over-all, organized group is, of course, the faculty group, which may be a district-wide group or a school-wide group. Whether the group is an inter-school or intra-school group, membership is implied with employment and the duties assigned the teacher always include certain tasks that are related to coordinating work within both kinds of groups. Often the meetings of the district-wide group are annual or semiannual, coming perhaps before the opening of school in the fall and at some designated time during the year when the pupils are dismissed. Frequently, the district-wide meeting is enlarged to include a number of school districts in some geographical unit, perhaps a county. Often, local teacher groups cooperate with school administrators in planning and conducting meetings.

In the local school the number and kind of professional groups to which the teacher belongs will be determined somewhat by the size of the school and somewhat by the philosophy of the school. If the school is large and the policy is to encourage cooperation and participation, the teacher may belong to several professional groups, in addition to the general faculty group. These might include, for instance, all the social studies teachers in the system, all the freshman homeroom teachers, or a group made up of the teachers new to the system.

In addition to the groups to which the teacher is probably required to belong and that are directly related to his professional work, the teacher belongs to numerous groups which may be quite nebulous in their purpose and indefinite in their membership boundaries but which usually, nevertheless, have a significant bearing on the teacher's satisfactions and happiness in his job.

When a number of people are together for any considerable length of time, they tend to form small cohesive groups based on some shared purpose, common interest, or other factor that draws individuals together. For instance, a teacher may be a member of a married teachers' group. The group probably will not be related to any school activities; it may get together only after school hours. But the fact remains that it *is* a group and members talk things over and present a more or less common front on many matters, often matters pertaining to the school. The group may be comprised of those interested in a particular hobby. The golfers, for instance, may get together for dinner and golf or for weekend outings. Perhaps the teachers who live in a particular area have a car pool and discuss and develop a measure of unity as they share time spent in transportation. Perhaps a difference of opinion over some school policy divides the teachers into opposing groups. Those in an elementary school who believe, for instance, in traditional report cards and letter-grading oppose those who advocate written messages and parent conferences. They may form a group, a kind of clique, and sit together at faculty meetings and vote alike even on issues entirely unrelated to the report card matter.

The possibilities of group membership for the teacher, even in his school associations, are many and exceedingly varied. A point to remember is that such memberships may be a powerful factor in the teacher's satisfaction with his work. A teacher's pleasure in helping Johnny advance to sixth-grade reading level may be diminished by the knowledge that some other teachers are having a weekly card game to which he has not been invited.

A teacher, and especially a new teacher, should be conscious that it is possible to make errors of lasting effect by hastily affiliating with some social group or other. Groups cannot usually be judged at their face value; they may be in conflict with one another; potent feelings of security and respect may be involved. Social groups within the faculty, as social groups within any other group, represent a challenge to human relations, a problem requiring tact and consideration.

EVALUATING A TEACHER MEMBERSHIP GROUP

In evaluating the effectiveness of a school as an institution contributing to the requirements of its personnel for group membership, what criteria should be used? What should participation in a school group contribute to the members? For, just as each individual is expected to contribute to the institution so, likewise, should the institution be expected to contribute to the individual.

First, participation in the school group should entail fulfilling a clearly designated role which, when successfully and efficiently performed, brings to the individual a feeling that he is respected and considered to be important by those with whom he has institutional connections. It is particularly important for him to know that his superiors respect him, that they have ways of letting him know that his work is esteemed.

An individual's work in the institution should net a financial reward high enough to insure physical health and the fulfillment of reasonable desires with respect to food, clothes, housing, travel, automobile, and hobbies. The institution is responsible for meeting this need.

The school should not unduly inhibit the desire of an individual teacher to make his own decisions, shape the course of his own life, and direct the course of his own actions.

It is important that the institution make it possible for the individual to contribute his abilities to the fullest. Where, because of the narrowness of an assigned role, only a portion of a teacher's capabilities are permitted to function, both the school and the teacher lose.

The individual's desire for and his achievement of a well-integrated personality and wholesome morale among members of the group can be encouraged or discouraged by the institution. These will be discouraged in a situation where an excellent teacher is assigned unreasonable responsibilities—an unduly heavy teaching load, numerous extra-class and extra-school responsibilities, regular classes with a number of emotionally disturbed children in them. Where efforts of the personnel are thoughtfully and skillfully coordinated and teaching loads and school responsibilities wisely and equitably distributed, the satisfactions and welfare of individual teachers tend to be adequately cared for.

ADJUSTMENTS WITHIN THE GROUP

What adjustments must teachers make because they are guided in their actions by the goals of an institution and are thus subject to institutional restraints?

Institutional behavior is, to a considerable degree, regulated behavior. The school legislates this behavior through a social superstructure consisting of traditions, rules, regulations, school laws, and the like. In addition, a complex pattern of school administration is set up in every community to guarantee that the laws, rules, and regulations will all operate effectively. The individual in this structural pattern, then, must make certain accommodations or adjustments. For example, the school has its institutional goals which, in certain instances, may be at variance with those of the individual teacher. Since the individual cannot very well change the institutional goals, he must adjust to them. Occasionally, the goals of the individual may be so completely out of harmony with the institutional goals that the adjustment required is especially difficult and is accompanied by heightened tension. Likewise, an individual teacher may be out of harmony with certain administrative policies in the school and this also may produce a serious problem of adjustment.

The most desirable and fortunate situation is, of course, one in which the individual finds his personal goals in harmony with institutional goals and administrative policies. Since, however, complete harmony is not usually possible, how may the tensions of personal adjustment be reduced? Some social psychologists suggest that participatory action should be the basis of institutional patterns of behavior that are determined by rules, regulations, laws, and other structurized elements in the institution. For example, a school policy toward any and all of a school system's teacher security provisions should grow out of the thinking of all the personnel. This is one reason for teacher negotiations with school boards—teachers are participants in making decisions that affect their welfare. It should be noted that those who advocate participation in making school policy are not arguing that the resulting rules and regulations will be wiser because of the participatory procedure or that group judgment will be any wiser than the judgment of a single expert. What they argue is that participation in and of itself is a value wherever action within a group must be uniform or patterned. It should be fostered in every institutional situation because it contributes to better adjusted personalities and is an essential element in the maintenance and improvement of a satisfactory level of group morale. Although participation does not provide the entire solution to the problem of tension in individual adjustment, it nevertheless is a significant factor.

Through his various group memberships the individual seeks to promote his security and insure his respect. How can the individual make his adjustment to the group and within the group? How may *he* attempt to influence the adaptation of the group?

Each group—faculty group, departmental group, or even a bridge-playing or golf-playing group—has more or less definite goals. In the case of the organized, professional group, goals may be stated, perhaps broadly and generally, or may not be expressly stated. There may be long-term or short-term goals.

In addition to the goals of his group, each member also has his own short- and long-term goals. Individual and group goals may not always be in harmony. The individual may belong to a number of groups whose goals are in conflict. The teacher's problem, then, is to establish a proper relationship between his goals and the goals of the groups in which he holds membership. A new teacher who joins a faculty group whose goals are in conflict with his, whose ways of doing things are different, will make a temporary adjustment. Eventually, through interaction and discussion within the group, the new teacher may expect to achieve a degree of integration with the group that will lead to satisfaction and effectiveness in functioning through the school organization.

1. Interaction

Interaction within the group provides members with the opportunity to influence others and to be influenced by them. Two teachers may begin with conflicting goals, disparate views, or divergent opinions. In their direct relationships, afforded by the school, they have the opportunity for interaction. Each has the chance to learn about and to evaluate the other's views, an opportunity to exert mutual influence for mutual change. Interaction may not result in unamimous agreement, but it may lead to a modification of views which will result in substantial agreement either in terms of one view or another, or in terms of a compromise that includes something and eliminates something of each. The agreement, on the other hand, may be something new and different. Through the process of group interaction, not only is agreement reached but, through the process itself, enrichment of personal satisfactions accrues.

2. Discussion

Discussion is the basic procedure of group action, the tool of interaction which leads to integration. Discussion is the method of group deliberation. It is an observable manifestation of a group studying and learning together, a group thinking out loud, a group interacting within itself. The success of discussion in any school group in promoting interaction and achieving integration depends somewhat on the discussion leaders.

Discussion may degenerate into a kind of "bull session." Sometimes individuals turn a faculty meeting into an unproductive kind of parliamentary debate. Or it may be merely a meeting of listeners receiving institutional pronouncements or decisions and directions from a school authority. To insure faculty-wide participation in a discussion, it is usually necessary to have the topics well selected, pertinent to the interests of the members of the group, and appropriate to the time available. Usually they should be announced in advance so that the members are prepared. The discussion leader—the school administrator, the teacher chairman—at the faculty meeting, like any other discussion leader, has the responsibility of keeping discussion "on the track," encouraging effective participation, summarizing the main points, and directing the group toward sound conclusions.

In all group relationships, but especially in a faculty group and particularly during discussion, tact is of great importance. Tact does not imply weakness or lack of standards. It means, rather, treating other people in such a way that their self-respect as well as your own is preserved. The desire for prestige and importance is universal. In using tact in discussion, one is consciously sparing pride, developing confidence, and assuring the other person a sense of importance. Ridicule and sarcasm are anathemas to effective discussion.

The new teacher who is intolerant of experienced faculty members must realize that anything different from what he anticipated is not necessarily bad. It is only after one has acquired intimate personal acquaintance with a specific school situation that one is in a position to evaluate policies and practices. What might at first seem undesirable may, after careful examination in the light of a specific situation, appear to be very desirable. A new teacher from another school should not be tactless in references made to his previous employment. Both the experienced and the inexperienced teacher in group discussion, in personal conversations, and in other institutional relationships should be alert to the danger of appearing to feel superior, seeming to believe that it is his business to enlighten and to point the way. By failing to understand the merits of the institution in which he works and to recognize the importance of respect for the staff members' achievements, a teacher retards his own integration and cannot achieve the climate most favorable for his maximum success.

3. Integration

The goal of group action is integration. Integration is achieved when all members of the group are completely identified with the group, when individual pleasures and satisfactions accrue from the successes and achievements of the group as a whole. An integrated faculty group exhibits *esprit de corps*, has good morale.

Integration is particularly desirable in a school faculty group because a teacher's role is interlocking, never individual and independent. It is especially important that a teacher be completely identified with the institution. The goals of the school and his own goals should be harmonious and to some extent identical. If a teacher has been a participant in discussion which led to the agreement on matters related to these goals, he will probably have a sense of personal responsibility for his contribution. This will facilitate his acceptance of the goals and his identification with them.

It is essential that integration be achieved because even a teacher with superior teaching skill cannot make his best contribution to the institution's program unless he sees his job always in reference to the services of other staff members. The success of the school is determined by its total performance. A teacher who is integrated within the group will perform as a member of the group. He will not seek exclusive limelight apart from his achievements as a contributor to the institution's goals.

In many schools an effort is made to acquaint the entire faculty with what is being done throughout the school and within the system. This is done not only to increase understanding and cooperation but also to promote mutual respect among all staff members. Such acquaintance leads to an appreciation that many diverse tasks are performed by members of the school group and that the tasks are coordinate in importance. It also may contribute to the individual's confidence in his ability to contribute successfully to his school's program.

4. Functioning through organization

Interaction, discussion, integration can be promoted more effectively where there are local professional organizations. In the chapter on the teacher and his profession, teachers' organizations were discussed. Where there is a strong local teacher organization there are opportunities for wide-scale participation and avenues for channeling constructive suggestions and for airing grievances. In studying problems, suggesting solutions, and proposing plans for implementing change, the organization is, of course, more potent than an individual. As we have mentioned, in many large districts teacher organizations employ a full-time salaried executive who is available to receive individual complaints and to proceed with professional skill to study the problems and to see that they receive appropriate action.

Functioning through a teachers' organization, however, places a responsibility on the teacher. He must help build a justifiably strong organization, then he must learn when and how to act through the organization. In short, he must learn to behave organizationally. Once a problem is referred to an association, then its solution should be worked out through organizational channels. Sometimes an individual, dissatisfied with a policy of the local association, works individually and at cross-purposes with the organization to achieve personal ends. If a policy of the organization is not acceptable, then the correct procedure is to work wholeheartedly to have the organization change that

policy. Since it is the product of many different persons, no professional organization is ever perfect. Nevertheless, the association that
makes it possible for its members to share in an effective professional
organization is granting important opportunities to them.

Induction of new teachers

How is the new teacher to be directed and aided in fulfilling his role
in the school personnel group? What steps are taken to "induct" him
into a school system, a school group, a classroom group? This is a
problem that has been gaining more and more attention from school
administrators. When there is a shortage of teachers it is particularly
important to assist teachers in their initial adjustments, to avoid having
teachers drop out of the profession or change their positions because
of unhappy initial experiences.

HANDBOOKS

In many school systems, particularly the larger school systems,
handbooks are issued to all teachers. They are especially helpful to
teachers new to the system. This is an effective way of eliminating
indiscretions and uncertainties and disappointments that grow out of
ignorance about what is expected of the new teacher, what is available,
and what the teacher can expect to receive by way of advancement.
The handbook speaks for the institution. It usually tells something
about the community, its location, transportation facilities, resources,
and so forth. It describes the history and location of the schools and the
policies concerning salary, tenure, and sick leave. It gives the calendar
of events and holidays. Usually the handbook is very helpful. In some
cases, however, it is so detailed that the teacher tends to be over-
whelmed. Ideally, it is not considered the final word but rather the
basis for personal discussions with the teacher, whether old or new.

PRESESSION WORKSHOPS

Sometimes a new teacher attends a presession workshop, an orientation week, a get-acquainted period in advance of the regular

A teacher—a good teacher—never stops learning and exploring, from the day he takes up his first position to the day he retires. There is always a future for a teacher : so he is always preparing himself to meet its challenges. The future is real and immediate for teachers in an induction program, such as these new teachers (some accompanied by older teachers). With the help of older teachers, a handbook, and advice from administrators and supervisors, they will start their teaching with the confidence that comes from knowledge. Farther along in their careers, some teachers are learning from another teacher how to use a new mathematics teaching aid. This demonstration is at the Pacific Science Center, operated by the Seattle Public Schools to serve 72 school districts. It is one of a number of such centers financed by federal grants under the Elementary and Secondary Education Act of 1965. Another group of teachers is learning. These people, who teach in Spanish-speaking areas of Chicago, are receiving in-service education designed to enable them to work intensively and successfully with small groups of linguistically handicapped children. In this part of the program, they are developing an appreciation of Spanish culture. They will then find it much easier to understand—and teach—those who know only that culture. But, after all, teaching itself is what brings satisfaction and self-fulfillment to the dedicated teacher. The mathematics teacher, who has been teaching for 42 years, has obviously found both.

opening of the school session. Often the teacher receives extra compensation for this work, especially in those cases where it takes as much as a week's time. Customarily, the principals, supervisors, and certain others of the regular staff work with the new teachers during this period. The activities include tours of the community and discussions of school policies. The teacher is given an opportunity to become acquainted with his classroom, with the resources of the school—audiovisual aids, library, art facilities, and so forth—and also with community resources. He is given an opportunity to ask questions which would be inappropriate in a larger faculty meeting scheduled after the opening of school. Such minor questions as "Does the teacher lead his children in line to the lunchroom?" "With whom should I communicate when I am forced to be absent from school?" "Are children allowed to go to their lockers at any time?" would be a waste of time in a faculty meeting and would seem so petty in that setting that they would never be raised. Knowing the right answers to such seemingly insignificant questions might, however, be quite important to the teacher's initial adjustment.

FACULTY ADVISER

It is common practice for one experienced teacher to be assigned to advise one incoming teacher. This is an arrangement that continues throughout the school year. The incoming teacher knows where to go for directions and information, and the experienced teacher feels a responsibility for giving the newcomer hints, suggestions, and directions that he feels may be helpful.

OTHER PLANS FOR INDUCTION

Perhaps fortified with a handbook of information, the experience of a presession workshop, and the name of a faculty member to whom he may turn for advice, the new teacher arrives at school on the opening day. Typically the session opens with meetings—district-wide and school-wide, and then perhaps at the department or grade level. The new teacher is introduced to the groups. He meets most of his colleagues for the first time. He is informed of the plans for the opening of school and is supplied with the details of his assignment, with his textbooks, and with information about his pupils. At once, the duties of checking, organizing, reporting, and accounting begin.

Usually an effort is made to have a tea or some other social gathering where the new teachers can meet the other teachers informally. Sometimes the older teachers tend to get together to renew friendships and overlook their responsibilities to the new teachers. Thus the new teachers may sometimes find the tea of little value in furthering acquaintance with the group. Where the function of such teas is more clearly understood by all, however, this difficulty is alleviated.

Summary

The institutional aspects of a school have a bearing on what the teacher does and how he does it. Good schools in good communities contribute to the welfare, to the feeling of well-being, of teachers. The opportunities provided for participation in a group have an influence on the total adjustment of an individual teacher. The program of induction is important to a new teacher. His feelings of security and pleasure in his work may be directly related to his knowledge about what is expected of him and what traditions he should respect. There are important, continuing relationships that he will have with other members of the personnel on a social and professional basis which are exceedingly important to his success in teaching.

A teacher is likely to work more efficiently and discharge his duties with greater satisfaction if, at all times, he is conscious that the nature of the institution is an influence on both him and his work. The institution contributes to him while he is contributing to the institution.

The school must be viewed as a group enterprise. The teacher's attitude toward his own role in relation to all other roles has a direct bearing on group morale, on personal satisfaction, and even on the school's educational achievement. Although the teacher has an assignment that is largely individual and a great deal depends on his individual initiative, he also must perform as a member of a group. This means that he sees his own achievement in the light of the total achievements of the group and recognizes that the group has contributed to his achievements, that he is part of a system characterized by interlocking roles, and that he has group-wide, institutional responsibilities.

The group, in order to perform in the desirable climate of wholesome group relations, must be characterized by a high degree of mutual respect on the part of all staff members. The teacher must appreciate that all tasks contribute to the whole and that each contribution is different and must be so because functions and needs are different and also because individuals cannot follow stereotyped patterns in carrying out any educational assignment.

In working in an institution, one works within a framework that must permit adaptation to change. Institutional membership requires that teachers possess flexibility to adjust to institutional change.

Being a member of a teaching group implies the responsibility of adaptation leading to general understanding and a common acceptance of satisfactory goals. Adaptation depends on interaction within the group. Discussion is the important group method of communication leading to integration. Developing skill in discussion is a sure path to effective performance in one's institutional relationships.

Questions

1. How are American schools affected by the attitudes of the people?
2. What are some of the principal effects on the individual teacher that result from the institutionalization of education?
3. What are the principal ways in which institutionalization influences educational progress?
4. When may a school be said to be progressive? conservative? reactionary? stereotyped?
5. Assuming that institutional changes should be made, how may the direction for desirable change be discovered?

Projects

1. Explain the ways a school represents the common response of the people of a community.
2. Describe some of the adjustments that an individual member of the teaching profession must make by virtue of his membership in a group because he works in an institution.

Unit I   Suggested Readings

COLE, FAY-COOPER, "A Witness at the Scopes Trial," *Scientific American*, 200 (No. 1): 120–130, January, 1959. Describes the famous trial in 1925 which resulted in the conviction of a teacher for teaching the theory of evolution to his classes in biology and gives a realistic picture of the ways in which legislators and pressure groups sometimes influence American education.

DORROS, SIDNEY, *Teaching As a Profession*. Columbus, Ohio: Charles E. Merrill Co., 1968. This small, readable book gives an overview of the teaching profession. Chapters 7, 8, 9, 10, and 11 deal, respectively, with selection and orientation, certification, economic welfare, work climate, and professional organizations. This is an excellent supplement to the topics discussed in Unit I of this book.

English Journal, "An Issue Within an Issue: Guidelines for the Preparation of Teachers of English," 57 (No. 4): 475–565, April, 1968. Most of this issue is devoted to the preparation of teachers of English. "The Guidelines have been composed, not as a monument to mark the close of an era, but as the blueprint of a basic design for the promising future." The Guidelines were prepared by educators together with state directors of teacher education and certification. Charts on certification requirements are provided.

FRANKEL, CHARLES, "Philosophy," *NEA Journal*, 51:50–53, December, 1962. A scholarly review by a professional philosopher of what the study of philosophy is about. Prepared expressly for classroom teachers.

HUBBARD, FRANK W., "Millions of Children," *NEA Journal*, 52 (No. 3), 52–54, March, 1963. A study of class size in America's urban elementary schools. "In the opinion of classroom teachers, the 'breaking point' is reached when we begin to put more than 30 pupils in one room." The study finds that only 28.8 percent of America's urban school children are enrolled in classes of fewer than 31 pupils; it considers the effects of the overload on teachers and on teaching effectiveness.

HUGHES, MARIE M., "What Teachers Do and the Way They Do It," *NEA Journal*, 53 (No. 6): 11–13, September, 1964. Discusses some of the ways of doing things in the classroom that can make a difference in the over-all quality of teaching.

JANSSEN, PETER, "The Union Response to Academic Mass Production," *Saturday Review*, October 21, 1967, pp. 64–66, 86–88. A magazine editor analyzes what he conceives to be strengths and weaknesses of the American Federation of Teachers.

KENNAN, RICHARD BARNES, "Sanctions Are Effective," *NEA Journal*, 54 (No. 8): 3132, 67, November, 1965. Explains how Oklahoma teachers, through the technique of sanctions by local, state, and national associations, received salary increments ranging from $380 up to $1,000 and more instead of the $50 a year token raise offered by the governor. Other security provisions were also made mandatory by the legislature.

LAMBERT, SAM M., "Angry Young Men in Teaching," *NEA Journal*, 52 (No. 2): 17–20, February, 1963. Explains why so many young men leave teaching for other kinds of work.

MEAD, GEORGE H., *Mind, Self and Society*. Chicago: University of Chicago Press, 1934. A distinguished social philosopher explains the theory behind the establishment of social institutions. Pages 260–273 afford an insight into the relationship between the community and the institutions it establishes. This is an earlier but still quite up-to-date development of the theory of social institutions.

NAGEL, ERNEST, "Charles Sanders Peirce, a Prodigious but Little-Known American Philosopher," *Scientific American*, 200 (No. 4): 185–192, April, 1959. A critical review of the man and his works by a professional philosopher. ". . . there is a fair consensus among historians of ideas that Charles Sanders Peirce remains the most original, versatile and comprehensive philosophic mind this country has yet produced."

NATIONAL EDUCATION ASSOCIATION, Research Division, *Analysis of*

Salary Schedule Provisions, Washington. Each year the NEA issues a report dealing with salary structure and salary scales. The brief comments preceding each table will be most informative to a beginning student in education who is considering entering the profession and whose welfare will be affected by the salary structure and salary scale in the district where he will first find employment.

NEA Journal, "Strikes and Sanctions," 56 (No. 7): 38–39, October, 1967. This is an official statement of the position of the NEA on teacher strikes. The NEA believes that the sanctions procedure should make strikes unnecessary in settling disputes, but where strikes occur, "the NEA will offer all services at its command to the affiliate concerned to help resolve the impasse."

NEA Journal, "We Had No Idea," 50 (No. 10): 47–54, October, 1961. Describes the many services rendered to the teaching profession by the NEA.

PETER, LAURENCE J., "The Peter Principle: We're All Incompetent," *Phi Delta Kappan*, 48 (No. 7): 339–341, March, 1967. This humorous article with serious intent explains why excellent teachers are encouraged by the system of promotions to desert that which they can do best.

Phi Delta Kappan (editorial), 49 (No. 10): 553–554, June, 1968. Two editors of the magazine make an analysis of the militant efforts of the professional organizations of classroom teachers to elevate the status of teachers.

Phi Delta Kappan, "NEA Officials Explain Refusal To Talk Merger with AFT," 50 (No. 6): 319, February, 1969. A short summary of the six main stumbling blocks to a merger of the two influential professional teachers' organizations.

REISERT, JOHN E., "Migrating Educator? What About Your Teaching Credentials?" *Phi Delta Kappan*, 47 (No. 7): 372–374, March, 1966. This outlines the steps one should follow to be certified in all the states. Of help to one who is interested in the problem of reciprocity between the states.

RETTIG, SOLOMON, and BENJAMIN PASAMANICK, "Status and Job Satisfaction of Public School Teachers," *School and Society*, 87:113–116, March 14, 1959. A study of status and job satisfaction by two medical men. Analyzes why public school teachers seem to have an inferiority feeling and suggests remedies.

RHODES, ERIC, "What Index Scheduling Means," *Phi Delta Kappan*, 46 (No. 9): 459–460, May, 1965. This article, showing what an index salary schedule is, should be of special interest to teachers-in-preparation.

ROSS, LILLIAN, "Dancers on the Green," *The New Yorker*, July 18, 1964, pp. 35–90. A description of the work of a fifth-grade public school teacher in New York City. This is a rather long, but highly readable, photographic-style picture of the work of a dedicated teacher, with some sidelights on what she was paid, how she lived, and the like.

Saturday Review, "A Summary of NEA Recommendations," October 19, 1963, p. 60. Sets forth 15 recommendations emanating from a three-year NEA project for the improvement of the instructional program in the schools throughout the United States prepared by a national committee of distinguished educators. A clear statement of what teachers feel their true functions to be and what their attitudes should be toward the many innovations now being introduced into school instruction.

SCANLON, JOHN, "Strikes, Sanctions, and the Schools," *Saturday Review*, October 19, 1963, pp. 51–55, 70–74. A careful appraisal of the efforts of teachers working through organizational channels such as the NEA and the AFT to gain recognition for their claims to better working conditions. The author contrasts the methods of the AFT in New York City with those used by the Utah Education Association in their demands for increased salaries.

SCHILPP, PAUL, ed., *The Philosophy of John Dewey*, 2nd ed. New York: Tudor, 1955. Pages 3–45 contain an excellent biography of Dewey written by his daughters and edited by his daughter Jene. Gives a realistic view of the times as reflected in the education of one man.

SHANKER, ALBERT, "The Real Meaning of the New York City Teachers' Strike," *Phi Delta Kappan*, 50 (No. 8): 434–441, April, 1969. An excellent example of how a teachers' union leader trained in philosophy used the philosophical method to analyze a very difficult educational problem. The beginning student of education will profit, especially by reading the generalizations beginning on page 437 (with "In this brief chronology . . . ") and continuing to the end of the article.

STIEBER, GERTRUDE N., "Teachers' Salaries," *NEA Journal*, 56 (No. 7):

36–37, October, 1967. An analysis of the salaries paid school teachers and other personnel in the 1966–1967 school year.

Today's Education, 57 (No. 4): 83, October, 1968. A succinct one-page summary of the over-all program of the National Education Association, of particular interest to serious beginning students of education.

WARREN, EVA, ''Earth Being So Good Would Heaven Seem Best,'' *NEA Journal*, 53 (No. 3): 8–10, 83, 85, 87, March, 1964. A free-lance writer and editor surveys what teacher associations are doing to provide homes for retired teachers. ''From my contacts with retired teachers in these communal residences, I am convinced they are . . . some of the happiest.''

II

Ideas Influential in America

In Unit II we examine some historical and contemporary features of living that seem to have had a marked influence in shaping the character of education in America. A necessary background to a sound understanding of what education in this country is like and what it is attempting is a comprehension of the broad assumptions that have more or less determined its direction and an acquaintance with the widely disseminated ideas that served as guides in the development of what is, after all, one of man's most splendid modern achievements. Clearly, knowing these assumptions and ideas and having an appreciation of historical bases, trends, and educational experiences and experiments are an important foundation for analyzing and evaluating current issues.

The United States is a nation with roots in Europe ; it is natural, therefore, that the ideas that were most basically influential in shaping American education are European in origin. Some are associated with certain great social movements—the Athenian, the Christian, and the Renaissance. These three movements are explored in the first chapter of the unit. The most dramatic of population movements in all history, the American frontier movement, also has had a basic and, in this case, a characteristically American influence. It is the subject of another chapter. In addition to discussing the ideas that grew from the great social movements, in this unit we also examine some of the educational ideas that have been disseminated and implemented by European thinkers and writers. We have selected six of these leaders—Comenius, Rousseau, Pestalozzi, Froebel, Herbart, and Spencer—and we devote a chapter to a brief exploration of some of their ideas that have had a distinguishable influence on American education.

In the final chapter of the unit, we see how the ideas from the European social movements, from our frontier movement, and from European leaders affect various aspects of our contemporary scene. Selected areas of contemporary life in America are studied as illustrative of factors that have an influence—sometimes subtle, often very deep—on current trends in education.

Ideas that become incorporated in institutions do not come into the world spontaneously. They have originated at some time in history, from a combination of sources, and they have been propagated. Ideas are somewhat like large streams of water. They are in constant motion, are constantly being swelled by tributaries whose identity is more or less lost in the main stream. The ideas that contribute to the main stream of thought, however, do not entirely lose their identity in the way the waters of tributaries are lost in the main stream. Their identity and the degree of their influence wax and wane.

Institutions like the school result when certain ideas eventually crystallize, are widely accepted, and are incorporated into practice. It is from a confluence of ideas in motion that the fabric of modern educational thought has been created. An educator does not create or invent current ideas any more than an economist invents the ideas of inflation, devaluation, price supports, or social security. Some recognized need has gradually brought the ideas into being.

Two sources of ideas

Where did our ideas about education originate? What was their genesis? Educational thought can be traced to a flow of ideas from two general sources—from social movements and from educational leaders. When a series of ideas is adopted by a mass of people and leads to widespread action toward some socially significant end, we have a social movement. When the ideas and resultant actions affect large masses of people so significantly that the course of history is influenced, we have what we call a historical movement, such as the Renaissance or the Christian movement. In the wake of historical movements, through the impetus of social thought, all institutions, all marks of the culture are swept along. Out of such movements many influential ideas, in education and other fields, emerge.

Concurrent with historical movements, and sometimes in advance of them, learned men, thinkers and writers, have formulated more or less generally accepted ideas into a system of thought. We can trace certain current educational thought back to these individuals. They saw more clearly than others of their time what the ideas were that answered the needs felt by the people. They were more skilled than others in organizing the thought and in putting it into a form that made the ideas clear. Because of their superior intelligence and shrewder insights, they discovered new underlying principles or enhanced the attractiveness of older ones.

What educational ideas have come to us from these two sources? Since the beginning, America has never been isolated, politically or otherwise, from European influences. In this chapter, a brief examination of the ideas and the propelling forces of three great European movements will make clear that some social thought of the past is related to educational ideas that have survived and continue, to some extent, to exert an influence. In the succeeding chapter, by turning attention to the other source of educational thought, to certain representative thinkers and writers, it will become evident that what they produced also has been and is related, to a considerable degree, to current educational thought.

In examining the historical movements two limitations are imposed. First, we must be brief. A description of any one of the large-scale social movements, giving an adequate picture of its background, its unfolding, its ramifications, its consequences, its sweeping historical effects, would take the efforts of a specialized historian and result in a lengthy book. Obviously, that is not necessary. Our purpose can be achieved, not by focusing upon details pertaining to events, causes, and results, but by focusing directly upon certain ideas that are part of the movement—ideas that have been most vitally related to modern educational thought.

167

CHAPTER 7
Ideas from
European
Social
Movements

The second limitation is in the choice of movements. Only those movements that are mainly European are included. This seems to be a logical selection, inasmuch as it is the historical movements of Europe which have led to the emergence of ideas that have had the greatest impact upon education in the United States. The great movements selected, and discussed briefly, are the Athenian movement, the Christian movement, the Renaissance, particularly the Italian Renaissance, and the American frontier movement. The first three are studied as European movements and are included in this chapter. The American frontier movement is explored in a separate chapter because of its importance to American education.

The Athenian movement and critical thinking

The Athenian movement, characterized by some historians as an episodic and somewhat fleeting event in history, grows in its appeal and takes on added significance with the perspective provided by passing years. The important point to remember here is that an idea emerged—an idea that, eventually, was accepted by Western civilization, an idea that has been an influence in shaping American educational institutions. The idea is *that habits of critical thinking are dynamic elements in personal and social progress.*

The city of Athens was a center of early cultural and intellectual development. The number of persons who participated in the intellectual movement was, perhaps, never above thirty thousand. At the peak of intellectual development, the Golden Age of Pericles (500–400 B.C.), the population of Athens was only slightly over a hundred thousand, including slaves and women, who were denied citizenship.

Before the Athenian movement, before the advent of the method of critical thinking, criticism of a deep-seated, widespread tradition was considered offensive. If an institution was well established, no one dared to question its favored practices or even to inquire about the premises upon which the institution had been built. To question a religion, for example, was thought to invite the wrath of the gods. It definitely brought down the wrath of all the citizens who believed in the particular religion. To question a religion was to classify oneself as a heretic and to lay oneself open to persecution. To think critically was dangerous. To differ from existing popular beliefs, to do something in a way which differed from custom, resulted in extreme unpopularity, perhaps even in being publicly designated an unworthy citizen. Such were the social attitudes that characterized civilizations preceding the Athenian era.

Since, in these earlier civilizations, only the tried ways were right ways, since there were no alternatives to the ways considered right, all that education could do was to justify and intrench the existing ways of thinking and of doing. The pupils were told how to act. Schools extolled the virtues of the past. Schools never, intentionally, attempted to show how the ways of living could be improved. The task of the pre-Athenian school was to protect the way of life, to serve as a brake upon any attempt to change it.

CRITICAL THINKING IN THE EDUCATION OF A CITIZEN

Life among the people of Athens was changed when a new type of teacher, a Sophist, came among them. Sophists were teachers of superior skill and enlarged vision. They claimed that they were not attempting to prepare pupils for any particular profession or field of study but were teaching definitely and specifically to develop their pupils into intelligent citizens. They stressed liberal education as a supplement to the customary instruction in reading, writing, music, and gymnastics.

The Sophists—such as Protagoras (481–411 B.C.), the first of the Sophists, and Isocrates (436–388 B.C.), perhaps the greatest of them —were, above everything else, teachers. They contributed an education of positive merit. Because they were also orators, they taught their pupils and other listeners to place high value upon literary and oratorical excellence. It was the Sophists who helped Plato, author of *The Republic*, and Demosthenes, who delivered the Philippics, develop their consummate powers of expression.

With the advent of the Sophists, the citizens of Athens, for the first time in history, were taught to think critically. Teachers encouraged the boys, the future citizens, to be critical. The premise was that each social custom, each social belief was only one step toward a still higher form of social custom, toward a more mature development in social belief. Each custom and each belief, therefore,

169

CHAPTER 7
*Ideas from
European
Social
Movements*

should be subjected to continuous, critical scrutiny and to thorough, constant reconsideration. Critical thinking, in other words, should precede social reconstruction.

The Athenians developed the point of view that man's nature permits him, when properly educated, to attain an indefinite degree of perfectibility because man possesses an almost limitless capacity to improve. They believed that the only instrument that man can use to achieve the higher life is *trained intelligence*. Critical thinking is an essential method for developing trained intelligence. They succeeded, through a highly skilled application of the method of critical thinking, in developing intelligence among their Athenian students to a degree unknown to any earlier civilization.

Through the use of their opportunities to educate and train the citizens in the method of critical thinking, the Sophists truly wrought a revolution in the intellectual life of the Athenian people. They spread knowledge, but they also spread a new way of thinking through the use of knowledge. Books assumed an important place in the lives of the Athenians. The shelves of the citizens' libraries were filled with row upon row of cylindrically shaped baskets which held the books. Higher education became an accepted feature of civilization, and learning with the aid of professional teachers became the accepted mode of educating citizens.

CRITICAL THINKING AS A METHOD IN EDUCATION

Among the educational leaders of Athens is one whose name has always been associated in history with unsurpassed teaching. He was not a Sophist, but he built upon much that the Sophists developed. He personifies the teaching spirit of his age. Socrates (469?–399 B.C.) started with a basic principle of the Sophists—"Man is the measure of all things." He taught that, since this is so, the first and highest obligation of man is to know himself, that knowledge is the basis of all virtuous action, and that the best method for an individual to obtain knowledge is by use of the dialectical method, or logical disputation.

Socrates entered into conversation with other Athenian citizens and adroitly questioned them. He made it appear that he accepted the answers given him and then developed his subsequent questions in

*S*ocrates (*469?–399* B.C.) *was born in Athens. His parents were too poor to give him the education of a gentleman—training in music and dancing—but he learned to read and write. At an early age he took up sculpture as a vocation, following in his father's footsteps. We do not know when or under what circumstances he left sculpture for teaching, but he declared that he knew he was divinely commissioned to teach. Socrates' teaching was not conventional instruction or formal lecturing. Instead he went about Athens— to the market place, the gymnasia, or some other place where men gathered in numbers—and sought out some individual whose ideas needed modifying or whose technique or conduct called for expert guidance. When he discovered such an individual he plied him with question after question, often leading him to contradiction and confusion. Socrates did this to develop powers of reflection and self-criticism, to foster the ability to think consistently and comprehensively, and to grow in skill in reaching clear conceptions. He believed these powers and abilities were antecedents of a virtuous life.*

For 30 or so years Socrates followed this way of life. He consistently sought to develop the excellence of man as a universal being, rather than as a mere citizen of Athens. His most notable disciples, therefore, were thought to be dangerously lacking in old-fashioned patriotism, which many of his contemporaries believed was essential to the survival of Athens. The opposition to Socrates grew to such an extent that ultimately, in 399 B.C., he was accused by his enemies and indicted for "corrupting the young" and for "impiety." The court by majority vote assessed the death penalty, which was carried out by means of a cup of poison hemlock.

Socrates wrote nothing. It is his conversational method as recorded by Plato, his most distinguished pupil, that assures his immortality as a great teacher. Benjamin Jowett, the Greek scholar, wrote: "During a long and confidential intercourse, Plato penetrated so deeply into the spirit of his distinguished friend that the portrait of that spirit which he was able to bequeath to us is at once the most faithful and the most ideal that we possess."

terms of the answers given, until the person being instructed was brought face to face with the follies and absurdities of his own superficially formulated answers. The first aim of Socrates' method was to bring recognition of error. The second aim was, through critical questioning, to develop the whole of the truth, of which the original opinion might have been a fragment. So representative of this method of inquiry was Socrates that the method came to be called the Socratic method of teaching.

1 7 1

CHAPTER 7
*Ideas from
European
Social
Movements*

Socrates engages his friends in discussion. (This mural by John La Farge is in the Supreme Court Chambers of the Capitol in Saint Paul, Minnesota.)

Skilled use of the method of inquiry which Socrates developed is still considered a mark of a great mind. It takes understanding and intelligence to formulate a wise question. It takes serious study and reflection to arrive at an intelligent answer. Like the Sophists, Socrates did not believe that a teacher should merely impart knowledge to the pupil. Socrates and his followers, however, believed that in order to create minds capable of forming correct conclusions, of formulating the truth for themselves, in order to generate the *power* of thinking, the method of formal delivery, of lecturing, that the Sophists mainly followed had to be replaced by the dialectic method. Socrates showed by his example that the proper methods of teaching could generate powers of thinking in the learners. Critical inquiry was appropriate to every subject, be it the operation of natural laws, principles of economics, moral principles, or politics. Nothing should be exempt from the arena of public discussion. In numerous respects the method of Socrates is still a considerable influence in current educational thought.

THE STATE AND THE CULTIVATION OF CRITICAL THINKING

The Sophists, who expanded the functions of education and developed the field of higher education in Athens, and Socrates, the great teacher, had a marked influence on the renowned writer and thinker of the period, Plato. One educational aim that emerged during the Athenian movement, one which is associated with Plato and which contributed to the fundamental idea that habits of critical thinking are related to personal and social progress, is that education should lead the child to yearn to be a good citizen. This was not just the aim of teachers. It was the central aim of government, and the entire life of the state was organized to enable boys to live richly the life of the free citizen. The philosophy of government was that government should be used as a means for developing the individual, that the State existed to serve Man. This was a marked departure from the philosophy that Man existed to serve the State.

To carry out this aim, teachers taught that which was desirable for good citizenship. Only boys were included in the program; women were not citizens. Boys lived with adult men and shared in all civic activities. They mingled with the men in the market place, at the theater, and at the games. At every turn a boy was encouraged to ask questions, to raise and discuss vital issues, to pursue knowledge for the purpose of living a freer, a richer, a more morally satisfying life. And of all his intellectual pursuits, the most highly respected was the search for truth. To discover truth he was encouraged to think critically.

As a result of expert, professional instruction and firsthand experiences that young men had in the conduct of public affairs, including freedom to raise questions, for the first time in history a considerable body of people representative of those qualified as citizens took part in governing the State. The community life of the Athenians unfolded at an unprecedented rate. The results, as James Henry Breasted has described them, were indeed impressive.

> Here had grown up a whole community of intelligent men, who were the product of the most active interest in the life and the government of the community, constantly sharing in its tasks and problems, in daily contact with the greatest works of art in literature, drama, painting, architecture, and sculpture—such a wonderful community indeed as the ancient world, Greek or oriental, had never seen before.[1]

[1] James Henry Breasted, *The Conquest of Civilization*. New York: Harper & Row, 1926, p. 383.

CRITICAL THINKING IN MODERN EDUCATION

From the standpoint of modern education, the most notable contribution of the Athenians was their method of critical thinking. It has been widely accepted and adopted by the Western world, and the effects upon Western civilization and Western education are of incalculable magnitude. Leading historians believe that the Greek emphasis upon the method of critical thinking was responsible for the greatest intellectual revolution of all time.

What do we have in our present educational situation that bears witness to the Athenian pattern? How has the method of critical thinking influenced current educational thought?

With us, as with the Athenians, the habit of critical thinking is considered something that must be nurtured in realistic, community surroundings. The community, as such, is an educative agency. The problems of the educational theorist then and now are: What kind of education will make citizens intelligent and willing participants in the sphere of everyday social action? How can the schools realize this ideal and at the same time develop to the fullest extent the personality of the individuals?

We follow in the footsteps of the Athenians when we adopt as one of our principal objectives the development in the pupils of the power to think with knowledge, not just to absorb it, when we

"The community, as such, is an educative agency." At the Metropolitan Museum of Art in New York, teachers discuss with museum staff members the types of facilities and materials the museum can provide for enriching American history courses. At a variety store in Chicago, a high school girl serves as a part-time clerk under a work experience program involving cooperation between school officials and retailers.

utilize conversational methods for helping pupils to obtain knowledge, and when we stimulate pupils to ponder and classify their own experiences. We reflect the influence of the Athenian movement when we say that that knowledge is of most value which in some way affects the course of human conduct.

The Christian movement

EMPHASIS ON ETHICAL BEHAVIOR

The Christian religious movement followed in historical sequence the Periclean Athenian period just discussed. About this time many people in the Mediterranean area were turning from their traditional religions. The Oriental religions, especially, were becoming influential. The center of political power was shifting to Rome, where the people were susceptible to new religious doctrines. The old Roman faith did not stress higher forms of human conduct, nor did it give its followers any promise of a future life. The trials of the populace were heavy. The common people longed for some assurance of blessedness beyond the grave. They turned in increasing numbers to a new faith which gave them an enlarged vision of the brotherhood of man and the fatherhood of God. A Jewish tentmaker from Tarsus, named Paul, preached the new doctrine far and wide and left a train of converted cities stretching from Palestine to Rome. This new religion placed strong emphasis upon ethical behavior in the conduct of human affairs. An ethical strain became influential in the determination of goals of education. Again, an idea was set in motion—an idea that subsequently affected intellectual thought throughout the Western world.

The central personality in the Christian movement was Jesus, a Jew who was born in Palestine in the days of Augustus. Like the Sophists, he was a teacher. Like Socrates, he was one of the greatest of teachers. His teaching incurred the hatred of the Roman rulers, and he was accused of political conspiracy. Jesus was put to death, as was Socrates before him. So strong was the appeal of his religion to men in all walks of life that within two hundred years the new religion outstripped all others throughout the whole of the Roman Empire. The influence of Christianity upon subsequent formal education in

175

CHAPTER 7
*Ideas from
European
Social
Movements*

Jesus was a master teacher. The ethical emphasis of Christian teaching is reflected in present-day education. (The artist was a fourteenth-century Italian, Spinello Aretino.)

Western civilization is immeasurable. In the United States, teaching has at all times reflected certain of the ethical emphases placed on education by the religious leaders of the Christian church.

Jesus developed the sublime art of addressing the imagination by appealing alike to the emotions and reason. The parables are examples of his method. The language used is both colorful and dramatic. His subject matter was derived from the common incidents of life and from the ordinary objects of nature. He so directed these simple tales that they became vehicles for conveying the most profound of lessons.

PROFESSIONAL EDUCATION

In time the leaders of the Christian church became the spokesmen of the people. When the common man was denied the privilege of playing a part in the control of public affairs, large numbers of them turned to the leaders of the Christian church for spiritual and political guidance.

Library of Pope Sixtus IV (1414-1484). In libraries like this priests studied to prepare to Christianize schools already established in Western Europe. Teaching as a profession and modern elementary education are generally dated from the fifteenth century.

The educational methods used by the Christian church to develop leaders were those of teaching, debate, and discussion. History saw the rise of educated religious leaders, the Christian clergy, who built a powerful religious organization. By 311 A.D., Christianity had been legalized by the Romans. It continued to spread through Europe. Its spectacular growth in influence was supposedly due to its stress upon education and to its creation of a specialized clergy for the purpose of advancing education.

Throughout its history and continuing to the present time, the Christian church has depended upon education. This is evident, for instance, in the creation of parochial elementary and secondary schools, in the establishment of many colleges for training leaders in the Christian faith. Many of these educational institutions rank among the top of their kind in the United States.

THE ETHICAL STRAIN IN SECULAR EDUCATION

The Athenian philosophers advanced the idea that the key to the solutions of the problems of life was to be found in the intellectual

Ideas have a profound influence on education. Christianity stresses the importance of the individual : a teacher works individually with a child, striving to bridge the barrier of deafness. The inductive approach to learning stresses reasoning from a part to a whole : the children observing a Trippensee planetarium are making their own generalizations about the motions of the planets. Public education as it has evolved in this country stresses ethical behavior : an older child helps a younger one. The method of

critical thinking stresses the development of the power to think with knowledge : the children in class are eager to express their thoughts growing out of their knowledge.

nature of man. Because the level of intellectual attainment expected by them was very high, the aim of education could not be attained by the masses. They sought an aristocracy of brains. The Christian educators, on the other hand, offered a goal that was within the power of everyone's attainment. They argued that man's moral nature is common to all men and that, given proper instruction, it is within the power of every man to develop his moral nature. They offered a universally applicable solution. Stress was on ethics and morality rather than on intellectuality.

The ethical strain introduced by the earlier Christian leaders into educational thought and practice has persisted in educationa philosophy to the present day. Education is to build better behavior, to improve conduct, to advance the cause of human relations, to emphasize the higher traits of character. This kind of aim for educacation receives, perhaps, a greater emphasis in modern educational theory than at any other time in history. As will be pointed out in the chapter on aims, ethical character has been one of the principal aims stressed in various official statements of the aims of American education. Secular education, at least in the theories that guide it, has stressed the ethical factor, and there is no indication that the emphasis on ethical outcomes will not be stressed in the future as much as in the past.

Many different kinds of Christian groups settled in the United States. Each sect had its own notions about how children should be educated. Partly because of dividedness, public education in the United States became secularized; that is, it became an education that was conducted without reference to any particular religion. It was public education, free from religious control. The teachers, however, were convinced of the importance of stressing ethical behavior. Many who taught in public schools stressed ethical conduct as consistently as teachers in church schools. It is possible, according to a secular philosophy of education, for every man to develop his moral nature, and it is held that one of the first duties of teachers is to help individuals develop personalities that are permeated with those ethical characteristics, such as love and charity, that have been emphasized throughout the history of the Christian movement.

The Renaissance: a new method of inquiry

THE RENAISSANCE PERIOD

One of the most interesting periods in European history is that which culminated in the Renaissance at the close of the Middle Ages. The story of the revival of classical learning has been told many times. It is the story of the achievements of great artists like Da Vinci, Raphael, and Michelangelo, of the rebellion against the authority of the Christian church, of the mathematicians who infused new life into an old subject, of the astronomers who gazed at the heavens and made new discoveries about the universe, and of the physicists who abandoned the method of speculative theory in the study of nature for study through the techniques of controlled experimentation.

Actually the Renaissance encompasses an indefinite period of time. No year marks its onset. The middle of the fifteenth century is sometimes mentioned as being near the beginning of the break away from the older intellectual patterns, principally because by 1440 printing had been developed. No date can be assigned to the ending of the new movement, for the spirit of the Renaissance is a vital force today.

When the Renaissance originated, Italy consisted of city-states like Venice, Florence, Genoa, Milan, and Pisa. In his novel *The Romance of Leonardo da Vinci*, the Russian author Dmitri Merezhkovski (1865–1941) gives us what historians say is a fairly realistic picture of the times. He paints a vivid canvas of a great genius living in a civilization filled with intense contrasts, with extremes of extravagance and magnificence, with foibles of sensuality and of human frailty.

The flow of thought that stemmed from the Renaissance must be interpreted against a background of social organization as well as disorganization. In this Italian civilization, with its intense rivalries, political betrayals, and lust and licentiousness on the one hand, and on the other, a growing sensitiveness to the values of scholarship, of the arts and sciences, and of critical thinking and education, modern ideas found their greatest propagating force. The sea of inquiry was widened. Men were both tied to and cut adrift from their ancient intellectual moorings.

The movement was of such great breadth that its results made the modern world modern. But ideas that were set into motion and that have since affected thought in the United States were not altogether harmonious in character. There were crosscurrents of thought and variations in practice. There were classicists; there were naturalists; there were scholastics. One thread of events and thought did emerge, however, and resulted in the development and propagation of a new method of inquiry. In addition to the old, and very worthy, method of inquiry, the deductive method, a new pattern of thinking, the inductive method, gained prominence. In order to understand better its present ramifications in educational thought and practice, we must consider what brought the idea of the inductive method of inquiry into being, what it involves, and where it has led.

INFLUENCE OF CLASSICAL LANGUAGES ON MODES OF THOUGHT

1. Created a class

All books and legal documents in Italy at the time of the Renaissance were written in classical Latin, although the common people spoke regional Italian dialects. The learned teachers delivered their lectures in Latin. In time, skill in the use of classical Latin became the badge of the educated man. It separated him from the uneducated, gave him membership in a distinguished prestige group. Latin was the international avenue for international communication.

2. Made the past authoritative

Because of his mastery of classical Latin, the educated man was able to study the great works produced before the Renaissance. Many an educated man also mastered classical Greek. Through his command of Greek he had access to the works of the Athenian scholars—to their drama, their philosophy, oratory, poetry, and the great literature of the perfectionists. To the Italian scholars of this period there was no source of learning so rich in quality, so universal in application as that handed down by the Greeks.

The effects of this emphasis on Latin and veneration for the works of the Greek scholars have been far-reaching and long-lasting. The Italian scholars believed that the works produced by the Athenian

181

CHAPTER 7
*Ideas from
European
Social
Movements*

scholars were unsurpassable, well-nigh perfect, sufficient for exclusive study, and applicable to every aspect of human conduct. The knowledge of the ancients became the authoritative guide for man's every endeavor. In the books of the ancients were found all the answers to man's esthetic, ethical, and political problems. Thus a knowledge of Latin and Greek was the key to all the answers. The man with the key was in a position of intellectual power and consequently had social prestige.

3. Perpetuated a pattern

Naturally, classical Latin became the core of the educational curriculum. Methods of teaching it were developed into highly refined techniques which had the psychological advantages of being both logical and definite.

The effects of these methods upon teaching in general seem fairly clear. A definiteness was given to teaching methods. The selection and management of subject matter were made more logical. The effects were felt long after the classical languages ceased to serve as the official language of communication. Latin continued to hold the central place in the curriculum. Methods of teaching Latin were deemed suitable for teaching the subjects in most other fields.

The predominance of Latin also served to perpetuate the separation of scholars into a class apart from the practical affairs of life. Even after newer subjects came into the curriculum, teachers of the older subjects retained special prestige, were considered to be more erudite, and were ascribed higher social status.

A CHANGED EMPHASIS

With time, veneration of the past and viewing writers of the past as authorities waned. Fewer and fewer of the Italian scholars followed the classical pattern. They increasingly focused education upon current problems. Eventually the fundamental premise of the scholastics—namely, that the present could not be much different from the past—was no longer widely accepted. Scholars did not cease to study the past, however. Simultaneously with an effort to achieve understanding and appreciation of the past, teachers strove to achieve understanding and appreciation of current problems. Sometimes older ideas became gradually blended with newer ones. Sometimes they flowed separately. Sometimes they were antagonistic.

The new emphasis and its consequences resemble, in some respects, the curriculum situation in modern education, where social studies have been viewed in a somewhat unfriendly fashion by those who believe pupils should study historical episodes and not waste much time trying to acquire an intimate acquaintance with problems of modern life. The blending and reconciliation of old and new, a problem that dates back to the Renaissance, continues to be a sharply debated educational issue.

EMERGENCE OF THE INDUCTIVE METHOD OF INQUIRY

The inductive method of inquiry emerged during the Renaissance. This method and its application permeates the whole of modern educational philosophy.

1. What the inductive method is

The inductive method involves reasoning logically and methodically from a part to a whole, from particulars to generals, from the individual to the universal. Making generalizations is probably as old as human thought, but before this time the method used to arrive at generalizations had received little attention. In order to make the generalizations of mankind more authentic, more valid, and more likely to be true, the leaders in the Renaissance popularized the inductive method as a mode of study, as a manner of reasoning.

The inductive method is a model of simplicity. It involves two steps: first, observation, and then, generalization. Johann Kepler (1571–1630), reasoning inductively, proved mathematically that the orbit of Mars is elliptical. Subsequent observations proved his "laws" to be true. He first collected all the available facts about planetary motion. This fulfilled the first step in inductive reasoning. Through careful study and application of mathematics he arrived at a generalization that he believed was true and that would either refute or fortify the generalizations previously reached. In other words, he subjected the generalizations made by others about the orbit of Mars to the proof furnished by his own observations and by further application of

183

CHAPTER 7
*Ideas from
European
Social
Movements*

his knowledge of mathematics. The kind of orbit that was consistent with his observations, with the observations of others, and with mathematical proof was elliptical. Kepler's success helped "popularize" the inductive method and encouraged others to study and employ it.

2. Why the inductive method emerged

The intellectual powers of the most learned men of the Renaissance had been challenged by one novel, basic question to which the older sources afforded no satisfactory answer. The question involved two parts: What is man's relationship to nature? and What is nature? A modern way of seeking an answer to educational implications of the problem would be to ask, "What should be the relation between the education a child receives in school and the nature of that child?" The scholastics had given little recognition to the problem, and the best the later scholars of the early Renaissance could do was to raise the question. They could not find a satisfactory answer in what was already known to them.

So tenacious was the hold of tradition upon methods of inquiry that even as late as 1400, despite the use by the Athenians of critical thinking, which was a near approach to the method, it was actually dangerous to arrive at any generalizations about nature through an application of the inductive form of logic. So impelling was the question, however, and so strong was the intellectual interest in it that, despite the danger involved, the newly discovered method was used in certain quarters. Copernicus (1473–1543) was a scientist who proceeded to employ inductive logic despite personal danger. He questioned the validity of the generally held beliefs about the motions of the heavenly bodies—beliefs that had been popularly accepted as part of the so-called Ptolemaic system. Copernicus, reasoning inductively, concluded that the earth is spherical, rotates on its axis, and revolves around the sun. He explained for the first time the phenomenon of the seasons. He gave permission for his work to be published and he escaped certain persecution only because he died before the work was published.

This new method that was leading to discoveries about nature, as startling then as the present-day exploration of space, appealed increasingly to men of trained intelligence. The pace of discoveries, especially discoveries about nature, was greatly accelerated. Advanced thinkers, through the use of the method, became more proficient, and their ranks swelled.

Later on, as the inductive method became more highly refined as a process for arriving at more valid generalizations, it became a useful tool in all fields of human endeavor. To the natural scientists it has become the process of reasoning from which the general laws of nature are reached. Underlying the use of the inductive process is the tacit assumption and acceptance in science of the postulate of the uniformity of nature. Once, however, a general law of nature is established, then the process of deduction is used to draw inferences that apply to special cases. As an example, the solution of a problem of physics is an exercise in the use of the deductive process. Thus the two processes are supplementary.

In all areas of knowledge where generalizations are made—biology, sociology, history—the inductive process is a universally used tool in the formulation of more or less valid generalizations. When combined with the deductive process, it has led to many great advances in the world of modern knowledge.

3. Conflict aroused

While the inductive method rapidly became acceptable among scientific thinkers, differences arose about its application and implications. Is the method applicable to the study of every kind of problem? If not, then to what kinds of problems may it properly be applied?

The use of the inductive method of inquiry gained increased attention when Galileo (1564–1642) dropped two bodies of unequal weight but of equal densities from the top of the leaning tower of Pisa and based his generalizations about falling bodies upon what he observed. Even though Galileo demonstrated visually to all the professors and students at the local university that bodies of different weights fall with the same velocity, even though he showed that the path of a projectile is a parabola, his theories were reviled. He was forced to resign his professorship at the University of Pisa and to withdraw from teaching. His later discoveries, made through the same inductive method, were termed heresies because there was a seeming discrepancy between his new view of the solar system and certain passages in the Bible. He was subsequently subjected to extreme ecclesiastical censure.

185

CHAPTER 7
*Ideas from
European
Social
Movements*

The first experiments, which Galileo made while he was a young professor at Pisa, were decidedly dramatic. At that time the doctrine that the rate at which a body falls depends upon its weight was generally accepted as true, merely on the authority of Aristotle. It was even held that the acceleration varies as the weight. Prior to Galileo it did not occur to any actually to try the experiment. The young professor's tests went contrary to the doctrine held for two thousand years. Allowing for the resistance of the air, he found that all bodies fell at the same rate, and that the distance passed over varied as the square of the time. With all the enthusiasm, courage, and impudence of youth, the experimenter proclaimed that Aristotle, at that time believed by nearly everyone to be verbally inspired, was wrong. Galileo met with opposition, but he decided to give his opponents ocular proof. It seems almost as if nature had resorted to an extraordinary freak to furnish Galileo, at this critical moment in the history of science, with an unusual convenience for his public demonstration. Yonder tower of Pisa had bent over to facilitate experimentation, from its top, on falling bodies. One morning, before the assembled university, he ascended the leaning tower, and allowed a one-pound shot and a one-hundred-pound shot to drop together. The multitude saw the balls start together, fall together, and heard them strike the ground together. Some were convinced, others returned to their rooms, consulted Aristotle, and, distrusting the evidences of their senses, declared continued allegiance to his doctrine.

Florian Cajori, *A History of Physics*. New York: Macmillan, 1924, pp. 32–33. Quoted by permission of Florian A. Cajori.

The inquisition to which Galileo was subjected resulted from a conflict between two methods of thinking—the deductive, older method of arriving at generalizations, used by the classicists, and the inductive, newer, and perhaps more dependable method of arriving at valid generalizations. The conflict was an intellectual one. No one was expected to examine or question the laws of courts and the principles of government, politics, education, and ethics. The underlying premises on which conclusions in most areas of social endeavor were based were not to be discussed or investigated. Many people feared that if the new method were applied to revered social traditions, to cherished educational patterns, society would be undermined, man made insecure. Galileo, however, had taken an important pioneer step, the imprint of which could not afterward be erased. He has been called the father of our modern times partly because of his scientific

Both the development of the method of inductive verification of hypotheses by observation and experimentation and the use of the new mathematics were accelerated by such men as Copernicus, Galileo, and Kepler. Unquestioned dependence on Greek authority finally began to falter.

discoveries but mainly because he reinforced confidence in the inductive method of reasoning, which has become a distinguishing characteristic of our modern age. This idea from the central stream of Renaissance thought has had a deep and lasting effect upon all subsequent intellectual thought.

Summary: effects of the ideas from social movements

We have said that the ideas that led to the forming of social institutions, for example the school, emerged from a broad stream of ever-moving thought. Many of the most influential of our modern ideas originated in the sweeping changes caused by social movements. From the Athenian movement we gained a belief in the value of critical thinking; from the Christian movement an ethical strain became part of our educational philosophy; and from the Italian Renaissance we inherited the method of inductive reasoning.

American schools stress education for citizenship. Teachers emphasize the importance of making critical judgments and personal evaluations. Information and knowledge are acquired for use in

187

CHAPTER 7
*Ideas from
European
Social
Movements*

thinking and reasoning. Did these practices and beliefs come to us from the Athenians? We cannot say that the connection is direct and unbroken. We can say that the Athenians originated a belief in critical thinking, that the belief has survived throughout history, and that it is a characteristic of our present-day educational thought.

Christianity stressed the ethical aspect of living. The individual became the pivot of the universe. Teaching became the great conditioner of lives. There is little question that the emphasis in present-day educational philosophy on the importance of relating education to desirable conduct, of attempting to design all phases of our educational scheme in terms of the best interests of the individual child, was nourished by the Christian influence. Philosophy, for example, stresses accommodation to individual differences because it is the individual and not the mass of children on which we attempt to focus. Education is not only to serve all; it is to serve each.

Perhaps when we come to the ideas that emerged from the Italian Renaissance we recognize the ideas that unmistakably mark our schools as modern. Our modern schools do not limit themselves to the methods and the tools of the classicists. They go beyond. Many teachers in America's schools who teach subjects other than the classics are tremendously influenced by the inductive method of reasoning. They are influenced by it in the way they guide children and youth. They encourage pupils to raise questions, to investigate, to confirm, to generalize. What the expert educator supports as sound educational practice is based on research that follows the inductive method. Much that is known about the nature and development of children has resulted from an application of the inductive method. The introduction of the inductive method added a new dimension to thinking. Instead of one method, now two great methods, mutually supplemental, contribute to the advance of knowledge.

The importance of the ideas that grew out of the three great European social movements is so vast that it cannot be pinpointed. We know that certain ideas originated in great social movements. We know that these movements affected the thinking of great masses of people in the Western world and that all the succeeding generations of Western people have been influenced by their heritage from such movements. But great social movements are instituted by men and propagated through men, and it is only through the thoughts of men that the ideas behind the movements are made clear to succeeding generations. As we move into the next chapter, we shall see that certain individuals—thinkers and educators—have been essential in propagating the ideas, in clarifying and expanding them, and in bridging the gap between the results of the Athenian movement, the Christian movement, the Renaissance, and other great movements and modern practices in the schools of the United States.

Questions

1. Why is it that most of the social movements that affected early American education were European in origin?
2. What evidence may be offered to justify the belief that critical thinking is essential to social progress?
3. What have been the principal positive and negative effects upon American education of the Christian religious movement?
4. What are the deductive and inductive methods of thinking?
5. How did the exclusive study of the classics affect the educational viewpoints of the classical scholars?
6. What, in your opinion, might be the educational effects of an overemphasis upon some given field, say, science or mathematics?
7. What were the forces in the Renaissance that led to widening the sea of inquiry?
8. How have the modern refinements in the process of induction and deduction led to a greater degree of confidence in the validity of the general fields of knowledge? Illustrate with reference to a specific field of knowledge.
9. How do you account for the fact that when study in the schools was confined almost exclusively to a study of the classics, the area of investigation was being widened?

Projects

1. Consult some standard treatise, such as an encyclopedia, on the nature of deduction. Cite several examples of legitimate uses to be made of the method.

2. Consult a standard treatise dealing with the nature of induction. Cite examples of legitimate uses made of the method.

3. Explain why the Athenian citizens developed a critical attitude toward their own civilization.

4. List a number of common practices in present-day education that are suitable for critical analysis.

5. Explain what is implied by the assertion that building character is a major responsibility of classroom teaching.

6. Identify three present-day social movements that have an influence on modern education. Describe the educational conflicts that have arisen.

7. Give an example that illustrates how some modern discoveries are being made by a combined use of deductive and inductive logic.

8

Ideas from European Leaders

New, propulsive ideas were the mainsprings of the three great social movements referred to in the previous chapter. And the distinctive philosophies of life that emerged from each underlay the social fabric of the Europe of the time.

History records that individuals—thinkers, writers, orators—are inevitably associated with the dissemination and implementation of new ideas. Eminent leaders have shown the ability to see more clearly than most of their contemporaries, to distinguish the more significant trends, and to extract from these the most vital ideas. They have, perhaps, felt no more strongly than many others the social significance of some idea, but they have had the power to be articulate, have not been discouraged by timidity, and have not succumbed to the pressure for conformity. Such leaders are the life-blood of social movements. They are also the ideological pioneers who are in the forefront, preparing the way for new advances, removing obstacles, and setting up markers to give directions.

European leaders who have fulfilled this kind of role in relation to thought that has had an influence on our present school program are numerous. Many sensed the essence of educational problems and indicated promising solutions.

We have selected six representative leaders of European thought who still influence us today. John Amos Comenius (1592–1670), Jean Jacques Rousseau (1712–1778), Johann Heinrich Pestalozzi (1746–1827), Friedrich Wilhelm Froebel (1782–1852), Johann Friedrich Herbart (1776–1841), and Herbert Spencer (1820–1903) were conspicuous as contributors to and disseminators of ideas that have become

Comenius is generally considered the greatest educational theorist and practical reformer of the seventeenth century. This title page of a collection of his works reflects his three great interests: religion, the encyclopedic organization of all knowledge, and education.

part of the main current of educational thought in the United States.
Their ideas have had a striking influence on modern educational
theory and a lesser but important effect on current educational
practice.

What type of person has pioneered in educational thought? What do the six leaders selected have in common? Are the leaders in the field always educators? Actually, they come from all walks of life and have different interests and vocations. Comenius was a Moravian minister, Rousseau a writer on political theory, and Pestalozzi a practicing schoolteacher, as was his follower, Froebel. Herbart was a professor of psychology, Spencer a philosopher. Their lives spanned approximately three centuries. They differed in their point of focus on social problems, but they shared an intensive interest in social advancement. All contributed ideas that have proved helpful in con-
g our modern schools—ideas which, if we but grasp them, will lead us to a better understanding of our schools today.

Comenius: application of the technique of induction to teaching

In the sketch of historical movements we noted that the inductive method was developed during the sweep of the Italian Renaissance. It was Comenius who advanced the idea of applying this inductive technique to teaching.

In the time of Comenius, school leaders generally agreed with his definition of the primary aim of education—"The ultimate end of man is eternal happiness with God." It followed, then, that the methods of teaching in the schools should be such as to enable man to attain this end. Education was to help pupils cultivate moral and mental discipline. The method used completely ignored pupil interest, emotion, natural desires, specialized abilities, and background of learning. In fact, some of the pupils' most active interests were entirely suppressed.

COMENIUS' IDEAS

Comenius became director of a school where he observed the ostentatious display of knowledge by teachers, the lethargic if not contemptuous response of the pupils to what was taught, and the stress on memorization of information without reference to its application. He set about to devise improvement and in time published, among other books, *The Great Didactic*, which, even as late as 1907, was described by Paul Monroe, a careful student of educational history, in this way:

> . . . so sane and far-seeing are the precepts of this work that it may now be read with greater immediate profit to the teacher, sufficiently intelligent to avoid many minor errors, than the majority of contemporary writings.[1]

Comenius proposed changes that, for the most part, were consistent with the application of the principle of induction to classroom teaching. He did not disagree with the accepted religious aim of education, but he differed in the approach. He argued that moral control over oneself and consequently control of all things would grow out of the acquisition of knowledge, virtue, and piety, in this order. To knowledge, the one element relating directly to the school, Comenius gave a new and vastly different interpretation.

He started with the organization and selection of subject matter, which he decided must progress step by step from the familiar to the less familiar. He wrote textbooks in which, as he said, he aimed to give "an accurate anatomy of the universe, dissecting the veins and limbs of all things in such a way that there shall be nothing that is not seen and that each part shall appear in its proper place and without confusion."[2] The textbooks, instead of presenting a collection of facts, presented material arranged so that study could proceed step by step from what is best known to what is less familiar. Each chapter and each paragraph led to the next. Comenius stressed the soundness of connecting words with the objects for which they stand, of learning a

---

[1] Paul Monroe, *A Brief Course in the History of Education*. New York: Macmillan, 1907, p. 247.
[2] Ibid., p. 240.

The Great Didactic, *or Didactica Magna, was a theoretical treatise on education that contained all the views of Comenius upon education. It laid the foundation for educational development for all the succeeding centuries. Examples from the Table of Contents illustrate the nature of the educational topics he discussed :*

6. *If man is to be produced, it is necessary that he be formed by education.*
7. *A man can be most easily formed in early youth, and cannot be formed properly except at this age.*
8. *The young must be educated in common, and for this schools are necessary.*
9. *All the young of both sexes should be sent to school.*
10. *The instruction given in schools should be universal.*
11. *Hitherto there have been no perfect schools.*
12. *It is possible to reform schools.*
13. *The basis of school reform must be exact order in all things.*
14. *The exact order of instruction must be borrowed from nature.*
16. *The universal requirements of teaching and of learning ; that is to say, a method of teaching and of learning with such certainty that the desired result must of necessity follow.*
17. *The principles of facility in teaching and in learning.*
18. *The principles of thoroughness in teaching and in learning.*
19. *The principles of conciseness and rapidity in teaching.*
20. *The method of the sciences, specifically.*
21. *The method of the arts.*
22. *The method of languages.*
23. *The method of morals.*
26. *Of school discipline.*
27. *Of the fourfold division of schools, based on age and requirements.*

As given in Paul Monroe, *A Brief Course in the History of Education.* New York: Macmillan, 1907, pp. 247–248. Quoted by permission of The Macmillan Company.

language the natural way—that is, by topical conversation—of making generous use of pictures and natural objects as classroom aids to instruction, and of including singing, economics, world history, geography, science, politics, art, and handicrafts as everyday parts of the subject matter of classroom instruction.

The most remarkable and most successful of all the Comenian

textbooks for children was *Orbis sensualium pictus* ("The World of Visible Things Pictured"). Its method of dealing with things was that of leading by inductive process to a generalized knowledge. It was also the first textbook for children that utilized illustrations.

A NEW METHOD

Comenius considered subject matter and method as inseparable aspects of teaching. The nine principles of teaching method that Comenius stated reflect his devotion to the inductive method, his long experience as a teacher, and his sensitiveness to logical and psychological relationships:

1. Whatever is to be known must be taught by presenting the object or the idea directly to the child, not merely through its form or symbol.
2. Whatever is taught should be taught as being of practical application in everyday life and of some definite use.
3. Whatever is taught should be taught straightforwardly, and not in a complicated manner.
4. Whatever is taught must be taught with reference to its true nature and its origin; that is to say, through its causes.
5. If anything is to be learned, its general principles must first be explained. Its details may then be considered, and not till then.
6. All parts of an object (or subject), even the smallest, without a single exception, must be learned with reference to their order, their position, and their connection with one another.
7. All things must be taught in due succession, and not more than one thing should be taught at one time.
8. We should not leave any subject until it is thoroughly understood.
9. Stress should be laid on the differences which exist between things, in order that what knowledge of them is acquired may be clear and distinct.[3]

Besides improvements in subject matter and method, Comenius proposed improvements in the organization of the schools so that they might also be more consistent with his basic philosophy. He proposed an organization of schools providing four levels of education based on the growth and development of children. Each level was to be a

[3] Ibid., p. 242. Quoted by permission of The Macmillan Company.

More than three hundred years ago Comenius helped to lay the foundations of what we now think of as modern education. He was a teacher of teachers. He stressed methods of instruction that have since been embodied in the thinking of the teaching profession. He was both a great educational theorist and a practical reformer who was accorded international recognition in his time and who is still recognized as one of the earliest innovators, a forerunner of modern education. Comenius believed in universal peace, and he believed that proper education of the young was an avenue to the advancement of peace and the elevation of society. Like some other advanced social thinkers, Comenius underwent severe persecution. He suffered greatly in the religious persecutions that were inflicted on him and his fellow Moravians during the Thirty Years' War. His wife and children were murdered. His home was twice plundered, and his books and manuscripts were burned. He was exiled from his native land and then worked as an educational reformer successively in Poland, Sweden, England, Sweden a second time, Hungary, and Poland again, where he underwent severe persecution and was again exiled. He finally found refuge and support in Amsterdam, where he spent the later years of his life.

different kind of school, and each school was to be six years in length. This is basically the pattern of organization that we follow today. The system proposed a single program applying to all classes. He rejected the idea of one school system for upper-class children and another, poorer one for the children of the lower classes. The first level, for infancy, should be at the mother's knee; the second, for children at the vernacular school; the third, for boyhood at the Latin school or gymnasium; and the fourth, for youth at the university or in travel.

Other educators who were the contemporaries of Comenius seem to have been unaffected by his practices and by his educational philosophy. He was, however, without doubt the greatest educator of his century. Many of his ideas are incorporated in our present educational system. All of his ideals have not as yet been attained in the countries where he lived and worked. The ideas of Comenius, especially his application of the technique of induction to teaching, are important because of their profound effects upon the formulation of subsequent educational theory.

Rousseau: education in accordance with nature

The question of the relationship of man with nature, which came to the forefront near the end of the Renaissance, continued to be of growing interest. Eventually those who devoted themselves to the subject developed a belief that their answer should be translated into social practices in various areas. In terms of their understanding of nature, they advocated certain revolutionary social reforms. The movement became known as the "naturalistic movement." It marked a reaction against formalism in education, but it was much wider than an educational movement. The naturalistic tendency in education was part of a vehement and revolutionary reaction to the dominance of arbitrary authority as exercised in all institutional life, including the family, the church, and the government. The naturalistic movement has been as revolutionary in its effects on broad and general intellectual conditions and on specific educational thought and practice as the Renaissance.

In education the naturalistic movement contributed to undermining the deep-seated, widely entrenched conception that education consisted chiefly of the mastery of books. The highly formalized kind of teaching that fostered this conception was adopted by the clergy and teachers, who constituted an aristocracy of special privilege. The naturalistic movement, on the other hand, since it was opposed to all kinds of artificial conventionality and formalism, tended to conform to the tenets of the doctrine of the rights of common man. The leaders of the movement directed most of their criticism toward political and social practices which they expected to reform. It is not at all strange, therefore, that it was a political theorist interested in interpreting the naturalistic idea as it applied to social and political life who also devoted a fair proportion of his thought toward influencing education, which he believed to be an avenue for bringing about the social reform he so earnestly desired.

Jean Jacques Rousseau was born 120 years after Comenius. By that time the inductive method was much more popular. Reform in the method of arriving at generalizations had been great, at least in the field of scientific investigation. Progress in social reform, however, had not been impressive. The lot of the common man had changed but

Rousseau was a capricious man, but he was an industrious writer, with interests ranging over many areas. His great strength is in the cogency and eloquence of his writing and in the ideas, especially in the field of education, that he advanced.

The life Rousseau lived and the life he envisaged in his writings seem strangely and unexplainedly paradoxical. He possessed an acute intellect, and his powers of expression were unsurpassed. He was not an originator of ideas, but he could assess the importance of an idea and, as a proponent, develop it in a way that greatly furthered its influence. He was not wholly sane in the last 10 or 15 years of his life, during which time he wrote his Confessions, *an undependable although, perhaps, partly true story of a sordid and not-to-be-admired kind of personal life. His personal life aside, Rousseau holds an unrivaled place in literary history. His emphasis upon the doctrine that all education must be in accord with nature brought forth a new emphasis in education which up to his time had been almost totally disregarded. Subsequent developments in the fields of physiology, psychology, and biology have reinforced the doctrine he so forcefully set forth. He did not minimize the great significance of nurture. What he did was to emphasize that the inherent capacities of the child constitute the foundations for all human development.*

little. Rousseau revolted violently against the social absurdities and glaring social inequalities of his time. He was a man who had the unusual gift of clearly comprehending great ideas and of embodying these ideas in noble words. The great ideas that flowed along with the naturalistic movement were not originated by him, but he was their most forceful proponent. He had a unique ability to select the principal idea and to express it more clearly than others could. It was this ability that made him one of the most powerful figures not only in education but in all intellectual thought.

AN IDEA WITH A LASTING EFFECT

Rousseau set forth his educational theory in his well-known semifictional exposition *Émile*. According to the preface, *Émile* was written primarily as a book on child study to describe and analyze children's characteristics. Rousseau's fundamental thesis is clear-cut: "Everything is good as it comes from the hand of the author of Nature; but everything degenerates in the hand of man." Education, he held, is natural. It is development from within. It comes from the natural workings of instincts and interests. It is an expansion of one's natural powers. It is life itself, not a preparation for life. Deliberate, formal education must, therefore, be in accordance with nature. So clearly and so forcefully did Rousseau express his idea that his words can scarcely be improved upon. They will repay careful study.

> Education we receive from three sources—Nature, men and things. The spontaneous development of our organs and capacities constitutes the education of Nature. The use to which we are taught to put this development constitutes that education given us by men. The acquirement of personal experience from surrounding objects constitutes that of things. Only when these three kinds of education are consonant and make for the same end does a man tend toward his true goal. . . . If we are asked what is this end, the answer is that of Nature. For since the concurrence of the three kinds of education is necessary to their completeness, the kind which is entirely independent of our control must necessarily regulate us in determining the other two.[4]

Rousseau believed that education must be based upon recognition of the rightful place of nature, men, and things in learning. His ideas, as expressed in the above quotation, when properly interpreted would be accepted as sound by the most critical of our educational thinkers today.

Rousseau advocated that the education of a child should follow four principles:

[4] As quoted in John Dewey, *Democracy and Education*. New York: Macmillan, 1916, pp. 131–132.

1. The physical activity of children is important for the development of physical strength and of intelligence.
2. Sense perception connected with motor activity and with experimental investigation is fundamental in elementary education.
3. Children reason about matters related to their immediate experience and interests, and hence the reasoned solution of small scientific problems should be part of their education.
4. The premature memorizing of words spoils the child's judgment.[5]

The fundamental point in the psychology of children, according to Rousseau, is that they exhibit characteristic differences at different stages of maturing, and that appropriate activities should be provided for each stage; the child should be treated as a child and not as a miniature adult.

THE IDEA INTERPRETED

Rousseau accepted as fundamental to teaching the naturalistic principle that "the spontaneous development of our organs and capacities constitutes the education of Nature." Consider how a child develops his ability to talk and how, as he attends school, he improves in his ability to express himself intelligently. The larynx, at the entrance to the trachea, is the organ of the voice. It contains the vocal cords which are necessary to developing the power of speech. Sounds are formed by directing expiratory blasts of air across these cords. The physiological structure of the larynx and the activities which it is capable of performing condition all of the teaching that one can do toward influencing the child to use the organ of speech properly. The degree to which development takes place, even under the most expert pedagogical direction, is limited in the very beginning by that which nature has provided.

When Rousseau said that "the use to which we are taught to put this development constitutes that education given us by men," he wished to make clear that man determines the ends toward which all the natural forces shall be directed. The kind of language the child learns to speak and the kinds of thought he expresses are man-directed.

[5] As quoted in Samuel Chester Parker, *A Textbook in the History of Modern Elementary Education*. New York: Ginn, 1912, p. 181.

When he said that the acquirement of personal experience from surrounding physical objects constitutes the education of things, he was explaining that the child interacts with his physical environment as well as with his social environment and that from these interactions he derives a considerable amount of learning. Providing a child with a suitable physical environment is as important to the promotion of optimum learning as providing him with trained teachers to direct his learning.

When Rousseau wrote that "only when these three kinds of education are consonant and make for the same end" and that "the kind which is entirely independent of our control necessarily regulates us in determining the other two," he was emphasizing the necessity of consonance and cooperation between natural endowment, social environment, and physical environment in desirable education. Rousseau's emphasis, which led educators to a consciousness of the interrelationship of the three factors, changed the whole direction of teaching method. It brought about the slow death of the conception of education consisting almost entirely of the mastery of books. The attention of schoolteachers was directed to the need for recognizing, as they taught, the innate differences in the inherent abilities of the children, their differences in temperaments, and the wide variance among the pupils in their social and experiential backgrounds.

Educating in accordance with nature requires full recognition of the importance of attitudes, preferences, interests, likes, dislikes, and habits, because these become as much a part of nature as do the intellectual factors. For the first time in education the affective factors were emphasized as important influences in learning. Schoolteachers of young children realized more than ever before the need for building bodily tone and vigor, saw the relationship of their teaching to a child's health, and recognized the need for manipulative experiences and the necessity for a reasonable degree of physical mobility among children if they were to be properly taught in accordance with nature.

SOME EFFECTS ON MODERN EDUCATION

In a social field like education it is always hazardous to attempt to trace cause and effect. The influence of an idea cannot be accurately estimated. It can be said that the implications of the belief presented by Rousseau—the belief that education should be in accord with nature and should take full cognizance of the child's instincts and capacities—did have a marked effect on some schools of the time of Rousseau and has had a part in the thinking of subsequent educators, especially the theorists. We are perhaps justified in saying that although the systematic study of the nature of children and of the variations in their patterns of development is still in its infancy, it is being encouraged and is progressing as a result, partly at least, of Rousseau's pioneer writing.

It can also be said, with considerable assurance, that teachers generally accept the principle that nature certainly must be taken into account if teaching is to be sound, not only in terms of child welfare, but also in terms of social effectiveness. A wide discrepancy often exists between a principle and the incorporation of that principle into practice. The road to good teaching which Rousseau outlined so eloquently has not even yet broadened into a wide highway that teachers, by and large, attempt to follow.

Pestalozzi: experimenting to discover effective teaching methods

THE EXPERIMENTAL MOVEMENT

To state the principle that education should be in accordance with nature gives no indication of how to incorporate that principle into classroom teaching. How that principle can be connected with concrete teaching realities and made a part of teaching in a specific school setting with a whole set of customs and traditions remained a problem.

Following Rousseau's enunciation and elaboration of his principle, experiments in teaching were undertaken to discover the most promising methods for interpreting the principle through practice. Rousseau's ideas appealed to numerous European teachers, but it was Pestalozzi who established the first of the European experimental schools. Pestalozzi was a Swiss schoolteacher, the ablest of the advocates of Rousseau's ideas. Because his experiments with Rousseau's ideas set a pattern and his conclusions and theories had a wide circulation, the educational trend became known as the Pestalozzian movement.

The experimental schools that Pestalozzi conducted in Switzerland between 1799 and 1825 were visited by educational leaders from many countries. Through these schools and through his writings and the teachers he trained he exerted great influence over early educational reforms in America's elementary schools.

CHAPTER 8
Ideas from European Leaders

THE FIRST EXPERIMENTAL SCHOOL

Pestalozzi's first experimental school—he conducted several—was at Neuhof, near Zurich, Switzerland. He moved to a farm and combined the teaching of children of poor parents with work at agriculture. He failed financially and was thereby forced to discontinue his experiment. He had, however, made a beginning which strengthened his faith in experimentation in education. He had gained some insights into educational method appropriate for implementing the naturalistic principle. He began to publish his educational ideas, and his influence spread. The conclusions Pestalozzi arrived at as a result of these first experiments in teaching were consistent with Rousseau's principles. In *The Evening Hour of a Hermit* he wrote:

> Man driven by his needs can find the road to truth nowhere but in his own nature. . . . Man, if you seek the truth in this way of Nature, you will find it as you need it according to your station and your career. . . . Whoever departs from this natural order and lays artificial emphasis on class and vocational education, or training for rule or for service, leads men aside from the enjoyment of the most natural blessings to a sea of hidden dangers.[6]

[6] As quoted in Robert Ulich, *History of Educational Thought.* New York: American Book Company, 1945, pp. 259, 261. Translation is by Ulich.

He also said:

> Man can, at best, do no more than assist the child's nature in the effort which it makes for its own development; and to do this, so that the impressions made upon the child may always be commensurate, and in harmony, with the measure and character of the powers already unfolded in him, is the great secret of education.[7]

BASIC THEORY AND LATER EXPERIMENTATION

Pestalozzi and his followers continued with their experiments to discover better methods of teaching and to work out practical applications of the naturalistic educational principle. Pestalozzi, teaching

[7] As quoted in H. Holman, *Pestalozzi, His Life and Work.* New York: David McKay Company, 1908, p. 172.

Pestalozzi's methods began with observation and concrete experience—both illustrated in this science laboratory in a modern elementary school. Through the years this observation method has steadily gained in favor. Not only does the method successfully promote learning, but it also is basic to the discovery of the secrets of the nature of the universe.

without pay, experimented with various school subjects. His most productive period was from 1799 to 1804, when government and private financial assistance enabled him to conduct an experimental school in Burgdorf, Switzerland, an industrial community near Berne. The experimental school enrolled 72 pupils and employed 10 teachers. Here he participated also in a program for the training of teachers. In 1802 he had 102 teachers studying in his institute, among them a number of foreigners who were studying in order to take ideas about teaching methods back to their homelands. Thus experimentation in methods of teaching and the training of teachers were related through a single program.

The Pestalozzian movement was a direct continuation of the strivings for social reforms stimulated by Rousseau's revolutionary books. At first Pestalozzi's endeavors were directed toward an improvement of the social condition of the lower classes through

Pestalozzi was a Swiss educational reformer whose principles of teaching found manifold application in the United States. The principles of teaching that he developed in his experimental schools were especially influential in teaching elementary school subjects like language, science, domestic geography, and primary arithmetic. Partly as a result of Pestalozzi's influence, the methods of instruction that were developed in America in these subjects represented an enormous improvement over the methods that had been prevalent in the schools before 1800—methods that were highly routinized, mechanical, and flagrantly wasteful.

Following the French invasion of Switzerland in 1798, Pestalozzi collected in a deserted convent a number of children made homeless by the invasion and spent his energies reclaiming them. In 1781, he had written his educational masterpiece, Leonard and Gertrude, *and the indigent and forsaken children under his care now gave him an opportunity to test his educational theories.*

In his later years he was visited and consulted by many political and educational leaders who recognized him as one who had demonstrated the worth of his educational ideas.

Around 1860, Edward A. Sheldon of the Oswego, New York, Normal School introduced the new Pestalozzian procedures to American teachers. The school was visited by leading educators from all parts of the United States, and it has been said that within 20 years the "Oswego movement" had completely reshaped instruction in the better elementary schools throughout America.

Pestalozzian methods were popularized by the Reverend Charles Mayo (1792–1846), who spent three years in Yverdon teaching under the direction of Pestalozzi. Returning to England in 1822, he opened a private school for children of the upper classes that proved highly successful. In several subjects he used Pestalozzi's methods—definitely organizing object teaching. Mayo's sister, Elizabeth, wrote a manual for teachers outlining methods of object teaching. The manual was published in 1830, passed through 26 editions, and was influential in the widespread adoption in England and America of formalized object teaching. The formalization of object teaching eventually became so exaggerated that it was ludicrous. Literary satires dissecting the educational practices of the times were numerous. Perhaps the most biting was written by Charles Dickens in his novel Hard Times (1854). *The following excerpt describes how Mr. Gradgrind, school patron, demonstrates model teaching for the schoolteacher.*

"Now what I want is Facts. Teach these boys and girls nothing but Facts. Facts alone are wanted in life. Plant nothing else, and root out everything else. You can only form the minds of reasoning animals upon Facts: nothing else will ever be of any service to them. This is the principle on which I bring up my own children, and this is the principle on which I bring up these children. Stick to Facts, Sir!"

.   .   .

"Girl number twenty," said Mr. Gradgrind, squarely pointing with his square forefinger, "I don't know that girl. Who is that girl?"

"Sissy Jupe, Sir," explained number twenty, blushing, standing up, and curtseying.

"Sissy is not a name," said Mr. Gradgrind. "Don't call yourself Sissy. Call yourself Cecilia."

"It's father as calls me Sissy, Sir," returned the young girl in a trembling voice, and with another curtsey.

"Then he has no business to do it," said Mr. Gradgrind. "Tell him he mustn't. Cecilia Jupe. Let me see. What is your father?"

"He belongs to the horse-riding, if you please, Sir."

Mr. Gradgrind frowned, and waved off the objectionable calling with his hand.

"We don't want to know anything about that, here. You mustn't tell us about that, here. Your father breaks horses, don't he?"

"If you please, Sir, when they can get any to break, they do break horses in the ring, Sir."

*"You mustn't tell us about the ring, here. Very well, then. Describe
your father as a horsebreaker. He doctors sick horses, I dare say?"
"Oh yes, Sir."
"Very well, then. He is a veterinary surgeon, a farrier, and a
horsebreaker. Give me your definition of a horse."
(Sissy Jupe thrown into the greatest alarm by this demand).
"Girl number twenty unable to define a horse!" said Mr. Gradgrind,
for the general behoof of all the little pitchers. "Girl number twenty
possessed of no facts, in reference to one of the commonest of animals!
Some boy's definition of a horse. Bitzer, yours."
. . . "Quadruped. Graminivorous. Forty teeth, namely twenty-four
grinders, four eye-teeth, and twelve incisive. Sheds coat in the spring;
in marshy countries, sheds hoofs, too. Hoofs hard, but requiring to be
shod with iron. Age known by marks in mouth." Thus (and much more)
Bitzer.
"Now girl number twenty," said Mr. Gradgrind. "You know what a
horse is."*

Charles Dickens, *Hard Times*. New York: E. P. Dutton & Co. (Everyman's
Library), pp. 1, 2, 3.

industrial education. It was in later experiments that he attempted to
determine the psychologically soundest methods of teaching subjects
in the elementary school. He protested vigorously against teaching
children words and phrases that they did not understand, and insisted
upon the substitution of firsthand experience with natural objects as
the fundamental starting point of instruction. He believed that the
primary purpose in teaching through observation and concrete
experience was to have the children get real and clear ideas instead of
mere words and hazy notions. The teacher became an active instructor
of groups of children instead of a hearer of individual recitations.
Children were freed from the dominance of textbooks and given
training in oral expression. In all subjects—geography, science,
arithmetic—emphasis on training in oral expression was prominent.

THE EXPERIMENTAL IDEA IN MODERN EDUCATION

The Pestalozzian movement was an attempt to translate an
acceptable principle of teaching into actual practice. Pestalozzi's own
book, *How Gertrude Teaches Her Children*, based on his experiences at
Burgdorf, popularized some of the ideas and stimulated further

experimentation. Slowly, but with certainty, the Pestalozzian emphasis in teaching and in the training of teachers gained a firm and lasting foothold upon educational practice. Experimentation in education eventually led to a new philosophy of education known as the philosophy of experimentalism. This philosophy has been, and remains, a considerable influence in present-day education in the United States. Universities and colleges that educate teachers conduct experimental schools and combine pre-service and in-service education of teachers with direct study of the subject matter and the methods used by the teachers in the experimental schools.

Froebel: emphasis on social participation and self-activity

IMPORTANCE OF EARLY BEGINNING

Concern that education begin in early childhood directly followed Rousseau's principle that education should be in accord with the child's natural design. Froebel, who had studied Pestalozzi's experiments carefully and who was convinced of the soundness of both the principle upon which they were based and the conclusions drawn by the Pestalozzians, considered as most precious the waxing and waning of children's interests and the irregularities in the growth patterns in the development of the very young. Froebel believed it important that later education should never have to undo the evil effects of earlier, inferior education. He believed that, in order to avoid this, deliberate education should begin earlier than had been the custom. To test his theory he, like Pestalozzi, established an experimental school in which he experimented with programs for children too young for the ordinary elementary school.

The chief feature of this new school, to which Froebel gave the name *kindergarten*, was organized play. Little children were given instructive diversions and healthful games. Froebel's experiences led to a deep conviction that the kindergarten age is the appropriate time to begin deliberate education. Realizing that teachers, in general, had meager knowledge about early education to guide them into sound practices, he decided to devote his later life to studying the needs of very young children, to providing an educational program

*At 15, Froebel was apprenticed to
a forester ; this experience gave him
insight into the established order of
nature's creations. He taught that
man is by nature a doer and
originator who learns through self-
activity. Froebel acknowledged the
importance of these attributes
throughout the period of education,
but he concentrated his attention
on what came to be known as the
kindergarten age. Like Rousseau, he
believed that perfection in
education at a later age depends on
perfection at a very early age.*

suitable to their age, and to propagating the ideas that seemed justified by his studies.

Although many ideas about method accrue from Froebel's experiences and studies, two principles which he developed have had great effect upon modern education. These are, even today, of interest to the student of education in the United States, where the idea of kindergarten education has become so common that no one questions that it is essential in a good education program. These two ideas are called the principle of self-activity and the principle of social participation. The two were inextricably interrelated in Froebel's theory of teaching.

SELF-ACTIVITY AS A STARTING POINT

As Froebel emphasized in his teaching of the very young, the principle of self-activity, or motor expression, followed the logic that self-activity is *the* process through which one realizes his own nature. It is natural for a child to be active. Self-activity, however, is not just any kind of activity. It is that kind of activity that is strongly influenced by one's motives, the kind that arises out of one's own interests. In a word, it is the kind of activity that is compelled by one's own nature. It is the individual's response to forces within him, rather than to forces outside him. It is this kind of activity which is of the highest educative value to the growing child.

Froebel was a German educational reformer. As a boy he attended the village school in his native town, Oberweissbach, Thuringia, where he was classified by his teachers as a dunce. It was through his experiences in the forests that came with his apprenticeship to a forester at 15 that he gained his profound insight into the laws of nature. Throughout the remainder of his life he was dominated by the thought that his greatest and most propelling aim was to advance the good of humanity through education. Like Pestalozzi, by whom he was greatly influenced, he conducted experimental schools. He was much concerned about the education of the younger children, those under 7 years of age, whose education he thought had traditionally been greatly neglected. Froebel's greatest work, The Education of Man, *deals chiefly with the education of children in their early years. Although the principle he emphasized—that self-activity is the surest road to sound education—found its greatest acceptance among those who taught younger children, it was Froebel's belief that the principle applied to the education of all ages. Froebel stressed that the tendencies of early childhood become fixed fundamental dispositions according to the ways the young are taught in their early years. This teaching in the early years also affects deeply the turn taken by the powers that develop later. Froebel's insistence that the education of children in their earliest years is critically important has had a lasting influence upon all serious-minded educators since his time.*

Froebel first made these ideas concrete and meaningful in his experimental kindergarten. The children were permitted to use all those forms of self-expression that would further their development. Self-activity provided the starting point. What was learned was a result of this self-activity.

As his idea developed, Froebel learned progressively better ways of applying the principle. Some of the activities which he, along with his followers, found that children liked and which seemed to bring the best learning results were rhythms, music, singing, creative dramatics, handicraft, drawing, painting, modeling with clay, collecting art specimens or objects of nature, growing plants, bringing animals into the school, and playing on a suitably equipped playground. All the activities required the supervision of a teacher trained to teach and understand children of that particular age. The principle of having children learn *through* activities suited to their age became an accepted principle of education for children in their earlier years.

It was never Froebel's belief that the principle of self-activity

*Modern teachers follow Froebel's
educational theories. The second-
graders acting in a play they
themselves wrote are engaging in an
activity similar to the activities
Froebel invented which were play
but which also fulfilled definite
educational objectives. Froebel
interpreted "play" as any
occupation that delights children.
Using the outdoor environment as a
"laboratory" for learning is also a
direct application of his principles.*

applied to younger children only. He believed it was also applicable to education at later levels. In order for later education to be most effective it must be built upon sound earlier education. But it must also continue to apply the principle of self-activity.

The emphasis Froebel gave to social participation followed his belief that cooperation is a fundamental social necessity, that it should be one of the goals of all education and must be cultivated very early in a child's life. He made considerable use of play activities to achieve this end, but in all other activities as well, cooperativeness among the children was one of the outcomes for which he continually strove.

INFLUENCE ON MODERN EDUCATION

Froebel's recognition that children have natural cravings for activity and that this desire for activity can be utilized by teachers to promote the development of children in a natural way has been reinforced by all subsequent educational experience. When education was narrowly conceived to be a mastery of books, teachers practiced a deadening kind of pedagogical pedantry which resulted in sterile schooling, uninteresting to the child and lacking in challenge to those teachers who possessed fertile minds. Teaching then was largely a matter of enforcing restraints. Froebel's experimentation not only led to the establishment of kindergartens but added an element to educational theory that has never been questioned.

It is not easy to appraise the effects of his emphasis on cooperativeness as an aim of education. One can still find in modern educational practice the manifestation of the opposite belief—namely, that teaching should stress competition, that competition is the principal motivating force in encouraging pupils to learn. This tendency seemingly runs counter to the one that Froebel indicated was worthy of developing.

Herbart: education in how to think

TEACHING AND THE RECITATION

Reciting in various ways has been a part of the teaching process since ancient times. Early Greek story-tellers recited their poetry by singing it and interpreting it by pantomime. Prizes were given in the

Herbart was a philosopher-educationist of scholarly bent. He studied under Johann Gottlieb Fichte, the noted German philosopher. In 1809, he was called to a professorship at Königsberg and occupied the chair formerly held by Immanuel Kant, the great German philosopher. From the standpoint of his exactness in analysis and his penetration of thought, he ranks in importance as the equal of any of the great German philosophers, with the possible exception of his contemporary, Georg Wilhelm Friedrich Hegel (1770-1831).

Speaking of one of Herbart's contributions to methods of teaching, John Dewey says:

> *But few attempts have been made to formulate a method, resting on general principles, of conducting a recitation. One of these is of great importance and has probably had more and better influence upon the hearing of lessons than all others put together; namely, the analysis by Herbart of a recitation into five successive steps.**

Herbart placed strong emphasis upon the importance of instruction and instructional techniques in the classroom. In his own words, we indicate the nature of his influence: "Instruction will form the circle of thought, and education the character. The last is nothing without the first. Herein is contained the whole sum of my pedagogy."

*John Dewey, *How We Think*. Boston: D. C. Heath, 1910, p. 202.

early Greek schools for reciting such literary subjects as tragedy, comedy, and lyric verse. In the European schools of the Renaissance, the emphasis was on having young children recite certain religious exercises, short passages from the classics, and even their own compositions. In time, as schools became more organized, the child's school day provided for a definite period in which the pupils recited the materials they had been assigned to learn and responded orally to questions asked by the teacher. This was known as the "recitation" period, the time for "re-citation" of lessons learned. Teaching was a simple process. Learning was from books. The pupils recited back to the teacher what they had learned from a book. Sometimes the "re-citation" was almost a verbatim reproduction of the words used in the book. The nearer the pupil came to an actual reproduction, the more likely it was that he would be judged a good learner.

Memorizing was much emphasized, and methods for effective memorization were often explained to the pupils. Of course, children improvised all kinds of methods of study in the preparation of their

Herbart is considered the forerunner of educational experimentation and organized instruction in education in American universities. As a professor at the University of Königsberg he established a pedagogical seminar with a practice school attached to it. Much of his life was devoted to investigating, lecturing, and writing.

lessons. Some studied at home, where they could read aloud. Sometimes they read a few sentences and then tried to repeat them aloud. In the early American schools and extending, in some cases, to present-day schools, the organization of the school day and the equipment of the schoolroom were planned to be suitable for a full exploitation of this method of teaching. The seats were in rows and firmly anchored to the wooden floors. Children were seated one behind the other as though they were never to talk to one another but were always to address their remarks only to the teacher.

Many leading scholars of the Middle Ages practiced learning by memorizing. Some of them could recite the entire works of Aeneas or Ovid. Their writings were replete with verbatim quotations from memory from their favorite authors. The biographers of some of the great scholars of earlier times demonstrated that power of memorization was considered almost synonymous with great genius by pointing out with pride that the subject of the biography had memorized the whole of some classical treatise. This was the picture of formal education when Johann Friedrich Herbart advocated a change in the prevailing method of conducting the recitation.

EMPHASIS ON HOW TO THINK

Herbart was a professor of philosophy and psychology at universities in Germany from 1802 to 1841. He is sometimes referred to as the first of the educational psychologists. He advocated a method for the recitation period that would train pupils to develop habits of thought. It is not difficult to imagine how little a teacher had to know, how shallow his thinking could be, when all he had to do was to hear pupils faithfully recite their assigned lessons. It is also not difficult to imagine the kind of social attitudes people developed toward such teachers.

Herbart did not hold memorization in low esteem. He was concerned because the memorizing method was used almost exclusively. He advocated that other activities be introduced into the formal recitation—activities that would be planned for the express purpose of encouraging pupils to think. He made clear that the method of reproducing what had been learned from textbooks overlooked certain significant educational values that come from studying with a purpose in mind, supplementing thought from one's own experiences, arriving at definite conclusions, and organizing one's own ideas. As an educational psychologist, he saw great need for broadening the then current narrow concept of the function of a recitation period.

Herbart recommended the employment of a wider range of activities during the recitation period. Pupils should think about the ideas taught and judge their worth, not only in terms of their soundness, but also in terms of their relative worth to the individual pupil. Pupils should be encouraged to make applications of what they learned and to relate the applications to their own experiences. Instead of the learning in the recitation being a passive affair devoted wholly to the absorption of material, Herbart advocated that it be an active-reactive period in which the pupils gave consideration to what was being studied, supplemented what they were studying, and ultimately assimilated what they had been studying.

The time seemed ripe for a change, and Herbart's ideas were received with immediate enthusiasm. Nowhere were they more cordially accepted than among the educational theorists in the United States. The interest continued, and around the year 1890, close to half a century after Herbart's death, educators were giving expression to educational theories which today are still being considered and elaborated. These ideas of the American educators will be discussed later.

HERBART'S PRINCIPLE

In contrast to the other educators discussed, whose ideas applied to the whole of the educative process, Herbart made his greatest contribution by concentrating on a single aspect of the educative process—namely, the recitation. He advocated making the recitation methodical by conducting it in four steps: preparation, presentation, comparison, and generalization or conclusion. Later, a fifth step was added by his followers: application. These became known as the five formal steps in the recitation.

Herbart attempted to deliver classroom teaching method from the routine and accidental habits it had become heir to by setting forth a formula which, if followed, would lead to far more wholesome results. It would be just as ill-advised, however, to follow slavishly the five formal steps in Herbart's principle as it would be to embrace unquestioningly the principle of learning by memorization.

THE PRINCIPLE INTERPRETED

Herbart recognized that the period set aside for recitation brought the teacher into close and intimate contact with the learner. It was a period that gave the teacher his greatest opportunity to influence the pupils in what they learned from their textbooks, in their ways of thinking and the habits of language they would develop, in the observations they would make, and in the generalizations and conclusions at which they would arrive. Therefore, the recitation period should be a period for *reflection*, for stimulating and directing thought, rather than a period for rehearsing in detail all of what the pupils had learned.

1. Preparation

The first logical step in the recitation is that of preparation. In preparing the pupils the teacher asked questions to help them recall familiar experiences related to the new topic that they were starting to study. This topic was always to be related to what the pupils already knew. At the end, a statement of the purpose of the new material was formulated with the class.

2. Presentation

Presentation is the next step toward learning something new. Herbartians often took the pupils on excursions to see firsthand what they were studying. The pupils would then give vivid oral descriptions of what they had seen. Presentation was a period for challenging interchange of experience and for discussion.

3. Comparison

The third logical step is comparison. Comparison was used to establish important thought connections. Each new connection, Herbart believed, not only insured more lasting impressions of what was being presented for the first time, but it also established new and closer associations among the ideas that had previously been studied. This comparison was for the main purpose of making the one central object of the lesson clearer. Every comparison was made *deliberately* to clear up some obscure aspect of the central problem or object of the recitation.

4. Conclusion

Finally, one conclusion or generalization or definition was reached. The conclusion then served as a basis for the next logical step in the further adventure in learning.

5. Application

The step added by Herbart's followers is application. In this step the pupil applied or utilized his general conclusion growing out of the study. When a sufficient number of applications had been made, the conclusion or definition or generalization would remain indelible in the minds of the learners.

One additional point about the five formal steps of the recitation should be emphasized. The steps applied to the teacher's preparatory work as well as to the actual manner in which he would conduct the recitation. He had not only previously gained a mastery of his subject matter but had also, through careful advance work, arranged an approach that would enable him to conduct the recitation in a manner best suited to cultivating thought. He would carefully prepare himself by thinking through what might be done in each of the five steps. He would need to review: What do my pupils already know? What questions shall I ask in order to bring out what they know and think? What aids shall I use? What incidents shall I relate? What are the difficulties some of the pupils may have? What conclusions should be reached?

Through preparation the teacher freed himself from any necessity of further study during the recitation and was able to focus his entire attention upon skillfully conducting the recitation. The teacher could be flexible, teach as the occasion demanded, and still end with some order and organization in what had been learned by the pupils. He did not intend to blindly formalize the recitation into a pattern of five steps. Rather, it could be modified as needed by a teacher alert to the opportunities for stimulating pupil thought. In interpreting Herbart's principle this point should always be kept in mind.

Herbart's efforts have had a great and wholesome influence. For the first time, trained schoolteachers generally realized the importance of turning periods for reciting into periods for stimulating and directing reflection. In fact, in the modern school, perhaps because of Herbart's emphasis on thinking as an important part of teaching, the very word "recitation" has disappeared from current educational vocabulary.

Spencer: education as preparation

ESTABLISHMENT OF A PATTERN

By 1850, education was receiving considerable attention from leading philosophers. Educational theory was perceptibly changing. The English philosopher Herbert Spencer added still another emphasis. In 1859 Spencer published "What Knowledge Is Most Worth," an essay on education. In it he proposed that an analysis of life's activities be used to determine what subject matter should be included in the school curriculum. He advocated classifying adult life activities into five categories and then selecting subject matter that would prepare the young to engage successfully in all those activities. The five classifications, which would constitute the objectives of all education, were related to preserving life and health, earning a living, family duties

Spencer evolved a theory that education should be preparation for the activities of later life. His ideas had much influence on those who shaped secondary education in this country.

and the care of children, social and political responsibilities, and leisure-time activities.

Many educators in the United States seized Spencer's idea as a suitable pattern for the statement of educational objectives in American schools. In time, a pattern for building the school curriculum which followed rather closely that proposed by Spencer became established.

Spencer is usually not thought of as an educational philosopher. His contribution to education was somewhat incidental, although what he wrote about education has had far-reaching subsequent effect. He was a self-taught philosopher of the scientific movement of the latter half of the nineteenth century. He was influenced in his thinking by his friends Charles Darwin (1809–1882), the naturalist ; Thomas Henry Huxley (1825–1895), the biologist and writer ; and George Henry Lewes (1817–1878), the philosophical writer and critic.

Inquiring what knowledge is of most worth, Spencer contended that all considerations lead to the conclusion that scientific knowledge is the most valuable. He spoke for all those who believed that the chief purpose of education in the schools should be to give a practical preparation for life. To use his own words : ''. . . To prepare us for complete living is the function which education has to discharge ; and the only rational mode of judging of any educational course is to judge in what degree it discharges such function.''

The pattern set by Spencer fastened upon modern education the principle that education should be carried on mainly to prepare the pupil for adult life. Although there have been dissenters, the principle has had a conspicuous effect on the character of present-day American secondary education. It has also, but to a lesser degree, had a marked influence on teaching at the elementary level. Seemingly, there has been little question about the validity of the activity analysis method for selecting the subject matter that prepares for the vocations. There seems now, however, to be a growing sentiment among educational theorists that the method is used too generously when it is applied to the whole of education and at all levels, that it is not applicable to teaching when growth is made the one important over-all objective of all education.

Summary: intermingling of ideas

The six ideas—applying the technique of induction to teaching, educating in accordance with nature, experimenting to discover effective methods, emphasizing self-activity and social participation, considering education in how to think as of primary importance, and seeing education as preparation—have been potent in shaping the character of formal education in the United States. The eminent European scholars who propagated these ideas were all productive thinkers and prolific writers. Each covered other aspects of education in addition to those discussed. The ideas selected are those that seem to have had greatest influence upon modern education in the United States.

As these six broad educational ideas were carried westward, they took root and became intermingled with other ideas. Maintaining more or less their individual identities, they became part of the great stream of thought that continues to flow and make modern educational theory what it is.

How the ideas intermingled when transplanted to a wholly new cultural soil is one of the exciting stories of social history. It is one, however, that cannot be even remotely understood without first taking a careful look at what that new soil was like. To develop a true picture we must turn to a discussion of the American frontier movement—a movement that has had lasting effects upon American education.

Questions

1. What is your explanation of how Comenius became skilled in applying the inductive method to teaching?
2. What were the features of Comenius' textbooks that gave them their long-lasting quality?
3. Why has Rousseau's influence on education been so great?
4. Why did the schools of Rousseau's time place such great emphasis upon the use of artificial effort? Do the schools show any such tendencies today?
5. How does it happen that it was a political scientist instead of a leading educator who called the attention of educators to the need to recognize the nature of the child when directing his learning?
6. What are some of the obstacles to conducting worthwhile experiments in modern American schools?
7. Assuming that the conclusions drawn from research studies in education are valid, to what degree should a teacher permit himself to be guided by these findings?
8. In what ways were the teachings of Pestalozzi a logical sequence to the social reforms initiated or stimulated by Rousseau's books?
9. Which changes introduced into American education can be traced to the influence of Froebel?
10. Why was the influence of Herbart upon American education around 1890 of such magnitude? How far has modern teaching practice advanced beyond what he advocated?
11. Why were Spencer's ideas so enthusiastically adopted in American education by those working at the secondary level?

Projects

1. Contrast the ideas of the six educational theorists whose ideas have been discussed in this chapter.

2. Explain why it was so long before an idea that was accepted became incorporated into educational practice.

3. Estimate the influence upon modern American education of Spencer's contention that the teaching of the classics in the elementary and secondary schools should largely give way to the teaching of science.

4. Describe evidence of a currently growing concern over the education of the very young.

5. Explain in what ways the pedagogical idea of dividing the school day into recitation periods affected the organization of America's schools, including school architecture.

9

The Frontier
Heritage

The present educational system in the United States had its origin in the streams of thought that grew out of the great social movements of history and the theories expounded by European leaders. Both were adapted to frontier conditions and altered by pioneer thinking. Understanding the nature of those earlier European influences is crucial to any evaluation of education in the United States. It is equally impossible to make a sound assessment without first recognizing and appreciating the significance of features that were molded by the frontier movement. The broad outlines of the movement are known to most students, but its specific direct influence upon modern American education is not always fully understood. It is important to focus attention upon the effects of the movement, upon the character of what is, perhaps, America's largest social undertaking, its educational program.

The migration to America was only one of the numerous migrations of Europeans to many new, sparsely populated lands. Behind this European "invasion" lay one simple assumption, the assumption that the lands lying immediately ahead were free for the taking. This assumption was applied to the whole vast expanse of the American continent. It was the backbone of a philosophy of the people. It resulted in one of the most dramatic population movements in all history, and its effects on educational policy in the United States are inestimable.

As the frontier continually moved westward from the first settlements on the Atlantic coast, it was marked not only by the development of new areas but also by a return to primitive conditions

In America the word [frontier] is hardly used at all to indicate the nation's limits. No American would refer to the line separating the United States from Canada or that from Mexico as the frontier, and to apply it to them in this sense would lead to misunderstanding. The American thinks of the frontier as lying within, and not at the edge of the country. It is not a line to stop at, but an area inviting entrance. Instead of having one dimension, length, as in Europe, the American frontier has two dimensions, length and breadth. In Europe the frontier is stationary and presumably permanent ; in America it was transient and temporal. The concept of a moving frontier is applicable where a civilized people are advancing into a wilderness, an unsettled area, or one sparsely populated by primitive people. It was the sort of land into which the Boers moved in South Africa, the English in Australia, and the Americans and Canadians in their progress westward across North America. The frontier movement is the invasion of a land assumed to be vacant as distinguished from an invasion of an occupied or civilized country, an advance against nature rather than against men. On a frontier the invaders often have immediate and exclusive possession whereas in a nonfrontier the invaders have to contend with the original inhabitants whom they always find troublesome and frequently too much for them. Inherent in the American concept of a moving frontier is the idea of a body of free land which can be had for the taking.

Walter Prescott Webb, *The Great Frontier*. Boston: Houghton Mifflin, 1952, pp. 2–3. Quoted by permission of Houghton Mifflin Company.

for the settlers. American social development was continually beginning over again on the frontier. American life achieved a fluidity which was marked by a steady movement away from the influence of Europe, a steady growth in independence, a reliance on American strenuous endeavor, a remolding of the older ways of life.

The movement lasted nearly 250 years. Free land is not inexhaustible in a rapidly expanding population, and all exoduses end somewhere and at some time. Historians generally record 1890 as the year when almost all free lands in the United States had been settled. Thus the movement ended. However, the values established in the frontier period continue to be cherished, continue to influence the thinking and determine the action of modern Americans who are part of the postfrontier period. The philosophy of the frontier was adaptable to rapidly changing conditions. That kind of adaptation is still in process.

As the frontier moved westward across the plains, public schools were built. This sod school in western Kansas—typical of many in the uncompromising barrenness of its setting—served as a cohesive influence on the widely separated families whose children learned the "three Rs" there.

Educational institutions, and especially American educational philosophy, today reflect clearly the continuing influence of the philosophy of the frontier.

The philosophy of the frontier

LOVE OF FREEDOM

The frontier brought about changed relationships between individual man and his neighbor. In crowded Europe the density of the population in 1500 was about 27 persons per square mile or something like 24 acres of land, good and bad, for each person. On the frontier in America there was plenty of room, and all the land one might wish to occupy. This meant release for the individual. His way of living began to reflect a hitherto unknown independence built upon the challenge of opportunities, the privilege of choice. He had freedom. His biggest responsibility was to learn how to make the most intelligent use of the freedom he had more or less by accident become heir to. We do not pretend that he always used this newly discovered independence wisely. His ideas of democratic government, his sometimes extravagant exploitation of natural resources, the unconventional forms of behavior he sometimes engaged in, his rude manners, his raw language, and the like attest to the fact that he did not always make the best use of his freedom. The point is that the new frontier conditions granted him a degree of freedom that he had never known before, and his knowledge that he had this freedom changed both his ideals and his fundamental social beliefs. In time, the ideal of freedom of the individual became strong, and, as the meaning was made clearer, it became a cherished guide to action.

The frontiersman's esteem for freedom resulted in a reliance on his individual intelligence. He did not want someone to tell him what to do. He believed that the application of his own intelligence, whether trained or not, was the best method of arriving at conclusions. He did not have to appeal to the judgment of someone higher up in seeking a solution to his problems. His intelligence was sharpened by constant application to numerous everyday practical problems, some of which involved his very survival.

Freedom to arrive at his own conclusions and to use his own solutions led the frontiersman to place a high value upon the opportunity to develop his intelligence, to use it in solving the problems of his life and in advancing his own material welfare. Freedom was a gift which, to him, became a right. Only through the development of his intelligence could he learn to use his freedom wisely.

Freedom of intelligence became a kind of religion. As the philosopher and essayist Ralph Waldo Emerson (1803–1882) said in his essay on self-reliance,

> Who would be a man, must be a non-conformist. He who would gather immortal palms must not be hindered by the name of goodness, but must explore if it be goodness. Nothing is at last sacred but the integrity of your own mind. Absolve you to yourself, and you shall have the suffrage of the world.

What kind of school would such freedom-loving people build? What happened to the freedom philosophy as the frontier moved westward and the civilization advanced? As schools become systematized in a developing civilization, must a degree of freedom be correspondingly relinquished? How much freedom must Mr. Average Citizen

His supreme generalization [Frederick Jackson] Turner presented in an address delivered in Chicago in 1893, entitled "The Frontier in American History." Within a few years his generalization became the most influential single interpretation of American history. Hundreds of disciples, inspired by Turner, diffused it in every section of the continent; and in time Turner was called to Harvard, under the presidency of Charles W. Eliot.

What had Turner said at Chicago? He had declared that the frontier and free land accounted for the characteristics that differentiated the evolution of society in the United States from the evolution of society in the Old World:

"The existence of an area of free land, its continuous recession, and the advance of American settlement westward, explain American development." The statement, in its unqualified simplicity, was categorical and sweeping. Apparently Turner believed that if it had not been for the advancing frontier, for the free land on the frontier, if the English colonists had been hemmed in on the Atlantic seaboard, American development would have followed European patterns. If this was his belief, then American civilization, without the advancing frontier, would have duplicated the European process of civilization, at least in its main stream. . . .

This, however, had not been the main course of American history: "American development has exhibited not merely advance along a single line, but a return to primitive conditions on a continually advancing frontier line, and a new development for that area. American social development has been continally beginning over again on the frontier. This perennial rebirth, this fluidity of American life, this expansion westward with its new opportunities, its continuous touch with the simplicity of primitive society, furnish the forces dominating American character. . . . The frontier is the line of most rapid and effective Americanization. . . . The advance of the frontier has meant a steady movement away from the influence of Europe, a steady growth of independence on American lines. And to study this advance, the men who grew up under these conditions, and the political, economic, and social results of it, is to study the really American part of our history."

Charles A. Beard and Mary R. Beard, *The American Spirit* (*The Rise of American Civilization*, Vol. IV). New York: Macmillan, 1942, pp. 360–361. Quoted by permission of The Macmillan Company.

surrender, and what methods should be used to achieve the surrender as the educational system develops and as smaller educational units are intergrated into larger units? The frontier American cherished freedom, and he established a halo of inviolability about it. How are those highly cherished, lasting, and theoretically desirable attitudes to be acknowledged as a new type of education develops under changed and still rapidly changing social conditions?

REGARD FOR THE INDIVIDUAL

The picture of the frontiersman as a lonely, isolated individual is largely a myth. He was a man with a family and a man in a group. The pioneer was just as interested in having standing with the other members of his group as he would have been in a European setting. The difference was that on the frontier his standing depended on different factors—not so much on his ancestors, his education, or even the money he had available, as on his success in adjusting to his environment and in triumphing over current vicissitudes, and on his effectiveness in helping the group to do likewise. The frontiersman was not satisfied with a new culture that would barely meet his biogenic needs. He also strove for the satisfaction of his biosocial needs, including that for prestige. He was a highly sensitive, social creature with natural concern for what others thought of him.

The frontiersman expected the respect of other individuals; he also expected to accord respect to other individuals. This was a natural corollary to his love for freedom. Freedom of the individual must include freedom to attain prestige and standing, which, in turn, depend upon respect for individual personality. What did the frontiersman's respect for the individual imply? It implied first a recognition that each individual is unique. It implied also an appreciation that each must be allowed to develop his pattern of living in a way that gives full recognition to the need for individuality and for individual expression.

Rousseau would have felt at home in this kind of philosophical surrounding. The social soil that nourished the individual afforded limitless opportunity for self-development. It was thought that there was something incommensurable about every man and that every man should have the opportunity to develop all his natural endowments.

The whole idea of forcing the individual to conform to a norm, of reducing everything to an average, of emphasizing the mediocre as a reasonable standard for all was discarded as an untenable social theory. It was argued, instead, that each individual should be encouraged to develop to the limit of his capacities. People were, by nature, constituted differently. One person should be as highly respected as another. Since each was different from every other, the talents possessed by each should be developed differently from those of all the others.

On the frontier there were always more jobs to be done than

With characteristic attention to detail, Currier and Ives depicted a school house in a frontier settlement. Inside, there probably were benches for the "scholars" and a desk and chair in front for the teacher—a young man who had been to "normal school" for a few weeks during the summer or a spinster with only a common school education.

there was help available. All individuals, regardless of natural design, had the opportunity to be of worth. The frontiersman developed a philosophy toward the individual which recognized that worth. Everyone should and did respect the inherent worth of the individual.

BELIEF IN EQUALITY

Égalité is the French word for "equality." Under the influence of Thomas Paine and Thomas Jefferson, egalitarianism became a highly favored philosophy in the new land. Paine was a clever journalist, usually remembered as the author of an essay written during the French Revolution called "The Rights of Man." Jefferson, too, could write with impelling force. He was the author of the Declaration of Independence.

The attitude of the frontiersman was expressed in the Declaration of Independence and reiterated in the Bill of Rights. In essence, the American spirit was pledged to an extension of equality. Equality, it was held, was essential to the maintenance of the general welfare of the people and to raising the level of well-being of every American citizen.

Regard for the individual—with its implied appreciation of individual differences and recognition of individual needs for social standing—was woven into a philosophy broadly based on the principle of equality. On the frontier all men were important; each had a significant job to do; the worth of each was taken for granted. As the frontier moved westward, the frontiersman expressed his belief in equality by insisting on universal suffrage. Property restrictions on voting were removed. Frontiersmen gave women their first chance to vote. The common man, the man of the people, whether educated or not, was elected to the highest offices.

As the nation developed, educators were constantly faced with the question, What does egalitarianism mean when incorporated into educational practice? What does it mean in terms of educational opportunity and in terms of teaching in the classroom? In the lands from which pioneers had come, it was held that people were unequal and that they should be educated as unequals. It called for thought and courageous action to build new schools and to follow new practices consistent with a philosophical position almost the reverse of that assumed by most leaders in the other lands.

FAITH IN ONESELF

The pioneer's love for freedom, his respect for the personality of others, his recognition of individual worth, and his devotion to egalitarianism had certain correlative values. One of these was a deep and abiding faith in his own power and ability to meet whatever problems he might, in the course of common events, happen to encounter. The frontiersman possessed an almost unlimited and unbounded optimism, whether he was considering his own future or that of the nation whose destinies he was helping to shape. This is an attitude in sharp contrast to the pessimism that prevailed around 1700 among the individuals of Europe and that is reflected in the literature of such writers as Dryden, Swift, and Montaigne. Faith in oneself and one's future was a pronounced characteristic of the frontiersman.

FAITH IN THE COMMON MAN

Life on the frontier also deepened the pioneer's faith in the common or average man. Once the door of opportunity was opened, common people proceeded to build a new nation. So great was their success that, the European critics of the new American civilization, the European aristocratic leaders who had expressed misgivings about the ability of common men to build a great civilization, were confounded. To the frontiersman, who believed that the worth and welfare of every citizen was important, the achievements of the common man forcefully verified his confidence. The frontiersman simply assumed that the common man could achieve a stable government, develop and diffuse the material necessities of a civilized life, create literature, art, and music, develop education, recreation, and health—in short, do whatever he deemed important for making life worthwhile. He had a boundless faith in the possibilities of himself and every normal man if adequately encouraged and wisely influenced. This faith in the intelligence of the common man has often been expressed by liberal philosophers who have advanced the principle that individual man may, if he strives to do so, make an almost limitless advance toward perfectibility. This is true because man possesses individually and collectively an almost infinite capacity for making new discoveries and for adapting his knowledge to improving the quality of living. Like the frontiersmen, liberal philosophers today believe that man possesses the intelligence to achieve in an almost unlimited degree. He needs most to learn how to use that intelligence wisely. It is an important responsibility of education to develop that intelligence, not in a select few, but in all men.

BELIEF IN THE VALUE OF WORK

Out of the experiences of the frontier a high regard for the disciplinary value of work developed in America. To the frontiersman the value of actual work in educating the boy or girl was equal or superior to the training he received in formal education. Somewhat like the Athenians, the boy and girl on the frontier were educated most by living and working with others. The future of a boy or girl who would not work was in jeopardy. It was work that brought a measure of unity into life and was considered the source of all of man's enduring satisfactions. Not to *earn* one's living was like being a traitor to one's country. It followed, then, that a proper education of the young called for opportunities for the young to work, which they were given. Forcing or allowing the young to be idle was tantamount to leading them into paths of wickedness. From this came the now fully accepted principle of education that an individual develops more rapidly and more wholesomely when he is faced with and assumes responsibility. The frontiersman believed that education should be essentially practical, that is should have a direct relation to building character. He rejected the idea of education for ornament, for superficial polish, as appropriate only to a leisure class.

FAITH IN THE COMMON SCHOOL

As schools became a necessity on the frontier, the ideas about education that the settlers brought with them were modified and incorporated into new practices. It cannot be said that the early frontiersman believed strongly in formal education, but it is clear that some of the leaders did. Many expressed a conviction that the common school was the hope of our country.

Settlers in the earliest New England frontier communities unknowingly established a lasting pattern for educational organization in the United States. The unit of educational organization, the local school, was controlled and supported by the community. The one-room school that eventually led to one of America's most lasting, sentimentalized pictures—the "Little Red Schoolhouse"—was established in almost every community. It displayed inevitable and flagrant weaknesses, but it symbolized, nevertheless, the pioneer's acceptance of a plan to give his children the benefits of a formal education. It was a manifestation of the belief held by most of the frontier leaders that a school was necessary to raise the level of American civilization.

This small school, meager in outlook and thwarted by the inadequacy of available teachers, was nevertheless the kind of educational institution that fitted admirably with the conditions and spirit of the time. It was a *little* school, close to the people it served. It was controlled locally by those who had complete confidence in their own vision and their own skill in management. It was supported locally. It truly belonged to the people it served. The influence of the traditions built up around this little school, the idea of neighborhood schools, local control of the school, and local support took a firm hold upon the hearts and minds of all early Americans.

In studying the manner in which education is now conducted in the United States and in evaluating the paths being advocated for its future progress, it is important always to be conscious of the persistent philosophies of life and of education that were a natural and unquestioned part of the beliefs and attitudes of the frontier. The frontiersman's faith in the common man, his regard for the worth of the individual, his belief in equality and freedom, and his confidence in the common school are a significant heritage directly related to the qualities that make our present schools unique and culturally characteristic.

Education on the frontier

It is well known that the American frontier movement was one part of a series of events—the conquest of a new continent, the planting of colonies, the conflicts between the incoming Europeans and the American red man, the fighting among Europeans for control of the new continent, the fight of new settlers for their independence, and the establishment of a new nation. From the very first arrival of settlers, civilization moved steadily westward. As the nation expanded, sectionalism—the identification of the people of one section of the country with that section rather than with the nation as a whole—nurtured competition for control of the West. New lands were exploited.

What sort of educational plans did the frontiersmen make as they adjusted to the conditions of westward expansion? By examining briefly some details of the educational experiences of the Puritans and the Massachusetts colony we can see, in some measure, how the frontier philosophy, in its early form, was put into action.

PURITAN EDUCATION

In discussing Puritan education, we deal with the Puritanism of the American frontier, not, for example, the English Puritanism of John Ruskin, who defended puritanical ethics thus: "Observe, then, this Puritanism in the worship of beauty . . . is always honourable and amiable and the exact reverse of the false Puritanism which consists in the dread or disdain of beauty."

Within a few years after 1628, when the Puritans obtained a charter to establish a colony on the land between the Merrimack and Charles Rivers, a large group of immigrants had settled in the colony of Massachusetts Bay. Many of the settlers were middle-class businessmen and country gentlemen who belonged to a religious group known as Puritans. Although these people were dissatisfied with the Church of England and wanted to "purify" it of the elements to which they objected, they were actually sufficiently conditioned to life in a church which for decades had been identified with the state so that a shadow of ecclesiastical despotism was cast over the government they set up in the New World.

The Puritans believed that the principal reason why education was necessary was that one should learn to read the Bible. Of the many effects the earlier attitudes of the Puritan leaders had upon educational practice, perhaps the most enduring effect was upon classroom methods of teaching.

From our present perspective we conclude that Puritanism led to a way of life narrow and petty in its formalism. Hard work, approaching

FIRST INFANT SCHOOL IN GREEN STREET NEW YORK.

Imbert's Lithography.

VIEW FROM THE ROSTRUM

Monitor Nine & Six?   Scholars Fifteen! &c.

The schoolrooms of the past reflected the "no-nonsense" teaching that went on in them—strict discipline, much rote-learning, no "frills." These rooms seem forbidding to us, but the children of the time knew nothing else. The frontispiece of the constitution and by-laws of the Infant School Society of the City of New York (1827) vividly evokes an era long gone: the boys along one wall, the girls along the other, the teacher speaking from a "rostrum" while a "monitor" (older pupil) drills the "scholars," who answer in unison. (The ominous "&c" implies much—the addition drill

lasted for a long time!) The stove was essential in a school house built in 1869 in Kent County, Michigan. This "substantial wooden structure with a bell" is still used, though only for conferences and storage. In 1873, a group of first-graders and two teachers posed in their classroom in Grammar School No. 3 in New York. (Grammar school first grade was roughly equivalent to the modern seventh grade.)

Seven-year-old Abe walked four miles a day going to the Knob Creek School to learn to read and write. Zacharia Piney and Caleb Hazel were the teachers who brought him along from ABC to where he could write the name "A-b-r-a-h-a-m L-i-n-c-o-l-n" and count numbers beginning with one, two, three, and so on. He heard twice two is four. The school house was built of logs, with a dirt floor, no window, one door. The scholars learned their lessons by saying them to themselves out loud till it was time to recite; alphabets, multiplication tables, and the letters of spelled words were all in the air at once. It was a "blab school"; so they called it.

.   .   .

A few days of this year in which the cabin was building, Nancy told Abe to wash his face and hands extra clean; she combed his hair, held his face between her two hands, smacked him a kiss on the mouth, and sent him to school—nine miles and back—Abe and Sally hand in hand hiking eighteen miles a day. Tom Lincoln used to say Abe was going to have "a real eddication," explaining, "You are a-goin' to larn readin', writin', and cipherin'."

He learned to spell words he didn't know the meaning of, spelling the words before he used them in sentences. In a list of "words of eight syllables accented upon the sixth," was the word "incomprehensibility." He learned that first, and then such sentences as "Is he to go in?" and "Ann can spin flax."

Some neighbors said, "It's a pore make-out of a school," and Tom complained it was a waste of time to send the children nine miles just to sit with a lot of other children and read out loud all day in a "blab" school. But Nancy, as she cleaned Abe's ears in corners where he forgot to clean them, and as she combed out the tangles in his coarse, sandy black hair, used to say, "Abe, you go to school now, and larn all you kin." And he kissed her and said, "Yes, Mammy," and started with his sister on the nine-mile walk through timberland where bear, deer, coon, and wildcats ran wild.

Carl Sandburg, *Abraham Lincoln: The Prairie Years.* New York: Harcourt, Brace & World, 1926, pp. 19–20, 38–39. Quoted by permission of Harcourt, Brace & World.

slavishness, became a moral virtue. The arts were discouraged as needless and useless frills. Nurtured in such a soil, education sank to a low level. Traditional education was condemned as being associated with an aristocratic, idle, lazy type of citizenship. The Puritans felt

*A*s *visits and pleasure were interspersed with hard work for Robert, he*
developed rapidly in physique and in character, and by the time he was
thirteen he had learned all that could be conveniently taught him at home
and at Eastern View [a private elementary school]. Accordingly, by 1820,
possibly before that year, Robert entered the Alexandria Academy. This had
been established about 1785, and had been privileged to list Washington as
one of its trustees. Occupying a one-story brick house on the east side of
Washington Street, between Duke and Wolfe, the school was made free to all
Alexandria boys after January, 1821. Here Robert met at their desks the
boys with whom he had played in the fields, and here he came under the
tutelage of William B. Leary, an Irishman for whom young Lee acquired
enduring respect.
For approximately three years Robert studied the rudiments of a classical
education under Mr. Leary. He read Homer and Longinus in Greek. From
Tacitus and Cicero he became so well grounded in Latin that he never quite
forgot the language, though he did not study it after he was seventeen. Later
in life, he expressed deep regret that he had not pursued his classical course
further. In mathematics he shone, for his mind was already of the type that
delighted in the precise reasoning of algebra and geometry.

Douglas Southall Freeman, *R. E. Lee.* New York: Charles Scribner's Sons, 1934,
pp. 36–37. Quoted by permission of Charles Scribner's Sons.

that education as it had been conducted up to that time resulted in the
creation of a class more ready to exploit than to serve, that it had
acted as an alley of escape from the rigors of work, and that it did not
adequately educate the pupil to meet conscientiously the requirements of a responsible and participant citizenship which the times
demanded. It would be better for him to receive most of his education
in the home under the guidance of watchful parents than to receive it in
schools that divorced him from the values so highly respected in the
home.

The Puritans put into practice what they thought were educational
theories clearly dictated by the Scriptures. They modeled their laws
to conform with these. Their educational philosophies harmonized
completely with their religious convictions. In an atmosphere in
which education was viewed so narrowly, superstition and ignorance
thrived and opposition to learning in the schools flourished.   They

At that time [1830] there were no free schools in Ohio, but Georgetown, like many other communities, had a subscription school—so called because the parents of the scholars subscribed various sums for the support of the teacher. In this school a Professor John D. White, for three months in a year, scattered knowledge to his pupils as one scatters crumbs to sparrows. The crumbs were poor in quality and few in number, but this meant nothing to Ulysses, whose intellectual hunger was easily satisfied. The simple curriculum consisted of reading, writing, arithmetic, and nothing else.

W. E. Woodward, *Meet General Grant.* New York: Liveright, 1955, p. 16. Quoted by permission of Helen Woodward and Liveright Publishing Corporation; copyright 1955 by Helen Woodward.

limited formal education to the study of reading, writing, and arithmetic at an elementary level. The principal textbook was a religious text for lay people known as *The New England Primer.* Teaching methods were primitive and grossly inefficient. Equipment was limited and neglected. At least two-thirds of the pupils' time was wasted or worse than wasted. At this distance the picture is, at best, dreary and discouraging. But the Puritan strain survived, and although some of the lasting effects upon later philosophies have been harmful, some of them have been sound and helpful.

The emphasis of the Puritans on the principle that every future citizen should be a person who could read and write and cipher was antecedent to the acceptance in the United States of the principle that education should be compulsory. By 1918 each of the then 48 states had enacted a compulsory attendance law. Along with the increase in compulsory attendance went a gradual increase in the length of the school term. The school year averaged only 130 days in 1870, but by 1950 it had reached its present average—almost 180 days.

The insistence of the Puritans on shaping elementary education so that it would contribute to the building of character gave an ethical emphasis to classroom teaching that still permeates both the theory and the practice of teaching in the elementary schools. Behavior is one of the uppermost concerns of every present-day elementary classroom teacher.

The emphasis the Puritans gave to reading, and especially to the reading of the Bible, and their insistence that the reader be given freedom to interpret what he read according to his personal values paved the way for the belief that a similar freedom should be granted in the whole world of thought. Freedom to think and freedom to act in terms of one's own thinking led to an emphasis in education on granting freedom and on teaching pupils to use this privilege wisely. Building habits of self-direction and achieving self-control became the abiding aims of the elementary schools. Such values are still cherished. In current professional literature we read that every citizen should be an enlightened citizen, that education in the schools should stress the building of good character, and that those of stronger character are those who have learned the lessons of self-direction and self-control and have learned to act in the light of a progressively more insightful intelligence that has been trained to think and to act. These effects of the Puritan doctrine have been deemed good, and they have been lasting.

Some effects of the Puritan influence that were also potent and lasting are now considered to be negative and unfortunate when viewed from the perspective of modern educational theory. The Puritans had a deep-seated belief in the efficacy of coercion and punishment to promote learning. It was assumed that children could never learn anything of their own volition. Their own interests were considered worthless. Teachers were to force the child to learn, using severe and vindictive methods of punishment as the chief instrument of motivation. As history so vividly shows, this philosophy was not only the philosophy of the teachers in the schools, it was the philosophy of the whole of the Puritan society. Punishment, whether administered in school or out, was an ethical social instrument admirably suited to building the kind of society the Puritans desired. Believing that coercion is the most effective method of promoting learning is not surprisingly backward in a society that as late as the seventeenth century put 32 persons to death, some by torture, because they were accused of practicing witchcraft.

The nature of subject matter, its arrangement, the equipment of the classroom—all reflected the same severe, authoritarian atmosphere. All subject matter was laid out in advance, and all pupils were to master precisely the same material. The teacher's desk was in front. Pupils faced the teacher, never one another. The whole process of education was harsh, sometimes inhumane. Pupils generally developed a dislike for the teachers—a dislike often kept through adulthood. Everything done conformed to narrow interpretations placed upon the meaning of the Scriptures, with the approval of the most learned men of the times. On August 9, 1681, Cotton Mather wrote in his diary:

> This day I took my second degree, proceeding Master of Arts. My Father was president, so that from his hand I received my degree. Tis when I am Gott almost half a year beyond eighteen, in my age. And all the circumstances of my commencement were ordered by a very sensibly inclined Providence of God. My Thesis was *Puncta Hebraica sunt Originis Divinae.* ["Hebrew vowel points are of divine origin."]

Not only were the attitudes toward education deep-seated, but because Puritan Massachusetts was a colony of great influence its attitudes and practices prevailed rather generally throughout the rest of the New England colonies. The Puritans left enduring traditions, some of which can still be identified in many parts of the nation. This is, perhaps, because wave after wave of the descendants of the Puritans moved westward with the frontier until it reached the Pacific.

EDUCATION IN MASSACHUSETTS

Some features of the educational experiences of the Massachusetts colony are particularly significant because it was Massachusetts that, early in American history, initiated certain educational legal principles that have endured.

Massachusetts Bay towns sent deputies to represent them in the General Court, as the legislature was called. This General Court, which met in Boston, in 1642 enacted what is probably the first school law to be passed in what afterwards became the United States. Officers chosen in the local town were empowered to find out whether parents and schoolmasters were teaching the children "to read and understand the principles of religion and the capital laws of the country" and to levy a fine on those who failed to report on these matters when required. As it worked out, a new legal principle toward education was established by the law—namely, that *the education of children is a proper subject for legal control.* Thus a first step was taken toward building a legal system of education in the United

States. In a law passed in 1647, the General Court strengthened this principle. The student will profit from reading this law (page 304), as it contains a clear expression of both the Puritan theory and an early frontier attitude toward education.

The principle established by the two Massachusetts laws was generally accepted throughout the colonies. The Massachusetts plan of leaving control and support of the schools to the citizens was inefficient when local interest in maintaining good schools declined. The frontier practice of having small school districts had, however, become established. As we shall see later, largely because of deep-seated tradition no problem in education has, through the years, been more difficult to cope with than the problem of organizing state school districts logically. As pointed out in Unit III, it is only in recent years that progress has been made in solving this thorny problem.

Gradually, the small, local school districts in Massachusetts became centers of selfish political activity. Election of school committee-men, location of school sites, and the payment of teachers' salaries became intense local political issues. Poor districts remained poor. The richer districts fought any action that would assign them a part in alleviating the weaknesses of the poorer districts. Poor districts, settled by poor people, were expected to have poor schools. Since poor districts greatly outnumbered wealthy districts, the typical school of the day was a poor one. It was only after poor schools in Massachusetts became so numerous as to constitute a disgrace that a reform movement set in.

In 1826, the state of Massachusetts passed a law that required every town to choose a school committee that would have general charge of *all* the schools within the town. The authority of this school committee extended to the selection of the textbooks, the examination and certification of teachers, and other matters that hitherto had been left to the jurisdiction of the local school committee, which had authority over only one school in a town. The first significant step in regeneration of the schools had taken place. Control of and supervision over all the schools in a town had become centralized under a single authority. Thus was begun the policy of organizing school units into a school system. The reform movement had begun too late to change greatly the educational practices that by then had become fixed and had spread as the frontier moved westward to other colonies and to other states. The evil had mounted, and it would take a long time to eradicate its effects.

It is well to note, at this point, that efforts to regenerate education have many times been significantly influenced by far sighted laymen as distinguished from professional educators. The law of 1826 was a result of a vigorous, personally waged campaign conducted by James G. Carter (1795–1849), a skilled parliamentarian who had become deeply concerned over the flagrant evils that he, and many others, recognized were sucking whatever lifeblood had been left in the degenerate public school system. Once Carter got the reform movement started, regeneration of the schools continued. Instances of lay leadership to improve public education in the United States have been common in most of the states and throughout the history of American education. Lay leadership was, and still is, one of the sources of strength of American public education.

In 1837, the Massachusetts legislature created the first state board of education. The board had eight members appointed by the governor. Its function was to gather information about education in the state and to make recommendations to the legislature. The board employed a secretary to study the needs of the schools, point out these needs to the public, diffuse other information about the schools, and help the board formulate its recommendations to the state legislature. The first secretary was a lawyer, Horace Mann (1796–1859), whose achievements have captured the admiration of all succeeding generations interested in education.

In the law of 1837, Massachusetts had contributed another principle to the building of an educational system in the United States: *School administration is a branch of public administration.* The state is the unit of school administration and organization. It is the supreme authority. It can determine the conditions under which local schools operate. The implications of this principle, now accepted throughout the nation, are very wide and are not even today fully realized. Some of the implications will be discussed more fully in a later chapter. Once Massachusetts accepted the principle and created a state authority over its schools, regeneration proceeded rapidly, and it has continued and persisted to the present time.

The Massachusetts story is but one example of how the social processes that built our national system of education during the

*Both these buildings reflect the
severities of earlier times. One is a
typical "grade" school, built in the
early 1900s in Racine, Wisconsin.
Such schools, located in "wards,"
were only slight improvements over
one-teacher country schools.
Obviously, elementary education was
not yet thought to be vitally
important in itself. (The attitude
toward high schools was different;
they were highly selective and had
to be accredited.) Many older school
buildings, unfortunately, are still in
use, as is the one below, which is in
Chicago. Note that virtually no
outdoor areas were provided, even
though land values were relatively
low when the school was built.*

frontier period and made a public school district a corporate entity in social organization tended to operate. In any other state the story would be just as exciting and would illustrate, more or less, the same points. As would be expected, however, since each state is a unit of administration, in each state the story would be different in many respects from all the others. For instance, New York furnishes an excellent example of how education in America came to be secularized; Texas, an example of how free lands have influenced education; and California, an example of how nonmineral underground resources like oil have contributed to the building of a great system.

EDUCATION IN THE SOUTH

Despite hardships and failures at its onset, Jamestown, Virginia, the first permanent English settlement in America, grew steadily. Within thirteen years its population numbered 4,000, and by 1700 as many as 100,000 people lived in Virginia. In 1693 William and Mary College, the second college founded in America, was established at Williamsburg, a short distance from Jamestown. Many citizens of Virginia were men of culture, wealth, and refinement. From their ranks came some of America's greatest earlier political statesmen.

In Virginia and subsequently in other southern states, the development of education followed a distinctive pattern. This pattern was considerably different from that of the middle colonies, such as Pennsylvania, or of the northern range of colonies like New York and Massachusetts. Perhaps the views of the earlier Virginia settlers were somewhat like those which Governor Berkeley reflected in his reply to the authorities in 1671. He thanked God that there were no free schools and no printing presses in the Province of Virginia, and expressed the hope that there would be none for a hundred years. "Learning," he said, "has brought disobedience, and heresy, and sects into the world, and printing has divulged them, and libels against the best government. God keep us from both." It was in 1779 that Thomas Jefferson showed that he had an extremely different view when he suggested his educational plan "for a more general diffusion of knowledge" among the people of Virginia.

The southern colonies, it seems, were not markedly influenced by the educational viewpoints of either Berkeley or Jefferson. Instead they developed plans for education along lines dictated by economic and social conditions. Children in the southern colonies did not attend school as we think of school today. Large plantations, located far apart and supported by a system of slave labor, led to a distinctive pattern of living and a special kind of educational organization. The more affluent plantation owners employed private tutors to teach their children. Sometimes planters cooperated to build a small schoolhouse in which the children from several plantation families received instruction. Plantation owners, in general, believed that schools should not be provided at public expense for all children but only for the children of indigent or near-indigent families. The Church also separated those who could afford to pay for their education from those who could not by providing education for the poor and underprivileged. Those who were able to pay for the education of their children were expected to do so or suffer a decline in social prestige. In the southern colonies public education was definitely to meet the needs of the poor. In other sections of the country this came to be known as the charity conception of education. Such a conception virtually placed a stigma on public education. Actually the demands of work kept education away from a major part of the population. Negro slaves and poor whites were so occupied that only a few of them could take advantage of what school experiences were provided for them. The effects of this flagrant neglect are still felt throughout America.

As the American frontier moved westward, people in the newer sections were not strongly influenced by southern traditions and practices in education. Instead they tended to be influenced by the policies that had been developed in states like New York and Massachusetts.

The educational heritage

DOCTRINE OF FREE SCHOOLS

It is important that we neither exaggerate nor underestimate the amalgamation of peoples in colonial days. At the time of the Revolution probably three-fourths to nine-tenths of the white colonists were still of British blood; but the infusion of Dutch, German, French, and other continental stocks was significant. A happy unity of tongue and basic institutions coexisted with a remarkable diversity in national origins.

To assess all the contributions of the frontier to American education would be infeasible because it would require study of how the frontier affected the entire scope of American life, including not only its institutions but also the philosophy that guided the nation in establishing those institutions. It is practicable, however, to focus on public policy toward economic support of schools extending from the kindergarten through the university. This seems especially appropriate and fruitful because economic support of an institution is one of the major factors in shaping the character of the institution. Economic support not only marks certain boundaries and to an extent limits what can be accomplished, but it is also a reliable reflection of the philosophy of the rank and file of the citizens. One may learn a great deal about a man and a nation by observing what they spend their money for.

The frontier philosophy toward human beings made the doctrine of free education inevitable and easy to accept. Jefferson, at this time the foremost political philosopher, forcefully expressed the doctrine of free education as early as 1779 in his "Bill for the More General Diffusion of Knowledge" as follows:

> . . . And whereas it is generally true that the people will be happiest whose laws are best and are best administered, and that laws will be wisely formed and honestly administered, in proportion as those who form and administer them are wise and honest; whence it becomes expedient for promoting the publick happiness, that those persons whom nature has endowed with genius and virtue should be rendered by liberal education worthy to receive and able to guard the sacred deposit of the rights and liberties of their fellow-citizens, and that they should be called to that charge without regard to wealth, birth, or other accidental condition or circumstance; but the indigence of the greater number disabling them from so educating, at their own expence, those of their children whom nature hath fitly formed and disposed to become useful instruments for the publick, it is better that such should be sought for and educated at the common expense of all, than that the happiness of all should be confined to the weak or wicked.[1]

[1] As quoted in Paul Leicester Ford, *The Writings of Thomas Jefferson*. New York: G. P. Putnam's Sons, 1893, vol. II, pp. 220–221.

Jefferson's words constitute a liberal statesman's understanding of democracy as it was interpreted and applied to education. The sentiments he expressed were subsequently voiced by political leaders in almost every section of the nation.

Free schools, however, must be paid for, and it is the contribution of the frontier to a policy of economic support that we are primarily concerned with at this point. How were free schools paid for?

FREE LANDS FOR A FREE EDUCATION

Democracy seemed to demand free education. Theoretically, free education seemed ideal. Those who were unable to pay for education themselves, of course, favored it. Many of the richer people, however, objected to paying for the education of the children of other families. To them free education at public expense was a startling if not radical step toward national or state socialism.

The frontiersmen resolved the problem of school support by granting subsidies of land to finance education. The income from the land would largely, if not entirely, remove the burden of support for education from the backs of the American taxpayer. Since all thirteen of the colonies prior to the American Revolution had granted land at one time or another for the support of schools, the citizens of the new nation were accustomed to the subsidy idea. When the Revolution ended, all of the lands owned by the Crown—and the extent of them was astounding—became the property of the states. Income from these lands relieved taxpayers of some of their responsibility for financing free public schools. How land subsidy for the support of public education operated in just one section of the nation, in what has been called the Northwest Territory, illustrates the principle of federal support for schools that has since become a permanent policy. This also illustrates the policy, still in operation, of recognizing that funds given to a school in the form of an endowment cannot subsequently be taken away. An institution might be financed indefinitely from the income of a grant.

When the colonies finally won their independence in 1781, the western boundary of the United States was the Mississippi River. The great expanse of land known as the Northwest Territory—land that has since been made into the states of Ohio, Michigan, Indiana,

Illinois, and Wisconsin, and a part of Minnesota—became the property of the federal government. The federal government, forced to plan for the administration of this vast territory, expressed its policy in the well-known Land Ordinance of 1785 and the Northwest Ordinance of 1787. The Northwest Ordinance was to the frontier settlers of the territory what, later, the Constitution was to the states. It was the framework of their government. The statement of policy concerning school support was forthright and unequivocal. A precedent was established.

The Land Ordinance of 1785 provided that after the land was surveyed, one section (one square mile) of every township (36 square miles) was given to the people to help support the schools. During the last days of the Congress of the Confederation, the Northwest Ordinance of 1787 was passed. This ordinance contained, in Article 3, the sentence that is accepted as the charter of public education in the United States: "Religion, morality, and knowledge, being necessary to good government and the happiness of mankind, schools and the means of education shall forever be encouraged."[2] In a second ordinance passed later in the same year, provision was made for the sale of the lands. This repeated the 1785 provisions reserving lands for public education. Any income received from the school lands, whether by sale or from rent, was earmarked for support of the schools. Thus, even before the Constitution was adopted, a policy of federal support of schools was established. The federal government has never since withdrawn from the practice of participating in subsidizing schools.

As states were formed in the new territory, the lands of the Northwest Territory became the property of the individual states under agreements with the federal government. Since the lands then belonged to the central territorial government, or to the state, the schools, too, were viewed as belonging to the established central government. The subsequent story of education in the United States is largely a picture of how states have operated the schools under their authority. It is now an accepted principle of American education that the state, not the local government, is the unit of school

[2] As quoted in Henry Steele Commager, *Documents of American History*. New York: F. S. Crofts & Co., 1934, vol. I, p. 131.

administration. This principle, however, does not rule out certain of the interests of the federal government. The entire problem of the organization of schools is discussed in detail in Unit III.

HIGHER EDUCATION

Frontier thinking about school support for free public education did not end with the elementary and secondary schools. The federal land-grant policy also provided for the building of colleges. In 1862, President Lincoln signed a bill known as the Morrill Act which made generous gifts of federal lands to states for the purpose of establishing what have since become known as land-grant colleges. The act provided that each state was to receive from the public domain 30,000 acres of land for each member it had in Congress. The proceeds from the lands were to be used in establishing agricultural and mechanical arts colleges. Free frontier land was a wedge sufficient to influence state legislatures to establish colleges that have since blossomed into some of the best and largest of America's universities. Subsequent acts have further fortified the principle that federal support should also be extended to institutions of college level.

Summary

The frontier movement was a vast social movement that nurtured some of America's lasting educational traditions. Traditions brought from Europe were changed or abandoned as frontiersmen accommodated to a new civilization, a new way of life. Free schools, first supported through land grants and later through taxation, are important among the elements of our modern heritage from the frontier period.

As we proceed, it will become increasingly evident that the frontier has had a striking effect on present education. Contemporary problems of education still revolve largely around how best to modify traditions so that they may be appropriate to modern social conditions. We must understand our educational heritage and make no attempt to divorce ourselves from the past. We must recognize that the past lives in the present and that the wisest plan is to recognize and strive to build on the past.

Questions

1. In what ways were the effects of the American frontier movement on both America and Europe of a reciprocal nature?
2. How did the fact that the frontier movement in America was continuous affect the development of education?
3. What social ideals currently esteemed by the American people are associated with frontier development? In your opinion, how should these ideals be modified in the light of modern conditions?
4. Which had the greater influence on the character of education developed by the Puritans, religion or social conditions?
5. Why did the legal principles adopted in Massachusetts have such wide influence throughout the United States?
6. What were some of the lasting effects on education in the United States that can be traced to the fact that the frontier moved rapidly?
7. What are some of the difficulties that confront modern educators in their attempts to formulate a postfrontier educational philosophy?

Projects

1. Consult some standard work, such as an encyclopedia, for information on the meaning of Puritanism. Note the ways in which later generations have tended to interpret the Puritan and what he advocated. Point out inaccuracies in popular interpretations.
2. Trace the main events in the history of education in some typical state, such as New York. Note the nature of the issues that arose and how they were settled.
3. Cite several examples to show that the use of free lands operated to shape the course of American education.
4. Trace the historical steps in the origin of the Northwest Territory. Show why it became a great influence on subsequent education.
5. Trace the principal historical events in the westward advance of the frontier subsequent to the establishment of the Northwest Territory. Indicate the possible effects of each of the events upon the development of education throughout the United States.

6. Compare Jefferson's plan of education with the plans advocated today by those who favor complete state control of public education.

7. Explain in what ways the early policies of the southern states toward public education are considered responsible for some of today's educational problems.

Education in America can only partially be interpreted in terms of ideas derived from those European social movements or social theories discussed in the preceding chapters. European ideas were modified in the evolution of the new social order, on our frontier. The frontier had a clear and lasting effect on our schools, and from the frontier we inherited traditions that have become firmly established, customs so deep-seated that many, as we have seen, came to be written into law. The frontier also can give only a partial background for understanding education in America today.

Although in time ideas and policies become modified, organizational patterns tend to change relatively slowly. The result is that a sizable lag develops in terms of a total, current social picture between what is believed to be good and the actualization of that good. Because of difficulties encountered when effecting change, some ideas that shaped the pattern of earlier education in America ultimately led to some present-day persistent and perplexing problems. To understand contemporary problems of American education, to appreciate their magnitude and significance, to evaluate current suggestions for education and attempts to improve it, one must begin with attention to the current social problems that constitute the backdrop to problems in education. It is important especially that those who share the major responsibilities of direct involvement in education in America have an understanding of and appreciation for the nature of the dynamic aspects of the contemporary social picture which is modern America.

Time, place, and circumstance

Education is a function of time, place, and circumstance. Reflect first upon the element *time*. The difficult problems that confronted leaders in education in the 1960s were very different from those they faced in the 1950s. Not only were the problems different, but the techniques used in dealing with the problems of the 1950s were largely inapplicable to solving the problems of the 1960s. Procedures had to be modified or new ones discovered. As with social organizations in general, problems in education and appropriate solutions change with the times.

Education is also a function of *place*. Activities fully appropriate to education in one place may be wholly inappropriate in another.

"Education is a function of time, place, and circumstance." These children in an outdoor elementary school in Nigeria are studying the Koran. As part of its effort to increase the number of professional workers, the Nigerian government has initiated extensive teacher-training programs at all educational levels.

Education in lower Manhattan differs from education in schools on a Texas plain. Teaching in a small town in the rural South is very unlike teaching in a rich suburban community in the industrialized North. So much does education differ from place to place that it is even hazardous to compare the effectiveness of education in one place with that in another. Locale makes a difference.

Education is a function also of *circumstance*. It is affected by such afflictive events as war, inflation, deflation, racial riots, events that make a deep and lasting imprint on education. A social crisis, wherever and whenever it arises, produces an educational crisis. It is widely believed that, if the nation can build a peaceful, ordered society, it will then achieve ordered, constructive educational progress. This conclusion is not necessarily valid. Circumstances would then be favorable, but suitable conditions will not be a guarantee of educational progress. The most healthful social situation makes progress possible; a strong *motive* to improve is also required. Circumstance permits what education *may be*. It will not determine what it *will be*.

Recognition that education is a function of time, place, and circumstance is essential to any successful effort to solve a serious educational problem. It helps a people to identify trouble spots. It stimulates motive to make a more serious search for effective techniques, promising innovations, better procedures, improved facilities. It strengthens the desire to understand the social setting in which education must operate. Perhaps, most of all, it leads the school publics to appreciate more fully the great importance of the teaching profession. It makes vivid to teachers themselves the essentiality of their work to the nation's welfare.

What, then, are the situations that bring into focus the more dynamic of the contemporary social forces? For our overview we shall mention but a few, those that seem to be the more effectual, that impinge most directly upon the schools. For purposes of simplification we shall treat these forces as separate entities—knowing, as we do so, that all contemporary social forces are the outgrowth of a single, vast social complex in which all social factors are inextricably interrelated. Our discussion will be somewhat like the discussions of our earth which treat the earth as a separate entity even though it is known to be only an infinitesimal, inseparable part of a vast cosmic system.

The international picture

International relations seem never to reach a state of equilibrium. They are characterized by continuous conflicts among nations, by aggressive attempts by some nations to become dominant, by intense competition for trade, oil, and military advantages, and, in some instances, by actions justified as necessary to a nation's survival. Many nations are also plagued with an internal instability that is reflected in their external relations with other countries and that has an effect on the total world picture.

The scope of interaction among nations is rapidly expanding. While the importance of *physical* distances between nations has diminished, the *social* distances between peoples have been reduced only slightly; nations now geographically close continue to remain socially far apart. Here and there, however, a degree of getting together can be recognized, even among nations that appear antagonistic.

An ideal of cooperation in dealing with conflicts among nations is kept alive in the United Nations organizations. Although speeches among national leaders of the world in the General Assembly, for example, do not always achieve the ideal of promoting international understanding and are often, instead, a way of accentuating the division in world alignments, influencing world opinion in a propaganda sense, they are sometimes effective in forwarding movements for international welfare and their function in "letting off steam" is perhaps important. Among other agencies of the United Nations, the World Health Organization is an example of one dedicated to improving the welfare of peoples throughout the world that has effected noteworthy achievements.

Cultural exchanges among nations are also encouraged, and international visits among various statesmen and political leaders of the world are becoming commonplace. There is ample evidence that cooperation among the nations of the world is possible, despite great differences. So far only small beginnings provide a spark of hope that interactions among nations, bound to multiply, will be increasingly effective in achieving worthy ends.

The international picture raises certain questions about education. How do these relations between countries affect the thinking and

*The relations between countries are exemplified in microcosm at the United
Nations in New York. Education is an important part of the UN's activities.
At the UN International School, children are performing during an assembly
attended by their parents. The pupils at this school include not only the
children of UN staff members and delegates, but also the children of parents
who have come to New York from other countries to represent commercial
organizations and the children of internationally-minded American families
who may have no direct contact with the UN. The school is dedicated to the
ideals of international understanding and cooperation but at the same time
enables children of diverse backgrounds to retain the culture and values of
their own national heritages.*

*The UN also maintains a language laboratory, with 18 booths and more
than 700 reels of tape, which is equipped to give instruction in 36 languages.
Tapes in the five official UN languages (English, French, Russian, Spanish,
Chinese) are used for the UN language classes. There also are tapes in these
and other languages for use by those not attending classes; on many,
literature such as short stories and plays is recorded. Some of the other
languages taped are German, Arabic, Hebrew, Italian, and Amharic. The
laboratory is controlled by a console that permits playing various combinations
of tapes and UN proceedings, plus individual communication.*

influence the behavior of us all, especially parents, pupils, and teachers? Psychologists tell us that the world situation is ever-present, consciously or subconsciously, in the minds of every person concerned with the education of the young. How does this modify the responsibilities of classroom teachers? Will new emphases in America's schools on the study of foreign languages, science, mathematics, social studies, and the like contribute to making America a more understanding, more intelligent member of the world family of nations? Will such subsidized programs as teacher exchanges with foreign nations, study abroad, and tourism of classroom teachers reduce social distances, help improve international relations? Is tourism, in general, more commercially than socially significant? Is experience in the Peace Corps reflected in America's classrooms?

What America's teachers have sought in their classrooms has admittedly had a relation to the picture of how America has been and should be doing its part in improving world relations. As ideas about how best to get along in the family of nations develop and are implemented, these ideas will be reflected in education. In turn, hopefully through education, ideas will be nurtured and set in motion. Whatever may be the ups and downs in the world picture, the effects of this image on the classroom are direct and striking.

The social setting

Though social forces and effects are always more or less international in their scope, for purposes of brevity and clarity we shall look mainly at the forces that have an influence on education as they are seen in our own national setting.

Education is a derivative of the social setting in which it is provided. Since the beginning of the nation, the questions related to the quality of education throughout America have so grown in number and magnitude as to appear almost unanswerable. For example, why have large cities provided substandard education for those children who live in the inner city, for those who must live in a deprived social environment? Why has only substandard education been provided for many born and reared in an exceedingly poor rural environment? Why, in present-day America, have large numbers of children who live in the substandard homes of migrant workers been practically denied the privileges of good schools? Why has affluent America allowed this to continue? Why has education in America been conducted with such extreme inequalities of educational opportunity? Are social unrest, societal inefficiency, societal instability, prices that America pays for this? Are the social forces that are built up by and lead to such practices awaiting other release? Is it important that educational planning take these social forces into account?

Social forces are real forces, forces with magnitude and direction; but, somewhat like topological physical forces, they are not measurable. It is the business of schools to direct education so that the effects of social forces will be constructive and their desirable outcomes will be reinforced and exploited.

One of the first and most important steps in determining improvements needed in all aspects of education—support, organization, curriculum, personnel, etc.—is to have educators and a wide range of the citizenry examine the social forces from an educational point of view and to understand the great influence that they have on education. Such a study and understanding are basic to the accomplishment of sound and orderly change in education. A few of the social forces are discussed in this chapter. In later chapters, where various details and components of American education are studied specifically, social forces will be discussed in the subject matter of which they are a natural part.

INFLUENCE OF TECHNOLOGY

Since the beginning of our nation, a growing technology has generated potent social forces. It has virtually revolutionized the ways in which Americans live, perhaps without their being aware of it. During each decade an increasing number of patents has been registered with the national government which, taken together, have left indelible imprints upon such aspects of American society as industrial development, living conditions, education. Synthetic fabrics, prefabricated houses, huge air buses, processed foods, selective techniques in office management are representative of a few of the technological developments which have influenced the lives and the education of children and youth.

Some adaptations in operation in the school, and some only in the planning stage, are illustrative of those having their base in technological change: (1) a longer school year, perhaps 48 weeks, so that all will not be released from school attendance at the same time; (2) improved flexibility in curriculum and teaching to meet more adequately the individual needs of boys and girls with a wide range of backgrounds, interests, and ability; (3) improved design of buildings to permit a wider use of technologically developed teaching aids, and to allow for a greater degree of flexibility in programing and in instruction; (4) training in the use of technical equipment as a part of teacher education; (5) specific vocational education in the upper grades for those who may enter the trades upon completion of a high school education; (6) improved opportunities to prepare for a wise use of leisure time; (7) increased and more varied opportunity for young employed adults to continue their education; (8) improved education of the American public concerning education's needs. Those in charge of education must realize that social changes caused by technology make new demands on education to which the schools must adjust rapidly and to which, some think, the school needs to make radical accommodations.

The background of experience a child brings to school is influenced by a technology that will continue to influence him, make an indelible impression on him. Technology, in a sense, determines where his parents live, where and when they move, what he hears and sees, the quality and conditions of life that surround him. As for his school itself, technology influences where it is, the kind of building that houses it, the kind of facilities that are provided, the kind of neighborhood that surrounds it, and the standards of workmanship he will respect. Considering all these factors, one can say that technology even influences the formation of a child's life values.

In addition, there are negative effects of technology on the lives of children. For example, children are frightened by press, radio, and television descriptions of the destructive capacities of the modern instruments of war that technology has created; there is no way to escape the fact that hydrogen bombs, napalm, and long-range guided missiles are devices whose reason for being is to kill people and demolish property. Though the psychological effects on children cannot be measured, they certainly are pronounced. Some children are probably more affected than others. It might be said that when on August

*F*irst of all, there is the role that technology plays in our lives. In no other age have men lived with so dizzying a sense of change, or seen their basic material and social environment being made over, and made over again, so steadily. Technology, plainly, is the fundamental dynamic element in modern society. It affects everything from size, shape, look, and smell of our cities and suburbs to the mobility of populations, the character of social classes, the stability of the family, the standards of workmanship that prevail, and the direction and level of moral aesthetic sensibilities. The decision as to when, where, and how to introduce a technological change is a social decision, affecting an extraordinary variety of values. And yet these decisions are made in something very close to a social vacuum. Technological innovations are regularly introduced for the sake of technological convenience, and without established mechanisms for appraising or controlling or even cushioning their consequences.

A current example is the impact of television. It has affected education and home life, changed the patterns of congressional behavior and political discussion, and fundamentally altered, for better or worse, the operating conditions and purposes of traditional political institutions like legislative investigations and political conventions. But the decisions on how to use television, and how not to use it, have been made almost entirely by men whose area of responsibility is very narrow, and who have to think about only a very few, selected values. . . . The engineers and industrialists who make decisions concerning technological changes have enormous power to affect the quality and conditions of our lives even though they do not know they have this power and have no interest in exercising it. This does not change the fact that their decisions are often decisions about basic social policy, and that the traditional liberal mechanisms of public consultation and consent, on which the authority for such basic decisions has been supposed to rest, have next to no influence here. From the point of view of most of us these decisions just seem to happen ; and it is one reason why so many ordinary men and women have come to feel that they are being manipulated by invisible persons whom they do not know and cannot control.

Charles Frankel, *The Case for Modern Man*. New York: Harper & Row, 1956, pp. 197–199. Quoted by permission of the publisher.

5, 1945, an atomic bomb was dropped on Hiroshima, a new instrument for personal disorganization, born of technology, had been released; and its ultimate effects upon the lives of children can only be assessed some generations hence.

Automation and electronics

Popularly speaking, aside from theories on the behavior of electrons in a vacuum, the term "electronics" refers to those many
devices that utilize this behavior of electrons in a vacuum. Most children know about electron tubes used in radios, picture tubes in television sets, transistors, and the like. Children may see bacon cooked
on a paper towel in the electronic oven. The lights of the family car
may operate automatically and the garage door respond to an electric
eye. They hear much about the computer, know that it is an electronic
device that makes computations almost instantly and solves complex
problems with lightning speed, and increasingly they use computers
in school. ("Lightning speed" is an apt description of the computer's
action, since electrons attain a speed up to 99 percent that of light,
nature's maximum, generally constant, velocity of 186,284 miles a
second.)

In addition to devices that are electronic, our environment is
modified by a constantly growing range of automatic mechanical devices. These are based on the principle of automation (the word is
derived from "automatic"), when applied to manufacturing, and include a large class of mechanical devices in which machines—not men
—feed machines, the operation or control of a process is accomplished
by automatic means, and the need for men is reduced to a minimum.
The assembly line in the production of automobiles, the production
of flour in a mill where few men are to be seen, are examples. Our
main interest here is to explore the question, How have electronic
and mechanical automated devices, two developments of modern
technology, changed the lives of American people so that adaptations
are required in the schools?

The uses of electronics and automated devices reach to many
areas of life—manufacturing, housekeeping, office practice, entertainment, insurance, banking, missile projection, space exploration, medicine, dentistry, merchandising, vending machines, communication,
and teaching.

Automated devices and electronics have led to a higher standard
of living for many, but not all, American people. The rural poor,
certain tribes of American Indians, migrant workers, the citizens in
the ghettos, and some other groups are exceptions. The benefits to

those who are employed by most large corporations are very impressive: less taxing work, reduced work hours, a more pleasant and healthful working environment, increased income, vacations with pay, sick benefits, and a sizable retirement income.

The beneficial effects of electronics and automated devices are well known. But what about other social effects? Often social changes seem to arrive without much general awareness of their social effects. We discover them only when some kind of crisis occurs, something like a nation-wide strike or riots in the cities, a manifestation of extreme social unrest. Then we ask what has taken place to result in societal disequilibrium, widespread social disturbances. We inquire about the part technology has played in nurturing such crises, about the adaptations schools have made or should have made to such social changes.

Technology has contributed to some problems that are relatively new to education and has increased the intensity of some older ones. The need for many formerly highly regarded manipulative skills has been eliminated, and therefore many skilled workers have been displaced by machines; at the same time, fewer productive jobs are available for the unskilled worker. In other words, the unskilled working group has been augmented by a large group of people formerly considered skilled or semiskilled, just at a time when there is little demand for unskilled workers of any kind. Social problems are accentuated by a concentration of the unemployables in rural sections, the fruit- and vegetable-growing parts of the country, and in the inner segments of large cities. The school dropout, the scholastically "poor" student, and others who do not succeed in school for various reasons are added to this group.

Occupations requiring technical training, a college education, a high degree of specialization, are on the increase, and this applies to many fields—agriculture, manufacturing, engineering, medicine, dentistry, law, teaching, and others. In all, the pattern is the same: in occupations calling for specialization, the workers are upgraded in social status; this is accompanied by a downgrading of the unskilled. As they are socially downgraded, many tend to acquire the behavior patterns typical of the disgruntled, the frustrated, the angry. The abler among them—and there are many able people in this group— become leaders of organizations for some kind of dynamic action, sometimes constructive, sometimes destructive, to serve as a kind of release and also as a means of applying pressure on society for an improvement in their lot.

Emphasis in the schools is being placed on an earlier, more timely, beginning of specialization, in some cases at the end of the eighth grade. Efforts are made to identify the more talented children and, likewise, the disadvantaged child—the physically handicapped, the emotionally disturbed, the culturally deprived, the child with learning disabilities—and to provide the special opportunities appropriate for each. When they reach the senior high school the more talented are offered courses equivalent to those offered in the colleges and are given college credit for pursuing them.

At the same time, educators are conscious that the rapid changes accompanying advances in technology tend to render the specializations of today obsolete tomorrow. An effort is made to educate for change, to help the young people acquire the kind of background education, the basic understandings and insights, that equip them for flexibility, adaptation to new demands, the fulfillment of functions perhaps undreamed of today.

As we show in more detail in later chapters, efforts are being made to improve instruction and subject matter in mathematics, science, and foreign languages to make these areas more appropriate for the demands of present-day living and for personal adjustment to a future that is constantly changing. With the problems of dropouts in mind, the schools are improving textbooks, supplying more supplementary materials as a part of the effort to meet individual pupil needs, equipping classrooms with mechanical aids, providing teacher aids such as paraprofessionals, lay readers, and other nonprofessional help, and experimenting with a wide variety of innovations in teaching. Training high school youth so that they have skills needed to cope with problems of the technological age, decreasing the rate of school dropouts, retraining those who have dropped out of school—in brief, working to improve the plight of the unemployables—is receiving serious attention at all three governmental levels, and especially at the national level, where large sums are being allocated to local school systems for this purpose.

Citizens are evidencing more concern about their schools than ever before. It is typical for a school district to have a panel of select citizens studying the broader problems of education as well as local problems. The reports of such citizen groups agree with reports from other groups who have been studying problems in education. It is rather consistently recommended that tax policies for the support of public education be amended, that the outmoded local personal and real estate property tax be dropped as the district's principal source of funds for elementary and high schools, and that other sources of support be used. As the expertly prepared Rockefeller Report on Education asserted, "There seems to be only one alternative, a thorough, painful, politically courageous overhaul of state and local tax systems."

Although the present federal government, in comparison with the federal government of earlier days, is investing heavily in education, most experts believe it is obligated further and must invest far more money. As the Committee on Education appointed by President Eisenhower stated: "America's teachers at all levels of education have actually been subsidizing education at considerable sacrifice to their families." In view of the rapid attrition in the teaching profession caused in part by inadequate support, one might reason that the people of America, and especially their children, lose far more from a parsimonious support of education than does the teaching profession.

Since each state is a unit of public school administration, the policies of the various states have a direct bearing on the problems of support. More on this subject will be found in Unit III. It might be mentioned here that anything like a satisfactory solution to some of the modern problems of the states will require that some states adopt new constitutions. Such changes, as the reader knows, follow only after prodigious and prolonged efforts have been made to achieve such reconstructions.

Many other suggestions for meeting a changed world are conspicuous in the professional and public press: school days to be lengthened; school term extended to 48 weeks a year; teaching staffs doubled to provide more and better education; school buildings in large cities built in clusters—school parks—to eliminate the kind of inequalities in educational opportunities characteristic of large cities.

This listing of attempts designed in part to meet the weightier problems accruing from social change, including changes related to technology, is not meant to be complete; it is merely a sample adduced to show that schools are making serious efforts to meet the problems.

EFFECT OF ECONOMIC CYCLES

Economic conditions in the United States are fluid. Like technology, they are a part of a broad social picture, influencing and being influenced by many other social factors—wars, for instance. As production, employment, and national income fluctuate, the economy does likewise. The undulations of the economy are not rhythmic. They are very unpredictable and, like the wild horse on the prairie, seem, at times, uncompliant to all efforts at control. The magnitude of the cycles becomes greater the further the economy retreats from the self-sufficiency economy of the frontier toward the money economy of modern times. With each new phase, the crests rise higher and the troughs sink lower. For example, the Great Depression of the 1930s was a tragic historical episode. It was so disastrous as, at this time, to seem incredible. As an illustration, consider the effects of such an economic incident upon education. The birth rate in the early 1930s declined precipitately, leading five years later to sharp decreases in early elementary school enrollments. Around 1936 empty classrooms were common in elementary school buildings. Later the high schools, and still later the colleges, suffered sharp reductions in enrollments. These decreases continued for some fourteen years in the high schools and for as many as eighteen years in the colleges. In one large city, for example, in ten years the high school enrollment declined from 155,000 to 83,000. This would be equivalent to closing 36 high schools with enrollments of 2,000 pupils. What was to be done with all the unneeded teachers, with empty classrooms? How was the morale of pupils and teachers affected? With what spirit did planning education for the next decade proceed?

In the 1960s the economic picture was far different. The decade was marked by a continued, sharp inflation that had begun after World War II. A whole new set of educational problems developed. The birth rate rose rapidly. Elementary classrooms were no longer empty; they were overcrowded. The mushroom growth began in the early 1950s with the kindergarten, then, year by year, advanced to the higher grades. Many new school buildings had to be built not only because of the influx of more children but because older buildings had deteriorated and become outmoded during the period of no building during the war. There was now a dearth of qualified teachers, especially in the elementary schools. Increasingly, teaching was done by less-qualified, inexperienced, and younger teachers. In 1956, for instance, the median age of classroom teachers was 43. In 1966 it was 36. The median age of men teachers over the same years dropped from 35.4 to 33 years, and it became almost impossible to employ competent men teachers for the lower grades. This made the problem of obtaining men teachers especially acute in the inner city, where men teachers were gravely needed. A nation that had become economically affluent had become educationally impoverished.

Economic cycles affect the psychology of a people. Since in America the citizens control the schools, their attitudes are reflected in their feeling-states toward schools, teachers, educational programs, and especially educational costs. In the 1930s schools were permitted to drift. In the 1960s they were subjected to trenchant criticism by feature writers, radio and television commentators, the public press, professional sociologists, and students themselves. The suggested readings at the end of this unit include a few articles that illustrate the nature of these criticisms.

What will the next cycle be like? How shall the American people and the education profession prepare? What will be the effect on the schools, now so rapidly expanding, if the birth rate falls farther? (In 1910, the birth rate, for example, was 30.1 per 1,000 population. In 1967, the figure was 17.8). At present, the young adults in our population are those born in the depression years when the birth rate was low. This means that now the bulk of those in the reproductive years represent an abnormally small proportion of the population. Does this, in part perhaps, explain the current lower birth rate? Will those now approaching young adulthood, the children of the postwar "baby boom," create a great and growing increase in the total number of persons in the reproductive years, perhaps even an abnormally high proportion of the population? Should we anticipate a higher birth rate? Will the elementary school population increase or decrease? Will the secondary schools, increasing by 25 percent to 1975, have over-expanded? Since the children born in 1967 will, for the most part, enter school in 1972, what enrollment trends are foreseeable? Since we now know from past events that the educational problems of the 1970s will be far different from those of the 1960s, just as those for any decade are unique, can the differences be projected? The answer

Technological changes and the population increase—both have had profound effects on our schools. It takes money to cope with these effects and, unfortunately, lack of support in some school districts leads to obsolete buildings and equipment and overcrowded classrooms. A compromise is better than no improvement, however; even when old buildings cannot be replaced, they can be adapted to new uses. A modern scientific laboratory installed in an old high school in St. Louis is shown in two views; a new language laboratory in an old Michigan high school is also shown. Expensive electronic devices are becoming essential. In a New York high school, pupils studying computer mathematics—a relatively new subject—are learning to program the computer to perform specific tasks. Much other electronic equipment is now used in schools. Obviously, advancing technology will add new elements to both pre-service and in-service teacher training. Overcrowded classrooms present a desperate problem in our cities. In the one shown, there are so many children that only a few can see the teacher's demonstration properly. Even confronted by such conditions, however, many excellent teachers achieve much. When they do, they find particular satisfaction in knowing that they are succeeding in a useful—indeed, essential— profession.

*B*ut *what should concern us much more is how the passion for popularity translates itself into an almost universal tendency to conformity among our younger generation. It runs through all social classes. American teenagers show substantial class differences in many aspects of their behavior, problems and aspirations, but in their desire for popularity and their conformist attitude they are as one : low-income or high-income, their highest concern is to be liked.*

This is the most striking and most consistent fact that has emerged from our polls through the 17 years. Poll after poll among our youngsters has given statistical confirmation of the phenomenon of American life which David Riesman, in his book The Lonely Crowd, *named "other-direction"— extreme sensitivity to the opinions of others, with a concomitant conformity. As a nation we seem to have a syndrome characterized by atrophy of the will, hypertrophy of the ego and dystrophy of the intellectual musculature.*

This rather unpleasant portrait is an inescapable conclusion from the mass of data on the attitudes of the younger generation.

H. H. Remmers and D. H. Radler, "Teenage Attitudes," *Scientific American,* 198 (No. 6): 25–26, June, 1958. Quoted by permission of *Scientific American,* H. H. Remmers, and D. H. Radler.

is perhaps a modified yes. Future differences can be more or less accurately projected providing the visible trends are carefully noted and meaningfully interpreted by an alert citizenry and a highly selected, fully qualified educational leadership.

THE CORPORATE TREND

In business and in other areas of American life, there is a growing trend toward acting through corporations. A corporation is an association of persons that functions in many respects as an individual who possesses certain rights, privileges, and designated authority. The legal rights of the corporation are defined in its articles of incorporation granted by the state. These rights, it should be noted, are the rights of the corporation, not the rights of any individual members of the corporation. The corporation belongs to shareholders, and the ownership of shares in corporations is exceedingly widespread among the American people. If the corporation borrows money, perhaps by selling bonds, the corporation, but no individual, is responsible for meeting its obligations. A corporation, as long as it fulfills its functions and meets its legal obligations, has the right of perpetual succession.

How is the corporation trend reflected in public school districting? A public school district is a state government corporation. It is established by the state and operates under the authority of the state. In technical language, it is a quasi-corporation; that is, the school district does not need to file articles of incorporation, such as would be necessary for the conduct of a private business. However, many of the features that are commonly associated with a commercial corporation do apply to public school districts. There is a board of directors, and a chairman of that board. The board is empowered by the state legislature to do whatever the board deems necessary to ensure the proper conduct of public education within the district, with the restriction that its actions comply with those laws of the state that apply to the conduct of education within public school districts.

Details about how public education in America is administered, how education is carried on through the public school district, a social invention peculiar to America, are dealt with in a later chapter. Our concern here is with how education is affected by the trend in America toward corporations of increasing size and range and variety of interests.

With a few exceptions, public school elementary and secondary school districts operate as autonomous, independent corporations, even in those instances where boundary lines of the municipal corporation and the school district corporation are coterminous. Despite this legal separation, however, many citizens view the public school system in a municipality, such as a city—erroneously, of course—as being a subsidiary part of the city. To them identical boundaries imply that school government is a subsidiary of city government. They refer to the schools as "city" schools, and their allegiances conform to their belief. In many school districts it has been extremely difficult to keep public school organization and administration separated from municipal government and to divorce the government of public schools from the kinds of politics that characterize municipal government.

Seemingly, it has also been difficult, once the state has set up school districts, to reorganize them into logical, more manageable

In their Pocket History of the United States, *the historians Allan Nevins and Henry Steele Commager summarize the social effects of the corporation trend in America.*

> *What was the significance of the growth of combinations and the rise of trusts? It created a system of absentee ownership more far-reaching than anything known heretofore to history—vast properties of coal, copper, iron, timber, railroads, owned and directed by New York corporations. It centered in the hands of a few men power over the fortunes of millions of people greater than that wielded by many monarchs. It concentrated economic control of the nation in a small section of the Northeast, creating a new sectionalism to take the place of the old. It separated ownership from management, lodging it in tens of thousands of stockholders who had little sense of responsibility and knew little about the financial or labor policies of their companies. It created new aggregations of capital powerful enough to dictate policies to state and even to national legislatures and to influence foreign as well as domestic policies. It undoubtedly eliminated a great deal of cutthroat competition, achieved greater efficiency, released money for necessary improvements and for research, and made possible mass production and lower prices— but all at a heavy cost to society.*

Allan Nevins and Henry Steele Commager, *The Pocket History of the United States.* New York: Pocket Books, 1951, p. 280.

administrative units. Apparently reorganization must be done by degrees. In harmony with the nation-wide trend over the years to expand corporations in size, almost every state has made efforts to reorganize its elementary and secondary public school districts into progressively larger units. The states seemingly have not as yet invented or discovered a wholly effective procedure, since some states still have what seems to be too many school districts.

The corporate trend as it affects school districting gives rise to some unanswered questions. Are large state-city school districts and large city schools the answer to efficiency in education? What is the maximum size of an effective school? Have some districts already given proof of being too large? If state school districts become progressively larger, in harmony with the corporate trend nationally, will this result in an undesirable degree of impersonalization in education? In submergence of the needs of individuals and of groups? Will schools be too far removed from the people who support them? Does the trend promise to sacrifice many of the values traditionally associated with the American system of public education?

DOMINANCE OF PRESSURE GROUPS

A pressure group is an organized minority group that, generally speaking, seeks to influence legislation, government agencies, public opinion, or something else in its own interest. The goals and some activities of a pressure group may be well publicized in order to enlist public support; the goals may be camouflaged and pseudo-goals publicized; or the pressure group may be a secret group, a so-called "undercover" one operating behind a false or hidden front. The number of pressure groups in America is unknown, but it is very large. Among the better-known national organizations that serve in part as pressure groups are the National Association of Manufacturers, the American Farm Bureau, the American Medical Association, the National Education Association, and the American Federation of Labor with its education affiliate, the American Federation of Teachers. All these have headquarters in the national capital and make use of the political technique of lobbying in exercising their pressure on the government.

Through his own experience and observation and through his local professional organization, a teacher learns of the aims and techniques of pressure groups in his community. Some groups try to shape the curriculum, some to influence support of schools, some to determine the choice of textbooks, some to get men and women with particular qualifications elected to school boards. A PTA organization is often an effective pressure group that gets a community to vote approval of a proposed school bond issue.

Powerful pressure group methods are used to influence state and national legislation on education. Since everyone is a part of the "school public," pressure groups disseminate propaganda to a wide audience; and therefore school legislation often faces an uphill battle against opposition organized by a pressure group. This, at least in part, explains why school legislation tends to lag behind the practical needs of education.

In a nation strongly characterized by pressure groups, the profession needs to be effectively organized for the exercise of its own pressure—to influence education policy at all levels of government, to promote effective public relations, to disseminate information. A teacher acting alone can have only limited influence under present-day conditions. Acting in the typical American organizational way, through pressure groups, he can be well informed and actively effective.

Family life

The family life background from which children come to our schools is, of course, an important ingredient to include in educational planning. Consider, first, family life in general—how it has changed, how education has influenced these changes and been influenced by the changes, and what the implications are for the future.

IMPROVED STANDARD OF LIVING

The material standard of living, as pointed out in our discussion of the effects of technology, has been markedly raised in the past decade and seems destined to continue to rise. Home comforts of many kinds are widely distributed and, as a concomitant, children are better fed, better clothed, and healthier than their predecessors, and enjoy many more luxuries. Parents live longer—life expectancy is now 67 years for males, 74 for females, as contrasted with a life expectancy of 47.3 years in 1900. Theoretically, these factors should add to stability in family-life relationships.

There are, of course, great contrasts between homes in the possession of these material comforts. Such comforts are usually least abundant in the ghettos, among migrant workers, among the poor in such rural areas as Appalachia, and on some American Indian reservations.

The rise in the general standard of living has brought benefits to education that are reflected in school buildings and facilities. Buildings that would have been adequate in the early part of the century have little place in a modern school district. Parents accustomed to the higher standard of living expect, and get, beautiful, comfortable, properly equipped, and well-kept school buildings for their children. Parents are not reluctant to protest vigorously to the board of education if their children do not have what parents believe they should. Most parents expect their children to have such benefits as attractive textbooks, teaching aids, prompt medical and dental attention when needed, nutritionally balanced lunches in pleasant surroundings. It is reasoned that the children from families where physical comforts and attractiveness are not common need most of all to have pleasant, wholesome, educationally effective surroundings during the part of their time that is spent in school. The parents of these children are not always vocal or successful in their protests about overcrowding and other discrepancies and deficiencies. However, they have organized protest campaigns that have brought results.

CHANGED FUNCTIONS OF THE FAMILY

One important function fulfilled by the family in our frontier history was that of providing itself with the basic necessities of living. The family was, in a sense, a miniature, self-sufficient, familial, economic society. This does not mean that the families were isolated. They built communities, although, as in any agrarian society, families did not live in close proximity. Social status of families in a given community was relatively equal, and each family was a comparatively stable organization. Every member was a producer, a cooperative contributor to the family, a worker. The interrelationships between family members and between families tended to be wholesome and lasting.

As industrialization steadily advanced, this older pattern of family life underwent gradual change, until in most of today's families the family-shared economic function has disappeared or greatly lessened. Typically children today have few assigned work responsibilities—regular chores for the younger, productive work for the older. When youth are employed it is mostly to earn money to spend, generally on themselves, for movies, dates, a motorcycle, a secondhand car, or, in brief, for a "good time." "Why," reasons the youth, "should I contribute when my parents can purchase the family needs?" Frequently not only the father but also the mother works. Appliances, prepared and packaged foods, easy-care fabrics have lightened home-making, diminished the mother's work in the home, and set the stage for families to become accustomed to two salaries.

How do we evaluate changes in functions of family members? Do they operate to weaken the effectiveness of the family, contribute to problems of life adjustment? Take, for example, a family near a large urban center with a father who must commute to his work. He is separated from his children, not only physically but by virtue of the nature of his work, which denies the family any participation. The children have very little knowledge of what he does. This brings new status to the mother. She makes most of the family decisions concerning the care of the children. The family may live in an apartment, the kind of environment that provides all the comforts of life but is not conducive to satisfying, shared activities. Acquaintance with neighbors, business associates, and personal friends will probably not be sufficiently intimate to allow for the expression of one's deepest hopes and fears. All of this leads to an acute need within the family for relationships that are intimate, affective, intense, exclusive—family life in which mutual affection is an ever-present ingredient.

Change in family function does not involve deterioration in family relationships. Becoming different does not necessarily mean becoming worse. Changes in the function of the family do, however, change the responsibilities of the school. Personal counseling, school psychologists, PTA activities, courses dealing with the problems of marriage, home instruction for the ill and the handicapped, vocational education in high school with emphasis on work experiences, are examples of attempts to compensate somewhat for changes in family life. Wholesome relationships in the school help promote wholesome relationships in the home. The school here has an opportunity as well as a responsibility.

FAMILY DISORGANIZATION

Changes in the structure and function of the family have been accompanied by an increase in family disorganization. The reasons for this are not entirely clear. Nor can the degree of disorganization in any particular case be estimated. Perhaps the best indication of the extent of family disorganization is the number of legal dissolutions given by the courts each year. The care of children in such dissolutions

*T*he erratic behavior of the adolescent, then, which proves so irritating to
his elders, represents his clumsy attempt to balance between the pressure of his
growth and the constraint of his codes. It is not at all surprising that he
wobbles occasionally from the even poise of strict conformity. But to think
that he is making no effort or that he has no codes, is an assumption that is
not justified. Not that this anxiety about the behavior of youth is limited to
our particular part of the world. An anthropologist friend tells me that he
has never visited any tribe of primitive people where the elders of the village
did not tell him that the young people were going to the dogs.
In looking at the conflict between nature and nurture, we see succeeding
generations of young people driven on by the inherent forces of their growth, the
most vital of which are restrained and opposed by the solicitous efforts of
generations of adults who, ironically enough, have just gone through the
same struggle. Considered dispassionately, one might wonder why we humans
have to be so hard on ourselves.

C. Anderson Aldrich and Mary M. Aldrich, *Babies Are Human Beings*, 2nd ed. New
York: The Macmillan Company, 1954, pp. 117–118. Quoted by permission of
The Macmillan Company.

is decided by the court. The divorce rate in America gradually increased
over the earlier part of the present century, reaching its maximum in
1946. Although there were far more marriages following World War
II, the divorce rate declined. Somewhat like the economic cycles, it is
an unpredictable social phenomenon. In 1890, for example, the year
that marks the close of the American frontier, the divorce rate was 0.5
per 1,000 population; in 1946 the corresponding rate was 4.3, an
increase of 8.6 times. From 1956 to 1966 it held relatively constant at
around 2.2, but then the rate began to rise (2.7 in 1968). In the years
1965–1966, for example, 975,000 families were dissolved. A vast
number of children come from these homes where marriages were dissolved. All are, more or less, emotionally affected. Their family life
experience has been both bewildering and devastating. In some cases
they know they have been the cause of disagreements. If one parent or
both parents have remarried, they have still further adjustments to make.

To many children from disorganized homes, the school serves as
an avenue of escape. They may suffer, not from a lack of material
provisions, but from a lack of healthy social provisions. Fortunate is
the child or youth coming from a broken home whose teacher is

mature, well-adjusted, sympathetic, understanding, one who does everything he can to give the pupil a measure of security. Unfortunately even a sympathetic, understanding teacher cannot provide wholly satisfactory solutions to a pupil's problems created and endured in a disorganized family situation. Such wounds are slow to heal.

The high school can perhaps help in the problem of family disorganization, can provide courses on family relationships and especially courses that stress how to achieve a happy marriage, how to consumate a wholesome family life. Even though the school does all that it can to help children from broken homes to adjust, and to prepare young people for stable family life in their adult period, it cannot bring an immediate change in the social situations that lead to the dissolution of families. The school must, however, be aware of the kinds of problems it inherits from such family disorganization.

COMMUNITY RELATIONSHIPS

The psychologist E. L. Thorndike, after an extensive study of communities, concluded: "The recipe for the welfare of a community is . . . very simple. Put able and good people in the community and provide them with high incomes." Some communities, of course, approach this ideal closer than others. Some communities, like some families, experience a kind of disorganization. Such communities may manifest conflicting attitudes among the citizens, neighborhoods and neighborhood schools in stages of deterioration, lack of unanimity of action toward building and supporting schools, continuing conflicts over politics, government control, local taxation. There may be dissensions between older and younger generations. Youth become rebellious against social restraints, engage in bizarre forms of behavior —vandalism or riots, perhaps—express a strong aversion to building a good community to, as they say, supporting "the establishment." In some communities—such as large cities—the cost of insuring school buildings against vandalism is almost prohibitive.

Fortunate indeed is Thorndike's community of good people who earn high incomes, and fortunate are the children who live in such communities. Unfortunately, communities generally are not good or bad but have qualities of each. Perhaps a true evaluation would be made in terms of their potential.

What adaptations must be made to build successful schools in seriously disorganized communities? What changes in curriculums are needed? Should work experience be substituted for compulsory school attendance? Should the military assume a greater responsibility for training youth in various vocational skills? Will the traditional acceptance of the neighborhood school idea have to be discarded? Modified? Or broadened to include the whole of a district? Should some children in a disorganized community be sent by bus to schools in a "good community?" And should this policy be followed in reverse? Should enrollments be balanced by sending children from one neighborhood to another? Would abandonment of the community school idea in large cities and its replacement with a park system, all schools in a favorable location, overcome the disadvantages of having schools in disorganized communities? The problems have so long been overlooked in some school districts that the threat is a continuation of disadvantaged schools in disorganized communities.

The needs of the children in disorganized communities are identifiable and somewhat unique and call for immediate and far-reaching action. It appears that good schools cannot be built by disorganized communities; at least they cannot be built without generous and vigorous help from outside the local community, from both the state and federal governments. Nor can schools in good communities continue to be good without such help. Up to the present this aid, when considered in terms of the growing educational needs, has been scanty. Teachers and the children in the schools throughout America's educational history have been the unfortunate heirs of an inadequate public support.

Population changes

The United States is a populous nation with more than 200 million people. The percentage of its people in the youngest age group has steadily increased, as has the percentage in its oldest age group. The population is exceedingly mobile, with the biggest shifts to urban centers and, geographically, to the Pacific Coast states. Even though the birth rate in 1967 was at its lowest—17.8 per 1,000—the population, and especially the school population, continues to increase.

FACTORS IN GROWTH

Immigration and the lengthening of the life span have been important factors in the growth of population in America. In addition, population growth in the United States and throughout the world has been due to excess of births over deaths. It is the excess of births elsewhere in the world that has made immigration important in our population increase. The drop in infant and youth mortality rate has been a factor in adding to school enrollment. By 1955 the death rate per 1,000 for those aged 1 to 24 was 0.6. The rate was uniform for each of the age years included and, in fact, did not begin to increase until after age 34. This makes possible a fairly accurate prediction of school population several years in advance. The children born in a given year, say 1970, will almost all be ready for kindergarten in 1975, thus somewhat simplifying advance school planning. One factor, however, complicates the picture: the mobility of the population. Population growth has never been uniformly distributed. Urban centers, particularly, have become plagued with grave social and educational problems because of the great movement to such centers. Since Washington's day the population has increased 50 times over, but the problems of education in large urban centers seem to have multiplied many more times than that. These are discussed in a later chapter.

1950   20.1
1960   24.5
1964   25.4
1967   26.1

Fig. 10.1 School-age (5–17) population as a percentage of total population. (Data from NEA Research Report 1968-R1)

ABSOLUTE AND RELATIVE GROWTH

Both absolute and relative figures are used in interpreting population growth. When we compare the actual number of people in any classification at one time with the actual number at another time and note an increase, we are describing *absolute* growth. For instance, the absolute growth in the population of the United States—200 million in 1968 and a projected 260 million in 1980—is obvious. Much data, however, are more meaningful when related to other data, usually in terms of percentages, as *relative* growth. For instance, note in Fig. 10.2 that the school-age populations of both Alaska and Rhode Island increased by around 34,000 during the period. Those absolute figures are not very meaningful, but in one case the relative growth was 81 percent, in the other, only 18 percent. Here the increase in school-age population has been related to the total population of each state. Another example of relative growth would be a comparison of the rise in college enrollments in a certain period with the rise in the country's population in the same period.

Absolute figures of the population in the whole country or in a single public school district give a realistic picture of the number of people who must be afforded a means of making a living and also of the ratios existing among the various age groups. A great variety of this kind of information is produced by the comprehensive census conducted by the federal government every 10 years. One can compare the data in the different periodic surveys, whether national or local, and compute relative rates of growth and population changes. In studying the growth in total population or growth in various age groups in any geographical segment such as a school district, both the absolute figures and the relative figures are considered. Taken together, they give a fairly realistic picture both of the nature of the population and of the changes that have been taking place. In most public school districts a continuing census of the school population is taken; obviously, this serves many useful purposes.

GROWTH TRENDS

Benjamin Franklin noted that the population of the original 13 colonies doubled about every 20 years. From its beginning, the United States has been a constantly expanding nation, in population, in economics, in education, and in government. So used to expansion has the nation become, and so great has been the influence on the outlook of the people, that any aspect of life that is not expanding is viewed with some suspicion. The nature of the over-all trend in population may be seen from the following data:

UNITED STATES POPULATION TOTALS

1880	50,000,000
1890	63,000,000
1900	76,000,000
1910	92,000,000
1920	106,000,000
1930	123,000,000
1940	132,000,000
1950	151,000,000
1960	179,000,000
1970	214,000,000—est.
1980	260,000,000—est.

Gross increase in population, while it has a bearing on the expansion and support of education, does not give a full description of what has taken place. There are trends within these trends, such as shifts in age ratios. Fig. 10.1 shows the increase of school-age population as compared with the total population. More than one-fourth of the total resident population of the United States in 1967 was of school age (5 through 17), as compared with only one-fifth in 1950. (More than 57 million children and youth entered school in the fall of 1968, taxing the nation's classrooms.) All the states did not share alike in the rise, bearing out earlier estimates such as those shown in Fig. 10.2. But it is hazardous to make long-term predictions about the school-age population in any specific area or state because of the current population mobility—which seems, in fact, to be increasing. Thus most school systems conduct continuous studies of their school population, and on the basis of these they predict for only a few years ahead. The school-age population is also reflected in statistics on the number of young children *under* 5 years of age—20,364,000 in 1960, according to the Bureau of the Census. The Bureau estimates that there will be 33,048,000 children under 5 in 1985—a prediction that is likely to be reliable. But no one knows, or can guess, how these children will be distributed throughout the country.

Clearly, the age composition of the population has been changing. Since 1950, the two groups that have increased most, proportionately,

Fig. 10.2 *Estimated changes in the school-age population, 1957–1963. (Data from National Industrial Conference Board*, Road Maps of Industry, *No. 1245)*

		PERCENTAGE CHANGES		ABSOLUTE CHANGES (IN THOUSANDS)
Alaska	1	81.0	37	34
Nevada	2	59.0	37	34
Florida	3	45.0	7	421
Arizona	4	42.0	23	118
Delaware	4	42.0	33	41
California	6	39.0	1	1,209
Colorado	7	31.0	22	127
Michigan	7	31.0	5	573
Maryland	9	29.0	11	202
Ohio	9	29.0	4	616
Washington, D.C.	11	27.0	35	40
New Jersey	11	27.0	9	331
Connecticut	13	26.0	21	130
New Mexico	13	26.0	29	61
Texas	13	26.0	3	619
Utah	13	26.0	29	61
Illinois	17	25.0	6	532
Indiana	18	24.0	10	264
Kansas	19	23.0	24	113
Washington	19	23.0	17	148
Louisiana	21	22.0	14	177
Montana	21	22.0	36	37
Wisconsin	23	21.0	12	198
Minnesota	24	20.0	16	163
New York	24	20.0	2	685
Oregon	24	20.0	26	83
Virginia	27	19.0	13	186
Missouri	28	18.0	15	170
Nebraska	28	18.0	29	61
New Hampshire	28	18.0	42	23
Rhode Island	28	18.0	39	33
Wyoming	28	18.0	47	14
Hawaii	33	16.0	41	24
Pennsylvania	34	15.0	8	371
South Dakota	34	15.0	40	26
Georgia	36	14.0	19	146
Massachusetts	36	14.0	18	147
Iowa	38	13.0	25	88
Idaho	39	12.0	44	20
South Carolina	39	12.0	27	81
North Carolina	41	11.0	20	132
Maine	42	10.0	43	22
North Dakota	43	9.0	45	16
Tennessee	44	8.0	28	70
Vermont	45	6.0	49	6
Alabama	46	5.0	32	42
Kentucky	46	5.0	33	41
Mississippi	48	2.0	46	15
Oklahoma	48	2.0	47	14
West Virginia	50	−4.0	50	−20
Arkansas	51	−8.0	51	−39

have been the oldest and the youngest age groups. It is estimated that the burden of education resting upon the American people in 1960 was 35 percent heavier than it was in 1950. Following World War I and the depression of the 1930s, the birth rate dropped precipitately in the United States. Following World War II, the pattern of fertility among the population of child-bearing age steadily climbed until new heights in fertility were reached. Before these years net reproductive rates had been steadily falling. During the 1950s, this trend was reversed, and as a result the United States faced an acute problem of how to establish and maintain schools that were equal to the task of caring for the increase in school population.

POPULATION PREDICTION

Total school population fluctuates largely because of variations in the birth rate; these, in turn, reflect such social factors as wars and depressions, which are accompanied by intense psychological effects. Inasmuch as these causative factors cannot be predicted nor their psychological effects foreseen, it is obviously hazardous to make more than short-time predictions of school population. For example, in 1940 the birth rate was 19.4 per 1,000. Fifteen years later, in 1955, the rate had increased to 25.0. After this a decrease set in, and the birth rate in 1967 hit a new low of 17.8. To put this another way, whereas in 1960, 4,258,000 children were born, in 1967, only 3,533,000 were born. In 1960, or 1966, a fairly accurate prediction of the number of children to be provided with places in kindergartens five years later could be made. However, a similar prediction made, say, for 1980 would likely have a much larger degree of error because it would have to be based partly on guesses relative to such items as future social attitudes, economic conditions, governmental policy toward immigration and education (see Fig. 10.3). Despite these unknowns and uncertainties, there is no escaping the responsibility for planning education for the future.

DIFFERENTIALS

There are marked differences in birth rates between the communities within a state, between states, and between different regions of

*T*he National Center for Educational Statistics, U. S. Office of Education, regularly publishes 10-year projections of the most important educational statistics, including enrollment in public and private elementary and secondary schools. These projections, which are based on assumptions made about future fertility rates, are updated every year to incorporate new information and the trends it indicates. Thus the nation is kept well informed concerning its future responsibilities for elementary and secondary education. The Office of Education's projections are, of course, based on the population projections made annually by the Bureau of the Census; the Bureau of the Census, in turn, bases its projections on four slightly different assumptions with respect to birth rates—assumptions A, B, C, and D, with A representing the highest rate of fertility and D the lowest. As the years go by and the data are checked against the actual birth rate, the projections become increasingly accurate for public school enrollment.

The following projections from 1969 to 1977 are based on assumption D, which is that a fertility rate approximating that of the early 1940s will prevail throughout the period :

YEAR	K–8	9–12
1969	32,100,000	13,100,000
1970	32,100,000	13,500,000
1971	31,800,000	13,900,000
1972	31,400,000	14,300,000
1973	30,800,000	14,600,000
1974	30,300,000	14,800,000
1975	29,700,000	15,100,000
1976	29,200,000	15,200,000
1977	28,900,000	15,200,000

If the projections hold true, and they probably will not be far off, the maximum enrollment in Grades K–8 will be reached in 1969, after which there will be a slight decline. The high school enrollment, however, will continue to increase.

The projections for nonpublic schools show enrollment in K–8 constant at 4,500,000 from 1969 to 1977 and enrollment in 9–12 constant at 1,000,000 for the same period.

Incidentally, these data apply to the nation as a whole. States can, however, if they wish, project their school enrollments by using the techniques employed by the federal government.

National Center for Educational Statistics, Office of Education, U. S. Department of Health, Education, and Welfare, *Projections of Educational Statistics to 1977–78*.

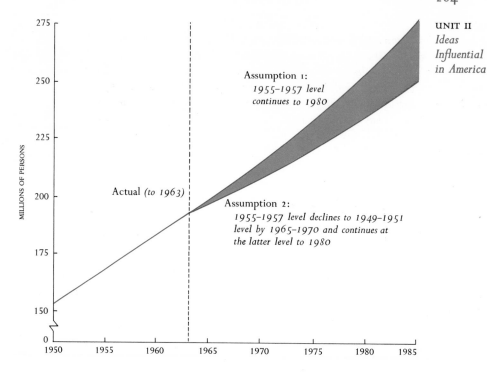

Fig. 10.3 Two population projections made in 1963 for the United States. In 1968, the actual population was 200 million; therefore, up to then, Assumption 2 seemed to be proving to be the more valid one. But later actual population figures will more definitely validate one assumption or the other. (Data from National Industrial Conference Board, Road Maps of Industry, *No. 1472)*

the nation. These differences have been great enough to create considerable inequality in education. No one can predict how long these regional and state differences in fertility will continue; however, it does seem logical to believe that there must come a time when they will level off. That time, however, seems to be in the somewhat unpredictable future. In the past, fertility rates have been lowest in the regions of highest income, thus accentuating the degree of educational inequality. Obviously, if future economic policies toward educational support tend to mitigate the effects of differentials in income in different regions, the regional and state differentials in birth rates will no longer present so great a problem for education. Currently the problem is a serious one. Where standards of living are the lowest, fertility rates are the highest; and where education should be strong, it is sometimes pathetically weak.

EFFECT ON EDUCATION

Population growth affects education in many ways. Noticeable is the very uneven demand for education arising at various educational levels because of precipitate fluctuations in the rate of growth. For example, the decline in high school population that followed the Great Depression amounted in some cities to school enrollment declines of 30, 40, and even 50 percent. At that time public school districts that had previously faced a shortage of well-prepared high school teachers found themselves with a large surplus of teachers on tenure. In 20 short years following 1940, the number of births in America rose from 2,360,000 to 4,258,000; and, by and large, schools had to be organized for all these children. In 1966, however, the number was back to 3,360,000 and continuing to decline. The year 1950 found kindergarten enrollments overflowing facilities. As they proceeded through the grades, many of these pupils discovered that crowded classrooms were always with them. The schools, relying as they do on public support, have often found it impossible to keep up with uneven educational demands.

A sharp upward trend in school enrollments, such as the ones in the 1950s and 1960s, makes necessary a general, rapid increase in material and human resources for education. To supply these needs quickly is difficult. To prepare and recruit the required additional teachers, for instance, takes time. New buildings and up-to-date equipment also take time to acquire. Rapid growth in school enrollments oftentimes, therefore, finds schools unprepared and the teachers less well trained, handling heavier teaching loads—perhaps outside their field of training or specialization—and teaching in overcrowded classrooms.

During inflationary times such as the 1960s, the cost of education rises precipitately, adding greatly to the problem of keeping pace with new demands and glaringly revealing that traditional systems of school support are inadequate and outmoded. If public education were the only problem the various governments had to meet, the problem of the cost of education would perhaps be solved. Unfortunately, education problems are only one kind of problem vying for financial help from federal, state, and local governments. Tax policies, often adopted many years ago when the state constitutions were written, are clearly out of date. A state tax system and a state's policy of financial aid to its school districts considered unsatisfactory to support its public school districts in, say, 1945, when most of the 2,360,000 children born five years earlier were entering kindergarten, was severely tested and in many cases shown to be patently inadequate when well over 4 million entered kindergarten in 1965. The same old taxes and formulas that have been the state's answer to school support for many years need to be adapted not only to population variations but also to rising costs. Tax systems are related to social unrest and social crises, though the necessity for changes is usually apparent considerably before it is politically possible to make them.

While many difficult educational problems are related to population changes, these very changes may also be related to a measure of continuing progress that is evident. The crises that at first were met with temporary emergency measures led to many wholesome changes that promise with time to be lasting benefits: better schools in financially poor districts, improved schools for the disadvantaged child of the cities, a move toward better racial balance in enrollment, teaching innovations and experimentation, improved facilities. At the same time, the teaching profession has become more militant, seeking to realize its long-established right to participate in decision making. Population changes and their concomitant problems have given impetus to modifications in the power structure in public education.

Perhaps the most hopeful of the positive results of social crises that are in part related to population problems has been a new and marked sensitiveness of the American people to their educational needs. At present, education has become a matter of first priority at all levels of government, of such vital importance that it can be expected to receive top consideration in future social planning. This planning will include answering such questions as: Will there be an expansion of average school attendance, say, through the junior college years? Will the school year be extended to 48 weeks to allow staggering of vacation periods and better use of school facilities? Will school districts be reorganized in terms of size and enrollment to improve school administration? Will the state and federal governments relieve the tax-burdened local citizens by revising the personal and property tax systems?

That such questions are in the minds not only of the education profession but of many lay people also indicates at least some predisposition toward changes that promise increasing future improvements. It seems likely, also, that the population will include an increasing proportion of educated people—see Fig. 10.4. This will automatically increase the number of lay people who will not only be predisposed toward, but will actively work for, improvements in our educational system. As the Bureau of the Census put it, in commenting on the data used in Fig. 10.4,

> Rising rates of enrollment in the past have been accompanied by a lengthening of the number of years spent in school. Increased schooling will lead in turn to a rising level of educational attainment for the American people as older generations are replaced by younger ones with more education.

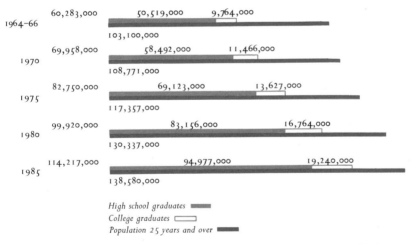

Fig.10.4 Educational status in the United States. Actual and projected numbers of high school and college graduates compared with the actual and projected population aged 25 and over. The combined totals—high school and college graduates—are to the left of the bars. (Data from U. S. Department of Commerce, Bureau of the Census, Projections of Educational Attainment, 1970–1985, Series P-25, No. 390)

Contemporary frontiers

Our brief examination of the contemporary social scene shows the dynamic nature of the social picture but leaves us with a somewhat uneasy feeling. Where will the trends lead?

In one sense the trends are facts. They are the bases upon which action must be built. They are factors that should be taken duly into account but that are nonetheless ignored or slighted. We know in advance, for instance, that the children who are two years of age are destined to go to school three years hence. We know, too, that the chances are that when they go to school, the schools will not be ready for them. It is true that societal change is somewhat unpredictable, but that is no excuse for a complete lack of preparation for probable changes.

Contemporary frontiers are not in the form of free lands and abundant natural resources. They are not the border lines between settled and unsettled regions of a country. They are the unexplored regions of knowledge, the untried institutional practices. Just as physical frontiers were pushed back, so likewise will new educational frontiers in America be explored and developed.

Education in America faces a new and somewhat uncharted frontier. The psychologists have strengthened Rousseau's contention that efficient education should be in accordance with the child's nature. In the face of antagonistic traditions, can the schools modify to conform with this now almost two-century-old dictum? Will technology, as some people seem to think, be able to individualize education? Are the principles of education for social living set down by Froebel accepted by current educators? What the Americans of today and of the future make of education may be as surprising as were the achievements of the earlier frontiersmen.

Emerging frontiers

Since education always has had to adjust to social changes, it seems sound to assume that such adaptations will continue in the future. What are some of the foreseeable future events that will lead to social

Telstar, the first communications satellite, raised hopes for the future. One may watch live television every day from around the world; see the rest of the world at work and play; see news as it happens around the world; see people all over the world—how they frown, how they smile. They'll see us— and we'll know each other a little better—which we critically need to do in these days when mass destruction has become possible.

Television by satellite will be everybody's window on the world—and bring us all closer together.

. . . let's look ahead for a minute to the day when our ventures into space will lead us to interplanetary traffic—when we'll be able to make round trips to far distant planets—you do hear some questions raised about what *might make such travel worthwhile.*

What commerce might profitably flow over such awesome distances? There is one commodity, a very special kind, well suited to interplanetary commerce. It weighs nothing. It travels cheaply at the speed of light. That commodity is communication.

To be of value, information requires communication.

From a television presentation by the Bell Telephone Company, "Telstar and Tomorrow," September 1, 1962.

change and necessitate educational adaptations? Coming events are said to cast their shadows before them. What are the events forecast by the shadows we see today?

First, consider the rapidity with which space exploration is developing. The earth has now been orbited many times—and men have landed on the moon itself. Plans are being made to send explorers to the planets. From this, it is expected that much will be learned about the age and origin of the earth. With an immense modern telescope man can see into space a distance of 200 million light years. Radio telescopes enable him to see much farther. From the moon his vision will be even clearer. Space exploration, now in its infancy, will bring much new knowledge. Can we anticipate, from what we now know, what kind of new knowledge we shall attain? What changes in thinking and learning by children will result? Will children need to learn more in less time? If new knowledges are brought into the curriculum, some of the older subject matters will have to be dropped. How will these new knowledges affect the preparation of teachers? Will the present classifications of subject matter remain unchanged? Will new names be used to identify the new subject matters?

Think of some of the developments man has made in the realm of energy. The energy famine that threatened mankind for many years is past. Man need no longer depend wholly upon the resources nature stored beneath the surface of the earth millions of years ago—resources which man has lavishly wasted, largely in waging wars. The potential effect of nuclear power on man's future can only be conjectured. In addition to nuclear energy there remains for man the possibility of creatively appropriating the energy of the sun and of the ocean waves.

How about travel in the future? Will new means of transportation affect man's relations throughout the world? His educational requirements? Speed is now the key emphasis in travel. The jet plane has diminished physical distance in earth travel. As the wheel and axle eliminated the skid some thousands of years ago, so are modern developments in modes of travel eliminating the wheel. The so-called VTOP (vertical take-off plane) and huge airplane buses, presage still further changes in travel.

We have noted that the home is a changed and changing place. Mechanization and the availability of processed foods have eliminated much of the drudgery of housekeeping. Short wave, hi-fi, and television have made the home a center for entertainment. It is said, perhaps with some degree of truth, that American people spend as much time watching television as they spend on their jobs. Will the future find families with more leisure becoming more closely knit as family units centered in the home?

What does the future promise in the area of human relations? We see the "Dark Continent" emerging to a place of prominence. We see nations becoming increasingly aware of the necessity of working together on tasks to achieve modernization, to formulate joint policies for economic and social progress, to open wide the doors for education of the masses, to develop a climate of peace, and to create a new and brighter picture of international cooperation for the elevation of mankind. Will the efforts be fruitful in raising the level of human relations among all the peoples of the world? How will the schools fit into the picture?

How will new knowledge and understandings accruing from areas like those mentioned affect education? New knowledge so

*In 1921 James Harvey Robinson, a historian, discussed how far the human
race has advanced in applying the method of critical thinking to human
affairs.*

> *Human affairs are in themselves far more intricate and perplexing than
> molecules and chromosomes. But this is only the more reason for bringing
> to bear on human affairs that critical type of thought and calculation
> for which the remunerative thought about molecules and chromosomes
> has prepared the way.*
> *I do not for a moment suggest that we can use precisely the same kind
> of thinking in dealing with the quandaries of mankind that we use in
> problems of mechanical reaction and mechanical adjustment. Exact
> scientific results are, of course, out of the question. It would be
> unscientific to expect to apply them. I am not advocating any particular
> method of treating human affairs, but rather such a* general frame of
> mind, such a critical open-minded attitude, *as has hitherto been
> but sparsely developed among those who aspire to be men's guides . . .*

James Harvey Robinson, *The Mind in the Making*. New York: Harper & Row, 1921,
p. 12. Quoted by permission of the publisher.

tested that it merits the appellation "scientific knowledge" is rapidly
accumulating in all fields of learning. Much knowledge that now exists
was not included in the textbooks studied by many of today's adults.
Much that today's adults have learned has been learned after they left
school. The expansion of knowledge promises to continue. What will
this mean for education in the future? Note the characteristics of new
knowledge as described by a renowned scientist.

> To sum up the characteristics of scientific knowledge today, then, I
> would say that it is mostly new; it has not been digested; it is not part of
> man's common knowledge; it has become the property of specialized com-
> munities who may on occasion help one another but who, by and large,
> pursue their own way with growing intensity further and further from
> their roots in ordinary life.[1]

In one's own picture of the foreseeable future one may include

[1] Robert Oppenheimer, "Tree of Knowledge," *Harper's Magazine*, 217: 57, October,
1958.

such details as travel beneath the oceans by nuclear-propelled sub-marine, cities transforming sea water into usable fresh water, a nation of people with leisure time so increased by the development of automation that citizens are largely free to engage in self-chosen occupations. Regardless of how one looks at the future, however, of how one predicts man's ascendancy over his physical environment, it is inevitable that the problem of what happens to the individual will be a major concern of education. As invention and discovery force man to reorganize his way of life, how will he use his time? Will he learn to be creative? to rise to new heights in science, in the arts, in the human-ities, to develop a higher level of social intelligence? In short, will new knowledge lead to enrichment, or will it lead to frustration, impover-ishment, and conflict? The responsibility for providing guidance and doing the very best possible to develop insights and understandings to equip generations to meet new challenges and cope with new problems rests with education.

Summary

The contemporary social scene, along with influences of streams of thought from the past and from various leaders, plays its dynamic part in making education what it is today and in shaping what it will become. The contemporary is, after all, only episodic; it is fleeting and changing. Each generation, in each decade, has its own peculiar problems, problems that appear to be crucial at the time. The problems and their solutions are inevitably related to time, place, and circum-stance.

Features of the contemporary social scene are selected to illustrate their impact on today's education. Problems of international relations continue in a somewhat paradoxical setting. The world is shrinking, but social distances among the peoples of the world may even be increasing. How do the schools respond? What new responsibilities are produced?

Expanding technology and its growing influence on education are significant. The changes affect relative prestige on a social scale, changes in methods of teaching, and changes in goals for an education that must take into account greater leisure for all people and the necessity for flexibility for rapid changes in career requirements. Economic cycles, the prosperity of business, and the economic welfare of the people are reflected in the schools. Pressure groups play their part in determining the contemporary setting of the schools and in influencing education. Family disruption and community disequilibrium affect the lives of boys and girls and require many adaptations in the schools. Throughout the following chapters of the book, aspects of education are studied in the light of these and other features of the contemporary social scene.

Being conscious of the importance of seeing education against the backdrop of contemporary social life, noting the changes that have followed such social factors as those selected for this chapter, the student may go on to reflect on ever-changing features of a dynamic society. Such current issues as "black power," the "generation gap," "campus unrest," "urban reorganization," "federal funds"—terms associated with some of today's problems—may tomorrow give way to another list of problems. Always, however, the schools will be influenced by all such factors; they will be challenged to adjust to changes and they will be responsible for preparing oncoming citizens to solve *their* contemporary problems and to aid in social progress.

Questions

1. How are the two social phenomena, mobility and technology, related?
2. How have the two current social trends, uniformity and standardization, seemingly affected educational practice?
3. In your opinion, how far should education go toward contributing to the solution of a contemporary social problem?
4. In what respects does education contribute to increased social mobility?
5. To what degree and in what ways should teachers give social direction to the achievements of pupils?

6. What are some present-day mental hazards of American youth? What are some of the problems these mental hazards introduce into the high schools?
7. Why is it difficult for a state to change its system of taxation to meet new educational demands?
8. What are the implications for education of the travel times made possible by faster planes as predicted by the diagram below?

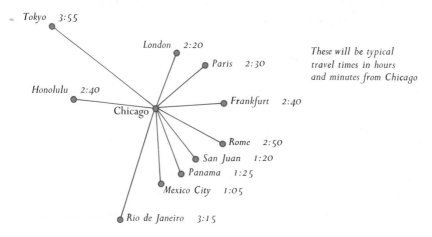

Tokyo   3:55

London   2:20

Paris   2:30

Honolulu   2:40

Frankfurt   2:40

Chicago

Rome   2:50

San Juan   1:20

Panama   1:25

Mexico City   1:05

Rio de Janeiro   3:15

These will be typical travel times in hours and minutes from Chicago

Projects

1. List eight major social trends and show some effects of each on education in America's schools.
2. Explain how the later discoveries about hydrogen in the universe influence the education of the young.
3. Give an illustration of automation and explain how this kind of development may affect education in the future.
4. Read one of the following books: *Death at an Early Age* by Jonathan Kozol (Houghton Mifflin, 1967); *Thirty-six Children* by Herbert Kohl (New American Library, 1967); *How Children Fail* or *How Children Learn* by John Holt (Pitman, 1964 and 1967). Discuss the difficulties in teaching the culturally disadvantaged that are portrayed. Discuss the deficiencies in teaching such children that are also described.

5. Explain what steps need to be taken to make the education of children in the economically depressed areas of America's larger cities socially and educationally effective.

6. Alfred North Whitehead once said, "The major advances in civilization are processes that all but wreck the societies in which they occur." Describe
   (a) how new inventions in communications—e.g., electronics—have affected what pupils have learned;
   (b) how this widened learning influences their learning in school;
   (c) problems that confront the teacher who attempts to adjust his teaching to the educative effects of the present media of communication.

7. If, as the historians Nevins and Commager contend, the American people have suffered great losses because of the corporation trend, explain what these losses are.

Unit II   Suggested Readings

ADAMS, JAMES TRUSLOW, *The Epic of America*. New York: Blue Ribbon, 1931. Chapter 10 tells the story of the end of the frontier.

ANGLE, PAUL M., *The American Reader*. Chicago: Rand McNally, 1958, Chap. XXII and pp. 555–558. Dr. Angle dramatically describes the plight of the farmer in the depression years of 1931–1933. Even with the aid of such an analysis, it is difficult for those who did not experience the Great Depression to realize how deeply a generation can be affected by an economic cycle such as characterized the United States in the early thirties.

BREASTED, JAMES HENRY, *The Conquest of Civilization*. New York: Harper & Row, 1926. Chapter 15 contains a scholarly description of Athens in the Age of Pericles. Shows how education was related to the training of citizens.

BUFFUM, WILLIAM B., "The UN at Twenty: An Instrument for International Cooperation," *Social Education*, 30 (No. 1): 13–18, 27, January, 1966. The author, Deputy Assistant Secretary of State for International Affairs, reviews some of the accomplishments and problems of the United Nations. Teacher responsibility in helping to achieve world peace is pointed out.

CLARK, BURTON R., *Educating the Expert Society*. San Francisco: Chandler, 1962. Chapter 2, "Education, Occupation, and Status," explains how education defines the "life chances" of individuals and groups.

COLES, ROBERT, "What Migrant Children Learn," *Saturday Review*, pp. 73–74, 88–89, May 15, 1965. This analysis of the plight of the children of migrant workers made by a child psychiatrist is based upon a two-year study of this disadvantaged group. ". . . regional networks of schools are badly needed, many of them mobile, all staffed by teachers specifically concerned with the customs and beliefs of the rural poor, white and Negro."

CONANT, JAMES B., *Slums and Suburbs*. New York: McGraw-Hill, 1961, 147 pp. The author contrasts public school education received in two kinds of neighborhoods: city slums and wealthy suburbs. "The lesson is that to a considerable degree what a school should do and can do is determined by the status and ambitions of the families being served."

EBY, FREDERICK, and CHARLES FLINN ARROWOOD, *The History and Philosophy of Education, Ancient and Medieval*. New York: Prentice-Hall, 1940. This thorough and authoritative treatment constitutes an excellent source for reference to any specific period. The effects of the three social movements described in Chapter 7 of this text—the Athenian, the Christian, and the Renaissance—are covered in the best of scholarly tradition. The student should consult the table of contents for specific reference.

EGGLESTON, EDWARD, *The Hoosier Schoolmaster: A Story of Backwoods Life in Indiana*. New York: Orange Judd, 1871. A novel that gives an authentic description of a frontier school.

FRANKEL, CHARLES, *The Case for Modern Man*. New York: Harper & Row, 1955. Chapter 10 contains an excellent analysis of the causes and effects of modern social change. In just 13 pages Frankel shows the impact of contemporary social change on institutions.

GOODLAD, JOHN I., "The Schools vs. Education," *Saturday Review*, pp. 59–61, 80–82, April 19, 1969. The author attempts to answer: Where are the schools today? What kind of changes will be needed in the 1970s? What lies ahead for the rest of the century? Emphasis is on the elementary schools, especially the earlier grades.

JAMES, MARQUIS, *Andrew Jackson*. Indianapolis: Bobbs-Merrill, 1933. Chapter I gives a vivid picture of the kind of environment in which many children of early settlers developed.

JENNINGS, FRANK G., "It Didn't Start with Sputnik," *Saturday Review*, pp. 77–79, 95–96, September 16, 1967. By tracing the history of educational change the author shows that the revolution in education has been and will be continuous. He concludes "Although progressive education died, as all movements must, it left a modest but most precious legacy."

NEA Journal, "Education and the Disadvantaged American," 51 (No. 4): pp. 8–12, 33–40, April, 1962. Shows that there are still schools in America as barren as the worst of the frontier schools.

Heavily illustrated pages 33–40. This is a summary of an extensive report by the Educational Policies Commission of the NEA. It shows that some of the problems of providing satisfactory education to the disadvantaged are beyond the powers of educators alone to solve.

PAGE, WALTER HINES, *The School That Built a Town.* New York: Harper & Row, 1952. Reprints of two addresses and one article by Walter Hines Page which explain the basis for his strong faith in democracy, and in education to strengthen democracy. An example of the kind of thinking done by the most intelligent of lay leaders.

PARKER, SAMUEL CHESTER, *A Textbook in the History of Modern Elementary Education.* Boston: Ginn, 1912. Chapter 5, "Development of American Secular School Systems," is an excellent treatment showing how the schools became secularized during the frontier period of American history. Parker's description of secularization as it took place in New York State is especially revealing.

ROBINSON, JAMES HARVEY, *The Ordeal of Civilization.* New York: Harper & Row, 1926. Pages 184–193 describe the Italian cities of the Renaissance, in which learning and art developed to a height undreamed of north of the Alps.

SCHRAG, PETER, "Kids, Computers, and Corporations," *Saturday Review*, pp. 78–80, 93–96, May 20, 1967. An analysis of the entrance of large corporations into the field of education in the manufacture of programed learning devices. Predictions for the future are made in the last three paragraphs.

ULICH, ROBERT, *History of Educational Thought.* New York: American Book, 1945. Pages 61–71 contain an excellent discussion, by a historian, of Jesus Christ as a teacher.

WEBB, WALTER PRESSOTT, *The Great Frontier.* Boston: Houghton Mifflin, 1952. Chapters 1 and 12 and pages 84–85 contain, respectively, an analysis of the frontier factor in modern history, a description of education in its relation to the corporate age, and a discussion of how the frontier influenced education.

WEINBERG, MEYER, *Integrated Education.* Los Angeles: Glencoe Press, 1968. This collection of some 50 articles, addresses, and documents selected from issues of the magazine *Integrated Education* surveys various aspects of this increasingly important contemporary problem in American education.

III

The Schools in America

Up to this point we have studied, first, the teacher in his place in American education, noting some elements that tend to increase his satisfaction in his work and others that tend to diminish it. Second, we have studied certain ideas, customs, traditions, and laws that have shared in making contemporary education in our country what it is. Now, in Unit III, we study directly, in three chapters, the three closely interrelated, interdependent levels of government—state, local, and federal—in their relationships with education. Each state has the heaviest responsibility for education within its boundaries; therefore, we examine first what the states do with respect to control over and support of education, following this with examinations of local aspects of educational organization and administration and then educational activities of the federal government.

Authority over education in America is divided, and this characteristic alone causes some confusion among average Americans about where the ultimate authority should be and what should be the relative roles of the three levels of government. Up to the present, in the minds of the citizens, the issue over relative roles has never been even partially settled. The issue is, in fact, livelier than it ever has been. Although these roles are constantly shifting in clearly identifiable directions, where the trends will ultimately lead seems to be anybody's guess.

In an earlier chapter it was pointed out that members of the teaching profession need to be sufficiently informed so that they may lead the public to a mature and intelligent view of what education in the United States should and could be, what it needs in order to build and maintain an excellent system of schools. The average classroom teacher is often so absorbed in his daily teaching duties that he tends to overlook his personal responsibility to help build a strong, potent education profession that can render broad educational leadership. Nevertheless, it is those who are responsible for the everyday duties of directing the vast educational undertaking who are in the best position to influence educational trends. The profession must be able to count on informed members who are actively concerned, and this concern must be based on sound understandings, including the kinds of understandings of the school system explored in the first three of the following chapters.

State
Public
School
Systems

The Constitution of the United States separates the powers of the federal and state governments. The Tenth Amendment to the Constitution (1791) reads: "The powers not delegated to the United States by the Constitution, nor prohibited by it to the States, are reserved to the States, respectively, or to the people." The power of education is not delegated by the Constitution to the Congress, nor is it prohibited by the Constitution to the states. It therefore remains legally the right of the state legislatures to organize and administer education within the respective states.

Each state legislature has developed its own plan for administering education, and consequently state systems vary. It is obviously beyond the scope of this book to describe each state system. Instead, what states have done in general about education, paths followed, common structural elements, common problems, and some proposed plans for the future are explored. We begin by considering the legal structure that guides or controls actions of the state legislatures.

Legal structure

As each state provided for education in its own constitution and from time to time passed laws relating to education within the state, it developed a legal structure. This legal structure includes the constitution, which is the fundamental or basic law of a state, subsequent legislation, and the decisions and precedents established by judicial review.

STATE CONSTITUTIONS

Each state has a written constitution which follows, in general, the pattern set by the federal government. It provides for the popular election of a legislature and an executive—a governor—and for a system of state courts. Theoretically, the governor is free from the dominance of legislators because he is elected directly by the people. He is the titular head of his political party in the state. What the executive head favors with regard to public and private education, therefore, will be influential in determining how education will fare under his executive and his partisan leadership. Thus education in a state depends somewhat upon the party in power. In all the states the welfare of education, especially in the long run, is determined by the kinds of citizens who, by popular vote, are elected to the state legislatures.

All the state constitutions contain provisions for public education. Some of our current attitudes and prevailing traditions can be traced to statements about education found in some of the original state constitutions. Section 44 of the Pennsylvania constitution, adopted in 1776, said:

> A school or schools shall be established in every county by the legis-
> lature, for the convenient instruction of youth, with such salaries to the
> masters, paid by the public, as may enable them to instruct youth at low
> prices; and all useful learning shall be duly encouraged and promoted in
> one or more universities.

The constitutions of North Carolina of 1776 and 1835 contained an almost identical provision. The emphasis on ''low prices'' to the public occurs in the constitutions of several other states. The Vermont constitution of 1787, for instance, provided:

> Section XL. A school or schools shall be established in every town,
> by the legislature, for the convenient instruction of youth, with such
> salaries to the masters, paid by each town; making proper use of school
> lands in each town, thereby enabling them to instruct youth at low prices.

A different pattern is found in the constitutions of states admitted to the Union later. Section 2 of the Indiana constitution, adopted in 1816, read:

It shall be the duty of the general assembly, as soon as circum-stances will permit, to provide by law for a general system of education, ascending in regular gradation from township schools to a State university, wherein tuition shall be gratis, and equally open to all.

Although it is evident that the states borrowed from one another in their constitutional provisions for public education, the systems of education that evolved later are the product of various interpretations and implementations by successive state legislatures. Considering, for instance, that the present constitution of Illinois was adopted in 1870 and geared to conditions very different from those of today, it is perhaps fortunate that the actual educational policies of the state have been determined by its succession of state legislators.

STATE LEGISLATURES

Each legislature in each state passes school laws. Typically, citizens differ about how to solve specific problems of education—the trans-portation of pupils, for example. The state legislators may have public hearings, conduct research, weigh various suggestions, and then pass a law defining a uniform policy for the entire state. Throughout the state pupils will be transported for school purposes in a way that conforms to this law.

The laws in each state, determining such important matters as how public education shall be organized and administered, what the structure of authority shall be, how schools shall be financed, make it clear that actually the state legislature is the supreme policy maker for education in the state. Each new legislature, often characterized by considerable change in membership, passes new laws related to education or modifies old laws.

Generally speaking, these state laws are of two kinds: mandatory and permissive. Mandatory laws are to be followed uniformly through-out the state and concern such matters as districting, pupil transporta-tion, and school taxation. Permissive laws give local school-governing bodies the right, within state-established limits, to use judgment, make interpretations, and determine implementations in terms of a particular situation. Matters related to salary provisions, security provisions for

The attitude toward education characteristic of the times is reflected in a law passed in 1647 in Massachusetts which has often been called the "Old Deluder Satan Act." It is quoted with the original spelling.

> *It being one chiefe project of the ould deluder, Satan, to keepe men from the knowledge of the Scriptures, as in former times by keeping them in an unknowne tongue, so in these latter times by perswading from the use of tongues, that so at least the true sence & meaning of the originall might be clouded by false glosses of saint seeming deceivers, that learning may not be buried in the grave of our fathers in the church and commonwealth, the Lord assisting our endeavours,—*
> *It is therefore ordered, that every towneship in this jurisdiction, after the Lord hath increased their number to 50 householders, shall then forthwith appoint one within their towne to teach all such children as shall resort to him to write & reade, whose wages shall be paid either by the parents or masters of such children, or by the inhabitants in generall, by way of supply, as the major part of those that order the prudentials the towne shall appoint ; provided, those that send their children be not oppressed by paying much more than they can have them taught for in other townes ; & it is further ordered, that where any towne shall increase to the number of 100 families or householders, they shall set up a grammer schoole, the master thereof being able to instruct youth so farr as they shall be fitted for the university, provided, that if any towne neglect the performance hereof above one yeare, that every such towne shall pay 5 pounds to the next schoole till they shall performe this order.*

Two centuries later, Horace Mann paid eloquent tribute to the law in his tenth annual report (1846) as secretary of the Massachusetts State Board of Education. He said, in part : "It is impossible for us adequately to conceive the boldness of the measure which aimed at universal education through the establishment of free schools. . . . [This] was one of those grand mental and moral experiments whose effects could not be developed and made manifest in a single generation."

personnel, school building requirements, location of building sites, are the types of subjects covered in permissive laws. In all cases, however, local authorities are required to comply with both the spirit and the formal requirements of a law, whether mandatory or permissive.

STATE SCHOOL CODES

In time, all the school laws of a state are brought together and published, making them easily accessible. The systematic collection of all the laws in force, together with judicial opinions and court decisions, makes up the state school code. Usually this published volume is quite sizable, technical, and detailed. For example, there will be an accumulation of many laws regarding such matters as compulsory school attendance, maximum liabilities of school districts, standards for teacher certification, charters for private schools, consolidation of school districts, the building and maintenance of school buildings, taxation for the maintenance of the schools, and policies toward pupil transportation—to name but a few.

Broadly speaking, the relations of American private and public schools to American society and to the pupils in the schools are defined in the state school codes. Nowhere else is there so complete and dependable a source of information about schools. The state school code is a valuable book of reference but, since much of it is expressed in legal terms, it is usually consulted only when special problems arise that call for legal answers—for instance, "What is the teacher's obligation to children taken on a field trip?" By going through the state school code, however, a classroom teacher can discover the nature and extent of school law in the state and may profit especially by noting those laws that apply to activities of classroom teachers. Direct acquaintance with school codes will impress a teacher with the importance of always acting within the limits prescribed by the law.

The Research Division of the NEA annually reports and interprets certain selected state laws that have been reviewed by the courts in cases involving teachers or schools—in suits for negligence, for instance. These court decisions, together with the analyses made by the judges, give information of professional interest. The cases selected by the NEA concern specific situations that have arisen, but they are representative of situations that might arise in connection with other schools, classrooms, or teachers.[1]

---

[1] See NEA, Research Report 1967–R6, *The Teacher's Day in Court, Review of 1966*, and NEA Research Report, 1967–R7, *The Pupil's Day in Court, Review of 1966*.

The policy of an individual state toward public education is, then, expressed in the constitution and in the specific laws passed by legislatures. The state constitution is the fundamental law. State legislatures are subject to restrictions placed upon them by the constitutions. The final authority to decide whether a state law is constitutional or unconstitutional belongs to the state court of highest appeal, usually called the supreme court. The state supreme courts may also invalidate an action of a state board or department of education.

As we shall see in a later chapter, the United States Supreme Court sometimes gets into the picture. A conflict over the way in which some state legislature or some state supreme court has decided a matter may, under certain circumstances, be carried to the United States Supreme Court, where the justices render what is expected to be, at least for some years to come, a final decision. The word "final" is a relative term and should not be too strictly interpreted, especially in the case of court decisions concerning public education. State supreme courts have reversed themselves at times—and so has the Supreme Court itself.

State controls

BASIC ADMINISTRATIVE UNITS[2]

As pointed out, ultimate responsibility for public education is vested in the legislatures of the individual states. The controls over public education, therefore, vary from state to state. There are, however, common policies of control among the states, and one of these, familiar throughout the history of American education, is the policy of establishing basic administrative units for purposes of state control. The state exerts its legal authority through these units (as explored further in the next chapter). Since the framework of administrative units, or the structure for exercising state authority, is about

[2] This discussion is limited to public elementary and secondary school districts; junior colleges and state universities are briefly described in Chapter 15.

*These are both rural schools, but
that is all they have in common.
The La Porte, Indiana, Senior High
School, architecturally and
technologically modern, enrolls some
1,800. This regional school, which
replaces five old high schools,
resulted from district reorganization.
The one-room, one-teacher school
was built in Kansas in 1884. Most
of the pupils lived within a mile
and a half.*

the same in all the states, it is essential to understand the nature of these basic administrative units as a step toward understanding public education in America.

When the earliest schools were established, a political boundary line was set around each school, designating the area from which its children were to come; the citizens who would support and control the school would be those who lived within the area. This geographical area, or territorial political division, was called a school district. Essentially, this is what a school district still is. Over the years, of course, the states have seen fit to modify the character of school districts—to enlarge the area, include more schools, redefine the prerogatives, add to or take away some of the powers of control. This redefining of a district, as explained later, has been continuous throughout our history, and is even now proceeding at an accelerated rate.

The National Commission on School District Reorganization defines a school district thus:

> A basic unit of local school administration is an area in which a single board or officer has the immediate responsibility for the direct administration of all the schools located therein. Its distinguishing feature is that it is a quasi-corporation with a board or chief school officer that

has the responsibility for, and either complete or partial autonomy in, the administration of all public schools within its boundaries.

A clear understanding of this definition of the basic administrative unit requires some analysis. What is meant by referring to a state school district as a quasi-corporation? It operates like a corporation, as mentioned in Chapter 10, but it does not have articles of incorporation because it is an instrumentality of the state. It is operated under the laws of the state and is created to facilitate the administration of public education by the state government, to execute the state's policy. As the definition points out, the state's authority is executed through a board, or chief school officer, who, like any other important state school officer, is responsible to the state government.

Full agreement among the states as to the relationship between a public school elementary and/or secondary school district and other political divisions is lacking. It should be emphasized, however, that what the relationship is makes a great deal of difference in the way public school systems are organized and administered. The basic administrative units in 29 states are established by the respective state legislatures as *independent* of all other governmental units; in four states the school district has a dependent relationship to the political division in which it is located; in 17 states the relationship is a mixture of both, some being dependent while others are independent. Educational specialists in public school administration almost unanimously advocate the separation of public school districts from municipal corporations. They believe that the boundaries of school districts, the basic state administrative units, can be more logically defined if they can disregard political boundary lines, that the financing of education in the independent district is more favorably considered by a community when costs are not compared with those of other government departments, and that it is much easier to reorganize school districts that are independent of other political ties. Some political scientists, however, for very commendable reasons, believe otherwise. The fact that only four of our 50 states have established dependent districts seems to indicate that independent districts, at least in public opinion, seem best.

Before the present district system of elementary and/or secondary education began to prevail, the pattern set by the Massachusetts law of 1647 was followed. As the frontier moved westward, the northernmost states as far west as Kansas and the Dakotas established similar public school districts, typically one-teacher, one-room, eight-grade elementary schools, called "country schools." These contrasted with the school districts in small towns and in cities, which were allowed to establish complete systems, including secondary schools. Often the eighth-grade graduates of the rural schools were permitted to transfer to a nearby town or city school, their tuition being paid by the rural school district.

As the nation's population increased, the states were kept busy changing district boundaries to meet changing needs—about which more later. In the school year 1968–1969, however, there still remained 19,369 operating basic administrative units in this country. Six states—Nebraska, Illinois, Texas, South Dakota, California, and Minnesota, in that descending order—had almost 40 percent of these units (Nebraska alone had 1,589; Kansas, her "sister" state, only 330).

By and large, school districts in the states on the mainland vary greatly in size, school population, and financial support—that is, in quality of educational opportunities. One large city, for example, operates on a $400,000,000 budget, enrolls over 600,000 pupils, has 25,000 teachers, and 10,000 nonprofessional employees. In contrast, in 1969 there were still 1,037 nonoperating districts, districts that did not operate any school facility but functioned only to transfer their pupils to schools in operating districts.

All the states, in varying degrees, place responsibility for conducting the affairs of a school district on the citizens who live within the district. The way in which the states pass these responsibilities on to local citizens and how they are handled will be explained in the next chapter, which is devoted entirely to the subject of local school districts.

REORGANIZATION OF STATE BASIC ADMINISTRATIVE UNITS

Originally, except for the cities and towns, a district was just large enough to support a single one-room, one-teacher neighborhood

‒,507	
‒ 35,676	
04–65 28,777	
1967–68 21,890	
1968–69 20,406	

Fig. 11.1 Number of school districts, 1931–1969. The decline in the total number has been caused primarily by reorganization laws. (Data from NEA Research Report 1968-R16)

school. Eventually larger districts were organized and a number of eight-grade elementary schools were supported in one district. In Indiana, a whole township under a political trustee became the basic unit of school administration. Other states followed other patterns, but very early in American history the movement to enlarge public school districts got underway and has continued at an accelerating pace ever since. Thirty years ago there were more than 100,000 basic administrative units operating elementary and/or secondary schools. By 1969, as stated above, this had been reduced to fewer than 20,000 operating districts; and, as we have also noted, almost 40 percent of these were in six states, where reorganization started later and has proceeded more slowly than in some other sections of the country.

What criteria should be applied to determine whether an area is qualified to be or to continue as a basic state administrative unit to do the job of education? Most educational specialists would agree on the following:

1. a minimum enrollment of 1,500 pupils
2. a somewhat homogeneous population
3. sufficient taxing wealth to support:
    a. elementary schools and a high school
    b. such special services as health, guidance, and progams for the handicapped
    c. capable administrators and supervisors.

Organizing a school district so that it meets desirable standards of size and support-potential often means removing control over the

Fig. 11.2 Number of school districts, state by state, 1968–1969. (Data from NEA Research Report 1968-R16)

Nebraska	1	2,021
Illinois	2	1,279
Texas	3	1,244
South Dakota	4	1,210
California	5	1,095
Minnesota	6	1,000
New York	7	830
Montana	8	808
Missouri	9	750
Oklahoma	10	703
Michigan	11	654
Ohio	12	648
Pennsylvania	13	617
New Jersey	14	593
North Dakota	15	474
Wisconsin	16	465
Iowa	17	460
Massachusetts	18	405
Arkansas	19	391
Oregon	20	365
Indiana	21	357
Washington	22	337
Kansas	23	330
Maine	24	307
Arizona	25	297
Vermont	26	281
Kentucky	27	195
Georgia	28	194
Connecticut ⎫		181
Colorado ⎭ 29		181
New Hampshire	31	173
Wyoming	32	165
North Carolina	33	157
Tennessee	34	150
Mississippi	35	148
Virginia	36	134
Alabama	37	118
Idaho	38	117
South Carolina	39	93
New Mexico	40	89
Florida	41	67
Louisiana	42	66
West Virginia	43	55
Delaware	44	49
Rhode Island ⎫		40
Utah ⎭ 45		40
Alaska	47	28
Maryland	48	24
Nevada	49	17
Hawaii	50	1

*Transportation then and now:
Pupils used to be taken to school
by genuine horsepower. (As early
as 1869, Quincy, Massachusetts,
transported children to the public
schools; the appropriation that year
was $521.12.) Now school buses
have become a familiar feature of
American education in most parts
of the country, especially since the
number of school districts has been
reduced.*

schools farther and farther from the local citizens, placing it in the hands of fewer citizens, sacrificing some of the considerable advantages that accrue from fostering strong local interest in the schools. This has often led to conflict when efforts are being made to reorganize. The answer by the states seems to be to strike a reasonable balance between the size and efficiency of the district and the preservation of local interest and participation. As pointed out when we examined the contemporary scene, the trend toward consolidation of assets and resources of corporations is a typical current social development. The move by the states to centralize control over public education by enlarging the basic administrative units is consistent with this trend. Although this similarity does not prove that every effort to enlarge a school district is wise, it does indicate that the trend is not likely to be reversed.

The contemporary picture

The public school districts that have the greatest influence on education in America, that enroll by far the largest proportion of the pupils, can be classified into three groups: large-city school districts; suburban school districts; and reorganized districts in agricultural centers. Public education is peculiarly different in each of these.

The following discussion deals with these three kinds of districts, omitting the much smaller districts which, although rapidly declining in number and importance, still operate small schools in a number of states.

LARGE-CITY SCHOOL DISTRICTS

In present-day America, the school districts of large cities are to the educational world what the cities themselves are to the world in general. Usually, large-city school districts are laid out within the boundaries of the city, although, theoretically at least, they are independent quasi-corporations of the state. The responsibilities placed upon citizens who are appointed or elected to serve on a school board for the public school system in a large city are tremendous. The New York City School District enrolls well over a million pupils and administers a budget of over half a billion dollars. It takes a citizen of considerable ability and unusual civic dedication to share in the direction of such a system.

Currently, journalists—some are mentioned in the readings—are directing many harsh criticisms at America's large cities for their failure to provide adequate education for all pupils. Many criticisms are directed at the leadership of the schools, some at the teaching profession. It is often overlooked that, although educational leadership has at times been deficient, some of the problems faced in the schools today are the outgrowth of broad *social* problems. The city schools did not create the ghetto or disadvantaged pupils. They are not responsible for the extreme heterogeneity of the population. The schools can, with adequate financial and civic support, provide many new and increased services and improve their adaptation to the needs of all pupils. The schools cannot, however, revolutionize the current social climate. Among the biggest problems of the large cities are those related to the socioeconomic structure of their inner cities. Improvement in education in the inner cities is a challenge that the schools must meet.

It is not our purpose here to discuss or even list all the critical problems of education in large American cities today. The reader will find these problems pictured, discussed, analyzed in many current professional and popular journals and books. Some thought-provoking articles, presenting various points of view on controversial issues, are listed among the readings at the end of this unit. Some aspects of urban school problems are treated in our study of the activities of the federal government in Chapter 13.

SUBURBAN SCHOOL DISTRICTS

We have pointed out that more affluent and better-educated people move in great numbers from the large cities and settle in the suburbs, thus not only creating new, and presumably better, communities, but at the same time contributing to the social, economic, and educational impoverishment of the large cities.

The states have followed a variety of patterns in setting up new school districts in the new locations of rapidly growing populations. In some instances the new districts followed the pattern of the large cities, creating a single unified district with schools from kindergarten through high school and defining the school district boundaries as identical with those of the city-suburb. In other cases, the boundaries crossed over political boundary lines, thus allowing the school district to be more independent of the influence of a single municipal corporation. Others created small districts for the elementary schools but created enlarged districts for the sole operation of high school education. Generally speaking, the salary scale for teachers in the dual districts was lower in the elementary school district than in the high school district, reflecting, perhaps, the earlier practice of requiring a longer period of training for a high school teacher than for an elementary school teacher.

It is generally held that the best education in America is in the suburban schools. There is much truth in this—suburban districts have many advantages: greater wealth, state taxing systems that favor these wealthier districts, newer and more modern school plants, more favorable teacher salaries and working conditions, more extensive citizenship involvement in the work of the schools, and local pride at a high level. It does not mean, however, that all suburban school districts fare alike in the educational benefits derived from being apart from, but contiguous to, large cities. Some suburbs have so grown in size that they have taken on the characteristics of the large city, the difference being that the offspring has not yet developed an inner city, with its ghettos and substandard living conditions. The extreme range in quality of education provided in the large cities has not yet extended to these suburbs.

DISTRICTS IN AGRICULTURAL CENTERS

While the problems of education in large-city school districts have grown in number and become more weighty, state programs for establishing school districts in agricultural centers have been achieved more smoothly and successfully. In part because of improvements in roads and other pupil-transportation facilities, it has been possible to enlarge the agricultural school district to a point where it can support

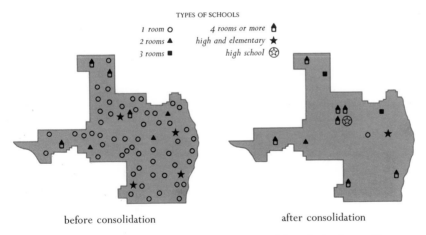

before consolidation   after consolidation

Fig.11.3 How the formation of Unit District No. 10, Pittsfield and Pike County, Illinois, reduced the number and types of school units. (Data from Pittsfield Community Unit School District No. 10)

schools that match the best programs offered in the cities in facilities and educational services. One can sense the change in education offered in agricultural centers merely by driving through the country-side. The elaborate school plants, beautifully landscaped, surrounded with ample space for parking and playing and, in many instances, located in a setting completely different from the crowded conditions of densely populated communities, are very impressive. From the standpoint of homogeneity of school population, modern facilities, and citizenship involvement, these schools are the greatest improvement in modern education in America. As reorganization in districting continues, the old "country school" or "small-town school" is rapidly fading from the contemporary scene.

If one may judge from these present trends throughout the nation, reorganization of the state's basic administrative units in agricultural centers will have three results:

1. A minimum enrollment figure or standard will be met in all except the more sparsely settled regions such as are found in the Plains and mountain states of the West;
2. Districts that maintain only elementary schools will be consolidated or augmented so that they will be large enough to maintain a complete system up through the twelfth grade, including nursery schools, kindergartens, junior high schools, and all the special services required by such a system;
3. Where districts operated only a four-year high school or a system of four-year high schools, these districts will gradually—and not without opposition—be combined with districts that operate elementary schools, thus creating conditions required for a unified system of schools with no salary differentials among elementary, junior high, and senior high school teachers.

The state educational authority

The state, with its units for educational controls, its school districts, has mandatory and permissive laws that *regulate* education. The state also has laws that *insure* the execution of the state's responsibilities for both public and private education. Such laws set up a structure of authority for the express purpose of administering the educational

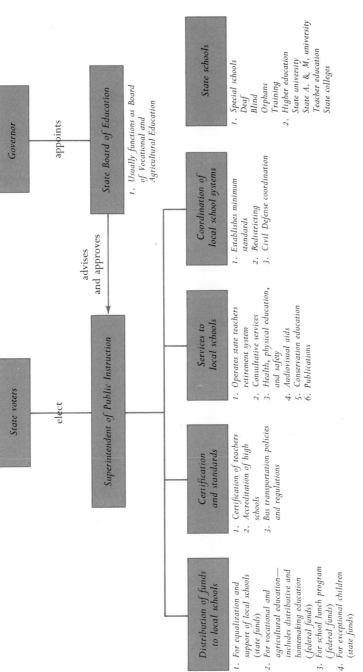

Governor

appoints

State Board of Education

1. Usually functions as Board of Vocational and Agricultural Education

State voters

elect

advises
and approves

Superintendent of Public Instruction

Distribution of funds to local schools

1. For equalization and support of local schools (state funds)
2. For vocational and agricultural education— includes distributive and homemaking education (federal funds)
3. For school lunch program (federal funds)
4. For exceptional children (state funds)

Certification and standards

1. Certification of teachers
2. Accreditation of high schools
3. Bus transportation policies and regulations

Services to local schools

1. Operates state teachers retirement system
2. Consultative services
3. Health, physical education, and safety
4. Audiovisual aids
5. Conservation education
6. Publications

Coordination of local school systems

1. Establishes minimum standards
2. Redistricting
3. Civil Defense coordination

State schools

1. Special schools
   Deaf
   Blind
   Orphans
   Training
2. Higher education
   State university
   State A. & M. university
   Teacher education
   State colleges

Fig. 11.4 A typical state educational organization. The general trend is toward increased state participation in and control over local educational functions. This chart shows one of the more common ways of organizing state authority. The student may find it valuable and interesting to draw a similar diagram for his own state and compare it with this one.

affairs of the state, ordinarily a state office or, in some cases, several offices, with specific and definite functions, with authority and responsibilities carefully spelled out. Characteristically, the states differ in the way the state educational office is organized and in the specific responsibilities assigned to it. There are, however, common elements in the national picture. Generally, the state's supreme authority over education begins with a state board of education, an office that greatly influences the character and tone of education within a given state.

STATE BOARDS OF EDUCATION

In 48 of our 50 states, a state board of education has authority over elementary and secondary school districts. (Illinois and Wisconsin are the two exceptions, although there are strong influences in both states that foreshadow change.) The state boards of education—sometimes called by other names such as the Board of Regents in New York State—uniformly constitute the highest educational authority in each of the states, although there is considerable variation in details related to powers, membership, methods of selection, and the like. Since some state policies are considered significantly better than others, a brief survey of current state practices may help in assessing proposed reforms.

1. Functions

Among the functions of the state boards of education, perhaps the most important are to appoint or have elected the chief state school officer, to designate the term of his appointment, to define his duties, and to state his salary. (Where there is no state board, as in Illinois and Wisconsin, this function is, of course, taken care of through state laws.) In broad outline, the responsibilities of a state board of education are somewhat analogous to those of local boards of education as described in Chapter 12. In general, the state board assumes responsibility for carrying out those aspects of education that must be administered at the state level and also for formulating educational policies related to the implementation, control, and supervision of state-wide education.

In most states these functions are divided among several boards, each with control over some segment of the state's education program.

In only 13 states, for example, are the state boards vested with general control over all elementary and secondary education. In many cases a separate board (or several boards) is responsible for universities, for junior colleges, for vocational education, for the education of the deaf and the blind, and so on. Boards originally set up to meet definite and timely needs have become deeply rooted, resistant to change. A more or less confused, diffused, and inefficient pattern of state boards of education, with overlapping functions and some of the evils that derive therefrom, persists.

2. Membership

The state board of education is an important factor in the welfare of education within a state. Who serves on the board is vital in determining how effectively the board fulfills its functions.

Currently the states follow different policies in selecting the members. At present the board is elected by popular vote in only 9 states; board members are appointed by the governor in 30 states; various methods of election and appointment are used in the remainder of the states.

The number of members on the state board varies, ranging from 21 in Texas to 3 in Mississippi. Nineteen states have from 8 to 11 members. Ten states have 7 members, while seven states have fewer than 7.

Numerous appointed commissions have made recommendations regarding the most acceptable membership of state boards. The commissions, almost without exception, have recommended popularly elected boards of five to seven lay citizens who serve without pay. No qualifications have been agreed upon other than that each member should be a prominent citizen who has an unselfish interest in the administration of education in his state. It is assumed that some kind of preliminary screening process will protect the office from citizens who are incompetent or have selfish designs. Obviously, expert opinion about what constitutes the ideal state board of education has so far had little influence.

CHIEF STATE SCHOOL OFFICERS

It is generally agreed by specialists in school administration that the state board should select the state's chief school officer, whose title is usually superintendent of public instruction or commissioner of education. In actuality, however, the chief state school officer is appointed by the state board of education in only 24 states. In 21 states he is elected by the people as a candidate on a political ticket. In the other five states he is appointed by the governor of the state, who, of course, is also elected on a political ticket. The trend, however, is toward a chief school officer appointed by the state board of education —since 1947 the number so appointed has risen from 11 to 24.

In those states where a nonpartisan state board is authorized to select the chief state school officer and to determine his functions, salary, tenure, and the like, it is then possible for the state to attract leaders of outstanding competence.

More than half the states still cling to partisan politics in connection with education. Politicians offer "good" arguments; they invent attractive slogans that influence people to oppose change: "Keep education close to the people"; "Make the chief state school officer independent of the board of education"; "Election by popular vote frees the chief state school officer from obligations to other officials, including the governor"; "If he proves incompetent, he can be recalled." Gradually, however, such political appeals are losing effectiveness—citizens are increasingly aware of the need for expert, not political, state-wide school leadership.

STATE DEPARTMENTS OF EDUCATION

In all the states the chief educational officer uses the services of a professional staff. He, with his staff, constitutes the state department of education. It discharges manifold responsibilities in connection with such matters as certificating all teachers of the state, distributing state aid to local school districts, assuming leadership in reorganizing school districts, enforcing various school codes, reporting the status of educational affairs to the public, and distributing large sums of money allocated to the state by the federal government for vocational education or other educational purposes. Responsibilities of a state department of education are indeed extensive. No school or school district in a state escapes its influences.

As is true of other aspects of education in America, there is wide variation among state departments of education in their relative importance in the over-all educational organization. Assuming that importance in, and power over, education are relative to the size of the department, the influence and the extent of responsibilities are much greater in some state departments than in others. All departments, however, are rapidly expanding in power, in size, and in influence. The state department of education in New York State, for example, now has a staff of more than 1,300 professional employees, California more than 435, Indiana more than 165, Wisconsin more than 130, and Connecticut, though a small state, also more than 130.

Judged in terms of time spent administering certain activities in the state, the most important areas are: vocational rehabilitation, vocational education, instructional services, handicapped children, veterans' education, adult education, finance, teacher certification, research, statistical services, and school lunch programs. Obviously, the state department in any state is important and influential.

Planning to improve the organization and services of the state department is in progress in all the states. All 50 states, and also Washington, D.C., the Virgin Islands, and Puerto Rico, have submitted to the United States Office of Education plans and requests for federal funds to help make such improvements. Federal funds are available for this purpose under Title V of the Elementary and Secondary Education Act of 1965 (the act is discussed in Chapter 13).

State involvement in public education

All the states face certain basic questions concerned with the degree of involvement that the state should assume in education and the areas of education where the state should expand its control. Old and new issues that confront state governments include: What is a reasonable balance between the district's control of its education and the state's control? What minimum standards should the state require each district to meet? What financial policy will insure adequate and equitable financial support to each of the school districts? From what sources should the state derive its financial support? What policies regarding distribution of funds to each of the districts are educationally most sound? What minimum, foundation program should be required of all public elementary and secondary schools? These are all urgent issues that challenge the most expert educational statesmanship. Each issue really merits extended analysis, but for our overview purposes, we necessarily choose only a few of the issues for brief discussion. These are, nevertheless, illustrative of the issues in general.

CENTRALIZATION

One of the most difficult problems as well as one of the longest duration concerns state power over local school districts. As has been said, when the Tenth Amendment to the Constitution was adopted, because there was no reference to education in the Constitution, the responsibility for education went automatically to the states. Each state became a unit for the organization and administration of education within its boundaries. Under this policy, the federal government had divested itself of control over a most important and costly social responsibility. The problem of how the state power over education should be exercised became, and to an extent continues to be, a problem for each state and, inasmuch as each state differs from the others, the problem was, and remains, in some measure unique with each state.

In the beginning the policy of the states was largely a let-alone laissez-faire policy. To start with, the Commonwealth of Massachusetts adopted what seemed to be the simplest solution by establishing very small school districts. Massachusetts' early system largely became the pattern for educational organization throughout the land. The citizens of the small administrative units truly exercised direct power over their schools. With time and changing social conditions, however, this simple solution became more and more impracticable and unacceptable. The various state legislatures had to face the problem of change, and the only direction that change could take was the removal of certain powers from the local school districts. Of course, when you begin to take powers from one group and give them to another, you introduce a degree of conflict. From the beginning to the present, one of the most difficult educational problems of the states has had two aspects: What powers can and should be removed from local districts? What procedures should be used to accomplish the change? At the center of the difficulty the enduring issue is: What degree of centralization of power should the state attempt to promote? Or, to put it a different way: To what degree and in what ways should the state proceed to decrease local control over public education?

A state can move control over education farther from the people in two principal ways. It can pass more mandatory laws naming specific functions to be administered at the state level (taxation, pupil transportation, and the certification of teachers are examples). Also, it can reorganize the public elementary and secondary school districts to make them much larger and more consistently able to maintain a full and complete system of elementary and secondary education. Many mandatory laws take much of the control of a function, although not necessarily complete control, out of local hands; they thus always reduce the extent of local control. Enlargement of public school districts, as previously discussed, would keep control over education in the hands of local people, but in the hands of fewer people.

MINIMUM STANDARDS

The state departments of education establish minimum standards which local schools must meet or else suffer such penalties as may be stated in the law—cutting down on state financial aid, for instance. As an example, a school may be required to employ only those teachers who possess minimum qualifications of training for state certification. Schools may be required to have pupils in attendance a minimum number of days each year. Some states require that certain subjects, like United States history or health education, be taught. Some states have established a minimum salary for beginning teachers. If a teacher, under contract, should perform services for a local school board and receive less compensation than the minimum prescribed by law, he is entitled to recover the deficiency.

The State Department of Education is one of the most important agencies in every state. This large headquarters building of the New Jersey department is tangible evidence of its place in the state administration—and of the size of the staff needed to carry out its many functions.

When the state establishes minimum standards, in theory it guarantees the individual pupil a basic standard of education regardless of where he lives within the state or which school he attends. All the states do not, of course, provide equal minimum standards.

FOUNDATION PROGRAM

Despite the establishment of certain minimum standards, studies show that marked inequalities in educational opportunity characterize the schools in all the states. The discrepancy in educational opportunities between the poorest schools and the best schools in a state is, in some cases, so great as to constitute a social threat. The discrepancies in some states are greater than in others, but they are wide in all states. It might logically appear that poor schools are in communities of substandard wealth and that the discrepancy can be explained by lack of money. When we consider, however, that the entire state is an educational unit, it seems clear that it is not the substandard wealth of a community that is responsible. It is the policy of the state toward raising and distributing revenue for public school purposes that creates and perpetuates the discrepancies. The state organizes school districts. If a school district has low taxing ability and insufficient income to support the schools, the state has the responsibility for equalizing the educational opportunities. This can be done, if the state desires, by first establishing a foundation program for every district and then adopting a policy of school support which will ensure each district's ability to maintain the foundation program.

How can a state do this? The state must begin by defining its foundation program—the minimum program of education to be available to each child in the state. Every state now prescribes some kind of foundation program for its schools, often a bare minimum, but many of these programs have been developed haphazardly, almost without plan. In many states, they have grown out of a long list of separate legislative actions. A legislature may decree, for instance, that every school in the state shall be open for a minimum of 180 days, that United States history shall be taught in all the secondary schools, and that all eighth-grade pupils shall be required to pass examinations testing knowledge of the federal and state constitutions as a condition for admission to the ninth grade. But can one call legal prescriptions such as these a "program"? Sometimes such foundation programs, if they deserve that name, do very little to reduce educational inequalities in a state. They may be legislated mainly to satisfy the passing fancy of legislators or to placate the persistent pressures of some highly vocal organized group.

The foundation program that will reduce educational discrepancies and equalize opportunities must be expertly planned and must be broadly acceptable to the school public. The state can act in either of two general directions. It can pass legislation defining in detail the standards each school district must meet. These standards might prescribe a school session of 180 days, a specified minimum salary for beginning teachers, and buildings and equipment which must meet definite quantitative and qualitative standards. The maximum size of a class might be established and the maximum teaching load stipulated. Many details of the state program are thus settled. They are defined by state fiat.

A simpler way, and one that is more in line with American local school tradition, is to set a minimum expenditure per pupil as the standard for all school districts. This leaves the planning of the details to the local district with a minimum of state intervention. The standard of expenditure may be changed from time to time as the occasion requires and as the state feels it is warranted.

Once the state requires that each public school district shall maintain a foundation program for all the children in the school district, it must collect and distribute school revenues so that the financial burden for this foundation program is no heavier in the districts of low taxing ability than in the districts with higher taxing ability. The cost factor must be equalized. (In fact, in 1968 the Detroit school system sued the State of Michigan in a demand for an *unequal* distribution of state school funds, with more money going to big cities, so that larger amounts could be spent there in building good schools in poor areas.)

FINANCIAL POLICY

What policy should the states follow in attempting to achieve a minimum program and at the same time to equalize the cost? It will require, initially, that each district in the state will make an effort to support the foundation program equal to the effort of every other district. The local tax rate for the foundation program in a poor district will be exactly the same as the local tax rate in a wealthier district. Obviously the returns from taxes will be much greater in the wealthier than in the poorer districts. The wealthier districts will be able to support the minimum program with considerable ease. They probably will pay for the entire foundation program and will go as far beyond the program as they wish and further tax themselves accordingly. No limit is set on how much they spend on their schools or how good they make them.

The poorer districts, when taxed uniformly with the rest of the state, may find that they have collected insufficient funds to meet the cost of the foundation program. Funds from the state, called state aid, make up the difference. The poorer districts will receive larger sums from the state than districts with more taxable wealth. All districts make an equal effort to pay, but some must receive more state aid than others. This is not consistent with general state practice, which is to base state funds solely on average daily attendance.

State aid equalizes the cost of education for the foundation program but leaves the control of schools in local hands. The state remains the unit for providing school revenue. The words "state aid" are appropriate, since they imply that the state will assist local school districts but will not dominate them.

The state has the major responsibility for a financial policy that will eradicate many of the inequalities in educational opportunity within the state. By first defining the foundation program that all public schools must provide, it lets the people of the state know the minimum education they can expect from any school. This minimum standard will be tailored to the state's over-all potential. Next, by establishing a foundation of financial support, the state will ensure that local public elementary and secondary school districts can maintain at least the accepted minimum program. Where a public school district is unable, through its own taxing powers with its own resources only, to support the foundation educational program, the state will provide the additional financial support needed. Wealthier districts may still, if they wish, provide education beyond the foundation minimum. The variable among the states will be the minimum or

Adequate state aid means modern facilities like the biology laboratory in an old remodeled school. Inadequate state aid means substandard schools. The teachers and pupils who use the biology lab may not realize that state distribution of public school funds is largely responsible for the up-to-date equipment. But without satisfactory state aid policies and without reasonable foundation laws setting forth minimum standards for schools, good laboratories will continue to be too rare, and antiquated classrooms will continue to be too frequent. Furthermore, the states should also pass laws prohibiting wealthy districts from operating schools with widely differing standards. Inner-city areas, especially, suffer from such unbalanced administration.

foundation program. This is a generally accepted plan, in broad outline. Working out the details of such a policy involves technicalities
that require educational experts to formulate the foundation program
and experts in state school finance to evolve the pattern for financial
support.

In 1968–1969, state aid to local schools averaged around 40
percent of available local funds, with a range from 84.8 percent in
Hawaii to 9.1 percent in New Hampshire (see Fig. 11.5). Perhaps, as
a beginning, all the states should move up to or above the 50-percent
point in providing state revenue. This might make a satisfactory
start toward the ideal of satisfactory educational opportunity for *all*
children.

SOURCES OF STATE SCHOOL REVENUE

Where does a state get the money for its education program,
including state aid? It is not possible to give a detailed analysis of all
the sources of public school revenue in each of our 50 states. In any
case, the picture is rapidly changing. A general trend is discernible,
however: an increasing proportion of the financing of education in
public elementary and secondary school districts is being assumed by
the state governments. Nevertheless, the states, in varying degrees,
still place a heavy responsibility for financing public schools on local
governments. In the school year 1968–1969, for example, nationwide,
about 53 percent of revenue receipts for public elementary and
secondary schools came from local sources, with a range from 86
percent in New Hampshire to 5.2 percent in Hawaii (see Fig. 12.2).

The principal source of these local revenues is the property tax,
both personal and real estate, a tax presumably conditioned on ownership of property and measured by its value. (The personal property
tax is a tax on automobiles, furniture, jewelry, and the like.) Although
specialists are generally agreed that the personal property tax is outmoded, it is still collected in some states, Illinois, for example. Making

*Fig. 11.5 Estimated percentages of revenue received by public elementary and secondary schools
from state governments, 1968–1969. (Data from NEA Research Report 1968-R16)*

Hawaii	1	84.8
Delaware	2	72.7
North Carolina	3	67.3
South Carolina	4	63.6
Georgia	5	63.2
Louisiana	6	62.8
New Mexico	7	61.8
Washington	8	60.8
Alabama	9	60.0
Florida	10	56.5
Arizona	11	55.2
Mississippi	12	53.1
Utah	13	52.0
Kentucky	14	51.3
West Virginia	15	50.2
Tennessee	16	48.7
New York	17	47.8
Texas	18	47.1
Arkansas	19	46.7
Pennsylvania	20	45.2
Alaska	21	44.7
Michigan	22	44.3
Minnesota	23	43.3
Idaho	24	40.9
Virginia	25	40.7
Nevada	26	38.8
Maryland	27	37.3
Ohio	28	34.9
Maine	29	34.7
California }	30	34.3
Missouri }		34.3
Indiana	32	34.0
Rhode Island	33	33.6
Oklahoma	34	32.7
Iowa	35	32.6
Connecticut	36	31.3
Vermont	37	29.7
Kansas	38	29.2
Montana	39	27.6
New Jersey	40	27.5
Illinois	41	26.7
North Dakota	42	26.1
Wisconsin	43	26.0
Wyoming	44	25.4
Colorado	45	24.0
Massachusetts	46	22.4
Oregon	47	17.7
Nebraska	48	17.6
South Dakota	49	11.4
New Hampshire	50	9.1

U.S.A.

53.7%
Local governments

8.1%
Federal government

37.8%
State governments

0.4%
All other (private) sources

the real estate tax the principal source of school revenue also is seriously questioned, partly because the tax tends to be rather inflexible and also because accurate and fair valuations of real estate are difficult to achieve. The property tax has become increasingly inadequate as real estate has become less of an income-producing item in the economy. Many groups who have studied tax problems over the years advocate diversifying sources of public school revenue, but the property tax remains the principal local base for support of schools in public school districts.

School costs are a large part of the budgets of local governments. Although the property tax burden increases during an inflation, American citizens, in many cases, continue to approve raising the property tax ceiling and issuing bonds for school improvements. In time of inflation, the problem of adjusting to increased school costs is especially difficult because few items in the budget can be reduced. Often the only alternatives are to make needed faculty replacements from younger, inexperienced teachers who are lower on the salary scale, to increase class size, or to eliminate or reduce the services of such personnel as psychologists, fine arts teachers, or supervisory help.

Where does the state go for its revenue to distribute to the local school districts? State plans vary. Revenue from almost any state tax source may be used for school purposes if the state legislature desires. There is more and more dependence on general sales taxes. Sometimes excise taxes are levied on special products like alcohol or tobacco. The objection to the general sales tax is that it imposes a greater burden on the lower-income group which spends a larger proportion of its income on necessary items for daily living and thereby pays proportionately more of the tax. Theoretically, the income tax is considered most equitable. State constitutions and public opinion, however, sometimes make it difficult for a state to impose a state income tax. Up to now, the reforms have developed at a snail's pace, probably because such reforms may call for constitutional changes which are difficult to get passed.

The whole problem of state revenue, and especially of providing

Fig.11.6 Total public school expenditure as a percentage of personal income, 1967–1968. (Data from NEA Research Report 1969-R1)

State	Rank	Value
Alaska	1	8.0
New Mexico	2	7.4
Wyoming	3	7.0
Utah	4	6.9
Montana	5	6.6
Arizona	6	6.2
Minnesota	6	6.2
North Dakota	6	6.2
Oregon	6	6.2
Louisiana	10	6.1
Nevada	11	6.0
Delaware	12	5.9
Arkansas	13	5.7
Maryland	13	5.7
Washington	13	5.7
Idaho	16	5.6
Mississippi	16	5.6
South Carolina	16	5.6
California	19	5.5
Colorado	19	5.5
Iowa	19	5.5
South Dakota	19	5.5
Vermont	19	5.5
Wisconsin	19	5.5
Hawaii	25	5.4
New York	25	5.4
West Virginia	25	5.4
Florida	28	5.2
Michigan	28	5.2
North Carolina	28	5.2
Virginia	28	5.2
Kansas	32	5.1
Maine	32	5.1
UNITED STATES		5.1
Indiana	34	5.0
New Jersey	34	5.0
Tennessee	34	5.0
Georgia	37	4.9
Texas	38	4.8
Missouri	39	4.7
Pennsylvania	39	4.7
Ohio	41	4.6
Oklahoma	41	4.6
Nebraska	43	4.5
Alabama	44	4.4
New Hampshire	44	4.4
Kentucky	46	4.3
Connecticut	47	4.2
Illinois	47	4.2
Rhode Island	49	4.1
Massachusetts	50	3.9

funds for public education, is a difficult one, the foremost problem in all the states. That education should be equalized throughout a state, and throughout any of the state's school districts, seems an essential, democratic principle. How to define the foundation program and how to raise the money to maintain it are, however, issues which arouse heated debate.

POLICIES OF STATE AID

All the states have programs of state aid, but the amount of state aid and the policy of distribution to the local public school districts differ vastly with the states.

Some states have moved further toward equalizing the cost of education than have others. In all probability, the state that has a lower level of state aid has had to reduce its minimum education program in order to avoid putting an impossible tax burden on some of the poorer local school districts.

It is not difficult to reason logically that the state aid fund in any particular state should be larger, that improved foundation programs should be required, or that the brunt of the burden for local and state school support should not be concentrated on property taxes. Methods for making such changes, however, are not so readily apparent. Should the local school districts be further modified? Should the kind of taxes levied be changed? Should the methods of assessing, levying, collecting, and distributing tax money be improved, and if so, how? Should the authority and functions of the divisions of the state school system be clarified, simplified, and made generally more effective? Where should we look for intelligent and dynamic leadership for necessary reorganization of a state school system? These are, as yet, unanswered questions.

The state is the educational unit. What may be done locally depends upon what the state constitution permits and what the state legislators feel inclined to do. The variations among the states regarding all details of state public school systems are imposing. Some states have advanced in their reorganization efforts, usually by gradual and continuous means. Some states have set up a permanent group, such as a commission on the reorganization of public school districts, to work on the problem.

From 1955 to 1964, the percentage of public school revenue from local, state, and federal sources remained fairly constant—about 4 percent from federal, 40 percent from state, and 56 percent from local sources. By 1968–1969, the percentage from the federal government had risen to more than 8 percent.

Summary

Each of our 50 states is the unit responsible for the administration of education within its boundaries. The states vary greatly in their policies toward education, some states placing a much higher priority on education than others. State educational policies vary in leadership, public school districting, financial aid to districts, how revenue is raised and distributed, the manner in which local citizens are involved, the transportation of pupils, and many other aspects of state and community interrelationships.

Each state has a constitution (some are considered quite antiquated) and this, together with laws passed by the legislature and decisions by courts, forms an extensive legal structure that determines policies for conducting education within the state. When laws concerning education have become part of this legal structure—known as the school code—they tend to be solidified and difficult to change.

Not all state educational problems are financial, although financial policy is perhaps the most important element in determining the quality of education within a state. Also of great importance is a state's policy toward districting. Of the three basic types of public elementary and secondary school districts—large-city, suburban, and agricultural-center—the agricultural-area districts seem to have evolved a better climate for education than either of the other two. Even in agricultural districts, however, when older ones are reorganized, the relocation of individual schools, the problem of transportation, and the difficulties of obtaining adequate specialized services have been and remain pressing administrative problems. In other words, the many perplexing questions presented by districting are far from being answered. Each kind of district has crucial problems that, in fact, may not be solved by the present generation.

Questions

1. What in your opinion is the responsibility of a state when it establishes a public school district that does not have the resources to provide the foundation program prescribed by the state?
2. What is meant by equalizing educational opportunity within a state?
3. What logical steps may a state take to equalize educational opportunities within its borders?
4. Is it possible for a state to equalize educational opportunity without violating the principle of local control over education?
5. Why was the power to certify teachers taken over by the state?
6. What provisions for public education are made in the constitution of your home state?
7. When should a state school law be mandatory? When should it be permissive?
8. When do you consider it right and appropriate for a state teachers' association to attempt to influence legislatures?
9. In your opinion, how should a state board of education be organized?
10. What should be the functions of a state board of education?
11. How should the state commissioner of education, or state superintendent of public instruction, be selected?
12. What powers and duties should be vested in the state department of education?

Projects

1. From a study of the state school code for your home state, list the major problems to which the legislature has given attention.
2. Describe the organization of the state board of education in your state and list suggested reforms.
3. Describe the organization of the state educational authority in your home state. Indicate the strengths and weaknesses.
4. Describe and evaluate the foundation program as prescribed in your state.

5. Explain, perhaps by using a table or a chart, why the state must be the unit for the administration of public education.
6. State the conclusions about school support that you believe are justified from your study of the data in Figs. 11.5, 11.6, 12.2, and 13.4.

*Local Aspects
of Public
School
Organization
and
Administration*

The student who is considering choosing public school teaching as his career may at this point say, "I'll give it a try!" He realizes he must graduate from college and, in the process, qualify for a state teaching certificate and perhaps meet the requirements set by the AACTE. He must think about the grade level at which he will begin teaching and consider the specific state and school district with which he would like to become identified. He knows that when he begins teaching in a public school, he will be part of a state school district system. What the school and the system are like will have much to do with his initial success and with his feeling of well-being. When he is first before his class of some 20 or 30 pupils, he may give little consideration to the school system as such. With time and experience, however, and with the growth that is sure to come, his professional horizon will expand, his views will broaden, and, ideally, they will continue this kind of enlargement throughout his career.

In this chapter we study certain matters of great importance to all teachers but of special significance to those making plans to enter the profession.

What is a local school district?

As we have noted, from the state view, local school districts are the units in the state through which the state governs its public elementary and secondary schools. In other words, the state system for organization and administration of a public school corporation functions

337

CHAPTER 12
*Local Aspects
of Public School
Organization and
Administration*

through those units known as school districts. As a part of the state-wide system, the local school district is one thing; as primarily a local organization, it also has a different set of characteristics, functions, and problems. It is the unit that encompasses a local area for the operation of schools for local boys and girls. It is the avenue through which local citizens act in establishing district-wide educational policies related to such important matters as financing, personnel, and curriculum. Local policies, of course, are always consistent with state-wide policies set forth in the state school code.

Originally, school districts were small, and the state legislatures permitted them to be almost autonomous. Gradually, through the years, the states assumed more powers of control over local school districts. In time, local districts were reorganized and consolidated into larger corporations, and thereby a measure of control was taken away from local people. Despite reorganizations, citizens of local areas still tend to think of local public schools as local possessions and of the operation of the schools as essentially a local responsibility. Some efforts at state reorganization have, therefore, encountered strong local resistance. Citizens, in general, wish to keep boundary lines constant so as to preserve what they believe is their rightful authority. Although, partly because of state district reorganizations, the meaning of the word "local" has undergone, and continues to undergo, change, what is done and what can be done in a school are matters of vital concern to people in the area that is a school district. Nevertheless, the way the local school operates has to change as the policies of the state and federal governments change. In other words, school districts have to be dynamic; despite conservative citizen effort to the contrary, they cannot be static.

The structure of authority

THE BOARD OF EDUCATION

1. Powers

For efficient, democratic, local operation of public elementary and secondary schools, a group of lay citizens called a board of education, school board, school trustees, school committee, township

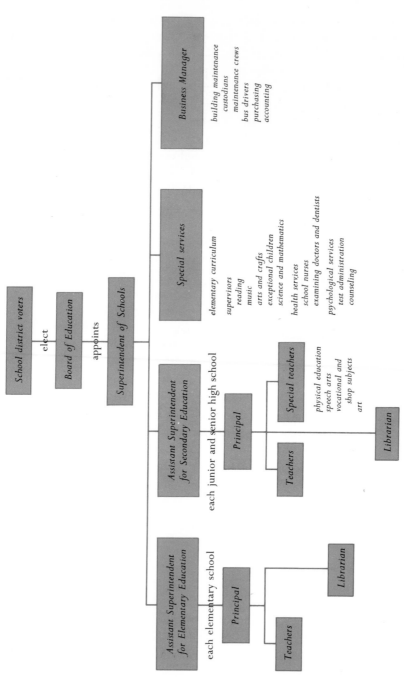

Fig.12.1 A typical local school system organization. The size and location of a system produce variations, but in all systems there are similarities in functions and in the way the functions are allocated and performed. Thus the pattern shown here is fairly common. The student may find it valuable and interesting to draw a similar diagram for a local system with which he is familiar and compare it with this one.

339

CHAPTER 12
*Local Aspects
of Public School
Organization and
Administration*

*School districts must move with the
trends. One trend : fewer districts,
with busing of children to
educational centers. A more recent
trend : compensatory education for
the disadvantaged. This enrichment
class is part of an intensive effort
in a Philadelphia "gray area" to
help deprived in-migrant children.*

board of education, county board of education, or something similar,
has been given definite powers. Nearly every public school district in
America is governed by such a board. In the school year 1968–1969,
the number of citizens serving on boards of this kind was estimated at
110,380. This great reduction from 423,974 in 1933 has been caused
in part by the great reduction in the number of local districts, but it
also reflects the decrease in citizen service to school boards; the latter
factor is more apparent when the growth in the nation's population
since 1933 is considered.

A board of education is the legal agent specified by the legislature
to be responsible for the conduct of education in the local district.
By court decision such a board has been held to be a state agency,
not an adjunct of local government—a fact often not recognized.

From the viewpoint of the state, the board's primary responsibility is to put into effect state and community plans of education.
The general power in the statute which states that the function of
a school board is "to do anything not inconsistent with this act"

provides a broad basis for action. School boards authorize many activities on the assumption that it is proper to do so unless specifically prohibited by statute, and since many of these activities go unquestioned, they gradually become a part of routine practice. Such broad powers permit flexibility in action and provide opportunity for experimentation in new areas.

2. Selection of members

The membership of boards of education is decided in a variety of ways. Popular election is the most common, approximately 85 percent of school board members being selected in this manner. The others are appointed, usually by the mayor, city council, city manager, judge, or some other city, county, or state agency. The proportion of board members elected is considerably higher in the smaller school districts than in the larger. In large-city school districts, where the boundaries of the school district are coterminous with those of the city, the board is usually appointed by the mayor. By and large American citizens have selected school board members in a manner consistent with the nonpartisan policy toward public education.

Whatever the method of selection, some kind of careful screening process often precedes the selection. Representatives of civic groups may meet in a district caucus to prepare the slate of nominees to be presented to the voters at the special school board election. The nomination of some outstanding citizen by the caucus is almost tantamount to election. In other instances school board nominations are made by petition, primary election, mass meetings, school district meetings, or by an individual announcing that he is a candidate. Perhaps the most able candidates are those who are invited to run after careful screening of a sizable group of qualified candidates. Without some such process, public apathy toward voting for school board members could result in election of weak, perhaps narrow or selfish, citizens.

3. Term of office

Since it takes time for a new board member to become informed respecting the needs of the local school district, it is desirable that he

Fig.12.2 Estimated percentages of revenue received by public elementary and secondary schools from local governments, 1968–1969. (Data from NEA Research Report 1968-R16)

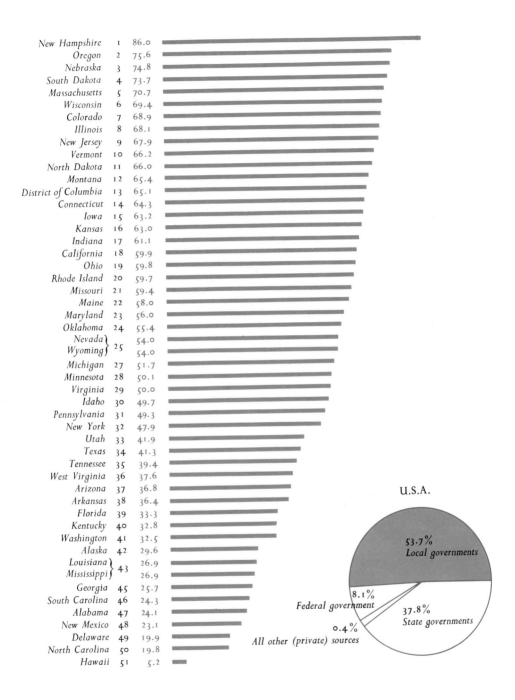

New Hampshire	1	86.0
Oregon	2	75.6
Nebraska	3	74.8
South Dakota	4	73.7
Massachusetts	5	70.7
Wisconsin	6	69.4
Colorado	7	68.9
Illinois	8	68.1
New Jersey	9	67.9
Vermont	10	66.2
North Dakota	11	66.0
Montana	12	65.4
District of Columbia	13	65.1
Connecticut	14	64.3
Iowa	15	63.2
Kansas	16	63.0
Indiana	17	61.1
California	18	59.9
Ohio	19	59.8
Rhode Island	20	59.7
Missouri	21	59.4
Maine	22	58.0
Maryland	23	56.0
Oklahoma	24	55.4
Nevada	25	54.0
Wyoming	25	54.0
Michigan	27	51.7
Minnesota	28	50.1
Virginia	29	50.0
Idaho	30	49.7
Pennsylvania	31	49.3
New York	32	47.9
Utah	33	41.9
Texas	34	41.3
Tennessee	35	39.4
West Virginia	36	37.6
Arizona	37	36.8
Arkansas	38	36.4
Florida	39	33.3
Kentucky	40	32.8
Washington	41	32.5
Alaska	42	29.6
Louisiana	43	26.9
Mississippi	43	26.9
Georgia	45	25.7
South Carolina	46	24.3
Alabama	47	24.1
New Mexico	48	23.1
Delaware	49	19.9
North Carolina	50	19.8
Hawaii	51	5.2

U.S.A.

53.7%
Local governments

8.1%
Federal government

37.8%
State governments

0.4%
All other (private) sources

serve a reasonable time—ordinarily a minimum of three to five years —and that, if warranted, he be allowed to serve a second term. For desirable continuity in board services, expiration of board member terms are generally staggered.

4. Size

The number of members of boards of education is related to efficiency in board action. A school board that is too small or too large has certain weaknesses. The number of members should be adequate to allow representation of the different points of view in the community. The one-member trustee, still found in some smaller communities, cannot fulfill this obligation. The question reduces to: What is the largest number that will assure a balanced judgment on school issues and will yet be small enough to work effectively as a single group? According to a National School Boards Association survey made in 1965 of 42 cities with populations of 300,000 and over, 17 had boards of 7 members; 12 had boards of 5 members; Milwaukee, Philadelphia, and Pittsburgh each had 15 members; Omaha and St. Louis had 12; Chicago had 11. Most experts in public school administration favor boards with 7 members. It is felt that 5 is too small because potentially a small political clique could gain control and 9 is too large to serve as a single group. There is a tendency for groups of 9 or more to act through committees. Therefore, 7 seems to be about the right number for a cohesive, representative unit. Because community traditions tend to be strong and the interests of the community and the schools to become intertwined, any practice, in the

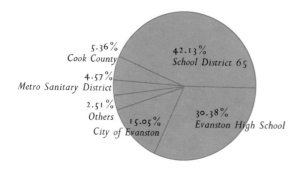

5.36%
Cook County

4.57%
Metro Sanitary District

2.51%
Others

15.05%
City of Evanston

42.13%
School District 65

30.38%
Evanston High School

Fig. 12.3 In Illinois, almost 70 percent of the funds available to public elementary and secondary schools comes from local governments. What this means to a local government is shown in this typical example from that state: the 1967 allocation of the Evanston taxpayers' tax dollars. Note that more than 72 cents of each dollar went to local schools.

343

CHAPTER 1 2
*Local Aspects
of Public School
Organization and
Administration*

best interests of schools and community or not, becomes exceedingly difficult to change.

5. Compensation

Membership on a school board has traditionally been considered as unselfish service to state, community, and children, and the chief reward has been the satisfaction of doing good work and receiving the respect of the community. In a few cities, however, the policy is to pay board members. In the 42 city school districts included in the National School Boards Association survey mentioned above, nine systems pay salaries to board members; seven pay expenses. In Atlanta, the president of the board receives $300 a month, the others $250. Memphis pays the president $5,000 a year, the others $75 a month. Like variations in amounts paid are found among the other systems that pay board members.

It is generally agreed within the profession that when compensation is provided, school board members tend to become executive in character in order to justify their pay. Serving on school boards might eventuate into a strange mixture of spoils, politics, and constant interference with the professional personnel in the actual operation of the schools.

6. Qualifications of board members

Usually the law specifies only that the candidate for board membership shall be over 21 years of age, a qualified voter, and a resident in the school district. Obviously, meeting only these minimum legal qualifications provides no guarantee that an individual can be an effective school board member, that the board will be broadly representative of popular interest in the public schools. Other factors that should be weighed in the selection of members include:

1. Whether the individual enjoys community-wide respect and is able to discuss educational problems intelligently and convincingly. Board members must cooperate with the community as well as with each other.
2. Whether the individual will be able to understand and direct the financial—business—affairs of the school system.

3. Whether the individual is willing and able to devote sufficient time and energy to the office.

4. Whether the individual is likely to minister to the educational needs of all the children in the district. The school board should be representative of and serve all the people in the district. It cannot fulfill its responsibilities if it is faction-ridden, comprised of individuals each concerned only with promoting the interests of one socioeconomic, racial, or religious group.

5. Whether the individual has children or grandchildren attending school or is active in youth work. An individual with such a background is more likely to be interested in and understanding of educational problems than, for instance, a middle-aged bachelor whose concern for children has not survived his own childhood.

Generally, the education of board members exceeds that of the total population—about 50 percent are college graduates. Typically the majority of the members are chosen from among the occupational groups called "successful men and women of business and professional affairs." Laboring groups and women are underrepresented. Women especially, it would seem, should be better represented, since as a group they have strong interest in and considerable insight into the education of their children, especially at the elementary level. Many women are qualified and have the time and energy required of a school board member. Of the 319 board members included in the survey mentioned above, 103 were businessmen; 66 were lawyers; 22 were physicians; 11 were clergymen; 70 were women, 51 of whom were housewives; 40 were non-Caucasian. In agricultural centers the representation would perhaps be different.

7. Functions

The functions of boards of education are implied in the broad powers, both specific and discretionary, granted them by the state legislatures. Ideally the school board acts as a kind of equalizer between the interests of the professional staff and the interests of the public. As state officers they also act as a counterinfluence to excessive state-centered authority over the public schools in their district.

More specifically, school boards hold meetings open to the public and to the professional staff, issue mimeographed or printed statements

Experience with children in schools is valuable in deciding whether or not to enter teaching and essential to the student teacher who has made the decision. A high school student works with a handicapped child during a summer program. (The NEA, through its Future Teachers of America, encourages this kind of activity.) A student teacher trains in an Appalachian region school.

of their policies, employ a professional administrative staff (superintendent, business manager, et al.) to whom they delegate executive functions, map out or approve an over-all educational program, fix salaries, draw up budgets, levy taxes, keep account of monies spent, decide the length of the school year, enforce compulsory attendance laws, determine where and when new buildings shall be erected, make rules and regulations for the management of the schools, purchase material, provide pupil transportation, and so on. The list of functions is indeed formidable.

In recent years board practices in formulating policies have changed considerably. Boards now spend far more time in holding meetings to hear expressions of public opinion before making final decisions. Probably because of the growth in membership and influence of the teachers' national organizations, the National Education Association and the American Federation of Teachers, today's school board willingly enters into professional negotiations with teachers through well-defined procedures before making final decisions with regard to teachers' security provisions such as salaries, sick leaves, and fringe benefits. In earlier times the teachers were expected to—and usually did—accept submissively whatever the school board decided to give them. At that time school boards took the position that their authority was established by law and could not, therefore, be delegated to others. That is no longer held to be true. Boards have learned that through a series of orderly procedures many of their decisions can be shared decisions. Among activities school boards have adamantly stood out against are mandated mediation, sanctions, strikes, boycotts, and the like. Nevertheless, these techniques are being used increasingly by classroom teachers in the interest of their rights at times when they feel that a state or a district is not treating them fairly.

General superintendent of schools

The school board consists of laymen who do not profess expertness in school management. It is their responsibility to see that the work of the school is properly performed by professional personnel. It is

347

CHAPTER 12
*Local Aspects
of Public School
Organization and
Administration*

essential that they employ a well-qualified professional educator to superintend the work of the schools. He is the chief executive. As superintendent of the school district, he occupies a central position in the over-all structure of authority. The boards of education delegate many of their own legal powers to him. His policies, of course, are subject to board approval.

Since the superintendent's powers are broad, his duties are many and varied. As administrative head of the district, he is professional adviser to the board of education as well as supervisor, employer, and organizer of the professional personnel and supervisor and employer of the nonteaching personnel, e.g., engineers and janitors. He is the expert in relations between the schools and the community and formulator of the policies that rule the selection, placement, and transportation of pupils. In other words, the superintendent of schools is charged with the final responsibility for the efficient management and effective organization and administration of all the public schools in the school district. His position is important, calling for a high level of administrative ability and professional leadership. The position has become so important in school administration that considerable study is devoted to defining the nature of the superintendent's work and to providing specialized training programs in the graduate schools of the universities.

In a smoothly running school organization only the chief executive is legally responsible to the board. In all but the smallest systems, however, he has administrative and supervisory assistants to whom he delegates important responsibility and authority.

There is a growing tendency to recognize the need for including the teachers and, in some cases, the public in defining school policy. In earlier years the superintendent was considered to be more sympathetic to the board than to the teachers. Today he is considered both the agent of the board and also the representative of the teachers. He tends to include teachers when he is formulating plans and policies and to encourage them to participate in making decisions. His authority has thus been reduced, his opportunities for leadership enhanced.

In simple terms, then, the public school district is a state corporation, the board of education is the governing body, the superintendent of schools is the chief administrative officer.

County superintendent of schools

The professional staff of the school district in agricultural centers is sometimes headed by a county superintendent of schools. From the title "superintendent," one might assume that this position is analogous to that of city superintendent of schools. Such, however, is not generally the case. In states where the school district in the agricultural centers is organized on the town or township basis, the county superintendent's functions are mainly of a clerical nature. Only a few executive responsibilities are delegated to him. For example, in Illinois the county school superintendent, who is elected on a partisan political ticket, visits the rural schools periodically. State monies are channeled through his office. As the legal representative of the state, he sanctions those who teach in county schools. He is the interpreter of school law when the need arises. As a rule, steps in the reorganization of school districts are cleared through his office. In the 12 states in which the school districts coincide with the county boundaries, however, the position is somewhat, but not wholly, like that of the superintendent in a city district.

County and district school boards look upon the county school superintendent as their professional adviser and leader. Whether he is appointed to be the chief executive officer for county boards of education, or is elected on a political ticket and possesses only remote executive authority over individual school units within the county district, or is selected by the elected trustees of the townships in the county, he is an important person in the direction and improvement of public education in the agricultural areas of the United States.

The trend toward the reorganization of school districts and the reduction or abolishment of one-teacher schools tends to change the functions of the county superintendent of schools. Perhaps the future of the office cannot be predicted at this writing. In some cases, where, say, the county is made the organizational and administrative unit, the powers and functions of the office might be expanded. In other instances the opposite effect might even lead to making the office relatively obsolete. Different policies of reorganization in different states will almost certainly affect the official state and local relationships of the county superintendent of schools.

349

CHAPTER 12
Local Aspects
of Public School
Organization and
Administration

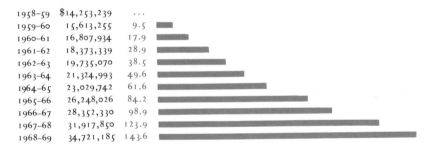

1958–59	$14,253,239	. . .
1959–60	15,613,255	9.5
1960–61	16,807,934	17.9
1961–62	18,373,339	28.9
1962–63	19,735,070	38.5
1963–64	21,324,993	49.6
1964–65	23,029,742	61.6
1965–66	26,248,026	84.2
1966–67	28,352,330	98.9
1967–68	31,917,850	123.9
1968–69	34,721,185	143.6

Fig. 12.4 Total expenditures for public elementary and secondary education, 1958–1959 to 1968–1969, with percentage increases over 1958–1959. Dollar amounts are in thousands. (Data from NEA Research Report 1968-R16)

Abiding traditions

The great variety in types of organization and administration results from (1) the unplanned development of education from semiprivate, short-term, low-cost schooling for the few to the huge public enterprise it is today and (2) the persistent emphasis on local initiative in educational planning. Despite this variety, however, traditions have persisted that cause schools throughout the nation to remain very much alike.

SELF-GOVERNMENT

An insistence on locally administered school systems is a manifestation of the deep-rooted American belief in the doctrine of popular sovereignty. The people elect school boards, vote bond issues, employ and live close to educational personnel, and in many other ways participate in school management. The degree of local control, however, is influenced by the policies of state and federal governments, and these shift with the times.

LOCAL INTEREST

Throughout the nation, citizens express pardonable pride in their local systems of free public schools. One way the professional staff fosters this interest is by encouraging wide, representative citizen involvement in public education. Furthermore, every proposal to shift responsibility and power from the local system to, for example, a state-wide system will always be examined closely to determine whether it may not weaken the system by diminishing the extent of local control and stifling the local public's interest in schools that they have come to regard as "theirs."

DISPERSION OF POWER OVER EDUCATION

Most Americans realize that power over education "equals" power over the nation's future. They know also that if this power were concentrated in a few "wrong" hands, education might be used to change the next generation's whole social outlook. Traditionally, we have rejected such concentration of power over education and, instead, have distributed control among many agencies and among many people. Of all traditions in American education, this, perhaps, is the one most likely to persist.

In 1969 there were 19,369 operating elementary and high school districts in the United States, and all of these were controlled by the local citizens. Some of these districts had boards with as many as 11 members—Chicago, for example. Some districts had only one school trustee, as in some township school districts in Indiana. The number of Americans who serve the schools on a voluntary basis is large indeed. Generally these people are capable and well-intentioned. Only rarely has control fallen into incompetent, corrupt, or selfish hands.

Teachers prefer to work in schools that are under the general control of local boards, principally perhaps because they are accustomed to this form of control and feel it can more readily reflect desirable local interests. Teachers cannot visualize what would be involved in adjusting to and influencing a highly centralized state educational system. Through their professional organizations teachers are encouraged to contribute to the formulation of school policies. Local school boards—which because they are local are accessible— are becoming more and more aware of the value of direct communication with teachers, of the value of consulting with teachers before defining policies. Teachers' relations with a nonlocal governing body would probably be too impersonal to permit such direct relationship.

The school and the community often cooperate in giving special help to those who need it to find success and self-fulfillment. In a school-community tutoring effort, educated housewives spend three hours a week trying to win the trust and build the confidence of high school students whose scholastic achievement has been seriously limited by cultural deprivation. A high school junior clerks in a record store under the Seattle

schools' work experience program. His on-the-job progress is discussed by the store's supervisor and a work experience counselor. A paraprofessional—one of a group of educated local people who do not fully qualify as teachers—works with a handicapped child. Such aides perform essential functions in many schools. The coordinator of the Seattle schools' disadvantaged student program arrives to discuss with the director of a community center ways to increase the help both schools and center give to socially and culturally deprived young people. (The other two men, the center's research director and the community relations secretary of the Seattle Urban League, also are active in the program.)

The public, of course, does not want the professional staff to conduct schools only as they, the staff, desire. On the other hand, the public does not want to dominate the schools. What they seek is partnership. Partnership recognizes that the interests of staff and public are mutual. The public and the staff are closely related in the same venture, the success of which depends on how each accepts and cares for the interests of the other.

NEIGHBORLINESS

Neighborliness is a cherished characteristic of the typical American community. The school is highly suitable for the promotion of neighborliness because it is the one community institution that can cut across lines of class, religion, race, or political affiliation. With the current practice of busing children within a city district to schools that are not geographically "neighborhood" schools for purposes of achieving racial integration, and with the reorganization of many schools in agricultural centers, the dedication to the neighborhood school has had to change. Even so, the spirit of the neighborhood school, neighborliness, continues. Although in many communities the present-day school is no longer a traditional neighborhood school in the sense that it is the main center of recreation and social life, the old spirit of neighborliness is still cultivated by such events as PTA activities, parents' night at school, after-school teas for teachers, athletic events, parades, concerts, exhibits, and so forth. To the extent that the school is used to strengthen the tradition of neighborliness, it too is strengthened.

FREE CHOICE

Parents are free to decide whether their children shall attend public or nonpublic schools. This is in accord with one of our democracy's central tenets: the individual has the right to believe in whatever he chooses. The individual's beliefs direct his choice among political parties, churches, clubs—or the school that his children will attend.

353

CHAPTER 12
*Local Aspects
of Public School
Organization and
Administration*

Summary

We find great variation among school systems in the public school districts, even within the same state. Differences among the states and differences among districts in the same state are due in part to the fact that many state legislatures grant considerable authority to district boards of education. In some cases, for example, the laws are permissive in character, granting the boards wide latitude in interpretation. This means that America really has an educational system based upon the principle of state-local cooperation. At present no complete or specific division of power has been developed. Experiments with local-state divisions of functions are going forward. There is a definite trend toward enlarging districts, especially in agricultural areas. Experiments with various patterns of enlarged districts, however, continue. Whatever the answer to the question of local-state relationships, it is generally agreed that the self-governing school community should not be sacrificed. Problems related to the local school district should be solved without weakening the local interest of the community in its schools. Lay leaders, as they function through boards of education, are vested with authority over the schools. Fundamental changes in education are dependent on aggressive lay leadership and an intelligently informed citizenry.

Under widespread control, no single agency, it is believed, can ever gain control of the public schools, nor can any one kind of selfish propaganda agency influence education throughout all the nation's public schools.

From the start it was believed that by leaving education in the hands of those who were most closely touched by it, the cause of education would be better cared for than if it were in the hands of those far removed from the community. A local school system is one that is more likely to respond quickly and sympathetically to a community's needs. Whatever the weaknesses of localism may be, it appears that the local school district, in some form, is likely to dominate the American educational scheme for years to come. There seems to be no strong desire on the part of the American people to discard the plan.

Questions

1. What are the principal advantages in the American policy of operating the schools largely through home rule? What are some disadvantages?
2. What have been the principal advantages and disadvantages to education of the district type of organization as it has functioned in the past?
3. What is a local board of education? What are its principal functions?
4. In what ways has local school management become more difficult in recent years? What may school boards do to compensate for the increase in their responsibilities?
5. How is the superintendent of a local district appointed? What, ideally, are his principal functions?
6. How is a county superintendent of schools selected? What are his principal functions?
7. In your opinion, should the functions of county superintendent rightfully parallel those of the city superintendent of schools?
8. What are the principal differences between a local municipal government and a local school district government?

Projects

1. Survey the pattern of school districting that prevails in your state. Point out where and how improvement has been brought about.
2. Draw up a list of standards for local school boards that should apply to such matters as selection, term of office, size, representation, qualifications, and compensation.
3. List the powers and duties of a local school board. Indicate how a community may guard against misuse of powers.
4. State the pros and cons of keeping school government separate from municipal government.
5. a. Explain why inequalities in educational opportunities have been allowed to develop in large-city school districts.
   b. Explain what should be done to erase them.

In the over-all picture of education in America, the relative roles of the three levels of government—federal, state, and local—do not remain fixed for any length of time. Changes in educational policy at the federal level produce changes at both the state and local levels. Likewise, a new state law may modify the relationships between the local and state levels. It seems, then, that the interrelationships that exist at any one time among the three levels of government will continue to be characterized by constant change.

The most significant change in the past quarter century in American education has been, perhaps, the steady growth in the concern, influence, and participation of the federal government in many aspects of both public and private education at all levels—for children, youth, and adults of all ages. As will become clear as we proceed, it is most difficult to come even close to making an accurate estimate of the extent to which the federal government contributes to education because its contribution takes so many forms. This is strikingly illustrated when we look at the growth in the amount of money the federal government spends on public education. In 1957–1958, the amount of public school revenue derived from the federal government was 4 percent of the total; 11 years later, however (1968–1969), it had increased to more than 8 percent. (The percentage remained fairly constant up to 1965–1966; then greatly expanded federal programs caused it to double.) When we consider that school expenditures were constantly increasing over that 11-year period, the federal expenditure in dollar amounts increased tremendously. As these new data show, the expansion, although continuous, has been uneven.

Because a classroom teacher's welfare is inevitably affected by changes in the federal government's activities, especially if the shifts in policy are sharp, no teacher will wish to remain a mere spectator to changes outside his classroom. As a member of the profession, he will wish to evaluate education changes, support those that seem desirable, skillfully implement those that are judged worthy from an educational point of view, and influence the direction of future changes. Government acts can produce good results only when the education profession provides the wise leadership needed to fulfill the provisions of the acts.

Since the influence of the federal government on education began even before the adoption of the Constitution, and since the long story of federal activities in the area of education has so many facets, we can select only a few of the more outstanding, more illustrative steps the federal government has taken. Let us consider first how the federal government justifies its considerable influence over education in America and note the ways it has, up to this time, limited its participation.

Constitutional provisions for education

Why did members of the Constitutional Convention omit any mention of education from the Constitution? For one thing, they were faced at that time with several other and more serious problems that had to be solved to preserve national unity. In the face of such emergencies it is not surprising that they should put less pressing matters in the background. We must remember, also, that at the time little thought had as yet been given to public education. The ideas and the theories developed by Pestalozzi, Herbart, and Froebel had not yet been born. Education in early America was largely a matter of interest only to those who could afford to pay for it.

In the preamble of the Constitution, however, the obligation to advance the cause of education is implied in the statement that it is the purpose of the Constitution to provide for the common defense and general welfare. The section of the Constitution that empowers Congress to levy and collect taxes likewise states that taxes shall provide for the common defense and general welfare of the

United States. Although the founding fathers did not specifically mention education, they made statements that unquestionably obligate the federal government to advance public education.

On the other hand, the Constitution, by implication, also makes clear that the power over education is to be delegated to the states. Since power over education was not specifically delegated to the United States nor prohibited to the states, it was, according to the Tenth Amendment, definitely to be left to the individual states. That has consistently been the construction placed upon the wording of the Tenth Amendment.

There is general agreement that the federal government in America has complete control over certain segments of education, segments that are wholly outside the jurisdiction of any other unit of government. These are:

1. The education of residents of special federal areas, such as government reservations and federal districts lying outside the legal jurisdiction of a state and other regional governments.
2. The education of the American Indians and other indigenous peoples within the national jurisdiction.
3. The education of the peoples of the territories and outlying possessions.
4. The training of persons in the service of the national government.
5. Scientific research and the collection and diffusion of information regarding education.
6. The intellectual and educational cooperation of the United States with other nations.[1]

The federal government thus assumes complete authority over a considerable part of education in America. In addition to these six areas of complete federal authority, the federal government increasingly participates in education in the states and in local districts and even gives educational aid to certain individuals. A review of the historical development of such federal activity will lead to a better understanding of current federal activity in education.

[1] National Advisory Committee on Education, *Federal Relations to Education*. Washington: National Capital Press, 1931, pp. 9–10.

Federal grants to education

UNCONDITIONAL LAND GRANTS

In 1785 and in 1787, the Continental Congress passed two ordinances which provided for surveying the Northwest Territory and planning the administration of the territory. The first of these ordinances (see p. 359) established the policy of reserving the sixteenth section in each township (one square mile out of 36) for the benefit of public schools. The precedent for this action was the reserving of land for school purposes by several of the former colonies.

The federal government did not put the land-grant policy into operation until 1803, when Ohio was admitted as a state. Vermont, Kentucky, and Tennessee, which were admitted to the Union as new states within a few years after the adoption of the Constitution, did not receive any land for common school purposes.

The provisions of the Ohio Act were extended in 1803 to the national domain south of Tennessee and in 1821 to the Louisiana territory. Only three states admitted since 1803 have never received some kind of federal land grant for public schools: Maine, where the federal government had no title to any territory because Maine had been part of Massachusetts; Texas, which was a sovereign state when annexed; and West Virginia, which seceded from Virginia during the Civil War. Since 1850, when California was admitted, two sections of each township have been given for schools in all new states except Utah, Arizona, and New Mexico, which were allowed four sections because of the low value of the lands.

It is evident that the early federal legislators did appreciate the importance of public education and were interested in helping the states establish public schools. However, fostering education was secondary to other desired achievements. Their first interest was in selling and settling western lands. They believed that making school land available would promote the sale of real estate.

The land grants to education, considered an acceptable and essential federal aid policy, were to be out-and-out grants to the states, with no strings attached. After the state received the land, the federal government did not interfere with its use or management. This is an

The policy of setting aside a portion of the public lands for school purposes, rather than selling all the land or homesteading it, was first established in the Land Ordinance of 1785, enacted by the Congress under the Articles of Confederation on May 20, 1785.

An Ordinance for Ascertaining the Mode of Disposing of Lands in the Western Territory

> Be it ordained by the United States, in Congress assembled, *That the territory ceded by individual States to the United States, which has been purchased of the Indian inhabitants, shall be disposed of in the following manner :*
> *A surveyor from each state shall be appointed by Congress.* . . .
> *The Surveyors . . . shall proceed to divide the said territory into townships of six miles square, by lines running due north and south, and others crossing these at right angles, as near as may be.* . . .
> *The plats of the townships, respectively, shall be marked by subdivisions into lots of one mile square, or 640 acres, in the same direction as the external lines, and numbered from 1 to 36.* . . .
> *. . . There shall be reserved the lot No. 16, of every township, for the maintenance of public schools within the said township ; also one-third part of all gold, silver, lead and copper mines, to be sold, or otherwise disposed of as Congress shall hereafter direct.* . . .

example of an early and prevailing attitude of the federal government—the principle of federal support without federal control.

In the states admitted early to the union, the general policy was to sell the land and to place the proceeds in a *permanent* fund. The interest from the fund was to be used for public school purposes. Often public land was the one source of support for education, and the lands could be kept or sold at the discretion of the state. Some states handled these permanent sources of income much more wisely than others. A few states virtually squandered their inheritance. Dishonest individuals and greedy corporate interests were allowed to exploit federal land grants for their own selfish purposes. However, in 1940, one-third of the land granted was still owned by the states. It is especially to the credit of the newer states that they have administered their share of public land for school purposes wisely. The value of their federal land grants is constantly increasing. The provisions of the early ordinances, which followed the policy of aid-in-general, stimulated sentiment for public education. In the older states the federal grants were especially helpful at a time when the idea of taxing citizens for the support of public schools was not generally acceptable.

The policy of depending on permanent school funds, in its application, has had great influence on both public and nonpublic education. At present almost every university, whether public or nonpublic, has its own tax-free foundation built from contributions from many agencies—private individuals, industrial and commercial organizations, and the like. Also many tax-free foundations with exceedingly large financial resources make liberal grants to education, both public and nonpublic, and thereby exercise far-reaching influence on the course of education in America. Where the principle of permanent funds, called endowments by some universities, has been tested in the courts, the Supreme Court of the United States has consistently sustained the validity of a corporate charter given by a state to a school, denying that the state subsequently has the right to amend it, thereby assuring preservation of educational capital and the continuity of educational foundations.

From the history of federal aid to education, it seems that the question of future policy will not be concerned with categorical versus general aid to the states. We may expect a continuation of both policies—specific aid where needed, and also general aid to the states to enhance their resources for designated state programs. Recent indications are, however, that categorical aid will receive first priority from the Congress.

FEDERAL GRANTS FOR A SPECIFIC PURPOSE

1. The Morrill Acts

The policy of no restrictions on management or uses made of the income from land grants was not followed in some of the later federal programs, notably in the Morrill Act of 1862. In part this was because the earlier grants had been squandered in some states and in part because the earlier universities had remained almost entirely academic.

A proposal to establish a national agricultural college, analogous

The principles of federal aid to higher education and of the legitimacy of permanent school funds, sometimes referred to as endowments, are recognized in the Morrill Act of 1862. The wording merits careful reading.

An Act Donating Public Lands to the Several States and Territories Which May Provide Colleges for the Benefit of Agriculture and Mechanic Arts

Be it enacted by the Senate and the House of Representatives of the United States of America, in Congress assembled, *That there be granted to the several States, for the purposes hereinafter mentioned, an amount of public land, to be apportioned to each State a quantity equal to thirty thousand acres for each senator and representative in Congress to which the States are respectively entitled by the apportionment under the census of eighteen hundred and sixty : Provided, That no mineral lands shall be selected or purchased under the provisions of this act. . . .*
Section 4. And be it further enacted, *That all moneys derived from the sale of the lands aforesaid by the States to which the lands are apportioned, and from the sale of land scrip hereinbefore provided for, shall be invested in stocks of the United States, or of the States, or some other safe stocks, yielding not less than five per centum upon the par value of said stocks ; and that the moneys so invested shall constitute a perpetual fund, the capital of which shall remain forever undiminished (except so far as may be provided in section fifth of this act), and the interest of which shall be inviolably appropriated, by each State which may take and claim the benefit of this act, to the endowment, support, and maintenance of at least one college where the leading object shall be, without excluding other scientific and classical studies, and including military tactics, to teach such branches of learning as are related to agriculture and the mechanic arts, in such manner as the legislatures of the States may respectively prescribe, in order to promote the liberal and practical education of the industrial classes in the several pursuits and professions in life.*

to West Point in the military field, had been defeated. The Morrill Act passed subsequently was intended to encourage the establishment in each state

of at least one college where the leading object shall be, without ex-cluding other scientific and classical studies, and including military tactics, to teach such branches of learning as are related to agriculture and the mechanic arts, in such manner as the legislatures of the States may respectively prescribe, in order to promote the liberal and practical education of the industrial classes in the several pursuits and professions in life.

This act, signed by President Lincoln, granted to each state

an amount of public land . . . equal to thirty thousand acres for each senator and representative in Congress to which the States are respectively entitled by the apportionment under the census of eighteen hundred and sixty: Provided, That no mineral lands shall be selected or purchased under the provisions of this act.

The act further established a measure of control by stipulating that each state claiming the benefits of the act should make an annual report "regarding the progress of each college, recording any improvements and experiments made, with their costs and results. . . ."

This act and another Morrill Act in 1890 led to the establishment of 69 land-grant colleges, some of which evolved into some of America's largest and most influential state universities. At least one such college was established in each state. In some states—e.g., Illinois, Wisconsin, and Minnesota—the colleges were combined with the state universities. In others, the federally aided colleges were established as separate colleges—e.g., Iowa State University, Michigan State University, and Purdue University.

Federal policy enunciated in the Morrill Acts was to give land grants to *higher* institutions, to state the principal objectives of the education for which the grants were to be used, and to require an accounting of the money spent. "Unconditional" grants did not constitute the only policy followed.

2. Smith-Hughes Act

A number of Congressional acts have authorized federal grants-in-aid to vocational education. The grants, in all cases, have been large and the effects upon public education have been far-reaching. The Smith-Hughes Act of 1917 was one of the first, and also one of the most influential, of a series of acts that gave aid to vocational education offered in the public high schools. It is a fairly typical example of how the federal government engages in educational activity.

The term "land grant" is significant, implying that land was the foundation on which the present structure of agricultural and mechanical and also military colleges has been erected. It would be more accurate, however, to call them "land bait" colleges, because the grants were relatively small moneywise. They were large enough, however, to induce the states to set up a system of colleges which are supported partly by state taxation and partly by federal funds. . . .
The purpose is to show how a relatively small gift of frontier land was used to establish a system of education that is nationwide, closely integrated, and now supported almost entirely by taxation, both state and federal. And it was created and raised by a little wedge of frontier land.

Walter Prescott Webb, *The Great Frontier*. Boston: Houghton Mifflin Company, 1952, pp. 402, 404. Quoted by permission of Houghton Mifflin Company.

Under the Smith-Hughes Act the federal government subsidizes high school vocational education in agriculture, home economics, and industrial education. The act also makes provisions for the preparation of teachers of those subjects. Money is apportioned to the state on the basis of total population, and in order to receive it "the state or local community, or both, shall spend an equal amount" for this work. Each state and local community is required also to meet certain other standards. Congress has never failed to make the appropriation for these purposes—but it could, of course, refuse at any time.

Certainly many favorable effects have accrued from the Smith-Hughes Act and from similar legislation. High schools have become more conscious of the great need for expansion in the vocational field. New instructional materials and methods have been developed. Shops and laboratories in the high schools have, for the first time, been well built and adequately equipped. Education and salaries of the high school teachers of vocational subjects have been greatly improved. Improving salaries for those who participate in the vocational education program at the state level also improves the personnel serving at that level.

The categorical-aid policy followed by the federal government in the Smith-Hughes Act and similar other acts called for the state to match federal funds to improve a single aspect of the educational program, perhaps at a given level. This was a departure from the

earlier policy of giving general aid. Some educational leaders questioned the wisdom of the change. It was argued that federal aid to a
given high school to help support a vocational education program, for
instance, gave certain advantages to some staff members in matters
like salary, training, and number of months employed during the year,
and was damaging to personnel relations. Also expressed was fear of
the power of the federal bureaucracy over state and local programs,
vocational or otherwise. Federal control was considered by some as a
threat to the principle that the state is the unit of school administration and to the general practice of having the states control the powers
given to the local school districts. With time, however, categorical
aid from the federal government has proved a powerful and more or
less welcomed stimulant which, once imbibed, continues to be
sought despite objections in some quarters that its acceptance is a bad
habit.

As the public and the teaching profession became accustomed to
a degree of federal control of education, it became easier to accept an
increase in federal power. For instance, the Morrill Acts extended a
measure of control at the college level, the Smith-Hughes Act of 1917
extended it to the high schools, and as noted later in this chapter, the
Elementary and Secondary Education Act of 1965 for the first time
included the elementary schools.

Clearly, the federal government has not followed a single policy
toward support of education. Politicians in particular seem to favor
the aid-for-specific-purpose policy. Each act, however, has been independent of all the others. Many of the federal grants-in-aid have
been crash programs, responses to sudden, pressing necessity. Each
act, therefore, must be viewed as a separate episode in the history of
the federal government's participation in American education.

RECENT FEDERAL MONEY GRANTS

1. Measures passed during the depression

During the depression of the 1930s, grants to education were
mostly outright, with no requirement of matching funds. Laws set
forth conditions under which funds must be used but did not exert
control over the programs.

"What's for lunch?" *Whatever the menu, this school lunch has been federally subsidized
and is provided at very low cost to each child.*

The National Youth Administration was organized during the
depression to provide aid for needy high school, college, and university students so that they might continue their education. The
funds were administered and the work was assigned by the individual
school in which the services were used. The federal grants-in-aid went
directly to the high school or college students through institutional
channels.

The Civilian Conservation Corps also was an emergency depression measure. Its purpose was "relief of unemployment through performance of useful public work." Camps were organized for young
men, and an education program was made an integral part of the plan.
The camps were under the administrative control of the army. So was
the education program.

The school lunch program was an emergency relief program also
started during the depression. With the passage of the National School
Lunch Act of 1946, however, it became a regular part of federal
participation in education. This act was designed "to safeguard the
health and well-being of the Nation's children and to encourage the
domestic consumption of nutritious agricultural commodities and

other foods." Under this act, the federal government gives the local schools, through the states, both direct grants of surplus commodities for use in school lunchrooms and money to facilitate the distribution and use of these food products. This enables local public schools to provide federally subsidized, low-cost lunches to their pupils. Although this is a direct form of federal aid to education, it was, in the beginning, designed primarily to help the farmers rather than the school children. Its value has been such as to assure its continuance as an accepted federal policy. In 1967–1968, 36.7 percent of the public and private school enrollments were participating in the federally subsidized school lunch program. The range by states was from 16.4 percent in Rhode Island to 67.1 percent in Louisiana.

Many other federal programs of education were initiated during the period of the depression, including the establishment of nursery schools, classes in avocational and leisure-time activities, special programs, and lectures. Funds for school buildings were also provided under the Works Progress Administration. It should be noted that federal aid to education has never been administered through a single agency such as the Department of Health, Education, and Welfare. Currently, as many as 20 agencies are dispensing funds for various kinds of aid to education.

2. Measures passed before and during World War II

In the period immediately before World War II and during the war, disruptions growing out of such emergencies as the demand for many people with certain highly specialized training, the relocation of masses of people, and the large-scale employment of mothers led the federal government to conduct some emergency education programs and to make grants for the administration of others. For example, the Lanham Act, passed in 1941, provided general appropriations for training war plant workers under the direction of the United States Office of Education, for constructing school plants in areas that were overburdened because of federal activity, and for maintaining child-care of the children of employed parents.

3. GI Bill of Rights

In terms of influence and cost, one of the great federal participations in education is contained in laws collectively and popularly

A law is not just words—it is hopes, intentions, actions, results. Here are three of the programs made possible by the federal government under the Elementary and Secondary Education Act of 1965. The actions are here ; the results meet expectations sometimes, sometimes not. But the hopes and the intentions endure. A child in a Title I speech development program uses a machine to listen to correctly pronounced words and phrases, then to her own efforts, then again to the model. Repeated practice will help her to improve her speech. Two views are shown of another Title I project—a cooperative learning program in Chicago for children aged 3 to 5 and their parents. Four child-parent centers were set up, each staffed by a principal, four primary teachers, four teacher aides, a

school-community representative, and others. In addition, a teacher-nurse, teacher-social worker, speech teacher, and two psychologists were hired to work in all four centers. Under a Title III program, a science kit produced during a summer elementary science institute for teachers is demonstrated to children in school.

known as the "GI Bill of Rights." The program began with the Vocational Rehabilitation Act and the Servicemen's Readjustment Act signed by President Franklin D. Roosevelt in 1944. Since then other laws have been added. In the peak year, 1948, nearly three billion dollars was spent in subsidizing programs of education for veterans. Incidentally, only very rarely was any charge raised of "government interference" in the educational programs of high schools and colleges that were involved in this GI schooling. The GI Bill of Rights guarantees to veterans payment of tuition as well as payment for board and room for a specified number of months, based on length of military service rendered. The GI Bill has enabled millions of young men and women to attend high schools, colleges, universities, specialized schools, and adult education classes throughout the land. Several hundred also have studied abroad under the GI Bill. In addition to increasing the numbers enrolled in our schools, the GI Bill tended to change the character of our school population. It became commonplace for married men and men with families to be full-time students. Temporary housing for young families mushroomed on college campuses. The GIs were older and more serious. Their presence raised the age level of those in school and gave an impetus to adult education.

4. Federal aid to higher education

Millions of dollars are now flowing annually from agencies of the federal government into educational agencies and institutions of higher learning. The National Defense Education Act, signed into law on September 2, 1958, strengthened American education at all levels. Within five years the federal government had expended $800 million to assist educational institutions of higher education, both public and nonpublic, and to aid state agencies with programs believed important to the nation's security. This included, for example, $330 million assigned to a student loan program, 70 percent of which was lent to students of superior ability who intended to teach in the elementary and secondary schools. Another $65 million was spent on the education of school counselors. Over the five-year period, 1958–1963, $181 million was paid to the states and territories to strengthen instruction in science, mathematics, and modern languages in the public elementary and high schools. The number of language laboratories in public high schools rose from 46 in 1958 to approximately 6,000 in 1963. Equally large amounts were spent in improving other services. Periodicially the U. S. Department of Health, Education, and Welfare issues a report on the National Defense Education Act, a report that describes in detail the many purposes for which federal funds are allocated. The annual report gives a vivid picture of the extensive scale of this federal excursion into a strengthening of American education, with the continuing support of the Congress.

5. Elementary and Secondary Education Act of 1965

In response to a rather belated awakening by the federal government to manifest, and extreme, inequalities in educational opportunity among school districts and among states, the Congress of 1965 passed a number of significant laws. The most far-reaching of these was the Elementary and Secondary Education Act of 1965, officially designated Public Law 89-10 and unofficially referred to as the federal government's billion-dollar educational venture. The law was designed to reduce certain long-time cumulative deficiencies in both state and local education—the neglected education of young children in underprivileged areas of large cities, for example. A brief description of each of the law's five original titles gives an understanding of the extent and intent of the act as a whole:

Title I. This title gives financial assistance to state school districts for the education of children from families whose income is less than $2,000 a year. Five-sixths of the entire federal appropriation goes for the implementation of this title of the law. In an area where there is a concentration of such families, an area clearly identified by administrators of public or nonpublic school systems, all children in that area are eligible to receive the benefits of the improved education made possible by federal funds.

Title II. This title allocates some $100 million to the states to provide state public school districts and nonpublic schools with certain specified resources, such as school libraries, textbooks, and a variety of other instructional materials.

Title III. The purpose of this title is to bring educational innovations into the school system. Application must be made to and approved by the United States Commissioner of Education. A wide variety of programs can be aided under this title. Basically, the hope is that the special and somewhat original local programs will make wide use of the community's resources, utilizing as never before its cultural advantages and talented leaders.

Title IV. This title provides $100 million over a period of five years for constructing and equipping national and regional research facilities. A rather broad interpretation is placed on the word "research." For example, funds are provided for building and operating national and regional laboratories, utilizing many existing resources such as universities, public schools, state departments of education, industrial research organizations, and the like.

Title V. This title gives grants to the states for the specific purpose of strengthening the state departments of education.

The five titles cover a wide area; taken together, they represent an energetic federal attack on the weakest points of education as it has functioned in the past.

6. Head Start programs

The Economic Opportunity Act, signed into law in 1964, was one of the key measures in the federal government's "war on poverty." One program under this act is Project Head Start, which was begun during the summer of 1965 and is continuing as a summer and also as a year-round activity. Head Start was designed

> to improve the health and physical ability of poor children, to develop their self-confidence and ability to relate to others, to increase their verbal and conceptual skills, to involve parents in activities with their children, and to provide appropriate social services for the family in order that the child of poverty may begin his school career on more nearly equal terms with his more fortunate classmates.[2]

In some cases Head Start programs are operated by public school systems and in others by private schools and by nonprofit private agencies, like settlement houses. About two-thirds of the summer programs and about one-third of the year-round programs are operated by the schools.

The government establishes criteria for selection of children but

---

[2] Office of Economic Opportunity, *Catalog of Federal Assistance Programs*, Washington, June 1, 1967, p. 554. (Head Start was moved to the Department of Health, Education, and Welfare in 1969.)

In this unique Head Start project, the "rules" are ignored and preschoolers are drilled intensively, with something of the old rote-type methods. A primary goal is just to get the children to talk in sentences. But success can be achieved only by a teacher who is dedicated, determined, and sympathetic, all at the same time. This is such a teacher.

allows some leeway by asking that 85 percent of the children meet the requirements. Government requirements include family income of less than $3,000. The age range of children included is 3 to 6.

Chapter 15, "Units of School Organization," contains a discussion of Head Start as a part of the total school organization.

PUBLIC REACTION TO FEDERAL GRANTS TO EDUCATION

It must be remembered that the major share of the nation's total educational program is still borne by the 50 states and the thousands of local communities that operate the schools of our country, even though the practice of making federal grants for the support of education is well established, widespread, and diversified. Even among those elements of the population who were, in the past, most vocal in their opposition to federal aid to education, the resistance has now subsided to a mere whisper. The questions now before the American public are: How much federal aid shall education be given? How shall it be administered? What agencies are best qualified to administer it? To whom shall grants be made? With what other governmental units should the costs be shared?

The Rockefeller Report succinctly states the problem:

> The proposals for the support of education have stimulated widespread public discussions; but there is an air of unreality about much of the debate. For a great deal of the debate centers around a doctrinal dispute over the dangers of such support. Over the years . . . practical-minded legislators and executives on the one hand and hard-pressed educators on the other have been hammering out compromises almost unnoticed. And out of these compromises over the years has come a great variety of well-established federal programs in education. . . . Federal programs in education now exist on a large scale and in variety. It is a stark fact that there are educational problems gravely affecting the national interest which may be soluble only through federal action.
>
> Under the circumstances, it is important for those who are apprehensive about the growth of federal support of education to examine the *direction* which it takes. There is no chance that we can turn back the clock and eliminate federal support of education. There is a chance that farsighted men may influence the *direction* of federal support or the *kinds* of federal support.[3]

James Cass, the education editor for *Saturday Review*, calls attention to some other kinds of problems:

> Too often, it appears, the new money in education is not searching out new and better ways to solve old problems, but is simply going into traditional channels to give us more of the same.
>
> The U. S. Office of Education is finding it virtually impossible to obtain qualified people, in sufficient numbers, to administer the massive funds for which it is responsible. . . .

---

[3] *The "Rockefeller Report" on Education, Special Studies Project*, Report V, Rockefeller Brothers Fund. New York: Doubleday, 1958, p. 35.

The lesson to be drawn . . . is that after years of penury, education suddenly finds itself with more money than ideas, more dollars than talent. However, this should be a cause for action, not despair. Money attracts talent and can stimulate its development; it can also provide an environment in which ideas germinate and flourish. But it does not do so automatically. Money alone is not enough. The question is whether, given the money, we can generate the ideas and attract the talent that are required. [4]

Other educational activity at the federal level

EDUCATION FOR NATIONAL DEFENSE

The United States Military Academy at West Point, New York, the United States Naval Academy at Annapolis, Maryland, the United States Merchant Marine Academy at Kings Point, Long Island, New York, and the United States Air Force Academy at Colorado Springs, Colorado, are all supported entirely by the federal government, and each is operated by an appropriate branch of the federal government. These are a few examples of federal education conducted for reasons of defense. The total program for such education is extensive.

EDUCATION UNDER SPECIAL FEDERAL JURISDICTIONS

Inasmuch as the District of Columbia is not part of any state, the operation of its education program is left to the federal government. Congress makes all the laws that govern the District of Columbia, including those that apply to the schools, makes all the appropriations, and provides the means for raising revenues, which are collected by a combination of direct taxes and direct appropriations from the federal treasury.

The citizens have the right to vote only in national elections for the president of the United States, and therefore, those who are placed in control of the schools are not responsible to the community to the

---

[4] James Cass, "More Money than Ideas or Talent," *Saturday Review*, p. 49, July 16, 1966. Copyright 1966 by Saturday Review, Inc.

same degree as in public schools that are part of a state system. The public schools in Washington, D.C., according to an act of Congress, operate under the authority of a board of education that is comprised of nine members, of whom three are women and, customarily, three are Negroes. The members are appointed for a term of three years by the justices of the District Court of the United States. The board appoints a superintendent of schools who performs the functions usually assigned to such an officer.

Where the federal government has complete control, it shows its skill and reveals its attitudes toward public education. Generalizing from the Washington, D.C., school system, we may say that federally controlled systems operate about as efficiently and in much the same manner as do public schools in the rest of the country. None of the federally operated schools have ever been thought of as providing models or patterns to follow. For example, the school system in the nation's capital is noted for a predominance of the typical "inner-city" school, for schools characterized by a large proportion of Negro disadvantaged-by-poverty children.

The federal government also assists in promotion of education in the federal reservations, territories, outlying possessions, and United States trusteeship territories. It aids other countries through the United States Point Four Program, the Foreign Operations Administration, the United Nations Technical Assistance Program, and the Peace Corps. The widely varying educational problems involved testify to the extensive range of federal activity in education.

INDIVIDUAL SCHOOLS

All of the executive departments of the federal government engage in some kind of educational activity. Some of them operate schools to train government personnel and to help improve the personnel once they are in the employ of the federal government. The Department of State, for example, gives instruction to all newly appointed diplomatic and consular officers. The Treasury Department maintains a training school for the Coast Guard service, one for stenographers, a correspondence school for the employees in the Bureau of Internal Revenue, and a number of others which the department considers essential to the proper performance of its functions. The Department of Justice's school to train its personnel and the schools maintained by the Social Security Board are other examples of the numerous individual schools set up and administered by various departments of the federal government. Their educational activities are of great magnitude, affecting in some form well over a million civilians.

The United States Office of Education

The chief educational agency of the federal government is the United States Office of Education. It is the only federal agency devoted solely to improving the education of about 60 million students in American schools and colleges and to making educational opportunities more equally available to all.

The legal foundation for the United States Office of Education was laid in 1867:

> *Be it enacted by the Senate and the House of Representatives of the United States of America, in Congress assembled,* That there shall be established at the city of Washington, a department of education, for the purpose of collecting such statistics and facts as shall show the condition and progress of education in the several States and Territories, and of diffusing such information respecting the organization and management of schools and school systems, and methods of teaching, as shall aid the people of the United States in the establishment and maintenance of efficient school systems, and otherwise promote the cause of education throughout the country.
>
> *39th Congress, 2nd Session :*
> *Approved by President Andrew Johnson, March 2, 1867.*

In spite of the use of the word "department," the agency was not intended to have Cabinet status; a little over a year later, its name was changed to Office of Education, and it was placed in the Department of the Interior. In 1870, the office was renamed the Bureau of Education, and that title was retained until 1929, when the title of Office of Education was restored. In 1939, the Office of Education was transferred from the Department of the Interior to the newly created Federal Security Agency. In 1953, the Office of Education became a part of the newly created Department of Health, Education, and Welfare, with a secretary in the President's Cabinet. In its present setting it naturally receives greater recognition than in earlier years.

Since 1918, bills for the establishment of a separate federal department of education and a secretary of education in the President's Cabinet have been proposed again and again. Those who favor these proposals believe that, at present, public education does not have sufficient prestige in the federal government and that a separate department could more effectively articulate the achievements and outstanding problems of public education. Opponents point out that placing a secretary of education in the President's Cabinet would move education into the arena of "politics" on a national scale and perhaps increase the danger of federal control over state and local education.

The Office of Education is one of seven operating agencies of the Department of Health, Education, and Welfare. Its early function— and a continuing one—was to collect and distribute statistical and other information on education in the United States. Today, however, its overriding responsibility is to administer financial aid to education, to channel federal funds allocated by Congress—several billion dollars annually in recent years—into programs developed by state educational agencies, local school districts, and colleges to upgrade the quality and broaden the scope of instruction. These programs cover the educational spectrum from kindergarten to postgraduate study, from vocational training in high school to adult education throughout life. Nearly all of some 19,000 public school systems and 2,300 colleges in the United States participate. Students in parochial and private schools at the elementary and secondary levels also benefit from some programs.

The change in emphasis dates from 1958, when Congress responded to the recent first successful launching of a Soviet satellite and the immediate concern in the United States about the quality of our educational programs in science and related fields. The National Defense Education Act of 1958 was the first step by the federal government to assist school administrators in their increasingly difficult task of trying to provide quality education largely with local tax dollars and, in the case of colleges, with state or private revenues.

Even more far-reaching were the congressional decisions of 1965. The Elementary and Secondary Education Act authorized a multibillion-dollar program of federal aid to elementary schools and junior and senior high schools. By far the largest part of these funds was marked for special programs to help raise the quality of education for children from low-income families. The Higher Education Act set up

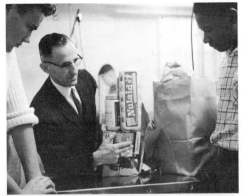

Various acts of the federal government have made possible both extended and intensified vocational programs in high schools throughout the country. At a school in California, a teacher using a transparent bag demonstrates proper bagging methods to trainee grocery clerks. At one of Chicago's nine vocational high schools, students experiment with resistive, single-time-element, and wave-shaping circuitry, using an audiogenerator, oscilloscope, and vacuum tube voltmeter. At the Aviation High School in New York, students learn how to repair aircraft.

seven new programs to strengthen colleges and universities and provide loans and grants to financially needy college students.

Other programs recently established or expanded by Congress and administered by the Office of Education include aid to vocational education, to the education of mentally and physically handicapped children, and to colleges and universities for construction or rehabilitation of classrooms, dormitories, and other facilities.

THE UNITED STATES COMMISSIONER OF EDUCATION

At the head of the United States Office of Education is the Commissioner of Education, who is appointed with the consent of the Senate by the President, upon the recommendation of the Secretary of Health, Education, and Welfare. He serves an indefinite term. Sometimes a change in Presidents is followed by the appointment of a new commissioner, although only 16 commissioners have served under 20 Presidents.

The commissioner's duties are listed in the act that established the Office of Education. In addition, his duties have been expanded over the years to include special tasks assigned by the President and imposed by congressional enactments, as well as voluntary cooperation with numerous educational agencies.

Judicial controls

While public education is a matter over which each state is sovereign, there are certain limitations on state action. State educational policy is in a most vital way subject to control by the Supreme Court of the United States.

Any state legislation, including educational legislation, is subject to review by the Supreme Court. If the Supreme Court decides that the law violates a provision of the United States Constitution, the law is declared unconstitutional and invalid. The authority to invalidate legislation affecting education is derived chiefly from the following provision of the Fourteenth Amendment:

> No state shall make or enforce any law which shall abridge the privileges or immunities of citizens of the United States; nor shall any state deprive any person of life, liberty, or property without due process of

law nor deny to any person within its jurisdiction the equal protection of the laws.

The Supreme Court of the United States is the final judge as to whether a person has been deprived of liberty or property. Since the terms "liberty" and "property" are extremely comprehensive, all manner of social and economic legislation, including educational legislation, may be invalidated. Obviously, state educational policy is in a large measure subject to control by the judges of the highest of our federal courts.

Supreme Court decisions have influenced the states in such problems as the relationship between schools and religion, uniformity of treatment of different races in the schools, and the matter of contractual relations with teachers. None of these matters have to do with federal power over education, but rather with federal responsibility for protecting individual rights.

When the Supreme Court hands down a decision that affects the policies of public education, the decision itself constitutes an interesting public statement of educational policy. The decision is always accompanied by the reasoning and the analyses behind it. These matters, broadly circulated by the press, radio, and television, serve to educate the American public effectively about fundamental issues in public education. In this way the Supreme Court has served as an educator to all the people of the United States.

The McCollum decision (1949) is one example of a Supreme Court decision concerned with the relationships of schools and religion. It grew out of the protest of Mrs. Vashti McCollum, a professed atheist, that her 7-year-old son, who attended a public school in Champaign, Illinois, was being subjected to ridicule and scorn because he remained in the classroom when the other children left to take part in religious exercises and training currently provided by the churches of the city on time released by the schools for this purpose. The school authorities, and then a series of lower courts, ruled against her plea that "released-time" practices be outlawed. The case finally went to the Supreme Court, which ruled against the released-time practices followed in this particular school system.

Another decision with respect to religious education in the public schools was made in 1952 in the Zorach case in New York City. This decision declared the practice of released time constitutional. The opinions in the two cases were not contradictory. In Champaign, those who were not excused to take religious instruction remained in school, whereas in New York, all pupils were released from school, presumably to receive religious instruction. The reasoning of the Court in rendering such judgments can be understood by a layman only after careful study of the complete decision. The important point is that, from the standpoint of the administration of public schools, the decisions of the Supreme Court are the final answers to controversies of a specific nature. Public schools may not be used to promote religious instruction, as was thought to be the case in Champaign. But where the public schools do no more than accommodate their schedules to a program of outside religious instruction, as was the case in New York, such action is deemed constitutional. Thus, religious instruction on released time is legal under certain conditions. Sometimes the distinctions between legal and illegal practices are so fine that only an experienced judge or lawyer can make them.

Another conflict that has received the attention of the United States Supreme Court is that over uniformity of treatment of different races. In past years the prevailing pattern of education in the states of the South was separate schools for Negro children. Both white and Negro schools were under the same board of education and the same superintendent of schools, were financed by a common tax structure. In many communities, however, inferior buildings, old equipment, and poorly paid teachers were provided for Negro children. In the cities of the North the policy of segregation was not as complete nor as openly advocated, but in many cases the education provided for Negro children in the North was not much better than that provided in the South and was equally segregated. This pattern of separate schools was made more permanent when the United States Supreme Court, in 1896, handed down a decision in the famous Plessy v. Ferguson case. The theory underlying this decision, that separate but equal facilities did not violate the Constitution, gave the highest governmental sanction to the pattern of organizational segregation but not to any practice that denied Negroes equal educational opportunities with white people. Any school district could segregate the races if it maintained schools that were equal. The separate-but-equal doctrine became the legal basis of segregated schools in the North as in the South.

Many cases involving the right to segregate the races have entered the courts since then. On May 17, 1954, the United States Supreme Court handed down the famous decision that declared an end to the segregation of school children on a racial basis:

> We conclude that in the field of public education the doctrine of "separate but equal" has no place. Separate educational facilities are inherently unequal. Therefore, we hold that the plaintiffs and others similarly situated for whom the actions have been brought are, by reason of segregation complained of, deprived of the equal protection of the laws guaranteed by the Fourteenth Amendment.

When Chief Justice Warren announced this decision, he said that the Court realized that the decree presented problems "of considerable complexity." In attempting to solve the very complex problems, educational and government authorities have encountered obstacles rooted in bitter hate and deep-seated prejudice in both the North and the South. School integration is difficult to achieve, in part because it is only one facet of the much wider problem of cultural integration, including such areas as housing and employment. Deep emotions have led to incredibly violent reactions, to assassinations, arson, looting, even to the murder of children in a church.

Many cities, especially those in the North, where segregation of the races has been related to or has grown out of segregated housing, are using buses to achieve racial balance among the schools of their jurisdiction. Opposition of whites to sending their children by bus out of a neighborhood school and into a school with mixed racial population, or sending Negro children into a formerly all-white school, has often led to some form of violence.

Federal programs like Project Head Start are operating with the hope that they may help the underprivileged child, black or white, to be prepared to take an equal place with his schoolmates in an integrated school.

Some leaders among the Negroes now advocate separate but *really* equal, or even superior, schools, schools in which the Negro will be the policy maker, where the power of the Negro will be equal to the power of white men in their schools.

Despite all the problems, many as yet unsolved, the movement toward school integration presses forward. Perhaps the ideal cannot really be achieved until racial discrimination has been removed from all our institutions—business, church, courts, housing, and, most important, from the attitudes and feelings of the members of each race toward the other.

On June 25, 1962, the Supreme Court rendered an opinion on the question of religion in the public schools. The Board of Education of Union Free School District No. 9, of New Hyde Park, New York, had directed the district's principal to have the following prayer said aloud by the teachers and pupils at the beginning of each school day:

> Almighty God, we acknowledge our dependence upon Thee, and we beg Thy blessings upon us, our parents, our teachers, and our country.

This daily ritual was backed by action of the state Board of Regents, thus making it a statement of authority by the State of New York. The parents of 10 pupils brought action against the regulation, contending that it violated both the New York State Constitution and the Constitution of the United States. The state courts of New York ruled the regulation to be constitutional. The Supreme Court of the United States held it to be unconstitutional.

That the Supreme Court has a vital influence over education in the United States cannot be denied. It makes the final decisions in many important cases as to what the laws pertaining to education mean. Since most Americans believe that law and not men shall rule, that known rules of procedure and not the whims of politicians or powerful pressure groups shall control in all exercise of governmental power, the judges of the Supreme Court are the final authorities who make the decisions that settle many concrete educational issues.

The future

EQUALIZATION OF EDUCATION

There is strong sentiment among educators favorable to having the federal government expand its efforts to equalize educational opportunities throughout the nation through some program of federal

Fig. 13.1 Estimated expenditure per pupil in average daily attendance, 1968–1969. (Data from NEA Research Report 1968-R16)

New York	1	$1,140
Alaska	2	987
New Jersey	3	913
Connecticut	4	826
Oregon	5	793
Wisconsin	6	787
Maryland	7	775
Rhode Island	8	756
Delaware	9	745
Pennsylvania	10	743
Illinios	11	742
Wyoming	12	715
Iowa	13	707
Arizona	14	698
California	15	697
Montana	16	696
Nevada	17	685
Minnesota	18	684
Hawaii	19	677
Massachusetts	20	673
Washington		673
Michigan	22	665
Vermont	23	660
Florida	24	647
Kansas		647
Indiana	26	640
Colorado	27	636
Ohio	28	634
Louisiana	29	632
New Hampshire	30	624
Missouri	31	619
New Mexico	32	611
Virginia	33	600
North Dakota	34	585
South Dakota	35	552
Maine	36	547
Idaho	37	545
Kentucky	38	535
Georgia	39	530
Utah	40	527
West Virginia	41	521
Nebraska	42	510
North Carolina	43	506
Oklahoma	44	496
Arkansas	45	486
Tennessee	46	485
Texas	47	480
South Carolina	48	478
Mississippi	49	465
Alabama	50	380

HIGHEST STATES

Alaska	$10,427
California	9,500
Michigan	9,288
Illinois	9,100

LOWEST STATES

South Carolina	5,875
Alabama	5,875
South Dakota	5,800
Mississippi	5,772

Fig.13.2 Estimated average salary of classroom teachers, 1968–1969. Note: In terms of actual purchasing power, the Alaska figure would be $7,820. If California were ranked as No. 1, New York would be No. 4, with $9,000. (Data from NEA Research Report 1969-R1)

grants to the states. There are, admittedly, great variations among the states in the quality of public education furnished and in their ability to support education. It is argued that the federal government has a responsibility to reduce such variations.

The quality of education furnished is not determined solely by the amount of money spent for education. The amount of money spent on education is, nevertheless, one very important factor. Perhaps it is the best single gauge to the quality of education. Those states that maintain inferior school systems are usually states that can raise little money, have little valuable school property, pay unreasonably low salaries to the teaching personnel, employ less well-qualified teachers, and assign large classes and excessive teaching loads to the teachers. According to data assembled by the NEA, New York spent $1,140 for each pupil in ADA (average daily attendance) in 1968–1969. During the same year, Alabama spent $380. (The expenditure in the United States as a whole was approximately $680.) By no combination of compensating factors could Alabama have offered its children educational opportunities equal to those of New York.

In 1968–1969, 19 states paid average annual salaries to classroom teachers of $8,000 and above, while the average for the United States was $7,908. The discrepancy between the states paying the higher salaries and those paying lower salaries is shown in Fig. 13.2; the lowest average salary was only $5,772—about 60 percent of the second highest, $9,500.

States also vary in birth rates and in the percentage of school-age children, aged 5 to 17, among the total resident population. In 1967, school-age children comprised 26.1 percent of the total population of the nation. New York, a wealthy state, with 23 percent of its total resident population of school age, ranked fiftieth among the states. Other affluent states, such as Rhode Island, New Jersey, Pennsylvania, Massachusetts, California, and Illinois, also ranked below the national average. On the other hand, some less wealthy states, such as North Dakota, South Dakota, Louisiana, South Carolina, and Mississippi, ranked above the national average: a larger percentage of school-age children was included in their total population.

Some states with limited resources available for public education must meet the greatest educational demand. Were such states as South Dakota, Mississippi, and Louisiana to adopt model tax systems and to assign the maximum amount they could afford to supporting public education, they would still be far short of the support needed for even an average state school system. It is evident from Fig. 11.6 (page 331) that many of the less wealthy states are making efforts relatively greater than some of the wealthier states, but they are still unable to raise sufficient revenue to support the kind of schools their children need.

Because our population has a high rate of mobility and because the rate seems to be increasing, the social evils resulting from substandard education in one section of the country are not confined to that area but spread to all sections of the country. The public school problems of New York and Chicago are accentuated because of the substandard education received by many who move into New York and Chicago from other sections of the country. It is not just for humanitarian reasons that the people of Oregon are asked to approve expenditures from the federal budget to help education in Mississippi. It is more than mere neighborliness. The quality of education in any section of the United States affects the welfare of the entire country.

Equalizing education on a national basis, it is argued further, is justified also on purely economic grounds. If it is true that the amount of education received by an individual increases his productivity and his other contributions to society as well as his desire and ability to consume more and better goods, then elevating the educational level in all sections of the country is economically advantageous.

If the federal government increases its efforts to equalize education through a policy of making larger grants-in-aid to economically poorer states, or to those cities with a concentration of large numbers of disadvantaged children, will that lead local authorities to relax in their own efforts to pay for schools? Will it be a case of "easy come, easy go," of careless wasting of federal money? This is one danger. Such laxity, however, would probably be corrected and perhaps prevented by an objective formula and a definite audit procedure. A national committee made this statement in 1931:

> The only restriction placed by federal legislation on such educational grants should be the provision that every State, when it accepts the grant, agrees to make each year to the federal headquarters for education a full report on all questions on which the federal headquarters for education may require information concerning the manner in which the State has used the grant.[5]

This should be broadened, perhaps, to include every district, individual, or institution that receives a federal grant.

TAX POLICY

For the federal government to tax wealth where it exists and to distribute funds where they are needed is in harmony with accepted principles of taxation. The federal government has tapped the most productive source of revenue—the individual income tax. A huge federal debt, made much larger by efforts to finance World War II and the subsequent continuing armament program, leads to the belief that federal taxes will probably be high for many years.

Local government agencies depend on the property tax for at least one-half of their total revenue. In most communities the expenditure for schools is the biggest item in the local budget. When property owners feel the pressure of adverse business conditions, they tend to demand relief first in property taxes. A reduction in school expenditures is a ready source of relief. The worst aspects of a demand for decreased school costs, it is believed, could be alleviated by having the states assume a greater share of the local school costs and,

[5] National Advisory Committee on Education, op. cit., p. 38.

Fig.13.3 School-age (5–17) population as a percentage of total resident population, 1967. (Data from NEA Research Report 1968-R1)

New Mexico	1	31.4
Alaska	2	30.8
Utah	3	30.6
Louisiana	4	29.0
Mississippi	5	28.7
Idaho	6	28.6
Montana	7	28.5
Arizona		28.3
South Carolina	8	28.3
Wyoming		28.3
North Dakota	11	28.2
Minnesota	12	28.1
South Dakota	13	27.9
Hawaii	14	27.8
Michigan	15	27.7
Delaware	16	27.5
Wisconsin		27.5
Colorado	18	27.3
Alabama		27.1
Georgia	19	27.1
Texas		27.1
Indiana	22	26.9
Maryland		26.9
Ohio	24	26.8
Maine	25	26.7
North Carolina		26.7
Vermont	27	26.6
Washington		26.6
Kentucky	29	26.5
Kansas	30	26.4
Iowa	31	26.3
Nebraska		26.3
Virginia	33	26.1
UNITED STATES		26.1
Nevada	34	25.9
West Virginia		25.9
Arkansas	36	25.8
Oregon		25.8
New Hampshire	38	25.7
Tennessee		25.7
Missouri	40	25.6
California	41	25.4
Illinois		25.4
Connecticut	43	25.0
Florida		24.9
Massachusetts	44	24.9
Pennsylvania		24.9
New Jersey	47	24.6
Rhode Island		24.6
Oklahoma	49	24.4
New York	50	23.6

in turn, having the federal government assist the states through a policy of equalization of the cost burden. Such a plan would, however, meet with considerable opposition, especially from those reluctant to minimize local community responsibility for local public education.

As early as 1949, President Harry S. Truman stated:

> It is shocking that millions of our children are not receiving a good education. Millions of them are in overcrowded, obsolete buildings. We are short of teachers because teachers' salaries are too low to attract new teachers or to hold the ones we have. All these school problems will become more acute as a result of the tremendous increase in the enrollment in our elementary schools in the next few years. I cannot repeat too strongly my desire for prompt federal financial aid to the states to help them operate and maintain their school systems.[6]

President Truman was supported by the great majority of professional voluntary organizations and by leading laymen. His Commission on Higher Education had gone even further by including aid to local school districts. It said:

> The federal government assumes responsibility for supplementing state and local efforts in military defense against the Nation's enemies without; surely it may as justifiably assume responsibility for supplementing state and local efforts against educational deficiencies and inequalities that are democracy's enemies within.[7]

Of course, if the federal government's spending for education is increased without a corresponding increase in federal taxes, there must be a shift in spending. Money will need to be diverted from some other activities that are now publicly financed. Relative values will need to be reassessed. If we agree that education is vital to the welfare and defense of the nation, it should not be difficult to elevate education to a higher position on the scale of federal budget appropriations.

[6] As quoted in Malcolm S. MacLean and Edwin A. Lee, *Change and Process in Education*. New York: Holt, Rinehart and Winston, 1956, p. 182.
[7] U. S. President's Commission on Higher Education, *Higher Education for American Democracy*. Washington: U. S. Government Printing Office, 1947, Vol. I, p. 103.

Fig. 13.4 Estimated percentage of revenue received by public elementary and secondary schools from the federal government, 1968–1969. (Data from NEA Research Report 1968-R16)

District of Columbia	1	34.9
Alaska	2	25.7
Wyoming	3	20.6
Mississippi	4	20.0
Arkansas	5	16.9
Alabama	6	15.9
Kentucky	7	15.8
New Mexico	8	15.1
South Dakota	9	14.9
North Carolina	10	12.9
West Virginia	11	12.2
South Carolina	12	12.1
Tennessee	13	11.9
Oklahoma		11.9
Texas	15	11.6
Georgia	16	11.0
Louisiana	17	10.3
Florida	18	10.2
Hawaii	19	10.0
Idaho	20	9.3
Virginia		9.3
Arizona	22	8.0
North Dakota	23	7.9
Kansas	24	7.8
Nebraska	25	7.6
Delaware	26	7.4
Nevada	27	7.2
Maine		7.2
Montana	29	7.1
Colorado		7.1
Massachusetts	31	6.9
Maryland		6.7
Rhode Island	32	6.7
Oregon		6.7
Washington		6.7
Minnesota	36	6.6
Missouri	37	6.3
Utah	38	6.1
California	39	5.9
Pennsylvania	40	5.5
Ohio	41	5.3
Illinois	42	5.2
New Hampshire	43	4.9
Indiana	44	4.8
New Jersey	45	4.6
Wisconsin		4.6
Connecticut	47	4.4
Vermont		4.2
New York	48	4.2
Iowa		4.2
Michigan	51	3.9

U.S.A.

53.7%
Local governments

8.1%
Federal government

37.8%
State governments

0.4%
All other (private) sources

Congress has reacted to these demands by a marked expansion of appropriations for education.

STATEMENT OF BASIC POLICY

If any one conclusion stands out from our review of the federal government's participation and activities in education, it is that there has, in the nation's past practice, been little consistency in procedures or purpose and little uniformity in policy. Grants-in-aid have sometimes been made without strings attached. In other instances the states have been asked to match federal funds granted. Grants have been made for higher education and for special fields on the secondary level. Grants have been made to ease emergencies in agriculture and other fields. Grants have been made to individuals. There seems to have been no pattern, no consistent trend, no emergent policy. It has been suggested that in order to aid in formulating future plans for the federal government in relation to education, a broad and basic statement of national policy be enunciated. This, it is believed, would serve as a guide to educators and legislators, contribute to stability, and lend direction and assurance to those involved in various aspects of the federal government's education program and activities.

What are some of the matters upon which clarification of position is needed? It would seem reasonable to expect that government aims should be stated. The statement of basic policy might say in broad terms what the federal government desires to achieve by way of educational opportunities for all children in the nation. The policy statement should also set forth general procedures and types of activities to be carried on in implementing the general aims. The basic and general terms of the statement of policy will give it qualities of endurance and make it adaptable to changing social conditions and to national emergencies. Such a statement of policy will provide a stable foundation and a guide for lawmakers and will encourage a measure of consistency in future federal participation in education.

The difficulties of formulating a statement of basic policy are numerous and sizable. In a democracy the frequent changes in Congress tend to result in inconsistencies and in activities that do not fit into a stable and long-term plan. Then, there is the question of who would draw up so important a statement of national policy.

Perhaps Congress, which has the final say, might itself issue a statement of policy with regard to federal participation in education. To date, however, there has been little unanimity among members of the Congress in this matter. Since World War I there has not been a session of Congress that has not had at least one bill introduced providing money grants to the states for state school support.

As we have stated, there has been considerable support for the proposal that a Cabinet office be created to be devoted solely to education. The suggestion that a board of education at the national level be organized has received the support of the NEA and other influential groups. Perhaps the present organization, which includes a Commissioner of Education and an Office of Education under the Department of Health, Education, and Welfare, is potentially equipped to draw up a statement of federal policy. If this agency were endowed with adequate authority and were assigned considerable administrative responsibility, it could, perhaps, give the guidance that is needed and give it with sufficient weight to make it effective.

Another possibility is the appointment of a special group with specific responsibility for formulating a general policy and for making recommendations. Beginning with President Herbert Hoover, who appointed a group that made a report in 1931, every President has called together a special committee of experts to study the nation's education and present recommendations for federal action. The weakness of such commissions has been their lack of influence on the legislators. It is the lawmaking body of the federal government that decides on the future of education in our country. Any special group—a national board of education, a Cabinet department, a strengthened Office of Education, or any other kind of functionary—can only be as effective as the Congress permits it to be.

This brings us to the responsibility of individual citizens—and particularly members of the teaching profession. The whole business of the federal program of education is not something remote, something complicated and removed from teachers and parents. Teachers owe it to themselves and to their profession to be acquainted with government activities in education on the local, state, and federal levels. It is important that teachers understand current political issues regarding such matters as federal support of education, taxation for education, and equalization of educational opportunities and that they be willing and able to discuss and interpret these issues for local citizens. It is this "grass roots" approach to the Congress through local voters that is the responsibility of individual citizens.

Summary

It is generally agreed that the federal government should continue but improve its program of equalizing education throughout the nation. A broad statement of acceptable policy produced by a competent authority is a sound preliminary step to future plans. Such a statement will give direction and information to the Congress, and from Congress will come decisions about the future of the federal government in the education picture.

Questions

1. What are some of the educational problems of the federal government that result from having three levels of government?
2. What legal principles have been developed by the federal government to guide it in its administration of education? How do you explain the lack of uniformity in these principles?
3. How is the education authority organized at the federal level? In what directions do you think improvements could be made?
4. What part does the United States Supreme Court play in shaping the policies toward education in the United States?
5. Do you consider the principal recommendations of the Hoover Commission with regard to federal aid to education to be sound? Why? How do you account for the small influence this report has had upon subsequent policy at the federal level?
6. How is the question of federal financing of education in the United States affected by the rapid growth in population?
7. How do you account for the extraordinary amount of attention that Congress has given to encouraging vocational education in the schools?

Projects

1. Appraise the effect of the Morrill Acts on higher education in America.
2. Appraise the effects on American education of the Smith-Hughes Act and other similar acts.
3. Analyze the arguments of the judges of the United States Supreme Court in some of their more notable decisions bearing upon education. Note particularly the social principles they used to justify their decisions.
4. Analyze the rankings of the states as given in Figs. 11.6, 13.1, and 13.4 (pp. 331, 383, and 389). Draw from your analysis what you believe to be a justifiable conclusion with respect to the desirable federal policy toward grants-in-aid to education.
5. Show why property taxes have, under present conditions, ceased to be a satisfactory base for public school support.
6. Show how certain problems like Americanization and illiteracy are essentially national problems. Draw an analogy with education.
7. List and briefly explain what you feel is required to correct the deficiencies in elementary and secondary education, in addition to the massive federal aid given in the Act of 1965.

14

The
Nonpublic
Schools

Many schools in the United States may be termed "nonpublic," a classification covering a wide variety of institutions operating at all levels of education. Generally speaking, nonpublic schools are supported by private funds and their control is vested in private individuals or nonpublic organizations. In a few instances, control and support may be both public and nonpublic. A laboratory school in a state university is an example. To achieve simplicity and clarity we shall focus our discussion on those schools that are mainly privately controlled and supported. Although the state has legal authority over nonpublic schools, in practice it normally exercises only a minimum of control, confining the use of authority to such matters as the competence of the teachers and the school's ability to satisfy certain minimum program requirements.

Enrollment figures are not available for all nonpublic schools. Little reliable data about specialized private vocational schools on the secondary level, for instance, are available. The ratio of nonpublic to public school pupils varies from state to state. Approximately 70 percent of the nonpublic school pupils are enrolled in schools in 10 states. The eight states that have the largest percentage of pupils attending nonpublic schools are Rhode Island, Wisconsin, Pennsylvania, New Hampshire, New York, Illinois, Massachusetts, and New Jersey (see Fig. 14.1). In these eight states the over-all ratio of nonpublic school attendance to public school attendance is about 1 to 5. In the country as a whole, the percentages range from 26.1 in Rhode Island to 1.7 in North Carolina.

In 1968–1969, the enrollment in Catholic parochial elementary and high schools was a little under 5 million (after reaching a peak of about 5.6 million four years earlier). Of all American elementary and secondary school pupils, some 10 percent attend Catholic schools. About 90 percent of the total elementary and secondary school enrollment of the parochial schools of America is in the Catholic schools. Of the remaining 10 percent, 4 percent are in Lutheran parochial schools, 4 percent in nonsectarian schools, and 2 percent in schools under the auspices of other religious sects. Since little is known of the large number of pupils enrolled in such nonpublic schools as the vocational, commercial, military, and technical trade schools that give high school and post-high school training, the picture of nonpublic schools in terms of statistics is not complete.

The ratio of attendance at nonpublic colleges to public colleges has been approximately 40 to 60. It has been changing, and the Office of Education estimates that by 1975 the ratio will be 30 to 70, assuming that the present trend continues. The ratio of resident attendance at nonpublic and public colleges and universities varies with the individual state. Close to 97 percent of college students in the District of Columbia attend nonpublic colleges, while none attend nonpublic colleges in Nevada or Wyoming. Other states that rank high in attendance at nonpublic colleges are Massachusetts, Pennsylvania, New Jersey, and Rhode Island.

Many of the institutions of higher learning in the United States enroll nonresident students. Some of them give courses for college credit by correspondence. Some give short courses, individual lessons, and other adult education programs without college credit. Hence many more students are enrolled than the numbers indicate.

Basic rights of nonpublic schools

The basic rights of nonpublic schools to operate in the United States are derived from two sources. First, the prevailing social philosophy of the people is pluralistic. It is an accepted American tradition that a citizen may have many loyalties—to his family, his church, his club, his lodge—and still be loyal to the state. Second, the right of the nonpublic schools to function was officially recognized by the United States in the Fourteenth Amendment to the Constitution. As discussed in the previous chapter, the United States Supreme Court is the final arbiter when individuals or groups feel that some law is unconstitutional because it infringes on personal liberty as guaranteed by this amendment.

The Supreme Court has decided that the right to attend a nonpublic school is a personal liberty guaranteed by the Constitution. Its first decision with respect to a violation of the spirit of the amendment was rendered in 1925. Oregon had legislated that all children must attend public schools. The Court ruled that the law was a violation of the Constitution because it interfered unreasonably with the liberty of parents to direct the education of their children. It was further held by the Supreme Court that a law requiring attendance at a public school would destroy the value of the property owned by the nonpublic schools. The wording of the decision is worth noting. It is a pointed statement of America's belief in the pluralistic philosophy.

> The fundamental theory of liberty upon which all governments in the Union repose excludes any general power of the State to standardize its children by forcing them to accept instruction from public teachers only. The child is not the mere creature of the State; those who nurture him and direct his destiny have the right, coupled with the high duty, to recognize and to prepare him for additional obligations.

The policy of the United States with respect to the basic rights of nonpublic schools seems clear. Parents are protected in their right to send their children to nonpublic schools. Freedom to choose is considered a fundamental right, one that is highly respected. The nonpublic schools are, in turn, protected in the ownership of their property and in their power to control that property.

Regulation of nonpublic schools

The nonpublic schools operate under the laws of the individual states just as the public schools do. The United States Supreme Court has consistently recognized the states' power to regulate schools. In the

Fig.14.1 Nonpublic school enrollment as a percentage of total elementary and secondary school enrollment, 1968–1969. (Data from NEA Research Report 1969-R1)

State	Rank	Value
Rhode Island	1	26.1
Wisconsin	2	23.5
Pennsylvania	3	22.6
New Hampshire	4	21.9
New York	5	21.7
Illinois	6	20.9
Massachusetts	7	20.3
New Jersey	8	18.4
Vermont	9	17.9
Minnesota	10	17.4
Connecticut	11	16.8
Hawaii	12	16.0
Nebraska	12	16.0
Missouri	14	15.8
Louisiana	15	15.7
Maryland	16	15.5
Ohio	17	15.4
Delaware	18	15.2
Michigan	19	15.0
Maine	20	14.4
Iowa	21	14.2
UNITED STATES		13.1
South Dakota	22	13.1
North Dakota	23	12.9
Kentucky	24	12.5
Montana	25	11.7
Indiana	26	10.9
Kansas	27	9.7
New Mexico	27	9.7
California	29	8.8
Colorado	30	8.5
Arizona	31	8.3
Washington	32	7.4
Oregon	33	7.2
Florida	34	7.0
Texas	35	5.9
Virginia	36	5.6
Idaho	37	5.3
Wyoming	38	4.7
West Virginia	39	4.2
Alaska	40	3.8
Nevada	40	3.8
Tennessee	42	3.7
Alabama	43	3.5
Oklahoma	43	3.5
Mississippi	45	3.3
Arkansas	46	2.7
Georgia	47	2.6
South Carolina	48	2.5
Utah	49	2.2
North Carolina	50	1.7

previously mentioned Oregon decision, the Supreme Court spoke as follows:

> No question is raised concerning the power of the State reasonably to regulate all schools, to inspect, supervise and examine them, their teachers and pupils; to require that all children of proper age attend some school, that teachers shall be of good moral character and patriotic disposition, that certain studies plainly essential to good citizenship must be taught, and that nothing be taught which is manifestly inimical to the public welfare.

In line with its rightful prerogatives, each state, as we have pointed out in a previous chapter, has passed laws governing the education that is conducted within its boundaries. These laws, as they affect the nonpublic schools, are of two kinds. There are general laws which apply to the activities of all individuals and organizations conducting businesses or charitable undertakings within the state. Unless specific exceptions are made, these laws apply to the nonpublic schools. Under these laws, an agency to which the state has delegated the responsibility must enforce regulations concerned with building codes, health laws, fire prevention, workmen's compensation, welfare of children in boarding schools, motor vehicle codes, codes regulating cafeterias and other boarding places, and any other provisions designed to protect public welfare. In other words, nonpublic schools, whether incorporated or not, are subject to all of the general regulations that have been prescribed by the state for corporations.

A second kind of state law applies specifically to nonpublic schools, although it may be general enough to apply also to some other organizations within the state. This type of law regulates details of the articles of incorporation of the nonpublic schools that constitute a contract between each nonpublic school and the state. The Constitution of the United States prohibits the passage of any state law that violates the agreements made in the contract. The privileges accorded the nonpublic school under articles of incorporation usually extend to such matters as holding property, the right to sue and be sued, the right to make contracts, and such other agreements as may be deemed necessary to achieve the objects for which the institution was established. The articles of agreement always presuppose the principle of self-government under state regulation and thereby have proved to be the most popular

Parochial schools educate a significant proportion of the children in America. Among the Protestant schools, the Lutheran ones outnumber those of any other denomination. These schools have excellent teachers and modern facilities. (As the picture indicates, the Lutherans try to staff each elementary school with a full quota of men teachers.) The Roman Catholic Church operates the largest group of parochial schools. The biology class at the Sacred Heart High School, Pittsburgh, is well equipped and expertly taught. The modern yeshivah—Jewish day school—is relatively new to the

American educational scene. An elementary class is shown receiving religious instruction from its Hebrew teacher.

and effective way a state has of regulating nonpublic schools. Incorporation also fully establishes the legal right of nonpublic schools to do what is deemed necessary to operate educational institutions under private auspices.

Besides basic legal regulations for nonpublic schools, state legislatures make interpretations that establish some limitations and privileges. The interpretations vary quite as much with respect to the conduct of nonpublic education as they do with respect to public education. These interpretations are found in the provisions made for education in the state constitutions, in the statutes passed by the state legislatures concerning nonpublic schools, and in relevant court decisions. This makes the state school code almost as important to the nonpublic school as it is to the public school.

Despite the variations among the states, two principles underlie state policy. The first is that, in general, a public tax may not be levied for the support of nonpublic schools. The second is that nonschool revenue may not be used for direct aid to nonpublic schools.

Even these principles, however, are subject to a variety of interpretations. Many of the differences arise in connection with the interpretation of the child benefit theory. This theory holds that benefits or services provided at public expense from revenue not collected for educational purposes should be given a child regardless of where he happens to attend school. Differences usually arise in a situation that involves indirect public aid to education—that is, the aid given to provide some service immediately for the individual pupil, not directly to the school. All children are entitled to the same free governmental services. In theory there should be no discrimination against children because they attend nonpublic schools. The question arises over whether the aid provided actually goes to the pupil or to the school. Among the services about which there has been this kind of disagreement are free textbooks, free transportation, health services, and other welfare services usually described as auxiliary educational services. If an auxiliary educational service is provided for all public school pupils, is it unjust discrimination to deny comparable services to all pupils in nonpublic schools? Some state legislatures say "yes." For example, the Michigan, New York, and Ohio legislatures have provided noninstructional services, textbooks, and transportation for pupils in church schools.

Many private schools are operated specifically to help in educating the handicapped. At the Lexington School for the Deaf, small classes are taught with the aid of technological equipment. Under the extensive program of the Hadley School for the Blind, a student learns braille at home. The Hadley School serves well over 2,000 students throughout the country. The curriculum, which includes more than 100 separate courses, is designed to teach blind persons of any age what they need or want to know. Students may qualify for accredited high school diplomas. The school achieves results that often seem almost miraculous.

Other services that have been centers of argument are commonly called quasi-instructional services. Examples of this kind of service are recreation; child accounting (the keeping of instructional and executive records of the child throughout the whole of his school life); psychological, psychiatric, and sociological diagnostic services;

and placement and follow-up of high school graduates. Should a social service considered vital to the welfare of every child of school age in a community be denied a child because he happens to attend a nonpublic school?

Decisions on such issues are related to the interpretation each individual state legislature makes of the child benefit theory when it is applied to a specific educational problem. What the interpretation may be cannot be predicted. In general, it is agreed that the state or the federal government may not directly make state or federal financial grants to nonpublic schools. It is expected, however, that certain social services rendered by the state to individuals will not be denied to an individual pupil, even though he attends a nonpublic school. The child benefit theory holds that the services of the state are to follow the child wherever he may be.

Classification of nonpublic schools

The great variety of nonpublic schools in the United States makes it difficult to arrive at a simple classification. The best we can do is to divide nonpublic schools into two main groups and state some of the features by which each group is identified. The parochial schools, one large group of elementary and secondary schools, are, as the name implies, operated by ecclesiastical organizations. A large majority of them are operated by the Roman Catholic Church; the Catholic schools now enroll approximately 90 percent of all the pupils officially reported to be attending the parochial schools in the United States. Because of the number and importance of these schools, more information about them is given in a later section.

The second large group of nonpublic schools is private schools. The term "private school" in some educational publications is synonymous with nonpublic school. In popular usage, however, and in our discussion, the private school differs from the parochial school in that it is largely nonsectarian and is controlled by an individual or a self-perpetuating board of trustees. The two classifications of nonpublic schools might well be sectarian and nonsectarian. However, most educational publications use the words "parochial" and "private."

PAROCHIAL SCHOOLS

Parochial schools are those nonpublic schools that operate on the elementary and secondary level under the control and with the support of an ecclesiastical organization. The largest group of parochial schools is operated by the Roman Catholic Church.

1. Roman Catholic schools

a. Origins. The Roman Catholic Church has followed a policy of establishing elementary parochial schools in communities that have a Catholic population and organization sufficient to support such a school. Organizing schools as a regular and permanent feature of parish work began with the establishment of the first Catholic parish in Philadelphia in 1730. Philadelphia had a larger Catholic population than any other city in the country, and the system of parochial schools established there and throughout Pennsylvania became a model subsequently followed by Catholics throughout the country.

The schools were aided by the founding of teaching orders such as, for example, the Sisters of Charity, the Sisters of Loretta, and the Sisters of Saint Dominic. Members of these orders established religious communities where some kind of productive activities, perhaps farming, made the community more or less self-sufficient. With the support of the religious order and of the Roman Catholic Church, the teachers were able to carry on their schools without aid from the state and to extend the Catholic educational system into new centers of Catholic life as fast as they became organized. Even before 1776, 70 Roman Catholic schools had been organized in the confines of what is now the United States. The Catholic Church expanded rapidly after 1840, when there was a rapid increase in the immigration of Catholics from Germany and Ireland. This increase in Catholic population, together with the action of the Third Plenary Council of Baltimore in 1885 making it obligatory for every parish to maintain a school, resulted in a rapid multiplication of Catholic parochial schools. The action of the Third Plenary Council made it clear that the church leaders considered education a vital factor in the internal development of the Roman Catholic Church in the United States.

b. Organization. The Roman Catholics followed the lines of their dioceses in their school organization. A diocese is the area and the population that fall under the pastoral care of a bishop. Each diocese has its school system with the bishop at its head. The bishops are bound by the legislation of the Third Plenary Council of Baltimore, which not only made schools obligatory but also prescribed a definite form of school organization for all the dioceses. Thus, it is accurate to speak of Catholic schools as constituting a system, and it is this systematization of their schools that has provided a measure of unity and a source of strength.

Control over the schools in the diocese is in the hands of a board of education presided over by the bishop. The members of the board, except for a few lay people, are elected from the clergy. The executive officer of the school board is a priest, specially trained as an educator and school administrator. He serves as superintendent of schools in the diocese. The priest of the local parish generally serves also as head of the individual school supported by his parish. Beyond supervising the financial and religious matters, he delegates the direction of the school to a superior of the sisters or brothers in charge. This superior is, in practice, the actual principal who administers the school.

c. Curriculum. The curriculum in the Catholic elementary and high schools is similar to the curriculum in the public schools in the same communities. The principal difference is in the emphasis upon religious education. The curriculum is planned to give a well-rounded general education and at the same time to give a special place to religious instruction, an area that is usually not recognized in the public schools, which must remain secular and nonsectarian.

d. Kinds of schools. The elementary schools are all diocesan schools and constitute the main part of the Catholic parochial school system. Some of the high schools are organized in the parish and are also members of the diocesan organization. Others are independent and are conducted by one of the religious orders of the church. The Catholic University of America at Washington, D.C., established in 1887 by Pope Leo XII and the American Catholic hierarchy, has as one of its purposes the preparation of teachers for the entire Catholic educational system.

e. Enrollments. The Roman Catholic school system in the United States has reached giant proportions. Specifically, in 1968–1969 there were almost 14,000 Catholic educational institutions: elementary schools, 10,603; secondary schools, 2,356; colleges and universities, 339; seminaries, 436; schools for atypical children, 260. They are organized in 147 different systems—one for each of the 147 archdioceses and dioceses in the country. About 40 percent of all these institutions, however, enrolling more than half of all the students, are in only 20 dioceses—Chicago, Boston, New York, and other metropolitan areas.

The total attendance at Catholic parochial elementary and high schools rose from about 405,000 in 1880 to almost 1.8 million in 1920 to 2.4 million in 1940 to a peak of about 5.6 million in 1964–1965. Around 10 percent of all American elementary and secondary school pupils are at Catholic parochial schools. There are difficulties ahead, however—a number of Catholic schools (most of them elementary schools) have been closed in recent years. Thus not only has the total enrollment not kept pace with the growth in the general school population—it has actually declined; in 1968–1969, the total Catholic elementary and secondary enrollment was down to a little under 5 million. Rising operating costs, decreasing revenues, and a scarcity of teaching priests and nuns are all factors. Moreover, more closings are predicted. The problems described in the following quotation, therefore, have become even more serious than they were in 1966.

> Merely to keep up with population growth . . . Catholic schools will by 1968–1969, have to take in a million more students than the number registered in 1962–1963—or more people than can be found in any one of 17 states in the Union. To hold the present line, 21,000 additional religious teachers and 10,500 lay teachers will be required. Additional school construction alone will cost more than $721 million. Even if all these miracles are accomplished, the schools will still be educating fewer than half the pupils in the United States baptized as Catholics. Even now the schools can find no room for about one-fifth of those who apply.[1]

f. Costs. The cost of attending Roman Catholic elementary and secondary schools, apart from services donated through the church, is borne by the parents. The annual costs of the elementary and secondary schools are well over a billion dollars.

[1] John Cogley, "Catholics and Their Schools," *Saturday Review*, p. 74, October 15, 1966. Copyright 1966 by Saturday Review, Inc.

g. Attitudes of Catholic leaders toward public education. Since those who send their children to Catholic schools must also pay taxes for the support of the public schools, the attitude of the Catholic leaders toward the public schools is of general interest. In the main, the parents of the children who attend the Catholic schools are appreciative of the privilege of freedom to make a choice between two kinds of schools and of being permitted to provide their children with religious education. The attitude both of the parents and of the clergy is positive, intelligent, and constructive. A short quotation expresses the sentiment that has long prevailed:

> Historically, we have had and, please God, we probably always will have a diversified system of education in this country. As American citizens, therefore, and especially as American educators, we must be interested in the improvement not only of our own unique kind of education, but of all kinds of American education—public, private, denominational—whatever it may be. . . . The public schools, as a complementary system to private education, are absolutely necessary for the thousands of Americans who are content with a purely secular educational pattern. Such schools deserve the interest and support of our Catholic population.[2]

2. Protestant schools

Some of the Protestant churches have, in recent years, conducted nursery schools for children who are younger than compulsory school and kindergarten age. These schools are operated by local churches more as a service to the members of the church than for religious reasons. Such schools diverge very little in their pattern of activities from those conducted under public auspices.

It is not easy to state the Protestant position toward elementary and secondary schools, because no official position has been taken. In general, and with notable exceptions mentioned later, it is the position of the Protestant groups that the parent should send his children to the public schools and that the child should receive his religious education in the home and in the church. Protestants, as a group, do not favor parochial education as an answer to the problem of religious education. Nevertheless, they "defend the right of all religious groups

[2] Very Rev. P. C. Reinert, S.J., "American Catholic Educators Face New Responsibilities," *Proceedings and Addresses, Forty-ninth Annual Meeting*. Washington: National Catholic Educational Association, 1952, p. 59.

Large industrial corporations conduct highly specialized courses, often using complicated and expensive equipment. The instrument shown is only one of many used in teaching electronics technology—it is designed to simulate, analyze, and visualize activated circuitry. For obvious reasons, such training is beyond the scope of most public school systems. The same corporation also maintains 36-foot trailer "classrooms," designed and equipped to keep its skilled workers up-to-date in such fields as electronics, computer concepts, pneumatics, hydraulics, and the like.

to carry on church-related education at any level, elementary, secondary, or higher, and the right of parents to send their children to these schools if they so desire."[3]

Although the majority of Protestants believe in sending their children to the public schools, they are favorable to church schools if member groups desire to have them. There are approximately 4,000 Protestant day schools which enroll approximately 385,000 elementary school pupils and 36,000 high school pupils. In the main, these are supported by the Christian Reformed Church members, Missouri Synod Lutherans—which is the largest group, with an elementary school enrollment of 193,000 pupils and a high school enrollment of 14,000—Seventh-Day Adventists, Mennonites, Episcopalians, and Baptists.

[3] D. Campbell Wyckoff, "The Protestant Day School," *School and Society*, LXXXII (October 1, 1955): 98.

3. Jewish day schools

Between 1940 and 1967 the Jewish day school (popularly known by its Hebrew name, *yeshivah*) has grown to include 305 elementary and secondary day schools in the United States. More than 90 percent of these were established between 1940 and 1967. During this period, the pupil enrollment increased almost tenfold, from 7,313 to approximately 65,000 students.

Jewish day schools are distinct educational units founded and supported by parents and interested individuals and communally conducted by autonomous, self-governing lay boards, responsive to the needs of the parents and community. As Alvin I. Schiff, noted authority on Jewish education, has said, "The Jewish day school was not founded in opposition to public education, since Judaism does not challenge the state's right to control education."

The establishment of the Jewish day school is predicated, first, on a deeply felt need for intensive Hebraic-religious schooling. Secondly, the American Jewish community strongly believes in the values of a sound secular education and emphasizes the importance of effective training in the skills of good citizenship. The advocates of the Jewish day School feel that this institution is the best means of achieving this dual goal, which is, in essence, the blending of the Hebraic and American cultures.

In line with these goals, the Jewish day schools are organized into two divisions: the secular or general studies department and the religious or Hebrew studies department. In the elementary school the pupils have two instructors, a Hebrew teacher and a general studies teacher; in the junior and senior high schools, where the programs are usually departmentalized, the students study under the guidance of two sets of instructors. Almost all schools are Bible-centered in the elementary grades. The concentration thereafter is divided between the study of Bible and Talmud and their major commentaries. The general studies programs are essentially the same as in the local public schools. The average Jewish day school has 225 pupils, although the range is from 50 to 1500. Some are all-boy and some are all-girl schools, but today 70 percent of the Jewish day schools either are coeducational or provide instruction for boys and girls under one roof.

Exposed to both disciplines in a congenial environment the child learns to integrate the traditional with the modern, the secular with the religious, his Jewish heritage with American civilization. Through meritorious educational attainment, in an enriched program, he grows intellectually and culturally; via a program of intensive Jewish study he grows spiritually. In all, he learns to be a good American Jew. He learns that to be a good Jew is to be a good American. On this frame of reference, he builds a wholesome set of values. He loves Israel and wants to help it grow, as he loves America and strives to become a useful citizen in his native country. He is part of his Jewish people as he is part of American democratic experience.[4]

PRIVATE SCHOOLS

The private schools are the most independent of the nonpublic schools. They are subject to very little public control and are permitted to operate with a minimum of state supervision. They are numerous, and they maintain widely varying standards.

1. Below-college level

   a. Vocational schools. Below-college vocational training, apart from the high schools, is almost exclusively the domain of the private school. Here vocational schools that are operated for profit prevail— technical institutes; business colleges; commercial or secretarial schools; art, interior decorating, drafting, design schools; charm, beauty culture, cosmetology, electrolysis schools; dramatic art, television, broadcasting, expression schools; trade, industrial, auto-mechanics schools; physical therapy, massage schools; baking, home economics, hotel management schools; jewelry and watch repairing schools. And there are many others that train specifically for some designated trade or commercial pursuit.

Information about such schools has not been collected thus far. Some notion of their magnitude, however, may be gained from estimates of enrollment made by the United Business Schools Association, with a membership of 500 institutions. It reports that in 1968–1969, the enrollment in these schools exceeded 150,000. One privately

[4] Alvin I. Schiff, *The Jewish Day School in America*. New York: Jewish Education Committee Press, 1966, p. 265.

owned technical institute in Chicago, whose students are trained to enter the field of electronics, enrolls more than 20,000 post-high school students every year. Undoubtedly, since the enrollments in these schools number in the millions, their influence is tremendous. They answer the need for a kind of education—such as, for example, short-term, concentrated training—that receives little emphasis in the public schools.

b. Parent-supported schools. Another type of private elementary and secondary school is sometimes endowed and supported by wealthy parents. These are nonsectarian and serve approximately the same purposes as public schools of similar grade. The children are often selected so that they comprise a more or less homogeneous group in terms of economic or social background or special interests or problems. When the children are likely to attend college, attention is given to college preparation. Some of the secondary schools are endowed boarding schools. Some are known as "country day schools," where typically some of the pupils are boarding pupils and others live at home. The purpose or purposes that justify the establishment and support of each of these private schools vary from school to school.

c. Academies. The academies, in part parent-supported and in part endowment-supported, are an important group of private secondary schools. Some of the academies have an illustrious tradition and history dating back to the early days of our country. Originally intended to provide a curriculum more flexible and enriched than was available elsewhere, the academies are now largely college preparatory. They are sometimes coeducational and are found in most parts of the United States. The military academies of high school grade emphasize military discipline.

d. Industry-supported schools. Private business has, during the past 50 years, greatly expanded educational opportunities in industry. This has resulted in another kind of private school. Large industrial corporations have provided extensive industrial training for their employees and in some instances have provided other kinds of education for the families of their employees. Some industries engage also in cooperative education programs with various engineering colleges in order to meet the nation's demands for citizens well grounded both in the common essentials and in the occupational abilities necessary to

*Benjamin Franklin (1706–1790) is known to every American boy and girl
as an American statesman, diplomat, author, scientist, and inventor. Few,
perhaps, realize that he also influenced American education.*

In 1749 Franklin voiced progressive ideas about education in Proposals
for the Education of Youth in Pennsylvania. *Two years later he opened
the Franklin Academy, which incorporated these ideas. His academy was far
different from the other institutions of the time. Students applying for
admission were offered a choice of three courses. They could enter one of
what he called three schools—the English school, the mathematics school, or
the Latin school. In typical Franklin manner he thus expressed his displeasure
over the narrow classicism that characterized the Latin grammar schools of
the time. Shortly after its establishment his academy was reincorporated as
a degree-conferring institution. In 1779, three years after the signing of
the Declaration of Independence, the University of Pennsylvania was
established in its stead.*

*Franklin's intention was to displace the unsystematic practices of the private
schoolmaster of the day with an institution organized and administered on a
public basis. He attempted, also, to offer, so far as was possible at the time,
a curriculum that was practical and useful. Even so great a man as Franklin,
however, could not overcome the deep-seated prejudices favorable to
educational emphasis on Latin. He saw English and other modern subjects
gradually ousted from the curriculum of the school he had established in order
to emphasize these very subjects.*

*Although Franklin's school was an initial failure, it was an expression of the
progressive educational thought of the time. The Franklin Academy passed
out of existence, but the ideas set in motion flowed on to exert a profound
influence on succeeding generations.*

insure economic and industrial efficiency. The number of people attending such schools is large, and it fluctuates greatly from time to time.

Since so many of the private schools operate quite independently
and since so little information has been assembled with regard to some
of them, few generalizations are possible except to say that they are
numerous and their influence is great.

e. Laboratory schools. Schools for children at the nursery, elementary, junior high, and senior high school levels are conducted on many
college campuses. These are variously called demonstration schools,
experimental schools, training schools, or laboratory schools. When

*T*he academy was introduced into America in recognition of the need for a
form of secondary education broader than that given by the Latin grammar
schools, with their highly restricted curriculum, which had dominated
American secondary education for nearly 200 years. The academy became
the principal institution in American secondary education, maintaining that
position from the latter half of the eighteenth century until the beginning of
the twentieth century, when the four-year high school began its rapid growth.
One way to get a picture of the purposes, programs, and achievements of the
academy and of its place in American secondary education is to read the
history of a successful one.* Phillips Exeter, for instance, one of the earliest
academies, continues to be a distinguished institution. Incorporated in 1781,
Exeter now has a campus of 775 acres—100 acres used for the school, 75
for playing fields, and 600 left in woodland. It has 125 school buildings
and a faculty of 125 men. Enrolled in the regular session are 825 boys from
all the states. In addition, there is a coeducational summer school attended
by 250 boys and 225 girls.

Tax-supported high schools have grown rapidly in this century, but the
number of able students who apply for admission to academies like Exeter has
also increased. The quality of instruction offered by the academies has
constantly improved. Also, their function has changed ; in the late eighteenth
century and for some time thereafter, the academies provided terminal
education, as very few graduates went on to college ; now, however, most
academy graduates continue their education, many of them at private
universities. For instance, for some time about one-third of the graduates of
Exeter have entered three of the most prestigious private eastern universities—
Harvard, Yale, and Princeton. (The 260 members of the Exeter class of 1968
went to more than 60 colleges and universities, but almost half entered five
private institutions : Harvard, 50 ; Yale, 20 ; Stanford, 20 ; Princeton, 19 ;
Dartmouth, 10.) The academies have, then, become college-preparatory
schools.

The academies in the United States are relatively inconspicuous in the total
picture of secondary education ; nevertheless, they perform significant and
unique functions that give them great influence and prestige. They offer
programs consistent with the ideals of high scholarship and they are dedicated
to close, personal guidance of the individual pupil, with particular emphasis
on character development.

* For a vivid account of the traditions, support, and functions of the academies, see
Myron R. Williams, *The Story of Phillips Exeter.* Exeter, N.H.: The Phillips Exeter
Academy, 1957.

they are associated with nonpublic institutions, they are private schools. Sometimes, however, they are part of a public teachers college or public university. Then they are public schools, which, however, differ from ordinary public schools in that they are not a part of any particular local school system. They are schools administered by the college or university for experimental and demonstrational purposes. Under Title III of the Elementary and Secondary Education Act of 1965, designed to establish or enrich exemplary elementary and secondary school programs, the federal government has given aid to demonstration or laboratory schools that are operated in public school systems.

Ideally, the laboratory school demonstrates the best modern educational theory in actual practice in the classroom. The philosophy of the school is carefully worked out; the curriculum is designed to meet the vital needs of its pupils; the teachers are skilled artists in teaching; the organization and the administrative machinery demonstrate arrangements that best serve the pupils and teachers and that foster wholesome human relations; and the building and equipment are thoughtfully planned.

Laboratory schools have contributed significantly to the improvement of education in both private and public schools. One main diffi-

The Academy Building, one of three main classroom buildings at Phillips Exeter Academy, is the headquarters for the mathematics, history, and classical languages departments. It contains 36 classrooms and also houses the chapel, which serves as the central assembly hall for meetings of the whole student body.

culty is that they sometimes operate on insufficient budgets. To supplement their budgets, they frequently charge tuition or fees, even though they may be part of a state university. This tends to result in an economically and sociologically favored enrollment of pupils, which makes the results of laboratory school research less applicable to a typical cross section of the general population. In addition to their contribution through experimentation and research, the laboratory schools have improved teaching in America's schools by providing opportunities for teachers in training to observe and to have actual daily experience in much better than average classrooms.

2. College level

a. Colleges and universities. No criterion has been established as a guide in the classification of higher-level institutions. The most dependable classification available shows that there are 132 universities in the United States, of which 70 are public and 62 are nonpublic. Since many public universities have numerous branches, the actual number of these far exceeds 70. Because of federal aid to nonpublic as well as public universities, the differentiation between the two types has diminished as far as support and control are concerned. With the increase in tuition in all universities, the distinction between public and nonpublic colleges and universities from the point of view of the student is also less.

The nonpublic four-year liberal arts college, usually just called a "college," dominates the four-year college scene. There are well over five hundred such colleges in the United States, all of which are fully accredited. Very few such colleges are publicly controlled and supported. The dominance of the private liberal arts college is perhaps due in part to the fact that it was the earliest kind of organization for higher education in this country and also to the respect and faith that the American people place in these institutions.

The nonpublic institutions of higher learning have exerted and continue to exert great influence upon the thinking of the American people. Their programs penetrate almost every aspect of American life. Since it is estimated that currently well over 2 million students attend these institutions, it seems that the American people will continue to accord nonpublic institutions of higher education a prominent and permanent position in the educational system of the United States.

b. Technological institutes. There are between 60 and 65 private technological institutions of higher learning in the United States. Among them, to name a few, are such distinguished institutions as the Massachusetts Institute of Technology, the Carnegie Institute of Technology, the California Institute of Technology, the Case Institute of Technology, and the Illinois Institute of Technology. As their names imply, their contributions are mainly to the fields of science and applied science. The number of full-time students attending such institutions is well over 250,000—a figure that attests to the general popularity of these institutions in the American scheme of education.

Contributions of nonpublic schools

The size and scope of the nonpublic school undertaking in the United States is in itself evidence of the high regard the people of the United States hold for nonpublic education. The debt the nation owes to nonpublic education is indeed very great. While it is not easy to assess the total contributions made by the nonpublic schools to the contemporary educational scene, a few of the more obvious contributions can be identified.

First, the nonpublic schools have furthered the preservation and strengthening of the cherished American ideal of freedom of choice and of the pluralistic philosophy which nourishes that ideal. Although in some communities competition between the public and nonpublic elementary and secondary schools creates a degree of friction, in most communities a healthy and friendly rivalry exists—rivalry to excel in the quality of services rendered. Cooperation between public and nonpublic schools is common.

Second, the nonpublic schools have educated so large a proportion of the American school population that they have appreciably lowered the burden of public support. Since the nonpublic schools seek to achieve all the functions striven for in the public schools and, as is the case especially with the vocational schools, to answer certain needs not recognized in the public schools, the lessening of the costs to the public is accompanied by an actual increase in the breadth of education available.

Third, the nonpublic schools have made distinctive contributions to educational practice. Many of the forward-looking practices in the public schools have first been developed in the nonpublic schools. The nonpublic schools have contributed particularly to experimentation at the elementary level. Nursery school and kindergarten education were first tested in nonpublic schools. Vocational education at the high school level was first introduced and developed in the nonpublic schools. A great deal of research in scientific and professional fields has emanated from the nonpublic universities.

These are only a few of the contributions made by nonpublic schools. Enough has been said, however, to show that public and nonpublic education in the United States have advanced together, with a minimum of conflict and a maximum of mutual appreciation. In the minds of the citizens, both kinds of schools are essential to the preservation and continued advancement of American civilization.

Summary

The term "nonpublic schools" applies to many kinds of schools operating in America under various controls and methods of support and serving all ages and levels from nursery school through post-graduate education. The magnitude of the entire nonpublic school undertaking cannot be accurately or even approximately assessed. All one can safely say is that the enrollment is large.

Nonpublic schools are favorably accepted. The pluralistic philosophy of the American people and of their government encourages the establishment of many kinds of nonpublic schools. The states may, if they wish, issue regulations for such schools but, generally speaking, the regulations are not highly restrictive.

Appraisal of the nonpublic schools reveals that they have made a sizable contribution to education in America. The schools that have had the greatest influence on American culture are perhaps those under church control. By and large, these schools discharge all the functions performed by the public schools and maintain standards of professional excellence equal to those achieved in the public schools.

Although the over-all contributions of the nonpublic schools cannot be fully assessed, it is evident that they are serving specific educational needs and are valued as a vital feature of the complete system of education in America.

Questions

1. Why has it been the policy of the various states to exert so little control over nonpublic education?
2. What would be some uses that could be served by the states collecting complete information about all the nonpublic schools operating under their jurisdictions?
3. What are the principal justifications for the establishment of nonpublic schools and nonpublic school systems in the United States?
4. What evidences are there that nonpublic universities exert a great deal of influence upon life in America?
5. Why are the four-year colleges in the United States predominantly nonpublic schools?
6. How do articles of incorporation operate to protect a nonpublic school?
7. How do the articles of incorporation of nonpublic schools serve as a control over nonpublic schools?
8. In your opinion, what will the future development of nonpublic education in the United States be like?

Projects

1. Secure information on one of the industrial education programs conducted by some large industry. Appraise the nature of the program.
2. Read the advertisements of nonpublic schools as found in some influential magazine. Itemize the claims of the various institutions.
3. Research the problems the Amish sect has had in Iowa, Pennsylvania, or some other state, in connection with their private schools. Give your own conclusions about a sound and just solution to the problem.

*Units of
School
Organization*

Units of local school organization and the educational ideas that underlie them are the concern of this chapter. In examining local units of organization, either public or nonpublic, keep in mind that each of these units came into being as a response to widely recognized needs, and that the practices within each unit are the educators' answers to what they believe these needs call for. As time goes by and new needs arise, either the old units of organization are modified or new ones are established. Some school publics may be reluctant to accept modifications or to approve the addition of new units, while in other sections of the country changes may be accepted with alacrity. As modifications and new units gradually prove their worth, however, they tend to become widely accepted. We describe here what is generally typical. The picture, however, may not accurately reflect the particular pattern of organizational units in any one public or private school system. As with so many other aspects of education in America, the general pattern of school organizations varies in details from place to place.

Schools for the early years

THE NURSERY SCHOOL

The nursery school is the latest unit of educational organization to bid for public recognition. Its growth in public acceptance is illustrated by the facts that in 1920 there were but three recognized nursery schools in the United States and that in 1966, enrollment of 3-, 4-, and 5-year-old children in nursery schools had reached a total of 686,000. One impetus for extension of the nursery school has come from the federal government, most recently through the Economic Opportunity Act and the Elementary and Secondary Education Act, which provided funds for classes for preschool children, especially children from more concentrated population centers, where many homes are unable to provide for the needs of young children. New emphasis was thereby given to the role of early education. Although nursery education is now an accepted institution throughout the country and has been widely adopted both as a public and nonpublic school unit, it has not received legal status from state legislatures. It therefore operates as a nonstandardized unit under the sponsorship of a large number of different agencies.

Among the sources of early encouragement to the nursery school movement were public universities, such as the University of Iowa and the University of Minnesota, which operated nursery schools. In these schools, child-development specialists made studies, the findings of which emphasized the importance of providing a suitable environment for the mental and physical development of children 2 to 5 years of age. The studies also demonstrated the importance of parent

At Halloween time, these nursery school children are reciting "Five Little Jack-o'-Lanterns." They apparently have reached the second one!

education, indicating that parents are the most important teachers of young children, since they are with the child for a greater part of the time than anyone else and share with the child a wide range of activities and experiences. It is mainly from parents that a child learns certain skills (such as talking) and develops attitudes, emotional control, maturity in his relations to others, and, hopefully, ideals that contribute to good living. Somewhere along the line, a transition must be made from the narrower environment of the home to the wider social environment of the school. The shift from home to school is a major environmental change in the life of a child. It is often a time when the child feels his security threatened, a time when he must make major adjustments. The studies of the psychologists conducting nursery schools in the universities showed that skillfully directed nursery schools made the transition from home to school easier and safer for many 4-year-olds and for some 3-year-olds.

Early expansion of the nursery school movement was also encouraged by the Works Progress Administration (WPA), an agency of the federal government that, among other things, sponsored nursery schools for working mothers during the depression of the 1930s. The WPA operated some 1,500 schools that enrolled well over 300,000 children. Being a branch of the federal government, it established a precedent by operating its schools in public buildings, including the public schools.

A third source of continuing encouragement comes from private, church, philanthropic, and other groups that have, with a considerable measure of success, operated nursery schools. During World War II, national defense was served by nursery schools that freed mothers of preschool children to work in industry or business. In the main these nursery schools have been well managed and have been fully accepted. In most cases the staff has been well qualified; often leadership has come from interested, dedicated experts who have volunteered their services.

Nursery school eduation serves two broad educational purposes —childhood education and adult, or parent, education. The location and equipment must be suited to the two purposes. An appreciation of the facilities required for such education can best be gained by a visit to a well-equipped nursery school. One will find that the selection of the room and equipment is dictated by what child development specialists have learned is appropriate for 3- and 4-year-olds. Psychologists who have studied the effects of nursery school education upon children are agreed that a nursery school that is not adequately equipped and conducted by a competent staff can do more harm than good. In a genuine nursery school, playground and schoolroom are a single unit, separate from units provided for older children. Playground equipment is specially designed. A roofed area just outside the room is provided for special outdoor activities. The room windows face the playground. The room is large, well lighted, and properly ventilated. The equipment is fairly expensive. It includes drinking fountains and toilets of suitable height, washrooms, sinks and other kitchen equipment, musical instruments, and facilities for caring for plants, animals, and birds. Cots are available for rest periods.

Nursery schools must also provide daily inspection by a nurse. Medical examinations and dental care are essential. The help of a nutritionist and of a psychologist is also needed to guarantee adequate attention to health needs. Most of all, of course, specially trained teachers are needed.

Not all children will need or will profit from attendance at a nursery school. In deciding who shall attend, parents and teachers weigh many factors. Is the child an only child? Does he live in an apartment? Does the mother work? Does the mother feel that the child will do better if he is apart from her for some time each day? Does the mother feel that the child should have increased opportunity to expand his social adaptability? Attendance at nursery school is never required. It need not be regular.

The nursery school is here to stay. Social conditions such as increased employment of mothers, crowded housing, urbanization, poverty, and the like appear to justify both a continuation and an expansion of the movement. Apart from social expediency, future expansion of nursery school education can be justified in terms of the immediate value to the children who attend and to their parents, who also participate in the program. Where nursery schools facilitate the transition from home to school, where they help parents understand and guide their children, where, all things considered, they help children make the adjustments required of them, the services and benefits justify the establishment and maintenance of nursery school units as a regular part of both the nonpublic and public school systems.

Head Start program

The statements made about nursery schools in general apply to the Head Start program also: that it serves childhood and also parent education and that it requires specially adapted facilities, highly trained teachers, medical attendants, and so forth. Although the Head Start program is not always a part of the public school organization, in many cases it is.

When the Office of Economic Opportunity initiated Head Start as a part of its war on poverty, the idea was to take youngsters from disadvantaged neighborhoods and give them preschool experiences so that they might more readily fit into the school picture and relate better to classmates from more advantaged homes when they started kindergarten or first grade. It was felt that what these children needed most was individual attention, to feel that someone cared about them.

The classes have usually included about 15 pupils with one highly trained teacher assisted by a number of teacher aides and volunteers. Doctors, nurses, psychologists, social workers, and nutritionists share also, especially in testing, guidance, home visits, and parental education. An effort is made to give the children a wide range of enriching experiences including conversation, simple tasks they can do with satisfaction, group play activities, well-planned lunches often including food items new to the children, bus trips, and excursions. Enrollment is voluntary, and the 3- to 6-year-olds are selected from homes whose annual income does not exceed a certain figure (usually $3,000).

That children entering kindergarten with experience in Head Start have had less trouble adjusting and seem happier is generally agreed. What happens, however, if the child finds that the pleasant surroundings and individual attention of the Head Start program are not part of the regular school? Perhaps in the regular school the teacher has to care for 30 or 40 children without all the aid, facilities, and equipment that were part of Head Start. Perhaps this teacher has preconceived notions about the limited potential of disadvantaged children. Will the early compensatory education be of limited, short-term benefit without consistent school experiences following? Hopefully, Head Start will call attention to the really crucial sectors in educational reconstruction—the primary and secondary inner-city schools—and will serve as the spark to bring about essential changes.

This is Head Start in action. Look at the faces of these preschoolers. Some seem puzzled, some seem awed, a few seem frustrated, but there is an over-all impression of striving—striving to understand, to grow, to express. It is a new, larger world these children are striving to enter. That is what Head Start is all about.

Even if we admit the important part preschool education can play, and even if the desirable features of Head Start could be continued throughout the school, do we still perhaps overestimate the value of preschool education in American education? Can these experiences offset the effects of poverty, provide a substitute for the broad range of healthful, normative home and family experiences of small children? Just as it has never been demonstrated that preschooling is essential to the future educational success of typical middle-class youth, may we possibly find that it is not essential to school achievement for disadvantaged youth—once we provide really adequate buildings, teachers, and educational programs, as well as the genuine promise of future success in life?

THE KINDERGARTEN

In an earlier chapter the idea of kindergarten education for children of preschool age was traced to Froebel, who demonstrated the practicality of the idea by conducting an experimental school. He moved his experimental school to Blankenburg, Germany, and in 1840 gave it the name "kindergarten"—a garden of children. So rapidly did the idea take hold that in the 25 years following Froebel's death kindergartens were established in the leading cities of Germany, Holland, Belgium, Switzerland, Austria, Hungary, Canada, Japan, and the United States. The name "kindergarten" has become synonymous, in many parts of the world, with the kind of education program suited to preschool-age children.

St. Louis made kindergarten education a part of its public school system in 1873. A demonstration kindergarten was established at the Philadelphia Exposition in 1876. These two ventures are credited with demonstrating to the American people, many of whom had previously been skeptical, the merits of kindergarten education. Within 10 years, kindergartens had been established in all the major cities of the United States. All of these, with the exception of St. Louis, were under private control. As people became convinced of the value of the kindergarten, public schools enthusiastically adopted the unit.

Comenius had argued that at 6 the child was at the best age to enter school. We still accept 6 years as the logical age for entrance into the first grade. The kindergarten precedes first grade and, from the standpoint of organization, remains a more or less separate unit in the school system. The kindergarten is neither fully integrated with the nursery school unit, where one exists, nor with the first grade. The separation is not considered undesirable. Psychologists believe that rapid maturation takes place between the ages of 4 and 5 and between the ages of 5 and 6, and that this must be taken into account in planning suitable programs for each of the three ages. For example, in contrast to the 4-year-old, the child at 5 is clear and complete in his answers to simple questions. He is more adept at building with larger blocks, more skillful in acts of simple drawing, more critical of his own inability to do something he would very much like to do, more likely to finish what he starts, and more self-reliant in the performance of his personal duties. He is ready for wider experiences than either the home or the nursery school can provide. Since the kindergarten must provide an environment quite different from other school units, the rather general practice of keeping it as a separately organized unit, even though in the same building, will probably be continued.

All large cities in the United States now have kindergartens, at which attendance is voluntary. Since there is considerable variation in the ages of children who attend the earlier grades—all children do not arrive at the age of 5 on the same day—it is not easy to interpret data on kindergarten attendance. It appears, however, that slightly over half the children of 5 years or thereabouts attend kindergarten. This means that not all of the communities in the United States that would be able to support kindergarten education do so, and also that not all parents are inclined to send their children to kindergarten even when one is readily accessible. It seems that the acceptance and development of kindergarten education, like nursery school education, will depend on the wishes of the American public. Where kindergartens have been conducted according to the best known educational standards of practice, experts report that some of the most effective education in the nation has been accomplished.

The elementary school

The common school, district school, or grade school in the early United States enrolled pupils from the first grade through the eighth. After that, if the pupil continued his schooling he transferred to a four-year high school. Since around 1910, there has been a strong tendency to reduce the unit of elementary education from eight to six grades. Even now, however, the eight-grade type of organization still enrolls more pupils than does the six-grade type. In discussing the education program at the elementary level, regardless of type of organization, it is common practice to consider Grades 1 through 6 as the logical unit.

THE CURRICULUM

Elementary school pupils ordinarily follow a single curriculum, the chief aim of which is *general education*. In some schools the subject matter is classified under broad fields like language arts or social studies. In others the classification is more restricted, and reading, writing, spelling, penmanship, and grammar are classifications. This is discussed more fully in a later chapter. Since the elementary school must be adapted to the needs of children who vary widely in both abilities and interests, the curriculum is never considered a set one, a laid-out-in-advance path, to be followed at all costs. The curriculum is more a suggestion to the teacher of what is desirable. The teacher, in most American elementary schools, is given freedom to modify and adapt as the conditions in his classroom warrant. To the well-trained teacher this freedom to devise the most fruitful environment in terms of the needs of the pupils as he learns to know them is what makes teaching in the elementary school a most challenging kind of work.

THE TEACHER

The elementary teacher is a specialist in teaching at a particular grade level, for which he must have well-rounded training and experience. This is recognized both within the profession and in the community. It has strong implications for the preparation of elementary teachers. The elementary teacher must teach a very wide range of subject matter. He must, therefore, strive for broad, well-rounded preparation in his college work, which is sometimes difficult within a rigid system of required majors and minors. The elementary teacher is so important an influence on the formation of early habits that help shape the future character of the pupils that the ideals he exemplifies must be part of a wholesome personality. He must have an understanding of how young children grow. He must be able to take their interests into account and make what he teaches continuous with what the child has previously learned. He must be prepared to confer with and direct parents. His relationships with parents place him in an excellent position to influence their thinking on educational problems.

THE SCHOOL BUILDING

The modern elementary school building is typically designed along functional lines and is surrounded with attractively landscaped grounds and outdoor play facilities. It is one of the most attractive buildings in many American communities. By visiting such a building and noting the details that have been incorporated to serve the educa-

Many school districts conduct summer schools at both the elementary and secondary levels. These Spanish-speaking children are in an intensive summer course in English.

tional needs of pupils and teachers, one gets a reasonable appreciation of what modern architectural school-building science can contribute to the improvement of the elementary school.

ORGANIZATION OF THE CLASSROOM

The organization within the elementary school generally follows the self-contained classroom pattern, the service and resource-unit pattern, or some modification of these. In either case, the furniture in the classroom is completely movable so that discussion, laboratory activities, individual projects, and "research" by children can be conveniently cared for within the room. Many kinds of teaching-aid materials are available—not resting on shelves in neat arrangements but carefully catalogued and circulated throughout the school.

Although the self-contained classroom has a rather recently acquired name, it is the oldest form of educational organization in the United States. It is still considered by many educators to be the most desirable plan for elementary school organization. Under this arrangement, one teacher is responsible for the whole range of activities, and the equipment in the classroom is complete. Ideally, toilet and washroom facilities are included, as well as shop facilities, cupboards, work tables, art equipment, a piano, a record player, and perhaps a movie projector.

The service and resource-unit pattern may shift some responsibility for teaching from the classroom instructor. To facilitate instruction, teachers at least have access to a library, a workshop, an auditorium, and other specialized facilities. A specialized staff of resource persons may also be available to help all classroom teachers. This may include a teacher-librarian, a psychologist, a teacher of dramatics, of music, of art, of crafts, of physical education, and a remedial teacher. The efforts of specialists are coordinated with those of the classroom teacher who, with the help of the principal, plans the activities so that there is no break in the unified development of the education program of a pupil. Coordination and scheduling of the use of the building and the personnel resources are the responsibility of the principal.

Whether the school is organized around the principle of the self-contained classroom, which is a more costly form of organization, or around the service and resource-unit pattern, or some variation of either, personnel organization is kept simple. All the teachers are specialized, but in different ways. Ideally, there are only two ranks among the staff, that of the teachers and that of the principal.

There are still a few schools in the United States that include all eight grades, all under the direction of one teacher and all housed in a one-room building. In some cities, Grades 7 and 8 are included in the same building with the first six grades. In some instances the practice of having subject matter departmentalized and the instruction in each subject handled by a specialized teacher in that area is carried down as far as the fifth grade. Sometimes departmentalization is only partial. In these cases children may have one teacher for most of their school-work but have specialized teachers for something like music, physical education, or art.

AREAS FOR IMPROVEMENT

The elementary school is a fertile area for educational improvement. The success of any plan to build a continuous, organized, developmental program to serve all who attend schools through the twelfth grade is contingent upon the program built for children while they are in the elementary school. One indicated change in the elementary school is a better balance of men and women on the teaching staff. Elementary teachers now constitute about two-thirds of all the public elementary and secondary teachers in America, and approximately 85 percent of these elementary teachers are women. Perhaps the growth of young children should be directed and stimulated by mature, emotionally well-balanced men *and* women. A number of changes in such areas as social attitude, salaries, and organizational pattern will necessarily precede this kind of improvement.

Middle, intermediate, and junior high schools

The middle grades—Grades 5, 6, 7, 8, and 9—united in the schools in various grade combinations, are the present-day answer to the problem of providing an organized school unit that will logically follow the one-curriculum lower-grade school and also facilitate transsition into the more specialized programs of the secondary school. Most commonly, this in-between school unit embraces either Grades 7, 8, and 9, or Grades 6, 7, 8, and 9. This is not always the case, however. In fact, having no in-between school at all, but having the first eight grades together as one unit, is still typical in some agricultural areas and in some larger cities. Sometimes legally established high school districts determine the grades included in the secondary school. In some parts of Illinois and California, for instance, the ninth grade is in a four-year high school that operates in a district independent of the district caring for the elementary levels from kindergarten through Grade 8. Education specialists indicate that, for psychological reasons, it is desirable to include the ninth grade in any middle school. Their opinions vary on the inclusion of sixth-graders.

Typically the junior high school has cared for the educational needs of 12-, 13-, and 14-year-old children, has directed teaching away from a single curriculum, from a uniform program for all pupils, toward an offering providing choice and opportunities for specialization. Ordinarily, opportunities for pupils to individualize their programs have been moderately introduced in the seventh grade and gradually increased through the eighth and ninth grades.

In the modern junior high school, pupils are usually provided a wide range of direct exploratory experiences. Although exploratory experience is not peculiar to the junior high school—basic science at the college level, for instance, may be exploratory—it is introduced in the junior high school as a special method of study through appropriate curriculums. Also, for the first time a pupil in an intermediate school ordinarily has the privilege of selecting an elective from among such areas as general shop, printing, crafts, ceramics, art, electricity, music, dramatics, or a foreign language. School marks are not usually given in the elective field, or, where they are assigned, they are not considered marks of relative achievement. Teachers are on the alert to discover special interests, aptitudes, and skills.

General science, mathematics, language arts, and social studies may be taught in the spirit of exploration and discovery. This consumes more time than conventional methods. Pupils are encouraged to observe, to read widely, to investigate independently, to write creatively, and to get a broad view of some field of learning before entering detailed study of it.

Extracurricular activities, under expert direction, in the athletic, social, musical, and dramatic fields are also provided. These, like the other features, are especially designed to meet the needs of the preadolescent.

The work of pupils in junior high schools is customarily planned around homerooms. Homeroom teachers generally combine the function of counseling with their teaching. Large junior high schools usually make available the services of a trained psychologist also. The principal aim of the homeroom teacher, and of the other people on the professional staff as well, but perhaps to a lesser degree, is to help pupils solve problems peculiar to their respective ages. The teacher must have an understanding of the problems typically associated with the dawning of a social consciousness—physical development, recreation, home relationships, religion, school relationships, personal conflicts, and the like. At the junior high school level, partly because of these guidance needs, it is important that men teachers should be as well represented as women teachers.

A majority of pupils of preadolescent age now attend some kind of intermediate, middle, or junior high school that differs from the traditional eight-grade elementary school. Studies by psycholgists recommend that in the future even more attention should be given to discovering better solutions to the ever-widening gap of individual differences that especially characterize pupils of the sixth-, seventh-, eighth-, and ninth-grade age groups. A potential weakness of the junior high school program is the tendency to veer too far and too rapidly from the older one-curriculum, elementary school program toward too much departmentalization. A pupil from a five- or six-grade, one-curriculum school, from a self-contained classroom with one teacher, going into a school where he may have as many as eight teachers, may find his problems of adjustment aggravated.

Psychologists, and particularly the child-development experts who have focused their studies and attention upon the children of the in-between, preadolescent ages tell us that the physical, emotional, and intellectual characteristics of these youngsters leave little doubt that their needs and interests must be given special consideration.

Henry Suzzallo (1875–1933), a distinguished educator and president of the University of Washington, expressed his thoughts on the constantly recurring social phenomenon, criticism of public elementary schools.

> The argument for the adequate maintenance of our common schools does not require much repetition to insure acceptance ; but the argument for much that goes on in their classrooms does. Nothing is more atonishing than the reforms which have been made in elementary education. The last decade or two have witnessed great changes, not all of them wise perhaps. For the most part, however, they have been worthy responses to changed conditions or to the demand for a larger realization of democratic ideals.
>
> These modifications have been so rapid and extensive that the older generation often judges current practice by a personal experience which has been left far behind. The schools can scarcely be judged by such naïve methods. It would be just as fair to judge contemporaneous medical practice by that of a generation ago without knowing anything of intervening scientific discovery. Psychology and experimental teaching have developed many new scientific facts unknown to the teachers or parents of a generation ago. Sociological science, too, has indicated many new adjustments that have had to be made.
>
> One constant recurring criticism suggests that our present-day schools do not teach the fundamental subjects as well as earlier schools did, meaning that children cannot read as intelligently or as quickly as they did, or that they cannot figure or spell as accurately as a previous generation.
>
> While such statements are based on rather plausible deductions, they are the product of a faulty psychology. The "good old days" have left most of their evils behind and the present remembrance of them is hallowed by a selective sentimentalism which retains only the agreeable. When based on any kind of reasoning, such conclusions assume that it would be impossible for a child to know the few basic formal subjects as well when they are pursued in connection with a half-dozen other studies as when they were studied exclusively. Hence the inference, that so many new "fads and frills" are certain to interfere with a thorough acquisition of the fundamentals. The argument is plausible enough, but it happens not to be true to the facts as scientifically determined.
>
> . . . Wherever it has been possible actually to compare past and present results, the comparison has been most favorable to current schooling.

Henry Suzzallo, *Our Faith in Education*. Philadelphia: J. B. Lippincott Company, 1924, pp. 74–77. Quoted by permission of J. B. Lippincott Company.

This is a crucial period in the life cycle, a period marked by the child's growth toward physical and mental independence, a period of widening gaps in individual differences. The age is considered the most difficult from the standpoint of discipline. Teaching at the junior high school level calls for special understanding and for specialized teaching skills. It promises commensurate teaching satisfaction.

The senior high school

The senior high school, as we discuss it, embraces Grades 10, 11, and 12, although some high schools include Grade 9 as well. When the ninth grade is included as a part of the high school, the attitudes toward the pupil and toward appropriate education for him are approximately the same as when the ninth grade is located in a junior high school. The pupil is still the same age, and has the same psychological characteristics and the same educational needs.

Americans believe that an enlightened citizenry is necessary to the survival of our democracy. They believe that equal educational opportunity for all children and youth is a correlative requirement. At the beginning of the century, however, many communities prided themselves on the fact that very few pupils who entered the ninth grade ever finished the twelfth. Modern senior high school practices emerged from a social atmosphere where selection was a favored policy. At the beginning of the century, fewer than 8 percent of the 17-year-olds graduated from high school. The high schools actually were *high* schools. Only a few years ago the chances of graduating from high school were greater for those pupils who had intelligence quotients of 110 and above. A pupil's chances of obtaining an education were enhanced if he came from an economically favored home, if his parents were in the highest income brackets in the community. In other words, the high school program was planned with highly selected college-bound pupils in mind. Traditions that accompanied that kind of policy became very deeply established. Now, typically, at the completion of 12 years of school attendance each pupil receives a high school diploma. The diploma is the same for all, regardless of the quality of work or the subject matter studied. In most communities, completion of the twelfth grade is the terminal point of education for many pupils. The activities of commencement are a universal recognition of this achievement.

With the extension of universal education it has become necessary to cut the academic cloth to fit the needs, abilities, and interests of every educable youth who may wish to take advantage of a senior high school education. If education at the senior high school level is to serve all American youth, then it must be so planned and administered that all American youth can profit from it. High school teachers have moved energetically in the direction of attaining this ideal. Though their progress has been commendable, the conflict of new with old continues partially unsolved. One obstacle to progress has been the deep-seated tradition, firmly intrenched in many minds of the older generation, that high schools should select the fit from the unfit. Another obstacle to fitting the high school program to all American youth is related to disrupting social crises—the depression of the 1930s, World War II in the 1940s, the sharp upturn in population growth in the 1950s, the Vietnam war of the late 1960s. A faculty may favor making indicated changes but may be hampered by lack of funds and lack of available personnel. In times of international conflict, industry and the government tend to exert pressure for a special kind of training in the high school. The rapidity of social change scarcely gives high school teachers a chance to keep up to date in their analyses of the adjustments currently needed.

THE CURRICULUM

Typically, the modern four-year high school is developed to serve the needs of students from 14 to 18. It offers in one administrative unit all of the programs for the education of all the youth who attend high school in a given community or school district. There are, however, some exceptions in a few of the larger cities. In New York City, for example, there are a number of specialized high schools, such as those giving vocational education. Specialized high schools are generally found in large, wealthy school districts. Most districts of ordinary size cannot afford them. Even though a high school may specialize in a particular kind of vocational training, it still remains comprehensive in that the pupils take a balanced program and can, therefore, continue on to college.

The problem of building a satisfactory curriculum to serve all American youth has two main facets. There must be, on the one hand, a reasonable degree of specialized education and, on the other hand, a reasonable emphasis on general education.

No term has been coined to designate the program that achieves an adequate balance between integration and specialization, between general education and specialized education. The pupil, with the help of his counselors, may in most cases select studies that will prepare him to enter some field of his own choosing. This is referred to as fulfilling the preparatory function of the high school. The program of studies can be planned in terms of a future goal. Some high schools have been very ingenious in finding ways to meet the differentiated needs of the young adults. Others have not been ingenious enough. They have stressed certain kinds of preparation, such as preparing the pupil to enter college, but have not succeeded as well with meeting needs of pupils who wish to follow other lines of endeavor.

Every high school curriculum should also give reasonable emphasis to fostering cultural compatibility. It is not easy to say how a heterogeneous population of young adults should be educated so that they become sufficiently like-minded to guarantee the perpetuation and improvement of the present American society. That is, nevertheless, a responsibility of every American high school.

The high school's answer to what it believes are the activities that lead to a well-integrated personality can be judged by what all the pupils are required to study. All pupils are usually required to study English for three years and United States history, civics, mathematics, science, and health and physical education for at least one year each. To this minimum or foundation program, the pupil can add, through his own selection, other courses in general or specialized education to complete his requirements for graduation. In other words, approximately one-half of his program is general education and one-half is specialized education. The four subjects most important in achieving general education are, in order of the emphasis they receive, English, social studies, mathematics, and science.

THE CORE PROGRAM

One example of how high schools sometimes adjust to new demands has been the development of the core program, sometimes called core courses, corerooms, or core studies. The core program includes all the instruction thought to be needed by all pupils of a given grade level. For example, oral expression, written expression, and citizenship training would be integrated into a single course taught by the core teacher, who has received appropriate special training.

Traditional subject-matter classification is generally disregarded in planning work. The work may be planned around a study of the problems of the immediate community. A given project may reveal the important part individuals play in the community, the principles that underlie the American way of life, and problems connected with developing responsible citizenship. The project may teach how to cultivate the art of oral expression and how to participate in planning and conducting certain social activities. The group—the core teacher *with* the pupils—determines the aims of the project and the resources and activities needed to achieve them as the study progresses. The period of working together is longer than a traditional class period. This allows sufficient time for use of laboratory techniques and for pupil-teacher planning. It permits use of the community, makes it possible to complete comprehensive projects, and allows participation in activities necessary for a realistic program of citizenship training.

Work accomplished in core studies varies considerably from school to school. But in all schools it is recognized that the core teacher must be with the pupils longer and that he must know them well. He must be assigned a moderate teaching and counseling load. The core teacher will teach a heterogeneous group, not pupils classified in terms of native ability or academic achievement. He will be responsible for giving individual and group guidance to the pupils and will be free to plan the activities of the core program. Subject-matter examinations will largely be replaced by an evaluation that is planned by both the teacher and the pupil. This newer evaluation will focus upon citizenship, work habits, and ability to solve problems, to contribute to group thinking and planning, and to master subject matter. While the coreroom is a unit in the high school plan of organization, it is also a unit of organization in which the teacher strives to fulfill certain functions with fairly definitely determined and generally accepted practices.

The core program is one recent attempt to improve the high school's effectiveness in achieving social integration. Other high school efforts at securing both specialized education and general education include the offering of extracurricular activities, counseling procedures, and special services like psychological testing. The American high school is becoming a truly comprehensive school. It is being modified to serve well the needs of all the children and young adults of the nation between the ages of 14 and 18. The "core" program, disregarding nomenclature, since it has various names, is an effort to make high schools that are comprehensive also socially unified, integrated schools.

The nongraded school

For some time educators have been struggling with various plans to meet specific needs and to adjust to definite abilities of individual pupils. Such plans as the Winnetka Plan, the Platoon System, and the Pueblo Plan have been tried, and for various reasons given up. A present plan is an organizational plan and is called the *nongraded school*. It differs from its predecessors in details, but it seeks to achieve the same service to individual pupils.

In the traditional units of school organization, the pupils of any one grade are usually of about the same chronological age. The pupils in any one classroom, however, exhibit a wide range of differences in ability. Teachers have, of course, always made adjustments within the classroom to these variations. Special materials have been supplied for various purposes and levels of learning ability. In the nongraded school, however, an *organizational* plan is followed which creates a framework that allows for flexibility and continuity.

Nongraded schools are to be found more often at the elementary school level, although there are nongraded plans to be found in some disciplines in some secondary schools. As is true of all features of our American schools, the details of the nongraded plan vary from place to place.

The nongraded elementary school, for the most part, relies on levels of accomplishment in reading as the basis for advancement and

The over-all system of education in this country is most readily studied in terms of units of school organization, but what it all adds up to is Education in America— *a vitally important undertaking that is almost bewildering in its scope and in the ways it responds to our ever-growing demands on it.* Adult education: *numerous subjects are offered, including printing.* Public junior colleges: *they are multiplying ; this one serves 13,000 students.* Curriculum materials centers: *many state universities maintain them ; they are used by school*

teachers and others. School libraries: *almost every public school has one, staffed by a teacher-librarian.* Acceleration by place-out: *this is a way to solve the problem of articulation between elementary school and high school ; eighth-graders with special aptitudes (here, mathematics) attend special high school classes ; when they enter high school, they are ready for study in depth.* Unit high schools: *this is a way to break down huge regional high schools into smaller units ; the three schools at left share the many special facilities at right.*

assignment in a program of vertical progression through the six years of the elementary school organization. No grade designators are used. The nongraded sequence usually consists of a three-year program (primary nongraded) or a six-year program (elementary nongraded). Levels of sequential reading content are most often the first organizational basis for nongradedness. For instance, the children may all start together at level 1, and progress through to level 20, to a traditional sixth-grade reading book. At each level there are possibilities for lateral movement with enrichment materials and also for reinforcement materials if a child needs more work before moving on to the next level.

The pupil either moves on into the intermediate nongraded unit from the primary unit or has his program enriched in depth. The amount of time it takes a child to complete a level varies. The slow learner may take four years to accomplish three. He does not have to repeat a whole year, as is the case in the graded school. Instead, he takes up in the fall where he left off at the beginning of summer. This is not retention, nor does it carry the stigma of retention. The decision about whether to enrich or advance the child who finishes three years in two is a basic one which involves many variables including age, size, intellect, and many other social and psychological aspects concerning the child's life situation.

Nongradedness in the secondary school is linked with team teaching. It usually provides for as much as 45 percent of the student's time for independent study. Of the other 55 percent, 30 percent might be given to large-group instruction and 25 percent to small groups. This allows for flexibility in the time students spend on each course, depending on their rate of progress and the modifications the teachers make in it for individual students.

The junior college

In America, the junior college—sometimes public and sometimes private—is a two-year post-high school institution. Currently, there is a dramatic increase in the number of public junior colleges and in their services. The establishment of such a junior college is typically initiated in the area to be served and may depend on approval in a referendum in the area. In some states the public junior college is part of the state system of higher education; in others it is part of the local school district. At the beginning of the century, there were fewer than 10 junior colleges in the United States; and only one—the junior college established at Joliet, Illinois, in 1902—was public. Now every state has one or more public junior colleges, the total number in 1968 reaching 708, with a total enrollment of 1,747,453. In contrast, the number of private junior colleges in 1968 was 273, the same number as in 1961, with, however, a modest growth in enrollment.

In the junior college a large proportion of the program typically is devoted to courses ''baccalaureate-oriented''—that is, courses that may be transferred to a four-year college or university and that fit into a program leading to the bachelor's degree. However, especially in the public junior colleges, there is also emphasis on two-year terminal curricula in the occupational, semitechnical, and technical fields such as business and secretarial, nursing, data processing, and electronics. The junior college also serves as a center for the administration of a program for adult education through evening schools, adult forums, and the like.

All who graduate from high school are eligible to continue their education in a public junior college. Tuition usually is charged. In addition to local tax funds, the support generally is shared to a relatively high degree by state funds and also by federal funds allocated to vocational and technical education and other areas of higher education. Federal funds are directly applicable to junior colleges under the Higher Education Act of 1965 and its 1968 amendments.

The junior college has a position of unquestioned acceptance in America, and present trends suggest that it will have a prominent place in future plans for extending educational opportunities to the youth of America.

The state university

One of the most spectacular developments in American education is the state university, the apex of the public educational system. The state university—the answer to the American public's demand for

*Walter Hines Page (1855–1918) is remembered as a distinguished ambassador
to Great Britian, an office to which he was appointed by President Woodrow
Wilson. Page was also a writer with an intense passion for democracy. One
of the institutions that he believed would make democracy strong was the
public school. In one of his speeches he described ''the school that built a
town.'' This excerpt illustrates the trend of his thinking :*

In the first period of Northwood's history, you will observe, the town
carried the schools—carried them as a burden. The schools of the
cultivated widow, the strenuous young lady and the old fashioned
scholar and the young ladies' seminary, much as the several sets and
sects each boasted of its own institution, were really tolerated rather
than generously supported. The principals had to beg for them in one
form or other. The public school was regarded as a sort of orphan
asylum for the poor. The whole educational work of the town was on a
semi-mendicant basis : or it was half a sort of social function, half a
sort of charity. It really did not touch the intellectual life of the people.
They supported it. It did not lift them. The town carried the schools
as social and charitable burdens.

Now this is all changed. The school has made the town. It has given
nearly every successful man in it his first impulse in his career and it
has given the community great renown. Teachers from all over the
country go there to see it. More than that, many pupils go from a
distance to enter the high school. More than that, men have gone there
to live because of the school. They go there to establish industries of
various sorts, because the best expert knowledge of every craft can be
found there. The town has prospered and has been rebuilt. The architects
are high-school men ; the engineers who graded the streets and made a
model system of sewers are high-school men ; the roads were laid out by
high-school men. There is a whole county of model farms and dairies
and good stock farms. High-school men have in this generation made
the community a new community. They conduct all sorts of factories—
they make furniture, they make things of leather, they make things of
wrought iron ; they have hundreds of small industries. It is said that
a third of the houses in the town contain home-made furniture after
beautiful old patterns that the owners themselves have made. And there
is one man who does inlaid work in wood. And all this activity clusters
about the public schools. The high school now not only affects but it
may be said to dominate the life of the town ; and this is the school
that has built the town, for it has given everybody an impetus and has

*started nearly everybody towards an occupation. It enables them to find
their own aptitudes.*

*Now there is all the difference in the world between the Northwood of
this generation, and the Northwood of the generation before. It is a
difference so great that it cannot be told in one morning. But the change
is simply the result of a changed view of education.*

Walter Hines Page, *The School That Built a Town*. New York: Harper & Row, 1952,
pp.59–60. Quoted by permission of the publisher.

higher education—has no counterpart in any other country. It is
indigenous to the American cultural soil and suited to American
tradition.

All the state universities have four-year colleges, which award a
bachelor's degree upon graduation. Superimposed on the college is
the graduate school which (1) affords specialization beyond that given
in the four-year undergraduate college, (2) awards degrees, the
master's degree for one year of study beyond the bachelor program
and the doctor of philosophy degree for three or more years of study
and research beyond the bachelor program, and (3) offers numerous
degrees designating fields of specialization—doctor of education,
doctor of laws, doctor of science. The faculties are made up of highly
trained specialists who combine teaching, scholarly writing, and
original research.

Professional schools of law, medicine, dentistry, agriculture,
library science, education, engineering, business, journalism, architecture, theology, and speech and a nonprofessional school of arts
and sciences are all administered within the common university
organization.

The public universities in some cases have become organizational
giants. The comprehensiveness of their programs may be inferred
from their size. For example, the University of California, with its
seven campuses, enrolls well over 125,000 students. Its Berkeley
campus alone has a teaching staff equal in number to a sizeable university
student body early in this century. So large have university enrollments
become that some state legislatures—Illinois, for example—have
established a system of independently administered state universities at
strategic locations throughout the state. It is not at all uncommon for a
state university to enroll more than 20,000 students. The projection of

future over-all enrollment is in excess of 6 million students by 1975. How large the state universities will be allowed to become is a matter of conjecture. One thing seems certain: their influence on American life and education will greatly increase.

The combination of college and university instruction under a single administration is the principal distinctive characteristic of the American state university and is considered one of its chief sources of strength. In some cases, technical institutes within the university framework operate primarily for research purposes, for issuing learned publications under the direction of the teaching staff, for conducting programs contributing to the national defense, and for carrying on a variety of other undertakings deemed essential enough to call for recognition at the university level.

Many state universities have programs set up to serve special needs of the state. Extension divisions, organized in most state universities, provide credit and noncredit courses in various centers of the state for training in many fields. The state universities distribute visual materials and maintain lending libraries throughout the state, and offer short-course seminars, lectures, conferences, and other similar services.

Some state universities have branches in convenient centers in the state, making education more accessible and less costly to the people of the state.

State universities are supported mainly by direct taxation. They also, however, derive considerable revenue from federal funds, endowments, alumni foundations, private foundations, student fees, athletics, and the like. The annual expenditure for all state institutions is very substantial. Their plans are extensive. Their educational influence is very great. The state universities are large, colorful, liberally supported, constantly expanding institutions which make a very popular appeal to the people of each state. They are the top rung of the educational ladder.

Summary: the educational ladder

The educational ladder in the American public school system has been the pride of the American people. It has made a major contribution to the maintenance and improvement of the American idea of civilization.

The ladder constitutes a continuous progression of instruction from the kindergarten through the most advanced training given by the universities. In the main, the costs are borne by the public, and the opportunity of advancing to the higher levels is constantly being extended to more people.

The elementary school, the junior high school, and the senior high school are viewed as institutions for everyone. The desire of the American people to extend educational opportunities at the higher level is answered in part by the junior college, the newest extension of free, or nearly free, popular education.

Questions

1. What factors should a parent consider before deciding whether to send his child to a nursery school?
2. How much should one expect a child's attendance at nursery school or kindergarten to contribute to his subsequent achievement in subject matter?
3. Why have the factors of continuity, gradation, and transition received such serious consideration in the establishment of school units of organization?
4. What kinds of specialized services would you expect to find in the better-organized elementary schools?
5. What are some of the instructional resources you expect to find in the better-organized elementary schools?
6. How is the transition idea reflected in the organization of the junior high school?
7. How has the movement to decentralize education affected the organization of the junior college?
8. What are some of the problems the high school faces when it attempts to provide an education for all American youth?

Projects

1. From a table of ages of the children in some particular grade of a school system, generalize on what some of the problems of teaching in that grade may be.

2. Describe the expanding role of the junior college and estimate the future of this public school unit.

3. Set forth what you consider the principal problems of teaching caused by individual differences among the pupils in the different units of school organization.

4. In view of the fact that the federal government provides generous aid to nonpublic higher institutions, state the pros and cons for its providing aid to nonpublic secondary schools; to nonpublic junior colleges; to nonpublic elementary schools.

5. Visit a local Head Start program. Evaluate the work in terms of specific observations.

Unit III Suggested Readings

ALDEN, VERNON R., "Planning for Education's Forgotten Men," *Saturday Review*, pp. 68–69, 85–86, May 15, 1965. Explains the hoped-for fruits of some 82 Job Corps education and training centers established under the Economic Opportunity Act passed by Congress in 1964. The author believes that experience with the Job Corps may lead to development of new techniques and teaching materials and also provide a training school for future teachers in depressed city areas.

ALEXANDER, WILLIAM M., "The New School in the Middle," *Phi Delta Kappan*, 50 (No. 6): 355–357, February, 1969. Explains why the middle school idea has grown so rapidly. "For the foreseeable future middle schools of grades 5–8 or 6–8 are destined to replace the traditional grades 7–9 junior high schools as the schools in the middle." Explains the rationale of the developing middle school idea.

ALFORD, ALBERT L., "The Elementary and Secondary Education Act of 1965," *Phi Delta Kappan*, 46 (No. 10): 483–488, June, 1965. Explains the provisions of the acts and explains what local leadership must do to implement it.

American Education, December 1968–January 1969, pp. 12–22, 30–31. A series of short articles on the growth and development of junior colleges. Data on growth and enrollment are on pages 30–31.

American Education, "Federal Funds," 5 (No. 4): 22–25, April, 1969. A breakdown of the $3.5 billion distributed by the U. S. Office of Education to the states. Shows how the states used the money to improve education.

American Education, "Federal Money for Education: Programs Administered by the U. S. Office of Education," 5 (No. 2) : 20–24, February, 1969. This lists 118 federal aid programs administered by

447

the U. S. Office of Education. Of particular interest to the beginning student of education are the column "Authorization," which lists the specific act upon which a program rests, and the column "Purpose." It should be kept in mind that this vast endeavor is only one part of the federal activity in education. The list grows each year. In 1969, for instance, the Head Start program was added to the Office of Education list.

American Education, "National Defense Education Act—Years of Progress," 4 (No. 8): 2–15, September, 1968. Progress in American education after 10 years of administration of the National Defense Education Act of 1958 is reviewed.

BARATZ, STEPHEN S., and JOAN C. BARATZ, "Negro Ghetto Children and Urban Education: A Cultural Solution," *Social Education*, 33 (No. 4): 401–404, April, 1969. A perceptive statement on the problems of teaching reading in the urban Negro ghetto. "Progress in school depends on the constant development of reading skills. Yet, the one major fault of our urban educational system is its failure to understand why teaching an urban Negro child to read is so difficult. But the explanation is really quite simple. A cultural variable is at work. . . ."

BERSON, MINNIE PERRIN, "Early Childhood Education," *American Education*, 4 (No. 9): 7–13, October, 1968. The Coordinator of Early Childhood Education in the US Office of Education gives an excellent report on what is being accomplished in such federally created childhood education programs as Head Start, Follow Through, and Parent-Child Centers.

COGLEY, JOHN, "Catholics and Their Schools," *Saturday Review*, pp. 72–74, 94–96, October 15, 1966. This is a comprehensive survey of the status of parochial education in the United States as conducted by the Roman Catholic Church.

COLES, ROBERT, "How Do Teachers Feel?" *Saturday Review*, pp. 72–73, 90, May 16, 1964. A research study by a child psychiatrist who spent two years in the deep South studying the problems of classroom teachers in desegregated schools.

COLES, ROBERT, "Some Children the Schools Have Never Served," *Saturday Review*, pp. 58–60, June 16, 1966. A psychiatrist who has worked with and lived among deprived groups explains why the present trends in organizing school districts and having school governments that are relatively autonomous fail to meet the educational needs of disadvantaged groups, such as migrants, and children in Appalachia, in the ghettos, and even in wealthy surburbs. "Millions of American children still find both their rights and their needs ignored."

CRONIN, JOSEPH H., "School Boards and Principals—Before and After Negotiations," *Phi Delta Kappan*, 49 (No. 3): 123–127, November, 1967. Discusses where administrators stand if and when teachers negotiate directly with school boards. "Principals all over the country have been allowed to drown in a sea of paperwork."

DASHIELL, DICK, "Teachers Revolt in Michigan," *Phi Delta Kappan*, 49 (No. 1): 20–26, September, 1967. Describes action of organized groups in Michigan to use the right, granted them by state law, to negotiate with boards of education on equal terms. "Pressure . . . was the only means teachers had to force scores of school boards across the state to negotiate in good faith and reach reasonable agreements with local associations." Describes also the results achieved.

DE YOUNG, CHRIS A., and RICHARD WYNN, *American Education*, 6th ed., New York: McGraw-Hill, 1968, chap. 17. Issues in American education are discussed by two of America's most insightful educators.

DREW, ELIZABETH BRENNER, "Education's Billion-Dollar Baby," *Atlantic Monthly*, (No. 1): 37–43, July, 1966. An analysis of the effects of the Elementary and Secondary School Act of 1965 on local schools. Special attention to Title I of the act, which states that each school district would be given funds based on the number of children in families with incomes of less than $2,000 or on welfare, this money to be over and above the already existing programs. Centers especially on the problems characteristic of large cities.

FABER, CHARLES F., "The Size of a School District," *Phi Delta Kappan*, 48 (No. 1): 33–35, September, 1966. Reviews the thinking of the past thirty years on the most desirable size of a school district.

FLEMING, THOMAS J., "The Crisis in Catholic Schools," *The Saturday Evening Post*, pp. 19–24, October 26, 1963. A survey of the problems facing the Catholic parochial schools in the United States along with various solutions being proposed and certain solutions being tried.

FULLER, EDGAR, "Government Financing of Public and Private

Education," *Phi Delta Kappan*, 47 (No. 7): 365–372, March, 1966.
A scholarly analysis is made by a lawyer-educator of the status of
legal review. He explains how the First Amendment is now applicable
to all three levels of government. "It is in the national interest to
have judicial definitions of the boundaries of the First Amendment in
education as soon as possible." Each new law raises serious legal
problems. The article gives an overview of some of these problems.

GOODLAD, JOHN I., and ROBERT H. ANDERSON, "The Nongraded
Elementary School," *NEA Journal*, 47 (No. 9): 642–643, December,
1958. Presents a report on the movement in some American communities to set up schools without following a grade-level pattern.
This movement is presently on the upswing.

GOSNELL, CULLEN B., LANE W. LANCASTER, and ROBERT S. RANKIN,
Fundamentals of American Government, New York: McGraw-Hill, 1957.
The student of educational organization may wish to review some
dependable text in political science that sets forth the fundamentals
of American political theory. Natural rights, popular sovereignty,
the separation of powers, and judicial review are all treated briefly
in chapters 1 through 4.

GRANT, GERALD, "Developing Power in the Ghetto," *Saturday
Review*, pp. 75–76, 88, December 17, 1966. A reporter analyzes how
the $1.3 billion spent in 1965–1966 on schools in city slums failed
to convince citizens who lived in the disadvantaged areas that better
schools were the result, explains why, and gives his opinion as to
what should be done.

HAZELTON, PAUL, "Education and Politics," *Saturday Review*, pp.
62–63, 81–83, June 15, 1963. An analysis of the relationship
between politics and the conduct of education.

HECHINGER, FRED M., and GRACE HECHINGER, "Panic Among the
Privileged," *Saturday Review*, pp. 70–72, 81, March 16, 1968.
This is an analysis of private elementary and secondary school
education in New York City and its environs. Why do teachers
prefer to teach in private schools even though they receive lower
salaries? If the private school is to prosper in American society,
what role should it assume in America's education?

HILL, HENRY H., "School Desegregation North and South," *Saturday
Review*, pp. 54–56, 71, July 16, 1966. A scholarly educationist
makes an analysis of the desegregation problem in the cities and

shows how extremism is harmful. "A militant moderate accepts school desegration in spirit, as well as in law, and is willing to help desegregation succeed. On the other hand, he resists those advocates of desegregation who would define good education only in terms of desegregation . . ."

HOLT, HOWARD B., "Are School Boards Necessary?" *School and Society*, 91: 349–350, November, 1963. An old question about the wisdom of placing the control of education in the hands of amateur citizens is analyzed. No one seems to have come up with a better practice.

HORN, WILLIAM A., "It's Safer on the Bus," *American Education*, 4 (No. 9): 2–6, October, 1968. This explains how industry, government, and the schools are striving to safeguard the 17 million children who ride buses to school. Practices vary from state to state.

HOWE, HAROLD, "Growth and Growing Pains," *Saturday Review*, pp. 68–70, 87, December 17, 1966. A former United States Commissioner of Education explains the difficult problems confronting his office because of rapid expansion of federal aid to education. "In December of 1964 the United States Office of Education was responsible for an annual budget of $1.5 billion. Now, two years later, its budget for the current fiscal year is $4 billion."

HUNTER, MADELINE C., "Teachers in the Nongraded School," *NEA Journal*, 55 (No. 2): 12–15, February, 1966. A teacher in a nongraded school explains problems in attempting to give each child a tailor-made education.

JACOBY, SUSAN L., "National Monument to Failure," *Saturday Review*, pp. 71–73, 89–90, November 18, 1967. A reporter for the *Washington Post* describes the schools in Washington, where the system operates under federal-government control. As the title implies, "the failure of public education is particularly shameful in a city filled with marble monuments proclaiming that this is, indeed, 'the greatest country on earth.'"

JACOBY, SUSAN L., "New Power in the Schools," *Saturday Review*, pp. 59–60, 70–72, January 18, 1969. This analyzes the position of black teachers in inner-city schools. "Black teachers and administrators are beginning to emerge as a power in the nation's city school systems at a time when the bitterness of black parents toward these schools is overflowing."

KAMINETSKY, JOSEPH, "The Jewish Day Schools," *Phi Delta Kappan*, 45 (No. 3): 141–144, December, 1963. ". . . Jewish Day Schools today are the fastest growing and the most dynamic of all Jewish schools." Explains the values seen in the nonpublic Jewish day school movement.

KOHLBRENNER, BERNARD J., "Some Practical Aspects of the Public Character of Private Education," *School and Society*, 86: 348–351, October 11, 1958. An examination of state constitutional and statutory provisions reveals that there is little public control over teachers in nonpublic schools.

LA NOUE, GEORGE R., "The Establishment Clause: Requiem or Rebirth?" *Phi Delta Kappan*, 50 (No. 2): 85–89, October, 1968. This analysis of the U. S. Supreme Court's 1968 decisions on church-state relationships from the viewpoint of federal policy in financing education clearly highlights the issues involved in using public revenue for private and parochial schools. For example, is the Pennsylvania law requiring the state to set aside horse-racing revenue to support instruction in mathematics, foreign languages, physical sciences, and physical education in nonpublic schools a wise law? Sound? Constitutional? A policy likely to be followed in other states? A lawyer analyzes the issue.

LEESON, JIM, "The Deliberate Speed of Title VI," *Saturday Review*, pp. 74, 87–88. December 17, 1966. Explains how efforts in southern school systems in 1965–1966 to comply with requirements of the Department of Health, Education, and Welfare in the enforcement of Title VI of the 1965 Elementary and Secondary Education Act to desegregate the public schools are working out. Also explores principal problems involved in desegregating southern schools.

MARCONNIT, GEORGE D., "State Legislatures and the School Curriculum," *Phi Delta Kappan*, 49 (No. 5): 269–272, January, 1968. This is an excellent survey of the requirements imposed on classroom instruction by state statutes or state constitutions. The number of limitations varies from 1 in Alaska to 31 in Indiana, 36 in Iowa, 37 in California, and so on. Hawaii is listed as having no state limitations.

MAUCH, JAMES E., "Breaking Traditions Forges School-Community Ties," *Phi Delta Kappan*, 50 (No. 5):270–274, January, 1969. The former administrator of Title I of the 1965 Elementary and Secondary

Education Act explains the many accomplishments made possible in city schools by this program of federal aid.

MCMANUS, MSGR. WILLIAM E., "The Administration and Financing of Catholic Schools," *Phi Delta Kappan*, 45 (No. 3):132–135, December, 1963. "There can be little doubt that the administration of the nation's Catholic schools has been more than adequate. They successfully meet the same standards as the public schools. . . ."

MCMURRIN, STERLING M., "The U. S. Office of Education: An Inside View," *Saturday Review*, pp. 78–81, February 16, 1963. A former Commissioner of Education discusses some of the problems that confront that office.

NATIONAL EDUCATION ASSOCIATION, Research Division, *Estimates of School Statistics*. An annual report of public school statistics, including pupils, professional staff, revenues, and expenditures for the 50 states, the District of Columbia, and the nation as a whole.

NATIONAL EDUCATION ASSOCIATION, Research Division, *Nursery School Education, 1966–67*, pp. 1–9. The introduction to this research report gives an overview picture of the nursery school movement in America.

NATIONAL EDUCATION ASSOCIATION, Research Division, *Rankings of the States*. An annual report that ranks the states in terms of teachers' salaries, relative wealth of the states, the financial effort made by each state to support schools, per pupil expenditure, and the like.

NEA Journal, "Project Head Start," 54 (No. 7): 58–59, October, 1965. A short illustrated article that clearly explains the Head Start program as operated in a Lancaster, Pennsylvania, elementary school. It is much like programs now carried on in many American cities.

PARK, JOE, ed., *Selected Readings in the Philosophy of Education*, New York: Macmillan, 1963, parts 5 and 6. Part 5 deals with Catholic philosophy of education. Part 6 discusses the philosophy of education in Protestant and Jewish thought.

PARKMAN, FRANCIS, "The 'Typical' Independent School," *Phi Delta Kappan*, 45 (No. 3): 128–131, December, 1963. Explains the administrative structure, nature of financial support, attitude toward federal aid, and other characteristics of nonpublic schools.

Phi Delta Kappan, "An Interview with James E. Allen, Jr.," 50 (No. 8: 468–473, April, 1969. The U. S. Commissioner of Education answers a long list of direct questions about the role of government in public education. From his successful experience as State Commissioner of Education in New York and from much study the new Commissioner derives his answers to questions about education in America.

REMSBERG, CHARLES, and BONNIE REMSBERG, "Chicago: Legacy of an Ice Age," *Saturday Review*, pp. 73–75, 91–92, May 20, 1967. Two free-lance writers analyze the dark sides of education in a large city, emphasize the job of the general superintendent, and by implication draw attention to the responsibilities of citizens who serve on boards of education.

RICHEY, ROBERT W., *Planning for Teaching*, 4th ed., New York: McGraw-Hill, 1968, chap. 17. This chapter discusses the current problems and issues in American education about which there is considerable controversy.

ROBERTS, WALLACE, "Can Urban Schools Be Reformed?" *Saturday Review*, pp. 70–72, 87–91, May 17, 1969. "The liberal reformers have tried to make the schools into institutions that can cure the diseases of society, but the schools are a direct reflection of society and can't be changed until the society itself is ready to change." The author illustrates his thesis with reference particularly to Philadelphia and its effort to solve city problems.

ROBINSON, DONALD W., "Commissioner of Education, Our Least/ Most Important Government Post," *Phi Delta Kappan*, 44 (No. 3): 106–115, December, 1962. A scholarly analysis of the work of the Commissioner of Education: what he does; why the Office of Education has so many vacancies; why the Office is ineffective; some of the proposals to improve the work of the Office.

ROGERS, DAVID, "New York City Schools: A Sick Bureaucracy," *Saturday Review*, pp. 47–49, 59–61, July 20, 1968. An analysis of the problems of education in a large-city school district serving more than 1,100,000 pupils and employing more than 59,000 classroom teachers. "The sooner the nation is willing to allocate its resources to these matters, the sooner there will be hope for the future."

Saturday Review, "Education in the Ghetto: A Search for Solutions," pp. 33–61, January 11, 1969. An excellent analysis of the problems of inner-city schools, consisting of a series of fully illustrated short articles prepared by the Committee for Economic Development (an organization of socially concerned businessmen) and the *Saturday Review*.

SCHRAG, PETER, "Pittsburgh: The Virtues of Candor," *Saturday Review*, pp. 82–84, 99–102, November 19, 1966. "... in 1958, ... Pittsburgh began to turn its attention to human renewal and especially to public schools." In this article the author describes what the citizens and the educational staff have done to make their attempt achieve a measure of success.

SHAW, FREDERICK, "The Educational Park in New York: Archetype of the Future?" *Phi Delta Kappan*, 50 (No. 6), 329–331, February, 1969. Explains what the park system is ("a number of educational divisions grouped together in a common campus") and what the primary goals of such school organizations are.

SHEED, WILFRED, "Don't Junk the Parochial Schools," *The Saturday Evening Post*, 6, 10, June 13, 1964. A young journalist makes a plea that America continue to permit its pluralistic philosophy to govern the education of its children.

SIZER, THEODORE R., "Reform Movement or Panacea," *Saturday Review*, pp. 56, 71, June 19, 1965. Explains how Title IV of the Elementary and Secondary Education Act of 1965, with grants totaling $100 million over five years for constructing a network of public school laboratory facilities, may lead to important improvements in teaching methods and school curriculum materials.

SILBERMAN, CHARLES E., "Give Slum Children a Chance," *Harper's Magazine*, 228: 37–42, May, 1964. Proposes an answer to the question, "Can the nation afford a public school system which is failing to educate between 50 and 80 percent of its Negro and slum white children?"

STELLHORN, A. C., "Schools of the Lutheran Church—Missouri Synod," *School and Society*, 87: 225–227, May 9, 1959. A statement of the educational program of this denomination. "Lutherans believe—and the other supporters of church schools share this view —that, besides greatly benefiting the individual and the church, they are rendering the state the best possible service . . ."

WOODRING, PAUL, "A View from the Campus," *Saturday Review*, p. 76, March 16, 1968. An analysis of the actions of student activists on college campuses and the ultimate effects on higher education.

Aims and Methods in America

We began our discussion of education in America with a study of the key figures in the educational picture, the classroom teachers—who, let us remember, number well over two million carefully selected, professionally trained men and women. Unit I centered on the teacher as an individual—his duties; his qualifications; his membership in a large profession; his personal philosophy; and his strategic institutional role. Now, in Unit IV, we return to the work of the teacher, focusing this time specifically on his most important responsibility: stimulating and directing the growth and development of pupils. The word "growth" is used to convey the idea of a process that results in a gradual increase in capabilities, while the word "development" refers to the stage or product attained in the process of growing. An important and broad objective of every classroom teacher is the continuous growth of the learners in desirable directions, progressing by gradual steps from one stage of development to the next higher one. Unit IV is intended principally to give a somewhat comprehensive overview of this most significant feature of a teacher's work by concentrating on three important aspects: the aims, objectives, or hoped-for results; the subject matter involved; and the methods used in attempting to achieve the desired pupil growth and development.

We recognize fully that these three features of the educative process are inseparable, are inextricably interwoven parts of a unified process. A teacher, when teaching, does not think separately about selecting an aim, then subject matter, and then the method of directing the pupils in using the subject matter. Nevertheless, for practical convenience we treat them as separate entities. (Similarly, a physicist discusses protons, neutrons, and electrons as separate entities, though in fact they are the three constituents of an atom.)

Before a teacher can effectively determine what any of the three elements should be, however, he must know and understand the pupils whose growth and development he is to stimulate and direct. Obviously, it is not within the purpose of this book to discuss fully all that is involved in understanding pupils. However, since aims, subject matter, and methods are predicated on the principle that pupils must first be understood, an overview of the subject is presented to make clear some of its important implications.

Clearly, the aims that are selected to guide in education must be related to the pupils, to unique and distinct individuals. Likewise, in determining what subject matter and teaching procedures are appropriate and promising, the decisions must be related to the pupils, to their capacities, interests, and needs. Understanding the pupils, then, is the prelude to the following chapters. This chapter describes some of the sources to which a teacher turns for information about children and also for help in interpreting and comprehending what he learns about pupils—in refining his own insights.

Getting information about pupils

SCHOOL RECORDS

All schools collect and record more or less specific information about pupils. Generally, such information is included in a continuous, cumulative record that gives a picture of an individual as he progresses through the school grade by grade. Before the opening of the school year, a teacher often looks over these records before making tentative plans.

What kind of information is on the official record? Actually, this varies considerably from one school district to another, but, in general, the records include the following:

459

1. Attendance

This will give the date of enrollment in the district and attendance by years in the school. Sometimes a record of tardiness is also included. This information may be an important item in understanding a child because attendance is sometimes related to health, to delinquent behavior, to home problems, or to something else equally significant. The pattern of attendance over the years may be enlightening.

2. Out-of-school background

Such items as where and when the child was born, where he lives, where his parents were born, the language spoken in the home, whether the parents are employed and what kind of employment they have, the number of brothers and sisters, older and younger, and with whom the child makes his home are recorded. The importance of this kind of information in understanding the child is obvious.

3. Health

This will include results on hearing and vision tests as well as any other pertinent information about such matters as surgery. Some schools require dental reports, and these are also recorded. This part of the record should be scanned early because it is important for the teacher to know at once if a child is epileptic, for instance, or even if he should be seated near the front because of a hearing disorder or requires some other minor classroom adjustment.

4. Academic record

This may include report card grades over the years. Usually achievement test scores are also recorded. Where some kind of intelligence or academic potential test has been given, usually this score is also recorded as a help in interpreting the achievement test scores. This part of the record will also show whether the child has been retained or double-promoted at any time throughout his school career.

5. Special services

Many schools provide various kinds of remedial and guidance services such as remedial reading, speech correction, counseling. Usually the agency providing the service prepares a report of what activities have been completed, what progress has been made, and a recommendation for future assignment, and this is included in the cumulative folder.

6. Teacher comments

By means of a check list or brief comments, generally one teacher, annually, records his impressions of the child's behavior and achievement in terms of personal adjustment, social adjustment, qualities of leadership, special aptitudes, creativity in various fields, and the like. Of course, the advantage of the insights and understandings of a pupil's previous teacher is inestimable. It is well to remember, however, that children do change, often go through "stages." An old record of problems should not be allowed to predispose a teacher unwisely.

A more extensive record is found in some schools, but in essence this is the information given to the teacher about each pupil. Without this kind of information supplied by the school, the teacher would be somewhat like a ship without a compass. A ship does not sink because it lacks a compass; nor does a teacher fail because he lacks adequate initial information about pupils. Both, however, are safer with the guidance of dependable instruments. Of course, each instrument must be intelligently used.

PERSONAL OBSERVATION

In learning to know a pupil, no approach is more rewarding than direct observation in a situation involving normal relationships with a peer group. Information from other sources becomes more meaningful as it is interpreted in the light of firsthand, everyday observation. With the pupil in the classroom the teacher observes evidences of maturity—personal, social, and academic. It may be significant to note, for instance, whether a pupil takes initiative in beginning an assignment, in going ahead on his own. How friendly, thoughtful, and helpful he is in his relations with fellow students, how alert he is in contributing to the class as a whole, are the kind of reactions that may be significant, especially as observed over a period of time. Evidence of a probable need for help in relation to emotional problems may be discovered initially through the teacher's observation in the

"In learning to know a pupil, no approach is more rewarding than direct observation in a situation involving normal relationships with a peer group." These junior high school boys are gathered outside their school before class time. What kinds of insights might a teacher begin to gain by observing them in an outwardly casual manner?

classroom. Fears that seem to manifest themselves in such behavior as withdrawal or hostility or in excessive aggressiveness are usually identifiable in a classroom situation.

The teacher's direct observation of the pupil need not be limited to the classroom. In fact, quite important observations may be made of a pupil in the cafeteria, in the halls, at the lockers, in extracurricular activities. In situations of this kind the pupil is making decisions on his own. That a pupil chooses to sit by himself, to seek always to be with a particular group, or to attempt consistently to draw certain others around him may be significant. The pupil who has an untidy, crowded locker, the one who puts the lock on upside down to tease his locker mate, the one who regularly shouts to those across the hall, the one who races down the corridor without thought for the safety of others, may be exhibiting behavior that is symptomatic, worthy of noticing.

CONFERENCES WITH THE PUPIL

The most important of all the conferences a teacher holds are the conferences with an individual pupil. These conferences are related to any interests or problems about which either the homeroom teacher or the pupil wishes to confer. In conference the teacher learns of the general progress one child is making. The conference may reveal certain pupil needs, such as improvement in study habits or budgeting time. It may reveal information pertinent to changes in instructional materials, procedures, or some specific aim of current work. It is during these conferences that the teacher devotes his attention to a single pupil, establishes rapport with the child. Most children and young people respond to evidence of a personal interest in their activities and concern about their progress. The teacher has an opportunity to discover how the pupil feels about his academic, personal, and social life at the school. Incidentally, the conference includes plans for a follow-up time, a time when the pupil will have an opportunity to report on any plan made during a conference, to continue it if it seems to be working well, to abandon it for some other plan if that seems desirable.

CONFERENCES WITH THE PUPIL'S PARENTS

In some schools at least one 20-minute conference with the parents of each child is required during each school year. In addition parent conferences are arranged at other times when a need for them is indicated. In general, all schools encourage parents to visit the school or the teacher at any time that they feel it is desirable. In the conference the parent is encouraged to talk about the pupil—his interests, needs, and problems. The parent is also informed about the child's progress, his strengths and the areas in which he might be expected to improve. Where the child's major academic work has been in a team teaching situation, the regular conferences are sometimes group conferences including the parent, the pupil (for a part of the conference), and a teacher from each of the disciplines represented on the team. Getting to know the parents directly from conferences, and also from association in the PTA or at some gathering where teachers and parents get together, enhances the teacher's knowledge of the background of the pupils. In addition, what the parents tell about such matters as the pupil's out-of-school interests and activities, home relationships, or problems adds significantly to the teacher's understanding. If the pupil is present for a part of the parent conference, the relationship exhibited between parent and child may be enlightening.

CONFERENCES WITH PROFESSIONAL SPECIALISTS

There are a number of professional specialists with whom the teacher confers to get help in understanding pupils. Professional services are typically rendered by a health department usually represented in the school by a school nurse, a speech correctionist, a school social worker, and a remedial reading teacher. Sometimes psychologists are available. Also among the specialists with whom a teacher may confer are teachers who give special instruction to the orthopedically handicapped or the partially sighted or who give instruction at home or in the hospital. Although information related to the special services will perhaps be in the school records, a personal, direct conference with the specialists usually gives the teacher further help. The school social worker, for instance, typically has a series of conferences with a pupil who has an adjustment difficulty, confers with the pupil's parents, visits in the home, and confers with various community agencies dedicated to social service that have had association with the pupil. The social worker has much to add to what the teacher has been able to learn through his own direct conferences and observation.

Using information about pupils

The sources of information discussed above are not meant to be complete or exhaustive. They are typically the outstanding sources. Most teachers will also have other avenues to use in learning about their pupils—perhaps tests which they adminster to reveal aptitudes, social adjustment, or something else. From whatever source—direct observation, conferences, school records, or something else—all this information helps the teacher in his quest for understanding of his pupils. To make proper use of what he has learned about his pupils, the teacher must know the meanings of certain terms ordinarily used in reports about pupils, and in order to comprehend the import of the entire collection of information from all sources, the teacher also needs to know some important generalizations that scientists in fields like psychology, biology, and sociology have evolved over the years.

TWO ASPECTS OF THE PUPIL

Learning by a pupil, in school as elsewhere, is an individual process. The pupil's interaction with his physical and social environment, however, significantly influences what he learns as an individual and how well he learns it. For example, a pupil may enlarge his vocabulary through personal, independent reading, but the actual meanings he attaches to the words he acquires, his pronunciation of them, his manner of speaking, and his conversational skills are largely the result of his interactions with those about him. The language of the child of the ghetto may be very different from the language of the child of the suburb. Think of a pupil solving a mathematics problem. He learns about mathemetics as he works the problem. He also, however, probably interacts with his teacher, with his fellow pupils, and, through the printed page, with the writer of the textbook. What results from working a mathematics problem or reading a story is thus a complicated, personal, inner change, a change that embraces different kinds of learning. Simultaneously, while adding insights into mathematics or increasing vocabulary, the pupil develops certain social attitudes—likes, dislikes, prejudices, for instance. Thus, to understand a pupil adequately, the teacher must interpret him both as an individual and in terms of his social environment.

MEANING OF TERMS

When it comes to the meaning of terms used in material reported about pupils or information gained in conferences with professional specialists, the general importance of having an accurate understanding of technical terms cannot be overemphasized. Definitions and explanations of such terms, however, are beyond the purpose of this book. Ordinarily technical terms will be explored in other professional

Lewis M. Terman (1877–1956)
pioneered in and popularized the
measuring of intelligence in the
schools. He revised the Binet-Simon
intelligence tests in 1916 and again
in 1937 to make them applicable to
American school children. The 1937
revision resulted in the familiar
Revised Stanford-Binet Intelligence
Scales (again somewhat revised by
others in 1960). This test and the
Wechsler Intelligence Scale for
Children are the two most widely
used in testing children.

courses, or their meanings will be discovered by the teacher through
his own research as the need to understand the terms arises.

It seems that every profession, as it develops, finds a need for
words that carry more precise meanings than those conveyed by the
everyday language of social communication. As pointed out earlier, in
an effort to promote a kind of standardization of terms related specifically to education, a dictionary of specialized vocabulary of professional
education has been produced (see page 24). In addition to technical
terms directly associated with education, the technical terms employed in relating information about pupils cover a wide range of
areas. Each fact, quantity, or statement used to describe growth and
development of pupils is concrete information about growth and
development—mental age, vision acuity, or any one of numerous
items. As we have noted, recorded information about pupils usually
begins with the kindergarten and continues as long as the pupil is
enrolled in school, perhaps through the twelfth grade. Of course, the
teacher cannot appreciate the meaning and implication of the terms
used in the entries unless he knows their technical meaning.

One example of the kind of technical term whose meaning a
teacher needs to understand is *mental age* (MA). A brief description
of the concepts implied by this term will, perhaps, show why mistakes are easy to make if technical terms are not accurately understood.

The term "mental age" is frequently used in schools where intelligence tests have been administered to pupils. It expresses the mental maturity of a child without regard to how long it took him to reach it. Technically defined, it is the level of a child's mental ability expressed in averages based on the median test scores of a large group of children (called the standardization group) having the same chronological age. The procedure in determining the mental age of a pupil— always described in months—is to find the *chronological* age of the standardization group whose average score on a given test was the same as his. This is his mental age, regardless of his own chronological age. If a pupil whose chronological age is 74 months makes a score corresponding to the average score made by a standardization group whose chronological age is also 74 months, then his mental age is 74 months. If the same pupil makes a score corresponding to the average score of a standardization group whose chronological age is 80 months, then his mental development is equal to that of the average child of 80 months. Since his chronological age is 74 months, he is judged to be abler than the average of his chronological age.

IMPORTANT GENERALIZATIONS

Besides knowing the meaning of terms used in referring to items about pupils, it is essential for teachers to know some of the important generalizations and conclusions regarding human growth and development that specialists have derived from researches, especially from researches in the life sciences such as psychology, sociology, pediatrics, psychiatry, biology, dietetics, education, and others that have focused on some aspect of the growth and development of children and youth. Each valid generalization made by a qualified specialist serves as a background which the teacher can use to make an intelligent interpretation of the specific information that the testers, dentists, nurses, caseworkers, and others provide about pupils.

We choose a few of the many important generalizations to illustrate their value to the teacher. The generalizations selected are related to concepts which are part of the broad concept of learning: habit, memory, forgetting, attention, and motive.

We are told that learning consists of the changes in behavior that follow behavior. When confronted by a situation a second time, one

*W*hat is learning? What is the nature of the psychological process by which learning takes place? A psychologist explains the process as follows :

> *In many ways, learning is the most vital phase of the whole psychological process—vital for the occurrence of the necessary changes in the behavior of adjusting organisms.*
> *The motivated organism senses its world, interprets it, responds to it, and then* responds to the consequences *of its own response. Once the organism has passed through this cycle, it is never again the same. Its first behavior has consequences ; there is resultant comfort or relief or satisfaction. These consequences of its own behavior, registered and stored, become a part of the organism. It has gained experience. It is never again the same, and its behavior begins to show it. Tomorrow the organism interprets the world differently than it did today because it is different. It responds differently. It continues to register the consequences of its own behavior. It is well embarked on the spiraling, dynamic process of living, a process in which growth and change, over a period of time and with experience, play a central role.*

Filmore H. Sanford, *Psychology, a Scientific Study of Man*. Belmont, California: Wadsworth Publishing Company, 1962, p. 303.

behaves differently from the way one did when meeting the situation the first time. To say this another way, learning is the modification in behavior that results from an earlier response to the same stimulus. A person responds differently to a stimulus situation because he profits from his previous experience. A child will not be likely to touch a hot stove a second time. It is relatively easy to define learning and to provide simple examples, but some learning—like, say, learning to be a great teacher, an outstanding novelist, a proficient surgeon, or a highly skilled mechanic—is very complex and occurs in many forms. The generalizations that follow are about concepts that help to clarify this broad meaning of learning.

1. Habit

Current extensive study of habit as a kind of learning reflects the great importance professional psychologists attach to the subject. The generalizations derived from the many scientific investigations of habit are worthy of careful study by the classroom teacher. Those who take a professional sequence of courses in preparation for teaching are likely to find that their psychology studies give major attention to this aspect of learning. For our overview purposes however, we merely introduce the subject by briefly exploring the answers to two questions: What is habit? What is its relation to learning?

A habit is a form of learned behavior that is engaged in without conscious thought. It is a pattern of behavior that has become stereotyped and hence is highly predictable. Habit is a kind of learning that is thorough. It is not a simple reaction, but a complex system of reactions. That the whole organism is involved in habit response is obvious as one watches a pupil walking, playing, talking, reading, or working a problem. By and large, one can roughly classify habits in three categories: motor habits, language habits, and emotional habits; all three are interrelated. In *deliberate* efforts at habit formation, the emotional factor must be emphasized, because consistent emotional reinforcement tends to make a habit an ingrained part of the organism.

Since many habits are readily acquired (some, in fact, result from a single response), it is important that, wherever possible, a pupil's first performance on a task be a correct one. There is always the chance that a pupil will repeat his first performance over and over again. Thus, one cannot overemphasize the crucial importance of the teaching a pupil receives in his early years and the habits he then establishes. Accordingly, psychologists currently are intensifying their study of early intellectual development, and schools are emphasizing the need for identifying as precisely as possible a child's particular style of learning. These trends are reflected in the recent concentration on Head Start programs, nursery schools, and the like.

The skilled teacher notes a pupil's habits from information supplied and from his observation and then tries to influence the pupil to form good habits in the right sequence. The teacher shows the pupil that every step in the right direction tends to make learning easier, to increase his self-mastery, to expand his personal freedom, to help him achieve his best. Efforts are directed toward getting pupils to channel their energies into directions that lead to the formation of desirable habits.

What should be done about the bad habits pupils—in fact, all of us—possess? The time-honored teaching device used to deter the development of bad habits and to encourage the building of good ones is punishment. Nevertheless, punishment in this connection does not always produce the results expected. For one thing, research has demonstrated that punishment, to be effective, must be so timed as to interrupt the course of the act and must be severe. Unfortunately, in school situations, punishment usually has to take place some time after the response that it is expected to disrupt. Furthermore, the degree of severity is very hard to judge. Punishment that is unnecessarily severe may lead to aversion, withdrawal, and other undesirable responses that may be worse than the bad habit the punishment is intended to correct. On the other hand, mild punishment may merely arouse interest and excitement among pupils, thereby actually reinforcing the bad habit.

In general, the principles that apply to the formation of good habits apply equally to the formation of bad habits. Neither good habits nor bad habits are formed in a day (with the exception of those formed under unusual environmental conditions that give strong emotional reinforcement). When incorrect responses are met with nonreinforcement, they are likely to decline. The emphasis, so far as possible, should be on immediate reinforcement of correct responses and, so far as possible, no reinforcement of incorrect responses. In time, and with considerable patience, incorrect performance is likely to decline without reinforcement. *Correct* performance, however, is also likely to decline without reinforcement. In other words, the same principles apply to the formation of all kinds of habits—good, bad, or indifferent.

2. Memory

Memory is another area about which experts have given us helpful generalizations. Memory is the recall of past behavior or, more accurately, behavior that is reconstituted, or mentally revived, or adapted. Some cue in the present environment, perhaps a substitute cue within the body itself, partially revives or reconstitutes some form of behavior that the learner has executed in the past. The recollection is available as knowledge, the possession of which prompts the individual to behave—differently, if the recollection is adverse, or in the same way, if the recollection is pleasant.

Ability to reconstitute past behavior is strengthened by repetition. The pupil strengthens his ability to recall an event or an experience through narration, by telling his parents about something learned in school, by repeating what is to be learned to himself, or by just thinking it. Intention to remember is also a factor here, since the pupil will remember more vividly, verbalize more often, repeat more accurately, if he is aware that he is expected to narrate later what he learns.

Pupils are frequently required to memorize subject-matter materials such as spelling words, definitions, rules of grammar; basic formulas in mathematics, chemistry, phsyics; vocabulary in foreign languages; and the like. Repeated verbalization, going over the material orally, silently, in writing, are indispensable reinforcements to efficient recall. Thorough, long-remembered learning is not a hurried process, nor does it proceed without conscious effort.

3. Forgetting

Forgetting, the inability to recall, is a kind of learning in which new learning weakens older learning. This concept of forgetting leads to practices different from those resulting from the concept that prevailed in earlier times—that memory is a kind of storehouse of knowledge and that forgetting is caused by a lapse of time between learning and attempted recall.

The current explanation of forgetting is that when a pupil makes two or more different responses to the same stimulus—assuming that the same stimulus recurs—the last response has a physiological advantage over the first. New and different responses to older stimuli diminish and eventually almost erase much of the earlier learning. What happens to what pupils learn in the early years of school depends, therefore, upon what they learn in the later years. A child may learn to say "am not" in school. If later he is constantly with people who say "ain't," he tends to forget the earlier learned response because when he makes the new response, using "ain't," the former response is weakened— forgotten. Thus we may conclude, as Thorndike did at the beginning of this century, after many studies of forgetting, that "there is no validity in the assumption that there is some magical curve of forgetting which every function at every stage will somewhat closely follow." How much one forgets depends upon the new learning that takes place, the conditions under which it takes place, and how many new responses take precedence over old responses.

4. Attention

There are also important generalizations about attention—called *stimulus selection* by psychologists. If the pupil's attention is given to a fly buzzing in the window instead of to the teacher's explanation of the meaning of a word, he learns about the fly and not about the word.

The teacher recognizes the importance of stimuli in the classroom and is alert to those which he may exploit to encourage pupils to give their attention. Stimuli that most favor attention are those most likely to arouse and hold interest, such as change and variety, which have the greatest advantage in attracting attention; definite form as contrasted with degrees of vagueness; striking quality, such as wisely selected, skillfully presented illustrations involving something extraordinary in color, sound, or shape; size at least sufficient to make clear the details (older textbooks presented the more technical and sometimes important materials in fine print that pupils usually skipped reading); strengths, such as a teacher who speaks with a clear, firm voice.

Repetition or frequency of response under many, but not all, conditions, may favor attention and reinforce learning generally. The more often a given stimulus is responded to within a limited period of time and under favorable conditions, the more firmly learning is established. The effectiveness of this principle is illustrated in politics and advertising, where slogans, phrases, claims are repeated over and over again. In teaching (the reader may think here of learning to type or learning the multiplication table) the repetition of an appropriate response should occur under conditions that utilize other reinforcements, such as words of approval from the teacher, concrete evidence of progress made toward attainment of the goal-object, desire on the part of the pupil to improve, and the like. Without these, repetition becomes dull and can lead to a decline in attention and in performance. In classroom practice, therefore, teachers construe repetition to mean the repeating of an appropriate response under conditions that afford the pupil other reinforcements when needed.

Since elementary teachers are with younger pupils throughout the school day and since the attention span of their pupils is short, sustained attention is not easy to obtain. Teachers of young pupils must give much thought to the problem of developing teaching skills.

The concepts about which generalizations have been given are

Attention, motivation, and information—they all must be taken into account by the teacher who is striving to help children learn up to their capacities. The complete attention of this group of pupils is captured by a lesson on closed-circuit television. A special class in repairing electronic equipment gives a special impetus to motivation, which is connected with needs, abilities, and interests. Sometimes sophisticated instructional aids are used to try to insure attention. The students in carrels (to minimize distractions) are listening to the teacher through earphones as they

watch a televised lesson. Is there an element of coercion in such a learning situation? In this column

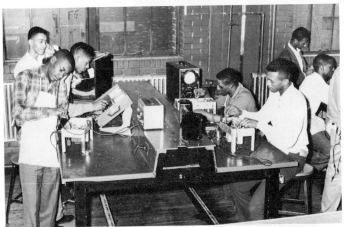

are shown two of the tests that produce valuable information for a teacher. One is a typical routine hearing test. The other is less routine ; it is given by a speech therapist to a child who has an obvious or suspected speech handicap. (This test is used to identify one of the more common speech problems— a protrusional lisp.)

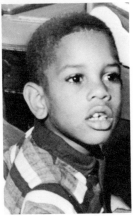

not mutually exclusive. Pupils can form the habit of making desirable stimulus selection, giving attention to what is expected of them, learning what is most worth attending to, and, conversely, learning not to attend to stimuli of little or no importance to them. The teacher, in addition to wisely selecting and managing the stimuli he uses, tries to get pupils to be conscious of their own responsibility in forming good habits of attention. In fact, teaching pupils how to study consists mostly of instructing them in how to develop good habits of attention.

It should be mentioned that undesirable behavior is often an effort to gain attention, and that redirecting attention is frequently dependent on a desirable learning climate in the classroom.

5. Motive

A motive is something that prompts a person to act in a certain way. The psychologist Woodworth defined motive as "a tendency toward a certain end-result or end-reaction, a tendency which is itself aroused by some stimulus, and which persists for a time because its end-reaction is not at once made." This seems to reduce the problem of teaching to the wise selection of a stimulus that arouses a strong tendency in the pupil, say, to read *Hamlet*, which persists until the reading of *Hamlet* is completed. How comforting! But—a qualification is in order. A pupil never has *a* motive. He has *many* motives; some of them harmonize, some compete, some conflict. Picture the teacher confronted with 30 pupils, each of whom may have a tendency to act in many different ways because he has a multiplicity of motives. It is this kind of situation that challenges the efficient teacher every day. The teacher knows that he can more intelligently interpret the behavior of his pupils if he has some basic understanding about how motives operate to condition behavior.

Motives are closely related to, and possibly emerge from, the fundamental needs of the human organism, the more basic of which are air, food, water, sex, and perhaps exercise. Even these are not always of the same level, the same degree of urgency. At different times varying ones take priority over others. It is believed that when the basic needs are met, higher needs emerge. A ravenously hungry growing boy will not be deeply interested in studying his mathematics just before lunch time. Nor will he be patient during a long wait in the lunch line. Food is the end result he seeks, and he does not like

*M*otivation originates in human needs. The psychologist explains the process :

> *Motivation, contrary to the popular usage of the term, is not a bag of tricks which the teacher uses to produce learning. Rather it is a process which belongs to the pupil. It is similar to vision in that it involves external stimulation, appropriate mechanisms of response, and an internal force which energizes the response. The basic substratum of motivation may be found in the needs of the child. The first important characteristic of motives is that they have an energizing function. They stir up behavior. Besides releasing energy, motives have a character of directionality. Energy produced by needs seeks a discharge in relevant incentives, or goal objects which satisfy needs. In brief, motivation may be described as a process in which energies produced by needs are expended in the direction of goals.*
>
> .　　.　　.
>
> *Motivation of school learning depends upon such factors as the learner's purpose or intent to learn, his self-concept and self-confidence, his levels of aspiration, and his knowledge and appraisal of how well he is doing in relation to his goals. It is the job of the teacher to create an atmosphere which provides desirable outlets for needs in the direction of worthwhile incentives—an atmosphere in which interests will as a consequence flourish.*

Glenn M. Blair, Stewart R. Jones, and Ray H. Simpson, *Educational Psychology*, 2nd ed. New York: Macmillan, 1962, pp. 208–209.

waiting to get it. The last period in the school day may seem dull to those pupils who feel a growing need for release of tension built up by a too-long period of inaction. Improper management of the motive-to-exercise sometimes leads pupils and teachers alike to look with a feeling of dread upon what they think of as the most difficult period in the day—the last one. Perhaps it has been preceded by too much physical inaction and the desire to exercise has intensified because the end-reaction has been too long delayed.

Human needs seem usually to follow a kind of hierarchical sequence in which the learner seeks to satisfy the lower-ranking or more urgent needs first. Once the basic needs are satisfied, further needs such as the needs for physical security, affection, self-esteem, feelings of independence, desire for adult and peer approval, pride in superior achievement, may then receive attention. Somewhere in the upper reaches of this hierarchy come responses such as appreciation for the beautiful, desire to write creatively, intention to specialize in some field of interest to a point where one can utilize all his abilities.

.   .   .

The generalizations explored above are only illustrative. They relate to learning and help the teacher to understand information about pupils in terms of the learning situation. Knowing about motives, for example, may shed light on some adjustment problem reported. Generalizations about the pupil as an individual, about his physical growth, his psychological development, and many other areas of growth are equally important tools for the teacher seeking to improve his understanding of pupils. Fortunately, there are reliable sources a teacher may consult for sound, guiding generalizations. Professional specialists like the school nurse or social worker, for instance, are helpful in stating generalizations in their areas. Well-indexed professional literature can be readily utilized. Many teacher organizations in specialized fields, such as the National Council of Teachers of English and the Association of Childhood Education, attempt to present through their publications significant research findings of special interest in their field, including the more recent investigations devoted to matters related to understanding pupils.

Neither of these two kinds of knowledge—an understanding of the specific information about a pupil and a comprehension of scientific generalizations that serve as a frame of reference—would be of any practical value without the other. Generalizations are derived from conclusions about many pupils; they are representative of none. They serve principally as a basis for studying one individual's performance in terms of what the scientists have said is generally true. With both kinds of information, the specific and the general, a teacher has a part of what is needed to judge the educational needs of each of his pupils, to gauge his possibilities more accurately, to influence his pattern of behavior, and to guide and stimulate his growth and development with greater wisdom.

Heredity and environment

Up to this point in our discussion of understanding pupils, it has sounded as if a teacher's interpretation of what he knows about a

To a biologist, one of the most remarkable features of the human population of this planet is its enormous variety. Here among the 2,500 million members of the one species, HOMO SAPIENS, *we find no duplicates, except those rare cases of identical twins, which, since they arose from one egg, count as one individual. Literally each person is biologically unique and declares this fact not only in his gross and obvious physical features, but in the individual properties of his blood and other body fluids, in the operation of his sense organs, and in numerous details of chemical constitution and behavior.*

What is the biological meaning of this vast variety? The biological study of man and of other animal and plant species has established that it arises out of the interplay of two influences to which every living being is subject. One is the heredity transmitted to an individual by his parents through egg and sperm; the other is the varied conditions of life, the environments in which different individuals develop. The causes of hereditary variety are known in outline; they originate in accidents (mutations) which occur in the self-reproduction of the units, the genes, through which the continous transmission of heredity takes place. The thousands of units which each parent transmits to the children are then shuffled and recombined in all possible combinations. . . .

The variety thus engendered is then acted upon by the sifting effects of the varied environments in which the species live. . . .

What is the implication for education?

. . . If increased ability to adapt by using our wits is the best hope of the future for human evolution, then the provision for varied opportunities for putting the great variety of human minds to use will be an important goal of future societies. Hardy, Weinberg, and their successors have shown us that human beings are never going to be uniform. Minds as well as bodies may be expected to retain their great variety. Any system of education based upon the assumption of uniformity will defeat its ends.

L. C. Dunn, *Heredity and Evolution in Human Populations*. Cambridge, Massachusetts: Harvard University Press, 1959, chap. 1, "Variety," pp. 1–2, 146.

pupil—assuming he is well trained—would be infallible, or at least highly dependable; as if a well-trained teacher could feel almost certain that his judgment about what to do with, for, or about this pupil or that pupil would be correct. That ideal might be a reality were it not for two factors that condition learning. We feel certain that learning is conditioned by these two factors—*heredity* and *environment*—but they introduce an element of uncertainty, of possible error, into every action that we take because we are never sure in any given situation how much relative influence the two factors exert. This has never been established with certainty. Our interpretations and our plans for pupils, nevertheless, rest to a considerable extent upon what we *believe* to be true about the relative importance of the two factors. In any discussion of what proportion of the wide differences in intelligence and achievement test scores, to take these as examples, should be attributed to genetic factors and what proportion to environmental influences, debate tends to become irrational and to be dominated by strong emotions and prejudices. These differences of opinion are not limited to matters involving allocation of relative importance to heredity and environment, but are, in fact, quite usual in many areas of human logic.

It is well to remember that often, in any area of human reasoning, when we state a principle or fact, in order to understand that principle or fact fully, we must go back to a broader principle or fact that formed the basis of our first statement. Then, if we go back to still further principles, we eventually come to a region in logic about which there is a degree of uncertainty. We do not discard the principle, however, any more than the physicist ceases to explain the universe because he does not know what gravitational energy or magnetic lines of force are. The best that we can do in our brief overview is to indicate how the two factors somewhat complicate the picture when we attempt to understand pupils and make choices on how to stimulate them and direct their learning.

HEREDITY

Accepting, then, that personal interpretation is a necessary ingredient in understanding pupils, and that such interpretation rests, in part, upon judgment about heredity and environment, we shall briefly explore both of these factors, turning our attention first to the natural forces that influence pupils—the inherited, genetic features. We approach this by an examination of what we call *maturation*.

From the biologists we learn that a close relation exists between natural forces that operate within a pupil and his over-all pattern of growth and development, that one cannot fully understand a pupil without recognizing that some characteristics of his growth are biologically determined. A teacher's assessment of what a pupil can achieve must give appropriate consideration to the hereditary factor, to the inner forces that influence the course of his growth and development.

The growth and development that result from forces that are purely hereditary are maturative; that is, in a friendly environment they produce maturation. The mechanisms of heredity are well understood, and the reader might profit by spending a few minutes reviewing the basic knowledge that biologists have supplied.[1]

The biological concept of maturation is that certain changes in the human organism are paced to a considerable extent by heredity. Succinctly stated, this means that certain kinds of learning will not take place, certain kinds of behavior will not emerge, until structural changes within the organism make such kinds of learning or behavior possible. What a pupil obtains, then, from instruction, from stimulation and direction, from favorable environmental influences, is determined by an inward, biological growth and development that are independent of environmental factors, that proceed at a rate that is *predetermined* by hereditary factors. What a pupil *can* learn at a given time is dependent in part upon the growth and development of certain mechanisms within him, upon his stage of biological maturation.

Because of biologically inherited characteristics related to maturation, pupils learn at different rates. In every sizable age group, learning rates range from slow to rapid, and as pupils advance from grade to grade the differentials in rates of learning result in progressively widening divergencies in learning achieved. The persistent and perplexing problem of giving adequate recognition to individual differences

---

[1] See, for example, Douglas H. Fryer, Edwin R. Henry, and Charles F. Sparks, *General Psychology*. New York: Barnes & Noble, 1954, pp. 131–134, 143–144. This is a condensed explanation of heredity and maturation in simple language.

caused both by heredity and by other factors, including previous learning experiences, receives and will continue to receive major consideration in America's schools.

With the exception of identical twins, no duplicates are to be
found among the people of the world. Each newborn child inherits a
natural design from his parents; his intrinsic growth will follow a
unique pattern. No pupil escapes developing in accordance with the
law of heredity. Each was unique when he entered school; each will
continue unique all his life.

In one respect, however, all pupils are alike: *Each stage of growth
follows the previous stage in a fairly well-defined sequence.* While all normal
pupils can, within reason, progress and achieve the same developmental
tasks and, when older, can master certain subject matter and develop
particular skills, they will not arrive at the same stage of development
at the same age because of the unique pattern of individual growth.
Knowing the present stage of development of a pupil, a teacher can,
within limits, predict what the next *stage* will be. Inasmuch as natural
growth patterns are not uniform, however, he cannot predict very
far in advance the specific *time* of full development in any area for a
particular pupil. A child may be expected to creep or crawl before he
learns to walk, but the prediction of the ages at which a particular
child will creep and then walk is subject to varying degrees of error.
All normal pupils can, within limits, learn to perform similar tasks.
Each, however, will learn in accordance with his own natural design.

ENVIRONMENT

Turning to the other of the factors whose relative effect on learning is so controversial, we examine some features of a pupil's physical
and cultural environment and note the relationship these seem to have
to some aspects of the child's growth and development. As pointed
out earlier, the pupil is in constant interaction. Someone has said that
through continuous social interaction a child is "able to traverse in a
short lifetime what the race has needed slow, tortured ages to attain."

The cultural background of a child includes material things such
as superhighways, ranch houses, and swimming pools (or dark, narrow
streets, tenements, and poolrooms). It includes also nonmaterial things
such as folk-singing, birthday parties, church attendance, and loyalty

to the Democratic or Republican party (or drunken brawls, crap games, and loyalty to the gang). Throughout man's history a vast complex of social practices has evolved with so many variations that today certain cultural characteristics identify regions, others identify nations, and others are associated with class membership within a common community. These influence the social climate of even the smallest classroom.

1. Regional and national differences

The cultural differences that characterize various geographical regions of our country may be trivial or fundamental, ranging from marked differences in pronunciation, in preferences for certain kinds of food or clothes, to differences in attitudes toward classes and minority groups and in ways of earning a living. In moving from one section of the country to another, a pupil becomes aware that he is different from those who have spent their lives in the new location. To avoid disagreeable tensions and to win approval of his peers, however, the pupil usually adapts rather quickly and satisfactorily to his immediate cultural environment, even if in doing so he encounters family disapproval. Regional cultural differences tend to create more of a classroom problem in instances where a large migration results in a block of "minority" group members, like the Cubans in Florida or the Mexicans in California.

2. Class differences

Cultural differences associated with regional or national differences do not usually, however, influence learning as much as differences that arise from membership in a particular class. Although many American citizens hesitate to admit that their society *has* classes, one can discern on a somewhat amorphous basis about six social classes: upper upper class; lower upper class; upper middle class; lower middle class; upper lower class; and lower lower class. Sociologists have identified the distinguishing characteristics of each class and have observed that class is important in determining, for example, an individual's associates, living quarters, churchgoing habits, reading materials, and quality of clothes worn, and that it greatly influences his educational interests and aims. In their choice of life plans, friends, leisure activities, and educational goals, pupils show that they pattern

*E*volving effective methods to help the educationally disadvantaged child is a problem that remains acute, in spite of the extensive and expensive programs that have been set up. These programs in general focus on compensatory services—remedial classes, counseling, cultural experiences, and so on. Many concerned people suspect, however, that a little-studied aspect of the problem—teacher attitudes and behavior—may deserve more attention than it has been given.

Robert Rosenthal, professor of social relations at Harvard, and Lenore Jacobson, principal of a San Francisco school and a former teacher, investigated the effect of teacher attitudes; they reported on their study in a thought-provoking book, Pygmalion in the Classroom. *At a public elementary school in a lower-class community, they led the teachers to believe that the results of a test showed that certain pupils would "spurt" in achievement. Actually, the designated children were picked at random. Later testing showed that these children had improved in their school work to a significant degree, while those not designated as "spurters" had made far smaller gains. Some of the achievements of minority-group children who had been designated as "spurters" were particularly dramatic. (The authors describe their procedures, their careful scientific methods of analysis, their results, and their conclusions in detail in their book.)*

Nothing was done directly for the disadvantaged children at the school—no crash programs, no tutoring, no museum trips. There was only the teachers' belief that certain children had competencies that would become apparent. Rosenthal and Jacobson speculate that the teachers who brought about intellectual competence simply by expecting it must have treated those children in a more pleasant, friendly, and encouraging way. In other words, they must have indirectly communicated their expectations to the children. Such behavior is known to improve intellectual performance, probably because it increases motivation. They speculate further that additional research might show exactly how teachers can effect dramatic improvement in their pupils' competence without changing their teaching methods. Then other teachers might be taught to do the same. They eloquently conclude:

> *As teacher-training institutions begin to teach the possibility that teachers' expectations of their pupils' performance may serve as self-fulfilling prophecies, there may be a new expectancy created. The new expectancy may be that children can learn more than had been believed possible. . . . The new expectancy, at the very least, will make it more difficult when they encounter the educationally disadvantaged for teachers to think, "Well, after all, what can you expect?" The man on the street may be permitted his opinions and prophecies of the*

*unkempt children loitering in a dreary schoolyard. The teacher in the
schoolroom may need to learn that those same prophecies within her may
be fulfilled ; she is no casual passer-by. Perhaps Pygmalion in the
classroom is more her role.*

Robert Rosenthal and Lenore Jacobson, *Pygmalion in the Classroom: Teacher
Expectation and Pupils' Intellectual Development*. New York: Holt, Rinehart and
Winston, 1968, pp. 181–182.

themselves after members of their own social class. As one sociologist
has said:

> Everyone knows that students come to school with widely varying
> interests and aspirations, but the social categories to which these differ-
> ences are generally linked are less well known. The most important of
> these background differences, leaving race and ethnicity aside, is the
> socioeducational level of the family—a combination of father's (and
> mother's) occupation, income, and education.[2]

Studies of the specific attitudes and forms of behavior of middle-
class and lower-class children and of the effects of these upon learning
show that there is an increased divergence among the classes both in
social attitudes and in specific forms of behavior as the children grow
older. Class differences influence the motivation of pupils to learn
in many ways.

America's schools are largely under middle-class leadership. Most
classroom teachers reflect middle-class values, and their instruction
favors middle- and upper-class children. Children who come from
middle-class homes have the values, manners, habits, and attitudes
that teachers share and stress at school. The vocabulary used by the
teachers is the vocabulary with which upper- and middle-class children
and youth are familiar. Even tests typically contain items more readily
recognized by children of the middle and upper classes than by children
of the lower classes.

3. Influence on the curriculum

Unless a definite effort is made to overcome it, the curriculum
prepared by middle-class personnel contains a middle-class bias. In

[2] Burton R. Clark, *Educating the Expert Society*. San Francisco: Chandler, 1962, pp.
58–59.

the lower grades, especially, the curriculum has often included material that gave little recognition to the cultural backgrounds of pupils from lower classes. Newer textbooks, however, particularly readers for the elementary schools, do show changes. The material is no longer as completely oriented to middle- and upper-class traditions, reflecting ethnic and class bias. Americans used to be consistently pictured as almost exclusively North European in origin and appearance, almost exclusively blonds, and always quite well-to-do. An attempt is made now to have the materials deal with ideas and experiences that include the lives of lower-class children. An effort is made to lead children of Negro, Puerto Rican, South European, and possibly Jewish origins not only to feel that they belong, but to be proud.

Pressure from Negro groups has been successful in calling attention to deficiencies in the treatment of the Negro's part in American and world history, and in bringing about curriculum changes to include more emphasis on these matters in the regular courses or special, definite courses to include Negro history and contributions.

The pupil who comes from a middle- or upper-class home where reading is a common pursuit, where books, paintings, music, and the like are important parts of the home surroundings, has an educational advantage. Perhaps this weighting of the curriculum explains, at least in part, the positive correlation of high school marks and dropouts with class membership.

4. Influence on school attendance

Poor school attendance and dropouts are definitely greater among lower-class and lower-lower-class children. This may be caused in part by the fact that pupils from the lower classes usually receive a greater proportion of the lower and failing grades. Studies of school records show that pupils who drop out of school early usually had a difficult time while in school. Studies also show that, on the average, the less competent a pupil has shown himself to be in meeting school tasks, the more quickly he is released to face out-of-school problems. The youngsters who are least able to acquire socially useful habits, information, and points of view without formal instruction are those to whom the school has given the poorest preparation. (The exception to this general rule is the athlete. Because of success in athletics, a pupil, regardless of social class, is given enhanced social recognition and his school attendance, therefore, is likely to continue.)

. . .

The teacher must know and appreciate the background of his pupils. Otherwise, he may unknowingly permit his own cultural biases to color his interpretation of pupils' needs and interests. Each pupil must be recognized as the product of his family, school, and community. It must be remembered that his personality is in large measure molded by forces beyond his control and that what he believes should be his goals in life will be influenced by the goals and marks of success that dominate in his social environment. Lower-class and lower-lower-class goals differ from those of middle- and upper-class families. Clearly, social factors such as these must be taken into account in the aims and in the selection of curriculum materials and methods used in the classroom, if America's schools are going to recognize individual differences adequately.

"READINESS," THE INCLUSIVE TERM

Returning to the unanswered question of the degree to which heredity conditions the learning of a child and the degree to which learning is conditioned by environment, we add another generalization important to teachers. The teacher starts where the child is and then proceeds, developmentally, keeping in mind all that he knows about the pupil. From this starting point the teacher seeks to stimulate the pupil's growth in harmony with his demonstrated capabilities, not attempting, at least for the time being, to determine whether these capabilities have resulted from heredity or environment. He will proceed slowly toward any tentative conclusions with respect to the relative influence of these two factors on the child's learning ability.

To help teachers, E. L. Thorndike coined the inclusive term "readiness," a term whose meaning makes no reference to the two determinants. "Readiness" merely describes the level of development of the pupil, the stage reached as a result of *both* environmental and heredity factors, and from which direction and growth must begin. Thorndike, in 1913, stated readiness as a law. "When an individual is ready to act in a particular way, it is satisfying to do so, and annoying

Edward Lee Thorndike.

*E*dward Lee Thorndike (*1874–1949*) *was a distinguished scientist in the field of educational psychology. He received honorary degrees from leading universities in both America and Europe in recognition of his achievements. His scholarly writings and penetrating researches extended to many areas, as a list of some of his more important publications shows :* Mental and Social Measurement (*1904*) *;* Elements of Psychology (*1905*) *;* Animal Intelligence (*1911*) *;* Educational Psychology (*1913–1914 ; three volumes entitled* The Original Nature of Man*;* The Learning Process*;* Mental Work and Fatigue and Individual Differences and Their Causes*);* Psychology of Arithmetic (*1922*) *;* Psychology of Algebra (*1923*) *;* The Measurement of Intelligence (*1926*) *;* Human Nature and the Social Order (*1940*).

Thorndike was also a professional lexicographer. He applied his knowledge of both language development and educational psychology to the compilation of a dictionary for children which—with some modernization by others—is still widely used. In 1942 he gave the William James lectures at Harvard (published the next year as Man and His Works*), in which he used his wide range of knowledge of various aspects of language, political science, law, and sociology. Writing for the most part in the early stages of the evolution of educational psychology, he pioneered in the development of methods of educational research that are still of considerable significance.*

not to do so; conversely, when an individual is not ready to act in a particular way, to do so is annoying.'' This law gives recognition both to the factor of biological maturation and also to the willingness of the learner to learn: his desire, his mental set, the effects of environmental influences. Any theoretical explanation of the *cause* of readiness is irrelevant in considering teaching practice; what is important is the *fact* of readiness. There are many kinds of readiness, one for almost every act: a readiness to walk, a readiness to talk, a mathematical readiness, a reading readiness, a writing readiness, and so on. The teacher begins with this, knowing that a pupil will profit very little from instruction for which he has not reached the appropriate readiness stage—the stage at which he can learn from that instruction with a reasonable amount of effort.

Summary

This chapter is the first of four that deal with aspects of the central problem of all formal education—stimulating and directing the growth and development of pupils. To fulfill his teaching responsibilities with reasonable skill, the teacher must understand each pupil, and to do this he must be in command of two kinds of information considered fundamental. He must have a reasonable grasp of generalizations the scientists have formulated that concern learning and human growth and development in general. He must, in addition, know the technical meanings conveyed by specific items of information assembled about the pupils. These will aid him in determining teaching methods, materials, guidance needs—the host of activities related to stimulating and directing the growth and development of *each* pupil.

Questions

1. What are some possible mistakes with and misuse of information from a pupil's cumulative record that a teacher may make?
2. What do you see as problems related to an upper-class person teaching in a school in a disadvantaged area of a large city?

3. Someone has referred somewhat sarcastically to the technical language educators use in intercommunication as "pedegese." In your opinion, is this implied criticism justified? Why, or why not?
4. What are some of the problems related to the fact that differences in learning rates increase with chronological age?
5. What is the effect on classroom procedures of acceptance of Thorndike's concept of readiness?
6. Does an educational program like Operation Head Start, for instance, imply adherence to a point of view toward the relative importance of the influence of heredity and environment? Explain your answer.

Projects

1. Study a pupil's cumulative record kept in some school. Write in as precise a way as you can what the record reveals about the pupil.
2. Observe two college students at study in the school library. Outline the nature of their habits of attention. What conclusions can you draw from the habits of attention in these cases?
3. Make a list of what it is necessary for a school system to provide in order that a classroom teacher will have the resources to know his pupils well.
4. In terms of an imagined or an observed classroom activity, point out how the generalizations about attention have been exploited or overlooked.

In our chapter "The Teacher and His Philosophy," it was pointed out that what a teacher attempts to achieve in his classroom and the way he goes about this are based on, and reflect, his educational philosophy, his educational values. We focus now, in this chapter, specifically on educational *aims*, not this time from the viewpoint of their philosophical base, but in terms of all the other factors that have an influence on educational aims in the restricted setting of an individual classroom or in the expanded setting of a school district or even of the nation.

In comparing two individuals, both well informed, we may discover that one is expert, efficient, and esteemed, and that the other is a bore and ineffective. They have had different aims for acquiring the knowledge that made them well informed. The efficient, interesting man accumulated knowledge for a purpose, so he had direction and his information is organized and useful. The boring, ineffective man lacked purpose and organization. His information is like scraps of metal in a junk yard. He is a man of motion without direction.

In exploring how learning takes place in the preceding chapter, the importance of motivation was highlighted. A desire to learn is the magic that leads to learning. We have said that the teacher's job, in essence, is to stimulate and direct the growth of pupils. Successful stimulation leads to self-motivation, and self-motivation implies accepted aims or goals.

Some self-made, or at least self-directed, men who have achieved expert or leadership status despite having no college degrees and perhaps even no formal schooling, show that a definite aim can unify and direct learning to a point of rather dramatic achievement.

What determines educational aims?

THE INDIVIDUAL TEACHER'S PHILOSOPHY

The teacher's aims, then, are related to his values, to his philosophy. He will seek, within the limits discussed in Chapter 5 and later in this chapter, to achieve those ends which to him, personally, are worthy and practicable. Some of the teacher's aims will be broad and sweeping. He may seek, for instance, to promote attitudes of fair play. Such aims underlie all his teaching. In addition, he will have immediate aims associated with what he seeks to achieve in a single activity. He may also have a specific aim for a particular child. For example, he may set as a goal for one child the development of the habit of paying attention to instruction. The teacher might have a conference with this child during which the wording of this goal could be worked out by the child. Checking with the child on the advancement toward that goal might occur weekly. When the goal is satisfactorily achieved, another goal may be adopted. Such immediate and specific goals give direction to effort and provide a measure for judging progress.

Sometimes the work in a specific area of teaching is organized in a unit. Such a plan includes a statement of aims to be achieved in the unit. The aims, in this case, help the teacher to select relevant material and to unify teaching. In such a unit in English, for instance, the aims might be (1) to participate courteously in a group discussion, (2) to build up understanding and consideration of others, and (3) to use concrete and vivid words in speaking and writing. The teacher is guided usually by *sets* of aims, not by a single aim. These aims, moreover, will be ineffectual if the pupils do not share, whenever possible, in their formulation, or do not feel that they are acceptable. The teacher's individual aims must always be flexible so that they can be readily modified in terms of the unexpected, in the light of changed conditions.

As America's schools are administered, however, the teacher is not always completely free to decide on his aims. Various influences and pressures affect his choice. Some of these are from external authorities—the school board, the local teaching group, state and federal governments, and accrediting agencies. There are also pressures from various groups, from the home, and from commerce and industry. The press may exert a strong and significant influence. Professional commissions set up to establish general educational aims, or supervision within a system, may also affect what the teacher attempts to do in his classroom. Sometimes, in fact, except for details related to an immediate situation, the choice of goals is made *for* the teacher, rather than *by* the teacher. When the influences do not operate in a consistent direction, a measure of confusion is introduced and then each teacher must decide, in his own way, to which influence he shall yield. Perhaps his teaching will be a compromise between his own aims and those of others.

EXTERNAL AUTHORITIES

1. Professional groups

In order to promote unity and give consistency to the direction of teaching at a given grade level or in a particular subject, a group of teachers, or their representatives, frequently get together and produce a general plan of work. The plan is typically preceded by a statement of aims or objectives which the group agrees should be striven for and toward the promotion of which the curriculum or other material worked out should lead. Often an instructional group looks for guidance to some national organization, like the American Society for Childhood Education or the Modern Language Association.

As an example, representatives of the English teachers in three junior high schools drew up a proposed English curriculum in which they set forth the following objectives:

1. Instruction in the language arts should prepare pupils to use efficiently the skills of listening, speaking, reading, and writing requisite to effective learning.
2. The language arts are avenues to all learning; therefore, a good language arts program should (*a*) integrate the language arts courses, (*b*) integrate with other courses of the school, (*c*) enrich personal living.

3. All good teaching in the language arts results in the development of individual personalities in the direction of their highest potentialities.[1]

Although such aims are general in the sense that they must be interpreted by the individual classroom teacher, they are sufficiently specific to give direction to the teacher's immediate aims.

2. School staffs

In many cases individual school staffs formulate statements of aims for their own school. Such goals will have an influence on the aims adopted by individual teachers. The following is an example:

We aim to help each pupil—
1. to succeed in school.
2. to learn to get along in the school where he is and in the classes of which he is a part and with the people with whom he works.
3. to form the habit of doing what is known to be right.
4. to be of service to other pupils and to the needs of the school.
5. to expect to abide by the rules and regulations that are made for the good of all.
6. to recognize and use the abilities, talents, and creative thinking of individuals in all lines to make an interesting school.

Sometimes this kind of statement of school aims is worked out by pupils in collaboration with the faculty and perhaps with parents.

3. State and federal governments

The aims of the school and of the individual teacher are influenced significantly by the state and federal governments. The federal government, we have noted, has often influenced aims by means of such acts as the Smith-Hughes Act of 1917, which gives grants-in-aid to high schools that meet certain federal requirements. The grants are administered through the state departments of education, thus giving some power over the program to the states. The grants-in-aid given by the federal government under Titles I, II, III, IV, and V of the Elementary and Secondary Education Act of 1965 are made for many different

---

[1] These objectives were based on the teachers' interpretation of the philosophy expressed in *Language Arts for Today's Children*, National Council of Teachers of English. New York: Appleton-Century-Crofts, 1954, vol. 2.

purposes and distributed in various ways. However, as pointed out earlier, the federal government, through this act, has become an active participant in education to an unprecedented extent. The Office of Education, especially, now has a greater degree of authority than it had ever before been given. Through these two acts alone—Smith-Hughes and the Elementary and Secondary Education Act of 1965—the federal government influences the aims of the schools significantly. The Smith-Hughes Act determines to a considerable extent the aims of agricultural education, home economics, and industrial arts in the high schools. The Elementary and Secondary Education Act further extends federal influence, now for the first time, into the elementary school. These are but two of the many avenues through which our national government influences the aims of American education.

State legislatures and state educational authorities also influence the aims of the school. For example, state laws stipulate that schools teach, and pupils study, certain subjects. In some states it is required that American history be studied for a full year in high school. In some states pupils in the elementary school are required to participate in physical education for a stated number of periods each week. Sometimes, through the office of the chief state school authority, the states have been prescriptive in the matter of study required of teachers who desire certification. The state foundation program is an influence on the aims of the school. Each governmental act is motivated by an aim, and the act in turn almost, if not entirely, legislates an aim for teaching.

4. Institutions of higher learning

Colleges and universities exert some influence on the aims and objectives of the high schools by their admission requirements. Sometimes high school pupils feel that the all-inclusive aim of their high school education is to prepare for college board examinations. Pressure on the high schools from institutions of higher learning may be cause for the high schools to attempt to influence what is taught in the junior high schools and even in the elementary schools.

It has been stated that high schools tend to credit the colleges with being more of an influence than they actually are. In defending the emphasis placed on the study of grammar in high school, it has been said, "Our children must be well prepared in grammar in order to do well on the college entrance examinations.'' A review of some of the college entrance examinations used, however, shows that little stress is actually placed on formal grammar. Some high schools are using college entrance examinations to justify something they include in their teaching for some other reason. This is not to imply, however, that the colleges do not influence the aims of the high school teachers considerably.

5. Accrediting agencies

Accrediting agencies like the North Central Association of Colleges and Secondary Schools determine to some extent what subjects a pupil in high school must pursue for graduation. In this sense, they, too, have an influence on the school's aims and on the aims of the individual teacher.

SOCIETAL PRESSURES

Pressure groups are characteristic of modern America—there is no escape from them (this was discussed in Chapter 10). It is up to the teaching profession, then, to work out ways of dealing intelligently with those groups that have the greatest influence on the schools. There are many such agencies; here we will briefly examine four of them as examples—the home, industry, the press, and professional organizations.

1. The home

If the home does not fulfill certain needs related to achieving maturity, then the school will be expected to add the fulfillment of these needs to its aims of instruction. The home or the community may, for instance, expect the school to undertake activities related to sex education, social dancing, grooming, or the like. In some instances the objectives of the school will be tied in with certain activities in the home. In an agricultural community, for example, the school may teach the conservation of food by correlating work in methods of freezing, canning, and otherwise preserving food with the materials and facilities the children have in their homes and the instruction they have received at home.

2. Industry

Industry, both through many organizations and through individual enterprises, shows a strong interest in education in America. Sometimes attempts are made to bring pressure on a particular segment of education, as when the public utilities, through advertising and printed materials, have tried to persuade social studies teachers to emphasize the advantages of private ownership of public utilities and, by implication, to minimize the values of, say, the Tennessee Valley Authority.

In a more positive direction, some American industries are spending large sums on developing and manufacturing teaching materials such as teaching machines and many kinds of classroom aids. The promise of ultimate profit is a factor in such expenditures, of course, but the executives who authorize these programs are also motivated by a genuine desire to advance modern education. Each year many large industrial corporations make sizable contributions to educational institutions, to university foundations, and for the establishment of scholarships for students in certain selected fields. Through their expertly directed public relations departments many large corporations—without any thought of influencing the direction they wish education to take—provide schools with a wide variety of skillfully prepared materials on many subjects of interest to teachers and pupils. The principal intent seems to be to build and maintain a favorable public image, an image that includes an abiding interest in encouraging education. There also is an obvious, and logical, factor of self-interest behind all these activities—better education for all results in more qualified workers for industry and in more consumers of its products; in other words, when industry aids education, it anticipates long-range benefits.

3. The press

Journalists, television commentators, and news analysts exert pressure on the public and also directly on the schools to shape their programs to fulfill objectives that come into the public limelight, usually because of current crises. When Russia surpassed the United States in the development of space satellites, journalists led the hue and cry for education to be patterned more on the Russian plan. Our assumed inferiority to Russia was attributed to inadequate education.

"Our children should work harder, be more serious." "Stress mathematics and science and foreign languages." "Select the gifted children early; see that they are adequately motivated to pursue the required subjects."

One trouble with journalists is that they quite naturally tend to be dramatic, to distort the true picture. They may overemphasize some of the aims of education because they are devoted to promoting a "cause." Often they are not completely informed about education but make an impression on the public by mounting emotional or irrational assaults on the waste of school funds in elaborate school buildings, on the school's failure to teach Johnnie to read, on the school's failure to keep America abreast of Russia in technical advances —matters that lend themselves to the journalist's art. Often, however, the effect of journalistic efforts—urging, for instance, that teaching be made more attractive as a means to alleviate teacher shortages—are socially very desirable. The restrictions of authoritative external bodies and the pressures of official statements, the press, and industry will be greater in fields of specific subject areas, especially in vocational fields. In the areas of the basic education that is given to all children— that is, the education of the elementary school and that portion of the high school program that is not differentiated—the teacher has more freedom in making the final decision as to aims and the subject matter that he believes is potentially most profitable in terms of those aims.

4. Professional organizations

From time to time groups of outstanding educators have taken up the task of formulating statements of the aims or purposes for education in America. Such statements may contain many helpful suggestions for the teacher. They may indicate what the teacher should emphasize, what results he may expect, what kinds of materials are best to choose, in what directions the pupils' energies may be influenced, and the like. For instance, the Educational Policies Commission of the NEA issued *The Purposes of Education in American Democracy* in 1938. The following is quoted from this classic statement, which is generally endorsed by public schools.

The Objectives of Self-Realization

The inquiring mind. The educated person has an appetite for learning.
Speech. The educated person can speak the mother tongue clearly.

Reading. The educated person reads the mother tongue efficiently.

Writing. The educated person writes the mother tongue effectively.

Number. The educated person solves his problems of counting and calculating.

Sight and hearing. The educated person is skilled in listening and observing.

Health. The educated person understands the basic facts concerning health and disease.

Health habits. The educated person protects his own health and that of his dependents.

Public health. The educated person works to improve the health of the community.

Recreation. The educated person is participant and spectator in many sports and other pastimes.

Intellectual interests. The educated person has mental resources for the use of leisure.

Esthetic interests. The educated person appreciates beauty.

Character. The educated person gives responsible direction to his own life.

The Objectives of Human Relationships

Respect for humanity. The educated person puts human relationships first.

Friendships. The educated person enjoys a rich, sincere, and varied social life.

Cooperation. The educated person can work and play with others.

Courtesy. The educated person observes the amenities of social behavior.

Appreciation of the home. The educated person appreciates the family as a social institution.

Conservation of the home. The educated person conserves family ideals.

Homemaking. The educated person is skilled in homemaking.

Democracy in the home. The educated person maintains democratic family relationships.

The Objectives of Economic Efficiency

Work. The educated producer knows the satisfaction of good workmanship.

Occupational information. The educated producer understands the requirements and opportunities for various jobs.

Occupational choice. The educated producer has *selected* his occupation.

Occupational efficiency. The educated producer succeeds in his chosen vocation.

The Purposes of Education in American Democracy *consists of four types of objectives. Here are some of the ways they are reflected in the schools. "The objectives of* economic efficiency" *are the central inspiration for the vocational preparation that is one important aim of all our high schools. "The objectives of* self-realization" *include building a healthy body. The schools carry on extensive physical education programs—both outdoors and indoors. "The educated person appreciates beauty" is another self-realization objective. Here second-graders are introduced to the work of local artists at an exhibit at their school. "The objectives of* civic responsibility" *are achieved by the educated citizen who "seeks to understand social structures and social processes." The citizens touring local schools, under the auspices of their PTA, are becoming familiar with the schools' aims and needs. "The objectives of* human relationships" *involve some of the fundamental purposes of America's schools. The members of a student council at an elementary school learn to cooperate as they meet regularly to make plans for class trips and parties. Sometimes they also discuss "the amenities of social behavior"—school dress and regulations.*

Occupational adjustment. The educated producer maintains and improves his efficiency.

Occupational appreciation. The educated producer appreciates the social value of his work.

Personal economics. The educated consumer plans the economics of his own life.

Consumer judgment. The educated consumer develops standards for guiding his expenditures.

Efficiency in buying. The educated consumer is an informed and skillful buyer.

Consumer protection. The educated consumer takes appropriate measures to safeguard his interests.

The Objectives of Civic Responsibility

Social justice. The educated citizen is sensitive to the disparities of human circumstance.

Social activity. The educated citizen acts to correct unsatisfactory conditions.

Social understanding. The educated citizen seeks to understand social structures and social processes.

Critical judgment. The educated citizen has defenses against propaganda.

Tolerance. The educated citizen respects honest differences of opinion.

Conservation. The educated citizen has a regard for the nation's resources.

Social applications of science. The educated citizen measures scientific advance by its contribution to the general welfare.

World citizenship. The educated citizen is a cooperating member of the world community.

Law observance. The educated citizen respects the law.

Economic literacy. The educated citizen is economically literate.

Political citizenship. The educated citizen accepts his civic duties.

Devotion to democracy. The educated citizen acts upon an unswerving loyalty to democratic ideals.[2]

Statements of aims

One of the first difficulties encountered in attempts to state the aims of education in American schools is terminology. The words used have had various meanings.

[2] Quoted from pp. 50, 72, 90, 108 by permission of the National Education Association.

TERMINOLOGY

In various lists of aims prepared as guides to teaching, many different kinds of terms have been used. This has led to some confusion and misunderstanding. Because of the subtleties of learning it may be that some confusion is unavoidable.

Consider the basic word "aim." The meaning of this word seems clear when one uses it to describe a physical object at which one is shooting a gun, or when, in war, the object is to destroy a certain bridge. When the act, however, is a mental one, no one word can describe all of the different kinds of objectives, and sometimes different words are used interchangeably to describe precisely the same objective. In most instances where mental processes are concerned, each of the various terms used carries a slightly different emphasis. Let us note how this is true in the following sentence: The student whose *aims* are worthy, whose *aspirations* are high, whose *designs* are wise, and whose *purposes* are steadfast may reach the *goal* of his *ambition* and surely will win some *object* worthy of life's *endeavor*. Writers who attempt to describe the direction education should take by stating what it should seek to achieve have to make a choice among such terms. All of the terms refer to mental acts in which aim plays a part. The choice of a particular word, however, results in slightly different emphasis.

It is, perhaps, not surprising to find writers in education using such phrases as "purposive learning," "objectives of education," "object lesson," "purposeful effort," "ends in view," and others that reflect a philosophical viewpoint toward the relation of aim to teaching. It would be easier, of course, if all the writers used the same terminology. In the present stage of terminology development, however, the best we can do is remember that all of these phrases are related to aim and not attempt to disentangle the meanings or to distinguish shades of emphasis. In all the lists the attempt has been to do the same thing—to make carefully formulated suggestions to guide teaching practices in schools, even though there have been different approaches that have led to different kinds of statements.

Although there have been a number of approaches to arriving at official statements of the aims of American education, two approaches have been most favored. The first involves the activity

John Dewey emphasized that aims and means are related, that ends are always pluralistic, and that all the consequences of an act, not just one, must be considered.

> *. . . ends arise and function within action. They are not . . . things lying beyond activity at which the latter is directed. They are not . . . termini of action at all. They are terminals of deliberation, and so turning points in activity. . . .*
>
> *In being ends of deliberation they are redirecting pivots in action. . . . A mariner does not sail towards the stars, but by noting the stars he is aided in conducting his present activity of sailing. . . . Activity will not cease when the port is attained, but merely the* present direction *of activity. The port is as truly the beginning of another mode of activity as it is the termination of the present one. . . . We know without thinking that our "ends" are perforce beginnings. . . . Common sense revolts against the maxim, . . . that the end justifies the means. There is no incorrectness in saying that the question of means employed is overlooked in such cases . . . that overlooking means is only a device for failing to note those ends, or conseqences, which, if they were noted would be seen to be so evil that action would be estopped. Certainly nothing can justify or condemn means except ends, results. . . . Not the end—in the singular—justifies the means ; for there is no such thing as the single all-important end. . . . It is not possible adequately to characterize the presumption, the falsity and the deliberate perversion of intelligence involved in refusal to note the plural effects that flow from any act, a refusal adopted in order that we may justify an act by picking out that one consequence which will enable us to do what we wish to do and for which we feel the need of justification.*

John Dewey, *Human Nature and Conduct.* New York: Holt, Rinehart and Winston, 1922, pp. 223, 225, 226, 228, 229. Quoted by permission of the publishers.

analysis method, a method similar to the vocational analysis method described in Chapter 2. The second emphasizes growth of the learner.

ACTIVITY ANALYSIS METHOD

In "What Knowledge Is Most Worth," an essay published in 1859, the English philosopher Herbert Spencer first proposed the use of the activity analysis method for arriving at aims of teaching.

*The eminent child development psychologist, John E. Anderson, after
directing the Child Welfare Research Institute at the University of Minnesota
for many years, arrived at the conclusion that the principal goal of education
should be the enhancement and enrichment of personality.*

> It is difficult, indeed, for one who has followed children and has seen
> at first hand the vitality, energy, and strength of the young human
> being to believe that their existence is without purpose and that humans
> are tiny bits of matter in a universe that is without meaning and
> significance. Through and through, the developmental process seems to
> be creative; the problems and situations which are old and hackneyed
> to the adult are new and interesting to the child. And the social
> organizations of adolescents, even though they are like those of earlier
> generations, are new creations to those who form them. Neither the
> person nor society is quite the same at successive moments—life goes on
> even while we think about it.
>
> In the enhancement and enrichment of personality and the mutual
> creation of a good life for all is found the measure of a full life.
> Some make money a symbol of a good life, some make power, some
> material goods, some social position. As more is learned about
> personality, the primary goal becomes the desirability of using the
> capacities of persons to the fullest degree, and of searching out the
> talents which all possess and giving them opportunities to manifest
> themselves. Society proceeds most rapidly when it utilizes its human
> resources most fully and gives each other member some opportunity for
> self-realization through the essentially creative process of broadening
> his own life space and finding in interests and activities the
> opportunities for development and appreciation. Wasted ability is
> forever lost, both for the person and for society. Emphasis, then, goes on
> living a full life, not so much in terms of status and rewards as in
> terms of contribution, development, and personality enhancement. Thus,
> we seek a society in which there will not only be a concept of the
> dignity of the human being, but also the opportunity for the person to
> manifest that dignity.

John E. Anderson, *The Psychology of Development and Personal Adjustment*. New York:
Holt, Rinehart and Winston, 1949, p. 675. Quoted by permission of the
publishers.

He classified the activities of life in which adults engage under five
categories: (1) those related to preserving life and health; (2) vocational activities, or those related to earning a living; (3) domestic

The goals of a curriculum in American schools in the middle of the twentieth century are determined finally by the purposes for which the schools are established. It is clear that the American people want the children and youth of the nation to be educated to the extent of their highest potentialities ; that they want them to be self-reliant individuals who are at the same time good cooperating members of society ; and that they want them to be able to make their own livings. In other words, the major purposes of American education are in general : (1) cultivation of satisfying and wholesome personal lives, (2) development of social sensitivity and effective participation in the life of the local community, the nation, and the world, and (3) preparation for vocational competence.

The English Language Arts, prepared by the Commission on the English Curriculum of The National Council of Teachers of English. Copyright 1952 by The National Council of Teachers of English. Reprinted by permission of Appleton-Century-Crofts.

activities, or those related to family duties or care of children; (4) social and political activities; and (5) leisure activities, art, etc. The school, he said, should improve the preparation of children to perform the activities related to each of these areas of adult life.

This method of arriving at the guiding aims of education was widely followed by groups in America. In 1918, for example, a commission of leading American educators was appointed by the NEA to formulate an official statement of the aims of American education. The commission, known as the Commission on the Reorganization of Secondary Education, prepared a report that was published by the United States government under the engaging title, "The Cardinal Principles of Education." The report proposed that the following seven objectives serve to guide the teaching process in American schools: health, worthy home membership, vocational efficiency, citizenship, worthy use of leisure time, ethical character, and command of the fundamental processes. Since 1918, attempts have been made to improve upon the statements contained in this report. In essence, the same activity analysis technique has been followed. The aims so derived generally bear some resemblance to the cardinal principles.

Those who are critical of this method point out that the activities analyzed and classified are typical of the society of the adult world outside the school. The objectives are not stated in terms of learners, are not indigenous to classroom situations, do not recognize the active, participatory nature of learning.

GROWTH CONCEPT APPROACH

Another and widely different approach, as described in Chapter 16, begins with focus on the learner and his desirable growth. The all-inclusive aim of education is the development of continued capacity for growth. In the words of John Dewey, who contributed much to a clarification of this approach,

> Since growth is the characteristic of life, education is all one with growing; it has no end beyond itself. The criterion of the value of school education is the extent to which it creates a desire for continued growth and supplies means for making the desire effective in fact.[3]

The growth concept requires that the teacher take conditions in his classroom into account and rely upon his knowledge of the pupils in his formulation of aims. Daily aims worked out in terms of this growth philosophy of education (or its sister, the developmental psychology of human development) would be too numerous to list and too varied for classification. Growth, self-direction, and self-control are very general and all-inclusive aims that must be implemented through the selection of more specific goals.

Criticisms of aims

ABSTRACTNESS AND IMPRACTICALITY

Statements of aims based on an analysis of activities should be expressed as specifically and concretely as possible, as are the aims quoted on pages 496–500. In this kind of sociological approach the aims are classified and divided into categories. Typically, the categories are kept at a minimum, somewhere between four and 10, a number thought small enough to preserve the unity of the educative

---

[3] John Dewey, *Democracy and Education*. New York: Macmillan, 1916, p. 62.

process but large enough to include all important phases of adult life. In the Educational Policies Commission statement there are four main classifications: (1) self-realization, (2) human relationships, (3) economic efficiency, and (4) civic responsibility. Each of these four main divisions is broken down into more specific statements. It was hoped that this arrangement would suggest aims to teachers of all grades and would provide guides for daily tasks and assistance in selecting subject matter, in evaluating pupils, and in directing extracurricular activities.

Still, some teachers feel that even a detailed classification, like the one quoted, is too general. Health and citizenship are abstractions. As they are stated they seem nebulous and isolated from the needs and capacities of individual boys and girls. In addition, they are considered by many too philosophically neutral, too subject to personal interpretation. Some teachers feel that they need help in applying these objectives to work with individual children in the classroom. Others discount such statements as idealistic wishes of adults rather than day-to-day guides for practical use. For these reasons, partly, the general trend has been toward greater use of the growth concept approach, toward stating only the general objective of education and allowing the aims to grow out of the classroom situation.

QUANTITY OF SUBJECT MATTER

One common criticism of teaching aims is that American schoolteachers sacrifice a desirable concern with the total product of their teaching—understanding, interest, desirable attitudes—to a concern with covering a certain amount of prescribed subject matter. In literature, pupils are expected to read a specified *quantity* of material; in algebra, all ninth-grade pupils are expected to advance rapidly enough to arrive at quadratics by the end of the year. Teachers are criticized for adopting too completely the aim to "cover so much ground in so much time."

PROMOTION POLICIES

Sometimes a teacher whose principal concern is with the total needs of an individual child will promote a pupil without giving

These pupils in Puerto Rico are reading a Spanish-language school newspaper during their recreational reading period. English is, of course, a second language for these children. But it is also a second language for many children in schools in the continental United States, especially in inner-city areas. In one situation, however, English is the language of the minority ; in the other, it is the language of the majority. How must the aims in the teaching of English be modified to take account of the educational needs of both types of pupils?

primary attention to the subject matter mastered. The teacher's aim is influenced, of course, by the objectives of the school. Formerly as many as 10 to 30 percent of the pupils were retained in a given grade. In recent years the tendency has been to pass on to the next grade all those who promise to profit more by promotion than by being required to repeat the grade. The practice has greatly reduced the number of retentions in each grade of the elementary school. In some of today's elementary schools there are, in fact, no "failures," and this comes as a shock to some of the older citizens. (The nongraded school eliminates grade classifications; the idea is to remove promotion and retention as influences on school or teacher goals or aims.)

Schools where pupils have been promoted freely have been criticized by some for "wholesale" promotion. Criticism stems from a difference in philosophy—a difference in conception of the aims of the school. Should the teacher follow practices deemed desirable in terms of the total growth needs of the child? How about the needs of the group being taught? To what degree should the achievements of a group be subordinated to the needs of an individual child? Can individual needs be fully met without unduly sacrificing the needs of a group? Before proceeding with his age group, should a child be required to master certain subject matter? Should the aims be in terms of this required mastery, or should they be wholly in terms of the individual's total needs? In terms of social needs? Should aims be formulated by the individual teacher or dictated by external authority? These are questions which, obviously, do not lend themselves to easy, offhand answers.

SCOPE OF SOCIAL STUDIES

Teachers who turn to the various specialized fields of the social sciences for sources of teaching materials—to take this subject-matter field as an example—rather than to one specialized field, such as history, are sometimes criticized for diluting the materials of history when history, in the critic's opinion, should receive the main, if not the sole, emphasis. Those who favor placing the main emphasis upon history or economics or political science, referred to as "study-in-depth," argue that it is better to probe one subject intensively than to skim the surface of a number of them. Arguments like this one sometimes become quite heated.

Teachers who follow a generalized approach to social studies maintain that they do not disparage the contribution of history or any subject to the understanding of modern social problems and interpretation of modern social movements. They feel, however, that social problems, economic problems, labor issues, political issues, and the like should be studied in their modern setting, too.

What should the aim of social studies teaching be? If the social studies teacher aims to cultivate the pupils' understanding of present-day issues and social conditions, then, perhaps, it does not matter from which of the major social science disciplines the subject matter comes. Those who feel that the stress should be on one particular social science will, of course, question—somewhat vociferously at times—the validity of the teacher's approach.

PURPOSE OF EXAMINATIONS

When examinations have been used to diagnose pupils' weaknesses, to reveal individual needs, when they have aided the teacher in increasing his effectiveness with individual pupils—in other words, when they have facilitated learning, examinations have been favorably viewed as helpful instruments of learning. When examinations have been used to compare the achievements of one pupil with another, to select the fit from the unfit, to classify and stratify the pupils, to determine who shall receive highest approval and honor awards, then they have come in for considerable criticism.

American educators, by and large, favor an increased use of examinations *as instructional aids*. This aim, it is contended, should guide the construction of examinations and determine how and when they shall be used. This is what a critic of examinations in English schools had in mind when he wrote:

> . . . no educational system is possible unless every question directly asked of a pupil at any examination is either framed or modified by the actual teacher of that pupil in that subject.
>
> .　　.　　.
>
> The best procedure [of examination] will depend on several factors, . . . namely, the genius of the teacher, the intellectual type of the pupils, their prospects in life, the opportunities offered by the immediate surroundings of the school, and allied factors of this sort. It is for this reason that the uniform external examination is so deadly. We do not denounce it because we are cranks, and like denouncing established things. . . . Our reason of dislike is very definite and very practical. . . . When you analyze in the light of experience the central task of education, you find that its successful accomplishment depends on a delicate adjustment of many variable factors. . . . The evocation of curiosity, of judgment, of the power of mastering a complicated tangle of circumstances, the use of theory in giving foresight in special cases—all these powers are not to be imparted by a set rule embodied in one schedule of examination subjects.[4]

[4] Alfred North Whitehead, *Aims of Education*. New York: Macmillan, 1929, pp. 7–8. Quoted by permission of The Macmillan Company.

Summary

It is perhaps obvious that teaching aims cannot be static, rigid, or fixed. As one aim is achieved, the next aim is defined. Each accomplishment leads to a definition of the next aim. When one end is achieved, it becomes the means to the next. Ends that are worthy function to free learning activities, to direct them, but never to freeze them.

This generalization is true of aims that are set by the school, by government authorities, by nations. History tells the story of Greece, a nation at one time alive with new and noble ideas that engendered aims which led the whole nation to socially desirable action. At a later time the people of the same nation found themselves no longer motivated by appropriate and collective aims. The nation lost direction and floundered. For education to have direction it must be guided by aims, but the aims must be appropriate, must make an appeal strong enough to evoke strong individual and collective action. The failure to recognize that effective aims are not static explains in part why Greece flourished at one time in its history and declined at another.

Forward-looking and active institutions sometimes, with the passing years, become stagnant and lose their strength and popular appeal. The early leaders in the schools of the Christian church were inspiring teachers. Later, much of the teaching by churchmen became pedantic, catechistic, formal, and uninspirational. Such deterioration is caused, in part at least, either by adherence to aims that are outmoded and therefore inappropriate, by the adoption of new aims inappropriate for some reason, or by a change in social conditions that renders all the general purposes of the institution obsolete.

Aims will influence education, will constitute a challenge to action, only when the aims are acceptable because they can be and are adapted to current conditions. The dynamic nature of the complete educational picture calls for a constant reinterpretation and reappraisal of the aims sought. Changing social conditions bring new educational demands into focus. Changing conditions in the classroom bring new demands into focus also. Conditions are never static. Effective aims also cannot be static.

Questions

1. How does the advancing age of the pupils affect the aims of instruction?
2. How are teachers to formulate aims that reflect the social viewpoints of the people when these viewpoints are sometimes in conflict?
3. How are the aims of education in American schools affected by the character of the community?
4. What functions are served by statements of aims carefully formulated by official bodies?
5. Under what conditions are educational aims apt to be static in nature? Dynamic?
6. How do you account for the great variety in the manner of stating aims? Would it be advantageous to have a single statement of the aims of education? How can one select from among the many statements?
7. When may a statement of educational aims be an aid to teaching? A hindrance?

Projects

1. Explain how one's educational philosophy shapes the character of his educational aims.
2. Give an example that illustrates the interrelationships of aim, subject matter, and method.
3. Summarize how one of the official statements was derived and show how the validity of the aims is established.
4. Illustrate by example how an educational aim directs the whole of the educative process.
5. State the aims that guide you in your professional study. Justify your professional studies and activities in terms of these aims.

18

Subject Matter
in America's
Schools

Subjects of study probably date back to the earliest schools. The Babylonians had schoolhouses in 2100 B.C.; other civilizations may have had them earlier than that. Archeologists have established that one of the skills taught in the early schools was writing. Words and phrases and, later, complete sentences and quotations were copied from old documents. Inasmuch as the documents were available for copying, writing—using symbols—must have predated even these very early schools. It also can be assumed that someone had been taught to read these early documents and that there were some who could teach others to read. In all likelihood, when the earliest schools were set up over 4,000 years ago, they aimed to perpetuate and extend the ability to read, to write, to interpret, to appreciate, and eventually to add to the store of manuscripts. No doubt these ancient manuscripts were the earliest forerunners of the subject matter in today's schools.

As time passed and it was recognized that certain social groups— especially at first the priests—needed knowledge in particular areas before beginning their work, pertinent information and skills were selected and organized for instructing potential members of these groups. It appears now that the advance from barbarism to civilization was marked by stages of development in the classifications of knowledge —classifications made partly to facilitate instruction of an oncoming generation.

The orderly organization of subject matter into classifications that were generally considered appropriate for young pupils was quite advanced by the time America began to be a settled country. When the first colonial schools were opened, there was available a great deal of material that those in charge felt was, with very little modification, ideally suited to their aims.

Evolution of subject matter in the United States

IN ELEMENTARY SCHOOLS

Initially, American elementary schools borrowed their classifications from Europe. Our first educators and those who supported the schools were religious leaders and other church members. Children were viewed as the children of the church. Schools were established to teach children to read and write so that they might read the Bible, which, in turn, might lead them to be better church members.

Many different religious groups set up schools that varied somewhat because of differences in religious beliefs. By the time the Declaration of Independence was signed, however, the elementary schools were essentially alike in that they all emphasized the study of reading, writing, spelling, and arithmetic. In all these subjects, they utilized scriptural quotations and moral platitudes.

After the passage of a half century, there were discernible changes in the common subjects. Although reading, writing, spelling, and arithmetic remained the chief subjects, modifications took place within each, both in content and in organization. English grammar became a separate subject equal in importance to the others. Knitting and sewing were included for girls in some schools.

By 1876, the subject matter of the elementary schools had been greatly expanded. Conditions had changed and some of the new ideas from European educators had filtered into practice. Following a trend toward secularization in the schools, education became less concerned with religion. In teaching reading the teachers helped the children not only to develop proficiency in reading the Scriptures but also to develop skill in reading and appreciating literature other than the Bible. Declamation, oral language, geography, United States history and the Constitution, elementary science, music, drawing, and physical education were now among the subjects. Many textbooks were rewritten. In addition to textbooks, actual objects were used for instruction. Such direct experiences as field trips and laboratory experiments were added.

The expansion of subjects of study continued, and by the end of the century, manual training, nature study, and a new outgrowth of reading—a subject called "literature"—had made their appearance. In fact, by the beginning of the present century, all the elements of the modern subjects had been introduced into the elementary schools. As our aims, our conditions, our knowledge, and our understanding change, the evolution continues, and our classifications, our emphases, and our textbooks continue to change.

IN FOUR-YEAR HIGH SCHOOLS

The evolution of subjects in the American four-year high school constitutes a story almost as independent of the evolution of the subjects in the elementary schools as though the two had never belonged to the same family of institutions. The effects of this earlier disregard of articulation of eighth-grade and ninth-grade subject matter are still a rather acute problem in America's schools, especially where the elementary and the high schools are in different, independently organized school districts.

When the Declaration of Independence was signed, the subjects in the high school were almost exclusively Latin and Greek. The dominance of what was studied is implied by the name of the school—Latin grammar school. The aim of the secondary school was largely vocational—to prepare individuals for further study for entrance into the ministry of the church. The transition from elementary school to high school was so abrupt that it amounted to an almost complete break.

Fifty years after the Declaration of Independence, high school subjects had undergone considerable change. By 1825, the Boston Public Latin School, considered in that day an extremely progressive school, had included in its program such well-defined subject matters as arithmetic, geometry, trigonometry, geography, declamation, reading, English grammar, English composition, debating, chronological history, and the constitutions of the United States and of Massachusetts. Slowly but surely the subjects covered by the high schools continued to undergo modification.

The influence of the Latin grammar schools waned after 1800, and the private academy became the dominant secondary school institution. The number of subjects expanded amazingly, reflecting the rapid development of new subject matter, especially that related to the development of the specialized sciences. By 1837, the academies in New York State were offering 73 different subjects, including architecture, astronomy, chemistry, botany, conic sections, embroidery, civil engineering, French, geology, analytic geometry, German, Hebrew, Italian, law, logarithms, vocal music, instrumental music, mineralogy, political economy, statistics, surveying, painting, Spanish, trigonometry, and principles of teaching.

After 1890, the date that coincides with the end of the American frontier movement, the private academy ceased to be the dominant institution and its influence rapidly waned. The four-year public high school became the prevalent institution. As the high schools grew in number and enrollment, new subjects were rapidly introduced into the curriculum. The passage of the Smith-Hughes Act of 1917, which gave federal grants-in-aid to those high schools giving training in vocational education, spurred expansion of vocational education programs. In some larger, comprehensive high schools, the entire program of some pupils was built around study in one of the areas of vocational education. The new subjects included motor mechanics, machine shop, radio, advanced electricity, agriculture, business law, stenography, beauty culture, commercial cooking, and aeronautics. Music and art subjects also multiplied. The older fields— such as English, science, mathematics, and foreign languages—also were expanded. As many as 19 different subjects were offered under the broad heading of "homemaking." Not all of these, of course, were offered in a single school. Driver training and mathematics and chemistry for nurses are further examples of the trend both toward completeness in curriculums to meet today's needs and toward selecting subject matter specifically and directly related to an explicit aim.

No attempt has been made here to establish relative importance or prominence among the many subjects offered. This is partly because no reliable data showing the percentage of pupils enrolled in the various subjects are available. Moreover, since there is no consistency in high school policies in requiring the pupils to pursue certain subjects, generalization about their relative prominence would be unreliable.

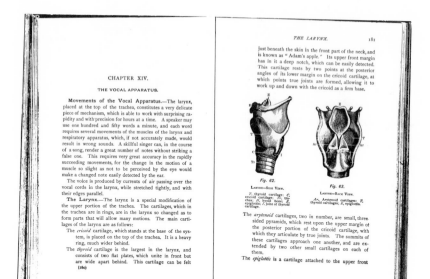

*L*ate-nineteenth-century textbooks drew material directly from the writings of specialists; some, in fact, were written by specialists, who made few concessions of the kind we now consider necessary to their intended readers. Advanced Lessons in Human Physiology by Oliver P. Jenkins—two pages are reproduced here—is a good example of the type. This text, published in 1891 by the Indiana School Book Company, was adopted by the State of Indiana as the curriculum in science for the seventh and eighth grades in all the elementary schools of the state. Note the precise, inclusive nature of the subject matter. Everything to be taught in science was in the book, and, in addition, the best methods to be used in teaching it were suggested. A text had to be more or less ''self-teaching'' in this way because the elementary school teachers of the time—most of them in one-teacher rural schools—could be certified merely by completing the eighth grade and passing an examination.

Many of America's early scientists of the modern era were ''graduates'' only of one-room, eight-grade rural schools. Furthermore, the school terms often lasted for only six months. It seems likely that those who were really interested in science were somewhat self-taught from books like the Jenkins book and then continued their studies on their own.

Selection of subject matter

The brief review of the history of subject matter in the schools in the United States reveals significant and continuous changes over the years in scope, content, organization, and emphasis. Apart from actual classroom instruction, perhaps more teacher time and energy have been given to selecting subject matter appropriate to the learning needs of pupils than to any other one activity. Reconstruction of the curriculum is a continuous process and is so complex that only a brief treatment is possible in this chapter.

Subject matter is a tool designed and selected to help children move in the direction defined by a school's educational goals. The relative values of various areas of subject matter have always been judged in terms of their probable potential contribution to the desired ends. As the aims, from colonial times on, changed for various reasons, subject matter likewise changed.

When educators began to state aims for education and were asked to justify subjects in terms of aims, the question of the relative values of different subjects also came up for serious consideration. Even assuming that all the subjects had value, the extent of that value, the relative value of one subject as compared to all the others, had to be determined.

If, as the great English philosopher John Locke (1623–1704) believed, the mind at birth is like a blank piece of paper with nothing written upon it, a *tabula rasa*, with inherent powers that can be strengthened by "exercising" with subject matter, then it could be argued that certain kinds of subject matter better serve this need for exercise than others. From this, it follows that subject matter for all pupils should be uniform. Teaching each learner the same spelling or grammar or mathematics is all right because these subjects provide the best kind of mental exercise for all learners. "The faculties of our souls are improved and made useful to us just after the same manner as our bodies are . . . would you have a man reason well, you must use him to it betimes, exercise his mind in observing the connection of ideas and following them in train."[1] Actually, the "blank paper"

[1] John Locke, as quoted in Paul Monroe, *A Brief Course in the History of Education*. New York: Macmillan, 1907, p. 265.

*John Locke is usually accorded the distinction of being the most influential
of all the English writers who addressed themselves to education. If the
degree of his influence is rivaled by that of Herbert Spencer, it should be
recalled that he preceded Spencer by almost 200 years.*

*First of all, Locke was a great philosopher generally admired by all
educated Americans, and it is easy to minimize his importance by singling
out his view toward education and presenting it as though it were the whole
of his philosophy. In fact, his second book,* Two Treatises of Government,
*contains the terms of the American Declaration of Independence. His views on
education did not accord with his philosophy, and this should be kept in
mind in judging the contributions of the man. He revealed his conception of
the intellectual aspect of education in his* Conduct of the Understanding.
*The entire treatise was a defense of the idea that the intellect is best trained
through exercise and discipline, and that mathematics is the most suitable
kind of subject matter to furnish the desired kind of discipline. ". . . Nothing
does this better than mathematics, which therefore I think should be taught
all those who have the time and opportunity* not so much to make them
mathematicians, as to make them reasonable creatures. . . ."

theory was not accepted for very long, so it had little influence on the
selection of subject matter.

Another belief that came to be known as faculty psychology had
more of a following. It explains, in part, some of the perplexing lack
of direct value in subject matter, especially in the high school. For
instance, early spelling textbooks contained many words that would
never be useful to most of the pupils, even in adult life. English
grammar, emphasizing sentence structure, seemed to have little
connection with developing powers of expression. Those who were
faculty psychologists believed that the mind was composed of a series
of distinct and separate faculties—such as thinking, memorizing,
feeling, willing—and that each of these could be trained through
exercise just as a muscle could be strengthened through exercise.
Moreover, it was assumed that training received in one area of subject
matter was transferred to another. This meant, for instance, that the
powers developed through memorizing poetry would be transferred
to memorization of grammar or multiplication tables. The study of
Euclidean geometry was considered particularly valuable because it

developed prowess in logical reasoning which could be used in studying other subjects and in out-of-school activities. When we recall that Euclid's *Elements*, a very early textbook on geometry (300 B.C.), has served as a model for all the later textbooks on the subject, we get some notion of how long this approach to learning and subject matter survived in at least one area.

Knowledge about how children learn, about the nature of child development and growth, and about differences in capacities and interests today influence the selection of subject matter much more than in the past. Currently the trend is to select subject matter that is as flexible as possible, is *directly* related to the achievement of aims, and is appropriate to the age, nature, and needs of the learners. Knowledge and insight are required in deciding what subject matter will contribute most. Usually the teacher in the classroom has more or less broad boundaries of subject matter determined for him by the school district, the school, or some other authority. Where textbooks are supplied or prescribed, the extent of teacher choice is further limited. In most systems, however, teachers participate in developing the curriculum, in determining subject-matter-to-be-taught, and also usually any prescribed materials will allow the teacher in the classroom some freedom or leeway to make reasonable adaptations. Today, the American people tend to become progressively more dependent upon formal education to educate youth for citizenship obligations. The selection of subject matter, therefore, becomes increasingly important. In earlier times much of the education of the young was received outside the school. At that time, because of social conditions, advanced education was highly selective, largely on the basis of ability to pay. Higher education was almost monopolized by specially privileged people who used graduation from higher institutions as a stepping-stone to rising on the social scale. That tradition is gradually disappearing in the United States. Formal education is becoming a requirement for entrance to most adult activities. The trend is toward greater attention to what graduates of high schools and colleges have learned or have learned to do and less attention to how long the graduates have attended school or from what units they have been graduated. There is greater interest in *what* children in the elementary and high schools study and in the degree to which efficient learning is promoted. The future promises even more emphasis on the practical values of the subjects provided in our schools.

Classification of knowledge

Perhaps one of the greatest advances man has made in his attempts to achieve a high level of civilization through education has been in the classifications he has made of accumulated knowledge. His ability to organize and to systematize his knowledge into such broad classifications as physics, geology, and mathematics and to make systematic classifications within these subjects has contributed to research, to the preservation of knowledge, and to learning. Man's future, it seems, will depend largely upon the uses he makes of his growing accumulations and classifications of knowledge. These uses hinge, in part, upon the way young people in America are taught to apply and expand knowledge. And knowledge in this context does not mean merely information that is immediately and obviously useful. Man's future also depends on the way he uses his knowledge of the humanities.

FOR PRESERVATION

Preservation of knowledge is essential to the continued existence of any civilization. Classification and organization of knowledge into logical, usable, understandable systems are essential for its preservation and transmission to succeeding generations. In botany, for example, material may be classified into progressively more select groups, beginning with broad divisions and proceeding to successively smaller units such as class, order, family, genus, species, and, finally, variety. Geology or zoology or history will follow some other pattern, each appropriate to its own field. In each of the divisions, organization is a value in itself. The practical purpose served is determined by the one who uses it. The more logical the classification and the more logical the various divisions within the organization, the more suitable is the whole for preservation for the future.

FOR RESEARCH

Logically classified categories of subject matter serve as a ready reference for those who wish to extend the range of human knowledge. Diligent and systematic research demands a previously well-organized

Bertrand Russell, the distinguished English philosopher, has written :

. . . *For the first time in history, it is now possible, owing to the industrial revolution and its by-products, to create a world where everybody shall have a reasonable chance of happiness. Physical evil can, if we choose, be reduced to very small proportions. It would be possible, by organization and science, to feed and house the whole population of the world, not luxuriously, but sufficiently to prevent great suffering. It would be possible to combat disease, and to make chronic ill-health very rare. It would be possible to prevent the increase of population from outrunning improvements in the food supply. The great terrors which have darkened the sub-conscious mind of the race, bringing cruelty, oppression, and war in their train, could be so much diminished as to be no longer important. All this is of such immeasurable value to human life that we dare not oppose the sort of education which will tend to bring it about. In such an education, applied science will have to be the chief ingredient. Without physics and physiology and psychology, we cannot build the new world.*

We can build it without Latin and Greek, without Dante and Shakespeare, without Bach and Mozart. That is the great argument in favour of a utilitarian education. I have stated it strongly, because I feel it strongly. Nevertheless, there is another side to the question. What will be the good of the conquest of leisure and health, if no one remembers how to use them? The war against physical evil, like every other war, must not be conducted with such fury as to render men incapable of the arts of peace. What the world possesses of ultimate good must not be allowed to perish in the struggle against evil.

. . . *What I suggest is that, where a difficult technique is indispensable to the mastering of a subject, it is better, except in training specialists, that the subject should be useful. In the time of the renaissance, there was little great literature in modern languages; now there is a great deal. Much of the value of the Greek tradition can be conveyed to people who do not know Greek; and as for the Latin tradition, its value is not really very great. I should, therefore, where boys and girls without special aptitudes are concerned, supply the humanistic elements of education in ways not involving a great apparatus of learning; the difficult part of education, in the later years, I should, as a rule, confine to mathematics and science.*

Bertrand Russell, *Education and the Good Life.* New York: Boni and Liveright, 1926, pp. 26, 27, 28, 30. Quoted by permission of Liveright Publishing Corporation and George Allen & Unwin Ltd.

body of subject matter to serve as a springboard for new discoveries, which, in turn, may modify previous classifications.

FOR LEARNING AND TRANSMISSION

The major classifications of knowledge have formed the bases of the subjects offered by the schools. Modifications in classifications have been evolved to make them more practical and more usable in teaching the young. By the end of his first grade, the pupil is aware of fairly sharp distinctions between reading, writing, spelling, and mathematics. As he advances through the grades, he rapidly learns to distinguish numerous other subjects. Usually the distinctions are emphasized by the way the subject matter is prepared for his use—in textbooks, workbooks, study guides, and the like.

It would be a mistake, of course, to conclude that all the child learns in school is a result of exposure to what is ordinarily thought of as subject matter. What the child learns before he begins school and what he learns in school apart from the materials in the subjects of study are thought by teachers to be quite as important as what he learns through association with organized subject matter.

There is one division of subject matter that is quite different from the rigid, logical classifications associated with the preservation of knowledge and the advancement of research. This is the classification of subject matter in terms of its relation to direct and indirect experiences of the child. Subject matter in books, for instance, would be classified as part of the indirect experience material. The subject matter is part of direct experience, however, if the child comes into direct contact with the original material. For example, the child learns as he sees a house burn down, climbs a mountain, watches a plane take off, observes a mother bird feeding her young, sees a TV program. His growth is promoted along desirable lines by the opportunity to preside at an assembly, make a dress, dissect a frog, or write a poem. The subject matter may be unorganized, lacking in sequence, and unplanned. It is not, however, without momentary or even long-range purpose. Learning in this way is natural and, perhaps, most rapid and most efficient.

Learning that is related indirectly to the experiences of the child utilizes subject matter that is more or less systematically arranged in a way to facilitate learning. The pupil learns through vicarious, not direct, experience. He reads, listens, observes. He learns through participating in the experiences of others.

Both kinds of learning, both kinds of subject matter, have a place in the school. In the earlier grades, particularly, direct learning, associated with personal experience, the method of direct discovery, is emphasized. In the field of science or mathematics, for example, the pupils work with objects at first hand, experience them as concrete realities. As the child progresses through the grades, the subject matter tends to be related more to indirect experience. Gradually a conceptual order in subject matter is introduced as a substitute for the perceptual order that preceded it. The important point to remember is that the perceptual precedes the conceptual.

There is a natural limit to the amount of subject matter that can be learned through firsthand experience. The time element must be considered. It becomes necessary to expand the world of the pupil through learning subject matter that depends upon language, pictures, mathematical symbols, stories, historical episodes, and maps. Sufficient direct learning experience makes the indirect learning more meaningful. A perceptual background is a sound base for a conceptual understanding. In mathematics, for instance, pupils may learn about symbols in such a way that symbols have no meaning apart from purposes associated with the mathematics lesson. In science, pupils may work with subject matter that has little relation to their everyday lives. On the other hand, the symbols used in mathematics can be so related to direct experience that they will be meaningful. If the materials of science provide an opportunity for direct experience in observation and manipulation, are related to, or are built upon, direct experience in the everyday life of the child, then the child has a background for the understandings that are conceptual. He can read and understand and learn about the matters of science. He has a background of percepts from direct learning upon which he builds. Thus, the two kinds of subject matter are complementary. When learned with a reasonable balance, the one reinforces the other.

Organization of subject matter for teaching purposes

In discussing the organization of subject matter for teaching purposes, the two terms "curriculum" and "course of study" are used frequently and are, therefore, explained here. Keep in mind that such terms as "integration," "correlation," "core," and "interdisciplinary team approach" are used to refer to various plans for unifying subject matter for teaching purposes.

1. *Curriculum.* The term "curriculum" is now commonly used to include all the activities and experiences that have been planned for the pupil in school, or that are sponsored by the school, to advance his desirable growth. Originally "curriculum" referred only to those activities that had been planned for the classroom. This left outside-of-the-classroom activities to be "extracurricular." The current trend is to consider the entire school experience of the pupil as a unit and to determine the emphasis on any particular kind of activity in terms of the needs, interests, and abilities of an individual pupil. As progress has been made in discovering pupils' needs and adapting to their needs, the curriculum, the total school offering, has been enriched by visual aids, plays, excursions, and various types of pupil activities in and out of the school. A specific plan of organization is implied when we talk about core curriculum, subject-matter curriculum, or integrated curriculum.

2. *Course of Study.* A course of study is usually worked out in a particular subject area to serve a variety of purposes. The area covered might be something like United States history, or it might cover a broader area like social studies. Typically the course of study begins with a statement of aims that the teacher will be expected to implement in his instruction. Organization, time allotments, teaching materials, methods, and activities are suggested. In a sense, the course of study sets a minimum common denominator for a grade level or a certain subject within a school system or a school. Besides these purposes, it serves as a tool for guidance workers who counsel high school pupils in their choice of subjects and helps a teacher by providing information relative to what a child has studied last year and what he probably will study next year.

A course of study is usually developed by teachers and supervisors working together. Sometimes they have the help of a curriculum specialist in a particular area or given grade level, and sometimes they also have the help of scholars in the field. For instance, in developing the course of study in United States history, an outstanding scholar in the field of Negro history might work with the committee.

Unfortunately, the course of study becomes an educational hazard when it is overly specific instead of suggestive, when it is too mandatory to allow for adaptations in terms of all aspects of a learning situation. It is a help but never a substitute for the kind of teacher planning that is built on an understanding of the pupils involved.

LANGUAGE ARTS

The emphasis in this broad field is upon the word "language." The raising of language to the level of an art signifies the attempt to cultivate language so that it may be used as an expression of beauty, be appealing, and have more than commonplace significance. Language arts is concerned mainly with developing skills in expressing ideas and in receiving ideas from others, through both the written and the spoken word.

In earlier American schools, subject matter was suited to

Textbooks are, of course, among the most important teaching materials. Here teachers who have been experimenting for a year with several sixth-grade social studies texts compare notes and preferences as they prepare to recommend one of the books for city-wide adoption. They have filled out evaluation sheets rating the trial books on content, adaptation to pupil needs, and format.

developing the mechanical skills of reading, speaking, spelling, and writing. Listening, appreciations, and habits were largely disregarded. The current trend is toward selecting subject matter that will contribute to much wider growth. It is assumed, for example, that the development of the powers of communication is closely related to the development of a rich, attractive, well-adjusted personality. The trend is toward emphasizing the values as well as mechanics of communication in the wider aspects of social living.

As the broader concept of the language arts has been adopted, subject matter has been increasingly diversified. As yet, no clear agreement has been reached among America's language arts teachers as to the relative emphasis different aspects of the program should receive, nor has a logical sequence in specific areas been developed. Some teachers deviate very little from the older practices of teaching reading, writing, and spelling as separate mechanical skills. Others place the greatest emphasis upon well-rounded development. Most teachers feel that a realignment of the subject matter of the language arts field is inevitable.

SCIENCE

Subject matter in science is selected in terms of an integrated-general approach for the elementary school through the eighth grade and for ninth grade where science is adapted to certain students who are not preparing for college. The really crucial problem in the selection of appropriate science subject matter is related to these early grades, where the integrated-general course is expected to include a range of nonspecialized science material. The emphasis in these grades is on the selection of material relevant to basic concepts-to-be-explored, concepts considered appropriate to an individual school population and its particular community. The curriculum and courses of study outline units prepared by the school as well as for the school. This results in the subject matter of science in early grades strongly reflecting the locale of the school and obviously rules out a standard subject matter for a state, as was once a common practice, or a standard sequence even for one large school system. In terms of concepts-to-be-learned, each school selects subject matter appropriate to its own pupils and to the environment of the school. It attempts to choose

*F*ormal grammar was greatly emphasized in the early elementary schools.
*The following is an excerpt from a text that was widely adopted and
generally used in the seventh and eighth grades.*

Exercise 72

Study the pronouns in the following sentences and :
1. *Classify each into the smallest known class.*
2. *Decline it.*
3. *Give its antecedent.*
4. *Give its gender.*
5. *Give its number.*
6. *Give its person.*
7. *Give its use in the sentence.*
8. *Give its case.*
9. *Tell how you determined these properties.*
10. *Explain any irregularity which you may discover.*

[*Thirty sentences are given. These are representative.*]

10. *He desired to pray, but it was denied him.*
11. *He has squandered his money, but he now regrets it.*
17. *It thundered as it seemed to me.*
19. *Well, then, Mistress Dudley, since you will needs tarry, I give
    the Province House in charge to you.*

John B. Wisely, *An English Grammar*. Boston: Atkinson, Mentzer and Company,
1906, p. 236.

subject matter that *is* inherently interesting as contrasted to materials
the teacher is asked to *make* interesting. This approach tends to build
favorable attitudes toward science by utilizing what is close to the
pupils, exists in their surroundings: seasonal changes, animals, plants,
airplanes, food, air, water—literally hundreds of items. This practice
of selecting subject matter in science that is closely related to the
lives of the pupils is generally advocated by leaders in science education. This obviously invalidates the idea of having a rigid science
sequence in the elementary schools.

The science courses in the secondary school, selected by or for
students preparing for college, are specialized courses like biology in
the ninth grade, followed by courses in physics, chemistry, the earth

sciences, and, for some, college-level courses in physics and chemistry. With the great expansion in knowledge, subject matter in all the specialized sciences has been greatly modified during the past decade, although the topics studied in each of the specialized science fields are fairly well standardized.

MATHEMATICS

Mathematics is what educators call a constant in the curriculum— that is, a subject to be studied by all pupils for a considerable length of time. Education in mathematics begins with the very young and continues, with varying degrees of emphasis, up through all the grades of the elementary school and in some grades of the high school. Mathematics is a *tool* subject, an essential instrument with which to think. Its value continues to increase as civilization advances. This is dramatically true in our current age of electronics. Knowledge of mathematics and skill in its application are essential nowadays to *advanced* study in most major subject fields: science, economics, geology, psychology, sociology, education, and so on.

Judged in terms of time devoted to mathematics in the schools, one would expect the graduates to have a high degree of competence and an ability to apply their knowledge where quantitative thinking is required. Actually, there has been a wide discrepancy between what is expected and what has been achieved. Hence, mathematics educators in recent years have been investing great effort to discover and rectify the mistakes of the past. They tackle such questions as: Why do high school graduates show glaring mathematical deficiencies? Why do many pupils exhibit a strong antipathy toward mathematics—even fear of it? Why do many elementary school teachers dislike teaching mathematics? Why are many elementary school teachers inadequately prepared to teach mathematics effectively? The first approach to the problem was to examine critically the subject matter traditionally studied in mathematics courses, subject matter considerably standardized: arithmetic in the elementary schools, algebra in the ninth grade, plane geometry in the tenth grade, solid geometry and advanced algebra in the eleventh grade, trigonometry, in larger schools, in the twelfth grade. Most teachers adhered closely to adopted texts, so the writers of mathematics textbooks really determined the subject matter taught. Textbooks written in the early 1890s in algebra and geometry were still in common use in the 1920s and 1930s and are in use in some places even today. For example, the popular textbook by Wentworth and Smith, *Plane and Solid Geometry*, was copyrighted in 1888, 1899, 1910, 1911, 1913, and 1939.

By 1950, the entire teaching profession had become aware that the subject matter of the old mathematical sequence should be revised and a different approach made. A much concerned federal government and numerous private foundations made large contributions for the support of projects to improve both mathematics and science in the schools. The federal government subsidized the re-education of mathematics teachers. In addition, numerous colleges and universities, the United States Office of Education, manufacturing corporations, and other agencies joined in an all-out effort to improve the subject matter and the methods of teaching mathematics in the schools. Experiments, perhaps influenced by the training programs of the National Science Project financed by the National Science Foundation, are now being conducted in elementary and secondary schools throughout the nation to improve both the subject matter and the methods of teaching mathematics.

The so-called *New Mathematics* is subject-matter-in-development. Concepts that constitute the central theme of mathematics are introduced early. Unifying ideas such as sets (any well-defined grouping of distinguishable objects) receive emphasis with the very young. Pupils are introduced to sets of objects, pictorially perhaps, before being introduced to symbols. The basic idea is first learned through direct experience; symbols and terminology follow later. Structure is a concept that is introduced early. The subject matter of structure sets forth principles and properties traditionally associated with the classifications of later mathematics, not excepting college calculus. A child can visualize a line as an infinite number of points. He can grasp the idea of infinity. Space, time, and distance are realized intuitively. As he advances the subject matter includes measurement, systems of enumeration, the meaning of operations, logical deduction, graphic representation, valid generalization, and, as the pupil develops, other unifying themes.

Throughout his elementary and high school experiences with mathematics, subject matter is so selected and the pupil so directed that from the beginning mathematics is a series of unifying concepts and integral relationships. The future of this new mathematics seems most promising; it has been a challenging innovation in modern American education.

SOCIAL STUDIES

As long as social studies was confined to a study of only one aspect of social living, the classification into specialized fields like geography or history was considered quite adequate. Teachers became increasingly aware, however, that within such a scheme of classification many important phases of social living were not even being touched. They reasoned that pertinent subject matter related to the whole of a current social process, not just a small segment of a process, should be included if pupils were to develop an intelligent appreciation of the broad area of human relations in modern society. In locating materials that would shed light upon crucial and urgent present-day social problems it was necessary to investigate all fields, not just the social sciences. The reorganized subject matter, focused upon selected problems of social living, was called the *social studies*.

The trend is for teachers, perhaps in terms of a curriculum or a district or school course of study, to formulate the course pattern, to direct the selection and organization of the subject matter, and to use any materials that promise to develop insight into human relations problems, to promote a better understanding of the nature of the social processes, and to build competence in living and dealing with one's fellows.

Sometimes as a preliminary step to the achievement of the kind of social aims named above, the development of definite, specific social concepts is assigned to be developed at a particular grade level. Such concepts might include, among others, colonialism in the seventh grade, for instance. Subject matter to assist in developing this concept will be social studies materials as defined above—not confined to history or to the United States or to any other limited area of time, place, location, or discipline. In fact, emphasis on the world, on international relations and international aspects of areas of study, is now replacing the older pattern of restricting study largely to the United States and Western Europe.

Whether the social studies is concept-oriented or not, the subject matter is selected to develop competence in intergroup relations, skills in group action, concern for the welfare of others, tolerance for the viewpoints of others, respect for and ability to work with others who have different cultural backgrounds, and understanding of the elements that contribute to the increasing interdependence of human beings everywhere. In other words, the social studies emphasize skills, traits, attitudes, and understandings needed for the improvement of human relations everywhere.

The subject matter of the social studies in the elementary and secondary schools has perhaps departed more radically from the older and more specialized patterns of organization than has that of any of the other fields. This is, it seems, partly because social problems are so numerous and varied that they, more obviously than other problems, can be approached only through the avenues of more than one kind of specialized subject matter.

Social studies in our schools, however, have never been organized uniformly according to any definite scheme or pattern or logical sequence. This is one criticism made by those who advocate the more traditional, specialized, schematic arrangement.

FINE ARTS

The fine arts include painting, the dance, music—any mode of expression thought to be significant and beautiful. The expression may be in the form of both appreciation and actual production or creation. Fine arts are emphasized throughout the elementary school, including the kindergarten, and also through most of the grades of the secondary school. They are recognized, also, as important in adult education.

The attention given to the fine arts at all levels of education in the United States is a recent phenomenon. In the past the tendency was to consider the fine arts as a "frill." Music in the nursery school and kindergarten, rhythms for younger children, handicrafts for all ages, including those who are handicapped or suffering from some nervous ailment, are now typical. Perhaps the relatively recent social changes—shorter work week, mandatory retirement, mechanical housekeeping aids—bringing about increased leisure have been responsible, in part, for the upsurge of interest in the fine arts.

The subject matter of the fine arts, drawn from many fields, is neither highly systematized nor standardized at any of the levels of education. In selecting and organizing the subject matter, the interests and the maturity levels of the pupils serve as the main criteria. Thus, a ninth-grader with no background in art and a fourth-grader who studied art in second and third grades might be able to handle the same subject matter. The subject matter is determined largely by the needs of the individual pupil as they are revealed to the teacher, not, as is the case with mathematics, by a progressively increased level of difficulty arbitrarily allocated to grade levels.

Children, particularly those in the elementary school, use a great variety of forms of expression—drawing, painting, singing, listening to good music, acting out stories, playing in a school orchestra, playing musical instruments they have made. The subject matter may include almost anything thought to be beautiful and esthetic, anything that will provide an outlet for children to communicate in a creative or in a receptive, appreciative way.

HEALTH

In all the official statements of aims of education in the United States, high priority is given to health. Sometimes the aim is divided into two aspects—physical health and mental health. This is one of the dualisms first introduced into educational philosophy in the Middle Ages. The use of the two terms indicates the emphasis desired in the education program and probably causes little harm, providing one remembers that the two terms merely designate the health aim from two different angles. Health is health of an organism. When there is a threat to good health, the whole of the organism is involved.

Study in the health area is varied. Children in the grade schools often make a special study of diets, record and rate their own diets, study the relative numbers of illnesses pupils have, and look for a relationship between illness and diet. Study of science at some grade levels will also include nutrition. It is not unusual for elementary school pupils, in their home economics classes, to carry on projects in nutrition. The classroom and the school building with its lighting,

Subject matter must be organized. Then it is taught, in countless different ways. Here are only a few. "*Mathematics is a tool subject.*" In later grades, when mathematics is used as a tool in understanding map-reading and income-tax forms, graphic representation and operational processes become relevant and therefore interesting. Second-graders learn about numbers themselves—a two-place numeral

really is tens and ones. Firsthand experience is emphasized in vocational education, as in a chemistry class for girls going into nursing or home arts. As one child weighs mice and the other records her findings, both begin to become interested in science. Teaching and learning go on far from textbooks and classrooms at times. Some students from Texas see where American history happened as they tour the nation's capital. (Their principal assembles them by blowing a whistle!)

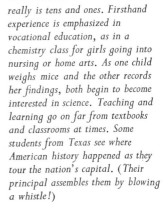

sewage disposal, and the like may also provide subject matter for health education. Sometimes the health services of the school are used as source material. School dental services have led science classes to study the fluoridation of water, the relation of diet to good teeth, and the relation of eating sweets or drinking sweetened liquids to the preservation of teeth.

Much of the subject matter of health studies involves direct experience from actual activities. Free play, particularly in the elementary school, may, for instance, make a significant contribution to self-control, fair play, and physical efficiency.

Health, as a major object of education, cannot be achieved by studying logical categories of subject matter. It is an aim that embraces the needs of every pupil at all levels of education. What is studied in health education even in a single grade cannot be standardized. Perhaps in this field more than in any other, expert planning is of paramount importance. The subject matter must be flexible—adaptable to the growth characteristics and primary interests of the individual pupils.

GENERAL TRENDS

The trend in organizing subject matter is toward larger units. Traditional organization is in terms of more or less isolated subjects. The teacher in the elementary school conducts a class in reading, a class in arithmetic, or a music class. In the high school one teacher has a class in geography, one a class in algebra, and another a class in chemistry.

To overcome the disadvantages of too great emphasis on the separateness of subject matter, to move from fragmentation toward greater unity, various plans have been followed. One such plan is called "correlation." Interested teachers working together discover relationships in their subject matter. The teacher of literature, for instance, may correlate Dickens' *Tale of Two Cities* with the history teacher's treatment of the French Revolution. Teachers and administrators tend to like this plan since no subject loses anything and traditional organization is not basically upset. Actually, the barriers between the subjects are not eliminated. Rather, they are adjusted to; teacher-planning achieves some unification despite them.

Another approach to unifying small areas of subject matter is called "integration." This type of organization is more readily adapted to the lower grades of the elementary school than to the secondary school. The teacher selects, or directs the selection of, projects that will give the child experiences educationally desirable, promote learning specifically suited to his academic level, and provide an opportunity for the teacher to give the kind of guidance that promises to lead to social and personal maturity. If, for instance, the project selected is the operation of a grocery store, in setting up the store and running the business the children would read, draw, add and subtract, and engage in many learning activities that ordinarily are taken up separately. They would also have such experiences as planning and working together, sharing, and cooperating.

Sometimes the fragmentary character of traditional subject-matter organization is lessened by combining areas and having an expanded unit. Typical large divisions are social studies, general science, language arts, health, physical education, general mathematics, and general arts. The subject matter area known as "unified studies," embracing English and social studies, is an even broader kind of classification.

The core program as a part of the junior and senior high school organization was described in Chapter 15. The term "core studies" is used to describe another plan for unifying work in the elementary school. Under this plan, a basic unit or problem on such subjects as housing, family, or civil liberties is the "core." Children who pursue the core give to this phase of their work all the time that is allocated to "general" education, that is, to education that is common to all students as differentiated from specialized education or vocational training. In working on the basic problem children use material from any subject. Emphasis is on pupil activity. A wide range of reading materials as well as the resources of the community are used.

Among the aims of the various forms of team teaching is that of unifying instruction by using the interdisciplinary resources of all the members of a team in developing a concept. Contributions from mathematics, science, social studies, and language arts may be utilized in a single unit of work.

Within the general plans called correlation, integration, unified studies, team teaching, and core studies, the variations are numerous. They all mark the trend toward organizing subject matter in larger units. They are of increasing interest to those who wish to improve the instructional programs.

Subject matter in America's schools

AT GRADE LEVELS

Subject matter has long been organized into levels paralleling the grades of our schools. In the Middle Ages, subject matter was limited to the knowledge systematically organized in books somewhat like encyclopedias for the purpose of being learned. Eventually the easier parts of accumulated, organized knowledge became the subject matter of the earlier grades. The more abstract, the more conceptual, and the more difficult to comprehend became the subject matter for the later grades. The most difficult to assimilate was to be taught by the graduate schools in the universities. Grade placement of subject matter was determined on an empirical basis. Eventually, for example, Euclidean geometry was placed regularly in the curriculum for sophomores in high school. Adaptations of Euclid's textbook are still used in some high school geometry classes at the sophomore level.

It was believed that subject matter, in time, found its own natural level and settled there. Its natural level was that stage of educational advancement at which it could be understood. Any other reasons for why it should be studied at a predetermined level were never probed. From earliest time a systematic, arbitrary arrangement of subject matter was accepted as appropriate apart entirely from utilitarian or interest values. It is related that even about 300 B.C. a pupil, having learned the first proposition of demonstrational geometry, raised the question of what he would get by learning these things and was answered by Euclid, who called his slave and said, "Give him threepence, since he must needs make gain by what he learns."

In the ninth grade, algebra begins with the intuitively conceived axioms and proceeds to quadratics. Demonstrational geometry, which follows, is a tenth-grade subject and also takes a full school year to learn. Advanced algebra is learned in the first half of the eleventh grade, and solid geometry is learned in the second half of the eleventh grade. The subject matter of Latin is grammar in the ninth grade,

Caesar's *Commentaries* in the tenth, Cicero's *Orations* in the eleventh, and Vergil's *Aeneid* in the twelfth.

Subject matter in American schools thus became crystallized. Materials in numerous fields have been systematically sifted, sorted, and organized, and their pedagogical uses have been prescribed according to grade-level sequence. Currently, however, traditional grade-level classifications are being modified. The determination of grade-level placement of subject matter is still made on an empirical basis, but improved understanding of pupils, of learning, and of subjects themselves has led to some drastic changes—to the teaching of geometry in the primary grades, for example. Because there has perhaps been most resistance to change in the grade-level placement of subjects in the secondary schools, pupils at present in the elementary schools may need accommodations in grade-level placement of some subjects when they reach the secondary schools.

TOTAL LEARNING

A somewhat expanded notion encompasses as subject matter *all* that a pupil learns. This concept does not exclude the idea that subject matter is organized in grade levels or that it includes what is in the textbooks. Subject matter, however, is not limited to that which is in a book. It also includes what goes on within the pupil, the reaction to what is studied. In this case the subject matter consists of the facts and ideas that are communicated to the pupil. Here the subject matter is only that which the pupil assimilates. In this sense no two pupils ever study the same subject matter, even though they use the same textbook and are taught by the same teacher.

PURPOSIVE LEARNING

Clearly, an individual's belief about what the subject matter of a school is, is directly related to what he thinks the aims of the school should be and how he can take into account what he knows about his pupils. If he believes that learning should contribute to purposes shared by the teacher and the pupils, then he might define subject matter broadly as the "facts observed, read, recalled, and talked about, and the ideas suggested, in course of a development of a situation having a purpose.''[2] This definition emphasizes that a classroom constitutes a special place for deliberate education and that there is more to the mastery of subject matter than learning what is included in the textbook. Importance is placed on the management of a situation so that learning proceeds with a purpose. It is the aim or purpose that is uppermost in the minds of the pupils and the teacher that dictates what and how subject matter shall be learned. In this concept, the subject matter varies with the individual pupil, since individual reactions to what is read or talked about will vary. In addition, it is recognized that how the pupil organizes what he learns depends on various factors, only some of which are within the pupil himself.

The teacher and subject matter

In our discussion of the qualifications, training, and experience necessary for teaching, it was pointed out that the successful teacher has acquired a breadth of knowledge far wider than that possessed by even the most advanced of his pupils. This knowledge is like a huge reservoir —it stands ready at all times to be drawn upon as needed.

The teacher's knowledge of subject matter and of pupils is a necessary complement to textbooks. Frequently, textbooks are divided into sections, and perhaps into subsections, for purposes of organization, reference, clarity, and emphasis. The textbook is a tool, and the divisions, sometimes quite minute, may be a definite aid to instruction. If, however, the teacher does not have a wide range of knowledge, the textbook with its detailed subdivisions tends to give subject matter a quality of rigidity, to make it less adaptable to momentary situations and less appropriate to teaching with a purpose. The teacher's knowledge must extend beyond the limits of the subject matter established in the textbook, limits unavoidable in the preparation of specialized books. The boundaries of a textbook are never the boundaries of the most fruitful subject matter.

The chances are that the teacher will organize his knowledge in a way somewhat paralleling the organization of subject matter of the specialist because the teacher has studied under and mastered that

[2] John Dewey, *Democracy and Education*. New York: Macmillan, 1916, p. 212.

kind of arrangement. The physics teacher, for instance, tends to think of physics around words like measurement, mechanics, heat, static electricity, electricity-in-motion, sound, light, and invisible radiations.

The pupil's orientation to subject matter is different from the teacher's. The pupil's organization, growing out of his past experiences, is inchoate. The successful teacher is aware of the discrepancy. He is alert to the opportunities and to the importance of providing avenues for a pupil to follow in developing his own organization and application. In drawing upon the reservoir of knowledge, the teacher will not be influenced by the kind of organization characteristic of his own school experience. He will tend to draw from any area, whether in textbooks or in the world of practical affairs, appropriate to achieving the end desired. For instance, the teacher's knowledge may influence the subject matter of the literature class to include something that might traditionally be classified as history, philosophy, economics, or something else. In our review of the current trends in the organization of subject matter, it will be noted that the importance of organizing subject matter in larger units is recognized.

Subject matter, it has been pointed out, may include direct experience and indirect or vicarious learning. In advancing educationally the tendency is to move from emphasis on the direct toward progressively greater emphasis on the indirect. A learning situation may include both direct and indirect features in varying degrees. In the biology laboratory the pupil may have such direct experiences as learning about circulation by dissecting a rabbit. He will also use the textbook, library reference materials, and perhaps filmstrips and movies. Sufficient direct experience is necessary to make indirect learning effective. The indirect must be associated with the direct by meaningful symbols, vocabulary, and examples. The successful teacher is resourceful in making appropriate connections. For instance, in teaching mathematics, it will be less difficult for a farm boy to make a meaningful connection between the symbols of measurement applied to a bushel of oats or an acre of ground than it will be for a city pupil who buys oats in a cereal box and thinks of land divisions as city blocks and 50-foot lots.

Unfortunately, students often arrive at college, even at the graduate level, without having built firsthand experiences with quantitative subject matter sufficient for clear understanding of the meanings various words and symbols are expected to convey. For enjoyment or real appreciation, a meaningful connection between subject matter and human living is essential.

Summary

It is important to remember that, of course, selection and organization of subject matter are never isolated activities. They are closely related to the educational aims of the school and of the teacher, which, in turn, are influenced by his understanding of his pupils. In deciding what is worthy and desirable subject matter and what would be the best organization of that subject, just as in selecting methods of instruction, the criteria used have a philosophical base.

At present, subject matter designed to promote specialized and vocational competences tends to be relatively adequate and satisfactory because the specialized areas have immediate and definite aims and the subject matter appropriate to advancing these aims is readily available. The path of progress leads toward selecting subject matter potentially more significant in advancing the aims of general education. There is a current tendency to give unwarranted emphasis to specialized subject matter and to give too little emphasis to subject matter that contributes to the aims of general education, to a sound cultural background. Chemistry teachers, for instance, tend to stress the kind of subject matter that prepares chemists, not the kind that makes citizens intelligent about the physical world. Unfortunately, there is a continuing lack of agreement about what subject matter best contributes to the general education of all learners. The development of materials appropriate to general education in all subjects, selection of suitable subject matter, and planning adequate curriculums are among important areas for study and leadership.

Another path to progress is unmistakably indicated in the selection of subject matter that is more adaptable to the vast range in the pupils' backgrounds, interests, and learning abilities. Balanced reading programs, textbooks suited to different levels of ability, and workbooks and other instructional aids that permit pupils to advance at individual rates are becoming increasingly effective. Including more direct experience, particularly in the high school, is another improvement in the selection of subject matter that may be profitably extended.

Present trends indicate that in the future, organization of subject matter will continue to be progressively more in terms of unity and less in terms of specialized, fragmentary fields. Specialists in the psychology of learning, in child development, in social psychology, and in social biology have effectively challenged the soundness of a theory in which education is viewed mainly as the acquisition of material as it is arranged in textbooks.

Regardless of the way subject matter is selected or organized, its value in the educational experiences of the pupil depends largely on the effectiveness of the teacher. Progress here lies in the direction of improved training and experience. In order to exploit fully the potentialities of the entire learning situation, the teacher must not only understand the learning process and be thoroughly acquainted with his pupils; he also must have both a broad, general background and an extensive reservoir of information and understanding in the particular field in which he is teaching.

Questions

1. What is your definition of subject matter?
2. What is the curriculum? the course of study? a subject of study?
3. How may one judge the relative values of the various subjects of study?
4. What should be the relationship between school textbooks and the subject matter used in a given classroom?
5. What are the characteristics of a suitable textbook?
6. How, in your opinion, is continuity in a subject such as the fine arts or social studies to be achieved?

Projects

1. Consult some specialized publication on the subject matter of your chosen field. Set forth what seem to be the principal trends in the selection of subject matter.
2. Look over materials in the curriculum resource center or consult professional publications—yearbooks, periodicals, etc. Make a list of changes that have occurred in a field other than the field of your major interest since you were a pupil in elementary school.

Four kinds of understandings are essential to effective teaching: first, basic understandings, knowledges, and generalizations about pupils; second, knowledge of the part played by aims and objectives in giving direction to the educative process; third, knowledge that is classified as appropriate subject matter; fourth, understandings related to methods, procedures, and skills required to utilize effectively, in directing learning, the knowledge of subject matter and understandings about pupils. In a sense, these four kinds of understandings constitute a unified whole in that they are inextricably interrelated, each constituting one component of the educative process.

For a teacher-in-preparation or an experienced teacher to keep informed about educational developments, it is important that he maintain a reasonably balanced interest in all four aspects. Since each kind of understanding is of such breadth and magnitude as to sustain a lifetime of study, it is relatively easy, even tempting, for a teacher to allow his interests to become one-sided. That a balanced interest in the four essential aspects—knowledge of pupils, of aims, of subject matter, and of methods—is a valuable goal for teachers-in-training and for teachers-in-service cannot be overemphasized.

Methods, a deepening concern

Problems relating to teaching methods have become a matter of rapidly expanding interest in recent years. This seems due, in part at least, to an intensified awareness on the part of teachers after they have gained

543

CHAPTER 19
*Methods of
Teaching in
America's
Schools*

teaching experience that all they knew about human growth and development and about subject-matter-to-be-learned could be translated effectively into learning only with wise use of skillful methods. Without the ability to select and utilize appropriate procedures, without the requisite skills to communicate effectively with pupils, a teacher is somewhat comparable to a family with a swimming pool that is only an ornament because no one in the family can swim.

The expanded interest in teaching methods is due in part also to the accelerated change in curriculum, to the expanded background of interests and experiences of pupils, and to the extensive variety of teaching aids now available. A teacher today looking back at the days before TV, plane travel, automated manufacturing, Cold War international maneuvering, recognizes at once that many classroom methods geared to conditions of a decade ago are now out of date. Also, there is the realization that technology is contributing to increased effectiveness of teacher communication. In the wake of current rapid change, teaching methods are inexorably swept along.

That the teaching profession is responding to the current demand for improvement in methods of teaching is attested in part by the great amount of time and money that industry feels can be wisely invested in developing and producing a wide range of teaching aids. Attention is given to improving teaching methods by numerous groups of educators—for instance, the National Council of Teachers of English and the National Council of Teachers of Mathematics. Information about teaching problems, experiments, recommendations, and innovations is widely disseminated by many such organizations through their national publications. A teacher will find among these much material to stimulate his interest in teaching methods and also to guide him in determining the methods and procedures appropriate or adaptable to his teaching responsibilities.

APPROACHES TO STUDY OF METHODS

One may approach a study of methods of teaching by focusing on so-called general methods. General methods include the basic principles, generalizations, and concepts that are, presumably, applicable to teaching in general, to the teaching of all subjects. In his five formal steps to conducting the recitation, for example, Herbart

B. F. Skinner (1904–   ) of Harvard is one of our foremost behavioral psychologists, noted for his pioneering work on teaching machines. Much of what he writes about the process of learning bears directly on classroom practice. Here are some of his thoughts on methods.

The most widely publicized efforts to improve education show an extraordinary neglect of method. Learning and teaching are not analyzed, and almost no effort is made to improve teaching as such. The aid which education is to receive usually means money and the proposals for spending it follow a few, familiar lines.

. . . Pedagogy is not a prestigious word. Its low estate may be traced in part to the fact that under the blandishments of statistical methods, which promised a new kind of rigor, educational psychologists spent half a century measuring the results of teaching while neglecting teaching itself.

. . . High-school and grade-school teaching is taught primarily through apprenticeships, in which students receive the advice and counsel of experienced teachers. . . . Any special knowledge of pedagogy as a basic science of teaching is felt to be unnecessary.

The attitude is regrettable. No enterprise can improve itself to the fullest extent without examining its basic processes. A really effective educational system cannot be set up until we understand the processes of learning and teaching. Human behavior is far too complex to be left to casual experience, or even to organized experience in the restricted environment of the classroom. Teachers need help. In particular they need the kind of help offered by a scientific analysis of behavior.

. . . a true technology of teaching is imminent. It is beginning to suggest effective alternatives to the average practices that have caused us so much trouble.

B. F. Skinner, "Why Teachers Fail," *Saturday Review*, pp. 80, 102, October 16, 1965. Copyright 1965 by Saturday Review, Inc.

assumes that teachers in general conduct recitations and that they can use the five formal steps as a guide regardless of the subject matter they are teaching. Likewise, Dewey in his *How We Think* assumes that all teachers are attempting to help pupils learn how to think. All teachers are assumed to ask questions, evaluate pupil achievement, engage in telling, and the like. A study of general methods would be expected to

545

CHAPTER 19
*Methods of
Teaching in
America's
Schools*

cover what teachers do in general to stimulate and direct the learning of pupils.

Another approach to the study of methods focuses on special methods. This approach relates to problems inherent in the teaching of a specialized subject-matter field or in the teaching of a particular age group, usually very young children. It assumes that there are methods which apply particularly to the teaching of English, mathematics, and the like, and that these can better be studied in special courses. The study of special methods is thought to have the added advantage of providing an opportunity for the logical combination of a study of teaching methods with a study of subject matter. Thus, colleges now give such courses as Intermediate Mathematics, Physics for Teachers, Chemistry for Teachers. Furthermore, in some universities the study of special methods and student teaching in the subject field are closely correlated.

No attempt will be made here to evaluate the two approaches to the study of methods. It seems that both have certain advantages. There is some advantage in the broader approach that gives consideration to such topics as the aims of education, how rewards and punishments operate to condition learning, how interests, motivation, and other affective factors can be utilized. On the other hand, concentration on a study of the problems peculiar to the primary or preschool level is likely also to result in certain advantages. Certainly it is profitable to explore under the guidance of a skilled college teacher problems related to any special field. Perhaps a study of both general and special methods may be needed for a satisfactory command in any one field.

A COMPREHENSIVE FIELD

Methods of teaching cover a comprehensive field. This is due first to the fact that education is established for the very complex purpose of promoting human improvement. As pointed out in Chapter 16, this involves a twofold continuing problem—on the one hand, problems related to the biological character of each human being, which is the product of the interaction between the individual and his environment, and on the other hand, problems related to the environment, including the school with everything that makes it an important part of that environment.

Paul Monroe (1869–1947) was a scholar whose special interest was the history of education. His influence over education was considerable at the beginning of this century. The following paragraph shows his view on the meaning of method.

> *Method is the process of using this culture material so as to produce the desired development of the child. This development must include the expansion of his own powers, the creation of control over them and the direction of them to the necessary, to the useful, and to helpful social activities. Method is the guidance of the child in his activities by the teacher so that he may incorporate into his own experience that portion of the experience of the race which, to those who have the direction of his education, seems valuable; that is, suitable for his stage of development and similar in complexity to his own interests and activities. The sole effort of the teacher should be directed toward the guidance of this process; his sole interest should be in the expanding consciousness of the child, in furnishing experiences appropriate to the power of the child and properly related to his interests and activities. The teacher should be so equipped by previous training that he can give undivided attention in this process. Hence the necessity of* method, *as the term is ordinarily used. This method should be possessed by the teacher, but it is of most value when most unconsciously used. Method in the broader sense requires upon the part of the teacher a knowledge of the child; a knowledge of his existing interests, activities and possessions; a mastery of the material or the subject-matter dealt with; an understanding of the process through which the child incorporates the novel experience into his own; and an ability to use and to make subordinate the machinery of the schoolroom and the technique of the process of instruction. This last one is considered method* par excellence, *but it is only one phase of method.*

Paul Monroe, *A Brief Course in the History of Education.* New York: Macmillan, 1907, pp. 407–408. Quoted by permission of The Macmillan Company.

The great breadth of the area of teaching methods is also due to the extended range of subject matter, each element of which presents its own novel teaching problems. Take, for example, the field of English. Some of the questions a teacher might need to answer are: What is the best method for the study of words? Children seem to learn slang terms easily, but have difficulty learning legitimate words.

547

CHAPTER 19
*Methods of
Teaching in
America's
Schools*

Why? How should punctuation be taught? Will a single method like phonemics suffice? Can a poem be taught to high school pupils by programed instruction? If so, how does one program a poem? One might similarly proceed to other elements of English such as reading, writing, grammar, spelling, listening, viewing, mass media, only to find that each presents peculiar problems of teaching, none of which is easy to solve. In seeking an answer, a teacher may recognize the need for knowing, in general, about available teaching aids, team teaching, programed learning, curriculum construction, program evaluation, and so on.

In the fields of language arts, social studies, science, and mathematics, a great deal of emphasis is at present given to the inductive method of teaching. This method allows students to *discover* knowledge, skills, understandings. The teacher's role is to provide students with structured situations, to pose questions which call upon the student to make the discoveries. An example is the teaching of the concept of the noun. Instead of telling the students "a noun is the name of a person, place, or thing" the teacher will perhaps give the class a sentence with nonsense words used as nouns and then ask the pupils what the words have in common, will let them discover clues that indicate how the words used as nouns function in the sentence. Later other examples will be given without nonsense words, and by careful

Extensive changes often are necessary in buildings and equipment before modern methods can be used. Here part of an old high school building has been remodeled. The result is an up-to-date laboratory-classroom.

analysis, by asking well-planned questions, the teacher will help the student strengthen his grasp of the concept.

Those who favor the inductive method contend that a student will learn and retain facts and rules best when he has put forth effort to discover or build them himself. Modern psychology tends to favor the inductive method, the presentation of arranged learning situations so that the student may discover through his own activity the facts, principles, and structures of the subject he is studying. He may thus attain understanding and intellectual growth by engaging in an activity through which he discovers structures of knowledge.

Since methods of teaching is such a comprehensive field of study, the survey that follows in this chapter and the next makes no attempt to deal with concrete analyses of the many problems of teaching method. Since our objective is to give a brief overview, the treatment is necessarily limited to over-all trends in various subject-matter fields.

Teaching subject matter

LANGUAGE ARTS

The aim in teaching language arts is twofold—the development of the abilities to express ideas and feelings and to receive and interpret messages. Writing and speaking constitute the media of expression of ideas and feelings. Listening and reading constitute the media through which the ability to receive and interpret messages is developed.

1. Written expression

After judging a pupil's present capacity to write clearly and effectively, the teacher next concentrates on finding ways to encourage growth in this skill. Growth is emphasized rather than expertness, which is held in mind as a remote goal. The pupil should always have a clear notion of the next step in the development of his abilities.

The material best suited for study, discussion, and rewriting is the sentences and paragraphs from a pupil's own written expression. Variations in word meanings receive attention, with a view to selecting words that express the precise meaning desired. Published paragraphs, which may be read by the pupils at home and which serve as

549

CHAPTER 19
*Methods of
Teaching in
America's
Schools*

examples of better forms of written expression, are also discussed in the classroom. The contributions made to expression by correct spelling, punctuation, and grammatical structure are made an integral part of the instructional procedure.

How does the assignment contribute to the growth of an individual's powers of expression? This is the paramount criterion for the selection of a method. For example, teachers help their pupils see that socially acceptable forms of written expression are important, not because they represent the ends of good written expression, but because they make a pupil a more effective social individual. An effort is made to help the pupil recognize that there is a place for the language, especially the oral language, that is a natural part of his everyday conversation, even though this may be different from the so-called "formal" language that is considered socially correct. The pupil is helped to understand that the informal language, or the dialect of a group or a neighborhood, is not *wrong*, is actually the most appropriate medium of communication under some circumstances, but that there is, however, a place where the socially correct language, the language characteristic of the educated people of the community, is needed. Younger children are taught to know words, to use them, and to write them in proper context. Knowing words helps them to think and adds to their development of capacity to deal with other persons and to provide solutions to individual personal problems. A pupil learns that his potential powers cannot be developed in a day, that they, with some effort on his part, will develop gradually.

One of the problems in attempting to promote growth in the abilities of written expression is the pupils' lack of interest. To encourage them to develop their capacities, teachers use as many lifelike situations as possible. Pupils write useful letters, prepare scripts for an assembly program, devise school posters, or originate captions to announce special events in the school. Pupils may be asked to read a written digest of something they have read in order that the class may also know about it, to write an occasional verse just for fun, to write a formal composition in order to demonstrate how one should be written, or to take notes on a talk they will hear in order to transmit effectively and faithfully the ideas of the speaker to the class. The use of lifelike situations has been effective because it brings into play the pupils' interests and helps the pupils to see that they write in school

The following is an excerpt from a lecture to prospective teachers given by William G. Perry, Jr., a professor at Harvard.

Now since the teacher is someone who has been hired by the community to engage full time in this transmission of the culture, you will find that you are not just a Ganymede or a Hebe standing at the fountain of knowledge with a little cup, but rather you will find that your students are quite properly responding to you as if your other hand, the one you have behind your back, had brass knuckles on it. They will be responding to you as if you were saying, as you must say—as you cannot escape saying whether you put it into words or not—not only, "Come and drink from the fountain of knowledge," but also, "And while you are at it, bud, you do it our way on time ; if you don't, you will not only not get these lovely things, but you will be sent shamefully home, a failure."

Now what do people do under stresses and threats like that? They resist, just as Sally resists eating those beans, not because she doesn't like beans, but because she is afraid that by liking them, now that you have told her to eat them, she will somehow be losing something. She doesn't know quite what, but she feels that something dreadfully important will be lost. So what students do in their resistance is to conform to the letter of what you say. They will eat two spoonfuls of beans, with one bean in each. They will say the letter of what you require them to repeat, but they will reject the spirit, even if they think it will be good for them.

. . .

It is in the student's sense of the warmth of being understood, of being therefore personally related, that he is set free from his anxiety so that he can do his academic work productively.

And it is not possible that it is through the warmth that you may convey this way that the student may come to feel that it may be worth while to grow up. If grown-ups are impersonal, authoritative, and intellectual, then it is perfectly clear that being mature means to give up having fun. It means to the student that to grow up and be a Self must carry with it an absolutely intolerable loss, the discard of all his impulses and desires, and that to be a Self will not only mean to be alone, but to be lonely indeed. But if you are warm and attentive to your students' feelings, then they will realize that you, too, put some value on feelings, and that maybe it would be possible to grow up and still have feelings

551

CHAPTER 19
*Methods of
Teaching in
America's
Schools*

*and still have fun. In that case, since you eat beans, maybe they will
try them, too.*

Reprinted by permission of the publishers from William G. Perry, Jr., "Conflicts
in the Learning Process: The Student's Response to Teaching," in *A Handbook for
College Teachers*, Bernice Brown Cronkhite, ed. Cambridge, Massachusetts: Harvard
University Press, 1950, pp. 20, 35.

for the same reasons that people write outside school. Resistance to
writing is easier to overcome if the pupils are encouraged to write
about things of concern to them and if writing can be done in ways of
some immediate use.

The question of methods in teaching spelling, punctuation, grammar, and handwriting often arises. Teaching written expression includes all these subject matters. Spelling is combined with, and is a
part of, written expression, but the central emphasis is upon word
study—the meaning of words and the form in which they convey the
meaning. Both the words studied and the spelling of the words are
taken from the words the pupils use. Meaning and structure are considered together. A word wrongly spelled usually does not carry its
true meaning. "It reigned yesterday" is an example. Teachers focus
attention upon words. A number of words are examined, analyzed,
and reviewed each week, but always by a method that leads to growth
in the powers of expression. Both punctuation and grammar are given
careful attention—but, again, as means to developing powers of
written expression.

Many current changes in methods of teaching language arts are
consistent with recommendations by scholars in the field of linguistics.
The language arts teacher oriented to the linguistic approach, instead
of presenting a collection of facts for rote learning, instead of teaching
rules for spelling and punctuation and grammar, shows students how
to examine and test the facts of language and expression for themselves.
The teacher frequently uses nonsense sentences to illustrate grammatical structure and emphasizes position as a means of identifying parts of
speech. There is some new terminology. For instance, *determiners* and
noun-markers are what traditionally have been called *articles* and *adjec-
tives*. In teaching spelling and word comprehension the phonemic
principle is stressed for a clear understanding of the difference between

letters and sounds. The oral language factors of pitch and stress are utilized for help in understanding and using punctuation. Common, basic sentence patterns are examined and the pupils have experience with the infinite variations that can be made in terms of these patterns. It is contended that this kind of language arts teaching will pay off in a noticeable improvement in the students' handling of the language in writing and oral work, that understanding the system of the language plus purposeful practice will result in improvement of language use.

2. Oral expression

In helping pupils develop the powers of oral expression, teachers must realize the importance of full recognition of the child's native resources and his level of maturation. The native capacities are developed by putting natural organs—ears, vocal cords, larynx—to use. The way the child is taught to use the organs determines the nature of the development that takes place.

Teaching speech in school is important because speech is man's basic mode of expression. It is his most effective way not only to give expression to his wants but to preserve his techniques and knowledge and to pass them on to the next generation.

Unfortunately, methodical teaching of speech in the schools has been somewhat neglected. This may be, in part, a legacy from the past when schools were places where children were forced to be quiet. Studies show that a 4-year-old speaks 10,000 words a day, a 5-year-old speaks 12,000 words a day, and the longest period for either age group without audible speech is 19 minutes. The average length of periods of inactivity—and these are infrequent—is four minutes. Children are naturally highly stimulated to talk, and if silence is not enforced, speech in the schoolroom is an almost continuous process. The methods for correcting, modifying, and directing the pupils' speech are continuously in use.

Considerable attention is given to the development of a speaking vocabulary. There are many differences between a speaking and an understanding vocabulary, and the problem of developing one differs from the problem of developing the other. Each entails different methods.

Training the voice has received much attention. Schools often provide specialists to direct the speech instruction of pupils with

553

CHAPTER 19
*Methods of
Teaching in
America's
Schools*

*A distinguished American philosopher, George Herbert Palmer (1842–1933),
analyzes the doctrine of giving praise.*

> . . . *When is conduct praiseworthy? When may we fairly claim honor
> from our fellows and ourselves? There is a ready answer. Nothing is
> praiseworthy which is not the result of effort. I do not praise a lady for
> her beauty, I admire her. The athlete's splendid body I envy, wishing
> that mine were like it. But I do not praise him. Or does the reader
> hesitate; and while acknowledging that admiration and envy may be
> our leading feelings here, think that a certain measure of praise is also
> due? It may be. Perhaps the lady has been kind enough by care to
> heighten her beauty. Perhaps those powerful muscles are partly the result
> of daily discipline. These persons, then, are not undeserving of praise, at
> least to the extent that they have used effort. Seeing a collection of
> china, I admire the china, but praise the collector. It is hard to obtain
> such pieces. Large expense is required, long training, too, and constant
> watchfulness. Accordingly I am interested in more than the collection. I
> give praise to the owner. A learned man we admire, honor, envy, but
> also praise. His wisdom is the result of effort.*
> *Plainly, then, praise and blame are attributable exclusively to spiritual
> beings. Nature is unfit for honor. We may admire her, may wish that
> our ways were like hers, and envy her great law-abiding calm. But it
> would be foolish to praise her, or even to blame when her volcanoes
> overwhelm our friends. We praise spirit only, conscious deeds. Where
> self-directed action forces its path to a worthy goal, we rightly praise
> the director.*

George Herbert Palmer, *The Nature of Goodness*. Boston: Houghton Mifflin,
1903, pp. 241–242. Quoted by permission of Houghton Mifflin Company.

exaggerated defects. Methods that have proved very effective in speech
correction are adaptable to teaching the normal pupil in the school.
In normal classroom situations, a few simple rules are followed. Good
speech calls for good listeners. The teacher sets an example with his
own speech habits. A pupil is directed to speak plainly and loudly
enough to be heard. He speaks to the class, not just to the teacher.
Good articulation is striven for. Careless speech, even in the most informal discussion, is discouraged. The pupil is made conscious that he
is speaking his thoughts, that others are thinking with him, and that

they are occupied with the thoughts he is trying to express, not with their own thoughts.

Most of the methods that teachers use are informal and are selected to help a certain pupil or to fit some special situation. As with written expression, as many true-to-life situations as possible are used, such as assemblies, announcements, presiding over the class, and discussion. Teachers find the tape recorder particularly helpful.

The linguists stress the importance of oral language, and recommend beginning with what students, as native speakers, already know, what they have learned from imitating those around them. The great variations in oral speech are not necessarily undesirable, something to be stamped out, and there are no permanent, absolute rules to follow in language arts, because language is constantly changing.

3. Reading

Reading is language development that interprets what is seen on the printed page. Reading English is the reverse of writing and speaking English. Writing and speaking are processes in which meaning is translated into words, while reading is a process in which words are translated into meaning. Both are active processes, but they differ; hence the methods of teaching the two must differ.

The discovery of printing brought reading into prominence. Hopefully, printed symbols cause one to think. Ideas come to the students through their eyes rather than through the medium of sound. The response a pupil makes to a symbol depends upon the ideas and emotions that are aroused in him by the sight of the symbols. No two pupils make the same response to a symbol because the symbol carries different meanings to different people.

How children are taught to read obviously influences the nature of their ability to comprehend and to interpret what they read. Reading is not taught as an absorptive process. It is treated as an active process in which the reader expresses himself through the interpretation of what he reads. It is a process that stimulates his thinking, feeling, and acting.

Powers of expression, whether oral or written, expand as the ability to read develops. The development of this ability is a constant and continuous process. It begins when the small child first points to a picture in a book and continues throughout the course of his life.

555

CHAPTER 19
*Methods of
Teaching in
America's
Schools*

Growth patterns in ability to read, to comprehend what is read, and to interpret more meaningfully what is read vary in different individuals. Thus the student who reads with ease the most difficult technical treatise is one who has gradually sharpened his powers of distinction, enlarged the scope of his knowledge of meanings, and developed a highly specialized vocabulary. What he reads may be easy for him and difficult for someone else. A pupil's ability to read depends not only on how well he has learned to read previously, but also on the lines along which growth has been directed. He may read one kind of material expertly and read and comprehend another kind poorly. In reading, the over-all growth pattern of each pupil is unique. A method of teaching that takes into account the natural design of the learner gives promise of contributing the maximum to the development of the ability to read.

In view of the nature of reading development, the efforts made in earlier schools to classify reading into grade levels and to establish standards for each of the grades seem rather hopeless gestures. The range of reading abilities in each of the grades is inevitably very wide. Method, to be effective, must take into account the extensive differences among pupils of the same age in reading interests, abilities, and all-around reading competence.

Teachers in the lower grades of the American schools have developed and use highly successful methods of teaching reading, principally because they have accepted the guidance of child development specialists. The quality of teaching reading deteriorates somewhat in the higher grades; teachers too often use methods that largely disregard the findings of the psychologists. Consequently, high school and college students do not read as well as they should. Their progress in language facility has been slower than it should be, considering the amount of training these pupils have had. Since the methods of teaching have been partly responsible for the situation, language arts teachers at all levels have made the improvement of methods of teaching reading one of their goals.

Thus, the reading process, as is the case with the learning process itself, should not be considered as isolated from other conditioning factors. The teacher should keep this in mind when he decides whether to have pupils read orally or silently and whether to use the word method, the telling method, phonetics methods or one of the several phonetic systems, the questioning method, the discussion method, or some other system. He may often have to make arbitrary decisions—simply because some decision has to be made. In the final analysis, as has been said, methods are inseparable from other factors. Indeed, one can think of the choice of a reading method as the end of a sequence: understanding pupils and knowing their needs and interests; evolving and following definite, specific, and worthy objectives for each of the lesson units; having a diversity of suitable materials available; and then choosing those methods that are best suited to directing the learning of the pupils effectively toward the desired ends, using, when needed, appropriate instructional aids (such as those described in the next chapter).

4. Listening

Attentive, sympathetic listeners are necessary to the cultivation of good oral expression. Listening is also a form of expression on the part of the one who listens. It is a somewhat neglected area of language arts. In teaching children to be good listeners the teacher is concerned with the impact the spoken word makes upon the listener, the ideas it arouses, and the reactions to which it leads.

Pupils are taught that listening may have different purposes—for example, listening carefully to a question to answer it, to a record just to be entertained, to a persuasive advertisement on the radio to criticize the logic of the argument, or to the reading of a beautiful poem to appreciate it. Life presents many opportunities for listening, and the school has an obligation to encourage growth and development in the skills of listening quite as much as in the skills of reading. Just as, at times, spelling, punctuation, and sentence structure are made the focus of direct instruction, so also is listening. The subject matter is carefully chosen, the purpose is agreed upon, and the procedures are defined just as carefully as they would be in any other language arts instruction.

5. Trends

Language arts teachers are aware of the individual differences among their pupils and know that the differences expand as growth in language arts progresses. Individual needs are given as close attention as are group needs. Much thought is devoted to choice of material and

Here are methods in action. Play-acting is often used by language arts teachers to promote self-expression and self-confidence. Classroom teachers are trying out programed text material increasingly in their efforts to individualize instruction. A junior high school boy studies the new mathematics from a programed textbook with accompanying geometric models. In three very different situations, modern methods of teaching science are shown. A teacher in a New York school has taken her pupils to a park, where she describes the scientific characteristics of a wild mustard plant as she prunes it. Two boys, re-enacting one of the basic experiments of physics, discover for themselves some of the principles relating to the Newtonian laws of motion. A boy, whose project evolved from his own interests, exhibits the results of his investigations at a Science Fair. Annual Student Science Fairs are held throughout the country, from local to national levels.

to deriving ways whereby subject matter may be effectively directed toward desired ends. Currently the inductive, linguistics approach is in vogue.

Language arts teachers carefully analyze the language development of preschool children, of children in the primary grades, and so on up through the graduate school of the university. Observation of growth in large numbers of children does not obscure their vision of individual differences. It does help in setting up levels that can be used as standards or guides in planning instruction.

The language arts teachers, whose methods are based on current educational theories, tend to be nonconformists in the profession. They ignore some practices that were sacred to the older language arts teachers—such practices as adhering to established grade-placement of subject matter and demanding standard achievement for promotion. These teachers insist that good language arts teaching can proceed only when the individual pupil is fully understood, when an attempt is made to discover his individual requirements. Only then can appropriate subject matter and methods be selected.

These language arts teachers are not, however, the educational rebels they are sometimes pictured. They are, in fact, realists. They are practicing psychologists. They are convinced by their studies of human growth and development that their methods of teaching are better, that these methods are essential to the proper promotion of human growth.

The language arts teachers seek to coordinate their classroom work with the social experiences of the school and with the experiences the pupil may have in other subjects like geography and social studies. Language is a social instrument, and a broadened range of social experience widens the range of the subject matter that can be used in teaching language arts. When correlating the language arts with other subjects, the language arts teachers may be accused of overlapping the other fields. If they do, it is with a distinct instructional aim in mind. When pupils read, they cannot just read "reading." Growth in reading implies a broadening of the range of experiences as well as growth in reading skills.

The language arts teachers have been especially resourceful in choosing functional subject matter. In reading, for example, schools

559

CHAPTER 19
*Methods of
Teaching in
America's
Schools*

have placed great emphasis upon having suitable library materials readily accessible to teachers and pupils alike. Paperbacks, popular with pupils, enhance the breadth of reading materials available. The librarian, who is usually also a language arts teacher, serves mainly as a resource person to help teachers or pupils. Single textbooks for reading have almost disappeared from the better schools. The wide range of pupil needs, interests, and abilities demands a wide range of reading materials. Efforts are made to develop balanced reading programs. A wide range of sources is made available. The differences in cultural backgrounds, interests, and abilities of the pupils are taken fully into account. This change in methods has impregnated many language arts classrooms with new spirit, has ventilated them with a breath of fresh air.

All teachers in the school are, in a sense, language arts teachers. Pupils are taught to read in mathematics and science classes. There they learn the use of specialized words. Language arts teachers attempt to coordinate the language arts of all the classes. When school work has been compartmentalized into rigid divisions of subject matter, the work of the language arts teachers to coordinate language arts skills with other school subjects tends to be more difficult. Critical reading, vocabulary building, spelling, sentence structure, and collateral reading become submerged in many of the classes in specialized subject matter because of the dominance of other aims. The trend at all levels, however, is to stress growth in the communicative arts through the conscious efforts of the teachers of all the subjects.

Planning a sequence in the language arts area remains an unsettled problem. There is agreement, however, that methods should place greater emphasis upon written and spoken communication, less upon isolated drill. Speaking opportunities should far outnumber writing opportunities. Overt attention should be given to developing the skills of listening. Both practical and imaginative writing should be taught. What a pupil reads should be in answer to his interests, needs, and abilities. The teaching of reading should emphasize reading with a purpose. Ordinarily the purpose of reading for information and enjoyment should outweigh, but not displace, reading to improve the mechanics of reading. Pupils should share their reading experiences with others as often as possible. To set forth in advance specifically what is to be covered in the language arts instruction or to define the methods of directing the instruction is not possible. Much is left to the intelligence of the well-trained language arts teacher.

SCIENCE

A precipitately heightened interest in science education among the American people has been reflected in the school program. Our discussion deals with the methods of teaching science only in the area of general education, where all pupils, regardless of interest or ability, are studying the same subject matter.

Much thought and effort have been devoted to the formulation of a developmental program of teaching science. The old problem of sequence is still unsolved, but instruction in science now begins in the first year of school and continues as general science up to the seventh grade. In the seventh, eighth, and ninth grades, science is usually still general science, but the instruction is given by a specialized teacher. The subject matter after that becomes more specialized. There are classes in physics, chemistry, and biology.

Teaching general science has two principal purposes: (1) to lead the student to an accurate understanding and appreciation of the physical world and (2) to cultivate the student's ability to use the scientific method.

One of the age-old stumbling blocks to teaching in this area is the complex form in which the sciences have been organized by the specialists. The connections of the highly systematized subject matter with the experiences of everday life have often been hidden from both the pupils and the teacher. Teachers in the earlier grades now teach science without the use of textbooks. The inductive approach is generally followed. Much attention is given at first to obtaining concrete experiences and to connecting the subject matters studied with those experiences. Even in the first grade, the pupil begins to recognize the nature of a lever or the relationship between sunlight and life. The teacher begins with what the pupil has learned from his previous experience and develops from that experience the proper modes of scientific treatment. Time is sacrificed to understanding and to fostering a vital interest. The cue to method is that nothing is learned by the pupils unless they understand it fully.

561

CHAPTER 19
*Methods of
Teaching in
America's
Schools*

The teacher in general education never assumes that he is obligated to produce a scientific specialist. He leaves that to the later years, when selection operates. He does assume that everyone should learn something about the method scientists have used to perfect their knowledge as well as something about the results they have achieved. A pupil's understanding grows as he learns *how* to look and for *what* to look.

Facilities for teaching science, generously furnished by most schools, are as highly varied as the methods that they are expected to serve. Laboratories, library materials, visual aids, books suited to the age of the pupils—all contribute to and influence the teacher's methods. The selection of science teaching methods is ideally left to the discretion of an able teacher who has considerable knowledge of pupils' needs.

MATHEMATICS

Methods in the teaching of mathematics in America's schools might have been included in the preceding discussion, except that American schools treat mathematics as a specialized subject apart from science. This specialization begins in the very early grades and continues through all the remaining grades. The subject matter of mathematics traditionally has been organized in relatively narrow areas like algebra and plane geometry. Changes which have resulted in the so-called "new mathematics" have brought about an organization into more comprehensive fields.

Perhaps in no field of teaching have the results been more subject to critical scrutiny. Criticisms have been heeded, and great changes have been made in methods of teaching mathematics in recent years. One of the common criticisms was that most pupils at the elementary and high school levels did not learn mathematics, and that what was learned about mathematics was largely forgotten as soon as the pupil left school and entered adult life. Another criticism was that in studying mathematics many pupils developed a fear of it, or an antagonistic attitude toward doing any kind of quantitative thinking. As already pointed out, quantitative thinking becomes increasingly important in this age of computers.

Teachers were the first to admit that the methods of teaching mathematics for the purpose of general education have not been as effective as desired, and efforts to improve these methods over the past years are continuing. Traditions, however, have a strong hold, and changes have not been easy to make. If, as some contend, the teachers of mathematics have placed too much emphasis upon manipulation, such as applying formulas, and upon getting the right answers, rather than upon processes of thinking out answers, then a key to progress seems to be a change in the emphasis of teaching. Setting up equations in the ninth grade will become just as important as solving an equation that has been set up. Teachers complain that in systems where city-wide standardized tests are administered, the tests are scored right or wrong, sometimes with a machine, according to the correctness of the answer, regardless of whether pupils can think through the processes or not. This places a pressure on teachers to emphasize rapidity and manipulation rather than thought processes. The emphasis is shifting to methods that train pupils to think quantitatively as well as to manipulate accurately and rapidly. The accuracy and speed are considered a follow-up to thinking rather than an antecedent.

The subdivisions of mathematics—algebra, geometry, and the like—have been taught in the general education programs as isolated, distinct, specialized subject matter, little related to one another or to the experience of the pupils. Current stress is, therefore, on the development of a unified mathematics field which emphasizes relationships and attempts to make all that is taught meaningful. It has become more important to have the children comprehend basic structures inductively than to have them advance through established, gradated steps, often going on to a new step without mastery of what went before. The emphasis is now being placed on developing an understanding of mathematical concepts through the pupils' own directed discovery, rather than on studying specialized arithmetic, algebra, or geometry. The trend is to strive to have the pupil fully understand those fundamental mathematical concepts that are part of his own living and those that are common to mathematics generally. There is also an increased concern with the child's growth pattern, with his background and his readiness. Teaching conceptual thinking without regard to whether the concept should be labeled "algebra" or "calculus" is a path to progress in teaching mathematics. All children, with adequate instruction, can learn mathematics, and many will

563

CHAPTER 19
*Methods of
Teaching in
America's
Schools*

enjoy it. Meaning, relationships, and processes will serve as a truer guide than emphasis on the so-called fundamentals so necessary to the manipulative tradition.

SOCIAL STUDIES

The social *sciences* are the orderly, systematically arranged bodies of knowledge that deal with various aspects of social living. The social *studies* of the elementary and high school consist of portions of the subject matter of the specialized fields that have been selected and organized for instructional purposes in general education.

Although the content of the social studies is similar to that of the social sciences, the methods of teaching are different because the purpose is different. The subject matter in social studies is simpler, less compartmentalized, and less logically organized. The methods of teaching social studies strive to utilize broader generalized interests of the pupils rather than the specialized interests that may later develop.

One area of life in which the teachers of the social studies seek to promote growth is that of social relationships and understandings. Civil rights, human relations, intercultural and interracial relations, and the like are very lively topics in present-day society. The methods used in teaching subject matter related to topics like these demand considerable skill. Obviously, this area cannot be wholly separated from the language arts. Nor can the social studies assume the whole of the responsibility for achieving growth in social development. They can merely give more emphasis to the problem. The methods of the social studies teacher will be selected to help pupils develop greater maturity in the socialized aspects of their behavior.

The affective factors involved in social development present one of the most difficult problems of method. Teachers and pupils alike have social attitudes, feelings, prejudices, and biases which they bring to school with them. Recognizing deep-seated predispositions among pupils, social studies teachers promote social interaction in the classroom that leads pupils to consider the bases of their opinions, beliefs, and prejudices and to understand and respect differences.

As in science, mathematics, and language arts, the inductive method is used increasingly in social studies instruction. The students discover for themselves answers to such questions as what something is, how it got that way, why it got that way, why it is important, what its current effects are, what its future effects may be. In this inductive method, in structuring the pupils' activities, the teacher may use as a base or goal the development of understandings of a broad social concept, thinking of a concept as a group of meanings that cluster around or belong to a social term. Such a concept might be democracy, nationalism, or rebellion, for example. A range of suggested methods and activities may be given the teacher in a course of study or curriculum outline.

In building a comprehension of a broad social concept, pupils may be directed to seek understandings related to various subconcepts —perhaps mercantilism, for example, as a step in the process of discovering what colonialism is and has been. Sometimes the concepts to be developed in a social studies program are organized in a sequential manner, building consecutively from kindergarten through the junior high school. Sometimes the geographical areas or historical or current events to be utilized in helping the students acquire the conceptual understandings are also suggested in the curriculum or course of study.

Social studies teachers have developed considerable skill in dealing with controversial problems. The technique is one of getting the pupils to understand both sides of a question and to make their

When the members of a small group share in an activity, they not only gain in understanding of the subject matter, but they also gain in the ability to cooperate with others.

565

CHAPTER 19
*Methods of
Teaching in
America's
Schools*

own decisions. This teaches pupils to deal intelligently with controversial aspects of life. The teacher is free to express his bias, but purely as a matter of opinion.

Social studies teachers at all levels of education have many opportunities to use lifelike situations. They make contact with issues in home life, study firsthand the operations of the police, fire, judicial, and other departments of local government, study the safety department programs and school board and municipal elections, participate in school government and other school activities, and hold mock political conventions. Study of such situations is combined with the study of the more formal kinds of subject matter. The two kinds of activities are complementary. Study of the causes of poverty, for example, may lead to a trip to several sections of the city where poverty is most prevalent, to the clubs, community organizations, settlement houses, and the like that work with the poor. Pupils are carefully prepared for the trip in advance through the study of pertinent books and pamphlets and by discussions. After the trip a scheduled follow-up lesson is devoted to reviewing what was learned on the trip, to making conclusions and generalizations, and perhaps to applying the generalizations to other situations or problems.

As mentioned earlier, the problem of developing a logical sequence in the subject matter of the social studies is similar to the problem encountered by the language arts teachers, and the same generalizations apply. There is a trend in the school to integrate the subject matter of social studies and language arts for the purposes of general education. The core program of the junior and senior high schools, which was described in Chapter 15, is an attempt to do this. The student of education will encounter a considerable amount of discussion of this trend in his future courses. The integrated approach, shown by the increased number of schools in which the curriculum includes integrated studies, interdisciplinary team teaching, and core programs, seems likely to continue. The movement now reaches from the first years of the elementary school through college.

FINE ARTS

The purpose of the fine arts is to develop the pupil's sensitivity to, and appreciation of, what creative artists seek to express. The teacher of fine arts seeks to provide an environment appropriate to this end and to cultivate the powers of expression.

We have noted that the logically organized subject matter of mathematics is used in directing pupils to develop their powers to think and express their thoughts quantitatively. In marked contrast, when directing growth in the area of the fine arts, loosely organized, and sometimes unorganized, subject matter is used.

The trend among teachers of the fine arts at all levels of education is to stress direct participation as a means to enlarging the scope of the esthetic experiences of the pupils. Painting, singing, acting, and playing instruments can add a great deal to the pupils' understanding and appreciation of what the arts are about. Listening and observing, too, have their place, but overly emphasized they can dull the pupils' interest in the fine arts. They can have a superficial or even a negative, effect.

While the emphasis in the fine arts is on creativeness and participation, the element of the technical is not omitted. As the children work to improve their acting in the play, or to sing in unison, or to perfect the rendition of instrumental music, they, of course, consider with the teacher the technical problems involved. As they study the technical aspect of the art, however, it is not just to learn more about the art. Always the purpose of technical study is to develop a higher level of expression.

Esthetic responsiveness and expression are closely bound up with emotions. The teacher, therefore, takes into full account the personal nature of responsiveness and expression and their emotional foundation. Respect for personality should be high on the scale of values of the teacher of fine arts, and his methods and the complete learning environment should reflect this at all times. Children will not sing or paint or act if they are ashamed or embarrassed or fearful. Teachers of the fine arts, themselves conscious of the values that lie in the arts, tend to demonstrate what teaching is like when teaching is viewed as an art. They follow their own, perhaps untraditional, methods in creating conditions most productive of the kind of pupil growth they seek to achieve.

When teachers of other subjects imply that fine arts is a somewhat inferior or unnecessary field of study, it is usually because they do not understand the purposes of the teachers of fine arts. Persistent

567

CHAPTER 19
*Methods of
Teaching in
America's
Schools*

traditions associated with other fields of teaching tend to set fine arts apart. For example, if a teacher of fine arts attempted to give pupils numerical or letter grades in music or art appreciation, not only would he find it impossible to evaluate a child's appreciation of music or of art, but he would damage the climate for advancing such appreciation by introducing competitiveness, desire to please the teacher, anxiety, and other undesirable attitudes. The moment a teacher of fine arts attempts to emulate the evaluation techniques of, say, the mathematics teacher, his effectiveness in achieving growth in fine arts starts to wane. Creativeness, free expression, and appreciation of the beautiful flourish only in a sympathetic atmosphere.

Summary

At all levels of education there is an increasing concern for improvement in the methods of effectively directing subject matter to desired ends. As Skinner points out, ". . . human behavior is far too complex to be left to casual experience. . . ." In line with the overview purpose of this book, the over-all trends in both general teaching methods and methods in specific fields are explored. Trends in teaching language arts, science, mathematics, social studies, and fine arts are given extended treatment because they are studied by all pupils—that is, they are the subjects that together ordinarily constitute the bases for general education.

The great breadth in teaching methods is caused in part by the complexity of the human organism and in part by the range in materials included in each subject field. Wherever possible, however, the inductive method of teaching is favored. It is believed that a pupil will attain better understandings if learning situations are arranged so that the facts, principles, structures of the subjects studied are discovered through his own activities. It is believed that, if there is a general method applicable to teaching in all subject-matter fields, the inductive method comes closest to meeting the requirements. Nevertheless when used in specific fields, its applicability has to be decided in terms of each new unit of subject matter. Perhaps teachers can err by placing too much emphasis on any one teaching method, either deductive or inductive. Both have their places.

Questions

1. What are some of the dangers in separating method from subject matter for purposes of analysis?
2. What purpose is served by an acquaintance with several methods of teaching in a given field?
3. Why is a teacher more likely to be effective with his teaching methods if he knows the subject matter well?
4. What is remedial instruction? When should it be used?
5. What is meant by the inductive method of teaching?

Projects

1. Analyze a recent publication of a subject-matter professional organization such as the National Council of Teachers of Mathematics or the National Council of Teachers of English. List the suggestions made on methods of teaching. State your conclusions as to what experienced teachers think is of greatest significance.
2. Set forth what preparation is necessary for teachers who are to engage in team teaching.
3. Explain what obstacles are encountered in any attempt to individualize instruction completely.

Related to subject matter and methods of teaching are instructional aids, aids that help the teacher achieve the aims he has set up for the lesson or the unit of study. There has been a great increase in the variety and refinement of instructional aids in recent years. Some people predict that even the chalk board, oldest of the instructional aids, may disappear from the classrooms of the future, to be replaced by the perhaps more effective overhead projector.

Certainly instructional aids help to bring teaching more closely in line with factors that psychologists say encourage effective learning, help instruction to capitalize on factors of attention and reinforcements to learning, and also help make possible a fuller recognition of wide divergencies in learning rates. Instructional aids, teacher and pupils alike agree, tend to make both teaching and learning more interesting. Every year shows an increase in their popularity, in confidence in their effectiveness.

The kinds of teaching aids available are very numerous. One college textbook devoted 500 printed pages to describing audiovisual aids. Several manufacturing companies list hundreds of such usable items as long-playing records, filmstrips, tape recordings, and models. One company alone lists, for example, 52 long-playing records that reproduce Shakespearean plays as recorded by the most famous Shakespearean actors. Another company specializes in making records for the elementary schools that reconstruct history through dramatizations of such themes as Riding the Pony Express, the California Gold Rush, and the building of the first transcontinental railroad. Each year more than 6,500 sound-motion pictures are produced and

Instructional aids range from those that have long been standard equipment to the latest electronic devices. Laboratories have been included in schools for years, though they are now used for teaching many subjects to all ages of children. The equipment is increasingly expensive because it has become increasingly specialized. The teaching aid console at right also is expensive. Such machines are so new that they have been tested in only a few schools so far. The variety of their equipment and their mobility make them adaptable to many different kinds of teaching.

adapted by several manufacturing companies for use in every grade and in almost every subject-matter field. Perhaps this stress on variety and quantity in instructional aids stems from a heightened recognition of the part played in effective learning by the senses, from an increasing knowledge of how perceptions are formed and of how perception and thought are related. The accepted assumption—that mental images result from sensations—reinforces the belief that variety in the stimulation of the senses in the classroom greatly enriches learning, and hence contributes to more reliable and mature thinking.

When the teacher makes his selection and decides on the use of instructional aids he is guided by the same consideration of definite and worthy purpose which guides in all other decisions related to the stimulation and direction of learning. Some aids are designed to serve but a single purpose; a slide rule is used for computation; a lifelike model of the human heart is used to explain the design and physiological functioning of the heart. An overhead projector, on the other hand, is an instructional aid adaptable to many purposes. The discussion of instructional aids in this chapter is intended to acquaint the student with some that teachers use, to give an overview. For obvious reasons, the purposes that guide teachers in the selection and use of aids are omitted.

Books and periodicals

The well-prepared teacher uses textbooks and workbooks as valuable aids to his teaching. He does not make the mistake of thinking that within the pages of the textbook he will find subject matter complete. He will not use the textbook and workbook as substitutes for his own knowledge or resourcefulness, but will, instead, use the textbook as a supplement, a guide, and a source of suggestions. In addition, the teacher does not restrict himself to one textbook but selects one or more books, perhaps books geared to different reading abilities, as basic texts and several others for the classroom reference shelf. The pupils use the basic textbook for study and the others as supplementary reading materials.

Paperbacks are taking an increasingly important place on the classroom list of reading materials. Their colorful covers make an appeal to young readers, especially if they can be displayed on the kind of wire revolving rack that the salesmen have found so appealing in the corner drugstore. Paperbacks are relatively inexpensive and are an effective answer to the problem of prohibitive costs in making a wide range of reading materials available. As Daniel Fader has pointed out in a report on his work with delinquent youth, the paperback appeals to young people who have had only unpleasant experiences with the hardcover textbook or library books displayed on a shelf with only the dull title on the spine showing.[1] It is sometimes good to have a book that fits well into a hip pocket to be taken out for reading at any time. The tremendous range of titles in paperback provides the teacher with ample choice and the opportunity to appeal to the interests of the

[1] Daniel Fader and Elton B. McNeil, *Hooked on Books*. New York: Berkley Publishing Company, 1968.

*I*t has been said that with the exception of the Bible no books had more
influence over the lives of early Americans than McGuffey's readers and
spellers. These books, begun in 1836, were revised many times, and the last
copyright was issued in 1901. It is said that the sales of the books totaled
over 100 million copies.

The Reverend William Holmes McGuffey (1800–1873), who edited the
books, was a Presbyterian minister and a professor at Miami University in
Ohio. McGuffey grew up with the frontier. He was born near the western
edge of Pennsylvania and moved with his family to Ohio.

McGuffey believed that the child should be taught to read from the start and
should not begin with spelling, as had been customary. He used many
illustrations and adapted the material to the level of the pupils. He
emphasized correct pronunciation and the precise use of words in everyday
speech.

His stories combined experiences of the frontiersmen with traditional types
of stories for children in a way that appealed to the entire frontier
population. From the standpoint of education, the new West was a simple
country. There were few books, but there was a zeal for a kind of education
that combined learning to read with learning the dominant cherished virtues
—thrift, hard work, morality, temperance, and religion. Many of the stories
McGuffey included in his books were so told that they unmistakably
emphasized a moral or extolled a virtue.

> *"If you find your task is hard,*
> *Try, try again ;*
> *Time will bring you your reward ;*
> *Try, try again."*

Since McGuffey's books were the principal reading material for the average
American of the time, the extent of McGuffey's influence on reading tastes,
points of view, common standards of conduct, morals, propriety, and
attitudes can well be imagined. His influence persisted for a long time and
extended to many facets of everyday life.

pupils as well as to reach their individual ability and to further the
aims of the course.

Newspapers and magazines are also a valuable aid to the classroom
shelf. In some cases they are used as a core and lessons are prepared

around them. Often they are supplementary, used for class work or for individual and committee work. Some of the city newspapers have "education editions" which contain material especially adapted to the classroom.

Frequently classes use a periodical prepared for boys and girls in school, perhaps *Junior Scholastic* in the upper elementary and junior high grades. Such a magazine has interesting material on current affairs, history, geography, arithmetic, social living, and science, together with easy-to-take exercises in reading, grammar, and vocabulary building.

How are textbooks selected? In approximately half of the states the local school district has jurisdiction over textbook selection. Usually a committee made up of teachers, supervisors, and administrators selects one or more books in a field or level. Unfortunately, under this plan there is no uniformity of textbooks, so that children who move from one district to another may be handicapped because they have become used to different books. In the remaining half of the states, statutes require uniform textbooks throughout the state. In some of these states the state department or an authorized committee selects several books or series of books for each subject, leaving the final choice from among these to the local district.

To aid in selecting textbooks, committees frequently use a check list containing such items as authorship, date of publication, content, vocabulary, organization, suggested pupil activities, recommended teaching aids, illustrative material, format, and durability. No matter how high a particular book may rate on all the check list items, however, the most important deciding factor will be how well it will contribute to the needs of the pupils who will use it. (As we have noted, it is in connection with adopting textbooks that pressure groups frequently try to use their influence to determine what students will or will not read and study.)

The textbooks today are far superior to those used even 50 years ago. In early America the hornbook, a paddle-shaped contrivance which hung from the pupil's neck, usually contained the Lord's Prayer and the alphabet. *The New England Primer* is an example of the small, morally slanted, compact textbook also used in colonial days. McGuffey's *Eclectic Readers* emphasized the Bible and morals by means of interesting stories. Until relatively recently, geography textbooks described countries merely by listing their boundaries, principal cities, rivers, mountains, and products; and history textbooks focused on dates, battles, and strictly political events without much attention to their implications.

The author of today's textbook determines content through experiment based on knowledge of child psychology. He attempts, as nearly as the pages of his book will permit, to enter the classroom and assist in the instruction. As with other teaching activities, the author sets up his goals and then draws upon his knowledge and experience as a teacher to meet the goals. The better present-day textbook is proficiently written, attractive, usable, and long-wearing. The improvement in appearance, format, durability, and illustrations has come about through research and advancement in publishing generally. The modern textbook is an invitation to learning.

Library and library materials

The typical elementary and secondary school has a central library within its own building, often one of the most inviting places in the building. In larger schools the school library is administered by a trained teacher-librarian; in smaller schools a classroom teacher doubles as school librarian. The resources housed in the library for both pupils and teachers vary with the policies of administration. In some the resource materials are limited to books and graphic materials, while in others they include teaching aids such as films and records.

In general, school libraries are administered by trained individuals who fulfill a coordinating function and serve teachers and pupils in many ways. Supplementary materials flow from library to classroom and back again. Pupils use the libarary for round-table discussions, group study, individual reading, research, and study, and as a place to learn to locate and use such resource materials as indexes, reference books, bibliographies, catalogs, encyclopedias. Pupils have the opportunity to browse among many books. They are guided and encouraged to choose books in harmony with their individual interests and abilities.

Administrators, teachers, and librarians cooperate to make the library a rich center for many kinds of resources and educational activities. Wisely coordinated, the library and the teacher-librarian are indispensable adjuncts, one might say handmaidens, to effective classroom teaching, vital in wisely planned programs of every classroom.

Audiovisual materials

The human organism constructs images that are a consequence of seeing and hearing. Since the nature of one's perceptions is closely related to one's ability to think, learning from a wise use of audiovisual materials in the classroom may be of paramount importance to effective teaching. From the images constructed by the pupils upon being exposed to wisely selected audiovisual material, understandings of the true nature of external objects and of spatial, social, and temporal relationships are expanded. Furthermore, the learning so acquired tends to be vivid and lasting. Perceptions resulting from effective audiovisual experiences are integrated by the human organism through some process the nature of which as yet is unknown. It is by some such reasoning as this that the wide use of audiovisual materials in American education has been justified.

In recent years, and particularly in the elementary schools, serious attention has been given to encouraging good habits of listening. Besides being an effective learning experience in general, good listening is precedent to effective speech. Skill in communication is considered closely related to habits of listening. Many audiovisual aids are so designed as to utilize to the fullest the advantages of good listening.[2] The Shakespearean records and the recorded dramatized historical incidents mentioned earlier, for instance, are excellent examples of a kind of device that promotes understandings and appreciations while also encouraging the habits of good listening.

The following cursory overview of some kinds of audiovisual aids that are frequently used by classroom teachers gives an idea of the great variety and educational potential of these aids. Teachers, guided by the purposes they have in mind, of course, use discrimination in selection of particular devices.

It has been suggested that the minimum equipment for each

[2] See the section on listening on p. 556.

classroom include dark shades, permanent screen, tape recorder, overhead projector, maps, and a globe. If the audiovisual aids are not easily accessible, teachers just do not have the time to round them up

FILMS AND FILMSTRIPS

Four types of projection machines are at present used effectively in the classroom. The *opaque projector* needs no special material for projection, but will reflect on a screen the image of any picture, printed page, or flat object of suitable size. It is used successfully in projecting pictures of which there is only one copy and in projecting pages of pupils' written work for discussion and criticism by a whole class. To make maps or drawings, students may project the map or picture on a tag board, follow the outline with a felt pen, and later add details or colors.

Because the *overhead projector* has the special advantage of being used at the front of the room by a teacher who is facing the class, it has proved useful at practically all grade levels and in all subject areas. This type projects materials prepared on transparencies by the teacher, the pupils, or commercially. The teacher can mark or write on the transparency while it is being projected, and this action will show on the screen behind him. Maps used in this way are very effective.

The *16-mm film projector* is widely used, and a large number of excellent sound films are available for use in all areas of the curriculum. Some of the films provide background or introduction, some add to appreciation or understanding. Many films are prepared for use in helping young people solve problems of getting along in school and in life, touching on such matters as study habits, personality, friendships, part-time jobs, and dating. Usually when a film is used in the classroom, some preparation should be made in advance, although some of the films, those related to personal and social problems, for instance, require little preparation because the motivation and introduction are included in them. Better films lead to discussion, criticism, and evaluation of their contribution by the class immediately after they have been seen.

Many large commercial organizations, such as Bell Telephone, Ford Motor, or American Oil, produce excellent educational films, sometimes as an outgrowth of a television program, and supply these without charge to schools as a part of their public relations programs.

At present most schools have available sound-motion equipment. In larger schools usually a teacher or a teacher-librarian or one who specializes in the use of sound-motion pictures serves as coordinator. Coordination is necessary partly because films and projectors are so expensive that their maintenance and use must be systematically provided for, and partly because it is wise to have someone in the school who knows what films are available and takes the responsibility for scheduling previews, obtaining the films, and returning them. For all teachers to know how to use such equipment as the movie film projector is highly desirable. Selected students in each class are often trained to be the "operators."

The *filmstrip projector* has largely replaced the simple slide projector although the instruments commonly used for filmstrips can also be used for slides. The filmstrip contains 25 to 100 "frames," or still pictures, which are projected on a screen in sequence by manual operation of the projector. Some filmstrips are accompanied by tapes or records containing commentary on each frame. A great many filmstrips, both single and in series, are available. They are especially helpful with material that the class needs to have time to discuss as the projection proceeds. Filmstrips are less expensive than regular movie films, so a library of filmstrips related to the curriculum will often be assembled in the school and be readily available at any time. A color slide is like one frame in the filmstrip. Such slides may be prepared by the teacher or purchased from commercial outlets. An entire biology class may, for instance, use a color slide to see in a greatly enlarged picture what each could see under an individual microscope, and the teacher can call attention to the parts that are especially significant. In the geography class a three-dimensional color slide may show a stereoscopic, lifelike view of an entire mountain scene and focus the attention of the students on such features as the terracing of farms on the mountainsides. (Also, both filmstrips and slides may be used individually by means of small portable viewers.)

RECORDINGS

The use of records has become an important part of teaching in recent years. In the language arts classroom, records serve as aids to understanding and appreciation, as enrichment, as supplementary material. Listening to literature read by professionals has proved valuable. In the music classes, by means of records students hear great works performed by outstanding artists. Dramatic readings of important episodes in history, a presentation of the music of a particular period, are the kinds of recording that bring color and a feeling of realness to the pages of the social studies textbook. Records are frequently used in the classroom, but they are also used for independent study, extra credit, or small group activities. Records, like the film-strips, are often a part of the library collection in the school. Sometimes the producers of the records supply text or workbook materials which the students may follow along with the sound.

The resourceful teacher will also find many uses for the tape recorder. Oral presentations of students may be recorded and later played back for student and teacher criticism. A panel discussion recorded in one class may be played in other classes. An address by a guest speaker in one class may be recorded and played to other classes. The teacher may record material that he wishes to use in several classes. The tape recorder may be stopped at any time for oral discussion or comment.

Many teachers feel that listening skills can be greatly improved through the use of the tape recorder. Students are asked to listen to recorded materials with a specific purpose in mind—listening for the main ideas, listening for supporting details, listening for "loaded" words, and the like.

From outside the classroom the sources of materials for tape recordings are unlimited. The best in radio and television programs can be brought into the classroom by means of the tape recorder. Public addresses and other performances of talented people of the community may be recorded for classroom use.

At present the greatest number of prepared tapes is related to social studies and language arts. There are, however, tape recordings that make the new mathematics meaningful even to young pupils, their parents, or teachers of other subjects who may wish to know what the subject is about. Some state universities maintain lending libraries of tape recordings to encourage the use of tape recorders in the classroom. They issue catalogs of available recordings that include valuable hints on how teachers can profitably use the recordings. The National Education Association, especially, has an extensive

An almost incredible number of instructional aids is now available —and more are constantly planned. Some are widely used; others are largely untried; still others are experimental. A teacher facing his class uses an overhead projector. A child learns from a very sophisticated teaching machine that combines programed learning and a computer; many educators think such machines may be the way to completely individualize instruction in at least some parts of some subjects. A boy experiments with a filmstrip projector. An expert teacher presents a mathematics lesson over closed-circuit television. In this case, the lesson is received by several schools in an inner-city area. The typical language laboratory has sound-absorbing partitions between the carrels. Computers like the two shown are not likely to be standard equipment in schools for some time. Their potential uses, however, are many—especially in mathematics. For instance, pupils can learn the binary system, programing languages, and computer technology itself. An aid that has become familiar is the simple type of commercial teaching machine shown.

The student answers a question in the space at right, then moves the slide to compare his answer with the correct one. Turning the knob reveals the next question.

tape-recording library located in the Audio-Visual Division of the University of Colorado. The great encouragement received by classroom teachers from agencies such as the NEA and the state universities attests to the confidence those agencies have in the educational values of tape recorders.

TELEVISION

For some years now, the classroom teaching uses and potential uses of television have been explored and discussed. The actual use of TV in schools indicates that though it can improve the effectiveness of classroom teaching in all subject-matter fields, the most valuable results so far have been achieved in social studies, mathematics, and science. Extensive experimentation is now being carried out to discover the most advantageous ways of using the new medium.

Teachers utilize television in a number of ways, but the most common procedure is to tell pupils, sometimes by means of a bulletin board, about programs they wish them to see. Since programs are announced a week in advance, any teacher has at hand a listing of a great many programs, some of which are likely to include the kind of material he wants the pupils to see. When commercial programs are of special interest to schools, the sponsors make available carefully prepared printed materials that can be placed on the bulletin board. Often, after a TV projection of an educational program, the material will be available on film for teacher use on a movie projector in the school.

Educational television, both open circuit and closed circuit, is an aid to direct classroom instruction. Open-circuit television refers to programs that originate outside the school system. These offer "front-row seats" to televised lessons by well-known professionals. Closed-circuit television has become an important adjunct in schools that can afford to install it. Here master teachers within the school broadcast to large audiences of students by means of receiving screens in various classrooms. The professional lecturer and the master teacher form "teams" with the regular classroom instructors. Lessons received either by open-circuit or closed-circuit television may be preserved on video tape and scheduled for use in the classroom at any appropriate time.

Televised lessons are organized in some places—in Chicago, for instance—in a so-called "cluster plan." The closed-circuit televised lessons are designed and taught by superior teachers in the Chicago public schools and are televised daily into the classrooms of approximately 30,000 children through the cluster plan, which links a studio school in a circuit with four or more adjacent schools by means of a coaxial cable. Televised teaching in five such clusters in Chicago located in areas of cultural disadvantage adapts the curriculum to the specific educational needs of the children in each cluster. In the cluster plan, all television teachers are also classroom teachers. Since the cluster links neighboring schools together, the teachers have a real understanding of the educational needs of the children to whom the lessons are telecast.

Experimentation with television as a medium of classroom instruction continues throughout the country. At present the trend is for the schools to obtain from both commercial and educational television stations special tapes or recordings that can be transmitted on the school's own closed-circuit equipment in any desired way or at any time. The effectiveness of television instruction, however, has not yet been adequately assessed, either from the educational or the relative cost standpoint. All that can be said with certainty is that it is a live innovation that will receive increasing emphasis.

THE LANGUAGE LABORATORY

The language laboratory now found in many high schools is an instructional aid to foreign-language teachers who stress building conversational skills. The equipment in the language laboratory enables pupils to listen to the spoken word and to repeat it in return and then listen again to their own pronunciation, thus comparing their own speech with that of the native.

It is general procedure to have the lessons taped and for all the pupils to listen to the same materials through individually provided earphones. The teacher also can join in with explanations. Each pupil may imitate what he has heard and have his own voice recorded. He may then play his version back, judge his response, then repeat the procedure until he is satisfied. As the reader probably knows, tapes can easily be erased and used over again many times. The language laboratory permits each pupil to proceed on his own and to practice building conversational skills in accordance with his own needs.

PICTURES AND CHARTS

For centuries flat pictures have been the means of effectively conveying a message, expressing an idea, portraying an event, reproducing the historical likenesses of persons and scenes. Pictographs in ancient caves and the large circulation of modern pictorial magazines attest to the everlasting appeal of flat pictures. Quite naturally, classroom teachers utilize all the advantages of their universal appeal.

Usually teachers in subject-matter areas like geography, social studies, history, literature, and science have a continuous but changing display of appropriate pictures in the classroom. Many such pictures are attractive, accurate as to detail, and instructionally sound. The pupils know what Ann Hathaway's cottage or the Wright brothers' airplane looks like, and the same holds true of many historical figures and places and scenes in the world. The effective use of color in modern photography adds to the vividness of the pictures. In addition to real pictures, there is a vast array of pictures that are wholly imaginative. An ancient battle, the sorrows of a displaced people, illustrations of literary themes are often shown in artists' imaginative drawings.

Some of the publishers make available to teachers charts that are excellent teaching aids. Such charts show, for instance, historical time lines for world history, how to use the dictionary, the evolution of the English language. Charts related to various aspects of science are on the market and tend to be valuable instructional aids. Book jackets make a colorful and stimulating bulletin board. Unfortunately, many other types of free material have been discontinued either temporarily or permanently because of higher operating expenses and postal rates.

An effective bulletin board display should be planned with and by the students. In fact, the best bulletin board display exhibits the students' own work—their writing, drawing, charting, painting.

MAPS AND GLOBES

Maps and globes are a part of the everyday equipment of the classrooms in America's elementary schools and in many classrooms in high schools. The maps and globes are made in attractive, contrasting colors to show areas of the earth or, in the case of globes, the whole earth itself. They are constructed so as to be readily accessible for classroom use, and are attractive and easy to read. They are accurately drawn to scale and can conveniently be used for such activities as locating places, measuring distances, computing areas, tracing great-circle air routes, ocean currents, and wind systems, or showing the number and position of heavenly bodies or the division of the country in the Civil War.

Often maps and globes are so constructed that they may be marked on with water-soluble felt pens and easily washed off. Manufacturers of school maps and globes recognize the principle of readiness through gradation of their product in detail and complexity. They make materials for younger children that show fewer details and acquaint the child with only basic map symbols. For older pupils all standard map symbols are used for details like elevation, rivers, falls, cities, railways. Often small desk globes give the pupil a chance to handle the globe individually, to experiment, explore, and follow directions on his own. Wall maps may be printed with few details and supplemented by transparent overlays which add the kind of details the teacher desires—population ,resources, battlefields, or something else.

The art of map making for educational purposes has been highly developed by a number of manufacturers who combine their know-how in the manufacture of maps with the knowledge and skill of professional cartographers and educational specialists. Through cooperative efforts a great variety of maps is available to serve in such special subject-matter areas as history, economics, and literature, as well as almost any particular branch of geography from world climate to geological evolution.

MODELS

Models, among the oldest of instructional aids, are still considered by teachers to be among the most helpful. Models appeal to all ages; children have played with them from infancy in the form of toys; adults flock to view and manipulate them in museums of science and industry, where they are used on an elaborate scale to elucidate a wide range of subjects. The gyroscope and pendulum, for instance, reveal the rotation of the earth.

Models are designed for use in elementary and secondary schools to aid in teaching in almost every subject-matter field and to serve a wide variety of purposes. True models are manufactured on an accurate scale and usually are three-dimensional representations of some principle, fact, or idea. An exact replica, for example, of an automobile or of any of its working parts is available to the high school teacher of auto mechanics to make clear his explanations or the explanations given in the text. A model may illustrate how the human heart functions or how the blood circulates in the body. With a skillfully designed model a pupil virtually "sees" the explanations.

Manufacturers often use true models (including full-sized mockups) to make clearer certain kinds of explanations. Sometimes they make models that utilize intentional exaggerations, as, for example, in size, color, or transparency. Thus, in the Chicago Museum of Science and Industry a viewer can stand inside a modified model of the human heart and study each working part at leisure. Another kind of modified model, the best examples of which are in museums, is the diorama. It consists of a combination of figures, background pictures, actual specimens, and symbolic materials, which, with the ingenious use of direct and indirect lighting, make a scene appear almost real.

In larger cities classroom teachers may supplement their own use of models with field trips to museums where skilled lecturers instruct the pupils on a great variety of subjects.

Models available in the schools usually are readily accessible, easily assembled and disassembled, and therefore conveniently adaptable to any logical teaching plan.

TACHISTOSCOPE

The tachistoscope is a device for projecting words, phrases, sentences, number combinations, formulas, and the like for short durations—as low as one-hundredth of a second. The image is either reproduced on a small viewing screen or flashed as a lantern slide on a larger screen. The viewer is warned when the shutter is about to be tripped; he looks at the screen and then reproduces what he has seen. As a rule, the device is used for remedial work, to speed up the reading of slow readers or to increase the rate and accuracy of computational skills.

Programed learning

Programed learning is a different kind of instructional aid. Learning is achieved by using subject-matter materials that permit an individual pupil to study efficiently without the continuous help of a teacher and independent of membership in a study group. To enable a pupil to learn independently, the subject matter to be learned is broken up into a series of small, psychologically related segments that are logically arranged in steps. With the aid of a teaching device, such as those described in the following pages of this chapter, a pupil proceeds independently, at his own rate, through each of the steps.

Since in programed learning the pupil learns at a rate commensurate with his ability, individual differences in learning rates are fully recognized, even though, theoretically, all pupils will eventually achieve at least a minimum standard of mastery. Programed learning is more satisfying to the pupil than learning through traditional processes because the results are immediately known to him. Since the programed learning activity is an individual one, a pupil who learns slowly does not feel the sting of competitive comparisons that make him feel inferior. Finally, programed learning utilizes the advantages of motivation. As one psychologist says:

> Human behavior is remarkably influenced by small results. Describing something with the right word is often reinforcing. Other simple reinforcers are to be found in the clarification of a puzzlement or simply in moving forward after completing one stage of activity.[3]

The proponents of programed learning in America's schools —a rapidly growing number—believe that it is an important step to correcting past omissions. Why, say the educational psychologists, do schools put forth such prodigious efforts to gain understandings of pupils, to discover their more urgent needs, and then give so little attention to their individual needs? Why should teachers learn about the psychological bases of education and then teach as though such bases did not really exist? If these omissions have been due to the lack

[3] B. F. Skinner, "Teaching Machines," *Scientific American*, 205 (No. 5): 97, November, 1961.

of a practical method, then, it is contended, programed learning will contribute to eliminating that lack.

Two difficult problems in programed learning are related to, first, selecting the kinds of material that can best be taught by this method, and second, arranging these materials into a series of steps that are reasonable and are psychologically related. Obviously, not all kinds of subject matter can be taught by the programed method. The selection must be carefully made. It is only by actual experiment with pupils that the soundness of the steps in a program can be evaluated. Many attempts are now being made in America's schools to select suitable subject matter and to program it. Although the method is relatively new, the results have been most promising.

Once the difficult tasks of programing are completed—the materials are selected and the logical steps for learning devised—the question remains: How shall the materials be presented to the pupil?[4] Three means of automated instruction are the programed textbook, the teaching machine, and the electronic learning laboratory.

PROGRAMED TEXTBOOKS

The programed textbook is an incomplete textbook that the pupil completes by filling in key sentences, words, or numbers in so-called "frames." He checks his own answers by comparing them with the correct answers given elsewhere in the book, usually on the succeeding page, where he also finds his next frame. Many attempts are being made currently in universities and in lower schools to produce improved automated textbooks. This calls for extensive tryouts of the materials and careful study of the results to refine the materials and improve the sequence.

A number of programed textbooks have been published for use in the schools. The books cover a wide range of subjects. Each presents the basic skills and information to be learned and allows each pupil to proceed at his own rate, evaluate his own progress, and correct his own weaknesses.

[4] See, for example, the explanation of difficulties encountered by an astute book editor in "An Adventure in Programing Literature," *The English Journal*, 52 (No. 9): 659–673, December, 1963.

TEACHING MACHINES

With teaching machines, instead of marking an answer in a frame
in a book, a pupil responds to the programed subject matter by making
the response on a machine that indicates immediately whether he has
chosen the correct answer. He cannot proceed to the next step until
a correct response is registered to the current one. A right response
is always a prerequisite to the next task. Like the programed textbook,
the value of teaching machines depends upon the skill in selecting the
subject matter and in arranging it in a logical series of steps. Like
experiments with programed textbooks, experiments with teaching
machines are being conducted in many schools, and there is considerable confidence that many kinds of learning can be achieved through
their proper use. In fact, numerous manufacturing concerns have
planned ambitious expansions and are building newer and better
teaching machines.

Research has given us no detailed information about the interactions of students with teaching machines and with their content
materials. As we have pointed out in connection with any kind of
programed learning, the practical value depends on the effectiveness
of content materials. At present, only a few instructional programs
have been adequately developed through a series of empirical trials
and revisions. Most of the well-developed programs today are short
sequences prepared for research purposes. Also, we do not have verified information about the effect of individualized instruction on children of varying abilities. For instance, a very bright child may be as
far along in his studies as another child several years older; the
student's scholastic peer group may thus be quite different from his
social peer group. Is it possible that the sociological and psychological effects could be harmful to the students?

ELECTRONIC LEARNING LABORATORIES

The electronic learning laboratory is an exciting innovation in
programed learning. The learning laboratory is a kind of wired classroom. Usually 30 or more students are seated in booths, each containing a tape recorder, earphones, a microphone, and master tapes. The
students can play and respond to master-tape lessons in English—such

areas as grammar, phonetics, vocabulary, remedial speech—and in foreign languages. From a master console, the teacher can direct the tape or hold a two-way conversation with one student or talk to all the students. In this technique the teacher is not replaced by machines; his capabilities are multiplied, and individual differences are handled adroitly.

Computers

It is easy to appreciate the potential of the computer in teaching high school mathematics students something about programing and computer operation and use, as well as in preparing them to use the device in more advanced mathematics work. The computer also has potentials in other areas of education, but many of these are highly technical, and many others require more research before they will become generally applicable. Computers can definitely be helpful in connection with more general school functions, such as counseling, relating census to budget, and distributing teacher loads.

The expense involved in installing computers has prevented their widespread use. For this reason and because the machines are constantly being changed and improved, even when they are used in the classroom or administrative office, they are often rented, rather than purchased. In the final analysis, present trends indicate that the cost of computers will decrease as their practical educational functions increase; thus their use is likely to become quite general within the next few years.

Resource center

As a facility particularly important for independent study as a part of team teaching, many schools are placing increasing importance on an area known variously as a resource center, an instructional materials center, a learning center, or something else. The center is usually located near the library and is, in a way, an extension of the library except that, in addition to the facilities of a regular library, the resource center also provides equipment for a kind of laboratory experience—individual work spaces and areas for individual and group activity.

The resource center contains books, magazines, pamphlets, pictures, maps, films, filmstrips, recordings, tapes, slides—all the learning aids and reference materials the school owns. Those items not located in the resource center are catalogued, and their school location is indicated.

The center is typically divided into three sections: a section provided with carrels for quiet reading, study, pursuing programed lessons; a section equipped for the use of various audiovisual materials and such aids as typewriters and office machines; a section for pupil-teacher or small-group discussion and conference. A specially trained personnel member is in charge of the resource center, and often he is assisted by paraprofessionals and other aides.

Pupils ordinarily go to the resource center to pursue independent study, sometimes for small-group study, in terms of their individual needs or special interests. As independent study is increasingly emphasized, the use of the resource center will likewise be increased. In time standard equipment will probably include carrels equipped with individual television screens; earphones and facilities for dialing for video-tape presentations and demonstrations; a signal device for notifying teachers when assistance is needed; tapes of lectures, lessons, speeches.

Aids requiring organizational modifications

Ability grouping, team teaching, and providing opportunity rooms are also ways of making instructional aids available to teachers. These differ from audiovisual aids and programed teaching in part because they require organizational modifications.

ABILITY GROUPING

The prevailing pattern of grouping children in America's schools is by age-grade. Ordinarily, children enter the kindergarten at age 5, then advance together from grade to grade, graduating from the high school at about 18 years of age. Ability grouping refers to classifying and regrouping pupils of a given age-grade for teaching purposes. This is usually done more or less in terms of ability to learn, in terms of relative intelligence.

Ability grouping in the lower grades is usually three, four, or five groups within one classroom. These groups may work at different rates on reading, spelling, and mathematics. The teacher works with one group while the others proceed with their individual activities. In the intermediate grades practices may vary from school to school and from subject to subject within the same school. For instance, classification and grouping may be used in mathematics and science but not in social studies or English.

For classification purposes within a grade level, intelligence scores are usually used for younger pupils. Achievement test scores, together with earlier measures of intelligence, are generally the bases for classifying older pupils, those above elementary school age.

No set pattern has been followed in the high schools in ability grouping. In some large high schools pupils who rank high on achievement tests are assigned to advanced placement. For them the subject matter studied is more advanced and the rate of progress is stepped up. College-level subject matter may be studied and college credit given for work in the last two years of high school. A second-level group may consist of the moderately gifted, who are assigned to courses, perhaps called "honor" courses, which are also advanced, both in subject matter studied and in rate of progress, but less so than the advanced-placement classes. The third level, which may comprise as many as two-thirds of the pupils of a given grade in high school, is more conventional in curriculum and methods of teaching. The lowest group is the smallest, and for this group the studies are largely limited to basic skills and vocational subjects.

It appears that, in general, the American people look with favor upon ability grouping in the schools when it is done to meet the educational needs of pupils at the extremes—those at very high ability levels and those at very low ability levels. The attitude toward the practice for pupils between these extremes is not clear. Some teachers say they find that ability grouping makes teaching easier and more challenging, and that it enables them to depart from the practice of teaching all the pupils the same kind of subject matter and of judging them by the same standards. At the same time, teachers generally recognize that the practice has unmistakable disadvantages, which, up to the present, schools have been unable to eliminate. In larger high schools, teachers and administrators have generally believed that ability grouping encourages a higher degree of achievement; in these schools, therefore, the practice has largely been taken for granted. Currently, however, community groups are challenging ability grouping, and in some high schools the number of different graduated groups has, because of this, been reduced.

Up to now research has not provided evidence that ability grouping, in general, is educationally more productive than heterogeneous grouping. Certain questions remain unanswered. What are the effects of the practice on the social attitudes of the pupils? of their parents? Will those labeled inferior have such a poor self-image that they are defeated to start with? Will they come to dislike those who are considered by school officials to be superior, to hate school, to build up a personal kind of protection against teachers? Will those labeled superior become smug? How do parents feel about having their children labeled slow learners, or fast learners? Might the lowest group consist mainly of children from disadvantaged homes who feel they are being degraded by the school? Are the criteria used in labeling the students infallible? Will teachers lessen their efforts to adapt subject matter and methods of teaching to the needs of individual pupils in an ability group? Is such a group really homogeneous? Will every group have some learners who, relatively, are slow learners? These are only a few of the many difficult questions related to ability grouping to which we do not at present have sound answers based on research. Questions of this kind need to be answered in any evaluation of ability grouping as an instructional aid. Perhaps the only valid conclusion we can draw from America's long experience with ability grouping is that it has been proved to have a number of worthwhile advantages but has not come even close to being the final answer to the problem of recognizing individual differences. The schools continue to experiment with and search for other answers to the problem.

TEAM TEACHING

Team teaching is a currently popular instructional aid that, at least in some forms, calls for somewhat basic organizational and

Each of the teachers in this cooperative team is efficiently performing a different function. Much planning has preceded this particular classroom meeting. The team approach is an example of the changes in classroom teaching that are enabling teachers to come ever closer to the ideal—understanding their pupils as individuals, recognizing their individual differences, meeting their individual needs.

structural modifications. Some features of team teaching are not entirely new; we have had some of them in some form to a greater or lesser degree for a long time. Now, however, under a team teaching organization, sharing of teacher resources by allowing teachers to specialize in fulfilling responsibilities in terms of talent and interest, cooperative planning, and flexible grouping are not a casual part of interteacher relations; they are definitely and specifically provided for, and their continuity is guaranteed.

Within these rather general characteristics of team teaching there are many differences about exactly what team teaching is and how it should operate. In the universities a general plan of team teaching has been followed for some time. There it has meant having a number of teachers, each with a different but related specialty, teach certain broad, basic or overview courses as a team. In some cases a similar kind of organization is followed in team teaching in the junior and senior high schools. Another plan is to have the teaching team comprised of a group of teachers in one field—say high school English—organize for and share the responsibility for high school English instruction for a specific group of students. Still another plan is to have the team organized in terms of a grade level and include, say, all seventh-grade teachers of specified fields—perhaps mathematics, science, language arts, and social studies. There are numerous variations to all of these plans.

Experience seems to indicate that team teaching is a profitable way to use teacher resources. A teacher on a team will have the opportunity to specialize when he plans units, develops materials, or conducts large-group instruction. This specialty will be decided in the light of his own interests and talents, and his personal choice as worked out cooperatively by the teaching team. It is important to remember, however, that the team teacher is also informed about what is going on in all the areas included in the team and is prepared to share in small-group and special-help activities in all team areas. He is alert to and capitalizes on all opportunities for worthwhile interdisciplinary integration. It seems reasonable to conclude that added incentive and increased satisfactions are among the rewards of the successful team teacher.

From the pupil's point of view, there are also potential advantages. It is expected that the pupil will have increased intellectual stimulation as a result of contact with several teacher personalities instead of one. With his learning experiences directed and stimulated through team teaching, he has an enhanced opportunity to develop skills in self-direction, perhaps partly through large-group instruction, but he also, however, has the considerable advantages of individual direction in small groups.

Flexibility in grouping and time allotments are among the essentials of team teaching. The team determines the time and grouping in terms of the nature of a particular learning experience. The pattern followed in a high school in Decatur, Illinois, is somewhat typical of a team devoted to English on the secondary school level: 20 percent of a week's time spent in large-group lectures (held two or three times a week); 50 percent of the time spent in small-group classes (held on days alternate to lecture days); and 30 percent of the time given to independent study (arranged according to the individual student's schedule.) This kind of flexible schedule eliminates the need for a teacher to make a boring repetition of instruction. Time saved by large-group presentations is utilized for individual conferences with pupils, for team planning, and for preparation of quality lectures.

Of special importance to the success of team teaching are adequate help from teacher aides and paraprofessionals and the provision of enough time in the team teachers' schedules to allow for team planning.

Many new schools and remodeled buildings incorporate architectural features adapted to team teaching, especially movable partitions for classes of various sizes. The instructional aids we have described as audiovisual aids are an important part of team teaching. For large-group instruction a microphone, an overhead projector, and a large screen are standard equipment. Other items such as an opaque projector, a record player, and film and filmstrip projectors should be readily available. Programed instruction, including electronic devices, will probably become a regular part of the team teaching of the future.

OPPORTUNITY ROOM

"Opportunity room" is the name given to a special room in a school set aside and specially equipped for the instruction of pupils who possess marked handicaps that make it impossible for them to learn in classes enrolling normal pupils. These handicaps may be either physical or mental.

In some states—Illinois, for example—a very successful state program affords leadership at the state level through a policy of financial aid and certification of specially trained teachers for the handicapped. Some school systems have specially designed buildings, provide suitable transportation, furnish teachers' helpers, and in other ways make the education of handicapped children a profitable and pleasant experience. At the same time, the removal of handicapped pupils from regular classrooms is an aid to teachers who, with many pupils to teach, would find caring for the handicapped a wearing additional responsibility.

Some schools have handicapped pupils spend part of their time in the regular classrooms and part in the opportunity rooms. This is advocated on the grounds that handicapped pupils should have as great an opportunity as possible to be a normal part of school life, since they will some day have to take a place in the everyday life of the community. There is also educational value in having normal pupils learn proper consideration for the handicapped.

Summary

Large sums of money are being spent on instructional aids to help teachers, make classroom teaching more rewarding, and encourage more effective and more significant learning. Instructional aids do not lighten the load of classroom teachers although they do help teachers to teach more effectively. Instructional aids emphasize the responsibilities of classroom teachers to adapt to methodological change. The traditional pattern of teaching was face-to-face verbal presentation and response. Today new media of communication require of the teacher additional specialization and extra preparation before teaching his pupils. All this requires extra time and energy. Instructional aids are

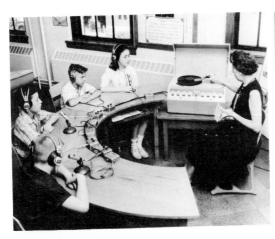
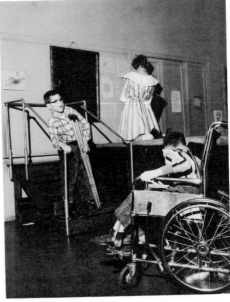

A great many different kinds of aids must be provided in schools that make special provisions for the education of the handicapped. A class for deaf children and an "opportunity room" for the physically handicapped are shown.

not contrivances that lessen the work teachers do. Other ways must be found to accomplish this.

Questions

1. What are some of the factors that must be considered by a classroom teacher in making a selection of teaching aids?
2. In what ways do teaching aids add to the direct experiences of the pupils?
3. What are some of the teaching advantages of mock-ups?
4. What are the advantages of programed learning? What are the possible dangers?
5. Which do you consider to be the better teaching device—programed textbook or teaching machine? Explain why.
6. To what extent do you believe that teaching methods will be changed by the introduction of automated learning materials in the classroom?
7. a. What, in your opinion, are the disadvantages of the state-wide adopted uniform textbook policy?
   b. What causes the state-wide adopted textbook policy to linger on?

Projects

1. After leafing through a textbook on audiovisual aids, write some of your conclusions about their uses in the classroom.
2. List the skills you feel you must develop while training to be a teacher in order to use teaching aids effectively.
3. Examine a programed learning textbook. Write your evaluation of the book.
4. Write the principal conclusions to be drawn from your study of the analyses of the 20 specialists writing in the *Phi Delta Kappan* on programed instruction. (See readings at the end of this unit.)
5. Give reasons why the 16-mm motion picture film has played and continues to play an important role in classroom learning.

6. Examine a teaching machine. Write what you conceive to be the advantages of teaching machines over other aids.
7. Some elementary schools are experimenting with nongraded rooms. Explain how this kind of grouping is achieved. Explain the advantages over ability grouping.
8. Write an evaluation of team teaching in terms of your own experience with team teaching or in terms of an interview with a teacher doing team teaching or a student in a team teaching situation.
9. List the many ways in which teaching aids promise to change the course of education in America.

The principal aim of this book has been to describe what the American people have done to provide adequate education for all American citizens and particularly for those who attend the schools. Trends in development have been noted, and in some instances future trends have been indicated. Selection of aspects of education to be included was made in the light of two criteria: the material chosen should contribute to an *overview* and should serve as an *introduction* to American education, especially for the reader getting his first view of American education. For some readers this book may be a terminal point. For others—students who have decided to enter teaching or who, for various reasons, wish to explore professional education further—the following brief view of some more specialized fields in education may be helpful. We have in mind here the freshman or sophomore—the student who has a few years of undergraduate work to do before entering teaching.

As described in our discussion of how the teacher qualifies, college programs for teacher preparation are made up of three parts. One is the general education, the liberal education, the common cultural knowledge and understandings expected of all college graduates. Another is specialized education. This includes work specifically selected to contribute to a specialized field of teaching. If the subject for specialized study is one that is included in the general education of all students, the courses pursued are more advanced than those required of all students. The third is devoted to professional training. It is to this third part that we now turn our attention.

Professional study

Professional education differs from other areas of study in three general ways. First, the subject matter is professional in nature. The aim is definitely vocational. It is assumed that the student has chosen teaching as his future vocation, as his chief means of earning a living. Second, the content of specialized methods courses in which the student learns to teach in his field of choice is not ordered on the principle of gradually advancing difficulty in the same degree as is content in fields like mathematics, physics, a language, or history. For example, a course dealing with the teaching of the new mathematics may use some simple mathematical materials that were learned by the teacher-to-be long ago but which he must now relearn with the new approach. He may also have to learn some mathematical concepts that are new to him. In the course in the teaching of physics in high school there is also a new physics: the whole field of physics, or any part of it, whether it is advanced or not, may be drawn upon for illustrative material. The main objective is to develop skill in teaching the physics that is modern. The assumption is that the student already has a good basic understanding of the subject he is going to teach, but that he will continue to learn more about it.

The third difference lies in the backgrounds of the professors of education in the college or university. In addition to their college work, which includes advanced training in professional education, they have had considerable practical school-teaching experience on the elementary and secondary levels. Their principal function is to help the teacher in preparing to become a *successful* teacher.

AIMS OF PROFESSIONAL STUDY

The all-inclusive aim of the professional program is to develop competent and interested teachers. Professional study is not always fully understood. Among students in professional education courses it is often possible to identify three quite different attitudes toward the work. There is, for instance, the student who thinks the work in professional courses, with the possible exception of student teaching, is abstract, theoretical, and quite unnecessary as preparation for his teaching career. He thinks that his native intelligence, his common sense, will be adequate support for him when he gets into the teaching world. He thinks he will guess about the things he has not studied and does not know about, will choose among alternatives after some trial and error in the classroom. In other words, he expects to get his professional training through experience in the classroom—obviously at the expense of his pupils.

Then there is the student who expects the professional courses to do so much by way of preparation that all he, as a beginning teacher, will need to do is to apply some rule-of-thumb method that he learned about in college. He expects the experts who teach him to give him specific solutions that he can apply to any difficult discipline case or to the selection of techniques in any particular learning situation. Of course, this student is destined for disappointment when he discovers he is not equipped with ready-made answers as he begins teaching; he will then tend to deny the value of any and all professional study. Perhaps he will even lose interest in teaching.

A third attitude is characteristic of the student who is not willing to begin teaching directed by caprice and depending upon trial and error, and who is also not willing to try to accumulate a collection of routine procedures to use in his teaching. Courses in professional education are designed to meet the needs of this kind of student, to help him improve his understandings of all aspects of teaching, to help him become intelligent about the problems of education, so that he may become an effective teacher.

Such understandings may be expected to reduce the number and seriousness of the errors that beset inexperienced teachers. The background of professional study may be expected also to add to the satisfactions of teaching. It is a common observation that, on the whole, no people are more seriously devoted to their work than teachers. The teacher who tends to be most devoted, to get the most gratification from teaching, is the one who understands the students, the materials, the aims—and all the other aspects of the complete educational picture. Courses in professional education are designed to build the understandings and insights that will enable him from the beginning to be an intelligent, fully informed member of the education profession, ready to play his role in whatever is required to discharge his obligations with professional skill.

"The teacher who tends to be most devoted, to get the most gratification from teaching, is the one who understands the students, the materials, the aims . . ." A great teacher combines many abilities and traits, some of which he continues to develop throughout his life. Both these teachers are totally involved— they project not only their subjects but themselves. Their students become equally involved. The teacher who is capturing the interest of a junior high school class is actually a professor at Teachers College, Columbia. While she was teaching for six weeks at this New York school, her classes were video-taped. She then returned to teaching her regular college course in Teaching Secondary School English, using the video tapes of her junior high school classes to illustrate important points. The other teacher is lecturing on poetry at a junior college. He is one of an elite group of teachers picked to teach in a comprehensive experimental program designed to produce intellectual independence and responsibility in the students.

Perhaps a part of the satisfaction in teaching comes from the kind of creativeness and independence that a teacher with a well-founded background in professional education enjoys. A teacher with confidence, assurance, and knowledge will have the incentive to use his own initiative. The textbook, the course of study, are his tools and his aids, and he knows how to utilize them in his own terms. In earlier days even the daily topics of classroom work were selected for teachers, and pages to be covered each day were indicated by overseeing authorities. Now it is the well-trained teacher who decides, within limits, what subject matter pupils will study, how much ground they will cover, how he will coordinate his work with that of his colleagues, and what his relationships with parents shall be. In general, he enjoys the privilege of deciding how he will advance the achievement of the aims he selects.

Professional study is also expected to help teachers become prepared to use their influence effectively—not only as leaders in the classroom, but as active members of the professional group and also as enlightened citizens. This does not necessarily imply holding elective offices, making speeches, or writing articles. These may be included, but not all teachers exercise their influence in these ways. The influence may come through activities that are individual, on a rather personal plane, and dedicated to long-term progress in education. People in the United States have all kinds of ideas for the improvement of education—some wise, some foolish, some constructive, some selfish. American schools are not all they should be, as has been made obvious in many of the discussions in earlier chapters. They fall short of what the teaching profession and the American people would like them to be. Many old educational traditions are outmoded. Methods of taxation need revising. The organization of schools needs overhauling. The curriculum needs reconstructing. Methods of teaching require improvement. Some colleges and universities have flagrantly neglected their most important function, training education leaders. Well-educated members of the teaching profession, though they may not dominate the future trends in American education, certainly must furnish some of the significant insights to help the American public make decisions about problems related to education.

The aims of professional study in education for the undergraduate are usually implemented through four main types of courses: foundation courses; specialized courses, including such areas as history of education, philosophy of education, and human development; student teaching; and specialized courses designed for advanced study.

FOUNDATION COURSES

All the beginning courses in any phase of professional education are foundational in character. This means that they provide an introduction to a particular field. They open the door to more advanced study in the area. The undergraduate student will study what deliberate education in America is about, will have "foundation" courses in philosophy of education and in child growth and development, for instance. In each of these areas, work advanced beyond the semiprofessional level will be offered to the undergraduate who is specializing in a professional area and to the graduate student who is doing work on a higher level. They differ from the more highly specialized courses, devoted to such topics as taxation, school law, school buildings, educational statistics, advanced child development, school supervision, and school administration, that are designed for experienced teachers.

Each state university has a school of education. The faculty and staff of each school devote themselves to serving the schools of their state, not only by giving the best possible training to the state's teachers, but also in many other ways. This large office building for the faculty of the School of Education at Indiana University is typical of those at many state universities.

Colleges and universities vary in their requirements of study in foundation courses. The foundational fields—education in America, history of education, philosophy of education, educational sociology, psychology of human development, methods of teaching, and student teaching—will, however, at some time and in some form be part of any program of professional preparation. In general, students will take at least the beginning course in these areas.

In some schools the courses named History of Education, Philosophy of Education, and Human Development or Educational Psychology, together with an Introduction to Education in America (such as the course for which this book is designed), are combined in a series of units each lasting for a semester and known as Foundations of Education. Usually such an integrated course is taught by a teaching team of specialists. It uses appropriate materials from sources like social psychology, sociology, political science, and anthropology. The integrated course has proved a successful base for more specialized professional study.

SPECIALIZED COURSES

In addition to so-called foundation courses in education—either basic, unified courses or more or less specialized beginning courses— undergraduate professional education offers beginning and advanced study in such fields as history of education, philosophy of education, and child development or educational psychology. Since this book itself illustrates the nature of the subject matter in the first course in professional education, Education in America, we need not further discuss the nature of that course.

1. History of education

In some teacher education programs a foundation course in the history of education is taught as a separate course. In others the historical aspects of some phase of education are included in the separate course devoted to that phase of education. If reading is studied, for instance, the student may begin with material related to the historical development of our present practices in teaching reading. Either kind of course, if taught by an able teacher, may achieve the desired understandings.

The general purpose in studying history of education is to make clear that the education of one generation is influenced by the education of the generation that preceded it. The student learns that it is profitable to study the thinking and practices of able educators throughout history, and he realizes that the key to what comes after is often found in what went before.

An eminent historian says:

> On every hand the past controls us, for the most part unconsciously, and without protest on our part. We are in the main its willing adherents. The imagination of the most radically minded cannot transcend any great part of the ideas and customs transmitted to him. When once we grasp this truth we shall, according to our mood, humbly congratulate ourselves that, poor pygmies that we are, we are permitted to stand on the giant's shoulders and enjoy an outlook that would be quite hidden from us if we had to trust to our own short legs; or we may resentfully chafe at our bonds and, like Prometheus, vainly strive to wrest ourselves from the rock of the past in our eagerness to bring relief to the suffering of men. . . . Whether we are tempted to curse the past as a sort of chronic disease, or bless it as the giver of all good things, we are inevitably its offspring; it makes us its own long before we know enough to defend ourselves. It is almost all that we have, and to understand it is to understand ourselves, our possibilities of achievement, our frustrations and perplexities.[1]

Education is a fundamental influence in the development of all civilizations, and the continuity in the development of education is a fundamental historical fact. Citizens of today, for instance, hear much about the educational programs of the national government, the programs of expediency, sometimes suddenly put into operation without any forward-looking planning. Yet this is not a new government attitude. The Morrill Act of 1862 was a crash program, as was the Smith-Hughes Act of 1917. Numerous other examples could be cited. The old traditions, like tenacious bulldogs, tend to hang on long after reason tells us to let go. The history of education indicates that the traditions of the past will only be changed after enlightenment is

---

[1] James Harvey Robinson, *The Ordeal of Civilization*. New York: Harper & Row, 1926, pp. 3–4. Quoted by permission of the publishers.

sufficiently widespread to make acceptable the fact that there are other and more efficacious ways of solving educational problems.

Study of the history of education can easily be dull unless attention is focused upon the future of education as it is understood in the light of the past. The history of education points to what education in the United States may become, as well as to what it has been. Knowledge and interpretation of the history of education can throw light on difficult educational problems and bring encouragement to those who might, without this understanding, be completely discouraged. A study of the history of education can do a great deal to improve our understanding of present education and to accent the challenge ahead.

From a historical perspective we get a notion of the relationship between an educational event, situation, or problem and certain other social events, situations, or problems. Further, we see the relationship between the educational events, situations, or problems and the whole of the American educational scene. By studying the history of education or some aspect of it, we get a picture of the relative place of education in the present scheme of social life in the United States.

2. Philosophy of education

The philosophy of education is a comprehensive, critical evaluation of the principles that underlie the practices in education in the United States. When organized into a system, these principles serve as a guide to intelligent practice. The study of educational philosophy helps each of us to formulate a consistent and comprehensive viewpoint toward education so that we may know why we do what we do and so that we may be able to give reasons for all that we do and be willing to examine our practices critically in order to assure ourselves that our practices are well founded. In other words, the philosophy of education is studied for the purpose of helping us clarify our own educational viewpoints.

The study not only will help the student formulate a comprehensive viewpoint toward education and educational practices but will also help him resolve within his own mind the conflicts that exist between the varied viewpoints Americans hold toward education. Some of the conflicts are rather troublesome to the beginning student in education and, as he begins teaching, may be a source of worry.

The conflicts exist not only among the citizens of a community but also among the members of the educational profession. Sometimes the sharpest critics of educational viewpoints and classroom practices are themselves teachers. At times the editors of popular, influential magazines and newspapers develop a philosophy of education for their publications and attempt to sway the American people to accept their views. These views are expressed with a positiveness and persistency that attract the attention of the public but that may disturb many classroom teachers whose fundamental views toward education are in direct conflict. Does a study of philosophy help resolve such conflicts?

After all, in the last two centuries the human race seems to have made little progress either in improving the quality of human relations or in working out universally accepted and generally effective ways of resolving conflicting social viewpoints. We must accept the fact that conflicts in viewpoints on almost every social issue exist. These a single individual cannot resolve. What he can do, however, is to resolve his own conflicting viewpoints. He can formulate a philosophy of education that, to him, is both justifiable in the light of what he knows and defensible in terms of its consequences.

There are three steps used by the educational philosopher in arriving at his judgments about what is the best educational theory and practice. The first is the establishment of a standard of values. The educational philosopher places a higher value on the path of action he follows than on the one he does not follow. He directs his actions in terms of widely accepted basic values such as democracy, morality, and so on. We constantly engage in selecting values to guide our action in everyday life. The process of establishing values and of evaluating education in terms of those values is no different in the school than outside, except perhaps that we formalize the process to a greater extent in the schools.

The second step involves a critical and methodical examination of the assumptions of each educational practice and an evaluation of these assumptions in terms of our chosen standards of value. What assumptions underlie using coercion? administering standardized tests to all pupils of a particular grade? giving marks to pupils? giving examinations? unionizing teachers? requiring demonstrational geometry in the tenth year of school? Every requirement in the school and every

technique of administration or of teaching is based on some fundamental assumption related to values.

The third step used by the educational philosopher is to evaluate
what is done in the schools in terms of its actual or possible effects.
Before one decides what it is good to do in school, one considers what
the consequences may be in terms of one's standard of value. The
teacher who contemplates keeping a student after school to study his
algebra must think of all the consequences. Might this student be led
thereby to dislike algebra, to dislike the teacher? All educational
philosophers are interested in the effects of what is done in the schools
on the character and personality of the pupils. They therefore consider
the possible outcomes of what is done in the schools and judge the
merit of what is done in terms of all the possible outcomes.

The practical and common problems of everyday classroom teaching are a rich source of subject matter for educational philosophy.
What are the ordinary beliefs of the members of the teaching profession about what is good education? What philosophical generalizations
about teaching do teachers draw from the knowledge of child growth
and development? On what kind of educational philosophy do practices
rest—such practices as marking pupils, classifying or refusing to classify
children into ability groups, awarding honors, withholding honors,
using the results of standardized tests, punishing children?

Educational philosophy examines all teacher activities critically,
with the purpose of testing the validity of all that is done. This does
not mean that teachers of educational philosophy find fault with everything that is done. Criticism is developed as a method of philosophy.
It is pursued methodically. Familiar practices are investigated beyond
what is ordinarily known about them. Inconsistencies in thinking are
revealed, confusions dissolved, conflicts resolved, and order, clarity,
and consistency introduced in knowledges, beliefs, and practices. The
philosopher in education goes to many fields for his information and
ideas. He examines the information and ideas critically, and as he does
this, he evolves both a method of criticism and criteria to use in
criticism.

Some of the greatest professional philosophers have addressed
themselves to educational philosophy. Some of the works of such men
as Charles S. Peirce, William James, Josiah Royce, John Dewey,
Bertrand Russell, A. N. Whitehead, Herbert Spencer, and others,

including even Plato, were directed to a discussion of education. It may well be that this linking of education and philosophy occurs because education is viewed as an organized, deliberate, conscious attempt to mold the viewpoints and the dispositions of the young. Truly professional philosophers can scarcely refrain from considering a matter that is of such social significance and ethical importance.

Educational philosophy can be as trivial or as deep as one wishes to make it. The foundation course, however, can only be the beginning of a study of a very extensive field. As a rule, the beginning courses deal with such philosophical topics as the aims of education, the nature of subject matter, appraisals of the methods used in teaching, and the various practices related to the organization and the administration of schools. Among the ideas that are critically examined may be those of grouping pupils, of promoting and failing pupils, of giving examinations, and many other practices commonly associated with teaching school.

The student who wishes to develop the art of critical thinking, who favors constructive change, who wishes to chart the paths to future progress, who believes that interests, attitudes, and emotions are factors to be considered in the education of people, who feels that what has been discovered by the specialists in human development and in the other fields of the social sciences should affect the practices followed in educating the young, will find his future study of educational philosophy a highly fascinating, practical, and significant experience. Above all, he will receive from such study help on one of the most important problems, one for which he must formulate a workable solution. That is the problem of his own reasoned, defensible point of view toward what the education of a growing, developing human being should be.

3. Human development

Human development is a fascinating field and one of undeniable importance to the individual who wishes to teach intelligently and to derive a great degree of personal satisfaction from his work.

The scope of the field of human development is wide. As a professional field of interest to teachers, however, the focus of the course, regardless of title, is on using education to promote growth in the quality of human behavior. Behavior and development of behavior patterns receive pronounced emphasis. A study leading to understanding of the learning acquired by the infant, the nature of childhood fears, the source of attitudes, the way children learn to talk or read or think or reason is helpful in planning classroom activities that promise maximum desirable growth among children.

The typical college textbook on human development devotes considerable attention to learning, growth, individual differences, personality development, emotions, attitudes, and the like. Perhaps the most fundamental idea underlying all the concepts is that of the total development of the pupil. Hence the textbooks include such topics as growth in ability to make generalizations, the effects of repetition on learning, how emotions promote or inhibit growth, what has been learned about memory, habit formation, the breaking of bad habits, the effects of approval, the effects of punishments and rewards on learning, how growth in skills is effected, how intention affects learning, how growth in habits of attention is encouraged, what the nature of thinking is, and so on. Each of these topics relates to factors that shape the character of total growth of the human individual. The subject matter of the course in human development may be almost as broad as life itself. All the topics included apply not only to the learners in the school, but to everyone who learns. It is, however, only when these findings are made directly applicable to the problems of learning in the school that we call the course Educational Psychology.

STUDENT TEACHING

As mentioned in Chapter 3, in his last year of training the student customarily spends part of his time as a student teacher. The course in student teaching is the most obviously practical of all the professional courses because it gives the student an opportunity to do on a limited scale what he has looked forward to doing and has prepared himself to do. The nature of the course varies greatly from institution to institution. Usually the student teacher is assigned to work with some teacher in a public school as an assistant or cooperative teacher. What the student does, of course, depends upon the teacher with whom he cooperates. Usually, the senior teacher has been selected because he is a successful teacher and because he is interested in helping in the education of teachers.

Various techniques are used to show teachers-in-training the best ways to teach in regular classrooms. Observation and experience are both essential. A nursery school teacher is shown in a laboratory school, one of many run by schools of education that give teachers-in-training valuable opportunities to observe experienced teachers. Teacher-training is more effective when a participation or demonstration class is video-taped for later play-back and study—this is being done in two situations here. Teachers-in-training act out a children's story, going through themselves what they will later lead children to do. The monitor screens show different views of an education professor as she gives a demonstration lesson—just as she would give it in an actual classroom —so that her students can study the techniques of an experienced teacher later. Many students take the more specialized courses in professional education that prepare them to deal with particular learning problems as teacher or diagnostician. Success in any type of effort to help children with specific difficulties brings its own rewards. A teacher and a student teacher give intensive remedial reading instruction to Spanish-speaking children. A boy is shown at a diagnostic reading center, being tested by a clinician who is trying to identify the reasons for his serious reading handicap. The boy tries to reproduce correctly a series of figures shown to him one at a time.

Under the immediate supervision of the classroom teacher, the student teacher gradually assumes more and more responsibility and engages in a constantly expanding number of practical activities. As he teaches, he continues to study with the object of personal and professional improvement. If the time is spent wisely, the student builds skills and understandings and develops a feeling of confidence that will be of inestimable value when he enters a school as one of the regularly employed teachers.

ADVANCED STUDY

The student in education will find many avenues open for advanced professional study. University catalogues list specialized courses given in departments and schools of education which deal intensively with almost every problem the teacher is likely to encounter. The teachers of nursery school, kindergarten, and the primary grades may study one kind of course grouping, the middle-grade teachers another, and the high school teachers still another. Courses are designed specifically for each of these levels in the teaching of reading, mathematics, science, social studies, geography, creative dramatics, arts and crafts, music, speech, physical education, and other related subjects. All such courses, when taught by able teachers, afford many insights into the handling of rather narrowly classified but important problems connected with the promotion of child growth. In the light of his interests and his choice of a field for specialization and with the aid of his adviser, a student will decide what advanced courses to pursue.

In contemplating future fields of study, if the student can select courses that are compatible with his vocational plans, not only will he enjoy them more but his profit will be much greater. By and large, the later courses in education, pursued for the purposes of professional preparation, include both subject matter and methods of directing the subject matter, combined in such a way as to promote human development to a maximum degree. Some may, however, emphasize one aspect much more than the other.

Most students find the more specialized courses in professional education a source of great interest, perhaps because these courses are then more closely related to the student's vocational objective and are usually taught by specialists who themselves are deeply immersed in their subject. If one is going to teach reading, for example, then a course in the teaching of reading, taught by an inspiring psychologist who has specialized in that aspect of child development, can indeed be most rewarding. The same is true in other fields.

Perspective for the future

In analyzing American education—what educators and the people are doing to provide American youth with an adequate formal education—we have examined primarily the past and the present. As this book closes we think back over some current trends, some current problems, and raise questions about the future. Will current trends continue in their present directions? How will vexing problems of education be solved? It has been said that coming events cast their shadows before. Can we peer into the shadows and identify a few outlines that seem to indicate what is emerging?

WILL FAITH IN EDUCATION PERSIST?

From our earliest frontier on the Atlantic coast, through various stages of western expansion to the Pacific coast, the American people have always manifested a faith in education. The early provisions for free public education were based on a conviction that education is a bulwark and indeed an essential in the foundations of democracy. Immigrants from Europe have recognized that education was the important portal to an improved life with extensive opportunities. Despite crosscurrents in educational theory, conflicts in educational philosophy, numerous diversions such as wars and depressions, distractions, intrusions, and criticisms from dissatisfied elements in the body politic, education has gradually and unmistakably improved from generation to generation. Are the pride and confidence of the American people in their educational institutions sufficiently strong so that they can withstand any future efforts to weaken or destroy them?

WILL CURRENT TRENDS IN EDUCATION CONTINUE?

Throughout the story of education in America we have observed trends, springing sometimes from ideas that go back to early movements and leaders in Europe, trends that have led to current practices.

Sometimes, as we have noted, trends have continued for a time and have then been reversed. Sometimes they have moved in cycles, recurring after an interval. Looking at some trends that seem current, what can we say about their future? Will they be maintained in their present direction? reversed? abandoned?

1. Adjustments to technology

We have noted many recent changes in education that have received their impetus from dramatic changes in social life in general, or that can be traced to rapid technological progress. These have included modifications in all aspects of the educational picture from building construction to curriculum and general aims.

Present predictions are that coming generations will have increasing time for their own personal use. Will the schools have to continue and expand their work in helping pupils build the kind of foundation that will equip them to utilize this free time in a satisfying manner? With shorter working days, shorter working weeks, longer

Exploration and informal discussion by teachers in charge of fully equipped and well-organized resource centers stimulate and increase the interest of pupils. A teacher discusses a specific project with students and suggests books they can read and films they can see. The other teacher, foreground, listens to music with pupils; he stops the tape at intervals to give explanations and interpretations. Films and tapes are important parts of a resource center—they can be used with almost any part of the curriculum.

vacations, and early retirement for the majority of employed people, will present trends of modification in the curriculum and other elements be adequate if continued? Should there be a more sensitive and insightful awareness of the school's responsibility in this area?

And how about preparation for actual careers or vocations? Are present trends appropriate for fulfilling the demands for a broad educational base, for training in skills needed today but training sufficiently flexible and broadly based so that the pupil is equipped to adjust to rapidly changing demands of science, industry, and business? Are present practices adequate to supply the pupil with a background that allows him to adjust to one of a number of employment opportunities if the specific one he has selected to prepare for has become obsolete even before he has completed his training?

Will the present trend in expansion of teaching aids that have been and continue to be produced in line with technological advances in other areas, be continued? accelerated? decelerated? Some of the aids have, apparently, proved themselves in the classroom. Many are still in a more or less experimental stage, although great achievement is promised for them. Will these benefits be realized? Will teaching machines, for instance, be the great help in meeting individual pupil needs that is predicted? Will their expense on a wide scale be so prohibitive as to counteract their value? Will they impersonalize instruction unduly? Will they reduce the number of teachers needed? What *is* their future?

2. Meeting individual needs and abilities

We have said that instructional aids are designed in part to assist the teacher in meeting individual needs and adjusting instruction to individual abilities. What about other current adjustments in schools to serve these purposes? Will the present trend toward increased numbers of nongraded classes and nongraded schools continue? How about team teaching? ability grouping? Have they proved themselves to be sound and practical? Should, or will, present trends continue? Are they still so new that they are really unproven, are still experimental, and the future cannot be predicted? Are there other trends in practices to meet individual needs and abilities that are more promising?

3. Trends caused by population shifts and expansion

We have noted that the current trend in school district organization is toward fewer and larger districts in agricultural areas. Has this proved to be desirable? Will the consolidation of smaller districts, the removal of control of education from a small community or neighborhood prove sound? How far will the corporate trend lead in district organization? Should it continue?

The great range of differences in neighborhood areas in large-city districts has led to a number of trends intended to eliminate racial segregation and minimize variation in educational opportunities due to cultural deprivation in such areas as the "inner city." Will the present attempt to achieve equality and racial integration by busing be continued? expanded? What is the future of the so-called "cluster school" plan? Will people become accustomed to, and reconciled to, having their children educated outside the immediate home neighborhood? Will the trend toward integration be reversed and the Negro children who live in highly concentrated Negro communities remain segregated in school as they are in life, but be supplied with schools that are better than the other schools in the city, so that they may be compensated for years of inferior education?

Will the size of large-city school districts reach a point where they can no longer be practically and efficiently administered, where they are weighted down with bureaucracy? Of the population in general, 71 percent now dwell in urban centers—in New Jersey more than 88 percent. The New York City District School System alone is responsible for educating more than 1,100,000 children and youth and employs more than 59,000 classroom teachers. Will the present trend toward expansion of districts be allowed to continue? Or will the states have to limit the size of large public school districts—force them to divide into a number of smaller administrative units (in much the same way as they have eliminated small districts by enforcing consolidations)?

HOW WILL CURRENT EDUCATIONAL PROBLEMS BE SOLVED?

Some current problems and what is being done about them are implied in the preceding section. What about other problems,

problems related to the financing of the school and to the personnel in the schools?

1. Financing

Many of the present problems in education go back to the problem of money. It cannot be said that unlimited funds would solve all the problems that beset the schools, but with greatly increased funds, over a period time, many of the present problems could perhaps be effectively attacked. Granted that, on the whole, more money is needed to improve education, where will the money come from? Should the tax base be changed? the tax system overhauled? Can local schools continue to get their main support from real estate property taxes? Should the basis for the tax resources of the states be changed so that the states will be in a position to contribute more to their local districts? Should the present formula for distribution of state public school funds be modified? Should required minimum educational programs be examined, improved, and utilized more universally as a basis for state aid? Should the federal government continue or expand its present trend of participation in education at all levels? Is it inevitable that the federal government share in much of education because the federal government has the greatest taxing power? Should the kind of participation be modified? Should the restrictions and limitations be changed? Is it time for the pendulum to swing the other way and for federal participation in education to be curtailed?

2. Personnel

Current problems with reference to personnel revolve largely around training, recruitment, and retention in the profession. Will the universities and colleges examine training programs and initiate improvements specifically related to the demands of the classroom? Will certificating authorities be alert to desirable modifications? What kinds of modifications in training and certification seem indicated?

Perhaps recruitment and retention in the profession are most closely allied to matters of status—to salaries, teaching load, relative position of teachers in the hierarchy, opportunities to share in policy making, and so forth. These in turn are part of the vital concerns of teacher organizations, the NEA and AFT. Is the increased influence of teachers through such organizations a practical answer to teacher status problems, to problems of training, recruitment, and retention in the profession? Will these two major organizations unite in the future? Will teacher militancy extend? Should it? Will all school boards accept teacher negotiators in matters that affect teacher welfare? Will the teacher organizations improve their internal organization to achieve greater effectiveness? Will teacher involvement in the organizations increase?

WILL COMPETENT EDUCATIONAL LEADERSHIP BE FORTHCOMING?

The subject of trends and problems is inexhaustible. The questions sketched above have many ramifications that may take the reader back to pertinent sections of the text. Perhaps what we hope most to see in the picture of the future is good educational leadership. Is this forthcoming, on the federal, state, local community, and school level? Are teachers assuming their responsibilities for active participation in professional affairs and also in leadership among citizens?

Past accomplishments, however worthy, must be but a prelude toward still greater educational achievements. Is this aim manifest, not only among intellectual leaders but in local communities, civic organizations, and at the state and federal government levels? If so, may we not say that the future of American education is bright with promise?

.   .   .

The reader will understand, I am sure, if I close this book on a personal note. I wish I were young again, starting a lifetime career in teaching, seeking answers to questions like those I have just asked, and expecting to share in solving educational problems. No work, no profession, offers a richer and more satisfying life for the person who genuinely wants to serve society well and proudly. What an exciting future, what a stimulating prospect, to have before you!

Unit IV Suggested Readings

ANDERSON, ROBERT H., *Teaching in a World of Change*. New York: Harcourt, Brace & World, 1966, chaps. 5 and 6. Chap. 5 treats of team teaching. Chap. 6 discusses the people who work with teachers—paraprofessionals, parent volunteers, and other teacher aides.

BALLINGER, STANLEY E., "Of Testing and Its Tyranny," *Phi Delta Kappan*, 44 (No. 4): 176–182, January, 1963. A review of a book by a professor of mathematics called *The Tyranny of Testing*. The review gives substantial analysis of the testing movement, reveals the major strengths and weaknesses of the movement.

BAREN, DAVID, "Do You Dare . . . Negro Literature and the Disadvantaged Student," *Phi Delta Kappan*, 50 (No. 9): 520–524, May, 1969. The author "challenges teachers, and particularly teachers of English, to examine in their classes the most fundamental and sharply probing studies of the Negro in America—made by Negro authors." Includes a short bibliography.

BECKER, JAMES M., and LEE F. ANDERSON, "Riders on the Earth Together," *American Education*, 5 (No. 5): 2–4, May, 1969. Explains some of the implications for education when the earth is viewed from afar. "Scrapping the segmented view of the earth that is our legacy from schools and maps and pre-space-age thinking, let us consider the lunar view of this world as a basic unity and examine its implications for education."

BEGGS, DAVID W., III, and EDWARD G. BUFFIE, eds., *Nongraded Schools in Action*. Bloomington: Indiana University Press, 1967, part II. Thirteen different nongraded schools are described by those connected with them.

BENNETT, MARGARET, "Teaching Is Better With," *Saturday Review*, pp. 82–83, February 16, 1963. A classroom teacher who began teaching without courses in education concludes, "My attitude toward education courses can be summed up with a paraphrase of that old saying about money: 'I have taught with education courses and without education courses, and, believe me, *with* is better.'"

BERKMAN, DAVE, "You Can't Make Them Learn," *Atlantic Monthly*, 210 (No. 9): 62–67, September, 1962. Analysis of the problems confronted by teachers who teach in schools in economically depressed areas.

BERLIN, I. N., "Desegregation Creates Problems Too," *Saturday Review*, pp. 66–68, June 15, 1963. Explains the problems created by teaching children who have widely divergent sociological origins.

BETTELHEIM, BRUNO, "Stop Pampering Gifted Children," *The Saturday Evening Post*, pp. 8, 10, April 11, 1964. "Segregating the gifted, I am convinced, harms both the advanced student and the not-so-advanced." A psychologist's analysis of the effects of ability grouping.

BIDWELL, JAMES K., "A New Look at Old Committee Reports," *The Mathematics Teacher*, 61 (No. 4): 383–387, April, 1968. Traces the suggestions made with respect to reform in mathematics subject matter beginning with a report made to a National Education Association meeting in 1892. "Thus we have seen that these reports in the nineties sometimes presented a point of view similar to what we consider good curriculum practice . . ." The pronouncements of committees are not always carried out in action.

BLOUNT, NATHAN S., "Fructify the Folding Doors; Team Teaching Reexamined," *The English Journal*, 53 (No. 3): 177–179, 195, March, 1964. Views team teaching as "the most exciting prospect in English." Explains why.

BROWNELL, JOHN A., and HARRIS A. TAYLOR, "Theoretical Perspectives for Teaching Teams," *Phi Delta Kappan*, 43 (No. 4): pp. 150–157, January, 1962. A rather complete analysis of what is required for team teaching, written by two men who are involved in an extensive experimental program of team teaching.

BRUNE, IRVIN H., "Some K-6 Geometry," *The Arithmetic Teacher*, 14 (No. 6): 441–447, October, 1967. An interesting article for the general reader who may not understand how geometry can begin at the kindergarten level and continue to be taught through all the grades of the elementary school. Clearly sets forth the basic concepts upon which mathematics is built.

BURNS, JOHN L., "Our Era of Opportunity," *Saturday Review*, pp. 38–39, January 14, 1967. Explains how the essential tools for improving the quality of education have become available through the development of a large number of teaching aids. "The first step toward improving quality would be to free the classroom teacher from much of his daily routine in order to give him time to help individual students." The author enumerates the devices he believes will accomplish this.

COULSON, JOHN E., "Automation, Electronic Computers, and Education," *Phi Delta Kappan*, 47 (No. 7): 340–344, March, 1966. This article is based on a presentation at a conference on cybernetics.

CRONBACH, LEO J., "What Research Says About Programed Instruction," *NEA Journal*, 51 (No. 9): 45–47, December, 1962. A clear explanation of what is involved in the current attempts to build well-designed programs of instruction, and some discussion of the difficulties encountered in arriving at a fair appraisal of the educational results.

DARLING, DAVID W., "Team Teaching," *NEA Journal*, 54 (No. 5): 24–25, May, 1965. A university consultant to an intern in team teaching in the University of Wisconsin Improvement Program explains his concept of team teaching in elementary school. "We believe that team teaching . . . offers a greater opportunity for achieving the objectives of elementary school education . . . than any other organizational plan that we know of."

DAWSON, KENNETH E., and MORRIS NORFLEET, "The Computer and the Student," *NEA Journal*, 57 (No. 2): 47–48, February, 1968. Explains how one computerized program works and its advantages. "The biggest advantage of the computerized program appears to be its ability to adapt to individual differences. . . . It automatically adjusts to the student's ability level and constantly leads him to more advanced problems as he progresses."

DU BRIDGE, LEE A., "Physics," *NEA Journal*, 52 (No. 9): 24–28, December, 1963. Shows in simple language the changes that are taking place in the field of physics and explains how the changes lead to many new developments.

ELDRED, DONALD M., and MAURIE HILLSON, "The Non-Graded School and Mental Health," *Elementary School Journal*, 63: 218–222, January, 1963. Discusses advantages of nongraded schools from the standpoint of mental health.

FISHER, MILDRED OGG, "Team Teaching in Houston," *The English Journal*, 51 (No. 9): 628–631, December, 1962. Describes the plan for modified team teaching which is working successfully in Houston.

GEDDES, DOROTHY, and SALLY I. LIPSEY, "Sets—Natural, Necessary, Knowable?" *The Arithmetic Teacher*, 15 (No. 5): 337–340, April, 1968. Explains why the idea of sets is fundamental to successful teaching of beginning mathematics. "The concept of set is an intuitive and natural one; every child has made use of it long before he enters school."

GIBB, E. GLENADINE, "Some Approaches to Mathematics Concepts in the Elementary School," *NEA Journal*, 48 (No. 8): 65–66, November, 1959. Analyzes the nature of the current discussions centering on the question of developing a better sequence of subject matter in mathematics.

GIBEL, INGE LEDERER, "How *Not* To Integrate Schools," *Harper's Magazine*, 227: 57–66, November, 1963. The writer, who is a mother in a large city, analyzes the effects of school policy, such as ability grouping, having mostly middle-class teachers, and the like, on the education of children.

GOSLIN, DAVID A., "The Social Impact of Standardized Testing," *NEA Journal*, 52 (No. 7): 20–22, October, 1963. A sociologist analyzes the effects of standardized testing both on the individual and on what is taught in the school.

GROBMAN, HAROLD, "Biology Is Changing, Too," *Saturday Review*, pp. 67–69, 75, September 21, 1963. Describes the new instructional practices and materials in biology that are being introduced into the schools, beginning with first grade and extending through the basic courses in college. Stresses particularly the trends in vitalizing the instruction at the high school level.

HANDLIN, OSCAR, "Are the Colleges Killing Education?" *Atlantic Monthly*, 209:41–45, May, 1962. A professor of history analyzes the stifling effects of the stress given to competition in college instruction.

INGRAHAM, LEONARD W., "Teachers, Computers, and Games: Innovations in the Social Studies," *Social Education*, 31 (No. 1): 51–53, January, 1967. The author gives a clear explanation of how a computer in a school can serve social studies teachers, points out that every social studies teacher should know something about computers, and appends a helpful bibliography.

JOHNSON, DONOVAN A., "Enjoy the Mathematics You Teach," *The Arithmetic Teacher*, 15 (No. 4): 328–332, April, 1968. Explains how enjoyment in learning mathematics is the key to success in teaching mathematics. Explains how many recreational topics can and should be used to discover mathematical concepts and to build positive attitudes toward learning the subject.

KLIGER, SAMUEL, "The Workbook and the Programed Text," *The English Journal*, 52 (No. 9): 674–676, December, 1963. Are programed textbooks merely old workbooks in new format? Answers the question from the programer's point of view.

KORB, SISTER MARY VICTOR, "Positive and Negative Factors in Team Teaching," *The Mathematics Teacher*, 61 (No. 1): 50–53, January, 1968. Reports on team teaching in high school mathematics, clearly explains how it was organized, and points out the benefits that accrue to teachers and pupils.

LANGE, PHIL C., "Selection and Use of Programed Learning Materials," *NEA Journal*, 53 (No. 4): 28–29, April ,1964. Sets forth the assumptions about teaching procedure that underlie programed learning.

LARRICK, NANCY, "The All-White World of Children's Books," *Saturday Review*, 63–65, 84–85, September 11, 1965. This analysis of children's books shows that they do not portray the lives of all kinds of racial groups but are representative mainly of the white group. Describes what the Council for Interracial Books for Children is doing to give direction to future children's books.

LEAR, JOHN, "What the Moon Ranger Couldn't See," *Saturday Review*, pp. 35–40, September 5, 1964. Shows the rapidity of change in the world of subject matter to which school children are exposed.

LEAVITT, WILLIAM, "Individuals, Front and Center," *American Education*, 5 (No. 2): 4–6, February, 1969. Explains how children in Washington, D.C., were used to demonstrate how innovative techniques employed in various school systems throughout the nation operate to individualize learning.

MAC KENZIE, VERNON G., "Health in a Changing World," *School Science and Mathematics*, 68 (No. 5): 380–384, May, 1968. Explains the impact of rapid social change on the health of the American people. "The giant and often conflicting scientific, social, and political forces within our society . . . move inexorably forward."

Decisions affecting public health are often made without reference to certain vital health concerns. A good problem to interest pupils in the study of science in school.

MANNING, JOHN, "Discipline in the Good Old Days," *Phi Delta Kappan*, 41 (No. 3): 94–99, December, 1959. A professor of humanities vividly and authentically describes how our ancestors handled the problems of school discipline not so long ago. The carefully documented references may serve as a bibliography.

MARKLE, SUSAN MEYER, "Inside the Teaching Machine," *Saturday Review*, pp. 58–60, November 18, 1961. Explains in detail the problem of programing instructional materials.

MICHELS, WALTER C., "The Teaching of Elementary Physics," *Scientific Monthly*, 298: 56–64, April, 1958. A new approach which emphasizes the understanding of basic principles. "The history of physics and mathematics supports the amalgamation of the two subjects."

MIZER, JEAN E., "Dear JM," *Today's Education*, 57 (No. 7): 18–25, October, 1968. Sage advice to beginning teachers is given in an informal and friendly way.

MUELLER, THEODORE, "Psychology and the Language Arts," *School and Society*, 87: 420, 422, 427, October 24, 1959. Shows why effective language training must center in audio-oral work.

MUSGRAVE, MARTHA L., "Seeing Double at Vero Beach," *American Education*, 4 (No. 8): 17–19, September, 1968. Numerous helpful ways closed-circuit television can be used in the school are explained. "Its versatility makes it suitable for use in many subject areas. . . ."

MUSS, ROF E., and others, "Discipline," *NEA Journal*, 52: 9–22, September, 1963. A series of discussions on the problem of discipline in the school.

National Education Association, Research Division, *Ability Grouping*, Research Summary 1968-S3. Of special interest are the pros and cons of ability grouping (p. 5) and the summary and conclusions (pp. 42–44). "The majority of teachers—close to three-fifths of the elementary-school teachers and nearly 9 of every 10 secondary-school teachers—favor the grouping of pupils for instruction according to ability." "Despite its increasing popularity, there is a notable lack of empirical evidence to support the use of ability grouping as an instructional arrangement in the public schools."

NEA Journal, "Denver's Home Teaching Program," 56 (No. 2): 14–16, January, 1967. A description of the program of the Boettcher School of Denver, organized for the education of the handicapped child. The program combines instruction in school, hospital, and home.

NEA Journal, "Teacher Opinion Poll," 53 (No. 6): 25, September, 1964. Maintaining pupil discipline remains one of the most persistent problems teachers face. It appears that keeping order in the classroom has become a more difficult problem than it was in past years.

NEA Journal, "How the Professional Feels About Teacher Aides," 56 (No. 8): 15–16, November, 1967. Report of NEA Research Division poll on teacher opinion. Most teachers—80 percent—do not have teacher aides. Those who do, find them of substantial assistance, and prefer that the duties of the aides be confined to noninstructional activities like clerical work. The survey reveals that aides perform a wide variety of services.

NOYES, KATHRYN JOHNSTON, and GORDON L. MC ANDREW, "Is This What Schools Are For?" *Saturday Review*, pp. 58–59, 65, December 21, 1968. The authors explain why "In sum, we run our schools almost totally without reference to the needs of the children who attend them."

OETTINGER, ANTHONY G., "The Myths of Educational Technology," *Saturday Review*, pp. 76–77, 91, May 18, 1968. A professor of linguistics and applied mathematics, after completing extensive research on problems connected with the application of technology (especially computers), warns of concluding that some teaching practices are much better than others. "Choice among existing practices cannot be made from data demonstrating the greater effectiveness of one over another. . . . We should plan for the encouragement of pluralism and diversity, at least in technique."

PETROQUIN, GAYNOR, *Individualizing Learning Through Modular-Flexible Programming*. New York: McGraw-Hill, 1968, chapter 1. This chapter, entitled "A Computer-Generated, Teacher-Developed, Modular-Flexible Schedule," explains what modular scheduling is and how it has evolved. A beginning student entering his professional preparation will do well to become acquainted with some of "the straws in the wind" that foreshadow future change.

Phi Delta Kappan, "Programed Instruction," 54 (No. 6), March, 1963. This issue is devoted entirely to the subject of programed instruction; 20 specialists write on the contributions such instruction can make to learning.

POSTMAN, NEIL, ed., *Television and the Teaching of English*. New York: Appleton-Century-Crofts, 1961, 138 pp. A report made by the Committee on the Study of Television of the National Council of Teachers of English. Part I deals with the educational significance of television. Part II deals with classroom study through television.

REED, JERRY E., and JOHN L. HAYMAN, JR., "An Experiment Involving Use of English 2600, an Automated Instruction Text," *Journal of Educational Research*, 55: 476–484, June, 1962. From this, one gets an idea of what an automated textbook is like.

REID, JAMES M., "An Adventure in Programing Literature," *The English Journal*, 52 (No. 9): 659–673, December, 1963. A veteran book editor explains the programing of poetry after what he calls his "two-year adventure" in programing literature.

ROSENTHAL, ROBERT, and LENORE JACOBSON, *Pygmalion in the Classroom: Teacher Expectation and Pupils' Intellectual Development*. New York: Holt, Rinehart and Winston, 1968. A report on a study showing that children whose teachers were led to believe they would improve in their school work *did* significantly improve. The authors describe in detail their careful scientific methods, their results, and their conclusions. Readable and thought-provoking.

ROWLAND, HOWARD S., "Using the TV Western," *The English Journal*, 52 (No. 9): 693–696, December, 1963. Shows how a teacher may use television "Westerns" to build a foundation for critical viewing.

SAVA, SAMUEL G., "When Learning Comes Easy," *Saturday Review*, pp. 102–104, 119, November 16, 1968. This is a strong argument for what the author refers to as "a massive investment in early childhood education."

School Science and Mathematics, 68 (No. 2): 148–153, 154–158, February, 1968. Perusal of these pages will illustrate the extensive efforts the federal government is making through grants to colleges and universities, private and public, to improve instruction in science and mathematics in the public schools. Note that grants are to help pupils as well as teachers. Official publications in other fields—

English, social studies, etc.—are just as extensive. These particular grants are through the National Science Foundation. Other extensive grants are under the National Defense Education Act.

SCOLLON, KENNETH M., "Why Art in Education?" *Saturday Review*, 70–72, 80. February 15, 1964. States many reasons why it is important to emphasize the fine arts in the schools.

SHAPLIN, JUDSON T., and HENRY F. OLDS, eds., *Team Teaching*. New York: Harper & Row, 1964. Gives an overview of the team teaching approach in classroom teaching as furnished by a number of writers who have studied the movement.

SHARP, EVELYN, "The New Math: You Don't Count on Your Fingers Anymore," *Saturday Review*, pp. 65–67, January 19, 1963. Describes the new mathematics being introduced into the modern school curriculum.

SKINNER, B. F., "Teaching Machines," *Scientific American*, 205 (No. 5): 90–102, November, 1961. Explains how teaching machines promote effective learning by enabling "the student to learn in small but rigorous steps, each of which is rewarding," and how they may introduce a new element to methods of teaching.

SKINNER, B. F., "Why Teachers Fail," *Saturday Review*, pp. 80–81, 98–102, October 16, 1965. An eminent psychologist analyzes the problem of teaching method. "Any special knowledge of pedagogy as a basic science of teaching is felt to be unnecessary. The attitude is regrettable. No enterprise can improve itself . . . without examining its basic processes." The author presents a strong case for the application of intensive study to methods of teaching.

Social Education, "Black Americans and Social Studies: Minority Groups in American Society," 33 (No. 4): April, 1969. The entire issue is devoted to the problem of adjusting education to the needs of various minority groups and ghetto children, including American Indians, Orientals, Spanish, and Negroes.

STEVENS, MARTIN, and WILLIAM R. ELKINS, "Designs for Team Teaching in English," *The English Journal*, 53 (No. 3): 170–176, March, 1964. Description of team teaching in a high school in which experiments have been conducted with different methods.

STREHLER, ALLEN F., "What's New About the New Math?" *Saturday Review*, 68–69, 84, March 21, 1964. Explains why mathematics as taught in the schools is being revised and explains why there is some confusion among educators as to what directions the revisions should take.

SUPPES, PATRICK, "The Teacher and Computer-Assisted Instruction," *NEA Journal*, 56 (No. 2): 15–17, February, 1967. Explains how computers can assist teachers in their instructional activities and answers some of the questions teachers commonly raise about the future of computers in the classroom.

THORNDIKE, EDWARD LEE, *Man and His Works*. Cambridge: Harvard University Press, 1943. Chapter 8, "The Psychology of Punishment," analyzes the psychological effects of the use of coercion.

TINCHER, ETHEL, "The Detroit Public Schools Present English on Television," *English Journal*, 56 (No. 4): 596–602, April, 1967. Explains how television can be used effectively to strengthen classroom teaching.

UNDERWOOD, BENTON J., "Forgetting," *Scientific American*, 210 (No. 3): 91–99, March, 1964. An experimental study of forgetting. "Summing up these observations in the form of a general theory, we can say that all forgetting results basically from interference between the associations a man carries in his memory storage system."

VOYAT, GILBERT, "IQ: God-Given or Man-Made?" *Saturday Review*, pp. 73–75, 86–87, May 17, 1969. This is a critique of a research study by Dr. Arthur R. Jensen, University of California at Berkeley, which concluded that heredity is a more powerful determinant than environment and that the IQ is a valid indication of inherited potential. Highly controversial.

WATSON, GOODWIN, "What Do We Know About Learning?" *NEA Journal*, 52 (No. 3): 20–22, March, 1963. A brief, readable summary of what psychologists believe to be true about learning.

WEINSTEIN, GERALD, and MARIO FANTINI, " 'Phony' Literature," *English Journal*, 84 (No. 4): 259–264, April, 1965. Finds most of the materials in English unsuitable for children from disadvantaged homes. Discusses how a teacher may develop his own materials.

WOODRING, PAUL, "Are Intelligence Tests Unfair?" *Saturday Review*, pp. 79–80, April 16, 1966. An eminent psychologist in a scholarly analysis sets the record straight on the right and wrong uses of standardized intelligence tests.

Index